LAWS
GODS
AND
HEROES

Thematic Readings in Early Western History

Third Edition

H.A. Drake   J.W. Leedom

 KENDALL/HUNT PUBLISHING COMPANY
4050 Westmark Drive   Dubuque, Iowa 52002

Copyright © 1994, 1999, 2002 by Hal A. Drake and Joe W. Leedom

ISBN 0-7872-9599-X

Library of Congress Control Number: 20021 12224

Printed in the United States of America
10 9 8 7 6 5 4 3 2

LAWS, GODS AND HEROES

THEMATIC READINGS IN EARLY WESTERN HISTORY

Contents

veggie cycle

the covenant

Part II: Defining The Individual: Greece And Rome

IV Greek Heroes

V. Sophistry And Illusion

VI. Great Individuals

Part III: Cause And Effect: The Fall Of Rome

X. Change And Continuity

Epilogue

Sources

PROLOGUE

WHAT DOES IT ALL MEAN?

Detail from *The Tower of Babel* by Peter Brueghel the Elder

Introduction: Using This Book

The following chapters consist of source material selected to correspond to the topics studied in each of the ten weeks of History 4A.

We would like to think that you, as a student of this subject, will be delighted and grateful that someone has gone to the trouble of selecting and editing this material for you, but previous experience suggests that the emotions of most of you will fall somewhat short of such bliss. You will, instead, regard these selections as an unpleasant assignment which must be performed, but from which you do not expect to derive either pleasure or profit. You will consider the selections arbitrary, too long and too many, designed merely to confuse and mislead you.

Actually, in a way, you're right! There are more questions in the following pages than there are answers, and if you use this book in a typical manner—which means putting off opening it until the last possible moment, and then doing the reading as quickly as possible, with no effort to think how it relates to issues raised in lecture or the textbook—you will certainly close it more confused and bored than you were before.

So, before this happens, we would like to suggest that you approach this book in a different way. This class, like all classes, is a war of sorts, and it might be well for you to consider these readings as "ammunition" for your side.

How is that? Let's look ahead to your first examination. In a question on the development of ancient religious beliefs—which you are almost sure to get—you might be inclined to write a statement such as, "The Pharaoh Ikhnaton was a monotheist," and to feel pretty pleased with yourself for knowing (1) what a pharaoh was; (2) what an Ikhnaton was, and (3) what a monotheist was. In which case, you surely will be surprised when your T.A. returns the exam with the comment, "What is your evidence for such a statement?" And if you should conquer your emotions sufficiently to complain that both the textbook and the lecturer have said that Ikhnaton was a monotheist, your surprise surely will change to frustration when your T.A. blandly replies, "That isn't evidence, either."

What, then, is "evidence"? It has to be something which directly testifies to the question at hand, not something somebody else already has concluded about it. In the case of Ikhnaton, it would have to be something he said or did, or that others in a position to know tell us he said or did, which justifies the conclusion that he believed in one god rather than many.

DO AS I SAY...

Because the lectures in this course are analytical and explanatory, and because they treat very large topics in each meeting, they tend to be fairly heavy on "conclusions" and fairly light on "evidence" of this sort. But if you look in the section of "Egyptian Hymns" in this book—and the lectures are based on the assumption that you have done so—you will find one attributed to Ikhnaton which contains such phrases as, "O sole God, like whom there is no other," which are pretty fair indications that the author believed in one god rather than many. Having read this, you can write in your examination, "Ikhnaton was a monotheist because in the hymn attributed to him there occur such phrases as 'O sole God, like whom there is no other.'"

In other words, you can use the readings as ammunition for your argument, and your T.A. will have no choice but to give you lots of points for doing so, no matter how much it may pain his or her shrunken heart to do so.

That is the first reason, then, for this readings book: it allows you to find materials on which to base statements you may wish to make about a person, a society or an event on an examination. If you approach the book in this light—what will this material tell me about ancient polytheism, say, or Greek culture or Roman government that I can use on an examination to show my T.A. what a smart sonofabitch I am?—you will be getting at the core of the course. You may also, incidentally, find the material much more interesting to read.

But why all this concern for "evidence"? If it is true that Ikhnaton was a monotheist, isn't that the important thing to know, at least in a freshman course? Maybe. But if learning to accept what other people have to tell you is what you came to college for, forget it. You can accomplish the same thing—and save your parents or the government or both a lot of money—by staying home and memorizing the Barnes & Noble College Outline Series. You are here to learn now to draw your own conclusions about events, and how to present the reasons for your conclusions to others in a way that doesn't make you look like an idiot. That means you have to learn first to ask for evidence, and then to evaluate and test that evidence for yourself.

LET'S PRETEND

Let's pretend, for instance, that we're in a court of law. Someone has been accused of murder, and the prosecutor has made introductory statements in which he has said, in effect, that murder is a bad thing, that it is against the law, that the very foundations of our social order will crumble if we do not severely punish persons who commit murder, and so on. He now brings forth a parade of expert witnesses to substantiate what he has said: a distinguished professor of law who confirms that murder is indeed against the law, a famous minister who says that murder is morally wrong, a historian who gives a long and boring discussion of the way murder has been dealt with since the beginning of recorded history, a psychiatrist who says that murderers are indeed dangerous people, and a sociologist who weeps and snivels for an hour. The prosecutor then returns and concludes triumphantly, "You have heard the charge and the evidence of a host of distinguished authorities. You have no choice but to turn in a verdict of 'Guilty as charged.'"

What do you do? Let's hope that you at least say, "Wait a minute. All the evidence so far has been from your side, and we don't expect you to present anything that will weaken your case. So let's hear from the defense before we decide." That at least is being fair. But if in addition you take the time to scrutinize the prosecution's case and the evidence presented for it, you will discover that not once did anyone ever say that the defendant—the particular person charged with the particular crime—committed the act of murder! Not only the charge, but all of the distinguished "evidence" is utterly worthless, because it does nothing either to prove or disprove the case at hand, no matter how eloquently it has been stated or how distinguished and numerous the witnesses.

This was an extreme example of bad evidence. We could give more normal examples—people who testify that they heard the defendant was a murderer, for instance, or people who say he looks like a murderer or who will offer statistics to show that persons of his race or class or religion commit more of this type of murder than others—but perhaps by now you get the point. It all may sound very plausible and it all may be true, but unless there is someone who saw the crime committed or pretty substantial documentation from ballistics, fingerprints and witnesses placing him at the scene of the crime with a plausible motive, you will not have the evidence you need for conviction.

It should also be clear that this kind of judging is important to more than history classes and courtrooms. Yet you probably will surprise yourself if you stop to consider how often you accept a conclusion after just hearing one side of a story, even when it comes from a person immediately involved in the controversy. From everything as major as a political campaign or as trivial as which brand of soap to buy, you are going to spend your life surrounded by people trying to get you to do what they want done, and if you don't learn to ask for evidence and then to ask questions about that evidence you are going to wind up with a closet full of junk soap and political leaders closely approximating those we now possess.

To evaluate evidence, you first must learn to distinguish *fact* from *interpretation*. This is not as easy as it sounds. Take the case of the student who once replied, when told that he would have to give evidence for the statement that Ikhnaton was a monotheist, "Wow! I'm also taking American history, and I had no idea I would have to prove it if I said, 'Franklin Roosevelt was President of the United

States.'" His surprise is a good example of failure to distinguish between fact and interpretation. Do you see the difference between the two statements?

The statement, "Franklin Roosevelt was President of the United States" is a fact which is either true or false on its face: either a person with such a name did or did not hold the office. There is no need for elaborate documentation. A similar statement about Ikhnaton would be, "Ikhnaton was a pharaoh of Egypt.." But suppose we said, "Franklin Roosevelt was a megalomaniac." This clearly is a different order of statement: one which may or may not be true, but in either case cannot stand or fall by itself. Why? Because it is a conclusion, presumably based on a number of things Franklin Roosevelt said or did. It is not a "fact," but an interpretation, based on study of a number of "facts."

The same is true of the statement, "Ikhnaton was a monotheist." It may be true, but it is not a "fact" the way any number of other statements about Ikhnaton are facts. Therefore, it is only as good as the facts on which, ultimately, it is based.

Conclusions, or interpretations, then, are statements based upon facts, but facts which have been chosen and evaluated in some way. There is nothing wrong with drawing conclusions or offering interpretations—indeed, it might be said that this is the function which (at present) most distinguishes human beings from computers. But unlike facts, which are readily documented, interpretations can vary widely, even when based on the same set of facts. Franklin Roosevelt was the only President ever elected to four terms. One person might say that proves he was power-hungry; but another might say it proves he was a selfless leader who sacrificed his personal life because his country needed him.

Now suppose you were asked to choose between these statements: what would you do? There is, of course, always the standard retreat of the unlearned to fall back on—"They're both opinions, and one opinion is as good as another." But if you've learned to distinguish between fact and interpretation, you will say instead, "That's a conclusion; I'd like to see the evidence on which it's based." Then you can start asking questions of the evidence: Does being elected to the nation's highest office, by itself, justify one conclusion more than the other? Or does it justify either? After all, lots of people have *run* for the Presidency more times than Roosevelt. Why did *he* get elected so often? Maybe the question calls for more information before a conclusion is justified.

ROOSEVELT'S PSYCHE

Although certainly a fascinating question in itself, Franklin Roosevelt's psychology is not really the issue before us. The point is that most historical questions are of this sort: they are interpretative rather than factual. Historians, of course, first need to find out what happened. But then they have to decide what is important about what happened, what it means. Therefore, a higher plane of reasoning is involved. You have to exercise analytical and evaluative powers, to be a lawyer, judge, and information specialist all rolled into one. Because historians also have to pose questions as well as answer them, you need to be a problem-solver as well.

Bear these thoughts in mind as you read works of historians. If they say something or someone was good or bad, a hero or a villain, do you realize you are being presented with a conclusion rather than a fact? Do they give you reasons for their conclusions? How good are the reasons? On the basis of them, would you have reached the same conclusion?

Once you start looking for it, you'll be surprised how often conclusions are offered with no supporting evidence whatsoever. Is that important? Maybe not if you know something about the subject. If I were to say a given rock group was made up of "a bunch of degenerates," you probably would know enough to agree or disagree. But if you know nothing about the subject, you must accept with that conclusion our standards for making it, which may not be your own. If my standard is that anyone who sings above a whisper is unspeakably degenerate, you might still agree or disagree, but then at least we both would know what we were talking about.

Bear in mind as well that this type of interpretation can be done solely with "facts" just as easily. A typical textbook, for example, seems to contain simply "the facts." But obviously it does not contain everything that ever happened. The author has selected facts she or he thinks important, and in so doing has interpreted the material for you. Are the author's standards for selection clear? Do they seem fair to you? Try a simple parlor game. Have each person write down the most important "facts" about the career of Richard Nixon, then compare them. Is each set of facts the same, or can you detect different emphases among them? Do these, in turn, lead to different conclusions? Facts, then, just like conclusions, must be tested, too. Interpretation is where the real pleasure, and challenge, of studying history resides.

All of this is a long and roundabout way of explaining how to use this readings book. There is, indeed, a great deal of material to be studied for each week. But the variety of selections in each chapter all have one thing in common: they were chosen because they each shed some light on the theme being discussed that particular week.

Keep this in mind as you read. In Week Three, for instance, you will find fragments from a Babylonian creation epic, the *Enuma Elish*. The story is filled with strange names, and the plot sometimes is obscure (to say the least). Before you start banging your head against a wall trying to memorize all these names, ask yourself why you are reading these fragments—To learn how to write creation literature? To learn the names of the Mesopotamian gods? Or to get some ideas about Babylonian notions of Creation? The answer will be different for different courses. You'll do better in this course (and in all others you take) if you know the answer to this question before you start reading.

Here, obviously, it's the last question that we're asking. So it's a waste of time of memorize the names of all the Mesopotamian deities. Instead, ask how their ideas about Creation compare with Egyptian and Hebrew ideas that you also are reading that week. Then ask what similarities and differences tell you about the peoples under study. Did these underlying assumptions affect their behavior or attitude toward life in significant ways? How?

In time, such thinking may even cause you to think about your own assumptions regarding Creation and the Universe, and the effects they may have had on your own attitudes and behavior. You might start comparing yourself to these ancient peoples, and wind up understanding both better as a result.

This is what people mean when they say that the study of history is a way to broaden your perspective and to grow as a human being. Insight into the human condition in general, and the working of your own mind in particular, is what the study of history is all about.

If you keep the weekly themes in mind as you study the readings, you will not only go through them more quickly, you also will learn how to extract common themes from seemingly dissimilar material. This will prove of great advantage to you in classes where these common themes are not identified for you in advance, as they are in this course, because most of the other students in the class won't have been trained to do so. It is a method that you will find useful not only for the classroom but for making your whole intellectual life more interesting and coherent.

I. Getting Started

Let's start things off right. Many of you have just entered the university, and are about to be exposed to an incredible amount of garbage, in the form of poor thinking and shoddy teaching masquerading as highly intellectual activity.

True, much of your college work will be confusing to you because it is new and difficult. But a lot of plain common sense and simple truth gets dressed up in fancy, obscure (and not-quite-English) language for no other reason than the academic impulse to make everything sound profound.

The problem is, most undergraduates lack the self-confidence to call a banality banal when it is expressed in jawbreaker words and sentences.

Your survival ratio probably, and your sanity certainly, will improve if you approach academia with some skepticism. To help you do so, Section A begins with an article by BRUCE D. PRICE, a novelist and advertising man who graduated from Princeton in 1963. You might store away some of the tricks he exposes here so you can spot them when they are used in your *other* classes. Following it, PAUL ST. PIERRE and BETTY ZISK have more insights into the quality of academic, and other, writing. Closing this section, advice from two veteran Western Civilization instructors. RICK KENNEDY (now a professor at Pt. Loma Nazarene College) gives some pertinent warnings about objectivity and grades, and LAURA WERTHEIMER (who is now writing her doctoral dissertation) with some pointed advice about writing analytical essays.

Finally, since so much of what you read will not be in the language it was written in, this chapter closes with an excerpt from an article on translation by PAUL WILLIAM ROBERTS. Roberts might not have been entirely fair to to the object of his scorn, but if nothing else his words keep you from making the mistake of thinking that translation is simply a matter of substituting a word in one language for one in another. It should start you thinking about all the subtle changes that occur when a document is taken out of its native context.

Since one aim of this book is to teach you to discern common themes and subjects in a set of readings, how about starting here: what common theme can you find in this chapter? What theme or themes can you imagine all three of these sections have? (Go ahead and take a wild stab—you can't possibly be any more confused than you are now, and you just might be right.)

❖   ❖   ❖

1. IN PRAISE OF STARK LUCIDITY

BRUCE D. PRICE

What I like to call Ph.D. illiteracy–impenetrable prose by those who should know better–has become more the rule than the exception. The "soft sciences" of sociology, psychology, linguistics, education, and dear old anthropology are safe ports for gibberish. Even respectable physicists and biologists and archi-tects are infected and fairly delirious with the babble of words in no hurry to say very much.

Here's a paragraph from a book by a noted sociologist:

Motoric reproduction processes. The third major component of modeling phenomena involves the utilization of symbolic representations of modeled patterns in the form of imaginal and verbal contents to guide overt perfor-

mances. It is assumed that reinstatement of representational schemes provides a basis for self-instruction on how component responses must be combined and sequenced to produce new patterns of behavior. The process of representational guidance is essentially the same as response learning under conditions where a person behaviorally follows an externally depicted pattern or is directed through a series of instructions to enact novel response sequences. The only difference is that, in the latter cases, performance is directed by external cues whereas, in delayed modeling behavioral reproduction is monitored by symbolic counterparts of absent stimuli.

When you understand something, you can give examples. Give two examples of what the famous sociologist is talking about.

An editor of one of the leading publishers of college texts recently told me: "I literally don't know what our authors are talking about sometimes. They meander. They use this terrible language. And their organization is so poor, I have to call them up and have them tell me what they mean."

In fact, some people have started to snicker. Not long ago, an anonymous cynic (apparently an anthropologist) sent me a "Folklore Article Reconstruction Kit" (FARK) which can quickly generate over 40,000 sentences of the kind I'd like to see on the wane. Any hundred of these sentences, say the instructions, will create "a Guaranteed Folklore Contribution to human knowledge. You will then be certain of Forging to the Front in the advancing horde of next year's Ph.D.'s, fighting it out for the cushier jobs in University and Government."

The kit consists of four groups of sentence fragments, numbered 1 to 10. You simply pick any four-digit number at random and then let each digit designate one fragment from each of the four lists. The number 3923, for instance, spits out this cut-glass gem: "From the intercultural standpoint, my proposed independent structuralistic concept maximizes the probability of project success while minimizing cross-cultural shock elements in improved subcultural compatibility-testing."

Unfortunately, my files bulge with examples of the real thing not much different from this

mechanically generated nonsense. Even more unsettling, I have the sensation I'm closer to understanding this kit-produced sentence than I am to understanding some of the man-produced sentences quoted earlier. What we're up against is stacks of 50-cent words and phrases that somehow add up to 5 cents worth of meaning. An inflation, I will argue, that we cannot afford.

The instructions, by the way, promise future kits "for Ph.D.'s in Sociology (SARK), Linguistics (LARK), Bio-Physics (BARK), and especially in Neo-Humanistics (NARK).... Computer-extrusion of Folklore articles, by the yard or until turned off, is also an obvious possibility through FARK."

Thomas Middleton, who writes "Light Reflections" for *Saturday Review*, once generated both amusement and hostility by a most gentle rebuke to obscurity in a new branch of sociology. He quoted a passage similar to the one I cited at the outset, and lamented that he had been unable to decipher it.[1]

One indignant professor, leaping to the barricades, wrote back arguing that sociologists and, indeed, all disciplines, have "a right to a technical language." A claim we must ponder. Certainly, there are technical terms—whether "neutron" in physics or "water column" in oceanography or "scale" in music—and one has to know these to read intelligently in the field. But technical terms do not a language make. And terms are not so much the problem in this kind of writing as grammar.

The problem, quite simply, is that the writer is illiterate in the peculiar way that 20 years of education makes possible. The kid on the street corner in Harlem who says, "I can't git no kinds work," is less illiterate than the sociologist quoted, since communication—how fast, how completely—must be the index of who's literate and who's not.

I submit that the professor's "right to a technical language" is brainless nonsense, on a par with your right—*undeniable, if you insist*—to express your thoughts in Pig Latin or dead languages or astrological symbols.

---

[1]Princeton Alumni Weekly (February 9, 1976).

What I'm arguing for here is that the best and the brightest have a special obligation to act like it. To set high standards of lucidity. To speak and write for the family of man, or at least the community of the educated and curious. The acid test is: can the writer improve the clarity of his prose without diminishing content? "Yes" means you're not ready to publish.

George Orwell offers a helpful insight: "One can write nothing readable unless one constantly struggles to efface one's personality." Scientists and scholars of all types, often loud in praise of their own objectivity, should not have to hear this admonition. And yet what does one sense in so much bad prose but a round-about groping for grandeur? Far from effacing themselves, too many of our intellectual leaders are saying: look at me, I've got something really, really profound to say, so deep and significant that you ordinary minds cannot dare hope to grasp my meaning. And to make sure this pompous declaration turns out true, they express their message more cryptically than Kabbalists.

What we seem to need is more love of knowledge and less love of effect. Orwell also said, "Good prose is like a windowpane."

Students, not knowing any better, are often awed by impenetrable prose. They don't question the tough going. Which is a big mistake.

At a party I spoke with an older student, a women who had worked for several years and then gone back to finish her B.A. in "early childhood education."

She said: "Well, some of these concepts are very complex. I have to read them two or three times to be sure I can understand them."

I said: "I just don't believe there are so many concepts that are hard to understand. Give me an example. I'll bet it can be put simply."

She said: "Oh, you mean—Oedipus complex, male child desires mother and this is resolved by age three; female child desires father and this is resolved by age three or never."

There she had taken one of those supposedly complex concepts and stated it in record time. "That," I said, "is my point."

She laughed nervously, *apparently at her own audacity.* She had never been so intimate with succinctness before and wasn't sure how it felt. Perhaps she feared that one of her professors would leap through the window and flunk her for failure to obfuscate.

That's no joke. *Harper's* recently ran an article about students who write as badly as their teachers in order to get good grades (not to mention grants). The writer called the students "straight-A illiterates." My own notion is that we can't hold 19-year-olds accountable for very much of anything. Department chairpeople and authors of books and scholars of renown we can.

There are two entirely different kinds of complexity, that of thought and that of expression. Ph.D. illiterates hope that we'll forget this distinction. They'd like us to see difficult, even totally obscure expression and think: Hey, this must be deep thought. Usually it's deep fraud.

Too many writers are specializing in what is, in practical effect, code. And too many readers are spending the bulk of their time deciphering these codes.

Ph.D. illiterates disdain simplicity of expression: the simpler the thought, the greater the exertions on behalf of obscurity or, if possible, total concealment. "It's hard to measure X" becomes, in a journal devoted to social psychology, "substantial measurement problems are encountered in evaluating X." I'm afraid the same magazine would translate "I love you" like so:

"The emotional intensity factors of my cognitive areas have been evaluated and the data permit the conclusion that your personality structure, and its continued proximity to my own, are of high quantitative value to my sustained happiness level rate."

Now this sort of writing is code, as surely as if each letter of "I love you" were replaced by its successor in the alphabet, making "J mpwf zpv." An honest code is respectable enough. What we can't have are all these closet cryptographers.

Unless we are at war or conversing among enemies, what justification can there be for codes or code-like writing? They waste our lives and our sacred energies. What excuse can there be for anything less than stark lucidity? When Ph.D. illiterates write codes, everyone else must expend a preponderance of strength on breaking those codes, and what little strength remains goes to absorbing the message and growing from it. You have certainly had that experience. Multiply your experience by millions and you can begin to assess the daily waste of a culture's most important natural resource, its intellectual energy.

I'd like to suggest a new field of inquiry: the sociology of prose. Its chief question is: why does any group of people write as they do? Specifically, why do so many of our most learned, particularly in sociology and psychology, write so opaquely? One likely theory states that nouveau intellectuals–very much like nouveau riche in feeling insecure about their rank in the community–will seek conspicuous proof of their arrival. To which one can only say: *how very tacky.*

From my vantage, however, Cadillac automobiles of even the most garish variety are far less injurious to the physical landscape than Cadillac prose is to the cultural landscape.

It would be only fair to apply the techniques perfected by sociologists to sociologists themselves, in the spirit of the injunction: "Physician, heal thyself!" Perhaps some intrepid researcher, indifferent to a career, could send questionnaires to our sociologists and psychologists by way of prying into their education, class, cultural anxieties, misgivings about their fields and attainments therein. Perhaps the data would explain the inevitable fascination that the newer disciplines, and unsure minds, find in the most Philistine prose.

For many years I've been monitoring a fairly new aspect of English usage–the stringing together of two or three or four or more nouns. I've dubbed this practice Nounspeak and written about it at length in *Verbatim: The Language Quarterly* (February 1976). There I objected to Nounspeak's wordiness, abstraction, and lack of vigor. It is, of course, beloved by Ph.D. illiterates.

I read that Princeton students now talk about their "grade point average" when everyone knows that "grades" or "average" says it all. A single sentence from *The Journal of Social Psychology* offers two exquisite examples of Nounspeak: "This study investigates group conformity influence on member grand choice." Just try to diagram that sentence.

I will speak here only of my more recent reflections on the subject. Nounspeak's most salient pretension is to precision and a sort of scientific solidity. Very often, however, it succeeds merely in introducing duplicities and confusions. A weatherman said that we should expect rain in "the southern California area." Is that identical with saying "in southern California"? Or does the addition of the noun "area" mean that Nevada and Mexico should also expect rain? The question is: what precisely did the speaker have in mind? The answer is: we don't know.

More and more these days people talk about "problem areas" instead of simple old problems, which are really what we have to face. My first reaction was that the only sin lies in adding an extra word where it's not needed. Then I heard someone speak of solving a problem area." And I thought: wait a minute– a problem is a thing, but a "problem area" is a category or territory, if it's anything. Although you can certainly solve a problem, you cannot solve a category, because a category is an abstraction. In short, "solving a problem area" may just be nonsense and not at all what the speaker meant.

A radio announcer said that Carter and his Cabinet were discussing "policy goals." And I thought: does that mean they discussed only the goals but not the policies themselves? What exactly is a "policy goal"? Give an example.

This sort of analysis is tedious and rarely conclusive. But that's my point. Nounspeak leaves the gate open for debates that should not even be imaginable. Each extra noun carries along its own baggage. And then if you place them in uncertain juxtaposition to each other, you have more confusion than you want. The result is that we are pushed back one step further from life, rather than led into it, which is properly the aim of language.

"Value system" has, unfortunately, become a cliché. But what is this thing, a "value system"? I don't have one in my life. I have values, surely, most of which don't fit together at all. "Value hodgepodge" is more like it. Such is the case, I suggest, with you and yours, General Motors, and the American public. Look all year and you won't find a "system." Maybe "value system"—that high-sounding theoretical abstraction—is in a class with "round square." You can mouth the words all you please, but that doesn't mean there is such a thing.

Nounspeak, like some pompous politicians, can look and sound impressive. But don't examine too closely. A phrase like "group conformity influence" will start shimmering before your eyes.

Language is not reality. Language points at reality. And it should point as directly as possible, like the pointer a lecturer uses to indicate cities on a map. Our problem is that our pointers are becoming wobbly.

Put this pointer on a table and push one end: the other end moves likewise. Now place a leather belt on the table and push one end: the other end moves only slightly and with little relation to the push. Now shove on a string of cooked spaghetti. The other end will ignore you.

In this image reality is doing the pushing. And the movement at the other end is the meaning that reaches your brain. The trouble with mushy language is that we no longer know what reality, if any, is being discussed. The language has ceased to point, has ceased to communicate any information about the hard push of reality.

In short, English becomes fettuccini.

This image is intended to illustrate the real horror of Ph.D. Illiteracy. Which is *not* that elaborately dense prose is an eyesore, an earsore, boring, hard to understand, and a blight on the intellectual community. No, the profoundly serious problem is that these people are wrecking our language, wrecking its ability to do its job. So that we now find English in the worst health of its long and fairly distinguished career.

From what I know of linguistics and the Sapir-Whorf hypothesis, we create our language and our language creates us. What alarms me is that we seem to be creating a particularly sloppy and boneless language. And in turn we find that our thinking and talking and writing will become as spineless as jellyfish pulsing in shadowy seas. What better setting can there be for the sly propagation of unstated premises, unfounded theories, malicious nonsense, and outright lies?

And so we reach my fundamental point, which is, broadly put, political. I coined the word Nounspeak in respectful tribute to Orwell, who was so remarkably insightful about the relationship between a debased language and a debased civilization. The totalitarian state he depicted in *1984* required a shrunken language—so that its citizens could not think their way to a better society. Of Newspeak, the language of *1984*, Orwell wrote: "It was designed not to extend but to diminish the range of thought." So it is with Nounspeak (often) and Ph.D. illiteracy (generally).

A healthy, strong democracy requires a healthy, strong language. I think each of us has a responsibility—and the greater the education, the greater the responsibility—to protect and refine our language precisely because we may need it to save our skins.

Those who have little to say, or evil to hide, will seek the friendly camouflage of fog-bound language. But let those who are confident of their contribution speak clearly.

It is fatuous to talk ever so grandly of Spaceship Earth and then to retreat into piddling specialized illiteracies. Technology is not going to slow. Politics will remain in ferment. It is more crucial than ever that all of the best and brightest minds speak lucidly to each other, educate each other, draw closer to one another. We need all the help we can give.

❖

2. A HANDY GUIDE

PAUL ST. PIERRE AND BETTY ZISK

Although it may have gone unnoticed by all except a few curmudgeonly old school teachers and some cranky ex-newspapermen, the English language is in large extent being replaced by jargon.

Jargon is not slang. Slang is sometimes witty. It is also usually understandable, within the context that it is delivered. A logger who lays down his chain saw and picks up an ax is understood when he announces that he is about to operate on the tree by the Armstrong Method. So is the man on the tide flats who calls his shovel a Clam Gun or the mechanic who drops his wrench, grabs a ball-peen hammer and announces that he is going to use his Persuader to Christianize a piece of machinery.

Slang is used for amusement. Jargon is used for confusion. Jargon words are heavy and ponderous. They are presented as the language of an elite. Unlike slang, jargon is considered to be much too good for the common people. It is the code of exclusive classes whose members use it to communicate with one another while politely putting down the unwashed masses who cannot understand the words.

Having observed the growth of jargon as a replacement for English during most of my lifetime, I confess that even today I hesitate to suggest which class of society relies most heavily upon it.

Armies make extensive use of jargon. (In army jargon, a target is not a target. It is a Pre-selected Impact Area). Jargon almost always takes longer to write than English, for which reason it is used by people to whom time and money are of little consequence.

Government bureaucracies dispense jargon in fountains. Academics, particularly those in economics or sociology, emit it in geysers and baptize one another in the thundering torrents. Businessmen and unionists are awed by the stuff and frequently hire people to write it for them under their own names, so that they may be confused by their own language instead of somebody else's.

Might I therefore put forward the suggestion that the cause of simple, Churchillian English has long since been lost and that those who love the language as a means of communication should accept their defeat gracefully and learn the jargon?

That is the purpose of this column. Here is the Handy Guide to Jargon. A simple formula. A child could use it. Many do. Please clip and save the following columns of words. The key to their use is provided at the bottom of the column.

HANDY GUIDE TO JARGON

0. integrated	0. management	0. options
1. total	1. organizational	1. flexibility
2. systematized	2. monitored	2. capability
3. parallel	3. reciprocal	3. mobility
4. functional	4. digital	4. programming
5. responsive	5. logistical	5. concept
6. optional	6. transitional	6. time-phase
7. synchronized	7. incremental	7. projection
8. compatible	8. third-generation	8. hardware
9. balanced	9. policy	9. contingency

To use the Handy Guide to Jargon, it is not necessary to have any thought whatever nor any understanding of the words. Just think of a three-digit number. Let's say 913. Read across the columns. 'Balanced organizational mobility.' Pretty impressive, wouldn't you say? Drop that into any letter, any speech, and your words will have the sonorous tone of authority.

Try 268: systematized transitional hardware, and 074: integrated incremental programming.

With the Handy Guide to Jargon, anyone who can write three figures on a piece of paper is equipped to deal with the highest mandarins of government, business, science, the arts or the radical left. In fact, you can cope with anybody. They won't understand what you're saying, but they will recognize you to be an intellectual and social equal.

❖

3.   *TRUTH AND EDUCATION*

RICK KENNEDY

I recently heard a physicist-friend say that the angles of a triangle do not actually add up to 180 degrees. I was shocked. I guess I should have expected it however, since in many ways, my whole college career has been an unlearning process rather than a learning one. Everything I think I know, I should hold suspect, knowing that some specialist is bound to tell me that what I thought was true is now not accepted by anyone smarter than a pineapple. The angles of triangle though! Isn't mathematics, at least, sacred? I mean, if you can't trust your tenth-grade geometry teacher, who can you trust?

Throughout this university, people seem to enjoy blowing away all those things–like geometry–that we naively believed when we entered. You can take a religious studies course and learn the Bible can be interpreted in hundreds of ways. You can take a physics course and find out that the law of gravity isn't much of a law. You can take a political science course and learn that the U.S. Constitution can be stretched, twisted, and broken–and it doesn't really matter. After a year or two here, it is amazing that anyone believes anything. Everything becomes more complicated and nothing seems to get easier.

The reason things do not seem to get easier is because no one at the university has any absolute knowledge of what is true and what is not. We do not absolutely know the nature of the universe, whether God exists, or, for that matter, whether we exist.

My philosopher-brother and I once spent an evening talking about this problem of absolute knowledge while sitting on the lawn outside his house. No respectable philosophic discussion can happen without cigars and technical language, so my brother produced two Santa Clara cigars (number twos with a maduro wrap), and we talked philosophically about "the problem of epistemology." We discussed Kant, Husserl, and such things as Logical Positivism as we watched our clouds of cigar smoke gather and dissipate. Neither of us understood what we were talking about, but, as our cigars became ash, we realized there can be no solution to the problem.

All sorts of professors here run around, bumping heads, producing good theories and discovering good facts. However, all they are actually improving is the smorgasbord of ideas and facts that we pick and choose from. For the student, college is basically four years of

standing in line at a large hofbrau that offers all sorts of meats, gravies, salads, and fattening desserts. No clear directions are given for how to fill one's plate with knowledge, nor is a guide given for the best meats and tastiest gravies. The student can only stand in line and try to do the best he can.

However, the university does offer something more than this; it offers an education in thinking. Knowledge is available here. It's not absolute, but it is knowledge nonetheless. In the history department we may not be able to prove absolutely that Napoleon existed, but we can give enough evidence to make it a good bet. Facts stack up on a scale of probability of being true. We gather and interpret all sorts of these facts in an attempt to get as close as we can to reality. This is what separates an educated guess from an opinion.

This is where grading fits in. A grade does not tell you how close you came to knowing the truth, it tells you how well you are using your education. A student who came in to my office to complain about his midterm grade took issue with the fact that I disagreed with him. He had no evidence to back up his statements and simply retorted, "That's your opinion!" This did not indicate that he understood the problem of epistemology; rather, it showed he had Jello for a brain.

The University of California is not in the business of teaching absolute truth; it is in the business of teaching people how to think in an analytical pattern in the context of certain fields. Do not expect too much from the university. Do not come here expecting to be taught good citizenship and how to follow the constitution. Do not expect to be taught whether Christianity or Buddhism is true. Do not even expect the scientists to tell you something ultimately true. Citizenship, religion, and truth have to be worked out individually. The university may offer a course in ethics, but it cannot teach ethics; it can only teach *about* ethics. The decisions are left up to the individual.

I was shocked to find that my tenth-grade geometry teacher was wrong, but that does not mean that there is no truth in geometry. Gravity may not qualify as a law anymore, but that does not mean physicists will not get closer to understanding it. The Bible may prove to be a shaky foundation, but Christianity can still be true.

Do not expect too much. There are no ultimate answers here; only small truths and methods of thought. There is no free lunch at this hofbrau; the burden is upon the student to fashion something coherent out of education.

❖

4. GETTING EVEN: HOW TO WRITE A CONVINCING ANALYTICAL ESSAY

Laura Wertheimer

Many of you will have trouble with the difference between an analytical essay and a descriptive one. To help you sort out this problem, here are some sample answers to an essay you are probably already planning.

Evaluate your teaching assistant's effectiveness as a teacher.

Essay 1.

I really dislike Laura.[1] Professor Drake, on the other hand, is fantastic. His lectures are organized, he has a commanding presence, and his slides are worth getting out of bed for every morning … [Four more paragraphs extolling Professor Drake].

This essay will get an F, or at best, a D. No matter how clear and analytical the discussion of Professor Drake is, it simply does not answer the question.

Essay 2.

Laura is the worst teaching assistant I have ever had.[2] She is disorganized. She can't teach.[3] She grades too hard. My roommate, who had her for 4A last year, says she never curves the grades.[4] She's mean. She has a bad haircut. I hate History because of her and think she should be kicked out of grad school.[5]

I know many of you would be proud to have written this evaluation, but it's only a "C" essay. While it lists a few of my bad qualities, it is entirely descriptive—it does not evaluate (or analyze) my performance. An essay that goes into greater detail with specific examples, but is still only descriptive, would get a C+.

Essay 3.

Having compared Laura with the grad students I had the last two times I took this class, I must regretfully say that her lack of organization, uncaring attitude toward the students, and inability to communicate the material force me to give her a poor evaluation as a TA.[6]

Laura is always very disorganized and clearly does not put much time into preparing her sections. This indicates that she does not take her teaching duties very seriously.[7]

Laura does not care about students. She grades too hard and is mean to us. She is not supportive of our efforts to learn. Since UCSB prides itself on its student-focused program, Laura's indifference towards students makes her a poor representative of this university.

Laura never understands questions and while she may know what she is talking about, this is not clear when she lectures. Since section is meant to clarify lecture, Laura fails her duties in this area.

This is a solid B essay. It doesn't just list my bad qualities: it analyzes them to give an evaluation of my performance.

---

[1] This is a very poor thesis statement. It does not answer the question.

[2] This is better than the previous thesis because it at least expresses an opinion relevant to the question, but it is not very analytical.

[3] You should not use contractions in formal writing. This statement is also too vague to be very useful.

[4] This is secondary evidence, similar to using the textbook or the introduction to a document in *Laws,* *Gods, and Heroes* as evidence in an essay. It is better than no evidence at all, but not as good as primary evidence (in this essay, primary evidence would be your own experience; in the class in general, the documents from *Laws, Gods, and Heroes,* such as *The Code of Hammurabi* or *The Iliad,* are primary sources.)

[5] Irrelevant: the question is on my teaching performance.

[6] This is getting to be a good thesis. It is analytical: it actually gives an evaluation, and sets up the criteria with which you are making this evaluation. The only thing missing is a brief mention of the specifics that will be discussed.

[7] This is an analysis. It takes a fact (disorganization) and draws a conclusion from it.

Essay 4.

Although Laura is a very nice person, she is not a good TA due to her lack of organization, uncaring attitude, and inability to communicate effectively. These flaws can be seen in her section planning, comments on homework, and her section lectures.[1] Laura is very disorganized, which makes it difficult for us to learn in section.[2] She skips from one topic to another, probably because she never has a lesson plan.[3] Half the time she loses our homework, so we can't learn from it. Sometimes she hasn't done the readings or gone to lecture. Her lack of preparation indicates that she does not take teaching very seriously.[4]

Laura's callous attitude towards students bruises our fragile egos and makes us afraid of her. She is rude to students, will not learn our names, and snickers when she passes back exams. Last week, she wrote "You are as dumb as a load of bricks" on my homework paper.[5] Her nastiness makes us unwilling to ask her for help. Since this university prides itself on its supportive atmosphere, Laura is not the sort of teacher we want here.

Finally, Laura cannot clearly answer questions or communicate what she knows. When I asked her to explain sophism, she gave me a ten-minute lecture on the later Middle Ages, but never answered the question. She also likes to respond to questions in Latin, and whenever anyone asks her to explain anything from lecture, she says "Go to class yourself, you bum!" Since her syllabus says that section is the place to clarify points from lecture and discuss the readings, she fails to carry out her responsibilities in this area as well.

Some people might say that Laura is a good TA because of her excellent penmanship, her willingness to squander History Department money on Xeroxing, and the fascinating vacation pictures she brings in to supplement section.[6] However, I feel that her flaws greatly outweigh these good points.

In conclusion, I would have to say that although I like Laura as a person, her performance is much worse than that of other TAs. Due to her cavalier attitude towards teaching, section was a complete waste this quarter. Since she fulfills none of the duties this department expects of teaching assistants, I must condemn her performance in the strongest terms and recommend that she not be allowed to teach anymore.

Now this is an essay that will get an A and might keep me from ever working in this field again. It gives a well-stated opinion is organized, analyzes rather than describes my performance, and gives clear supporting evidence. It has a solid thesis which sets up the organization of the essay, and even has a conclusion that not only summarizes previous points but also develops the essay. It is no coincidence that the better essays tend to be longer. While padding your response will not help, the exam questions can rarely be answered completely in less than two and one-half pages.

If you have further questions about writing analytical essays, don't hesitate to see your instructor or TA. She or he will be delighted to help, and if not, just memorize the "A" essay for use when you do evaluations.

❖

5. MY TRANSLATION PROBLEM

ROBERT PAUL WILLIAM

Let's face it: When it comes to ancient translations, you either know an idiom or you don't. And if you don't, a phrase like "the guitarist's too much, man" ends up getting translated as "The player of the guitar is excessive, O human" or even "The guitarist is excessively masculine." Imagine how the problem is compounded when dealing with long-dead languages written without the Roman alphabet—or without any alphabet —that convey not rock-and-roll fandom, but a profound system

---

[1] This is a very good thesis statement. It gives an evaluation (poor TA), gives the basis for the evaluation, and sets up the specifics with which you will support this analysis.

[2] Establishing a cause and effect relationship.

[3] Evidence of my disorganization.

[4] See note 7.

[5] Now *there's* good supporting evidence!

[6] Many evaluative or analytical essays will have two sides. You should always take and defend an opinion, but should briefly discuss the other side and explain why you found it unconvincing.

of metaphysics or philosophy. It isn't pretty, is it…?

Ever since 1821, when the young French linguist Jean-François Champollion, working with the Rosetta stone (a second-century B.C. inscription in classical Greek, Egyptian hieroglyphs, and Egyptian vernacular), persuaded himself and others that he could decipher those enigmatic Egyptian hieroglyphs, academics across a broad and varied terrain have unhesitatingly backed each other up over such issues as indeclinable nouns and unwritten vowels, frequently to the extent of endorsing the authority of a translation despite its implausibility. Champollion, one of the most formidable linguists of modern times, contributed to this problem. For all his undisputed brilliance, he insisted on assigning phonetic value to each Egyptian pictogram—a strategy that has effectively imprisoned Egyptology in a cage of literalism.

One of the more unfortunate exponents of Champollion's methodology was the eminent Victorian Sir Wallis Budge, keeper of Egyptian and Assyrian antiquities at the British Museum a century ago, and thus a man who probably wrote more books about ancient Egypt than he could have possibly read on the subject. No doubt he knew an awful lot about ancient Egypt, but in his published work, Budge flaunts his spectacular incompetence as a translator by publishing a so-called "transliteration," with a hieroglyph above a phonetic rendition above an English "translation. Since anyone familiar with pictographic languages knows that half, if not more, of their meaning—especially in the case of religious or ritual texts—lies in an understanding of symbols impervious to direct "translation," it seems scarcely believable that an astute scholar could convince himself that something like the following was an accurate rendering of a long-dead language used by a civilization whose monumental achievements 3,000 years ago continue to confound us:

Chapter of not allowing to be repulsed the
    heart of [Here comes name of deceased]
in the underworld. Says he, "O Heart mine of
    mother
mine. Twice. Heart mine of evolution mine.
    Not may be obstruction

against me in evidence. Nor may be repulsed
    to me by the Powers.
Nor may be made separation thy from me in
    the presence of the
guardian of the scale. Thou art genius my in
    body my, Chnem, making
sound limbs my. Mayest come forth thou to
    felicity [to which] go we
there. Not may overthrow name our the
    Shenit [who] make men firm.
Pleasant to us, pleasant [is] the hearing of joy
    of heart at the
weighing of words. Not may be told falsehood
    [against me] near
the god, in the presence of the god great, lord
    of the underworld. How
great art thou rising up in triumph!

This stupefying passage is from Budge's opus on funerary practices, *The Mummy* (1925). If a reader bothers to peruse Budge's annotations after ploughing through this drivel, he discovers that Budge admits that these texts are "very varied, but at present it is not possible to explain one half of them satisfactorily." The same could be said of Budge's translations. What we are being subjected to here is, in my view, an academic legerdemain. The transliteration masks the bald fact that, even with their words rearranged, most of these sentences would still be gibberish. The strategic use of brackets—to show where a word or phrase has to be fabricated or guessed at—belies the fact that virtually *every word* is scarcely more than fabrication or guesswork, all of it based on a context that is itself mere surmise.

Readers should remember that there is no such thing as "natural" gibberish: Even pidgin is grammatically and syntactically coherent. Therefore, to render a language, ancient or no, into gobbledygook and offer it as a "translation" is an act difficult to defend.

❖

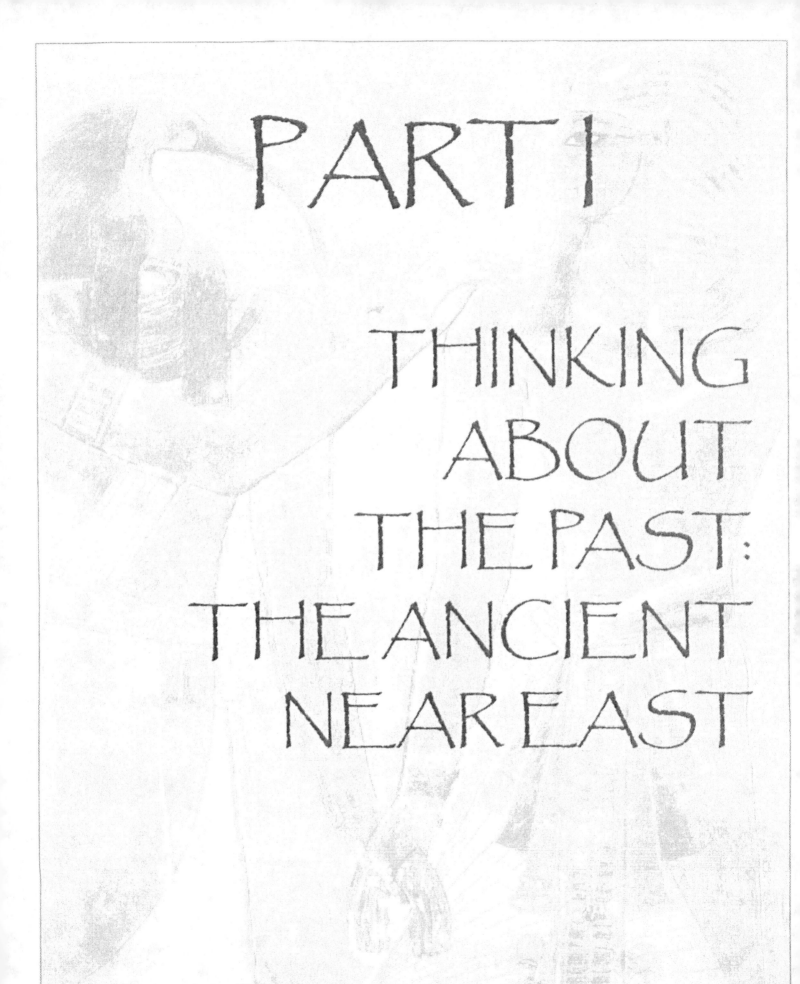

PART 1

THINKING ABOUT THE PAST: THE ANCIENT NEAR EAST

Pharoah Seti I and Thoth (c. 1300 B.C.)

II. In The Beginning...

Organized human activity–civilization–had its rise in the Ancient Near East, and with it came the problem of deciding how humans should live under such conditions, or even if it is "natural" for us to do so (a problem that will come up again when we look at the Greeks). When you think of the problem of civilization versus nature, you probably think of Jean-Jacques Rousseau, whose essays about the "noble savage" touched off a furious debate in the eighteenth century, and helped inaugurate the age of Romanticism. The ancients argued about this topic, too, though few of them came to as idealized a picture as Rousseau's.

Since this is a course about civilization, we start with a level-headed presentation of the issue by a Cambridge anthropologist. The one thing PATRICIA CRONE does not consider is the role of religion. Ironic, because of all the many contributions of the Ancient Near East to Western Civilization this is the one that has had the most lasting impact.

The remaining readings in this chapter (with one exception) come from a variety of ancient sources, including myths and law codes. Religion, science, and government usually are treated as separate and even mutually exclusive topics. But in one sense at least they are all the same, for all serve to explain, and thereby to rationalize, life. Like science–and unlike fable–ancient myths deal with perceived phenomena: why is there rain, or flood, or drought, or death? True, the answers are hardly scientific, nor do they use our techniques of analysis. But, as Henri Frankfort observed in *The Intellectual Adventure of Ancient Man* (Chicago, 1946), the difference is one of method, not of motive. The myths of the Ancient Near East are best studied as a form of speculative thought.

The urge to order and to rationalize is what underlies the seemingly disparate readings in this section. They are myths and laws for the most part, but look for common threads: what social functions did each of these readings fulfill, and how did they go about doing so? Do you have a sense of development between the earliest and the latest, and if so, in what way? Finally, in what way could you use these documents to illustrate differences between the societies which produced them?

❖   ❖   ❖

1. COMPLEX SOCIETIES

PATRICIA CRONE

Imagine that you and some friends and relatives of yours are shipwrecked on an uninhabited island with no hope of ever getting back. What would you do? Obviously, you would have to start by finding something to eat. The ecology of the Island might be such that you could feed yourselves by gathering fruit, berries and other edible plant material, supplementing your diet by hunting or fishing. But if you could, you would start growing things, for agriculture makes for a more dependable food supply than hunting and gathering: cereals such as grain, rice and millet can be stored; and your sedentary mode of life would enable you to store both these and other things on a scale impossible to those who have to move to wherever prey and plants happen to be available in a particular season. (You might of course still engage in some hunting or fishing from time to time.)

Having solved the problem of food, what sort of organization would you need? Given that you would be both few (indeed friends and relatives) and devoid of external enemies, you obviously would not need much organization at all. You might have to meet from time to time for decisions on issues affecting all of you (such as whether or not to set up a granary for use in years of shortage) and also for the settlement of disputes threatening to disrupt the general peace (such as your claim that your neighbor had stolen part of your harvest); and no doubt the opinions of some would carry greater weight than those of others; some would be leaders and others would be led. But you would hardly need a formal leader. Your society would be stateless, or indeed acephalous, *headless*. It would also be extremely primitive, that is to say lacking in social, economic, political and other differentiation on the one hand and poor in culture, both material and intellectual, on the other.

But now imagine that a very large number of you are shipwrecked on that island, or that the island is not uninhabited, but on the contrary full of hostile natives. If there were thousands of you, you might split up into several small acephalous societies, but then you might start quarreling over land, boundaries, noise or whatever. If so, you would need more in the way of political organization. You might also find that some societies had access to commodities that others lacked (such as salt, precious stones or metals), in which case you would start exchanging goods with each other, or in other words trading; some might then get very much richer than others, both within each community and between them, and some people might stop growing food altogether, earning enough by trade to buy it from others. Your internal homogeneity would be lost, meaning that disagreements between you would intensify; and the balance of power between the various communities would also be affected, meaning that some might try to dominate others. Under such circumstances, too, you would need much more in the way of organization. On the other hand, if the island were full of hostile natives, you would not be able to split up: you would have to stick together and coordinate your activities. And this would also force you to become more organized.

Let us assume that you have retained your internal homogeneity, but need a formal leader to coordinate your activities vis-à-vis dangerous outsiders: you elect a chief. Your chief might be able to go on producing his own food. (In fact, one would scarcely call him a chief, as opposed to a king or the like, if he did not.) But if his official duties were too time-consuming for him to engage in food production, how would he be able to live? Obviously, you would have to grow his food for him. But your chief might also need some people to help him on a full-time basis. For example, the natives might be so dangerous that it would be a good idea for some of you to form a standing army. If so, the rest of you would have to grow food for these soldiers too. But how much extra food should each of you produce, how should it be collected, how much should the recipients receive, and who should keep accounts of what is due and what has been handed over? Some of you would have to become administrators, and the rest of you would have to produce food on their behalf on top of everything else. But then you might find that you needed buildings for the quartering of the soldiers, the filing of administrative records, the storage of grain handed over, and so on; and the soldiers would need arms, clothes and cooking pots, while the administrators would need their pens and writing paper. So some of you would start producing buildings, pots, pans, clothes, arms, writing material and so on over and above your own needs, or indeed specialize in such production in return for some of that food which the soldiers and administrators have received from the rest of you; some would start trading in all these goods, and no doubt others would start specializing in the transmission of skills (e.g. teaching the administrators to read and write)....

I had better emphasize that the thought experiment should not be taken as an account of how the first civilizations in history arose. For one thing, we landed on our island fully aware of such things as agriculture, writing, administration and government. We reconstituted them in our new setting, but we did not invent them from scratch, and it is by no means obvious that we would have invented them if we had not known about them.... For another thing, the thought experiment completely fails to account for one element of fundamental importance in all human societies (and in the emergence of complex organization too), that is religion....

Whatever the circumstances behind the emergence of the first civilizations, however, all primitive societies develop into complex ones by division of labor, and this is the point which the thought experiment is meant to illustrate.

❖

2. THE DESCENT OF ISHTAR

One of the earliest, and most important, phenomena perceived by early man was the vegetation cycle: at some times of the year crops grow, at other times they do not. Why? The following myth, from ancient Mesopotamia, is an attempt to explain this phenomenon. How does it do so? Do you find the attempt successful? Why, or why not? Who is Ishtar? Why should she be involved in this myth? What does the myth reveal about the Mesopotamian attitude toward death? Do you know any other myths which deal with the same subject? How do they compare with this one? How are they different?

To the land of no return, the land of darkness,
Ishtar, the daughter of the Moon-God, directed her thoughts,
Directed her thought, Ishtar, the daughter of Sin,
To the house of shadows, the dwelling of Irkalla,
To the house without exit for him who enters therein,
To the road whence there is no turning.
To the house without light for him who enters therein,
The place where dust is their nourishment, clay their food.
They have no light, in darkness they dwell.
Clothed like birds, with wings as garments,
Over door and bolt, dust has gathered.
Ishtar on arriving at the gate of the land of no return,
To the gate-keeper thus addressed herself:
"Gate-keeper, ho, open thy gate!
Open thy gate that I may enter!
If thou openest not the gate to let me enter,
I will break the door, I will wrench the lock,
I will smash the door-posts, I will force the doors.
I will bring up the dead to eat the living.
(And) the dead will outnumber the living."
The gate-keeper opened his mouth and spoke,

Spoke to the lady Ishtar:
"Desist, O lady, do not destroy it.
I will go and announce thy name to my queen Ereshkigal."
The gate-keeper entered and spoke (to Ereshkigal):
"Ho! here is thy sister, Ishtar...
Hostility of the great powers (?)..."
When Ereshkigal heard this,
As when one hews down a tamarisk (she trembled?)
As when one cuts a reed, (she shook?):
"What has moved her heart, what has (stirred) her liver?
Ho there, (does) this one (wish to dwell?) with me?
To eat clay as food, to drink (dust?) as wine?
I weep for the men who have left their wives.
I weep for the wives (torn) from the embrace of their husbands;
For the little ones (cut off) before their time.
Go, gate-keeper, open thy gate for her,
Deal with her according to the ancient decree."
The gate-keeper went and opened his gate to her:
"Enter, O lady, let Cuthah greet thee.
Let the palace of the land of no return rejoice at thy presence!"
He bade her enter the first gate which he opened wide, and took the large crown off her head:
"Why, O gate-keeper, dost thou remove the large crown off my head?"
"Enter, O lady, such are the decrees of Ereshkigal."
The second gate he bade her enter, opening wide and removed her earrings:
"Why, O gate-keeper, dost thou remove my earrings?"
"Enter, O lady, for such are the decrees of Ereshkigal."
The third gate he bade her enter, opened it wide and removed her necklace:
"Why, O gate-keeper, dost thou remove my necklace?"
"Enter, O lady, for such are the decrees of Ereshkigal."
The fourth gate he bade her enter, opened it wide and removed the ornaments of her breast:
"Why, O gate-keeper, dost thou remove the ornaments of my breast?"

"Enter, O lady, for such are the decrees of
  Ereshkigal."
The fifth gate he bade her enter, opened it
  wide and removed the girdle of her body
  studded with birth-stones.
"Why, O gate-keeper, dost thou remove the
  girdle of my body, studded with birth-
  stones?"
"Enter, O lady, for such are the decrees of
  Ereshkigal."
The sixth gate, he bade her enter, opened it
  wide and removed the spangles off her
  hands and feet.
"Why, O gate-keeper, dost thou remove the
  spangles off my hands and feet?"
"Enter, O lady, for thus are the decrees of
  Ereshkigal."
The seventh gate he bade her enter, opened it
  wide and removed her loin-cloth.
"Why, O gate-keeper, dost thou remove my
  loin-cloth?"
"Enter, O lady, for such are the decrees of
  Ereshkigal."
Now when Ishtar had gone down into the
  land of no return,
Ereshkigal saw her and was angered at her
  presence. Ishtar without reflection threw
  herself at her.
Ereshkigal opened her mouth and spoke,
To Namtar, her messenger, she addressed
  herself:
"Go Namtar, (imprison her) in my palace.
Send against her sixty diseases, (to punish?
  Ishtar.)
Eye disease against her eyes,
Disease of the side against her side,
Foot-disease against her foot,
Heart disease against her heart,
Head-disease against her head,
Against her whole being, against (her entire
  body?)."
After the lady Ishtar had gone down into the
  land of no return,
The bull did not mount the cow, the ass ap-
  proached not the she-ass.
To the maid in the street, no man drew near,
The man slept in his apartment,
The maid slept by herself.
The countenance of Papsukal, the messenger
  of the great gods fell, his face (was trou-
  bled).
In mourning garbs he was clothed, in soiled
  garments clad.

Shamash [the sun-god] went to Sin, his father,
  weeping,
In the presence of Ea, the king, he went with
  flowing tears.
"Ishtar has descended into the earth and has
  not come up.
The bull does not mount the cow, the ass does
  not approach the she-ass.
The man does not approach the maid in the
  street,
The man sleeps in his apartment,
The maid sleeps by herself."
Ea in the wisdom of his heart formed a being,
He formed Asu-shu-namir, the eunuch.
"Go, Asu-shu-namir, to the land of no return
  direct thy face!
The seven gates of the land without return be
  opened before thee,
May Ereshkigal at sight of thee rejoice!
After her heart has been assuaged, her liver
  quieted,
Invoke against her the name of the great gods,
Raise thy head, direct (thy) attention to the
  khalziku skin."
"Come, lady, let them give me the khalziku
  skin, that I may drink water out of it."
When Ereshkigal heard this, she struck her
  side, bit her finger, "Thou hast expressed a
  wish that cannot be granted.
Go, Asu-shu-namir, I curse thee with a great
  curse,
The sweepings of the gutters of the city be thy
  food,
The drains of the city be thy drink,
The shadow of the wall be thy abode,
The thresholds be thy dwelling-place;
Drunkard and sot strike thy cheek!"
Ereshkigal opened her mouth and spoke,
To Namtar, her messenger, she addressed
  herself.
"Go, Namtar, knock at the strong palace,
Strike the threshold of precious stones,
Bring out the Anunnaki, seat (them) on
  golden thrones.
Sprinkle Ishtar with the waters of life and take
  her out of my presence."
Namtar went, knocked at the strong palace,
Tapped on the threshold of precious stones.
He brought out the Anunnaki and placed
  them on golden thrones,
He sprinkled Ishtar with the waters of life and
  took hold of her.

Through the first gate he led her out and returned to her her loin-cloth.

Through the second gate he led her out and returned to her the spangles of her hands and feet.

Through the third gate he led her out and returned to her the girdle of her body, studded with birth-stones.

Through the fourth gate he led her out and returned to her the ornaments of her breast.

Through the fifth gate he led her out and returned to her her necklace.

Through the sixth gate he led her out and returned to her her earrings.

Through the seventh gate he led her out and returned to her the large crown for her head.

✝

3. THE CODE OF HAMMURABI

In addition to natural phenomena, the Mesopotamians sought to rationalize human activity. Settled life greatly increased the complexity of this activity, and hence the number of disputes to be resolved, while growth in size of states made it impossible for the king to be everywhere at once. As early as c. 2200 B.C., kings were issuing codes of law so that judgments and penalties might be uniform throughout their domains. One such was issued by the Babylonian king HAMMURABI (c. 1792-1750 B.C.). It survives as a document of prime historical importance, for laws—by telling us what sort of situations required regulation— tell us much about the values and organization of a society. What do these laws tell you about Hammurabi's Babylon? Do they strike you as "fair?" What types of people do they deal with? In whose interests were they made? How highly civilized a society do they deal with?

There are other issues to consider. Laws depend for their force on something greater. What is the "something greater" in the Code? Are any principles of justice expressed? Are they implied? Are these what the laws derive from? Who guarantees and enforces these laws? What provisions, if any, has Hammurabi made for disobedience by his officials? How organized does the code seem: are the laws in random order, or can you perceive some categories? The answers to these questions can reveal much about the level of sophistication of Hammurabi's government.

PROLOGUE

After the lofty Anu, king of the Anunnaki, and Enlil, lord of heaven and earth, he who determines the destiny of the land, committed the rule of all mankind to Marduk, the chief son of Ea; after they made him great among the Igigi; after they pronounced the lofty name of Babylon and made it famous among the quarters of the world...at that time Anu and Enlil called me, Hammurabi, the exalted prince, the worshipper of the gods, to cause justice to prevail in the land, to destroy the wicked and the evil, to prevent the strong from oppressing the weak, to go forth like the Sun over the Black Head Race, to enlighten the land, and to further the welfare of the people. Hammurabi, the Governor named by Enlil am I, who brought about plenty and abundance...the descendant of Sumulailu, the powerful son of Sinmu-ballit, the ancient seed of royalty, the powerful king, the Sun of Babylon, who caused light to go forth over the lands of Sumer and Akkad; the king, who caused the four quarters of the world to render obedience; the favorite of Ishtar, am I. When Marduk sent me to rule the people and to bring help to the country, I established law and justice in the land and promoted the welfare of the people.

THE CODE

1 If a man bring an accusation against a man, and charge him with a (capital) crime, but cannot prove it, he, the accuser, shall be put to death.

2. If a man charge a man with sorcery, and cannot prove it, he who is charged with sorcery shall go to the river, into the river he shall throw himself, and if the river overcome him, his accuser shall take to himself his house. If the river show that man to be innocent, and he come forth unharmed, he who charged him with sorcery shall be put to death. He who threw himself into the river shall take to himself the house of his accuser.[1]

3. If a man, in a case (pending judgment), bear false witness or do not establish the testimony

---

[1]Cf. Exod. 22.18; Deut. 18.10; Jer. 27.9.

that he has given, if that case be a case involving life, that man shall be put to death.[1]

4. If a man bear witness for grain or money (as a bribe), he shall himself bear the penalty imposed in that case.

5. If a judge pronounce a judgment, render a decision, deliver a verdict duly signed and sealed, and afterward alter his judgment, they shall call that judge to account for the alteration of the judgment which he had pronounced, and he shall pay twelve-fold the penalty which was in said judgment; and, in the assembly, they shall expel him from his seat of judgment, and he shall not return, and with the judges in a case he shall not take his seat.

6. If a man steal the property of god (temple) or palace, that man shall be put to death; and he who receives from his hand the stolen (property) shall also be put to death.[2]

7. If a man purchase silver or gold, manservant or maidservant, ox, sheep, or ass, or anything else from a man's son, or from a man's servant without witnesses or contracts, or if he receive (the same) in trust, that man shall be put to death as a thief.[3]

8. If a man steal ox or sheep, ass or pig, or boat—if it be from a god (temple) or a palace—he shall restore thirty-fold; if it be from a freeman, he shall render tenfold. If the thief have nothing wherewith to pay, he shall be put to death.[4]

14. If a man steal a man's son who is a minor, he shall be put to death.[5]

15. If a man aid a male or a female slave of the palace, or a male or a female slave of a freeman, to escape from the city gate, he shall be put to death.

16. If a man harbor in his house a male or female slave who has fled from the palace or from a freeman, and do not bring him (the

slave) forth at the call of the commandant, the owner of the house shall be put to death.[6]

17. If a man seize a male or female slave, a fugitive, in the field, and bring that (slave) back to his owner, the owner of the slave shall pay him two shekels of silver.[7]

18. If that slave will not name his owner, he shall bring him to the palace, and they shall inquire into his antecedents, and they shall return him to his owner.

21 If a man make a breach in a house, they shall put him to death in front of that breach, and they shall thrust him therein.[8]

22. If a man practice brigandage and be captured, that man shall be put to death.

23. If the brigand be not captured, the man who has been robbed shall, in the presence of the god, make an itemized statement of his loss, and the city and the governor, in whose province and jurisdiction the robbery was committed, shall compensate him for whatever was lost.[9]

24. If it be a life (that is lost), the city and governor shall pay one mina of silver to his people.[10]

25. If a fire break out in a man's house, and a man who goes to extinguish it cast his eye on the property of the owner of the house and take the property of the owner of the house, that man shall be thrown into that fire.

42. If a man rent a field for cultivation and do not produce any grain in the field, they shall call him to account because he has not performed the necessary work in the field, and he shall give to the owner of the field grain on the basis of the adjacent (fields).

45. If a man has given his field to a tenant for crop-rent, and receive the crop-rent of his field, and later Adad (i.e., the Storm God) inundate the field and carry away the produce, the loss (falls on) the tenant.

---

[1]Cf. Deut. 19.19; Exod. 23.8.
[2]Cf. Gen. 31.32; Josh. 7.1f.
[3]Cf. Gen. 23.10f.; Ruth 4.2f.
[4]Cf. Gen. 40.9; Exod. 21.37, 22.1f, 9; 2 Sam. 12.6.
[5]Cf. Exod. 21.16; Deut. 24.7.

[6]Cf. Deut. 23.15f.; 1 Sam. 30.15.
[7]Cf. Gen. 16.7f; Deut. 23.16; 1 Kings 2.39.
[8]Cf. Exod. 22.2, 3.
[9]Cf. Deut. 21.1f.
[10]Cf. Deut. 21.1f.

48. If a man owe a debt, and Adad inundate his field and carry away the produce, or, through lack of water, grain have not grown in the field, in that year he shall not make any return of grain to the creditor, he shall alter his contract-tablet, and he shall not pay the interest for that year.

53. If a man neglect to strengthen his dike and do not strengthen it, and a break be made in his dike and the water carry away the farm-land, the man in whose dike the break has been made shall restore the grain which he has caused to be lost.

54. If he be not able to restore the grain, they shall sell him and his goods, and the farmers whose grain the water has carried away shall share (the results of the sale).[1]

55. If a man open his canal for irrigation and neglect it, and the water carry away an adjacent field, he shall measure out grain on the basis of the adjacent fields.

57. If a shepherd have not come to an agreement with the owner of a field to pasture his sheep on the grass; and if he pasture his sheep on the field without the consent of the owner, the owner of the field shall harvest his field, and the shepherd who has pastured his sheep on the field without the consent of the owner of the field shall give over and above 20 GUR of grain per GAN to the owner of the field.

102. If a merchant give money to an agent as a favor, and the latter meet with a reverse where he goes, he shall return the principal of the money to the merchant.

103. If, when he goes on a journey, an enemy rob him of anything he was carrying, the agent shall take an oath in the name of the god and go free.

108. If a wine-seller do not receive grain in payment of drink, but if she receive money by the great stone, or make the measure for drink smaller than the measure for grain, they shall call that barwine-seller to account, and they shall throw her into the water.

109. If outlaws collect in the house of a wine-seller, and she do not arrest these outlaws and bring them to the palace, that wine-seller shall be put to death.

110. If a votary, who is not living in a convent, open a wine-shop or enter a wine-shop for a drink, they shall burn that woman.[2]

117. If a man be in debt and sell his wife, son, or daughter, or bind them over to service, for three years they shall work in the house of their purchaser or master; in the fourth year they shall be given their freedom.[3]

126. If a man have not lost anything, but say that he has lost something, or if he file a claim for loss when nothing has been lost, he shall declare his (alleged) loss in the presence of the god, and he shall double and pay for the (alleged) loss the amount for which he made claim.[4]

127. If a man point the finger at a votary or the wife of another and cannot justify it, they shall drag that man before the judges and they shall brand his forehead.

128. If a man take a wife and do not draw up a contract with her, that woman is not a wife.

129. If the wife of a man be taken in lying with another man, they shall bind them and throw them into the water. If the husband of the woman would save his wife, or if the king would save his male servant (he may).[5]

130. If a man force the (betrothed) wife of another who has not known a male and is living in her father's house, and he lie in her bosom and they take him, that man shall be put to death and that woman shall go free.[6]

131. If a man accuse his wife and she has not been taken in lying with another man, she shall take an oath in the name of the god and she shall return to her house.

132. If the finger have been pointed at the wife of a man because of another man, and she have not been taken in lying with another

---

[1]Cf. Exod. 23.3; Lev. 25.39f.

[2]Cf. Gen. 38.24; Lev. 21.9.

[3]Cf. Gen. 31.41. 47.19; Exod. 21.2, 7; Lev. 25.39f.; Deut. 15.12, 14, 18; 2 Kings 4.1; Neh. 5.5f; Isa. 16.14, 21.16, 50.1; Jer. 34.8; Amos 2.6, 8.

[4]Cf. Exod. 22.9.

[5]Cf. Gen. 38.24; Lev. 20.10; Deut. 22.22f.

[6]Cf. Exod. 22.16; Deut. 22.23f.

man, for her husband's sake she shall throw herself into the river.[1]

134. If a man be captured and there be no maintenance in his house, and his wife enter into another house, that woman has no blame.

135. If a man be captured and there be no maintenance in his house, and his wife openly enter into another house and bear children; if later her husband return and arrive in his city, that woman shall return to her husband (and) the children shall go to their father.

136. If a man desert his city and flee, and afterwards his wife enter into another house; if that man return and would take his wife, the wife of the fugitive shall not return to her husband, because he hated his city and fled.

138. If a man would put away his wife who has not borne him children, he shall give her money to the amount of her marriage settlement, and he shall make good to her the dowry which she brought from her father's house and then he may put her away.[2]

139. If there were no marriage settlement, he shall give to her 1 mina of silver for a divorce.

140. If he be a freeman, he shall give her one-third mina of silver.

141. If the wife of a man who is living in his house set her face to go out and play the part of a fool, neglect her house, belittle her husband, they shall call her to account; if her husband say: "I have put her away," he shall let her go. On her departure nothing shall be given to her for her divorce. If her husband say: "I have not put her away," her husband may take another woman. The first woman shall dwell in the house of her husband as a maid-servant.

142. If a woman hate her husband, and say: "Thou shalt not have me," they shall inquire into her antecedents for her defects, and if she have been a careful mistress and be without reproach, and her husband have been going about and greatly belittling her, that woman has no blame. She shall receive her dowry and go to her father's house.

143. If she have not been a careful mistress, have gadded about, have neglected her house and have belittled her husband, they shall throw that woman into the water.

144. If a man take a wife and that wife give a maid-servant to her husband and she bear children; if that man set his face to take a concubine, they shall not countenance him. He may not take a concubine.[3]

145. If a man take a wife and she do not present him with children and he set his face to take a concubine, that man may take a concubine and take her into his house. That concubine shall not rank with his wife.

146. If a man take a wife and she give a maid-servant to her husband, and that maid-servant bear children and afterwards would take rank with her mistress; because she has borne children, her mistress may not sell her for money, but she may reduce her to bondage and count her among the maid-servants.[4]

147. If she have not borne children, her mistress may sell her for money.

148. If a man take a wife and she become afflicted with disease, and he set his face to take another, he may. His wife, who is afflicted with disease, he shall not put away. She shall remain in the house which he has built and he shall maintain her as long as she lives.

149. If that woman do not elect to remain in her husband's house, he shall make good to her the dowry which she brought from her father's house, and she may go.

150. If a man give to his wife field, garden, house, or goods, and he deliver to her a sealed deed, after (the death of) her husband, her children cannot make claim against her. The mother after her (death) may will to her child whom she loves, but to a brother she may not.

151. If a woman, who dwells in the house of a man, make a contract with her husband that a creditor of his may not hold her (for his debts) and compel him to deliver a written agreement; if that man were in debt before he took that woman, his creditor may not hold his

---

[1]Cf. Num. 5.12f.
[2]Cf. Deut. 24.1.

[3]Cf. Gen. 16.1f., 21.10f., 30.3f., 9f.
[4]Cf. Gen. 16.4f., 21.10; Deut. 21.14; 1 Sam 1.1f.

wife, and if that woman were in debt before she entered into the house of the man, her creditor may not hold her husband.

152. If they contract a debt after the woman has entered into the house of the man, both of them shall be answerable to the merchant.

153. If a woman bring about the death of her husband for the sake of another man, they shall impale her.

154. If a man have known his daughter, they shall expel that man from the city.

155. If a man have betrothed a bride to his son and if after his son have known her he (the father) lie in her bosom and they take him, they shall bind that man and throw him into the water.[1]

156. If a man have betrothed a bride to his son and his son have not yet known her, but he himself lie in her bosom, he shall pay her one-half mina of silver and he shall make good to her whatever she brought from the house of her father, and the man of her choice may take her.[2]

157. If a man, after the death of his father, lie in the bosom of his mother, they shall burn both of them.

158. If a man, after (the death of) his father, be taken in the bosom of the chief wife (of his father) who has borne children, that man shall be cut off from his father's house.[3]

159. If a man, who has brought a present to the house of his father-in-law and has given the marriage settlement, look with longing upon another woman and say to his father-in-law, "I will not take thy daughter," the father of the daughter shall take to himself whatever was brought to him.

160. If a man bring a present to the house of his father-in-law and give a marriage settlement, and the father of the daughter say, "I will not give thee my daughter," he (i.e., the father-in-law) shall double the amount which was brought to him and return it.

161. If a man bring a present to the house of his father-in-law and give a marriage settlement, and his friend slander him; and if his father-in-law say to the claimant, "My daughter thou shalt not have," he (the father-in-law) shall double the amount which was brought to him and return it, but his friend may not have his wife.

167. If a man take a wife and she bear him children, and that woman die, and after her (death) he take another wife and she bear him children, and later the father die, the children shall not divide (the estate) according to the rank of the mothers. They shall receive the dowries of their respective mothers and they shall divide equally the goods of the house of their father.

168. If a man set his face to disinherit his son, and say to the judges: "I will disinherit my son," the judges shall inquire into his antecedents, and if the son have not committed a crime sufficiently grave to cut him off from sonship, the father may not cut off his son from sonship.[4]

169. If he have committed a crime against his father sufficiently grave to cut him off from sonship, they shall condone his first (offense). If he commit a grave crime a second time, the father may cut off his son from sonship.[5]

175. If either a slave of the palace or a slave of a freeman take the daughter of a man (gentleman) and she bear children, the owner of the slave may not lay claim to the children of the daughter of the man for service.

178. If (there be) a votary or a devotee to whom her father has given a dowry and written a deed of gift; if in the deed which he has written for her, he have not written "after her (death) she may give to whomseoever she may please," and if he have not granted her full discretion; after her father dies her brothers shall take her field and garden and they shall give her grain, oil, and wool according to the value of her share, and they shall make her content. If her brothers do not give her grain, oil, and wool according to the value of her share and they do not make her content, she

[1]Cf. Gen. 24.4f.
[2]Cf. Exod. 22.16; Lev. 20.12; Deut. 22.28.
[3]Cf. Lev. 20.11; Deut. 22.30.
[4]Cf. Deut. 21:18f.
[5]Cf. Deut. 21.21.

may give her field and garden to any tenant she may please and her tenant shall maintain her. She shall enjoy the field, garden, or anything else which her father gave her as long as she lives. She may not sell it, nor transfer it. Her heritage belongs to her brothers.

179. If (there be) a votary or a devotee to whom her father has given a dowry and written a deed of gift; if in the deed which he has written for her, he have "after her (death) she may give to whomsoever she may please," and he have granted her full discretion; after her father dies she may give it to whomsoever she may please after her (death). Her brothers may not lay claim against her.

180. If a father do not give a dowry to his daughter, a bride or devotee, after her father dies she shall receive as her share in the goods of her father's house the portion of a son, and she shall enjoy it as long as she lives. After her (death) it belongs to her brothers.

181. If a father devote a votary or hierodule or virgin to a god and do not give her a dowry, after her father dies she shall receive as her share in the goods of her father's house one-third of the portion of a son, and she shall enjoy it as long as she lives. After her (death) it belongs to her brothers.

182. If a father do not give a dowry to his daughter, a votary of Marduk of Babylon, and do not write for her a deed of gift; after her father dies she shall receive as her share with her brothers one-third the portion of a son in the goods of her father's house, but she shall not conduct the business thereof. A votary of Marduk after her (death), may give to whomsoever she may please.

188. If an artisan take a son for adoption and teach him his handicraft, one may not bring claim for him.

189. If he do not teach him his handicraft, that adopted son may return to his father's house.

190. If a man do not reckon among his sons the young child whom he has taken for a son and reared, that adopted son may return to his father's house.

192. If the [adopted] son of a NER SE GA, or the son of a devotee, say to his father who has reared him, or to his mother who has reared him, "My father thou art not," "My mother thou art not," they shall cut out his tongue.

193. If the [adopted] son of a NER SE GA, or the son of a devotee, identify his [natural] father's house and hate the father who has reared him and the mother who has reared him and go back to his [natural] father's house, they shall pluck out his eye.[1]

194. If a man give his son to a nurse and that son die in the hands of the nurse, and the nurse substitute another son without the consent of his father or mother, they shall call her to account, and because she has substituted another son without the consent of his father or mother, they shall cut off her breasts.

195. If a son strike his father, they shall cut off his fingers.[2]

196. If a man destroy the eye of a man (gentleman), they shall destroy his eye.[3]

197. If one break a man's bone, they shall break his bone.

198. If one destroy the eye of a freeman or break the bone of a freeman, he shall pay 1 mina of silver.

199. If one destroy the eye of a man's slave or break a bone of a man's slave, he shall pay one-half his price.[4]

200. If a man knock out a tooth of a man of his own rank, they shall knock out his tooth.[5]

201. If one knock out the tooth of a freeman, he shall pay one-third mina of silver.

202. If a man strike a man who is his superior, he shall receive 60 strokes with an ox-tail whip in public.

203. If a man strike a man of his own rank, he shall pay 1 mina of silver.

---

[1]Cf. Prov. 30.17.
[2]Cf. Exod. 21.15, 17.
[3]Cf. Exod. 21.23-25; Lev. 24.20; Deut. 19.21; Matt. 5.38.
[4]Cf. Exod. 21.26f.
[5]Cf. Exod. 21.24.

204. If a freeman strike a freeman, he shall pay 10 shekels of silver.

205. If a man's slave strike a man's son, they shall cut off his ear.

206. If a man strike another man in a quarrel and wound him, he shall swear, "I strike him without intent," and he shall be responsible for the physician.[1]

207. If (he) die as the result of the stroke, he shall swear (as above), and if he be a man, he shall pay one-half mina of silver.[2]

208. If (he) be a freeman, he shall pay one-third mina of silver.

209. If a man strike a man's daughter and bring about a miscarriage, he shall pay 10 shekels of silver for her miscarriage.[3]

210. If that woman die, they shall put his daughter to death.

211. If, through a stroke, he bring about a miscarriage to the daughter of a freeman, he shall pay 5 shekels of silver.

212. If that woman die, he shall pay one-half mina of silver.

213. If he strike the female slave of a man and bring about a miscarriage, he shall pay 2 shekels of silver.

214. If that female slave die, he shall pay one-third mina of silver.

215. If a physician operate on a man for a severe wound (or make a severe wound upon a man) with a bronze lancet and save the man's life; or if he open an abscess (in the eye) of a man with a bronze lancet and save that man's eye, he shall receive 10 shekels of silver (as his fee).

216. If he be a freeman, he shall receive 5 shekels.

217. If it be a man's slave, the owner of the slave shall give 2 shekels of silver to the physician.

218. If a physician operate on a man for a severe wound with a bronze lancet and cause the man's death; or open an abscess (in the eye) of a man with a bronze lancet and destroy the man's eye, they shall cut off his fingers.

219. If a physician operate on a slave of a freeman for a severe wound with a bronze lancet and cause his death, he shall restore a slave of equal value.

220. If he open an abscess (in his eye) with a bronze lancet, and destroy his eye, he shall pay silver to the extent of one-half of his price.

221. If a physician set a broken bone for a man or cure his diseased bowels, the patient shall give 5 shekels of silver to the physician.

222. If he be a freeman, he shall give 3 shekels of silver.

223. If it be a man's slave, the owner of the slave shall give 2 shekels of silver to the physician.

224. If a veterinary surgeon operate on an ox or an ass for a severe wound and save its life, the owner of the ox or ass shall give to the physician, as his fee, one-sixth of a shekel of silver.

225. If he operate on an ox or an ass for a severe wound and cause its death, he shall give to the owner of the ox or ass one-fourth its value.

226. If a brander, without the consent of the owner of the slave, brand a slave with the sign that he cannot be sold, they shall cut off the fingers of that brander.

229. If a builder build a house for a man and do not make its construction firm, and the house which he has built collapse and cause the death of the owner of the house, that builder shall be put to death.

230. If it cause the death of a son of the owner of the house, they shall put to death a son of that builder.[4]

231. If it cause the death of a slave of the owner of the house, he shall give to the owner of the house a slave of equal value.

---

[1]Cf. Exod. 21.18f.; Num. 35.16f.; Deut. 19.4f.
[2]Cf. Exod. 21.18f.; Num. 35.16f.; Deut. 19.4f.
[3]Cf. Exod. 21.22.

[4]Cf. Deut. 24.16.

232. If it destroy property, he shall restore whatever is destroyed, and because he did not make the house which he built firm and it collapsed, he shall rebuild the house which collapsed from his own property.

240. If a boat under way strike a ferryboat (or boat at anchor) and sink it, the owner of the boat whose boat was sunk shall make declaration in the presence of the god of everything that was lost in his boat and (the owner) of (the vessel) under way which sank the ferryboat shall replace his boat and whatever was lost.

244. If a man hire an ox or an ass and a lion kill it in the field, it is the owner's affair.

245. If a man hire an ox and cause its death through neglect or abuse, he shall restore an ox of equal value to the owner of the ox.[1]

251. If a man's bull have been wont to gore, and they have made known to him his habit of goring and he have not protected his horns or have not tied him up, and the bull gore the son of a man and bring about his death, he shall pay one-half mina of silver.[2]

252. If it be the servant of a man, he shall pay one-third mina of silver.[3]

265. If a shepherd, to whom oxen or sheep have been given to pasture, have become dishonest or have altered the price, or sold them, they shall call him to account and he shall restore to their owner oxen and sheep tenfold what he has stolen.

266. If a visitation of god happen to a fold, or a lion kill, the shepherd shall declare himself innocent before the god, and the owner of the fold shall suffer the damage.[4]

278. If a man sell a male or female slave, and the slave have not completed his month, and the *bennu* fever fall upon him, he (the purchaser) shall return him to the seller, and he shall receive the money which he paid.

---

[1]Cf. Exod. 22.10f.
[2]Cf. Exod. 21.29f.
[3]Cf. Exod. 21.32.
[4]Cf. Exod. 22.10f.; John 10.12.

Epilogue

The righteous laws, which Hammurabi, the wise king, established and (by which) he gave the land stable support and pure government. Hammurabi, the perfect king, am I. I was not careless, nor was I neglectful of the Black Head people, whose rule Enlil presented and Marduk delivered to me....

The great gods proclaimed me and I am the guardian governor, whose scepter is righteous and whose beneficent protection is spread over my city. In my bosom I carried the peoples of the land of Sumer and Akkad...that the strong might not oppose the weak, and that they should give justice to the orphan and the widow...my weighty words I have written upon my monument, and in the presence of my image as king of righteousness have I established.

The king who is pre-eminent among city kings am I. My words are precious, my wisdom is unrivaled.... Let any oppressed man, who has a cause, come before my image as king of righteousness! Let him give heed to my weighty words! And may my monument enlighten him as to his cause, and may he understand his case! May he set his heart at ease!

In the days that are yet to come, for all future time, may the king who is in the land observe the words of righteousness which I have written upon my monument! May he not alter the judgments of the land which I have pronounced, or the decisions of the country which I have rendered! May he not efface my statues!.... Let him root out the wicked and evil-doer from his land! Let him promote the welfare of his people!....

If that man pay attention to my words...then will Shamash prolong that man's reign, as he has mine, who am king of righteousness, that he may rule his people in righteousness.

If that man do not pay attention to my words...may the great god, the father of the gods, who has ordained my reign, take from him the glory of his sovereignty, may he break his scepter and curse his fate!

May Enlil, the lord, who determines of destinies, whose command cannot be altered, who has enlarged my domain, drive him out from his dwelling through a revolt which his hand cannot control and a curse destructive to him! May he determine as his fate a reign of sighs, days few in number, years of famine, darkness without light, death staring him in the face!

May Ea, the great prince, whose decrees take precedence, the leader of the gods, who knows everything; who prolongs the days of my life, deprive him of knowledge and wisdom! May he bring him to oblivion, and dam up his rivers at their sources! May he not permit corn, which is the life of the people, to grow in his land!

May Shamash, the great judge of heaven and earth, who rules all living creatures, the lord (inspiring) confidence, overthrow his dominion; may he not grant him his right!... May the blighting curse of Shamash come upon him quickly! May he cut off his life above (upon the earth)! Below, within the earth, may he deprive his spirit of water!

May Ishtar, goddess of battle and conflict, who makes ready my weapons, the gracious protecting deity, who loves my reign, curse his dominion with great fury in her wrathful heart, and turn good into evil for him! May she shatter his weapons on the field of battle and conflict! May she create confusion and revolt for him! May she strike down his warriors, may their blood water the earth! May she cast the bodies of his warriors upon the field in heaps! May she not grant his warriors [burial (?)]! May she deliver him into the hands of his enemies, and may they carry him away bound into a hostile land!

May the great gods of heaven and earth, the Anunnaki in their assembly, curse with blighting curses the wall of the temple, the construction of the E-babbarra, his seed, his land, his army, his people, and his troops!

†

4. HEBREW LAW

The code of Hammurabi represents one type of law to come to us from the Ancient Near East. Another is the body of HEBREW LAW, parts of which are reproduced here for comparative purposes. Ask yourself the same questions you just put to Hammurabi's laws: where do these laws come from? Why should they be obeyed? What type of people do they seem to deal

with—the same as Hammurabi's? Are their concerns the same? If you were presented these two sets of laws without identification, what distinctions could you make between them? How do you account for the similarities between these laws and Hammurabi's? The differences?

Here, too, there is a question of enforcement. Compare Moses' words in Deuteronomy with those of Hammurabi in the Conclusion of his Code. How are they the same? How different?

A. THE BOOK OF EXODUS

CHAPTER 19

7 So Moses came and called the elders of the people, and set before them all these words which the Lord had commanded him. 8 And all the people answered together and said, "All that the Lord has spoken we will do." And Moses reported the words of the people to the Lord. 9 And the Lord said to Moses, "Lo, I am coming to you in a thick cloud, that the people may hear when I speak with you, and may also believe you for ever."

Then Moses told the words of the people to the Lord. 10 And the Lord said to Moses, "Go to the people and consecrate them today and tomorrow, and let them wash their garments, 11 and be ready by the third day; for on the third day the Lord will come down upon mount Sinai in the sight of all the people. 12 And you shall set bounds for the people round about, saying, 'Take heed that you do not go up into the mountain or touch the border of it; whoever touches the mountain shall be put to death; 13 no hand shall touch him, but he shall be stoned or shot; whether beast or man, he shall not live.' When the trumpet sounds a long blast, they shall come up to the mountain." 14 So Moses went down from the mountain to the people, and consecrated the people; and they washed their garments. 15 And he said to the people, "Be ready by the third day; do not go near a woman."

16 On the morning of the third day there were thunders and lightnings, and a thick cloud upon the mountain, and a very loud trumpet blast, so that all the people who were in the camp trembled. 17 Then Moses brought the people out of the camp to meet God; and they took their stand at the foot of the mountain. 18 And Mount Sinai was wrapped in smoke, because the Lord descended upon it in fire;

and the smoke of it went up as the smoke of a kiln, and the whole mountain quaked greatly. 19 And as the sound of the trumpet grew louder and louder, Moses spoke, and God answered him in thunder. 20 And the Lord came down upon Mount Sinai, to the top of the mountain; and the Lord called Moses *up* to the top of the mountain; and Moses went up. 21 And the Lord said to Moses, "Go down and warn the people, lest they break through to the Lord to gaze and many of them perish. 22 And also let the priests who come near to the Lord consecrate themselves, lest the Lord break out upon them." 23 And Moses said to the Lord, "The people cannot come up to Mount Sinai; for thou thyself didst charge us, saying, 'Set bounds about the mountain, and consecrate it.'" 24 And the Lord said to him, "Go down, and come up bringing Aaron with you; but do not let the priests and the people break through to come up to the Lord, lest he break out against them." 25 So Moses went down to the people, and told them.

CHAPTER 20

And God spoke all these words, saying,

2 "I am the Lord your God, who brought you out of the land of Egypt, out of the house of bondage.

3 "You shall have no other gods before me.

4 "You shall not make for yourself a graven image, or any likeness *of* anything that is in heaven above, or that is in the earth beneath, or that is in the water under the earth; 5 you shall not bow down to them or serve them; for I the Lord your God am a jealous God, visiting the iniquity of the fathers upon the children to the third and fourth *generation* of those who hate me, 6 but showing steadfast love to thousands of those who love me and keep my commandments.

7 "You shall not take the name of the Lord your God in vain; for the Lord will not hold him guiltless who takes his name in vain.

8 "Remember the Sabbath day, to keep it holy. 9 Six days you shall labor, and do all your work; 10 But the seventh day is a Sabbath to the Lord your God; in it you shall not do any work, you, or your son, or your daughter, your manservant, or your maidservant, or your cat-

tle, or the sojourner who is within your gates; 11 For in six days the Lord made heaven and earth, the sea, and all that is in them, and rested the seventh day; wherefore the Lord blessed the Sabbath day and hallowed it.

12 "Honor your father and your mother; that your days may be long in the land which the Lord your God gives you.

13 "You shall not kill.

14 "You shall not commit adultery.

15 "You shall not steal.

16 "You shall not bear false witness against your neighbor.

17 You shall not covet your neighbor's house; you shall not covet your neighbor's wife, or his manservant, or his maidservant, or his ox, or his ass, or anything that is your neighbor's."

18 Now when all the people perceived the thunderings and the lightnings and the sound of the trumpet and the mountain smoking, the people were afraid and trembled; and stood afar off, 19 and they said to Moses, "You speak to us, and we will hear; but let not God speak to us, lest we die." 20 And Moses said to the people, "Do not fear; for God has come to prove you, and that the fear of him may be before your eyes, that you may not sin."

21 And the people stood afar off, while Moses drew near to the thick darkness where God *was.* 22 And the Lord said to Moses, "Thus shall you say to the people of Israel: 'You have seen for yourselves that I have talked with you from heaven. 23 You shall not make gods of silver to be with me, nor shall you make for yourselves gods of gold. 24 An altar of earth you shall make for me, and sacrifice on it your burnt offerings and your peace offerings, your sheep and your oxen; in every place where I cause my name to be remembered I will come to you and bless you. 25 And if you make me an altar of stone, you shall not build it of hewn stones; for if you wield your tool upon it, you profane it. 26 And you shall not go up by steps to my altar, that your nakedness be not exposed on it.'

CHAPTER 21

"Now these *are* the ordinances which you shall set before them. 2 When you buy a Hebrew slave, he shall serve six years, and in the seventh he shall go out free, for nothing. 3 If he comes in single, he shall go out single; if he comes in married, then his wife shall go out with him. 4 If his master gives him a wife and she bears him sons or daughters, the wife and her children shall be her master's and he shall go out alone. 5 But if the slave shall says, 'I love my master, my wife, and my children; I will not go out free,' 6 then his master shall bring him to God, and he shall bring him to the door or the door post; and his master shall bore his ear through with an awl; and he shall serve him for life.

7 "When a man sells his daughter as a slave, she shall not go out as the male slaves do. 8 If she does not please her master, who has designated her for himself, then he shall let her be redeemed; he shall have no right to sell her to a foreign people, since he has dealt faithlessly with her. 9 If he designates her for his son, he shall deal with her as with a daughter. 10 If he take him another wife to himself, he shall not diminish her food, her clothing, or her marital rights. 11 And if he does not do these three for her, she shall go out for nothing, without payment of money.

12 "Whoever strikes a man so that he die shall be put to death. 13 But if he did not lie in wait for him, but God let him fall into his hand, then I will appoint for you a place to which he may flee. 14 But if a man willfully attacks another to kill him treacherously, you shall take him from my altar, that he may die.

15 "Whoever strikes his father or his mother shall be put to death.

16 "Whoever steals a man, whether he sells him or is found in possession of him, shall be put to death.

17 "Whoever curses his father or his mother shall be put to death.

18 "When men quarrel and one strikes the other with a stone or with his fist and he does not die but keeps his bed, 19 then if the man rises again and walks abroad with his staff, he that struck him shall be clear; only he shall pay for the loss of his time, and shall have him thoroughly healed.

20 "When a man strikes his slave, male or female, with a rod, and the slave dies under his hand, he shall be punished. 21 But if the slave survives a day or two, he shall not be punished; for the slave is his money.

22 "When men strive together, and hurt a woman with child, so that there is a miscarriage, and yet no harm follows, the one who hurt her shall be fined, according as the woman's husband shall lay upon him; and he shall pay as the judges determine. 23 If any harm follows, then you shall give life for life, 24 eye for eye, tooth for tooth, hand for hand, foot for foot, 25 burn for burn, wound for wound, stripe for stripe.

26 "When a man strikes the eye of his slave, male or female, and destroys it, he shall let the slave go free for the eye's sake. 27 If he knocks out the tooth of his slave, male or female, he shall let the slave go free for the tooth's sake.

28 "When an ox gores a man or a woman to death, the ox shall be stoned, and its flesh shall not be eaten; but the owner of the ox shall be clear. 29 But if the ox has been accustomed to gore in the past, and its owner has been warned but has not kept it in, and it kills a man or a woman, the ox shall be stoned, and its owner also shall be put to death. 30 If a ransom is laid on him, then he shall give for the redemption of his life whatever is laid upon him. 31 If it gores a man's son or daughter, he shall be dealt with according to this same rule. 32 If the ox gores a slave, male or female, the owner shall give to their master thirty shekels of silver, and the ox shall be stoned.

33 "When a man leaves a pit open, or when a man digs a pit but does not cover it, and an ox or an ass fall into it, 34 the owner of the pit shall make it good; he shall give money to its owner, and the dead beast shall be his.

35 "When one man's ox hurts another's, so that it dies, then they shall sell the live ox and divide the price of it; and the dead beast also they shall divide. 36 Or if it is known that the ox has been accustomed to gore in the past,

and its owner has not kept it in, he shall pay ox for ox, and the dead beast shall be his.

CHAPTER 22

"If a man steals an ox or a sheep, and kills it or sells it, he shall pay five oxen for an ox, and four sheep for a sheep.[1] He shall make restitution; if he has nothing, then he shall be sold for his theft. 4 If the stolen beast be found alive in his possession, whether it is an ox, or an ass, or a sheep, he shall pay double.

2 "If a thief is found breaking in, and is struck so that he dies, there shall be no blood guilt for him; 3 but if the sun has risen upon him, there shall be blood guilt for him.

5 "When a man causes a field or vineyard to be grazed over, or lets his beast loose and it feeds in another man's field, he shall make restitution from the best in his own field and in his own vineyard.

6 "When fire breaks out and catches in thorns so that the stacked grain or the standing grain or the field, is consumed, he that kindled the fire shall make full restitution.

7 "If a man delivers to his neighbor money or good to keep, and it is stolen out of the man's house, then, if the thief is found, he shall pay double. 8 If the thief is not found, the owner of the house shall come near to God, to show whether or not he has put his hand to his neighbor's goods.

9 "For every breach of trust, whether it is for ox, for ass, for sheep, for clothing, or for any kind of lost thing, of which one says, 'This is it,', the case of both parties shall come before God; he whom God shall condemn shall pay double to his neighbor.

10 "If a man delivers to his neighbor an ass or an ox or a sheep or any beast, to keep, and it dies or is hurt or driven away, without anyone seeing it, 11 an oath by the Lord shall be between them both to see whether he has not put his hand to his neighbor's property; and the owner shall accept the oath, and he shall not make restitution. 12 But if it is stolen from him, he shall make restitution to its owner. 13

If it is torn by beasts, let him bring it as evidence; he shall not make restitution for what has been torn.

14 "If a man borrows anything of his neighbor, and it is hurt or dies, the owner not being with it, he shall make full restitution. 15 If the owner was with it, he shall not make restitution; if it was hired, it came for its hire.

16 "If a man seduces a virgin who is not betrothed, and lies with her, he shall give the marriage present for her and make her his wife. 17 If her father utterly refuses to give her to him, he shall pay money equivalent to the marriage present of virgins.

18 "You shall not permit a sorceress to live.

19 "Whoever lies with a beast shall be put to death.

20 "Whoever sacrifices to any god, save to the Lord only, shall be utterly destroyed.

21 "You shall not wrong a stranger or oppress him, for you were strangers in the land of Egypt. 22 You shall not afflict any widow, or orphan. 23 If you do afflict them, and they cry out to me, I will surely hear their cry; 24 and my wrath will burn, and I will kill you with the sword, and your wives shall become widows and your children fatherless.

25 "If you lend money to any *of* my people with you who is poor, you shall not be to him as a creditor, and you shall not exact interest from him. 26 If ever you take your neighbor's garment in pledge, you shall restore it to him before the sun goes down; 27 for that is his only covering, it is his mantle for his body; in what else shall he sleep? And if he cries to me, I will hear; for I am compassionate.

28 "You shall not revile God, nor curse a ruler of your people.

29 "You shall not delay to offer from the fullness of your harvest or the outflow of your presses.

"The first-born of your sons you shall give to me. 30 You shall do likewise with your oxen and with your sheep: seven days it shall be with its dam; on the eighth day you shall give it to me.

---

[1]Restoring the second half of verse 3 with 4 to their place immediately following verse 1.

31 "You shall be men consecrated to me; therefore you shall not eat any flesh that is torn by beasts in the field; you shall cast it to the dogs.

CHAPTER 23

"You shall not utter a false report. You shall not join hands with a wicked man, to be a malicious witness. 2. You shall not follow a multitude to do evil; nor shall you bear witness in a suit, turning aside after a multitude, so as to pervert justice; 3 nor shall you be partial to a poor man in his suit.

4 "If you meet your enemy's ox or his ass going astray, you shall bring it back to him. 5 If you see the ass of one who hates you lying under its burden, you shall refrain from leaving him with it, you shall help him to lift it up.

6 "You shall not pervert the justice due to your poor in his suit. 7 Keep far from a false charge, and do not slay the innocent and righteous, for I will not acquit the wicked. 8 And you shall take no bribe, for a bribe blinds the officials, and subverts the cause of those who are in the right.

9 "You shall not oppress a stranger; for you know the heart of a stranger, for you were strangers in the land of Egypt.

10 "For six years you shall sow your land and gather in its yield; 11 but the seventh year you shall let it rest and lie fallow, that the poor of your people may eat; and what they leave the wild beasts may eat. You shall do likewise with your vineyard, and with your olive orchard.

12 "Six days you shall do your work, but on the seventh day you shall rest; that your ox and your ass may have rest, and the son of your bondmaid, and the alien, may be refreshed. 13 Take heed to all that I have said to you; and make no mention of the names of other gods, nor let such be heard out of your mouth.

14 "Three times in the year you shall keep a feast to me. 15 You shall keep the feast of unleavened bread; as I commanded you, you shall eat unleavened bread for seven days in the month of Abib, for in it you came out of Egypt. None shall appear before me empty-handed. 16 You shall keep the feast of harvest, of the first fruits of your labor, of what you sow in the field. You shall keep the feast of ingathering at the end of the year, when you gather in from the field the fruit of your labor. 17 Three times in the year shall all your males appear before the Lord God.

18 "You shall not offer the blood of my sacrifice with leavened bread, or let the fat of my feast remain until the morning.

19 "The first of the first fruits of your ground you shall bring into the house of the Lord your God.

"You shall not boil a kid in its mother's milk.

20 "Behold, I send an angel before you, to guard you on the way and to bring you into the place which I have prepared. 21 Give heed to him and hearken to his voice, do not rebel against him, for he will not pardon your transgression; for my name is in him.

22 "But if you hearken attentively to his voice and do all that I say, then I will be an enemy to your enemies and an adversary to your adversaries.

23 "When my angel goes before you, and brings you in to the Amorites, and the Hittites, and the Per´izzites, and the Canaanites, the Hivites, and the Jeb´usites; and I blot them out, 24 you shall not bow down to their gods, nor serve them, nor do according to their work; but you shall utterly overthrow them and break their pillars in pieces. 25 You shall serve the Lord your God, and I will bless your bread, and your water; and I will take sickness away from the midst of you. 26 None shall cast her young, or be barren in your land; I will fulfill the number of your days. 27 I will send my terror before you, and will throw into confusion all the people against whom you shall come, and I will make all your enemies turn their backs to you. 28 And I will send hornets before you, which shall drive out Hivite, Canaanite, and Hittite from before you. 29 I will not drive them out from before you in one year, lest the land become desolate and the wild beasts multiply against you. 30 Little by little I will drive them out from before you, until you are increased and possess the land. 31 And I will set your bounds from the Red Sea to the sea of the Philistines, and from the wilderness to the Euphrates; for I

will deliver the inhabitants of the land into your hand, and you shall drive them out before you. 32 You shall make no covenant with them or with their gods. 33 They shall not dwell in your land, lest they make you sin against me; for if you serve their gods, it will surely be a snare to you."

B. DEUTERONOMY

(*The speaker is Moses*); 5 Behold, I have taught you statutes and ordinances, as the Lord my God commanded me, that you should do them in the land which you are entering to possess it. 6 Keep them and do them; for that will be your wisdom and your understanding in the sight of the peoples, who, when they hear all these statutes, will say, 'Surely this great nation is a wise and understanding people.' 7 For what great nation is there that has a god so near to it as the Lord our God is to us? 8 And what great nation is there, that has statutes and ordinances so righteous as all this law which I set before you this day?

9 "Only take heed, and keep your soul diligently, lest you forget the things which your eyes have seen, and lest they depart from your heart all the days of your life; make them known to your children, and your children's children—10 how on the day that you stood before the Lord your God at Horeb, the Lord said to me, 'Gather the people to me, that I may let them hear my words, so that they may learn to fear me all the days that they live upon the earth, and that they may teach their children so. 11 And you came near and stood at the foot of the mountain, while the mountain burned with fire to the heart of heaven, wrapped in darkness, cloud, and gloom. 12 Then the Lord spoke to you out of the midst of the fire; you heard the sound of words, but saw no form; there was only a voice. 13 And he declared to you his covenant, which he commanded you to perform, that is, the ten commandments; and he wrote them upon two tables of stone.

14 And the Lord commanded me at that time to teach you statutes and ordinances, that you might do them in the land which you are going over to possess.

15 Therefore take good heed to yourselves. Since you saw no form on the day that the Lord spoke to you at Horeb out of the midst of the fire, 16 beware lest you act corruptly by making a graven image for yourselves, in the form of any figure, the likeness of male or female, 17 the likeness of any beast that is on the earth, the likeness of any winged bird that flies in the air, 18 the likeness of anything that creeps on the ground, the likeness of any fish that is in the water under the earth; 19 And beware lest you lift up your eyes to heaven, and when you see the sun and the moon and the stars, all the host of heaven, you be drawn away and worship them and serve them, things which the Lord your God has allotted to all the people under the whole heaven. 20 But the Lord has taken you, and brought you forth out of the iron furnace, out of Egypt, to be a people of his own possession, as at this day. 21 Furthermore the Lord was angry with me on your account, and he swore that I should not cross the Jordan, and that I should not enter the good land which the Lord your God gives you for an inheritance. 22 For I must die in this land, I must not go over the Jordan; but you shall go over and take possession of that good land. 23 Take heed to yourselves, lest you forget the covenant of the Lord your God, which he made with you, and make a graven image in the form of anything which the Lord your God has forbidden you. 24 For the Lord your God is a devouring fire, a jealous God.

25 "When you beget children, and children's children, and have grown old in the land, if you act corruptly by making a graven image in the form of anything, and by doing what is evil in the sight of the Lord your God, so as to provoke him to anger; 26 I call heaven and earth to witness against you this day, that you will soon utterly perish from the land which you are going over the Jordan to possess; you will not live long upon it, but will be utterly destroyed. 27 And the Lord will scatter you among the peoples, and you will be left few in number among the nations, where the Lord will drive you. 28 And there you will serve gods of wood and stone, the work of men's hands, that neither see, nor hear, nor eat, nor smell. 29 But from there you will seek the Lord your God, and you will find him, if you search after him with all your heart and with

all your soul. 30 When you are in tribulation, and all these things come upon you in the latter days, you will return to the Lord your God, and obey his voice; 31 for the Lord your God is a merciful God; he will not fail you or destroy you or forget the covenant with your fathers which he swore to them."

✝

5. *THE INSTITUTES OF JUSTINIAN*

The Code of Hammurabi and the Hebrew Law come at the beginning of our period. Here is the Introduction to the *Institutes* of the Roman Emperor JUSTINIAN (A.D. 527-565), who ordered the last great code of law to be compiled in antiquity. More than 2300 years separate Justinian from Hammurabi. What differences do you see in the approach to law of the two rulers? Are there any similarities? At the end of the term, both the similarities and the differences may help you understand what is meant by "the fall of Rome."

IN THE NAME OF OUR LORD
JESUS CHRIST

The Emperor Caesar Flavius Justinianus, vanquisher of the Alamanni, Goths, Francs, Germans, Antes, Alani, Vandals, Africans, pious, happy, glorious, triumphant conqueror, ever August, to the youth desirous of studying the law, greeting.

The imperial majesty should be not only made glorious by arms, but also strengthened by laws, that, alike in time of peace and in time of war, the state may be well governed, and that the emperor may not only be victorious in the field of battle, but also may by every legal means repel the iniquities of men who abuse the laws, and may at once religiously uphold justice and triumph over his conquered enemies.

1. By our incessant labors and great care, with the blessing of God, we have attained this double end. The barbarian nations reduced under our yoke know our efforts in war; to which also Africa and very many other provinces bear witness, which, after so long an interval, have been restored to the dominion of Rome and our empire, by our victories gained through the favor of heaven. All nations moreover are governed by laws which we have already either promulgated or compiled.

2. When we had arranged and brought into perfect harmony the hitherto confused mass of imperial constitutions, we then extended our care to the vast volumes of ancient law; and sailing as it were across the mid-ocean, have now completed, through the favor of heaven, a work that once seemed beyond hope.

3. When by the blessing of God this task was accomplished, we summoned the most eminent Tribonian, master and ex-quaestor of our palace, together with the illustrious Theophilus and Dorotheus, professors of law, all of whom have on many occasions proved to us their ability, legal knowledge, and obedience to our orders; and we have specially charged them to compose, under our authority and advice, Institutes, so that you may no more learn the first elements of law from old and erroneous sources, but apprehend them by the clear light of imperial wisdom; and that your minds and ears may receive nothing that is useless or misplaced, but only what obtains in actual practice. So that, whereas, formerly, the junior students could scarcely, after three years' study, read the imperial constitutions, you may now commence your studies by reading them, you who have been thought worthy of an honor and a happiness so great as that the first and last lessons in the knowledge of the law should issue for you from the mouth of the emperor.

4. When, therefore, by the assistance of the same eminent person Tribonian and that of other illustrious and learned men, we had compiled the fifty books, called Digest or Pandects, in which is collected the whole ancient law, we directed that these Institutes should be divided into four books, which might serve as the first elements of the whole science of law.

5. In these books a brief exposition is given of the ancient laws, and of those also which, overshadowed by disuse, have been again brought to light by our imperial authority.

6. These four books of Institutes thus compiled, from all the Institutes left us by the ancients, and chiefly from the commentaries of our Gaius, both in his Institutes, and in his work on daily affairs, and also from many other commentaries, were presented to us by

the three learned men we have above named. We have read and examined them and have accorded to them all the force of our constitutions.

7. Receive, therefore, with eagerness, and study with cheerful diligence, these our laws, and show yourselves persons of such learning that you may conceive the flattering hope of yourselves being able, when your course of legal study is completed, to govern our empire in the different portions that may be entrusted to your care.

Given at Constantinople on the eleventh day of the kalends of December, in the third consulate of the Emperor Justinian, ever August (533).

LIBER PRIMUS
TIT. I. DE JUSTITIA ET JURE

Justice is the constant and perpetual wish to render every one his due.

1. Jurisprudence is the knowledge of things divine and human; the science of the just and the unjust.

2. Having explained these general terms, we think we shall commence our exposition of the law of the Roman people most advantageously, if our explanation is at first plain and easy, and is then carried on into details with the utmost care and exactness. For, if at the outset we overload the mind of the student, while yet new to the subject and unable to bear much, with a multitude and variety of topics, one of two things will happen—we shall either cause him wholly to abandon his studies, or, after great toil, and often after great distrust of himself (the most frequent stumbling-block in the way of youth), we shall at last conduct him to the point, to which, if he had been led by a smoother road, he might, without great labor, and without any distrust of his own powers, have been sooner conducted.

3. The maxims of law are these: to live honestly, to hurt no one, to give every one his due.

4. The study of law is divided into two branches; that of public and that of private law. Public law is that which regards the government of the Roman Empire; private law, that which concerns the interests of individu-

als. We are now to treat of the latter, which is composed of three elements, and consists of precepts belonging to natural law, to the law of nations, and to the civil law.

The law of nature is that law which nature teaches to all animals. For this law does not belong exclusively to the human race, but belongs to all animals, whether of the air, the earth, or the sea. Hence comes that yoking together of male and female, which we term matrimony; hence the procreation and bringing up of children. We see, indeed, that all the other animals besides man are considered as having knowledge of this law.

TIT. II. DE JURE NATURALI, GENTIUM ET CIVILI.

1. Civil law is thus distinguished from the law of nations. Every community governed by laws and customs uses partly its own law, partly laws common to all mankind. The law which a people makes for its own government belongs exclusively to that state, and is called the civil law, as being the law of the particular state. But the law which natural reason appoints for all mankind obtains equally among all nations, and is called the law of nations, because all nations make use of it. The people of Rome, then, are governed by the laws which are common to all mankind. What is the nature of these two component parts of our law we will set forth in the proper place.

2. Civil law takes its name from the state which it governs, as, for instance, from Athens; for it would be very proper to speak of the laws of Solon or Draco as the civil law of Athens. And thus the law which the Roman people make use of is called the civil law of the Romans, or that of the Quirites, as being used by the Quirites; for the Romans are called Quirites from Quirinus. But whenever we speak of civil law, without adding of what state we are speaking, we mean our own law: just as when 'the poet' is spoken of without any named being expressed, the Greeks mean the great Homer, and we Romans mean Virgil. The law of nations is common to all mankind, for nations have established certain laws, as occasion and the necessities of human life required. Wars arose, and in their train followed captivity and then slavery, which is contrary to the law of nature; for by that law all men are

originally born free. Further, from this law of nations almost all contracts were at first introduced, as, for instance, buying and selling, letting and hiring, partnership, deposits, loans returnable in kind, and very many others.

3. Our law is written and unwritten, just as among the Greeks some of their laws were written and others not written. The written part consists of laws, *plebiscita, senatus-consulta,* enactments of emperors, edicts of magistrates, and answers of jurisprudents.

4. A law is that which was enacted by the Roman people on its being proposed by a senatorial magistrate, as a consul. A *plebiscitum* is that which was enacted by the *plebs* on its being proposed by a plebeian magistrate, as a tribune. The *plebs* differs from the people as a species from its genus; for all the citizens, not being patricians or senators. But *plebiscita,* after the Hortensian law had been passed, began to have the same force as laws.

5. A *senatus-consultum* is that which the senate commands and appoints: for, when the Roman people was so increased that it was difficult to assemble it together to pass laws, it seemed right that the senate should be consulted in the place of the people.

6. That which seems good to the emperor has also the force of law; for the people, by the *lex regia,* which is passed to confer on him his power, make over to him their whole power and authority. Therefore whatever the emperor ordains by rescript, or decides in adjudging a cause, or lays down by edict, is unquestionably law; and it is these enactments of the emperor that are called constitutions. Of these, some are personal, and are not to be drawn into precedent, such not being the intention of the emperor. Supposing the emperor has granted a favor to any man on account of his merits, or inflicted some punishment, or granted some extraordinary relief, the application of these acts does not extend beyond the particular individual. But the other constitutions, being general, are undoubtedly binding on all.

7. The edicts of the praetors are also of great authority. These edicts are called the *jus honorarium,* because those who bear honors in the state, that is, the magistrates, have given it

their sanction. The curule aediles also used to publish an edict relative to certain subjects, which edict also became part of the *jus honorarium.*

8. The answers of the jurisprudents are the decisions and opinions of persons who were authorized to determine the law. For anciently it was provided that there should be persons to interpret publicly the law, who were permitted by the emperor to give answers on questions of law. They were called jurisconsults; and the authority of their decisions and opinions, when they were all unanimous, was such, that the judge could not, according to the constitutions, refuse to be guided by their answers.

9. The unwritten law is that which usage has established; for ancient customs, being sanctioned by the consent of those who adopt them, are like laws.

10. The civil law is not improperly divided into two kinds, for the division seems to have had its origin in the customs of the two states Athens and Lacedaemon. For in these states it used to be the case, that the Lacedaemonians rather committed to memory what they were to observe as law, while the Athenians rather kept safely what they had found written in their laws.

11. The laws of nature, which all nations observe alike, being established by a divine providence, remain ever fixed and immutable. But the laws which every state has enacted, undergo frequent changes, either by the tacit consent of the people, or by a new law being subsequently passed.

12. All our law relates either to persons, or to things, or to actions. Let us first speak of persons; as it is of little purpose to know the law, if we do not know the persons for whom the law was made.

❖

III. Monotheism

Monotheism, the belief in one God, is a system we take for granted today, but for thousands of years polytheism, the belief in many gods, was much more normal. We tend to think of polytheism as wicked and depraved, but like monotheism it provided the fundamentals of religion: explanation and solace. In fact, in some ways it did so better, for in a polytheistic system there is no need to explain the existence of evil, or why God lets the wicked prosper and the good suffer. What, then, does monotheism have to offer? How can you explain its eventual triumph over polytheism?

A comparison of the following readings might give you some ideas. First, from Mesopotamia, the creation epic of the New Year's festival, ENUMA ELISH. Then a selection of EGYPTIAN HYMNS, followed by Hebrew writings from the HEBREW BIBLE (or "OLD TESTAMENT.") Some of these are monotheistic and some polytheistic. Can you identify which are which? Do the monotheistic ones have anything in common besides belief in one God? What questions do they address? How do these questions— and the answers given in monotheistic writings—compare with the questions and answers in the polytheistic writings?

Then EGYPTIAN HYMNS. To the Sun and To the Nile, and an account of the Egyptian myth of ISIS AND OSIRIS given by PLUTARCH, a Greek living in the Roman Empire, around A. D. 100. Compare these with the ENUMA ELISH at the start of this chapter and the DESCENT OF ISHTAR in the previous chapter. Can you find similarities and differences? The HYMN TO ATON is attributed to another reformer, the Egyptian Pharaoh IKHNATON (c. 1379-1362 B. C.) Can you identify parts of it that seem monotheistic? Why do you think the Egyptians did not accept Ikhnaton's changes?

The third section introduces writings from the HEBREW BIBLE. Compare the account of Creation with Enuma Elish, and the flood story with a similar story in the Epic of Gilgamesh. Besides many gods in one and one god in the other, do you differences that might help you explain why monotheism was so hard to accept? Look at the remaining excerpts, the story of ABRAHAM AND ISAAC, SODOM AND GEMORRAH, JONAH AND THE WHALE and THE BOOK OF JOB. Do these give you more ideas? Once you understand the difficulty of monotheistic belief, you can understand why it may legitimately be asked, "Why did the Hebrews accept it?" What's your answer?

Just so you don't think Hebrew monotheism was the only successful attempt at reform, this chapter ends with selections from THE GATHAS, attributed to the Persian sage ZARATHUSTRA, which comprise the oldest sections of the sacred books of the Zoroastrian religion. Dates for Zarathustra vary widely, from 1300 B. C. to 600 B. C. His teachings have been defined as dualism, a system in which there is not one chief god, but two (one good, one bad). Do not make the mistake of thinking of dualism as a stage between polytheism and monotheism. It is a separate, and very powerful, system of religious thought. In some ways, it seems clearly to have influenced Hebrew monotheism. Can you identify these? Why do you think Zarathustra was successful?

❖   ❖   ❖

1. MESOPOTAMIA

A. ENUMA ELISH

This dramatic epic was performed in Mesopotamia on New Year's Day every year for at least a thousand years. It recounted the First New Year as they conceived it, which occurred when the god Marduk defeated the forces of chaos led by Tiamat, the Great Mother. The epic survives only in fragments, but there is enough here for you to compare it fruitfully with ideas of creation with which you are more familiar. What causes the war? What motivates Tiamat? Marduk? How do these gods compare with your own concept of divinity?

TABLET I

When on high the heaven had not been
    named,
Firm ground below had not been called by
    name,
Naught but primordial Apsu,[1] their begetter,
(And) Mummu-Tiamat,[2] she who bore them
    all,
Their[3] waters commingling as a single body;
No reed hut had been matted, no marsh land
    had appeared,
When no gods whatever had been brought
    into being,
Uncalled by name, their destinies undeter-
    mined—
Then it was that the gods were formed within
    them.[4]
Lahmu and Lahamu[5] were brought forth, by
    name they were called.
For aeons they grew in age and stature.
Anshar and Kishar[6] were formed, surpassing
    the others.
They prolonged the days, added on the years.
Anu[7] was their son, of his fathers the rival;
Yea, Anshar's first-born, Anu, was his equal.
Anu begot in his image Nudimmud.[8]
This Nudimmud was of his fathers the master;

---

[1] God of subterranean waters; the primeval sweet-water ocean.
[2] A water-deity; the primeval salt-water ocean.
[3] I.e., the fresh waters of Apsu and the marine waters of Tiamat.
[4] The waters of Apsu of Tiamat.
[5] The first generation of gods.
[6] Gods.
[7] The sky-god.
[8] One of the names of Ea, the earth- and water-god.

Of broad wisdom, understanding, mighty in
    strength,
Mightier by far than his grandfather, Anshar.
He had no rival among the gods, his brothers..
The divine brothers banded together,
They disturbed Tiamat as they surged back
    and forth,
Yea, they troubled the mood of Tiamat
By their hilarity in the Abode of Heaven.
Apsu could not lessen their clamor
And Tiamat was speechless at their [ways].
Their doings were loathsome unto [...].
Unsavory were their ways; they were overbear-
    ing.

[Apsu decides to destroy the gods in order to have peace; Tiamat opposes, but Apsu prevails.]

When the gods heard (this), they were astir,
(Then) lapsed into silence and remained
    speechless.
Surpassing in wisdom, accomplished,
    resourceful,
Ea, the all-wise, saw through their[9] scheme.
A master design against it he devised and set
    up,
Made artful his spell against it, surpassing and
    holy.
He recited it and made it subsist in the deep,
As he poured sleep upon him.[10] Sound asleep
    he lay.

[Led by Ea, the gods slay Apsu. Ea takes Apsu's place among the gods]

In the chamber of fates, the abode of destinies,
A god was engendered, most potent and wis-
    est of gods.
In the heart of Apsu[11] was Marduk created,
In the heart of holy Apsu was Marduk created.
He who begot him was Ea, his father;
She who conceived him was Damkina, his
    mother.
The breast of goddesses he did suck.
The nurse that nursed him filled him with
    awesomeness.
Alluring was his figure, sparkling the lift of his
    eyes.
Lordly was his gait, commanding from of old.
When Ea saw him, the father who begot him,

---

[9] Apsu and his vizier Mummu.
[10] Apsu.
[11] Meaning now "the deep," not the god.

He exulted and glowed, his heart filled with
gladness.
He rendered him perfect and endowed him
with a double godhead.
Greatly exalted was he above them, exceeding
throughout.
Perfect were his members beyond compre-
hension,
Unsuited for understanding, difficult to per-
ceive.
Four were his eyes, four were his ears;[1]
When he moved his lips, fire blazed forth.
Large were all four hearing organs,
And the eyes, in like number, scanned all
things.
He was the loftiest of the gods, surpassing was
his stature;
His members were enormous, he was exceed-
ing tall.

[Upset by the death of Apsu, Tiamat creates an
army of monsters to do battle.]

She set up the Viper, the Dragon, and the
sphinx,
The Great-Lion, the Mad-Dog, and the
Scorpion-Man,
Mighty lion-demons, the Dragon-Fly, the
Centaur—
Bearing weapons that spare not, fearless in
battle.
Firm were her decrees, past withstanding were
they.
Withal eleven of this kind she brought [forth].
From among the gods,[2] her first-born, who
formed [her Assembly].
She elevated Kingu, made him chief among
them.
The leading of the ranks, command of the
Assembly,
The raising of weapons for the encounter, ad-
vancing to combat,
In battle the command-in-chief—
These to his hand she entrusted as she seated
him in the Council:
"I have cast for thee the spell, exalting thee in
the Assembly of the gods.
To counsel all the gods I have given thee full
power.
Verily, thou are supreme, my only consort art
thou.!

Thy utterance shall prevail over all the Anunnaki."[3]

TABLET II

[None of the gods can placate Tiamat. In fear,
they summon Marduk. Ea, his father, speaks:]

"My son, (thou) who knowest all wisdom,
Calm [Tiamat] with thy holy spell.
On the storm-ch[ariot] proceed with all speed.
From her [presence] they shall not drive
(thee)! Turn (them) back!"
The lord [rejoiced] at the word of his father.
His heart exulting, he said to his father:
"Creator of the gods, destiny of the great gods,
If I indeed, as your avenger,
Am to vanquish Tiamat and save your lives,
Set up the Assembly, proclaim supreme my
destiny!
When jointly in Ubshukinna[4] you have sat
down rejoicing,
Let my word, instead of you, determine the
fates.
Unalterable shall be what I may bring into
being;
Neither recalled nor changed shall be the
command of my lips."

TABLET III

[Anshar, father of the gods, summons an assembly to grant Marduk the supreme power he demands.]

They made ready to leave on their journey,
All the great gods who decree the fates.
They entered before Anshar, filling
[Ubshukinna].
They kissed one another in the Assembly.
They held converse as they [sat down] to the
banquet.
They ate festive bread, partook of [the wine].
They wetted their drinking-tubes with sweet
intoxicant.
As they drank the strong drink, [their] bodies
swelled.
They became very languid as their spirits rose.
For Marduk, their avenger, they fixed the de-
crees.
Tablet IV
They erected for him a princely throne.
Facing his fathers, he sat down, presiding.

---

[1]Cf. Ezekiel 1:6.
[2]The gods who joined Tiamat in her war.

[3]Here a collective name of the nether world gods.
[4]The assembly hall of the gods.

"Thou art the most honored of the great gods,
thy decree is unrivaled, thy command is Anu.[1]
Thou, Marduk, art the most honored of the
   great gods,
Thy decree is unrivaled, thy word is Anu.
From this day unchangeable shall by thy pro-
   nouncement.
To raise or bring low—these shall be (in) thy
   hand.
Thy utterance shall come true, thy command
   shall not be doubted.
No one among the gods shall transgress thy
   bounds!

[Marduk prepares for war.]

He constructed a bow, marked it as his
   weapon,
Attached thereto the arrow, fixed its bow-
   cord.
He raised the mace, made his right had grasp
   it;
Bow and quiver he hung at his side.
In front of him he set the lightning,
With a blazing flame he filled his body.
He then made a net to enfold Tiamat therein.
The four winds he stationed that nothing of
   her might escape,
The South Wind, the North Wind, the East
   Wind, the West Wind.
Close to his side he held the net, the gift of his
   father, Anu.
He brought forth Imhullu, "the Evil Wind,"
   the Whirlwind, the Hurricane,
The Fourfold Wind, the Sevenfold Wind, the
   Cyclone, the Matchless Wind;
Then he sent forth the winds he had brought
   forth, the seven of them.
To stir up the inside of Tiamat they rose up
   behind him.
Then the lord raised up the flood-storm, his
   mighty weapon.
He mounted the storm-chariot irresistible
   [and] terrifying.
He harnessed (and) yoked to it a team-of-four,
The Killer, the Relentless, the Trampler, the
   Swift.
Sharp were their teeth, bearing poison.

[Marduk challenges Tiamat.]

"Stand thou up, that I and thou meet in single
   combat!"

When Tiamat heard this,
She was like one possessed; she took leave of
   her senses.
In fury Tiamat cried out aloud.
To the roots her legs shook both together.
She recites a charm, keeps casting her spell,
While the gods of battle sharpen their
   weapons.
Then joined issue Tiamat and Marduk, wisest
   of gods.
They swayed in single combat, locked in bat-
   tle.
The lord spread out his net to enfold her,
The Evil Wind, which followed behind, he let
   loose in her face.
When Tiamat opened her mouth to consume
   him,
He drove in the Evil Wind that she close not
   her lips.
As the fierce winds charged her belly,
Her body was distended and her mouth was
   wide open.
He released the arrow, it tore her belly,
It cut through her insides, splitting the heart.
Having thus subdued her, he extinguished her
   life.
He cast down her carcass to stand upon it.

[Marduk captures the rest of Tiamat's band, then
returns to her body.]

The lord trod on the legs of Tiamat,
With his unsparing mace he crushed her skull.
When the arteries of her blood he had severed,
The North Wind bore (it) to places undis-
   closed.
On seeing this, his fathers were joyful and
   jubilant,
They brought gifts of homage, they to him.
Then the lord paused to view her dead body,
That he might divide the monster and do art-
   ful works.
He split her like a shellfish into two parts:
Half of her he set up and ceiled it as sky,
Pulled down the bar and posted guards.
He bade them to allow not her waters to es-
   cape.
He crossed the heavens and surveyed (its) re-
   gions.
He squared Apsu's quarter, the abode of
   Nudimmud,
As the lord measured the dimensions of Apsu.
The Great Abode, its likeness, he fixed as Es-
   harra,

---

[1]I.e., it has the authority of the sky-god, Anu.

The Great Abode, Esharra, which he made as
   the firmament.
Anu, Enlil,[1] and Ea he made occupy their
   places.

TABLET V

He constructed stations for the great gods,
Fixing their astral likenesses as constellations.
He determined the year by designating the
   zones:
He set up three constellations for each of the
   twelve months...
In her[2] belly he established the zenith.
The Moon he caused to shine, the night (to
   him) entrusting.
He appointed him a creature of the night to
   signify the days...

TABLET VI

When Marduk hears the words of the gods,
His heart prompts (him) to fashion artful
   works.
Opening his mouth, he addresses Ea
To impart the plan he has conceived in his
   heart:
"Blood I will mass and cause bones to be.
I will establish a savage, 'man' shall be his
   name.
Verily, savage-man I will create.
He shall be charged with the service of the
   gods
That they might be at ease!"

[Marduk uses the body of Tiamat's consort,
Kingu, to create humans.]

Out of his blood they fashioned mankind...
After Ea, the wise, had created mankind,
Had imposed upon it the service of the gods—
That work was beyond comprehension;
As artfully planned by Marduk, did Nudim-
   mud create it—
Marduk, the king of the gods, divided
All the Anunnaki above and below.
He assigned (them) to Anu to guard his in-
   structions.
Three hundred in the heavens he stationed as
   a guard.
In like manner the ways of the hearth he de-
   fined.

---

[1] The god of the wind, i.e., of the earth.
[2] Tiamat's.

In heaven and on earth six hundred (thus) he
   settled.

[The gods build a great shrine in Babylon for
Marduk, Esagila, in which Marduk, Enlil and Ea
reside. Here is where the gods come on the day
of the New Year's festival.]

✝

B. NABONIDUS AND BABYLONIAN RELIGION

i. THE STELE OF NABONIDUS

(This is) the great miracle of Sin that none of
the (other) gods and goddesses knew (how to
achieve), that has not happened to the country
from the days of old, that the people of the
country have (not) observed nor written down
on clay tables to be preserved for eternity, that
(you), Sin, the lord of all the gods and goddesses residing in heaven, have come down
from heaven to (me) Nabonidus, king of
Babylon! For me, Nabonidus, the lonely one
who had nobody, in whose heart was no
thought of kingship, the gods and goddesses
prayed (to Sin) and Sin called me to kingship.
At midnight he (Sin) made me have a dream
and said (in the dream) as follows: "Rebuild
speedily Ehulhul, the temple of Sin in Harran,
and I will hand over to you all the countries."

But the citizens of Babylon, Borsippa, Nippur,
Ur, Uruk (and) Larsa, the administrators (and)
the inhabitants of the urban centers of Babylonia acted evil, careless and even sinned
against his great divine power, having not (yet)
experienced the awfulness of the wrath of the
Divine Crescent, the king of all gods; they dis-
regard his rites and there was much irreligious
and disloyal talk. They devoured one another
like dogs, caused disease and hunger to appear
among them. He (Sin) decimated the inhabitants of the country, but he made me leave my
city Babylon on the road to Tema, Dadanu,
Padukka, Hibra, Jadiru even as far as Jatribu.
For ten years I was moving around among
these (cities) and did not enter my own city
Babylon.

Upon the order of Sin, the king of all gods,
the lord of lords, which the gods and goddesses living in heaven (then) executed, upon
the order of the Divine Crescent, Sin, they
appointed Shamash, Ishtar, Adad and Nergal

to watch over my well-being. (Thereupon) in one and the same year (twice), to wit in the month of Nisannu as well as Tashritu, the people of Babylonia and Upper Syria could collect the products of the (open) country and the sea, and throughout all these years, without exception, Adad, the dike warden of heaven and nether world provided them upon the command of Sin with rain even in the height of the summer, in the following months: Simanu, Du'uzi, Abu (and) Ululu, and so they could *bring* me (in order to support me) their abundance without hardship. Upon the command of Sin <and> Ishtar, the Lady-of-Battle, without whom neither hostilities nor reconciliation can occur in the country and no battle can be fought, extended her protection over them, and the king of Egypt, the Medes and the land of the Arabs, all the hostile kings, were sending me messages of reconciliation and friendship. As to the land of the Arabs which [is the eternal enemy] of Babylonia [and which] was (always) *ready* to rob and carry off its possession, (ii) Nergal broke their weapons upon the order of Sin, and they all bowed down at my feet. Shamash, the lord of oracular decisions, without whom no prediction can be uttered, made, in execution of a command of his own father, the Divine Crescent, the words and the hearts of the people of Babylonia and Upper Syria, who are in my charge, turn (again) to me so that they began to serve me and to execute my command throughout all the distant mountain regions and inaccessible paths I was moving about.

Then the (predicted) term of ten years arrived, it happened on the very day which the king of the gods, the Divine Crescent, had (in the dream) predicted, i.e., the 17th day of Tashritu, of which it is said (in the hemerologies): a day on which Sin is gracious.

O Sin, lord of the gods, whose name on the first day (of his appearance) is "Weapon-of-Anu," (you) who are able to illuminate the heaven and to crush the nether world, who hold in your hands the power of the Anu-office, who wield all the power of the Enlil-office, who have taken over the power of the Ea-office, holding thus in your own hand all the heavenly powers; Enlil among the gods, king of kings, lord of lords, whose command they

do not contradict, you who do not have to repeat your order, of whose great awe the heaven and the nether world are full, with whose sheen heaven and nether world are covered—who can do anything without you? You place religious awe of your great godhead in the heart of any country n which you desire to dwell and its foundation remains steadfast forever; you remove awe toward you from any country which you choose to destroy and you overthrow it forever. (You) are the one whose utterance all the gods and goddesses living in heaven observe; they execute the command of the Divine Crescent, their own father, who wields the powers of heaven and nether world, without whose exalted command, which is given in heaven every day, no country can rest in security and no light can be in the world; the gods shake like reeds and the Anunnaki quiver; those who [bow down] before his divine command which cannot be changed ...

* * *

(Thus) I fulfilled the command of Sin the command of Sin, the king of the gods, the lord of lords who dwells in heaven, whose name surpasses that of (all) the (other) gods in heaven, (i.e.) of Shamash, who is *installed* by him, Nushku, Ishtar, Adad (and) Nergal who have (only) executed the command of the Divine Crescent, who surpasses them (all).

ii. THE VERSE ACCOUNT OF NABONIDUS

(i)

[...law (and] order are not promulgated by him,
[...*he made perish the common people* through w]and, the nobles he killed in war,
[...for] the trader he blocked the road.

[...for the farmer] he made rare the *kuruppa*
[...] there is no ... in the country.
[...the harvester] does not sing the *alalu*-song (any more)
[...] he does not fence in (any more) the arable territory....

[...] their faces became changed/hostile,
[...] they do not parade along the wide street,

[...] you do not see happiness (any more);
[... is] unpleasant, they decided.

[As to Nabonidus] (his) protective deity be-
    came hostile to him,
[And he, the former favorite of the g]ods (is
    now) seized by misfortunes:
[... against the will of the g]ods he performed
    an unholy action,
[...] he thought out something worthless:

[He had made the image of a deity] which no-
    body had (ever) seen in (this) country
[He introduced it into the temple] he placed
    (it) upon a pedestal;
[...] he called it by the name of Nanna,
[it is adorned with a ... of lapis] lazuli,
    crowned with a tiara,

[...] its appearance is (that of) the eclipsed
    moon,
[... the gest]ure of its hand is like that of the
    god Lugal.SU.DU,
[...] its head of hair [rea]ches to the pedestal,
[... in fr]ont of it are [placed the Storm]
    (abûbu) Dragon and the Wild Bull.

(ii)

(Nabonidus said): "I shall build a temple for
    him, I shall construct his (holy) seat,
I shall form its (first) brick (for) him, I shall
    establish firmly its foundation,
I shall make a replica even to the temple Ekur,
I shall call its name é.hul.hu for all days to
    come!

"When I will have fully executed what I have
    planned,
I shall lead him by his hand and establish him
    on his seat.
(Yet) till I have achieved this, till I have ob-
    tained what is my desire,
I shall omit (all festivals, I shall order (even)
    the New Year's Festival to cease!"
✝

2. EGYPTIAN BELIEFS

The Sun and the Nile are unavoidable features of
the Egyptian landscape, and the following hymns
reflect their influence on Egyptian thought. But
the last of these, the HYMN TO ATON, said to
have been written by the Pharaoh Ikhnaton (c.
1379-1362 B.C.) is substantially different from the
others. Can you identify the differences? What is
significant about them? How do these hymns
compare with the selections from Mesopotamia
in the preceding section? Is their concept of the
gods the same? In what way do similarities and
differences between them help illustrate the
growth of religious beliefs in these two regions?

A. HYMNS TO THE SUN

To the morning sun.
Adoration of Rê, when he ariseth in the east-
    ern horizon of heaven.
Praise to thee, that ariseth in Nun and light-
    eneth the Two Lands, when he cometh
    forth.
Thee the whole Ennead praiseth - - - - thou
    goodly, beloved youth— when he ariseth,
    men live.
Mankind rejoiceth at him; the Souls of He-
    liopolis shout joyfully to him; the Souls of
    Buto and Hierakonpolis extol him. The
    apes adore him; "Praise to thee," say all
    wild beasts with one consent.
Thou rejoicest, O lord of gods, over them
    whom thou hast created, and they praise
    thee. Nut is blue alongside of thee, and
    Nun...for thee with his rays.
Give me light, that I may see thy beauty.

To the evening sun.
Adoration of Rê-Harakhti, when he setteth in
    the western horizon of heaven.
Praise to thee, O Rê, when thou settest,
    Atum, Harakhti! Divine divinity, that came
    into being of himself, primaeval god, that
    existed at the beginning.
Jubilation to thee that hast fashioned the gods;
    he that hath raised up the sky to be the
    pathway (?) for his eyes, that hath fash-
    ioned the earth to the extent (?) of his radi-
    ance, so that every man may discern the
    other.
Thou settest beauteous with gladsome heart in
    the horizon of Manun. The noble dwellers
    in the West exult. Thou givest light there

for the great god Osiris, the ruler of eternity.

The lords of the underworld, they are happy when thou bestowest light on the West. Their eyes open when they behold thee. How their hearts rejoice when they behold thee!

Thou hearest the petitions of them that are in the coffin. Thou dispellest their pain and drivest away their evils. Thou givest breath to their nostrils, and they take hold of the rope at the forepart of thy ship in the horizon of Manun.

B. TO THE NILE

Praise to thee, O Nile, that issueth from the earth, and cometh to nourish Egypt. Of hidden nature, a darkness in the day time — — — —.

That watereth the meadows, he that Rê hath created to nourish all cattle. That giveth drink to the desert places, which are far from water; it is his dew that falleth from heaven.

Beloved of Keb, director of the corn-god; that maketh to flourish every workshop of Ptah.

Lord of fish, that maketh the water-fowl to go upstream. — — — — ,

That maketh barley and createth wheat, so that he may cause the temples to keep festivals.

If he be sluggish, the nostrils are stopped up, and all men are impoverished; the victuals of the gods are diminished, and millions of men perish.

If he be niggardly (?) the whole land is in terror *and* great and small *lament.*— — — —

Khnum hath fashioned him. When he riseth, the land is in exultation and every body is in joy. All jaws begin to laugh and every tooth is revealed.

He that bringeth victuals and is rich in food, that createth all that is good. The revered, sweet-smelling— — — —. That createth herbage for the cattle, and giveth sacrifice to every god, be he in the underworld, in heaven, or upon earth— — — —. That filleth the storehouses, and maketh wide the granaries, and giveth things to the poor.

He that maketh trees to grow according to every wish, and men have no lack thereof; the ship is built by his power. . . .

All that is intelligible is: thy young folk and thy children shout for joy over thee, and men hail thee as king. Unchanging of laws, *when he* cometh forth in the presence of Upper and Lower Egypt. Men drink the water— — —.

He that was in sorrow is become glad, and every heart is joyful, Sobk, the child of Neith, laugheth, and the divine Ennead, that is in thee, is glorious.

Thou that vomitest forth, giving the fields to drink and making strong the people. He that maketh the one rich and loveth the other. *He maketh no distinctions, and boundaries are not made for him.* . . .

Men begin to play to thee on the harp, and men sing to thee with the hand. Thy young folk and thy children shout for joy over thee, and deputations to thee are appointed.

He that cometh with splendid things and adorneth the earth! That causeth the ship to prosper before (?) men; that quickeneth the hearts in them that are with child; that would fain have there be a multitude of all kinds of cattle. . . .

When the Nile floodeth, offering is made to thee, cattle are slaughtered for thee, a great oblation is made for thee. Birds are fattened for thee, antelopes are hunted for thee in the desert. Good is recompensed unto thee.

All ye men, extol the Nine Gods. and stand in awe of the might which his son, the Lord of All, *hath displayed,* even he that maketh green the Two River-banks. Thou art verdant, O Nile, thou are verdant. He that maketh man to live on his cattle, and his cattle on the meadow! Thou art verdant, thou art verdant; O Nile, thou art verdant.

C. ON ISIS AND OSIRIS

PLUTARCH

They say that Isis and Osiris, being in love with each other even before they were born, were united in the darkness of the womb. Some aver that Aroueris was the fruit of this union and that he is called the elder Horus by the Egyptians, and Apollo by the Greeks.

It is said that Osiris, when he was king, at once freed the Egyptians from their primitive and brutish manner of life; he showed them how to grow crops, established laws for them, and taught them to worship gods. Later he civilized the whole world as he traversed through it, having very little need of arms, but winning over most of the peoples by beguiling them with persuasive speech together with all manner of song and poetry. That is why the Greeks thought he was the same as Dionysus.

While he was away Typhon [Plutarch gives a Greek name to the Egyptian god Set, brother of Isis and Osiris] conspired in no way against him since Isis was well on guard and kept careful watch, but on his return he devised a plot against him, making seventy-two men his fellow-conspirators and having as helper a queen who had come from Ethiopia, whom they name Asô. Typhon secretly measured the body of Osiris and got made to the corresponding size a beautiful chest which was exquisitely decorated. This he brought to the banqueting-hall, and when the guests showed pleasure and admiration at the sight of it, Typhon promised playfully that whoever would lie down in it and show that he fitted it, should have the chest as a gift. They all tried one by one, and since no one fitted into it, Osiris went in and lay down. Then the conspirators ran and slammed the lid on, and after securing it with bolts from the outside and also with molten lead poured on, they took it out to the river and let it go to the sea by way of the Tanitic mouth [one of the five branches, or "mouths," by which the Nile empties into the Mediterranean], which the Egyptians still call, because of this, hateful and abominable. They say that all these events occurred on the seventeenth day of the month of Athyr, when the sun passes through the scorpion, in the twenty-eighth year of the reign of Osiris. But some state that this was the period of his life rather than of his reign.

The first to hear of the misfortune and to spread the news of its occurrence were the Pans and Satyrs who live near Khemmis, and because of this, the sudden disturbance and excitement of a crowd is still referred to as 'panic.' When Isis heard of it she cut off there and then one of her locks and put on a mourning garment; accordingly the city is called Coptos to this day. Others think the name indicates deprivation; for they use *koptein* to mean 'to deprive,' and they suggest that Isis, when she was wandering everywhere in a state of distress, passed by no one without accosting him, and even when she met children, she asked them about the chest. Some of these had happened to see it and they named the river-mouth through which Typhon's friends had pushed the box to the sea....

They say that she learned as a result of this that the chest had been cast up by the sea in the land of Byblos [Phoenicia] and that the surf had brought it gently to rest in a heath-tree. Having shot up in a short time into a most lovely and tall young tree, the heath enfolded the chest and grew around it, hiding it within itself. Admiring the size of the tree, the king cut off the part of the trunk which encompassed the coffin, which was not visible, and used it as a pillar to support the roof. They say that Isis heard of this through the divine breath of rumour and came to Byblos, where she sat down near a fountain, dejected and tearful. She spoke to no one except the queen's maids, whom she greeted and welcomed, plaiting their hear and breathing upon their skin a wonderful fragrance which emanated from herself. When the queen saw her maids she was struck with longing for the stranger's hair and for her skin, which breathed ambrosia; and so Isis was sent for and became friendly with the queen and was made nurse of her child. The king's name, they say, was Malcathros; some say that the queen's name was Astarte, others Saôsis, and others Nemanous, whom the Greeks would call Athenaïs.

They say that Isis nursed the child, putting her finger in its mouth instead of her breast, but that in the night she burned the mortal parts of its body, while she herself became a swallow, flying around the pillar and making lament until the queen, who had been watching her, gave a shriek when she saw her child on fire, and so deprived it of immortality. The goddess then revealed herself and demanded the pillar under the roof. She took it from beneath with the utmost ease and proceeded to cut away the heath-tree. This she then covered with linen and poured sweet oil on it, after which she gave it into the keeping of the king and queen; to this day the people of Byblos venerate the wood, which is in the temple of Isis. The goddess then fell upon the coffin and gave such a loud wail that the younger of the king's sons died; the elder son she took with her, and placing the coffin in a boat, she set sail. When the river Phaedrus produced a somewhat rough wind towards dawn, in a fit of anger she dried up the stream.

As soon as she happened on a deserted spot, there in solitude she opened the chest and pressing her face to that of Osiris, she embraced him and began to cry....

Having journeyed to her son Horus who was being brought up in Buto, Isis put the box aside and Typhon, when he was hunting by night in the moonlight, came upon it. He recognized the body, and having cut it into fourteen parts, he scattered them. When she heard of this, Isis searched for them in a papyrus boat, sailing through the marshes. That is why people who sail in papyrus skiffs are not harmed by crocodiles, which show either fear or veneration because of the goddess.... The only part of Osiris which Isis did not find was his male member; for no sooner was it thrown into the river than the lepidotus, phagrus and oxyrhynchus ate of it, fish which they most of all abhor. In its place Isis fashioned a likeness of it and consecrated the phallus, in honour of which the Egyptians even today hold festival.

Afterwards Osiris came to Horus, it is said, from the underworld, and equipped and trained him for battle. Then he questioned him as to what he considered to be the finest action, and Horus said, 'To succour one's father and mother when they have suffered wrong.' Osiris asked him again what he considered to be the most useful animal for those going out to battle. When Horus replied, 'The

horse,' he was surprised and he queried why he did not name the lion rather than the horse. Horus answered that the lion was helpful to some one in heed of aid, but that the horse routed the fugitive and so destroyed completely the force of the enemy. Osiris was pleased on hearing this, thinking that Horus had adequately prepared himself. When many were coming over, as they say, to the side of Horus, there came also Thoueris, Typhon's concubine; and a snake which pursued her was cut in pieces by Horus, for which reason they now throw out a piece of rope in public and cut it up. The battle then lasted for many days and Horus won. When Isis came across Typhon tied in bonds, she did not kill him, but freed him and let him go. Horus did not take this at all calmly, but laying hands on his mother he ripped off the crown from her head. Hermes however put on her instead a cowheaded helmet. When Typhon brought a charge of illegitimacy against Horus, Hermes helped Horus, and the latter was judged by the gods to be legitimate. Typhon was defeated in two other battles, and Isis, having had sexual union with Osiris after his death, bore Harpocrates, prematurely delivered and weak in his lower limbs.

❖

D. TO ATON

Thou appearest beautifully on the horizon of heaven,
Thou living Aton, the beginning of life!
When thou art risen on the eastern horizon,
Thou has filled every land with thy beauty.
Thou art gracious, great, glistening, and high over every land;
Thy rays encompass the lands to the limit of all that thou hast made:
As thou art Re, thou reachest to the end of them;
(Thou) subduest them (for) thy beloved son.
Though thou art far away, thy rays are on earth;
Though thou art in *their* faces, *no one knows thy* going.

When thou settest in the western horizon,
The land is in darkness, in the manner of death.
They sleep in a room, with heads wrapped up,

Nor sees one eye the other.
All their goods which are under their heads
    might be stolen,
(But) they would not perceive (it).
Every lion is come forth from his den;
All creeping things, they sting.
Darkness *is a shroud*, and the earth is in still-
    ness,
For he who made them rests in his horizon.

At daybreak, when thou arisest on the hori-
    zon,
When thou shinest as the Aton by day,
Thou drivest away the darkness and givest thy
    rays.
The Two Lands are in festivity *every day*,
Awake and standing upon (their) feet,
For thou hast raised them up.
Washing their bodies, taking (their) clothing,
Their arms are (raised) in praise at they ap-
    pearance.
All the world, they do their work.

All beasts are content with their pasturage;
Trees and plants are flourishing.
The birds which fly from their nests,
Their wings are (stretched out) in praise to thy
    ka.
All beasts spring upon (their) feet.
Whatever flies and alights,
They live when thou hast risen (for) them.
The ships are sailing north and south as well,
For every way is open at thy appearance.
The fish in the river dart before thy face;
Thy rays are in the midst of the great green
    sea.

Creator of seed in women,
Thou who makest fluid into man,
Who maintainest the son in the womb of his
    mother,
Who soothest him with that which stills his
    weeping,
Thou nurse (even) in the womb,
Who givest breath to sustain all that he has
    made!
When he descends from the womb to *breathe*
On the day when he is born,
Thou openest his mouth completely,
Thou suppliest his necessities.
When the chick in the egg speaks within the
    shell,

Thou givest him breath within it to maintain
    him.
When thou has made him his fulfillment
    within the egg, to break it,
He comes forth from the egg to speak at his
    completed (time);
He walks upon his legs when he comes forth
    from it.

How manifold it is, what thou hast made!
They are hidden from the face (of man).
O sole god, like whom there is no other!
Thou didst create the world according to thy
    desire,
Whilst thou wert alone:
All men, cattle, and wild beasts,
Whatever is on earth, going upon (its) feet,
And what is on high, flying with its wings.

The countries of Syria and Nubia, the *land* of
    Egypt,
Thou settest every man in his place,
Thou suppliest their necessities:
Everyone has his food, and his time of life is
    reckoned.
Their tongues are separate in speech,
And their natures as well;
Their skins are distinguished,
As thou distinguishest the foreign peoples.
Thou makest a Nile in the underworld,
Thou bringest it forth as thou desirest
To maintain the people (of Egypt)
According as thou madest them for thyself,
The lord of all of them, wearying (himself)
    with them,
The lord of every land, rising for them,
The Aton of the day, great of majesty.

All distant foreign countries, thou makest
    their life (also),
For thou hast set a Nile in heaven,
That it may descend for them and make waves
    upon the mountains,
Like the great green sea,
To water their fields in their towns.
How effective they are, thy plans, O lord of
    eternity!
The Nile in heaven, it is for the foreign peo-
    ples
And for the beasts of every desert that go upon
    (their) feet;
(While the true) Nile comes from the under-
    world for Egypt.

Thy rays suckle every meadow.
When thou risest, they live, they grow for
  thee.
Thou makest the seasons in order to rear all
  that thou hast made,
The winter to cool them,
And the heat that *they* may taste thee.
Thou hast made the distant sky in order to rise
  therein,
In order to see all that thou dost make.
Whilst thou wert alone,
Rising in thy form as the living Aton,
Appearing, shining, *withdrawing or approach-
  ing*,
Thou madest millions of forms of thyself
  alone.
Cities, towns, fields, road, and river—
Every eye beholds thee over against them,
For thou art the Aton of the day over *the earth*
  …

Thou art in my heart,
And there is no other that knows thee
Save thy son Nefer-kheperu-Re Wa-en-Re,
For thou hast made him well-versed in thy
  plans and in thy strength.

The world came into being by thy hand,
According as thou hast made them.
When thou hast risen they live,
When thou settest they die.
Thou art lifetime thy own self,
For one lives (only) through thee.
Eyes are (fixed) on beauty until thou settest.
All work is laid aside when thou settest in the
  west.
(But) when (thou) risest (again),
[*Everything is*] made to flourish for the king,
  …
Since thou didst found the earth
And raise them up for thy son,
Who came forth from thy body:
  the King of Upper and Lower Egypt, … Akh-
    en-Aton, … and the Chief Wife of the
    King … Nefert-iti, living and youthful for-
    ever and ever.

✝

3. THE HEBREW INTERPRETATION

A. CREATION

CHAPTER 1

In the beginning God created the heavens and the earth. 2 The earth was without form and void, and darkness *was* upon the face of the deep; And the Spirit of God was moving over the face of the waters. 3 And God said, "Let there be light"; and there was light. 4 And God saw that the light was good; and God separated the light from the darkness. 5 God called the light Day, and the darkness he called Night. And there was evening and there was morning, one day.

6 And God said, "Let there be a firmament in the midst of the waters, and let it separate the waters from the waters." 7 And God made the firmament, and divided the waters which *were* under the firmament from the waters which were above the firmament. And it was so. 8 And God called the firmament Heaven. And there was evening and there was morning, a second day.

9 And God said, "Let the waters under the heaven be gathered together into one place, and let the dry land appear." And it was so. 10 God called the dry land Earth, and the waters that were gathered together he called Seas. And God saw that it *was* good. 11 And God said, "Let the earth put forth vegetation, plants yielding seed, and fruit trees bearing fruit in which is their seed, each according to its kind, upon the earth." And it was so. 12 The earth brought forth vegetation, plants yielding seed according to their own kinds, and trees bearing fruit in which is their seed, each according to its kind. And God saw that it was good. 13 And there was evening and there was morning, a third day.

14 And God said, "Let there be lights in the firmament of the heavens to separate the day from the night; and let them be for signs and for seasons and for days and years, 15 and let them be lights in the firmament of the heavens to give light upon the earth." And it was so. 16 And God made the two great lights, the greater light to rule the day, and the lesser light to rule the night; he made the stars also. 17 And God set them in the firmament of the

heavens to give light upon the earth, 18 to rule over the day and over the night, and to separate the light from the darkness. And God saw that it was good. 19 And there was evening and there was morning, a fourth day.

20 And God said, "Let the waters bring forth swarms of living creatures, and let birds fly above the earth across the firmament of the heavens." 21 So God created the great sea monsters and every living creature that moves, with which the waters swarm, according to their kinds, and every winged bird according to its kind. And God saw that it was good. 22 And God blessed them, saying, "Be fruitful and multiply and fill the waters in the seas, and let birds multiply on the earth." 23 And there was evening and there was morning, a fifth day.

24 And God said, "Let the earth bring forth living creatures according to their kinds: cattle and creeping things and beast of the earth according to their kinds." And it was so. 25 And God made the beasts of the earth according to their kinds and cattle according to their kinds, and everything that creeps upon the ground according to its kind. And God saw that it was good.

26 Then God said, "Let us make man in our image, after our likeness; and let them have dominion over the fish of the sea, and over the birds of the air, and over the cattle, and over all the earth, and over every creeping thing that creeps upon the earth." 27 So God created man in his own image, in the image of God he created him; male and female he created them. 28 And God blessed them, and God said to them, "Be fruitful and multiply, and fill the earth and subdue it; and have dominion over the fish of the sea and over the birds of the air and over every living thing that moves upon the earth." 29 And God said, "Behold, I have given you every plant yielding seed which is upon the face of all the earth, and every tree with seed in its fruit; you shall have them for food. 30 And to every beast of the earth, and to every bird of the air, and to everything that creeps on the earth, everything that has the breath of life, I have given every green plant for food." And it was so. 31 And God saw everything that he had made, and behold, it

was very good. And there was evening and there was morning, a sixth day.

CHAPTER 2

Thus the heavens and the earth were finished, and all the host of them. 2 And on the seventh day God finished his work which he had done, and he rested on the seventh day from all his work which he had done. 3 So God blessed the seventh day and hallowed it, because on it God rested from all his work which he had done in creation.

4 These *are* the generations of the heavens and of the earth when they were created.

B. THE FLOOD

6.5 The LORD saw that the wickedness of man was great in the earth, and that every imagination of the thoughts of his heart was only evil continually. 6 And the LORD was sorry that he had made man on the earth, and it grieved him to his heart. 7 So the LORD said, "I will blot out man whom I have created from the face of the ground, man and beast and creeping things and birds of the air, for I am sorry that I have made them." 8 But Noah found favor in the eyes of the LORD.

9 These are the generations of Noah. Noah was a righteous man, blameless in his generation; Noah walked with God. 10 And Noah had three sons, Shem, Ham, and Japheth.

....13 And God said to Noah, "I have determined to make an end of all flesh; for the earth is filled with violence through them; behold, I will destroy them with the earth. 14 Make yourself an ark of gopher wood; make rooms in the ark, and cover it inside and out with pitch. 15 This is how you are to make it: the length of the ark three hundred cubits, its breadth fifty cubits, and its height thirty cubits.... 17 For behold, I will bring a flood of waters upon the earth, to destroy all flesh in which is the breath of life from under heaven; everything that is on the earth shall die. 18 But I will establish my covenant with you; and you shall come into the ark, you, your sons, your wife, and your sons' wives with you. 19 And of every living thing of all flesh, you shall bring two of every sort into the ark, to keep them alive with you; they shall be male and female....22 Noah did this; he did all that God commanded him.

7.1 Then the LORD said to Noah, "Go into the ark, you and all your household, for I have seen that you are righteous before me in this generation....4 For in seven days I will send rain upon the earth forty days and forty nights; and every living thing that I have made I will blot out from the face of the ground." ...

24 And the waters prevailed upon the earth a hundred and fifty days.

8.1 But God remembered Noah and all the beasts and all the cattle that were with him in the ark. And God made a wind blow over the earth, and the waters subsided; 2 the fountains of the deep and the windows of the heavens were closed, the rain from the heavens was restrained, 3 and the waters receded from the earth continually. At the end of a hundred and fifty days the waters had abated; 4 and in the seventh month, on the seventeenth day of the month, the ark came to rest upon the mountains of Ar'arat....

20 Then Noah built an altar to the LORD, and took of every clean animal and of every clean bird, and offered burnt offerings on the altar. 21 And when the LORD smelled the pleasing odor, the LORD said in his heart, "I will never again curse the ground because of man, for the imagination of man's heart is evil from his youth;"....

9.8 Then God said to Noah and to his sons with him, 9 "Behold, I establish my covenant with you and your descendants after you.... 11 I establish my covenant with you, that never again shall all flesh be cut off by the waters of a flood, and never again shall there be a flood to destroy the earth" 12 And God said, "This is the sign of the covenant which I make between me and you and every living creature that is with you, for all future generations: 13 I set my bow in the cloud, and it shall be a sign of the covenant between me and the earth. 14 When I bring clouds over the earth and the bow is seen in the clouds, 15 I will remember my covenant which is between me and you and every living creature of all flesh....

✝

C. ABRAHAM AND ISAAC

In antiquity it was assumed that gods and humans were interdependent: the gods gave fertility (as in *The Descent of Ishtar*) and humans provided sacrifices. This agreement was called a *berit*, or covenant.

The most famous such berit is that between Abraham and Yahweh, formed sometime around 1400 B.C.: Jews, Christians, and Muslim all trace the origin of their faith to this one covenant. But the berit of Abraham has some very peculiar elements, as this story demonstrates. What is Abraham seeking? What is God seeking? Do the events described here indicate that Judaism (and Christianity and Islam) will develop differently from other Mesopotamian religions? [From: *Genesis*, 17-18, 21-22; *New Revised Standard Version*.]

CHAPTER 17

When Abram was ninety-nine years old the Lord appeared to Abram, and said to him, "I am God Almighty; walk before me, and be blameless. 2: And I will make my covenant between me and you, and will multiply you exceedingly."

3: Then Abram fell on his face; and God said to him, 4: "Behold, my covenant is with you, and you shall be the father of a multitude of nations. 5: No longer shall your name be Abram, but your name shall be Abraham; for I have made you the father of a multitude of nations. 6: I will make you exceedingly fruitful; and I will make nations of you, and kings shall come forth from you. 7: And I will establish my covenant between me and you and your descendants after you throughout their generations for an everlasting covenant, to be God to you and to your descendants after you. 8: And I will give to you, and to your descendants after you, the land of your sojournings, all the land of Canaan, for an everlasting possession; and I will be their God."

9: And God said to Abraham, "As for you, you shall keep my covenant, you and your descendants after you throughout their generations. 10: This is my covenant, which you shall keep, between me and you and your descendants after you: Every male among you shall be circumcised. 11: You shall be circumcised in the flesh of your foreskins, and it shall be a sign of the covenant between me and you. 12: He that is eight days old among you shall be circumcised; every male throughout your generations, whether born in your house, or bought with your money from any foreigner who is not of your offspring, 13: both he that is born in your house and he that is bought with your money, shall be circumcised. So shall my covenant be in your flesh an everlasting covenant. 14: Any uncircumcised male who is not circumcised in the flesh of his foreskin shall be cut off from his people; he has broken my covenant."

15: And God said to Abraham, "As for Sarai your wife, you shall not call her name Sar'ai, but Sarah shall be her name. 16: I will bless her, and moreover I will give you a son by her; I will bless her, and she shall be a mother of nations; kings of peoples shall come from her."

17: Then Abraham fell on his face and laughed, and said to himself, "Shall a child be born to a man who is a hundred years old? Shall Sarah, who is ninety years old, bear a child?" 18: And Abraham said to God, "O that Ishmael might live in thy sight!"

19: God said, "No, but Sarah your wife shall bear you a son, and you shall call his name Isaac. I will establish my covenant with him as an everlasting covenant for his descendants after him. 20: As for Ishmael, I have heard you; behold, I will bless him and make him fruitful and multiply him exceedingly; he shall be the father of twelve princes, and I will make him a great nation. 21: But I will establish my covenant with Isaac, whom Sarah shall bear to you at this season next year."

22: When he had finished talking with him, God went up from Abraham.

23: Then Abraham took Ishmael his son and all the slaves born in his house or bought with his money, every male among the men of Abraham's house, and he circumcised the flesh of their foreskins that very day, as God had said to him. 24: Abraham was ninety-nine years old when he was circumcised in the flesh of his foreskin. 25: And Ishmael his son was thirteen years old when he was circumcised in the flesh of his foreskin. 26: That very day Abraham and his son Ishmael were circumcised; 27: and all the men of his house, those born in the house and those bought with

money from a foreigner, were circumcised with him.

CHAPTER 18

And the Lord appeared to him by the oaks of Mamre, as he sat at the door of his tent in the heat of the day.

2: He lifted up his eyes and looked, and behold, three men stood in front of him. When he saw them, he ran from the tent door to meet them, and bowed himself to the earth, 3: and said, "My lord, if I have found favor in your sight, do not pass by your servant. 4: Let a little water be brought, and wash your feet, and rest yourselves under the tree, 5: while I fetch a morsel of bread, that you may refresh yourselves, and after that you may pass on -- since you have come to your servant."

So they said, "Do as you have said."

6: And Abraham hastened into the tent to Sarah, and said, "Make ready quickly three measures of fine meal, knead it, and make cakes." 7: And Abraham ran to the herd, and took a calf, tender and good, and gave it to the servant, who hastened to prepare it. 8: Then he took curds, and milk, and the calf which he had prepared, and set it before them; and he stood by them under the tree while they ate.

9: They said to him, "Where is Sarah your wife?" And he said, "She is in the tent."

10: The Lord said, "I will surely return to you in the spring, and Sarah your wife shall have a son." And Sarah was listening at the tent door behind him. 11: Now Abraham and Sarah were old, advanced in age; it had ceased to be with Sarah after the manner of women. 12: So Sarah laughed to herself, saying, "After I have grown old, and my husband is old, shall I have pleasure?"

13: The Lord said to Abraham, "Why did Sarah laugh, and say, `Shall I indeed bear a child, now that I am old?' 14: Is anything too hard for the Lord? At the appointed time I will return to you, in the spring, and Sarah shall have a son."

15: But Sarah denied, saying, "I did not laugh"; for she was afraid. He said, "No, but you did laugh."

CHAPTER 21: 1: The Lord visited Sarah as he had said, and the Lord did to Sarah as he had promised. 2: And Sarah conceived, and bore Abraham a son in his old age at the time of which God had spoken to him.

3: Abraham called the name of his son who was born to him, whom Sarah bore him, Isaac. 4: And Abraham circumcised his son Isaac when he was eight days old, as God had commanded him. 5: Abraham was a hundred years old when his son Isaac was born to him.

6: And Sarah said, "God has made laughter for me; every one who hears will laugh over me." 7: And she said, "Who would have said to Abraham that Sarah would suckle children? Yet I have borne him a son in his old age."

8: And the child grew, and was weaned; and Abraham made a great feast on the day that Isaac was weaned. 9: But Sarah saw the son of Hagar the Egyptian, whom she had borne to Abraham, playing with her son Isaac. 10: So she said to Abraham, "Cast out this slave woman with her son; for the son of this slave woman shall not be heir with my son Isaac."

11: And the thing was very displeasing to Abraham on account of his son.

12: But God said to Abraham, "Be not displeased because of the lad and because of your slave woman; whatever Sarah says to you, do as she tells you, for through Isaac shall your descendants be named. 13: And I will make a nation of the son of the slave woman also, because he is your offspring."

14: So Abraham rose early in the morning, and took bread and a skin of water, and gave it to Hagar, putting it on her shoulder, along with the child, and sent her away. And she departed, and wandered in the wilderness of Beersheba. 15: When the water in the skin was gone, she cast the child under one of the bushes. 16: Then she went, and sat down over against him a good way off, about the distance of a bowshot; for she said, "Let me not look upon the death of the child." And as she sat over against him, the child lifted up his voice and wept.

17: And God heard the voice of the lad; and the angel of God called to Hagar from heaven, and said to her, "What troubles you, Hagar?

Fear not; for God has heard the voice of the lad where he is. 18: Arise, lift up the lad, and hold him fast with your hand; for I will make him a great nation." 19: Then God opened her eyes, and she saw a well of water; and she went, and filled the skin with water, and gave the lad a drink.

20: And God was with the lad, and he grew up; he lived in the wilderness, and became an expert with the bow. 21: He lived in the wilderness of Paran; and his mother took a wife for him from the land of Egypt.

CHAPTER 22: 1: After these things God tested Abraham, and said to him, "Abraham!" And he said, "Here am I."

2: He said, "Take your son, your only son Isaac, whom you love, and go to the land of Moriah, and offer him there as a burnt offering upon one of the mountains of which I shall tell you."

3: So Abraham rose early in the morning, saddled his ass, and took two of his young men with him, and his son Isaac; and he cut the wood for the burnt offering, and arose and went to the place of which God had told him. 4: On the third day Abraham lifted up his eyes and saw the place afar off. 5: Then Abraham said to his young men, "Stay here with the ass; I and the lad will go yonder and worship, and come again to you."

6: And Abraham took the wood of the burnt offering, and laid it on Isaac his son; and he took in his hand the fire and the knife. So they went both of them together. 7: And Isaac said to his father Abraham, "My father!" And he said, "Here am I, my son." He said, "Behold, the fire and the wood; but where is the lamb for a burnt offering?"

8: Abraham said, "God will provide himself the lamb for a burnt offering, my son." So they went both of them together.

9: When they came to the place of which God had told him, Abraham built an altar there, and laid the wood in order, and bound Isaac his son, and laid him on the altar, upon the wood. 10: Then Abraham put forth his hand, and took the knife to slay his son.

11: But the angel of the Lord called to him from heaven, and said, "Abraham, Abraham!" And he said, "Here am I." 12: He said, "Do not lay your hand on the lad or do anything to him; for now I know that you fear God, seeing you have not withheld your son, your only son, from me." 13: And Abraham lifted up his eyes and looked, and behold, behind him was a ram, caught in a thicket by his horns; and Abraham went and took the ram, and offered it up as a burnt offering instead of his son.

14: So Abraham called the name of that place The Lord will provide; as it is said to this day, "On the mount of the Lord it shall be provided."

15: And the angel of the Lord called to Abraham a second time from heaven, 16: and said, "By myself I have sworn, says the Lord, because you have done this, and have not withheld your son, your only son, 17: I will indeed bless you, and I will multiply your descendants as the stars of heaven and as the sand which is on the seashore. And your descendants shall possess the gate of their enemies, 18: and by your descendants shall all the nations of the earth bless themselves, because you have obeyed my voice."

❖

D. JONAH AND THE WHALE

CHAPTER 1

Now the word of the Lord came to Jonah the son of Amittai, saying,

2: "Arise, go to Nineveh, that great city, and cry against it; for their wickedness has come up before me."

3: But Jonah rose to flee to Tarshish from the presence of the Lord. He went down to Joppa and found a ship going to Tarshish; so he paid the fare, and went on board, to go with them to Tarshish, away from the presence of the Lord. 4: But the Lord hurled a great wind upon the sea, and there was a mighty tempest on the sea, so that the ship threatened to break up.

5: Then the mariners were afraid, and each cried to his god; and they threw the wares that were in the ship into the sea, to lighten it for them. But Jonah had gone down into the inner part of the ship and had lain down, and was fast asleep. 6: So the captain came and said to him, "What do you mean, you sleeper? Arise, call upon your god! Perhaps the god will give a thought to us, that we do not perish." 7: And they said to one another, "Come, let us cast lots, that we may know on whose account this evil has come upon us." So they cast lots, and the lot fell upon Jonah. 8: Then they said to him, "Tell us, on whose account this evil has come upon us? What is your occupation? And whence do you come? What is your country? And of what people are you?"

9: And he said to them, "I am a Hebrew; and I fear the Lord, the God of heaven, who made the sea and the dry land."

10: Then the men were exceedingly afraid, and said to him, "What is this that you have done!" For the men knew that he was fleeing from the presence of the Lord, because he had told them. 11: Then they said to him, "What shall we do to you, that the sea may quiet down for us?" For the sea grew more and more tempestuous. 12: He said to them, "Take me up and throw me into the sea; then the sea will quiet down for you; for I know it is because of me that this great tempest has come upon you." 13: Nevertheless the men rowed hard to bring the ship back to land, but they could not, for the sea grew more and more tempestuous against them.

14: Therefore they cried to the Lord, "We beseech thee, O Lord, let us not perish for this man's life, and lay not on us innocent blood; for thou, O Lord, hast done as it pleased thee." 15: So they took up Jonah and threw him into the sea; and the sea ceased from its raging. 16: Then the men feared the Lord exceedingly, and they offered a sacrifice to the Lord and made vows.

17: And the Lord appointed a great fish to swallow up Jonah; and Jonah was in the belly of the fish three days and three nights.

10: And the Lord spoke to the fish, and it vomited out Jonah upon the dry land.

CHAPTER 2

Then Jonah prayed to the Lord his God from the belly of the fish, 2: saying,

"I called to the Lord, out of my distress,
and he answered me;
out of the belly of Sheol I cried,
and thou didst hear my voice.

3: For thou didst cast me into the deep,
into the heart of the seas,
and the flood was round about me;
all thy waves and thy billows
passed over me.

4: Then I said, `I am cast out
from thy presence;
how shall I again look
upon thy holy temple?'
5: The waters closed in over me,
the deep was round about me;
weeds were wrapped about my head

6: at the roots of the mountains.
I went down to the land
whose bars closed upon me for ever;
yet thou didst bring up my life from the Pit,
O Lord my God.

7: When my soul fainted within me,
I remembered the Lord;
and my prayer came to thee,
into thy holy temple.

8: Those who pay regard to vain idols
forsake their true loyalty.

9: But I with the voice of thanksgiving
will sacrifice to thee;
what I have vowed I will pay.
Deliverance belongs to the Lord!"

CHAPTER 3

Then the word of the Lord came to Jonah the second time, saying,

2: "Arise, go to Nineveh, that great city, and proclaim to it the message that I tell you."

3: So Jonah arose and went to Nineveh, according to the word of the Lord. Now Nineveh was an exceedingly great city, three days' journey in breadth. 4: Jonah began to go into the city, going a day's journey. And he cried, "Yet forty days, and Nineveh shall be overthrown!"

5: And the people of Nineveh believed God; they proclaimed a fast, and put on sackcloth, from the greatest of them to the least of them. 6: Then tidings reached the king of Nineveh, and he arose from his throne, removed his robe, and covered himself with sackcloth, and sat in ashes. 7: And he made proclamation and published through Nineveh, "By the decree of the king and his nobles: Let neither man nor beast, herd nor flock, taste anything; let them not feed, or drink water, 8: but let man and beast be covered with sackcloth, and let them cry mightily to God; yea, let every one turn from his evil way and from the violence which is in his hands. 9: Who knows, God may yet repent and turn from his fierce anger, so that we perish not?"

10: When God saw what they did, how they turned from their evil way, God repented of the evil which he had said he would do to them; and he did not do it.

CHAPTER 4

But it displeased Jonah exceedingly, and he was angry.

2: And he prayed to the Lord and said, "I pray thee, Lord, is not this what I said when I was yet in my country? That is why I made haste to flee to Tarshish; for I knew that thou art a gracious God and merciful, slow to anger, and abounding in steadfast love, and repentest of evil. 3: Therefore now, O Lord, take my life from me, I beseech thee, for it is better for me to die than to live."

4: And the Lord said, "Do you do well to be angry?"

5: Then Jonah went out of the city and sat to the east of the city, and made a booth for himself there. He sat under it in the shade, till he should see what would become of the city.

6: And the Lord God appointed a plant, and made it come up over Jonah, that it might be a shade over his head, to save him from his discomfort. So Jonah was exceedingly glad because of the plant.

7: But when dawn came up the next day, God appointed a worm which attacked the plant, so that it withered. 8: When the sun rose, God appointed a sultry east wind, and the sun beat upon the head of Jonah so that he was faint; and he asked that he might die, and said, "It is better for me to die than to live."

9: But God said to Jonah, "Do you do well to be angry for the plant?" And he said, "I do well to be angry, angry enough to die."

10: And the Lord said, "You pity the plant, for which you did not labor, nor did you make it grow, which came into being in a night, and perished in a night. 11: And should not I pity Nineveh, that great city, in which there are more than a hundred and twenty thousand persons who do not know their right hand from their left, and also much cattle?"

❖

E. THE BOOK OF JOB

(Job, an upright and pious man, has been struck by a series of disasters which have destroyed his family, his great wealth, and finally his health, leaving him only his shrewish wife. In a society where it was believed that God rewarded the just and punished the evil, Job's sufferings presented a terrible problem.)

Now when Job's three friends heard of all this evil that had come upon him, they came each from his own place, Eliphaz the Temanite, Bildad the Shuhite, and Zophar the Naamathite. They made an appointment together to come and comfort him. And when they saw him from afar, they did not recognize him; and they raised their voices and wept; and they rent their robes and sprinkled dust upon their heads toward heaven.

After this Job opened his mouth and cursed
    the day of his birth. And Job said:
Let the day perish wherein I was born, and the
    night which said, "A man child is con-
    ceived."
Let that day be darkness! May God above not
    seek it, nor light shine upon it.
Let the stars of its dawn be dark; let it hope
    for light, but have none, nor see the eyelids
    of the morning; because it did not shut the
    doors of my mother's womb, nor hide
    trouble from my eyes.
Why did I not die at birth, come forth from
    the womb and expire?
Why did the knees receive me? Or why did
    the breasts, that I should suck?

For then I should have lain down and been
    quiet; I should have slept; then I should
    have been at rest, with Kings and coun-
    selors of the earth who rebuilt ruins for
    themselves, or with princes who had gold,
    who filled their houses with silver.
Why is light given to him that is in misery and
    life to the bitter in soul?
Why is light given to a man whose way is hid,
    whom God has hedged in?
Then Eliphaz the Temanite answered:
If one ventures a word with you, will you be
    offended?
Is not your fear of God your confidence, and
    the integrity of your ways your hope?
Think now, who that was innocent ever per-
    ished? Or where were the upright cut off?
As I have seen, those who plow inequity and
    sow trouble reap the same.
By the breath of God they perish, and by the
    blast of his anger they are consumed. Can
    mortal man be righteous before God? Can
    a man be pure before his maker?
For affliction does not come from the dust,
    nor does trouble sprout from the ground;
    but man is born to trouble as the sparks fly
    upward.
Behold, happy is the man whom God re-
    proves; therefore despise not the chastening
    of the Almighty.
For he wounds, but he binds up; he smites,
    but his hands heal.
Then Job answered:
Teach me and I will be silent; make me under-
    stand how I have erred.
How forceful are honest words! But what does
    reproof from you reprove?
You would even cast lots over the fatherless,
    and bargain over your friend.
Therefore I will not restrain my mouth; I will
    speak in the anguish of my spirit. I will
    complain in the bitterness of my soul.
Then Bildad the Shuhite answered:
How long will you say these things, and the
    words of your mouth be a great wind?
Does God pervert justice? Or does the
    almighty pervert the right?
Behold, God will not reject a blameless man,
    nor take the hand of evildoers.
Then Job answered:
Truly I know that it is so: But how can a man
    be just before God?

If one wished to contend with him, one could not answer him once in a thousand times.

How then can I answer him; choosing my words with him?

Though I am innocent, I cannot answer him; I must appeal for mercy to my accuser.

There is no umpire between us, who might lay his hand upon us both.

Let him take his rod away from me, and let not dread of him terrify me.

Then I would speak without fear of him, for I am not so in myself.

Then Zophar the Naamathite answered:

Should your babble silence men, and when you mock, shall no one shame you?

For you say, "My doctrine is pure, and I am clean in God's eyes."

But oh, that God would speak, and open his lips to you, and that he would tell you the secrets of wisdom!

If you set your heart aright, you will stretch out your hands toward him.

Surely then you will lift up your face without blemish; you will be secure, and will not fear.

Then Job answered:

No doubt you are the people, and wisdom will die with you.

But I have understanding as well as you; I am not inferior to you.

Who does not know such things as these?

I am a laughingstock to my friends; I, who called upon God and he answered me, a just and blameless man, am a laughingstock.

But I would speak to the Almighty, and I desire to argue my case with God.

Man that is born of woman, is of a few days and full of trouble.

He comes forth like a flower, and withers....

Since his days are determined, and the number of his months is with thee, and thou hast appointed his bounds that he cannot pass, look away from him and desist, that he may enjoy, like a hireling, his day.

Why do the wicked live, reach old age, and grow mighty in power?

Their houses are safe from fear, and no rod of God is upon them.

They say to God, "Depart from us! We do not desire the knowledge of thy ways. What is the Almighty that we should serve him?

And what profit do we get if we pray to Him?"

Behold, is not their prosperity in their hand? The counsel of the wicked is far from me.

As God lives, who has taken away my right, and the Almighty, who has made my soul bitter;

as long as my breath is in me, and the spirit of God is in my nostrils;

my lips will not speak falsehood, and my tongue will not utter deceit.

Till I die I will not put away my integrity from me.

I will hold fast to my righteousness, and will not let it go; my heart does not reproach me for any of my days.

Let me be weighed in just balance, and let God know my integrity!

Then the Lord answered Job out of the whirlwind:

Who is this that darkens counsel by words without knowledge?

Gird up your loins like a man, I will question you, and you shall declare to me.

Where were you when I laid the foundations of the earth?

Tell me, if you have understanding: Who determined its measurements? Surely you know!

Or who stretched the line upon it?

On what were its bases sunk, or who laid its cornerstone

when the morning stars sang together, and all the sons of God shouted for joy?

Or who shut in the sea with doors, when it burst forth from the womb;

when I made clouds its garment, and thick darkness its swaddling band, and prescribed bounds for it, and set bars and doors, and said,

"Thus far shall you come, and no farther, and here shall your proud waves be stayed"?

Where is the way to the dwelling of light, and where is the place of darkness, that you may take it to its territory and that you may discern the paths to its home?

You know, for you were born then, and the number of your days is great!

Do you give the horse his might? Do you clothe his neck with strength?

Is it by your wisdom that the hawk soars, and spreads his wings toward the south?

Is it at your command that the eagle mounts up and makes his nest on high?

Shall a faultfinder contend with the Almighty?
He who argues with God, let him answer
it.
Deck yourself with majesty and dignity; clothe
yourself with glory and splendor.
Pour forth the overflowings of your anger, and
look on everyone that is proud and abase
him.
Look on everyone that is proud and bring him
low; and tread down the wicked where they
stand.
Hide them all in the dust together; bind their
faces in the world below.
Then will I also acknowledge to you, that your
own right hand can give you victory.
Who has given to me, that I should repay
him? Whatever is under the whole heaven
is mine.
Then Job answered the Lord:
I know that thou canst do all things, and that
no purpose of thine can be thwarted.
Who is this that hides counsel without knowledge?
Therefore I have uttered what I did not understand, things too wonderful for me,
which I did not know.
Hear, and I will speak; I will question you, and
you declare to me.
I had but heard of thee by the hearing of the
ear, but now my eye sees thee; therefore I
despise myself, and repent in dust and
ashes.

❖

4. PERSIA AND ZARATHUSTRA: THE GATHAS

A. FROM YASNA 30

(1) Truly for seekers I shall speak of those things to be pondered, even by one who already knows, with praise and worship for the Lord of Good Purpose, the excellently Wise One, and for Truth .... (2) Hear with your ears the best things. Reflect with clear purpose, each man for himself, on the two choices for decision, being alert indeed to declare yourselves for Him before the great requital. (3) Truly there are two primal Spirits, twins renowned to be in conflict. In thought and word, in act they are two: the better and the bad. And those who act well have chosen rightly between these two, not so the evildoers. (4) And when these two Spirits first came together they created life and not-life, and how at the end Worst Existence shall be for the wicked, but (the House of) Best Purpose for the just man. (5) Of these two Spirits the Wicked One chose achieving the worst things. The Most Holy Spirit, who is clad in hardest stone, chose right, and (so do those) who shall satisfy Lord Mazda continually with rightful acts. (6) The Daevas indeed did not choose rightly between these two, for the Deceiver approached them as they conferred. Because they chose worst purpose, they then rushed to Fury, with whom they have afflicted the world and mankind. (7) With Power He came to this world, by Good Purpose and by Truth. Then enduring Devotion gave body and breath .... (8) Then when retribution comes for these sinners, then, Mazda, Power shall be present for Thee with Good Purpose, to declare himself for those, Lord, who shall deliver the Lie into the hands of Truth. (9) And then may we be those who shall transfigure this world. o Mazda (and you other) Lords (Ahuras), be present to me with support and truth, so that thoughts may be concentrated where understanding falters .... (11) O men! when you learn the commands which Mazda has given, and both thriving and not-thriving, and what long torment (is) for the wicked and salvation for the just—then will it be as is wished with these things.

B. FROM YASNA 46

(1) To what land to flee? Whither shall I go to flee? They thrust me from family and clan. The community with which I have kept company has not shown me hospitality, nor those who are the wicked rulers of the land. How then shall I propitiate Thee, Lord Mazda? (2) I know why I am powerless, Mazda: I possess few cattle and few men. I lament to Thee. Take heed of it, Lord, granting the support which friend should give to friend. let me behold the might of Good Purpose with Truth! ... (7) Whom, Mazda, hast Thou appointed protector for one like me, if the Wicked One shall dare to harm me! Whom but Thy Fire and Thy (Good) Purpose by whose acts, Lord, Truth is nourished. Proclaim this teaching to my Inner Self! ... (10) Whosoever, Lord, man or woman, will grant me those things Thou knowest best for life—recompense for truth, power with good purpose—and those whom I shall bring to Your worship, with all thee shall I cross over the Chinvat Bridge. (11) Karapans and kavis by their powers yoked mankind with evil acts to destroy life. But their own soul and Inner Self tormented them when they reached the Chinvat Bridge—guests for ever in the House of the Lie!

C. FROM YASNA 49

(1) Truly in my lifetime I have been condemned as the greatest defiler, I who seek to satisfy with truth those who are poorly protected, O Mazda! With good apportioning of gifts come to me, support me! ... (4) Those who with ill purpose increased with their tongues fury and cruelty, they the non-pastors among pastors, for whom evil deeds have prevailed, they having no good deeds, they serve the Daevas, which is the religion of the wicked man. (5) But he, O Mazda, is himself the sacrifice and oblation who has allied his Inner Self with Good purpose. Whoever belongs to Devotion is of the (same) good lineage as Truth, and as all those in Thy dominion (khshathra), Lord .... (10) This Thou dost guard in Thy house, O Mazda—good purpose, and the souls of the just, and reverence with which there is devotion and sacrifice—this Thou dost guard, O Thou of mighty power, with abiding strength. (11) But the wicked, of bad power, bad act, bad word, bad

Inner Self, bad purpose—(departed) souls will encounter (them) with ill nourishment, they shall be rightful guests in the House of the Lie. (12) What help hast Thou, through Truth, for him who invokes Thee? What help, through Good Purpose, for Zarathustra, who will celebrate You all, Lord Mazda, with praises, while longing for the best in Your possession?

✝

5. ANOTHER VERSION: "THE SCROLLS"

WOODY ALLEN

Without belaboring the point, to what extent does the following piece depend on the tradition elaborated in these pages? If you had to, how could you use this work to illustrate the way that tradition has developed in our own age?

Scholars will recall that several years ago a shepherd, wandering in the Gulf of Aqaba, stumbled upon a cave containing several large clay jars and also two tickets to the ice show. Inside the jars were discovered six parchment scrolls with ancient incomprehensible writing which the shepherd, in his ignorance, sold to the museum for 750,000 dollars apiece. Two years later the jars turned up in a pawn shop in Philadelphia. One year later the shepherd turned up in a pawn shop in Philadelphia and neither was claimed.

Archaeologists originally set the date of the scrolls at 4000 B.C., or just after the massacre of the Israelites by their benefactors. The writing is a mixture of Sumerian, Aramaic and Babylonian and seems to have been done by either one man over a long period of time, or several men who shared the same suit. The authenticity of the scrolls is currently in great doubt, particularly since the word Oldsmobile appears several times in the text, and the few fragments that have finally been translated deal with familiar religious themes in a more than dubious way. Still, excavationist A. H. Bauer has noted that even though the fragments seem totally fraudulent, this is probably the greatest archaeological find in history with the exception of the recovery of his cufflinks from a tomb in Jerusalem. The following are the translated fragments.

*One...*And the Lord made an bet with Satan to test Job's loyalty and the Lord, for no apparent reason to Job, smote him on the head and again on the ear and pushed him into an thick sauce so as to make Job sticky and vile and then He slew a 10th part of Job's kine and Job calleth out: "Why doth thou slay my kine? Kine are hard to come by. Now I am short kine and I'm not even sure what kine are." And the Lord produced two stone tablets and snapped them closed on Job's nose. And when Job's wife saw this she wept and the Lord sent an angel of mercy who anointed her head with a polo mallet and of the 10 plagues, the Lord sent one through six, inclusive, and Job was sore and his wife angry and she rent her garment and then raised the rent but refused to paint.

And soon Job's pastures dried up and his tongue cleaved to the roof of his mouth so he could not pronounce the word "frankincense" without getting big laughs.

And once the Lord, while wreaking havoc upon his faithful servant, came too close and Job grabbed him around the neck and said, "Aha! Now I got you! Why art thou giving Job a hard time, eh? Eh? Speak up!"

And the Lord said, "Er, look–that's my neck you have...could you let me go?"

But Job showed no mercy and said, "I was doing very well till you came along. I had myrrh and fig trees in abundance and a coat of many colors with two pairs of pants and many colors. Now look."

And the Lord spake and his voice thundered. "Must I who created heaven and earth explain my ways to thee? What hath thou created that thou doth dare question me?"

"That's no answer," Job said. "And for someone who's supposed to be omnipotent, let me tell you, 'tabernacle' has only one 'L.'" Then Job fell to his knees and cried to the Lord. "Thine is the kingdom and the power and the glory. Thou hast a good job. Don't blow it."

*Two...*And Abraham awoke in the middle of the night and said to his only son, Isaac, "I have had an dream where the voice of the Lord sayeth that I must sacrifice my only son, so put your pants on." And Isaac trembled and said, "So what did you say? I mean when He brought this whole thing up?"

"What am I going to say?" Abraham said. "I'm standing there at two a.m. in my underwear with the Creator of the Universe. Should I argue?"

"Well, did he say why he wants me sacrificed?" Isaac asked his father.

But Abraham said, "The faithful do not question. Now let's go because I have a heavy day tomorrow."

And Sarah who heard Abraham's plan grew vexed and said, "How doth thou know it was the Lord and not, say, thy friend who loveth practical jokes, for the Lord hateth practical jokes and whosoever shall pull one shall be delivered into the hands of his enemies whether they can pay the delivery charge or not." And Abraham answered, "Because I know it was the Lord. It was a deep, resonant voice, well modulated, and nobody in the desert can get a rumble in it like that."

And Sarah said, "And thou art willing to carry out this senseless act?" But Abraham told her, "Frankly, yes, for to question the Lord's word is one of the worst things a person can do, particularly with the economy in the state it's in."

And so he took Isaac to a certain place and prepared to sacrifice him but at the last minute the Lord stayed Abraham's hand and said, "How could thou doest such a thing?" And Abraham said, "But thou said...."

"Never mind what I said," the Lord spake. "Doth thou listen to every crazy idea that comes thy way?" And Abraham grew ashamed. "Er– not really...no..."

"I jokingly suggest thou sacrifice Isaac and thou immediately runs out to do it."

And Abraham fell to his knees, "See, I never know when you're kidding."

And the Lord thundered, "No sense of humor. I can't believe it."

"But doth this not prove I love thee, that I was willing to donate mine only son on thy whim?"

And the Lord said, "It proves that some men will follow any order no matter how asinine as long as it comes from a resonant, well modulated voice."

And with that, the Lord bid Abraham get some rest and check with him tomorrow.

Three...And it came to pass that a man who sold shirts was smitten by hard times. Neither did any of his merchandise move nor did he prosper. And he prayed and said, "Lord, why has thou left me to suffer thus? All mine enemies sell their goods except I. And it's the height of the season. My shirts are good shirts. Take a look at this rayon. I got button-downs, flare collars, nothing sells. Yet I have kept thy commandments. Why can I not earn a living when mine younger brother cleans up in children's ready-to-wear?"

And the Lord heard the man and said, "About thy shirts..."

"Yes, Lord," the man said, falling to his knees.

"Put an alligator over the pocket."

"Pardon me, Lord?"

"Just do what I'm telling you, You won't be sorry."

And the man sewed on to all his shirts a small alligator symbol and lo and behold, suddenly his merchandise moved like gangbusters and there was much rejoicing while amongst his enemies there was wailing and gnashing of teeth and one said, "The Lord is merciful. He maketh me to lie down in green pastures. The problem is, I can't get up."

Laws and Proverbs:

Doing abominations is against the law, particularly if the abominations are done while wearing a lobster bib.

The lion and the calf shall lie down together but the calf won't get much sleep.

Whosoever shall not fall by the sword or by famine, shall fall by pestilence, so why bother shaving?

The wicked at heart probably know something.

Whosoever loveth wisdom is righteous but he that keepeth company with fowl is weird.

My Lord, my Lord! What hast thou done, lately?

✝

PART II

DEFINING THE INDIVIDUAL: GREECE AND ROME

Departing Soldier, Attic red figure cup (c. 470 B.C.)

IV. Greek Heroes

From the ancient states of Greece and Rome come certain of our basic concepts of the state and the role of citizens in society. It is typical to say that the Greeks gave us democracy. While this is true, an even more important concept underlies it: that of the value of the individual. In earlier ages, the needs and goals of all were thought to be identical: there was no difference between the needs of the individual and those of the group. Our concept of a separation of interests between the individual and the group, and of a duty to ourselves as well as to the state, is something we derive in part from the Greeks.

The readings in this chapter illustrate the emerging idea of the individual in Greece. First, HOMER'S *Iliad*, long considered the foundation piece of Western literature. Following that, some verses from the Greek LYRIC POETS who wrote about a century after Homer. Finally, SOPHOCLES' *Antigone*, a classic of the genre of tragedy that flourished in the Golden age of the fifth century B. C.. You may already have read some or all of these works in literature classes. But now you need to think of them as historical documents. What values do they reveal? Do you see different values in them? What do the different values tell you about the different periods that produced them? What do all of them, together, tell you about the Greeks?

One way to approach a big question like this is to look at the traits of their heroes: How do Achilles, say, or Antigone compare with a great Near Eastern hero such as Gilgamesh?

Try the technique on yourself: Do you have a hero? What does this hero tell us about you? If we were studying you from some future age, how could we tell if your hero also is a hero for Americans as a whole? For that matter, who is the American hero? Do we have someone that other people could study the way we study the heroes of the Greeks and Romans? What sort of things do you learn about us from our heroes? From comparing our heroes with those of antiquity?

❖   ❖   ❖

The indiv. vs. state: Achilles the indiv. fights for his own glory and not ~~fore~~ for Greece. He stops fighting when Agamemnon takes away his prize.

1. THE ILIAD

HOMER

Homer (c. 800 B.C.) was the master of epic poetry, a key figure in the history of Western literature, and as much of a national character as the Greeks ever had. Greeks of all types would be expected to know most if not all of his works, *The Iliad* and *The Odyssey*, by heart—just as a century ago pious Americans knew the Bible.

The Iliad focuses on one episode of the great Greek war against Troy, or "Ilios," as it is often called in the epic. According to legend, Greeks besieged the famous city on the Hellespont in Asia Minor after a Trojan prince, Alexander (also called "Paris") ran off with Helen, the wife of Menelaus, the king of Sparta. Menelaus's brother was Agamemnon, an overlord who commanded

an army made up of troops from all the lesser kingdoms of Greece. After ten years, the Greeks finally captured Troy through a trick. Pretending to give up hope of taking the well-fortified city, they sailed away leaving behind a present for the Trojans—a giant wooden replica of a horse, the animal who represented Troy's patron deity, Poseidon. The horse was in fact filled with Greek soldiers who took control of the city after the jubilant Trojans dragged the horse inside their gates (hence the famous line, coined by Vergil in *The Aeneid*), "Beware of Greeks bearing gifts.

Homer's tale does not cover the whole ten-year period. Instead, it focuses on events near the end of that period, when Agamemnon provoked the wrath of the great warrior Achilles, son of Peleus and the goddess Thetis. Achilles in turn takes himself out of the fight. Before he eventually returned to battle, the Greek forces were almost destroyed by the Trojans, led by their hero, Hector. Consider Achilles' reasons for leaving and for coming back—what do they tell you about Greek heroes? Does Hector fight for the same reasons, or different ones? What do you learn by comparing Achilles and Hector? The end of the war—the story of the Trojan Horse—is not in the *Iliad*. What does that tell you?

In the following passages, Homer uses a variety of terms for the Greeks—"Danaans," "Achaians," "Argives." Agamemnon and Menelaus were both sons of Atreus, and they are sometimes called the Atreidai or Atreides (a name used again in a famous science-fiction novel).

From Book I: The Quarrel

[Homer begins the tale by telling of the events that led Achilles (Achilleus) to stop fighting, which begin when Agamemnon refuses to return the daughter of Chryses, a priest of Apollo. In return, Apollo sends a plague against the Greeks.]

Sing, goddess, the anger of Peleus' son
    Achilleus
and its devastation, which put pains thousand-
    fold upon the Achaians,
hurled in their multitudes to the house of
    Hades strong souls
of heroes, but gave their bodies to the delicate
    feasting
of dogs, of all birds, and the will of Zeus was
    accomplished
since that time when first there stood in divi-
    sion of conflict
Atreus' son the lord of men and brilliant
    Achilleus.
What god was it then set them together in bit-
    ter collision?
Zeus' son and Leto's, Apollo, who in anger at
    the king drove
the foul pestilence along the host, and the
    people perished,
since Atreus' son had dishonored Chryses,
    priest of Apollo,
when he came beside the fast ships of the
    Achaians to ransom
back his daughter, carrying gifts beyond count
    and holding
in his hands wound on a staff of gold the rib-
    bons of Apollo
who strikes from afar, and supplicated all the
    Achaians,
but above all Atreus' two sons, the marshals of
    the people:

"Sons of Atreus and you other strong-greaved
    Achaians,
to you may the gods grant who have their
    homes on Olympus
Priam's city to be plundered and a fair home-
    coming thereafter,
but may you give me back my own daughter
    and take the ransom,
giving honor to Zeus' son who strikes from
    afar, Apollo."
Then all the rest of the Achaians cried out in
    favor
that the priest be respected and the shining
    ransom be taken;
yet this pleased not the heart of Atreus' son
    Agamemnon,
but harshly he drove him away with a strong
    order upon him:
"Never let me find you again, old sir, near our
    hollow
ships, neither lingering now nor coming again
    hereafter,
for fear your staff and the god's ribbons help
    you no longer.
The girl I will not give back; sooner will old
    age come upon her
in my own house, in Argos, far from her own
    land, going
up and down by the loom and being in my bed
    as my companion.
So go now, do not make me angry; so you will
    be safer."
So he spoke, and the old man in terror obeyed
    him
and went silently away beside the murmuring
    sea beach.
Over and over the old man prayed as he
    walked in solitude
to King Apollo, whom Leto of the lovely hair
    bore: "Hear me,
lord of the silver bow who set your power
    about Chryse
and Killa the sacrosanct, who are lord in
    strength over Tenedos,
Smintheus, if ever it pleased your heart that I
    built your temple,
if ever it pleased you that I burned all the rich
    thigh pieces
of bulls, of goats, then bring to pass this wish I
    pray for:
let your arrows make the Danaans pay for my
    tears shed."

So he spoke in prayer, and Phoibos Apollo heard him,
and strode down along the pinnacles of Olympus, angered
in his heart, carrying across his shoulders the bow and the hooded
quiver; and the shafts clashed on the shoulders of the god walking
angrily. He came as night comes down and knelt then
apart and opposite the ships and let go an arrow.
Terrible was the clash that rose from the bow of silver.
First he went after the mules and the circling hounds, then let go a
tearing arrow against the men themselves and struck them.
The corpse fires burned everywhere and did not stop burning.
Nine days up and down the host ranged the god's arrows,
but on the tenth Achilleus called the people to assembly;
a thing put into his mind by the goddess of the white arms, Hera,
who had pity upon the Danaans when she saw them dying.
Now when they were all assembled in one place together,
Achilleus of the swift feet stood up among them and spoke forth:
"Son of Atreus, I believe now that straggling backwards
we must make our way home if we can even escape death,
if fighting now must crush the Achaians and the plague likewise.
No, come, let us ask some holy man, some prophet,
even an interpreter of dreams, since a dream also
comes from Zeus, who can tell why Phoibos Apollo is so angry,
if for the sake of some vow, some hecatomb he blames us,
if given the fragrant smoke of lambs, of he goats, somehow
he can be made willing to beat the bane aside from us."
He spoke thus and sat down again, and among them stood up

Kalchas, Thestor's son, far the best of the bird interpreters,
who knew all things that were, the things to come and the things past,
who guided into the land of Ilion the ships of the Achaians
through that seercraft of his own that Phoibos Apollo gave him.
He in kind intention toward all stood forth and addressed them:
"You have bidden me, Achilleus beloved of Zeus, to explain to
you this anger of Apollo the lord who strikes from afar. Then
I will speak; yet make me a promise and swear before me
readily by word and work of your hands to defend me,
since I believe I shall make a man angry who holds great kingship
over the men of Argos, and all the Achaians obey him.
For a king when he is angry with a man beneath him is too strong,
and suppose even for the day itself he swallow down his anger,
he still keeps bitterness that remains until its fulfillment
deep in his chest. Speak forth then, tell me if you will protect me."
Then in answer again spoke Achilleus of the swift feet:
"Speak, interpreting whatever you know, and fear nothing.
In the name of Apollo beloved of Zeus to whom you, Kalchas,
make your prayers when you interpret the gods' will to the Danaans,
no man so long as I am alive above earth and see daylight
shall lay the weight of his hands on you beside the hollow ships,
not one of all the Danaans, even if you mean Agamemnon,
who now claims to be far the greatest of all the Achaians."
At this the blameless seer took courage again and spoke forth:
"No, it is not for the sake of some vow or hecatomb he blames us,
but for the sake of his priest whom Agamemnon dishonored

and would not give him back his daughter nor accept the ransom.

Therefore the archer sends griefs against us and will send them

still, nor sooner thrust back the shameful plague from the Danaans

until we give the glancing-eyed girl back to her father

without price, without ransom, and lead also a blessed hecatomb

to Chryse; thus we might propitiate and persuade him."

He spoke thus and sat down again, and among them stood up

Atreus' son the hero wide-ruling Agamemnon

raging, the heart within him filled black to the brim with anger

from beneath, but his two eyes showed like fire in their blazing.

First of all he eyed Kalchas bitterly and spoke to him:

"Seer of evil, never yet have you told me a good thing.

Always the evil things are dear to your heart to prophesy,

but nothing excellent have you said nor ever accomplished.

Now once more you make divination to the Danaans, argue

forth your reason why he who strikes from afar afflicts them,

because I for the sake of the girl Chryseis would not take

the shining ransom; and indeed I wish greatly to have her

in my own house since I like her better than Klytaimnestra

my own wife, for in truth she is no way inferior,

neither in build nor stature nor wit, not in accomplishment.

Still I am willing to give her back, if such is the best way.

I myself desire that my people be safe, not perish.

Find me then some prize that shall be my own, lest I only

among the Argives go without, since that were unfitting;

you are all witnesses to this thing, that my prize goes elsewhere."

Then in answer again spoke brilliant swift-footed Achilleus:

"Son of Atreus, most lordly, greediest for gain of all men,

how shall the great-hearted Achaians give you a prize now?

There is no great store of things lying about I know of.

But what we took from the cities by storm has been distributed;

it is unbecoming for the people to call back things once given.

No, for the present give the girl back to the god; we Achaians

thrice and four times over will repay you, if ever Zeus gives

into our hands the strong-walled citadel of Troy to be plundered."

Then in answer again spoke powerful Agamemnon:

"Not that way, good fighter though you be, godlike Achilleus,

strive to cheat, for you will not deceive, you will not persuade me.

What do you want? To keep your own prize and have me sit here

lacking one? Are you ordering me to give this girl back?

Either the great-hearted Achaians shall give me a new prize

chosen according to my desire to atone for the girl lost,

or else if they will not give me one I myself shall take her,

your own prize, or that of Aias, or that of Odysseus,

going myself in person; and he whom I visit will be bitter.

Still, these are things we shall deliberate again hereafter.

Come, now, we must haul a black ship down to the bright sea,

and assemble rowers enough for it, and put on board it

the hecatomb, and the girl herself, Chryseis of the fair cheeks,

and let there be one responsible man in charge of her,

either Aias or Idomeneus or brilliant Odysseus,

or you yourself, son of Peleus, most terrifying of all men,

to reconcile by accomplishing sacrifice the archer."

Then looking darkly at him Achilleus of the
    swift feet spoke:
"O wrapped in shamelessness, with your mind
    forever on profit,
how shall any one of the Achaians readily obey
    you
either to go on a journey or to fight men
    strongly in battle?
I for my part did not come here for the sake of
    the Trojan
spearmen to fight against them, since to me
    they have done nothing.
Never yet have they driven away my cattle or
    my horses,
never in Phthia where the soil is rich and men
    grow great did they spoil my harvest, since
    indeed there is much that lies between us,
the shadowy mountains and the echoing sea;
    but for your sake,
O great shamelessness, we followed, to do you
    favor,
you with the dog's eyes, to win your honor and
    Menelaos'
from the Trojans. You forget all this or else
    you care nothing.
And now my prize you threaten in person to
    strip from me,
for whom I labored much, the gift of the sons
    of the Achaians.
Never, when the Achaians sack some well-
    founded citadel
of the Trojans, do I have a prize that is equal
    to your prize.
Always the greater part of the painful fighting
    is the work of
my hands; but when the time comes to dis-
    tribute the booty
yours is far the greater reward, and I with
    some small thing
yet dear to me go back to my ships when I am
    weary with fighting.
Now I am returning to Phthia, since it is
    much better
to go home again with my curved ships, and I
    am minded no longer
to stay here dishonored and pile up your
    wealth and your luxury."
Then answered him in turn the lord of men
    Agamemnon:
"Run away by all means if your heart drives
    you. I will not
entreat you to stay here for my sake. There are
    others with me

who will do me honor, and above all Zeus of
    the counsels.
To me you are the most hateful of all the kings
    whom the gods love.
Forever quarreling is dear to your heart, and
    wars and battles;
and if you are very strong indeed, that is a
    god's gift.
Go home then with your own ships and your
    own companions,
be king over the Myrmidons. I care nothing
    about you.
I take no account of your anger. But here is
    my threat to you.
Even as Phoibos Apollo is taking away my
    Chryseis,
I shall convey her back in my own ship, with
    my own
followers; but I shall take the fair-cheeked
    Briseis,
your prize, I myself going to your shelter, that
    you may learn well
how much greater I am than you, and another
    man may shrink back
from likening himself to me and contending
    against me."
So he spoke. And the anger came on Peleus'
    son, and within
his shaggy breast the heart was divided two
    ways, pondering
whether to draw from beside his thigh the
    sharp sword, driving
away all those who stood between and kill the
    son of Atreus,
or else to check the spleen within and keep
    down his anger.
Now as he weighed in mind and spirit these
    two courses
and was drawing from his scabbard the great
    sword, Athene descended
from the sky. For Hera the goddess of the
    white arms sent her,
who loved both men equally in her heart and
    cared for them.
The goddess standing behind Peleus' son
    caught him by the fair hair,
appearing to him only, for no man of the oth-
    ers saw her.
Achilleus in amazement turned about, and
    straightway
knew Pallas Athene and the terrible eyes
    shining.

He uttered winged words and addressed her: "Why have you come now,

O child of Zeus of the aegis, once more? Is it that you may see

the outrageousness of the son of Atreus Agamemnon?

Yet will I tell you this thing, and I think it shall be accomplished.

By such acts of arrogance he may even lose his own life."

Then in answer the goddess grey-eyed Athene spoke to him:

"I have come down to stay your anger—but will you obey me?—

from the sky; and the goddess of the white arms Hera sent me,

who loves both of you equally in her heart and cares for you.

Come then, do not take your sword in your hand, keep clear of fighting,

though indeed with words you may abuse him, and it will be that way.

And this also will I tell you and it will be a thing accomplished. Some day three times over such shining gifts shall be given you

by reason of this outrage. Hold your hand then, and obey us."

Then in answer again spoke Achilleus of the swift feet:

"Goddess, it is necessary that I obey the word of you two,

angry though I am in my heart. So it will be better.

If any man obeys the gods, they listen to him also."

He spoke, and laid his heavy hand on the silver sword hilt

and thrust the great blade back into the scabbard nor disobeyed

the word of Athene. And she went back again to Olympus

to the house of Zeus of the aegis with the other divinities.

But Peleus' son once again in words of derision

spoke to Atreides, and did not yet let go of his anger:

"You wine sack, with a dog's eyes, with a deer's heart. Never

once have you taken courage in your heart to arm with your people

for battle, or go into ambuscade with the best of the Achaians.

No, for in such things you see death. Far better to your mind

is it, all along the widespread host of the Achaians

to take away the gifts of any man who speaks up against you.

King who feed on your people, since you rule nonentities;

otherwise, son of Atreus, this were your last outrage.

But I will tell you this and swear a great oath upon it:

in the name of this sceptre, which never again will bear leaf nor

branch, now that it has left behind the cut stump in the mountains,

nor shall it ever blossom again, since the bronze blade stripped

bark and leafage, and now at last the sons of the Achaians

carry it in their hands in state when they administer

the justice of Zeus. And this shall be a great oath before you:

some day longing for Achilleus will come to the sons of the Achaians,

all of them. Then stricken at heart though you be, you will be able

to do nothing, when in their numbers before man-slaughtering Hektor

they drop and die. And then you will eat out the heart within you

in sorrow, that you did no honor to the best of the Achaians."

Thus spoke Peleus' son and dashed to the ground the sceptre

studded with golden nails, and sat down again. But Atreides

raged still on the other side, and between them Nestor

the fair-spoken rose up, the lucid speaker of Pylos,

from whose lips the streams of words ran sweeter than honey.

In his time two generations of mortal men had perished,

those who had grown up with him and they who had been born to

these in sacred Pylos, and he was king in the third age.

He in kind intention toward both stood forth and addressed them:

"Oh, for shame. Great sorrow comes on the
land of Achaia.

Now might Priam and the sons of Priam in
truth be happy,

and all the rest of the Trojans be visited in
their hearts with gladness,

were they to hear all this wherein you two are
quarreling,

you, who surpass all Danaans in council, in
fighting.

You, great man that you are, yet do not take
the girl away

but let her be, a prize as the sons of the Achaians gave her

first. Nor, son of Peleus, think to match your
strength with

the king, since never equal with the rest is the
portion of honor

of the sceptered king to whom Zeus gives
magnificence. Even

though you are the stronger man, and the
mother who bore you was immortal,

yet is this man greater who is lord over more
than you rule.

Son of Atreus, give up your anger; even I entreat you

to give over your bitterness against Achilleus,
he who

stands as a great bulwark of battle over the
Achaians."

Then in answer again spoke powerful
Agamemnon:

"Yes, old sir, all this you have said is fair and
orderly.

Yet here is a man who wishes to be above all
others,

who wishes to hold power over all, and to be
lord of

all, and give them their orders, yet I think I
will not obey him.

And if the everlasting gods have made him a
spearman,

yet they have not given him the right to speak
abusively."

Then looking at him darkly brilliant Achilleus
answered him:

"So must I be called of no account and a coward

if I must carry out every order you may happen
to give me.

Tell other men to do these things, but give me
no more

commands, since I for my part have no intention to obey you.

And put away in your thoughts this other
thing I tell you.

With my hands I will not fight for the girl's
sake, neither

with you nor any other man, since you take
her away who gave her.

But of all the other things that are mine beside
my fast black

ship, you shall take nothing away against my
pleasure.

Come, then, only try it, that these others may
see also;

instantly your own black blood will stain my
spearpoint."

So these two after battling in words of contention

stood up, and broke the assembly beside the
ships of the Achaians.

Peleus' son went back to his balanced ships
and his shelter

with Patroklos, Menoitios' son, and his own
companions.

From Book I: Zeus's Oath

[In his anger, Achilleus asks his mother, the goddess Thetis, to turn Zeus against the Greeks.]

But when the twelfth dawn after this day appeared, the gods who

live forever came back to Olympus all in a
body

and Zeus led them; nor did Thetis forget the
entreaties

of her son, but she emerged from the sea's
waves early

in the morning and went up to the tall sky and
Olympus.

She found Kronos' broad-browed son apart
from the others

sitting upon the highest peak of rugged
Olympus.

She came and sat beside him with her left
hand embracing

his knees, but took him underneath the chin
with her right hand

and spoke in supplication to lord Zeus son of
Kronos:

"Father Zeus, if ever before in word or action
I did you favor among the immortals, now
grant what I ask for.

Now give honor to my son short-lived beyond
all other

mortals. Since even now the lord of men
Agamemnon

dishonors him, who has taken away his prize
and keeps it.

Zeus of the counsels, lord of Olympus, now do
him honor.

So long put strength into the Trojans, until
the Achaians

give my son his rights, and his honor is increased among them."

She spoke thus. But Zeus who gathers the
clouds made no answer

but sat in silence a long time. And Thetis, as
she had taken

his knees, clung fast to them and urged once
more her question:

"Bend your head and promise me to accomplish this thing,

or else refuse it, you have nothing to fear, that
I may know

by how much I am the most dishonored of all
gods."

Deeply disturbed Zeus who gathers the clouds
answered her:

"This is a disastrous matter when you set me
in conflict

with Hera, and she troubles me with recrimi-
nations.

Since even as things are, forever among the
immortals

she is at me and speaks of how I help the
Trojans in battle,

Even so, go back again now, go away, for fear
she

see us. I will look to these things that they be
accomplished.

See then, I will bend my head that you may
believe me.

For this among the immortal gods is the
mightiest witness

I can give, and nothing I do shall be vain nor
revocable

nor a thing unfulfilled when I bend my head
in assent to it."

He spoke, the son of Kronos, and nodded his
head with the dark brows,

and the immortally anointed hair of the great
god

swept from his divine head, and all Olympus
was shaken.

From Book II: The Assembly

[Zeus inspires Agamemnon to launch an offensive, even without Achilles to fight for him.]

Now the rest of the gods, and men who were
lords of chariots,

slept night long, but the ease of sleep came not
upon Zeus

who was pondering in his heart how he might
bring honor

to Achilleus, and destroy many beside the
ships of the Achaians.

Now to his mind this thing appeared to be the
best counsel,

to send evil Dream to Atreus' son Agamemnon.

He cried out to the dream and addressed him
in winged words:

"Go forth, evil Dream, beside the swift ships
of the Achaians.

Make your way to the shelter of Atreus' son
Agamemnon;

speak to him in words exactly as I command
you.

Bid him arm the flowing-haired Achaians for
battle

in all haste; since now he might take the wide-
wayed city

of the Trojans. For no longer are the gods who
live on Olympus

arguing the matter, since Hera forced them all
over

by her supplication, and evils are in store for
the Trojans."

So he spoke, and Dream listened to his word
and descended.

Lightly he came down beside the swift ships of
the Achaians

and came to Agamemnon the son of Atreus.
He found him

sleeping within his shelter in a cloud of immortal slumber.

Dream stood then beside his head in the likeness of Nestor,

Neleus' son, whom Agamemnon honored beyond all

elders beside. In Nestor's likeness the divine
Dream spoke to him:

"Son of wise Atreus breaker of horses, are you
sleeping?

He should not sleep night long who is a man
burdened with counsel

and responsibility for a people and cares so
 numerous.
Listen quickly to what I say, since I am a
 messenger
of Zeus, who far away cares much for you and
 is pitiful.
Zeus bids you arm the flowing-haired Achaians for battle
in all haste; since now you might take the
 wide-wayed city
of the Trojans. For no longer are the gods who
 live on Olympus
arguing the matter, since Hera forced them all
 over
by her supplication, and evils are in store for
 the Trojans
from Zeus. Keep this thought in your heart
 then, let not forgetfulness
take you, after you are released from the kindly
 sweet slumber."
So he spoke and went away, and left
 Agamemnon
there, believing things in his heart that were
 not to be accomplished.
For he thought that on that very day he would
 take Priam's city;
fool, who knew nothing of all the things Zeus
 planned to accomplish,
Zeus, who yet was minded to visit tears and
 sufferings
on Trojans and Danaans alike in the strong
 encounters.
But Agamemnon commanded his clear-voiced
 heralds to summon
by proclamation to assembly the flowing-
 haired Achaians,
and the heralds made their cry and the men
 were assembled swiftly.

[Agamemnon decides to try some "reverse psychology," hoping that by proposing to abandon
the siege, his army will insist the war go on. Before speaking, he arranges for other leaders to
lead a "spontaneous" demonstration against his
false plan.]

So he spoke and led the way departing from
 the council,
and the rest rose to their feet, the sceptred
 kings, obeying
the shepherd of the people, and the army
 thronged behind them
and gave over their clamoring. Powerful
 Agamemnon

stood up holding the sceptre Hephaistos had
 wrought him carefully.
Leaning upon this sceptre he spoke and addressed the Argives:
"Fighting men and friends, o Danaans,
 henchmen of Ares:
Zeus son of Kronos has caught me fast in bitter futility.
He is hard; who before this time promised me
 and consented
that I might sack strong-walled Ilion and sail
 homeward.
Now he has devised a vile deception, and bids
 me go back
to Argos in dishonor having lost many of my
 people.
Such is the way it will be pleasing to Zeus,
 who is too strong,
who before now has broken the crests of many
 cities
and will break them again, since his power is
 beyond all others.
And this shall be a thing of shame for the men
 hereafter
to be told, that so strong, so great a host of
 Achaians
carried on and fought in vain a war that was
 useless
against men fewer than they, with no accomplishment shown for it;
since if both sides were to be willing, Achaians
 and Trojans,
to cut faithful oaths of truce, and both to be
 numbered,
and the Trojans were to be counted by those
 with homes in the city,
while we were to be allotted in tens, we Achaians,
and each one of our tens chose a man of Troy
 to pour wine for it,
still there would be many tens left without a
 wine steward.
By so much I claim we sons of the Achaians
 outnumber
the Trojans—those who live in the city; but
 there are companions
from other cities in their numbers, wielders of
 the spear, to help them,
who drive me hard back again and will not allow me,
despite my will, to sack the well-founded
 stronghold of Ilion.

And now nine years of mighty Zeus have gone
   by, and the timbers
of our ships have rotted away and the cables
   are broken
and far away our own wives and our young
   children
are sitting within our halls and wait for us,
   while still our work here
stays forever unfinished as it is, for whose sake
   we came hither.
Come then, do as I say, let us all be won over;
   let us
run away with our ships to the beloved land of
   our fathers
since no longer now shall we capture Troy of
   the wide ways."
So he spoke, and stirred up the passion in the
   breast of all those
who were within that multitude and listened
   to his counsel.
And the assembly was shaken as on the sea the
   big waves
in the main by Ikaria, when the south and
   south-east winds
driving down from the clouds of Zeus the father whip them.
As when the west wind moves across the grain
   deep standing,
boisterously, and shakes and sweeps it till the
   tassels lean, so
all of that assembly was shaken, and the men
   in tumult
swept to the ships, and underneath their feet
   the dust lifted
and rose high, and the men were all shouting
   to one another
to lay hold on the ships and drag them down
   to the bright sea.
They cleaned out the keel channels and their
   cries hit skyward
as they made for home and snatched the props
   from under the vessels.

[When Agamemnon's stunt backfires, the goddess Athena urges Odysseus to stem the rout.]

Athene of the grey eyes stood beside him and
   spoke to him:
"Son of Laertes and seed of Zeus, resourceful
   Odysseus:
will it be this way? Will you all hurl yourselves
   into your benched ships
and take flight homeward to the beloved land
   of your fathers,

and would you thus leave to Priam and to the
   Trojans Helen
of Argos, to glory over, for whose sake many
   Achaians
lost their lives in Troy far from their own native country?
Go now along the host of the Achaians, give
   way no longer,
speak to each man in words of gentleness and
   draw them backward,
nor let them drag down to the salt sea their
   oarswept vessels."
So she spoke, and he knew the voice of the
   goddess speaking
and went on the run, throwing aside his cloak,
   which was caught up
by Eurybates the herald of Ithaka who followed him.
He came face to face with Agamemnon, son
   of Atreus,
and took from him the sceptre of his fathers,
   immortal forever.
With this he went beside the ships of the
   bronze-armored Achaians.
Whenever he encountered some king, or man
   of influence,
he would stand beside him and with soft
   words try to restrain him:
"Excellency! It does not become you to be
   frightened like any
coward. Rather hold fast and check the rest of
   the people.
You do not yet clearly understand the purpose
   of Atreides.
Now he makes trial, but soon will bear hard on
   the sons of the Achaians.
Did we not all hear what he was saying in
   council?
May he not in anger do some harm to the sons
   of the Achaians!
For the anger of god-supported kings is a big
   matter,
to whom honor and love are given from Zeus
   of the counsels."
When he saw some man of the people who
   was shouting,
he would strike at him with his staff, and re-
   prove him also:
"Excellency! Sit still and listen to what others
   tell you,
to those who are better men than you, you
   skulker and coward

and thing of no account whatever in battle or
   council.
Surely not all of us Achaians can be as kings
   here.
Lordship for many is no good thing. Let there
   be one ruler,
one king, to whom the son of devious-devising
   Kronos
gives the sceptre and right of judgment, to
   watch over his people."
So he went through the army marshaling it,
   until once more
they swept back into the assembly place from
   the ships and the shelters
clamorously, as when from the thunderous sea
   the surf-beat
crashes upon the great beach, and the whole
   sea is in tumult.
Now the rest had sat down, and were orderly
   in their places,
but one man. Thersites of the endless speech,
   still scolded,
who knew within his head many words, but
   disorderly;
vain, and without decency, to quarrel with the
   princes
with any word he thought might be amusing
   to the Argives.
This was the ugliest man who came beneath
   Ilion. He was
bandy-legged and went lame of one foot, with
   shoulders
stooped and drawn together over his chest,
   and above this
his skull went up to a point with the wool
   grown sparsely upon it.
Beyond all others Achilleus hated him, and
   Odysseus.
These two he was forever abusing, but now at
   brilliant
Agamemnon he clashed the shrill noise of his
   abuse. The Achaians
were furiously angry with him, their minds re-
   sentful.
But he, crying the words aloud, scolded
   Agamemnon:
"Son of Atreus, what thing further do you
   want, or find fault with
now? Your shelters are filled with bronze,
   there are plenty of the choicest
women for you within your shelter, whom we
   Achaians

give to you first of all whenever we capture
   some stronghold.
Or is it still more gold you will be wanting,
   that some son
of the Trojans, breakers of horses, brings as
   ransom out of Ilion,
one that I, or some other Achaian, capture and
   bring in?
Is it some young woman to lie with in love and
   keep her
all to yourself apart from the others? It is not
   right for
you, their leader, to lead in sorrow the sons of
   the Achaians.
My good fools, poor abuses, you women, not
   men, of Achaia,
let us go back home in our ships, and leave
   this man here
by himself in Troy to mull his prizes of honor
that he may find out whether or not we others
   are helping him.
And now he has dishonored Achilleus, a man
   much better
than he is. He has taken his prize by force and
   keeps her.
But there is no gall in Achilleus' heart, and he
   is forgiving.
Otherwise, son of Atreus, this were your last
   outrage."
So he spoke, Thersites, abusing Agamemnon
the shepherd of the people. But brilliant
   Odysseus swiftly
came beside him scowling and laid a harsh
   word upon him:
"Fluent orator though you be, Thersites, your
   words are
ill-considered. Stop, nor stand up alone
   against princes.
Out of all those who came beneath Ilion with
   Atreides
I assert there is no worse man than you are.
   Therefore
you shall not lift up your mouth to argue with
   princes,
cast reproaches into their teeth, nor sustain the
   homegoing.
We do not even know clearly how these things
   will be accomplished,
whether we sons of the Achaians shall win
   home well or badly;
yet you sit here throwing abuse at Agamemnon,

Atreus' son, the shepherd of the people, be-
     cause the Danaan
fighters give him much. You argue nothing
     but scandal.
And this also will I tell you, and it will be a
     thing accomplished.
If once more I find you playing the fool, as you
     are now,
nevermore let the head of Odysseus sit on his
     shoulders,
let me nevermore be called Telemachos' father,
if I do not take you and strip away your per-
     sonal clothing,
your mantle and your tunic that cover over
     your nakedness,
and send you thus bare and howling back to
     the fast ships,
whipping you out of the assembly place with
     the strokes of indignity."
So he spoke and dashed the sceptre against his
     back and
shoulders, and he doubled over, and a round
     tear dropped from him,
and a bloody welt stood up between his shoul-
     ders under
the golden sceptre's stroke, and he sat down
     again, frightened,
in pain, and looking helplessly about wiped off
     the tear-drops.
Sorry though the men were they laughed over
     him happily,
and thus they would speak to each other, each
     looking at the man next him:
"Come now: Odysseus has done excellent
     things by thousands,
bringing forward good counsels and ordering
     armed encounters;
but now this is far the best thing he ever has
     accomplished
among the Argives, to keep this thrower of
     words, this braggart
out of the assembly. Never again will his proud
     heart stir him
up, to wrangle with the princes in words of
     revilement."

From Book VI: The Trojan Hero

[Exhausted from the day's fighting, Hektor returns to his home.]

Now as Hektor had come to the Skaian gates
     and the oak tree,

all the wives of the Trojans and their daugh-
     ters came running about him
to ask after their sons, after their brothers and
     neighbors,
their husbands; and he told them to pray to
     the immortals,
all, in turn; but there were sorrows in store for
     many.
Now he entered the wonderfully built palace
     of Priam.
This was fashioned with smooth-stone cloister
     walks, and within it
were embodied fifty sleeping chambers of
     smoothed stone
built so as to connect with each other; and
     within these slept
each beside his own wedded wife, the sons of
     Priam.
In the same inner court on the opposite side,
     to face these,
lay the twelve close smooth-stone sleeping
     chambers of his daughters
built so as to connect with each other; and
     within these slept,
each by his own modest wife, the lords of the
     daughters of Priam.
There there came to meet Hektor his bounti-
     ful mother
with Laodike, the loveliest looking of all her
     daughters.
She clung to his hand and called him by name
     and spoke to him: "Why then,
child, have you come here and left behind the
     bold battle?
Surely it is these accursed sons of the Achaians
     who wear you
out, as they fight close to the city, and the
     spirit stirred you
to return, and from the peak of the citadel lift
     your hands praying
to Zeus. But stay while I bring you honey-
     sweet wine, to pour out
a libation to father Zeus and the other immor-
     tals
first, and afterwards if you will drink yourself,
     be strengthened.
In a tired man, wine will bring back his
     strength to its bigness,
in a man tired as you are tired, defending your
     neighbors."
Tall Hektor of the shining helm spoke to her
     answering:

"My honored mother, lift not to me the kindly sweet wine,
for fear you stagger my strength and make me forget my courage;
and with hands unwashed I would take shame to pour the glittering
wine to Zeus; there is no means for a man to pray to the dark-misted
son of Kronos, with blood and muck all spattered upon him.
But go yourself to the temple of the spoiler Athene,
assembling the ladies of honor, and with things to be sacrificed,
and take a robe, which seems to you the largest and loveliest
in the great house, and that which is far your dearest possession.
Lay this along the knees of Athene the lovely haired. Also
promise to dedicate within the shrine twelve heifers,
yearlings, never broken, if only she will have pity
on the town of Troy, and the Trojan wives, and their innocent children,
if she will hold back from sacred Ilion the son of Tydeus,
that wild spear-fighter, the strong one who drives men to thoughts of terror.
So go yourself to the temple of the spoiler Athene,
while I go in search of Paris, to call him, if he will listen
to anything I tell him. How I wish at this moment the earth might
open beneath him. The Olympian let him live, a great sorrow
to the Trojans, and high-hearted Priam, and all of his children.
If only I could see him gone down to the house of the Death God,
then I could say my heart had forgotten its joyless affliction."
So he spoke, and she going into the great house called out
to her handmaidens, who assembled throughout the city the highborn
women; while she descended into the fragrant store-chamber.
But Hektor went away to the house of Alexandros,

a splendid place he had built himself, with the men who at that time
were the best men for craftsmanship in the generous Troad,
who had made him a sleeping room and a hall and a courtyard
near the houses of Hektor and Priam, on the peak of the citadel.
There entered Hektor beloved of Zeus, in his hand holding
the eleven-cubit-long spear, whose shaft was tipped with a shining
bronze spearhead, and a ring of gold was hooped to hold it.
He found the man in his chamber busy with his splendid armor,
the corselet and the shield, and turning in his hands the curved bow,
while Helen of Argos was sitting among her attendant women
directing the magnificent work done by her handmaidens.
But Hektor saw him, and in words of shame he rebuked him:
"Strange man! It is not fair to keep in your heart this coldness.
The people are dying around the city and around the steep wall
as they fight hard; and it is for you that this war with its clamor
has flared up about our city. You yourself would fight with another
whom you saw anywhere hanging back from the hateful encounter.
Up then, to keep our town from burning at once in the hot fire."
Then in answer the godlike Alexandros spoke to him:
"Hektor, seeing you have scolded me rightly, not beyond measure,
therefore I will tell, and you in turn understand and listen.
It was not so much in coldness and bitter will toward the Trojans
that I sat in my room, but I wished to give myself over to sorrow.
But just now with soft words my wife was winning me over
and urging me into the fight, and that way seems to me also
the better one. Victory passes back and forth between men.

Come then, wait for me now while I put on
my armor of battle,
or go, and I will follow, and I think I can overtake you."
He spoke, but Hektor of the shining helm
gave him no answer,
and in speed made his way to his own well-es-
tablished dwelling,
but failed to find in the house Andromache of
the white arms;
for she, with the child, and followed by one
fair-robed attendant,
had taken her place on the tower in lamentation, and tearful.
Hektor hastened from his home
backward by the way he had come through the
well-laid streets. So
as he had come to the gates on his way
through the great city,
the Skaian gates, whereby he would issue into
the plain, there
at last his own generous wife came running to
meet him,
Andromache, the daughter of high-hearted
Eetion;
Eëtion, who had dwelt underneath wooded
Plakos,
in Thebe below Plakos, lord over the Kilikian
people.
It was his daughter who was given to Hektor
of the bronze helm.
She came to him there, and beside her went an
attendant carrying
the boy in the fold of her bosom, a little child,
only a baby,
Hektor's son, the admired, beautiful as a star
shining,
whom Hektor called Skamandrios, but all of
the others
Astyanax—lord of the city; since Hektor alone
saved Ilion.
Hektor smiled in silence as he looked on his
son, but she,
Andromache, stood close beside him, letting
her tears fall,
and clung to his hand and called him by name
and spoke to him "Dearest,
your own great strength will be your death,
and you have no pity
on your little son, nor on me, ill-starred, who
soon must be your widow;
for presently the Achaians, gathering together,

will set upon you and kill you; and for me it
would be far better
to sink into the earth when I have lost you, for
there is no other
consolation for me after you have gone to your
destiny—
only grief; since I have no father, no honored
mother.
It was brilliant Achilleus who slew my father,
Eëtion,
when he stormed the strong-founded citadel
of the Kilikians,
Thebe of the towering gates. He killed Eëtion
but did not strip his armor, for his heart respected the dead man,
but burned the body in all its elaborate war-
gear
and piled a grave mound over it, and the
nymphs of the mountains,
daughters of Zeus of the aegis, planted elm
trees about it.
And they who were my seven brothers in the
great house all went
upon a single day down into the house of the
death god,
for swift-footed brilliant Achilleus slaughtered
all of them
as they were tending their white sheep and
their lumbering oxen;
and when he had led my mother, who was
queen under wooded Plakos,
here, along with all his other possessions,
Achilleus
released her again, accepting ransom beyond
count, But Artemis
of the showering arrows struck her down in
the halls of her father.
Hektor, thus you are father to me, and my
honored mother,
you are my brother, and you it is who are my
young husband.
Please take pity upon me then, stay here on
the rampart,
that you may not leave your child an orphan,
your wife a widow,
but draw your people up by the fig tree, there
where the city
is openest to attack, and where the wall may
be mounted.
Three times their bravest came that way, and
fought there to storm it
about the two Aiantes and renowned
Idomeneus,

about the two Atreidai and the fighting son of
　　Tydeus.
Either some man well skilled in prophetic arts
　　had spoken,
or the very spirit within themselves had stirred
　　them to the slaughter."
Then tall Hektor of the shining helm an-
　　swered her: "All these
things are in my mind also, lady; yet I would
　　feel deep shame
before the Trojans, and the Trojan women
　　with trailing garments,
if like a coward I were to shrink aside from the
　　fighting;
and the spirit will not let me, since I have
　　learned to be valiant
and to fight always among the foremost ranks
　　of the Trojans,
winning for my own self great glory, and for
　　my father.
For I know this thing well in my heart, and
　　my mind knows it:
there will come a day when sacred Ilion shall
　　perish,
and Priam, and the people of Priam of the
　　strong ash spear.
But it is not so much the pain to come of the
　　Trojans
that troubles me, not even of Priam the king
　　nor Hekabe,
not the thought of my brothers who in their
　　numbers and valor
shall drop in the dust under the hands of men
　　who hate them,
as troubles me the thought of you, when some
　　bronze-armored
Achaian leads you off, taking away your day of
　　liberty,
in tears; and in Argos you must work at the
　　loom of another,
and carry water from the spring Messeis or
　　Hypereia,
all unwilling, but strong will be the necessity
　　upon you:
and some day seeing you shedding tears a man
　　will say of you:
'This is the wife of Hektor, who was ever the
　　bravest fighter
of the Trojans, breakers of horses, in the days
　　when they fought about Ilion.'
So will one speak of you; and for you it will be
　　yet a fresh grief,

to be widowed of such a man who could fight
　　off the day of your slavery.
But may I be dead and the piled earth hide me
　　under before I
hear you crying and know by this that they
　　drag you captive."
So speaking glorious Hektor held out his arms
　　to his baby,
who shrank back to his fair-girdled nurse's bo-
　　som
screaming, and frightened at the aspect of his
　　own father,
terrified as he saw the bronze and the crest
　　with its horse-hair,
nodding dreadfully, as he thought, from the
　　peak of the helmet
and laid it in all its shining upon the ground.
　　Then taking
up his dear son he tossed him about in his
　　arms, and kissed him,
and lifted his voice in prayer to Zeus and the
　　other immortals:
"Zeus, and you other immortals, grant that
　　this boy, who is my son,
may be as I am, pre-eminent among the Tro-
　　jans,
great in strength, as am I, and rule strongly
　　over Ilion;
and some day let them say of him: 'He is bet-
　　ter by far than his father',
as he comes in from the fighting; and let him
　　kill his enemy
and bring home the blooded spoils, and de-
　　light the heart of his mother."
So speaking he set his child again in the arms
　　of his beloved
wife, who took him back again to her fragrant
　　bosom
smiling in her tears; and her husband saw, and
　　took pity upon her,
and stroked her with his hand, and called her
　　by name and spoke to her:
"Poor Andromache! Why does your heart
　　sorrow so much for me?
No man is going to hurl me to Hades, unless
　　it is fated,
but as for fate, I think that no man yet has es-
　　caped it
once it has taken its first form, neither brave
　　man nor coward.
Go therefore back to our house, and take up
　　your own work,

the loom and the distaff, and see to it that
  your handmaidens
ply their work also; but the men must see to
  the fighting,
all men who are the people of Ilion, but I beyond others."

From Book IX: The Embassy To Achilles

[The Greeks are unable to stop the onslaughts of
Hektor and the Trojans. Agamemnon decides
that he must placate Achilles and secure his return to the war.]

So the Trojans held their night watches.
  Meanwhile immortal
Panic, companion of Cold Terror, gripped the
  Achaians
as all their best were stricken with grief that
  passes endurance.
As two winds rise to shake the sea where the
  fish swarm, Boreas
and Zephyros, north wind and west, that blow
  from Thraceward,
suddenly descending, and the darkened water
  is gathered
to crests, and far across the salt water scatters
  the seaweed;
so the heart in the breast of each Achaian was
  troubled.
And the son of Atreus, stricken at heart with
  great sorrow,
went among his heralds the clear-spoken and
  told them
to summon calling by name each man into the
  assembly
but with no outcry, and he himself was at
  work with the foremost.
They took their seats in assembly, dispirited,
  and Agamemnon
stood up before them, shedding tears, like a
  spring dark-running
that down the face of a rock impassible drips
  its dim water.
But the son of Atreus led the assembled lords
  of the Achaians
to his own shelter, and set before them the
  feast in abundance.
They put their hands to the good things that
  lay ready before them.
But when they had put away their desire for
  eating and drinking,
the aged man began to weave his counsel before them

first, Nestor, whose advice had shown best before this.
He in kind intention toward all stood forth
  and addressed them:
"Son of Atreus, most lordly and king of men,
  Agamemnon,
with you I will end, with you I will make my
  beginning, since you
are lord over many people, and Zeus has given
  into your hand
the sceptre and rights of judgment, to be king
  over the people.
It is yours therefore to speak a word, yours also
  to listen,
and grant the right to another also, when his
  spirit stirs him
to speak for our good. All shall be yours when
  you lead the way. Still
I will speak in the way it seems best to my
  mind, and no one
shall have in his mind any thought that is better than this one
that I have in my mind either now or long before now
ever since that day, illustrious, when you went
  from the shelter
of angered Achilleus, taking by force the girl
  Briseis
against the will of the rest of us, since I for my
  part
urged you strongly not to, but you, giving way
  to your proud heart's
anger, dishonored a great man, one whom the
  immortals
honor, since you have taken his prize and keep
  it. But let us
even now think how we can make this good
  and persuade him
with words of supplication and with the gifts
  of friendship."
Then in turn the lord of men Agamemnon
  spoke to him:
"Aged sir, this was no lie when you spoke of
  my madness.
I was mad, I myself will not deny it. Worth
  many
fighters is that man whom Zeus in his heart
  loves, as now
he has honored this man and beaten down the
  Achaian people.
But since I was mad, in the persuasion of my
  heart's evil,

I am willing to make all good, and give back
gifts in abundance.
Before you all I will count off my gifts in their
splendor:
seven unfired tripods; ten talents' weight of
gold; twenty
shining cauldrons; and twelve horses, strong,
race-competitors
who have won prizes in the speed of their feet.
That man would not be
poor in possessions, to whom were given all
these have won me,
nor be unpossessed of dearly honored gold,
were he given
all the prizes these single-foot horses have won
for me.
I will give him seven women of Lesbos, the
work of whose hands is
blameless, whom when he himself captured
strong-founded Lesbos
I chose, and who in their beauty surpassed the
races of women.
I will give him these, and with them shall go
the one I took from him,
the daughter of Briseus. And to all this I will
swear a great oath
that I never entered into her bed and never lay
with her
as is natural for human people, between men
and women.
All these gifts shall be his at once; but again, if
hereafter
the gods grant that we storm and sack the
great city of Priam,
let him go to his ship and load it deep as he
pleases
with gold and bronze when we Achaians divide the war spoils,
and let him choose for himself twenty of the
Trojan women
who are the loveliest of all after Helen of Argos.
And if we come back to Achaian Argos, pride
of the tilled land,
he may be my son-in-law; I will honor him
with Orestes
my growing son, who is brought up there in
abundant luxury.
Since, as I have three daughters there in my
strong-built castle,
Chrysothemis and Laodike and Iphianassa,
let him lead away the one of these that he
likes, with no bride-price,

to the house of Peleus, and with the girl I will
grant him as dowry
many gifts, such as no man ever gave with his
daughter.
I will grant to him seven citadels, strongly-
settled:
Kardamyle, and Enope, And Hire of the
grasses,
Pherai the sacrosanct, and Antheia deep in the
meadows,
with Aipeia the lovely and Pedasos of the
vineyards.
All these lie near the sea, at the bottom of
sandy Pylos,
and men live among them rich in cattle and
rich in sheepflocks,
who will honor him as if he were a god with
gifts given
and fulfill his prospering decrees underneath
his sceptre.
All this I will bring to pass for him, if he
changes from his anger.
Let him give way. For Hades gives not way,
and is pitiless,
and therefore he among all the gods is most
hateful to mortals.
And let him yield place to me, inasmuch as I
am the kinglier
and inasmuch as I can call myself born the elder."
Thereupon the Gerenian horseman Nestor
answered him:
"Son of Atreus, most lordly and king of men,
Agamemnon,
none could scorn any longer these gifts you offer to Achilleus
the king. Come, let us choose and send some
men, who in all speed
will go to the shelter of Achilleus, the son of
Peleus;
or come, the men on whom my eye falls, let
these take the duty.
First of all let Phoinix, beloved of Zeus, be
their leader,
and after him take Aias the great, and brilliant
Odysseus,
and of the heralds let Odios and Eurybates go
with them.
Bring also water for their hands, and bid them
keep words of good omen,
so we may pray to Zeus, son of Kronos, if he
will have pity."

So he spoke, and the word he spoke was
   pleasing to all of them.
And the heralds brought water at once, and
   poured it over
their hands, and the young men filled the
   mixing-bowl with pure wine
and passed it to all, pouring first a libation in
   goblets.
Then when they had poured out wine, and
   drunk as much as their hearts wished,
they set out from the shelter of Atreus' son,
   Agamemnon.
And the Gerenian horseman Nestor gave
   them much instruction,
looking eagerly at each, and most of all at
   Odysseus,
to try hard, so that they might win over the
   blameless Peleion.
So these two walked along the strand of the
   sea deep-thundering
with many prayers to the holder and shaker of
   the earth, that they
might readily persuade the great heart of
   Aiakides.
Now they came beside the shelters and ships
   of the Myrmidons
and they found Achilleus delighting his heart
   in a lyre, clear-sounding,
splendid and carefully wrought, with a bridge
   of silver upon it,
which he won out of the spoils when he ruined
   Eetion's city.
With this he was pleasuring his heart, and
   singing of men's fame,
as Patroklos was sitting over against him,
   alone, in silence,
watching Aiakides and the time he would
   leave off singing.
Now these two came forward, as brilliant
   Odysseus led them,
and stood in his presence. Achilleus rose to his
   feet in amazement
holding the lyre as it was, leaving the place
   where he was sitting.
In the same way Patroklos, when he saw the
   men come, stood up.
And in greeting Achilleus the swift of foot
   spoke to them:
"Welcome. You are my friends who have
   come, and greatly I need you,
who even to this my anger are dearest of all
   the Achaians."

So brilliant Achilleus spoke, and guided them
   forward,
and caused them to sit down on couches with
   purple coverlets
and at once called over to Patroklos who was
   not far from him:
"Son of Menoitios, set up a mixing-bowl that
   is bigger,
and mix us stronger drink, and make ready a
   cup for each man,
since those who have come beneath my roof
   are the men that I love best."
So he spoke, and Patroklos obeyed his beloved
   companion,
and tossed down a great chopping-block into
   the firelight,
and laid upon it the back of a sheep, and one
   of a fat goat,
with the chine of a fatted pig edged thick with
   lard, and for him
Automedon held the meats, and brilliant
   Achilleus carved them,
and cut it well into pieces and spitted them, as
   meanwhile
Menoitios' son, a man like a god, made the
   fire blaze greatly.
But when the fire had burned itself out, and
   the flames had died down,
he scattered the embers apart, and extended
   the spits across them
lifting them to the andirons, and sprinkled the
   meats with divine salt.
Then when he had roasted all, and spread the
   food on the platters,
Patroklos took the bread and set it out on a
   table in fair baskets, while Achilleus served
   the meats. Thereafter
he himself sat over against the godlike
   Odysseus
against the further wall, and told his companion, Patroklos,
to sacrifice to the gods; and he threw the
   firstlings in the fire.
They put their hands to the good things that
   lay ready before them.
But when they had put aside their desire for
   eating and drinking,
Aias nodded to Phoinix, and brilliant
   Odysseus saw it,
and filled a cup with wine, and lifted it to
   Achilleus:
"Your health, Achilleus. You have no lack of
   your equal portion

either within the shelter of Atreus' son,
    Agamemnon,
nor here now in your own. We have good
    things in abundance
to feast on; here it is not the desirable feast we
    think of,
but a trouble all too great, beloved of Zeus,
    that we look on
and are afraid. There is doubt if we save our
    strong-benched vessels
or if they will be destroyed, unless you put on
    your war strength.
The Trojans in their pride, with their far-
    renowned companions,
have set up an encampment close by the ships
    and the rampart,
and lit many fires along their army, and think
    no longer
of being held, but rather to drive in upon the
    black ships.
And Zeus, son of Kronos, lightens upon their
    right hand, showing them
portents of good, while Hektor in the huge ✳
    pride of his strength rages
irresistibly, reliant on Zeus, and gives way to
    no one
neither god nor man, but the strong fury has
    descended upon him.
He prays now that the divine Dawn will show
    most quickly,
since he threatens to shear the uttermost horns
    from the ship-sterns,
to light the ships themselves with ravening
    fire, and to cut down
the Achaians themselves as they stir from the
    smoke beside them.
All this I fear terribly in my heart, lest immor-
    tals
accomplish all these threats, and lest for us it
    be destiny
to die here in Troy, far away from horse-pas-
    turing Argos.
Up, then! if you are minded, late though it be,
    to rescue
the afflicted sons of the Achaians from the
    Trojan onslaught.

[Odysseus offers Achilles the gifts.]

Then in answer to him spoke Achilleus of the
    swift feet:
"Son of Laertes and seed of Zeus, resourceful
    Odysseus:

without consideration for you I must make my
    answer,
the way I think, and the way it will be ac-
    complished, that you may not
come one after another, and sit by me, and
    speak softly.
For as I detest the doorways of Death, I detest ✳
    that man, who
hides one thing in the depths of his heart, and
    speaks forth another.
But I will speak to you the way it seems best to
    me: neither
do I think the son of Atreus, Agamemnon,
    will persuade me,
nor the rest of the Danaans, since there was no
    gratitude given
for fighting incessantly forever against your
    enemies.
Fate is the same for the man who holds back,
    the same if he fights hard.
We are all held in a single honor, the brave
    with the weaklings.
A man dies still if he has done nothing, as one
    who has done much.
Nothing is won for me, now that my heart has
    gone through its afflictions
in forever setting my life on the hazard of bat-
    tle.
For as to her unwinged young ones the mother
    bird brings back
morsels, wherever she can find them, but as
    for herself it is suffering,
such was I, as I lay through all the many
    nights unsleeping,
such as I wore through the bloody days of the
    fighting,
striving with warriors for the sake of these
    men's women.
But I say that I have stormed from my ships
    twelve cities
of men, and by land eleven more through the
    generous Troad.
From all these we took forth treasures, goodly
    and numerous,
and we would bring them back, and give them
    to Agamemnon,
Atreus' son; while he, waiting back beside the
    swift ships,
would take them, and distribute them little by
    little, and keep many.
All the other prizes of honor he gave the great
    men and the princes

are held fast by them, but from me alone of all
   the Achaians
he has taken and keeps the bride of my heart.
   Let him lie beside her
and be happy. Yet why must the Argives fight
   with the Trojans?
And why was it the son of Atreus assembled
   and led here
these people? Was it not for the sake of lovely-
   haired Helen?
Are the sons of Atreus alone among mortal
   men the ones
who love their wives? Since any who is a good
   man, and careful,
loves her who is his own and cares for her,
   even as I now
loved this one from my heart, though it was
   my spear that won her.
Now that he has deceived me and taken from
   my hands my prize of honor,
let him try me no more. I know him well. He
   will not persuade me.
Let him take counsel with you, Odysseus, and
   the rest of the princes
how to fight the ravening fire away from his
   vessels.
Indeed, there has been much hard work done
   even without me;
he has built himself a wall and driven a ditch
   about it,
making it great and wide, and fixed the sharp
   stakes inside it.
Yet even so he cannot hold the strength of
   manslaughtering
Hektor; and yet when I was fighting among
   the Achaians
Hektor would not drive his attack beyond the
   wall's shelter
but would come forth only so far as the Skaian
   gates and the oak tree.
There once he endured me alone, and barely
   escaped my onslaught.
But, now I am unwilling to fight against brilliant Hektor,
tomorrow, when I have sacrificed to Zeus and
   to all gods,
and loaded well my ships, and rowed out on to
   the salt water,
you will see, if you have a mind to it and if it
   concerns you,
my ships in the dawn at sea on the Hellespont
   where the fish swarm

and my men manning them with good will to
   row. If the glorious
shaker of the earth should grant us a favoring
   passage
on the third day thereafter we might raise generous Phthia.
I have many possessions there that I left behind when I came here
on this desperate venture, and from here there
   is more gold, and red bronze,
and fair-girdled women, and grey iron I will
   take back;
all that was allotted to me. But my prize: he
   who gave it,
powerful Agamemnon, son of Atreus, has
   taken it back again
outrageously. Go back and proclaim to him all
   that I tell you,
openly, so other Achaians may turn against
   him in anger
if he hopes yet one more time to swindle some
   other Danaan,
wrapped as he is forever in shamelessness; yet
   he would not,
bold as a dog though he be, dare look in my
   face any longer.
I will join with him in no counsel, and in no
   action.
He cheated me and he did me hurt. Let him
   not beguile me
with words again. This is enough for him. Let
   him of his own will
be damned, since Zeus of the counsels has
   taken his wits away from him.
I hate his gifts. I hold him light as the strip of
   a splinter.

[Thwarted, the couriers return to Agamemnon.]

Now when these had come back to the shelters
   of Agamemnon,
the sons of the Achaians greeted them with
   their gold cups
uplifted, one after another, standing, and
   asked them questions.
And the first to question them was the lord of
   men, Agamemnon:
"Tell me, honored Odysseus, great glory of the
   Achaians:
is he willing to fight the ravening fire away
   from our vessels,
or did he refuse, and does the anger still hold
   his proud heart?"

Then long-suffering great Odysseus spoke to
    him in answer:
"Son of Atreus, most lordly, king of men,
    Agamemnon.
That man will not quench his anger, but still
    more than ever
is filled with rage. He refuses you and refuses
    your presents.
He tells you yourself to take counsel among
    the Argives
how to save your ships, and the people of the
    Achaians.
And he himself has threatened that tomorrow
    as dawn shows
he will drag down his strong-benched, oar-
    swept ships to the water.
He said it would be his counsel to others also,
    to sail back
home again, since no longer will you find any
    term set
on the sheer city of Ilion, since Zeus of the
    wide brows has strongly
held his own hand over it, and its people are
    made bold.
So he spoke. There are these to attest it who
    went there with me
also, Aias, and the two heralds, both men of
    good counsel.
But aged Phoinix stayed there for the night, as
    Achilleus urged him,
so he might go home in the ships to the
    beloved land of his fathers
if Phoinix will; but he will never use force to
    persuade him."
So he spoke, and all of them stayed stricken to
    silence
in amazement at his words. He had spoken to
    them very strongly.
For a long time the sons of the Achaians said
    nothing, in sorrow,
but at long last Diomedes of the great war cry
    spoke to them:
"Son of Atreus, most lordly and king of men,
    Agamemnon,
I wish you had not supplicated the blameless
    son of Peleus
with innumerable gifts offered. He is a proud
    man without this,
and now you have driven him far deeper into
    his pride. Rather
we shall pay him no more attention, whether
    he comes in with us

or stays away. He will fight again, whenever
    the time comes
that the heart in his body urges him to, and
    the god drives him.
Come then, do as I say, and let us all be won
    over.
Go to sleep, now that the inward heart is
    made happy
with food and drink, for these are the strength
    and courage within us.
But when the lovely dawn shows forth with
    rose fingers, Atreides,
rapidly form before our ships both people and
    horses
stirring them on, and yourself be ready to fight
    in the foremost."
So he spoke, and all the kings gave him their
    approval,
acclaiming the word of Diomedes, breaker of
    horses.
Then they poured a libation, and each man
    went to his shelter,
where they went to their beds and took the
    blessing of slumber.

From Book XXIV: Achilles and Priam

[To prevent the Greek ships from being burned,
Achilles' companion, Patroklos, dons Achilles'
armor and fights the Trojans. He drives them
back, but finally is killed by Hektor. In grief and
anger Achilles himself returns to the fighting,
stalks and kills Hektor, and desecrates his corpse.
At last Priam, king of Troy and Hektor's father,
goes secretly to the Greek camp to plead for the
body of his son.]

The old man made straight for the dwelling
where Achilleus the beloved of Zeus was sit-
    ting. He found him
inside, and his companions were sitting apart,
    as two only,
Automedon the hero and Alkimos, scion of
    Ares,
were busy beside him. He had just now got
    through with his dinner,
with eating and drinking, and the table still
    stood by. Tall Priam
came in unseen by the other men and stood
    close beside him
and caught the knees of Achilleus in his arms,
    and kissed the hands
that were dangerous and manslaughtering and
    had killed so many

of his sons. As when dense disaster closes on
    one who has murdered
a man in his own land, and he comes to the
    country of others,
to a man of substance, and wonder seizes on
    those who behold him,
so Achilleus wondered as he looked on Priam,
    a godlike
man, and the rest of them wondered also, and
    looked at each other.
But now Priam spoke to him in the words of a
    suppliant:
"Achilleus like the gods, remember your fa-
    ther, one who
is of years like mine, and on the door-sill of
    sorrowful old age.
And they who dwell nearby encompass him
    and afflict him,
nor is there any to defend him against the
    wrath, the destruction.
Yet surely he, when he hears of you and that
    you are still living,
is gladdened within his heart and all his days
    he is hopeful
that he will see his beloved son come home
    from the Troad.
But for me, my destiny was evil. I have had the
    noblest
of sons in Troy, but I say not one of them is
    left to me.
Fifty were my sons, when the sons of the
    Achaians came here.
Nineteen were born to me from the womb of a
    single mother,
and other women bore the rest in my palace;
    and of these
violent Ares broke the strength in the knees of
    most of them,
but one was left me who guarded my city and
    people, that one
you killed a few days since as he fought in de-
    fense of his country.
Hektor; for whose sake I come now to the
    ships of the Achaians
to win him back from you, and I bring you
    gifts beyond number.
Honor then the gods, Achilleus, and take pity
    upon me
remembering your father, yet I am still more
    pitiful;
I have gone through what no other mortal on
    earth has gone through;

I put my lips to the hands of the man who has
    killed my children."
So he spoke, and stirred in the other a passion
    of grieving
for his own father. He took the old man's
    hand and pushed him
gently away, and the two remembered, as
    Priam sat huddled
at the feet of Achilleus and wept now for his
    own father, now again
for Patroklos. The sound of their mourning
    moved in the house. Then
when great Achilleus had taken full satisfac-
    tion in sorrow
and the passion for it had gone from his mind
    and body, thereafter
he rose from his chair, and took the old man
    by the hand, and set him
on his feet again, in pity for the grey head and
    the grey beard,
and spoke to him and addressed him in
    winged words: "Ah, unlucky,
surely you have had much evil to endure in
    your spirit.
How could you dare to come alone to the
    ships of the Achaians
and before my eyes, when I am one who have
    killed in such numbers
such brave sons of yours? The heart in you is
    iron. Come, then,
and sit down upon this chair, and you and I
    will even let
our sorrows lie still in the heart for all our
    grieving. There is not
any advantage to be won from grim lamenta-
    tion.
Such is the way the gods spun life for unfor-
    tunate mortals,
that we live in unhappiness, but the gods
    themselves have no sorrows.
There are two urns that stand on the door-sill
    of Zeus. They are unlike
for the gifts they bestow: an urn of evils, an
    urn of blessings.
If Zeus who delights in thunder mingles these
    and bestows them
on man, he shifts, and moves now in evil,
    again in good fortune.
But when Zeus bestows from the urn of sor-
    rows, he makes a failure
of man, and the evil hunger drives him over
    the shining

earth, and he wanders respected neither of
gods nor mortals.
Such were the shining gifts given by the gods
to Peleus
from his birth, who outshone all men beside
for his riches
and pride of possession, and was lord over the
Myrmidons. Thereto
the gods bestowed an immortal wife on him,
who was mortal.
But even on him the god piled evil also. There
was not
any generation of strong sons born to him in
his great house
but a single all-untimely child he had, and I
give him
no care as he grows old, since far from the
land of my fathers
I sit here in Troy, and bring nothing but sorrow to you and your children.
And you, old sir, we are told you prospered
once; for as much
as Lesbos, Makar's hold, confines to the north
above it
and Phrygia from the north confines, and
enormous Hellespont,
of these, old sir, you were lord once in your
wealth and your children.
But now the Uranian gods brought us, an affliction upon you,
forever there is fighting about your city, and
men killed.
But bear up, nor mourn endlessly in your
heart, for there is not
anything to be gained from grief for your son;
you will never
bring him back; sooner you must go through
yet another sorrow."
In answer to him again spoke a aged Priam the
godlike:
"Do not, beloved of Zeus, make me sit on a
chair while Hektor
lies yet forlorn among the shelters; rather with
all speed
give him back, so my eyes may behold him,
and accept the ransom
we bring you, which is great. You may have
joy of it, and go back
to the land of your own fathers, since once you
have permitted me
to go on living myself and continue to look on
the sunlight."

Then looking darkly at him spoke swift-footed
Achilleus:
"No longer stir me up, old sir, I myself am
minded
to give Hektor back to you. A messenger came
to me from Zeus,
my mother, she who bore me, the daughter of
the sea's ancient.
I know you, Priam, in my heart, and it does
not escape me
that some god led you to the running ships of
the Achaians.
For no mortal would dare come to our encampment, not even
one strong in youth. He could not get by the
pickets, he could not
lightly unbar the bolt that secures our gateway.
Therefore
you must not further make my spirit move in
my sorrows,
for fear, old sir, I might not let you alone in
my shelter,
suppliant as you are; and be guilty before the
god's orders."
He spoke, and the old mad was frightened and
did as he told him.
Then when the serving-maids had washed the
corpse and anointed it
with olive oil, they threw a fair great cloak and
a tunic
about him, and Achilleus himself lifted him
and laid him
on a litter, and his friends helped him lift it to
the smooth-polished
mule wagon. He groaned then, and called by
name on his beloved companion:
"Be not angry with me, Patroklos, if you discover,
though you be in the house of Hades, that I
gave back great Hektor
to his loved father, for the ransom he gave me
was not unworthy.
I will give you your share of the spoils, as
much as is fitting."
So spoke great Achilleus and went back into
the shelter
and sat down on the elaborate couch from
which he had risen,
against the inward wall, and now spoke his
word to Priam:
"Your son is given back to you, aged sir, as you
asked it.

He lies on a bier. When dawn shows you
    yourself shall see him
as you take him away. Now you and I must
    remember our supper.
For even Niobe, she of the lovely tresses, re-
    membered
to eat, whose twelve children were destroyed
    in her palace,
six daughters, and six sons in the pride of their
    youth, whom Apollo
killed with arrows from his silver bow, being
    angered
with Niobe, and shaft-showering Artemis
    killed the daughters;
because Niobe likened herself to Leto of the
    fair coloring
and said Leto had borne only two, she herself
    had borne many;
but the two, though they were only two, de-
    stroyed all those others.
But she remembered to eat when she was
    worn out with weeping.
And now somewhere among the rocks, in the
    lonely mountains,
in Sipylos, where they say is the resting place
    of the goddesses
who are nymphs, and dance beside the waters
    of Acheloios,
there, stone still, she broods on the sorrows
    that the gods gave her.
Come then, we also, aged magnificent sir,
    must remember
to eat, and afterwards you may take your
    beloved son back
to Ilion, and mourn for him; and he will be
    much lamented."

✝

2. GREEK LYRICS

The development of lyric poetry during the Greek Archaic Age (c. 800-550 B.C.) is an aspect of the growth of individualism in Greece. The subjects of these verses are more mundane than those of heroic epics like *The Iliad*, and perhaps because of that these verses sound particularly "modern." But there are other differences. Can you identify them? Which of these in particular contribute to your understanding of "individualism"?

A. ARCHILOCHUS OF PAROS (C. 680-640 B.C.)

I am two things: a fighter who follows the
    Master of Battles,
And one who understands the gift of the
    Muses' love.

✝

By spear is kneaded the bread I eat, by spear
    my Ismaric wine is won,
Which I drink, leaning upon my spear.

✝

Some barbarian is waving my shield, since I
    was obliged to
Leave that perfectly good piece of equipment
    behind under a bush.
But I got away, so what does it matter?
Let the shield go; I can buy another one
    equally good.

✝

On A Willing Woman

Wild fig tree of the rocks, so often feeder of
    ravens,
Loves-them-all, the seducible, the stranger's
    delight.

✝

Two Captains

I don't like the towering captain with the
    spraddly length of leg,
One who swaggers in his lovelocks and clean-
    shaves beneath the chin.
Give me a man short and squarely set upon his
    legs, a man
Full of heart, not to be shaken from the place
    he plants his feet.

✝

B. HIPPONAX OF EPHESOS (EARLY SIXTH CENTURY B.C.)

The God of Wealth, who's altogether blind,
     never
Came walking in my door and told me:
     "Hipponax,
I'm giving you three hundred silver mina
     pieces,
and much besides." Not he. He's far too
     mean-hearted.

✝

Hold my jacket, somebody, while I hit
     Boupalos in the eye.
I can hit with both hands, and I never miss
     punches.

✝

C. SAPPHO OF LESBOS (C. 600 B. C.)

To a Rival

You will die and be still, never shall be mem-
     ory left of you
after this, nor regret when you are gone. You
     have not touched the flowers
of the Muses, and thus, shadowy still in the
     domain of Death,
you must drift with a ghost's fluttering wings,
     one of the darkened dead.

✝

Like a sweet apple turning red on the branch
     top, on the
top of the topmost branch, and the gatherers
     did not notice it,
rather, they did notice, but could not reach up
     to take it.
Like the hyacinth in the hills which the shep-
     herd people
step on, trampling into the ground the flower
     in its purple.

✝

D. ANACREON OF TEOS (560-490 B.C.)

The love god with his golden curls
Puts a bright ball into my hand,
Shows a girl in her fancy shoes, and suggests
     that I take her.
Not that girl—she's the other kind,
One from Lesbos. Disdainfully,

nose turned up at my silver hair, she makes
     eyes at the ladies.

✝

E. EPITAPHS

When Learete died her father set up a monu-
     ment which has beauty.
But we shall nevermore see her alive.

✝

The tomb of Phrasikleia: I shall be called
     maiden forever.
This, not wife, is the title the gods gave me for
     mine.

✝

Whether you are a citizen or a stranger com-
     ing from elsewhere,
Take pity on Tettichos as you pass by; a brave
     man
Killed in battle, who there lost the pride of his
     fresh youth.
Mourn him for a while, and go on. May your
     fortune be good.

✝

F. ANONYMOUS LYRICS

The moon has gone down, the Pleiades
Have set; and the night's at halfway,
And the time is passing,
And I lie in my bed, lonely.

✝

Oh what ails you? Do not betray me, I implore
     you.
Before he comes back, get up, never ruin
yourself, do not ruin me a poor wretched sin-
     ner.
It is day now, see the light through the win-
     dow, do you not see it?

✝

3. *Antigone*

SOPHOCLES

Sophocles (496–406) was born in Athens to aristocratic parents, and he retained the taste for public life so characteristic of Athenian democracy in the fifth century. Much of his life was devoted to public service–he was twice elected a general–and it is important to see his plays as an extension of that service.

In 468 he entered his first tragedy in a drama competition, defeating Æschylus for the prize. In all he wrote 123 plays; 96 of them won a first-prize, the remainder second. Only seven of his plays survive, though there are fragments of others, as well as parts of poems, odes, and hymns.

Antigone was first performed in 441. The story was familiar enough: Œdipus' two sons, Polynices and Eteocles, died fighting one another at Thebes; Eteocles fought to defend his city, Polynices to capture it. From this simple legend Sophocles addresses a topic that had become a subject for debate among the philosophers of his time: what happened when different kinds of laws conflicted? The philosophers had dealt with the possibility of a clash between natural law and human law; Sophocles raised the stakes by casting the issue as a contest between divine law and public law. In *Antigone*, then, you can see different perspectives on a central problem: what was the role of the individual in the state?

INTRODUCTION

When Laïus, King of Thebes, planned to marry Jocasta, the oracle at Delphi foretold that if they had a son he would live to kill his father and marry his mother. In fear of this prediction, when the baby was born the king ordered that he should be exposed on the mountains and left to die. He was, however, found by a shepherd and taken to the King and Queen of Corinth, who adopted him and brought him up as their son. They called him Oedipus ("swollen-feet") because his feet had been pierced and tied together.

Though Oedipus did not know he had been adopted, it was known in the palace, and the destiny which the oracle had foretold about him. Overhearing some gossip one day, but believing that the King and Queen of Corinth were his father and mother, he decided to flee from Corinth, never to return, and so prevent this disaster. On he way, however, he met Laius, who was his real father, although Oedipus did not know this; they quarreled, and Laius was slain.

He then went on to Thebes, and after ridding the city of a terrible monster which had been plaguing the city for years, was chosen as King and married the widowed Queen, not knowing she was his real mother. They had two sons, Eteocles and Polynices, and two daughters, Ismene and Antigone. After some years the ghastly truth came out. The Queen killed herself, and Oedipus put out his own eyes.

This is the plot of Oedipus Rex of Sophocles.

Oedipus was banished and, attended by his two daughters, wandered to Colonus near Athens, where he died. His two sons agreed to share the throne, each ruling in turn for one year. Eteocles, ruling first, refused to hand over the throne to his brother when his year of kingship was over. Polynices in the meantime had been staying at the court of Adrastus, the King of Argos, and had married his daughter. Adrastus then collected an army in support of Polynices and attacked Thebes, led by the famous Seven Champions. In the battle outside the walls the army of Adrastus was routed and the two brothers killed.

Creon, brother of Jocasta and uncle of the four children, became King of Thebes and ordered that the bodies of the enemy, especially that of Polynices, should be refused burial on the grounds that he was a traitor, having led an army against his own city. This was a terrible wrong, not only because Polynices was partly right, since his brother had broken his promise, but much more because the Greeks believed that if a corpse were left unburied its spirit became earthbound and haunted the neighborhood.

The essential part of the burial ceremony was the sprinkling of a handful or two of earth on the corpse. Sometimes libations also were poured in the form of a drink offering. Antigone decides to defy her uncle's edict. At this point the play begins.

DRAMATIS PERSONAE

ANTIGONE, daughter of Oedipus and Jocasta, late King and Queen of Thebes
ISMENE, her sister
CREON, their uncle, brother of Jocasta, now Ruler of Thebes
HAEMON, Creon's son, betrothed to Antigone
EURYDICE, wife of Creon, mother of Haemon
TIRESIAS, a blind prophet
A SENTRY
Two MESSENGERS
CHORUS of Theban Elders
LEADER of the Chorus

Scene: Early morning, courtyard of the Royal Palace at Thebes. There are three entrances—one into either wing, and central doors into the palace. Enter Antigone and Ismene from the palace door. Time: early morning.

ANTIGONE: Ismene, my own sweet sister, can you imagine any suffering, any humiliation worse than we have already endured together? Of all the curses heaped upon the house of Oedipus, do you think there is a single curse that the gods will not work out upon us before we die?

And now comes this new edict which I hear our king has issued to the whole city. Surely you have heard that the punishment which our enemies have brought upon themselves is threatening those we love?

ISMENE: No, Antigone, I have heard no news—good or bad—about anyone we love, since the day our brothers killed each other.

Nothing since the Argive[1] army fled last night—nothing to bring me either joy or sorrow.

ANTIGONE: So I thought; and that is why I have been trying to bring you outside to talk to you alone.

ISMENE: What is it? What dark thought thunders in your mind?

ANTIGONE: You know that Creon has granted one of our brothers the honor of a state funeral, but has insulted the other by denying him the right of burial? They say that Creon buried Eteocles with all traditional ceremonies so that he should be honored by the dead. But he has decreed that the wretched Polynices (looks to right) must not be mourned, but shall be left, unwept, unburied, for vultures to batten upon.

This is the order of our gracious King—an order that binds you, yes—and binds me too. And should anyone not have heard it, he is on his way now to proclaim it, as he counts it no light matter.

Anyone who dares to disobey shall die—die by stoning in the market-place. There! Now is your chance to show the mettle of your royal blood.

ISMENE: If things are as bad as this, how could my meddling help them now?

ANTIGONE: Are you prepared to help?

ISMENE: What is it? Is it dangerous? What do you mean?

ANTIGONE: Will you help to give Polynices—

ISMENE: You mean—bury him (looking in the direction of the corpse). In defiance of the order?

ANTIGONE: He is my brother—and yours—unless you disown him. I cannot be false to him.

ISMENE: You are mad. Creon has forbidden it.

ANTIGONE: But he has no right to shut me away from what is mine.

ISMENE: Think back, ANTIGONE: Think how our father died, detested and disgraced. Think how he stabbed out his eyes with his own hands, when he discovered the full horror of his guilt. Then his mother who became his wife—his mother-wife—one person—took a rope and hanged herself in shame. And now, our two brothers—poor wretched men—have died on the same day, each at the other's hand.

We two that alone are left, how much more dishonorable will be our end if we break the law and defy the King's decree! We must remember that we are women, and women are not meant to fight with men. Our rulers are stronger than ourselves, and we must obey them in this, and in things more bitter still.

And so I shall obey those in power, since I am forced to do so, and can only ask the dead to pardon me, since there is no wisdom at all in going too far.

ANTIGONE: I will not press you to do it. Even if you should decide to help me, you would not do it with a good grace, nor would your help be welcome to me. Be true to yourself. I shall bury him. I could not die better than in doing this. Resting with the one I love, who loves me, I shall be a criminal most holy.

I owe a longer allegiance to the dead than to the living; for with them I shall sleep for all eternity. But you, dishonor the laws of heaven if you must.

ISMENE: I am not dishonoring them, but defy the country's laws I cannot.

ANTIGONE: Make this your excuse, if you wish. I am going to bury the brother that I love.

ISMENE: Poor girl—how I fear for you!

ANTIGONE: Don't fear for me. Look to your own fate.

ISMENE: At least, Antigone, tell no one of this. Breathe no word of it, and neither will I.

ANTIGONE: Oh! shout it from the house-tops! They'll hate you all the more, if you keep it quiet.

ISMENE: You are all on fire to do a deed that chills my blood.

ANTIGONE: But I know, Ismene, I am only serving where my duty lies.

ISMENE: If you can, then do. But you are in love with the impossible.

ANTIGONE: I shall only give up when my strength fails.

ISMENE: Why pursue the impossible at all?

ANTIGONE: Say that, and I shall hate you. The dead will hate you too—and justly. Go, leave me and my folly to suffer what you fear. That way I shall not die in disgrace.

ISMENE: Do it, if you must. But remember this at least, that foolish though you are, there'll be some who still will love you.

(Antigone goes right to bury the corpse. Ismene pauses and returns into the palace.)

(CHORUS of Theban Elders enters from left and takes up position in front of the stage.)

CHORUS: Ray of the sun, the fairest light
That ever shone on the gates of Thebes
We hail you, eye of the golden day,

Rising over Dirce's[1] streams
You have scattered in flight the Argive foe
The panoplied hosts with their long white shields
You have driven away in galloping rout.

LEADER: Polynices led this host
Angered by the claim refused him.
Down they swooped like screaming eagles
Shielded with wings as white as snow,
Tossing their crests of horsehair plumes
That fluttered from a thousand helms
They swooped upon our land.

CHORUS: Over our roofs he paused
Flashing spears athirst for blood,
Ravening round our seven gates.
But ere the torch had burnt our towers,
Or his jaws with our blood were glutted,
He fled, and loud was the roar of war
Of the Theban dragon[2] behind him.

LEADER: Zeus, who hates a braggart's tongue,
Saw that mighty host approaching
In the pride of clanging gold.
One he struck with lightning bolt,
As he scaled the wall and moved his lips
To raise the shout of "Victory."

CHORUS: Down he swung to earth with a crash,
With torch ablaze—madman! to breathe
Against us blasts of flaming hate.
In vain his threats! And thousands more
Were sent to their deaths
By the havoc-making War-god, our Protector.

LEADER: Their seven chiefs at our seven gates
Stood matched with ours, but they left to Zeus
The tribute of their brazen arms;
All save two brothers,
Who face to face, and spear to spear,
Went down in a common death.

CHORUS: The Goddess of Victory has come
To share the joy of glorious Thebes.
Let us now, the war forgotten,
Thank our gods with dance and song.

---

[1] Dirce, a fountain west of Thebes.
[2] Cadmus, the founder of Thebes, killed a dragon there. The Goddess Athena told him to sow its teeth. Soldiers sprang up from the soil and became the ancestors of the Theban race.

All night long let Bacchus[1] lead us,
Lead the dance till he shake the earth.

LEADER: Look! the King of our land is here—King Creon, newly crowned by the new fortunes that the gods have sent. What thoughts are in his mind, that he has summoned us to this conference?

(Enter Creon from the center door of the palace. He is dressed as a king and preceded by attendants.)

CREON: My friends, the gods have brought our ship of state safely to port after wild tossing on the stormy seas. We have summoned you here, of all our people, because we know how firm was your allegiance to King Laius, and how loyal you were to his successor, Oedipus, and when he died, to his children after him. As you know, his two sons killed each other, staining their hands with a brother's blood. So we now hold the throne and the supreme power as kinsman of the dead.

A man's character and ability can only be judged when he has been tried as a ruler. Him we will hold base, and always have done so, who when in charge of the state spurns the best advice, and through fear closes his lips. And if he puts his friends before his country, we have for him nothing but contempt.

Zeus, who sees all, knows that we cannot be silent, if we see our country heading for disaster. Our country's enemy could never be our friend. For we know well that this country is a ship that bears us safely, and, only if we steer her straight, shall we make real friends.

By such principles we will make this city great, and in accordance with them we have published a decree about the sons of Oedipus. Eteocles, who died fighting for his country, shall be given a soldier's funeral and honored with all the ceremony that the brave and glorious deserve.

But his brother Polynices, that runaway who came back to destroy with fire and sword the city of his fathers and our ancient shrines, who came to taste his brother's blood and make our people slaves, this man, we have decreed, shall be left unburied and unmourned. His corpse shall lie without a grave, for dogs and vultures to mangle and devour.

This is our decision. Never through act of ours shall a traitor share the honors of the brave. But whoever loves his country, him will we honor in life or death.

LEADER: If this is your decision, King Creon, about our country's friend and our country's enemy, we must accept it. you have the power to order what you will, both for the dead and for us, the living.

CREON: See then that you keep well our commands.

LEADER: Give that responsibility to younger men.

CREON: We have already chosen sentries to guard the body.

LEADER: What further order do you wish to give?

CREON: To give no ear to anyone who breaks my law.

LEADER: No one but a fool would want to die.

CREON: Yes, death will be his wages. But bribes have often led men to disaster.

(A Sentry enters from right.)

SENTRY: Please sir, it is not from running that I am out of breath—no, I am not, for I've stopped lots of times to think, and I kept looking back and wondering if I should come at all. I kept saying to myself, "Don't be a fool! Why go and look for trouble?" I said. And then again, "Why stand there like a fool?" says I, "if this gets round to Creon before you get there, you'll pay for it."

What with worrying over all this I dawdled, and a short road turned into a long one. In the end I made up my mind to come, and here I am, and even if I've nothing to say, I'll say it. I've come hanging on to the hope that …after all, as I said to myself, what's coming to me is coming.

---

[1] Bacchus, or Dionysus (he had many names), was the god, originally of the vine, and so of vegetation, and all the green life that bursts forth in spring. An annual spring festival of drama was held at Athens in his honor. He was specially connected with Thebes, because he was the son of Zeus and Semele, the daughter of Cadmus.

CREON: Yes—yes—but what is the trouble.

SENTRY: First let me speak for myself. I didn't do it—I didn't see who did it. It isn't right that this should get me into trouble.

CREON: How cleverly you hedge! You cover yourself well. You must have something very strange to say.

SENTRY: I have, sir. A man does not rush into trouble.

CREON: Well, let me hear it, and then be off.

SENTRY: Right, I'll tell you—it's the body—someone has just buried it and gone off—he sprinkled dust on it, and performed the rites.

CREON: What did you say? What living man would dare to do such a thing?

SENTRY: I don't know, sir. There was no mark of a pick-axe, or earth thrown up by a spade. The ground was hard and dry, unbroken, and there were no wheel tracks. Whoever did it left no clue.

When the first day-sentry showed us this, we were all too stunned to speak. The body was concealed not by a mound, but by a light layer of dust thrown on it, as if someone wanted to escape the curse of leaving a corpse unburied. There was no sign that any dog or wild animal had been near to maul it.

Then we started arguing—each sentry accused the other. We nearly came to blows, as there was no one there to stop us. We all blamed each other, and we couldn't prove who had done it; each one said that he knew nothing about it. We were ready to take red-hot iron in our hands, or to walk through fire, or to swear by all the gods in heaven that none of us had either done it or had any part in it.

In the end, when all our questions got us nowhere, one of us said something, and after what he said, we didn't dare look up. We didn't know how to contradict him, nor, if we followed his advice, how we could escape trouble. His advice was to report the matter to you and not to hush it up.

So we drew lots to decide who should tell you, and my luck was out. So here I bring you the news, which I do not want to tell, nor you to hear. No one likes a man who brings bad news.

LEADER: O King, I have been wondering, could this not be the work of the gods?

CREON: Enough! before I burst with rage, and you show yourselves foolish old men. Your suggestion is fantastic! That the gods should care about this corpse, that they should bury and honor as a patriot—a man who came to burn their temples, to destroy their sacred treasures, to scorch their land, and tear up their laws! Have you ever known the gods to honor evil men?

I have long known there are men in the city who murmur against me, shaking their heads in secret, and chafing with discontent under my yoke. These are the men, I know, who have bribed my guards to do this deed.

Nothing has brought more evil to mankind than money. Money brings cities to the dust and drives men from their homes. Money corrupts honest souls and lures them on to wickedness. Money leads men to crime and to every kind of sin.

But the men who have been hired for this deed have made their death inevitable.

Therefore, as Zeus lives, the god in whom I trust, I swear, that unless you find the man who carried out this burial and bring him here before my eyes, death alone will not be punishment for you. You shall be strung up alive, and left hanging until you reveal the author of this monstrous outrage. You shall learn the folly of hoping to profit from evil-doing and of seeking wealth by shameful practice. Ill-gotten gains bring not happiness but misery.

SENTRY (subdued) May I speak, or shall I go now?

CREON: Do you not see that every word you speak is torture to me?

SENTRY: Torture to your ears, or your conscience?

CREON: It is no concern of yours where my trouble lies.

SENTRY: The one who did it troubles your mind, I only offend your ears.

CREON: You are a born chatterer.

SENTRY: That may be so, but I am innocent of this charge.

CREON: Indeed! When you have sold yourself for money!

SENTRY: It is a pity that your opinion of me is so mistaken.

CREON: Quibble about opinions if you will, but if you fail to discover the culprit, you shall find that treachery leads only to disaster.

(Creon goes into the palace.)

SENTRY: I hope they find him, but whether he is caught or not (fate will settle that), you may be sure you won't see me here again. And now I thank the gods I am still alive, I never expected it.

(Sentry goes out right.)

CHORUS: Wonders are many, but the greatest of all is man.
The foaming windswept sea is his conquest.
His ships cleave through engulfing waves.
He has conquered the earth,
Earth, the unwearied and everlasting,
With ploughs that never rest from year to year.
He ensnares the careless birds, and nets the
    fishes of the deep,
And traps the savage beast.
Man, the ingenious,
Has mastered the mountain beat,
Has bridled the rough-maned horse,
And yoked the mighty bull.
He has found wind-swift thought,
He has learnt speech,
And taught himself to live with other men.
He has sheltered himself from frost,
And the shafts of rain.
Man, always resourceful,
Can escape all—but death.
Even disease he can master.
He has science beyond his dreams,
Which he uses for good or ill.
And when he lives by the laws of gods and
    men,
His country prospers.
But if he chooses evil
And defies the gods,
He destroys his country.
Such a man shall never cross my threshold,
Never shall I share his thoughts.

(The Sentry re-enters with Antigone as a prisoner.)

LEADER: What devil's work is this? I do not understand. It cannot surely be Antigone? How comes she to be under arrest, unhappy girl? She could not be so foolish as to defy the King's decree?

SENTRY: Here's the one who did it. I caught her at it. Where's Creon?

(Creon appears, preceded by soldiers.)

LEADER: Here he comes—just when we need him.

CREON: What is this? What has happened that my return should be so opportune?

SENTRY: Your majesty, there is nothing a man should ever swear he will not do, for often second thoughts belie the first. I vowed it would be long time before I ever came here again, buffeted by your threats as I was before.

But there's nothing like an unexpected success. And so I've come—although I swore I wouldn't—with this girl I found preparing a burial. We didn't draw lots this time. It was my own find, no one else's. And now, your majesty, cross-examine her, and deal with her as you will. But I am cleared now. You cannot charge me with this crime again.

CREON: Where did you find her? How? Where did you catch her?

SENTRY: She was burying the body. That's all there is to it.

CREON: Do you know what you're saying? Is it the truth?

SENTRY: To put it plainly—I saw her burying the body which you said was not be touched.

CREON: How did you come to see her? Did you catch her in the act?

SENTRY: It happened like this. When I got back to my companions with those terrible threats of yours still in my ears, we brushed away all the dust that covered the corpse, and laid the clammy body quite bare. Then we sat down on some high rocks out of the wind, away from the smell. There we were, nagging each other to keep awake, in case any of us should neglect his watch.

So we stayed until the sun was at its highest, and its heat grew fierce. Then suddenly a whirlwind raised a mighty storm from the earth, which blotted out the sky, swept the plain, and stripped the low-lying wood bare of its foliage. The wide expanse of heaven was black with dust. We shut our eyes to avoid this affliction sent by the gods.

And when at last the storm was over, we saw this girl. She was uttering shrill cries, as a bird in pain when it sees its nest empty and robbed of its young. When she saw the bared corpse, she sobbed bitterly and cursed the one who had done it. Then at once she brought dry sand in her hands, and three times poured a libation on the body from a bronze pitcher.

The moment we saw it, we dashed forward and caught her, She was calm and not afraid. We cross-examined her about the burial, and also about the first one. At this she stood her ground and denied nothing. In a way I glad to see this, in a way I was sorry—glad to get myself out of trouble, sorry to lead others into it. But what did all this matter as long as I could save my own skin?

CREON *(to Antigone)*. Do you deny or admit this? Look up and answer me.

ANTIGONE: I admit it. I will not deny it.

CREON *(to the Sentry)*. You may go where you like—you are cleared from blame.

CREON *(to Antigone)*. Tell me at once, and keep to the point. Did you, or did you not know that my order had forbidden this?

ANTIGONE: I knew it well enough. The whole city knew.

CREON: And yet you dared to disobey my law?

ANTIGONE: It was not the gods who made that edict; this is not the kind of law that divine Justice,[1] who rules among the dead, or-

dains for men. I did not think that a mere mortal could make decrees of such power that they could override the unwritten and eternal laws of heaven. For these live not today nor yesterday, but for all time, and no man knows when first they came.

I could not bring myself, through fear of one man and one man's pride, to incur the punishment that falls on those who break the laws of Heaven.

That I must die sometime I knew—edict or no edict. And if I am to die before my time, that I count a gain. When one lives, as I do, in the midst of sorrow, surely one were better dead.

So this fate is no calamity to me. But if I had allowed my own brother to lie in death unburied, that would indeed have been sorrow beyond words. This brings me no sorrow. And if what I do now seems foolishness to you, perhaps he who condemns my folly is …a fool?

LEADER: The girl is as headstrong as her father. She does not know how to bend before misfortunes.

CREON: Do you not know that stubborn spirits are most often broken? The toughest steel, hardened in the fire, is most often snapped. I have seen the wildest horses tamed by the lightest grip.

Proud thoughts are not for slaves. This girl was already a practiced hand in insolence when she transgressed my established law, but this is insolence redoubled when she laughs and gloats over what she's done.

Now she will be the man, not I, if she wins this victory and goes unpunished. Though she is my niece, and bound to me more close than all who worship at our family hearth, she shall not escape a death most shameful—no, nor her sister either. I accuse her, too, of plotting this burial.

Go, bring her out. I saw her just now, within, hysterical and wild beyond control. When men plot evil in the dark, their thoughts often con-

---

[1] The Greeks believed there were gods in two places, under the earth and above it. Their belief must not be confused with the Christian heaven and hell. Those in the nether world looked after the spirits of the dead. Their king was Pluto, sometimes called Hades. "That

divine Justice who rules among the dead" is the personification of the right of the gods of the nether world to claim funeral offerings and ceremonies from the living.

vict them before the deed is done. How I abhor the man who, when caught in evil-doing, tries to glorify his crime.

ANTIGONE: Now that you have caught me, do you want to do more than kill me?

CREON: Nothing more. Having that, I have everything.

ANTIGONE: Why delay then? Your words are as displeasing to me as mine must be to you. God forbid this should ever be otherwise. And yet, how could I have won greater glory than by burying my own brother? All here would admit this, if their mouths were not gagged by fear. But kings are most fortunate. They can say and do what they like.

CREON: No one in Thebes but you holds this opinion.

ANTIGONE: Oh yes, they do. But they cower before you and curb their tongues.

CREON: Do you presume to ignore their wisdom?

ANTIGONE: There is nothing shameful in honoring a dead brother.

CREON: Was not the one who died for Thebes your brother, too?

ANTIGONE: Yes, they both had the same mother and father.

CREON: Then why insult the one by honoring the other?

ANTIGONE: Eteocles in his grave would not think that I insulted him.

CREON: Indeed he would, if you pay the same honor to a traitor.

ANTIGONE: Polynices was his brother, not his slave.

CREON: He attacked his country. Eteocles gave his life for it.

ANTIGONE: May be, but there are rights that every dead man is entitled to.

CREON: Yes, but not the same for traitors as for patriots.

ANTIGONE: Who knows what the gods regard as good, and what is evil?

CREON: A traitor is a traitor, even in death.

ANTIGONE: To those who love me I give love, to those who hate me I return not hate.

CREON: If love you must, then go and love them in the world below. No woman shall rule me while I'm alive.

(Enter Ismene from the palace under escort.)

LEADER: See! here Ismene comes.

Her clouded eyes drop tears—tears of a sister's love.

Those cheeks are deeply flushed that were just now so fair.

CREON: You viper! lurking secretly in my house, sucking my life-blood! Little I knew that I was nurturing two pests—rebels against my throne. Answer me—do you admit you took a share in this burial, or will you swear on oath that you knew nothing of it?

ISMENE: I did it …*(aside)* if she will let me stand with her.

Part of the blame is mine, and I will bear it.

ANTIGONE: You? Truth will not allow you to say that. You never offered, nor did I ask for your help.

ISMENE: But now that you are in this trouble, I am not ashamed to brave the tempest at your side.

ANTIGONE: The dead know, and the gods who rule the dead know, whose deed it was. A friend who only talks is no friend of mine.

ISMENE: Sister, don't turn away from me. Let me but die with you and pay honor to the dead.

ANTIGONE: Die with me? Never! How dare you claim a deed you've never done. My death will be enough.

ISMENE: What life is worth living for me when you are dead?

ANTIGONE: Ask CREON: (Sarcastically) He's the one you really care for.

ISMENE: Antigone, why do you laugh? Why hurt me so? It does you no good.

ANTIGONE: I hurt myself, Ismene, if I laugh at you.

ISMENE: Then tell me how I can help you even now.

ANTIGONE: Save yourself. I don't grudge you your escape.

ISMENE: I beg you, Antigone, I beg you, let me share your fate.

ANTIGONE: No. You chose to live, I chose to die.

ISMENE: I did all I could to warn you first.

ANTIGONE: Warn me? Well, some may think you the wiser, but others will think I am.

ISMENE: But the guilt falls equally upon us both.

ANTIGONE: Take heart! You are alive, I died long since when I gave my life to help the dead.

CREON: These women are both mad; one has just become so, the other has been mad since she was born.

ISMENE: Misfortune makes fools of us all, O King, even the wisest.

CREON: A fool of you, when you chose to join criminals in crime.

ISMENE: But how could I go on living, were she not here?

CREON: "She"—"here?" Enough! She is as good as dead.

ISMENE: Will you kill the girl your own son loves?

CREON: My son can find another field to plough.

ISMENE: No, not another love like his and hers.

CREON: I want no shameless woman to wed my son.

ANTIGONE: Haemon, dearest! How your father wrongs you!

CREON: Enough of you and your marriage!

LEADER: Will you really rob your own son of his bride?

CREON: No, not I, but Death himself will end for me this love affair.

LEADER: So her death-warrant, it seems, is signed.

CREON: Yes, by you, as much as by me. (To the sentries) You men there, quick! take them inside and put them in chains. Women like these must not go out into the streets. When death comes near, even the brave are apt to run.

(The sentries take Antigone and Ismene into the palace. Creon stays thinking.)

CHORUS: Blest are they whose days have
　　　　never tasted sorrow.
When a house quakes that the gods have
　　　　shaken,
The curse never leaves it.
Like a mountainous surging wave,
Rolled on by blasts from Thrace[1]
Over the darkness of the deep,
It passes to each generation.
While the ooze is stirred from the ocean bed,
And the billows break on the wind-swept
　　　　cliffs,
And the headlands echo the roar.
Mine eyes have seen from ages past
The curse on the house of Oedipus
Mounting woe upon woe from the dead.
No generation can free the next,
But each is stricken by heaven,
And no respite comes to the race.
A ray of hope shone in that house
As the last shoot quickened,
But the light has been quenched by the gods
　　　　below,
By a sprinkle of dust, and a foolish tongue,
And a mind deranged.
Thy power, O Zeus, no pride of man can
　　　　shake;
'Tis stronger than sleep that ensnareth all,
More tireless than moons that wax and wane.
Age cannot touch thee, King enthroned
In the dazzling light of Olympus[2]

---

[1] Thrace, a part of northern Greece, now Macedonia.
[2] Olympus, a mountain in Northern Greece, on the summit of which the gods were thought to dwell. The word is sometimes used to denote the region of the sky where they were also believed to live.

Thy law prevails till the end of time
"The over-proud and the over-great
Are caught in the end in the toils of Fate."
Hope roaming afar to some brings blessings,
But others it tempts with vain desires,
And a man walks blindly
Till his feet are caught in the flame.
Wise was he of old who said:
"He whom the gods draw on to ruin
sees good as evil, evil good."
Few are his days without sorrow.

LEADER: See, Haemon comes, the last of your sons. Does he come in grief for the doom of Antigone? Is he angry at being cheated of his promised bride?

(Enter HAEMON from left.)

CREON: We shall soon know—more surely than any prophecy could tell us. You may have heard, my son, that your bride is sentenced to death. Have you come to rail against your father? Or can I trust you to be loyal whatever I do?

HAEMON: Sir, I am yours and I will follow the wise guidance which you, my father, have always put before me. No marriage could ever mean as much to me as your good opinion.

CREON: Well said, my son! For a man's most heart-felt wish should be to bow before his father's judgment. It is for this that a father prays to have obedient children, who will strike his enemies blow for blow, and honor the same friends. The man who begets worthless children, what has he gained but trouble for himself and derision from his enemies?

Oh my son, do not abandon reason through a passing fancy for a woman. Remember that the embraces of a worthless wife soon grow cold. Wickedness in one you love rankles more deeply than any running sore. So send away this girl as one you loath, to find herself a husband in hell. She alone of all the city defied my decree. I will not betray my people. She shall die.

No prayer to God, no tie of family, will help her. She can expect no mercy from me. How can I expect obedience from my subjects if I nurse rebellion in my own house? Surely the man who deals justly with his household will also be found just in affairs of state. He, I am

sure, would acquit himself well as ruler or as subject, and, amid the hail of spears, would stand his ground, a good soldier and a loyal comrade. I have no patience with a man who breaks the law and tells his rulers how to rule. The man whom the people put in power must be obeyed in matters great and small, just or unjust.

What evil is greater than anarchy? Anarchy destroys cities; anarchy desolates homes; anarchy breaks up armies in the stress of battle. Good lives are only made and saved by discipline.

So we must defend the laws with all our strength and not allow ourselves to be flaunted by a woman. If fall I must, then let it be a man that casts me down. Never let it be said of me that I was conquered by a woman.

LEADER: I am old; my age confuses me; yet I feel that there is wisdom in your words.

HAEMON: Father, the greatest gift that the gods implant in man is reason. I would not dare—far be it from me—to deny that all you say is right, and yet another's counsel might be of value. Your part is not to keep watch on what men say or do, and what they find to criticize. Your dread frown deters the citizens from speaking words that would not please your ear.

But I hear whispers in the dark, murmurs among the people in pity for this girl. " No woman," they say, "ever less deserved such a doom. None was ever condemned to die so shamefully for a deed so noble."

When her own brother fell in battle, she would not leave him unburied for carrion curs and vultures to devour. Is that a crime? "Does she not rather deserve," they say, "a crown of gold?"

Such are the dark rumors that are spreading secretly through the city. No treasure, father, is more precious to me than your welfare. What pleases a son more than his father's good name, or what delights a father more than his son's reputation?

(Creon sneers. Haemon changes his tone— finding every appeal useless.)

Must you always nurse this one idea in your heart, that what you think, and nothing else, is right? If you look into the heart of a man who thinks that he alone is wise, wise in all his thoughts and words, wise above all others, you will find nothing but emptiness.

It is no disgrace even for a wise man to be willing to learn and yield at times to reason. Look at trees in a wintry torrent, how those that bend keep safe every bough and twig, but those that resist the raging flood are destroyed root and branch. So, too, a sailor who keeps his sheet taut and never slackens it ends his voyage by capsizing.

So, father, stay your anger. Allow your mood to change. Though a younger man, may I offer you my counsel? I say that best by far is that in all things man should avoid folly. But if he cannot always be wise (and who of us always can?) it is good to learn from those who speak wisdom.

LEADER: Sir, it is right that you should profit by your son's words, if he has something opportune to say. And for you too, Haemon, to listen to your father. For in both there is good sense.

CREON: Am I, at my age, to be taught by a youngster like this?

HAEMON: Only if what he says is right. If I am young, you should consider not my years, but the merits of what I have to say.

CREON: Merit, is it, to respect law-breakers?

HAEMON: God forbid that anyone should respect a scoundrel.

CREON: But that is precisely what she is.

HAEMON: The people of Thebes think otherwise.

CREON: Shall Thebes dictate to me how I shall rule?

HAEMON: Who is talking like a youngster now?

CREON: Am I to rule at another's dictation?

HAEMON: A city is no city that is ruled by one man.

CREON: Does not the city belong to the ruler? I am the city.

HAEMON: A one-man city! It's a desert you should be ruling.

CREON: Champion a woman, would you, boy?

HAEMON: Who's the woman? You? It's you I have at heart.

CREON: Villain, how dare you wrangle with your father?

HAEMON: Only because I see you sinning against the light.

CREON: Against the light! A sin! To respect my own prerogative?

HAEMON: Respect! You talk of respect when you trample underfoot the reverence due to the gods!

CREON: You poor fool! You woman's slave!

HAEMON: You will never find me a slave to what is base.

CREON: In every word you utter, you plead for her.

HAEMON: Yes, and for you too, and for myself, and for the gods below.

CREON: Never shall you marry that girl in this life.

HAEMON (thinking of himself, but Creon misunderstands him) If she dies, her death will cause …another's death.

CREON: How dare you threaten me? What insolence!

HAEMON: Threaten? Is it a threat to oppose your nonsense?

CREON: You shall pay for this—daring to teach me wisdom.

HAEMON: In another man I should have counted it madness—but—you are my father.

CREON: You woman's plaything! Don't try and wheedle me.

HAEMON: Do you want to do all the talking, and hear nothing in reply?

CREON: Indeed? By all he gods on Olympus, you shall pay for your jeering. (To the guards) Bring out that hateful thing, that she may die before her bridegroom's eyes, nay, at his very side.

HAEMON: Before my eyes! no, never! My face you shall never see again. Go, rave among your friends, if they can endure a madman.

(Haemon goes out right, unseen by Creon.)

LEADER: See King, your son has gone in anger.

Beware a young mind brooding on its pain.

CREON: Gone? Let him go, and try to do what no man can. He shall not save these girls from their fate.

LEADER: Do you intend to them both to death?

CREON: No, not the one who took no part. You are right.

LEADER: And what death do you intend for the other?

CREON: I will take her to a desolate spot where man's foot never treads, and there seal her up alive in a rocky cavern, with only as much food as custom[1] prescribes to absolve the city of her death. There let her pray to the gods below, the only ones she worships, and (sarcastically) maybe they will rescue her from death. And if they do not, she may learn at last, though late, that to revere the dead is wasted toil.

(Creon goes out left.)

CHORUS: Love invincible, love irresistible,
Matchless in fight,
Love that sleeps in a girl's soft cheek,
Keeping vigil,
Love that riots among the flocks,
Over the sea Love seeks his prey,
In lonely cabins among the hills,
None can escape you—god or man—
Not deathless gods nor mortal man,
And he you enslave is mad.
You warp the minds of the good to sin,

And lure them to disaster.
Strife you sow in peaceful homes,
Embroiling sons and fathers.
The shaft of desire from a maiden's eyes
Who can resist? She sits enthroned
Beside the eternal laws triumphant—
Man-mocking Aphrodite.[2]

(Enter Antigone under escort. Quiet music is heard.)

LEADER. Now this tempts me beyond the law,
And I can scarce hold back my tears,
When I behold Antigone
Going to Death's bridal-bower
Where all must sleep a sleep unending.

ANTIGONE: Behold me, citizens of my land,
Going upon my last journey,
Never shall I see the sun again,
The King of Death, who puts all to sleep,
Leads me alive to Acheron's[3] cold shore.
No marriage-song for me,
No wedding-marches there
For the bride of Death.

CHORUS: With honor and praise you go
To the dark, deep vault of the dead,
Smitten not by wasting disease,
Tasting not the sword's keen edge.
'Tis of your own free will you go—
No other mortal has gone this way
Alive.

ANTIGONE: I have heard men tell of Niobe,[4]
Daughter of Tantalus, Queen of Thebes,
Turned to stone on Phrygia's mount.
Stone grew round her like ivy clinging.
From her eyelids drop sad tears,
Tears of everlasting rain—
On her frozen bosom lie
Drifts of ever-clinging snow.
So must I lie,
Turning to weeping stone like Niobe.

---

[1] The Greeks thought it wrong to starve a person to death, and therefore supplied a little food, so that if death ensued, it would be the work of Nature and not Man.

[2] Aphrodite, the Goddess of Love, called by the Romans Venus.

[3] Acheron, a river in the lower world.

[4] Niobe, the wife of Amphion, and early king of Thebes, who boasted that she had more children than Leto, the mother of Apollo and Artemis. Leto therefore persuaded her children to kill all Niobe's. Niobe went to her old home on Mount Sipylus, near Smyrna, and was turned into stone. The rock, which can still be seen, looks from a distance in heavy rain like a woman sitting on a throne and weeping.

CHORUS: Yet she was a goddess and a child
    of a god,
While we are mortal, mere children of men.
Glorious is the name of woman
Who shares in life and shares in death
The lot of a suffering god.

ANTIGONE: Ah, you mock me—to my face.
Can you not wait till I am dead?
City mine, and your mighty sons,
Springs of Dirce, bear witness all!
Thou sacred plain where chariots race,
Bear witness, by what cruel law
Unwept by friends
I go condemned to a prison-tomb—
A prison strange—a rock-built tomb—
An outcast among the living,
Homeless among the dead.

CHORUS: In daring you climbed to the ut-
    most height,
Climbed too high,
Before the altar-steps of Justice
You fell, my child, and lost and lay.
It must be for your father's sin
That you are paying now.

ANTIGONE: You have touched my most bit-
    ter pain—
My father's sin, and the doom it brought
On whole of our ancient house.
Oh! the horror of the incestuous bed
Where my mother slept in her son's em-
    brace—
Her son ...my father! Where I was conceived,
I and my hell! To them I must go
Accursed, unmarried, a homeless girl
To share their home in the world below.
Oh brother, ill-starred in your marriage,
'Tis your dead hand that has murdered me.

CHORUS: Respect should be paid where re-
    spect is due,
But he who rules must guard his laws
And punish the transgressor.
But you—your ruin springs from your own
self-will.

ANTIGONE: I am ready. No tear, no friend,
    no marriage-hymn,
To cheer me on my miserable road.
On me no more the sun will shed his holy
    light.
Alone I go—no friend, no tears.

(Creon returns impatient.)

CREON: Would men ever cease moaning and wailing, if moans and wails could postpone death? (To the guard) Take her away at once. Wall her up, as I have told you, in the vault, and leave her there alone, to die if she likes, or go on loving in a tomb. Our hands are clean of this girl's blood. But all I deny her is the right to live on this earth.

(Creon goes into the palace.)

ANTIGONE: O grave, my bridal-chamber! O rock-prison, my eternal home! To you I go, to meet again mine own, all those whom Perse-phone[1] has welcomed among the dead. Of them I am the last, and the most miserable of all, taken before my life's allotted span. But as I come, one hope sustains me that my coming will be dear to my father, and dear to you, mother, and dear to my brother Eteocles. For with my own hands I washed your dead bodies and shrouded them, and poured libations on your graves.

And yet I honored you as those that are wise will agree. For never, if I had been the mother of children or if I had had a husband moulder-ing in death, would I have chosen this task against the will of the people. To satisfy what law do I say this? If my husband had died, I might have had another and a child from an-other if I had lost one, but since both my mother and father lie in Hades, no other brother could ever be born to me. That was the law that led me to honor you before all others. Yet Creon thought I did wrong in this, daring a deed so evil, ah brother mine! And now he has taken me captive and is leading me away unwed, unsung, robbed of the joy of marriage and the bringing up of children. Thus bereft of my friends I go unhappy, alive, to the vaults of the dead.

And now, Polynices, for tending your dead body my reward is death.

Yet against what law of God have I offended? Why should I in my sorrow look to heaven again? To what friend can I appeal, when I am condemned as unholy for doing a holy deed?

If my doom is held among the gods to be right, when I have suffered death, I shall be-

---

[1] Persephone, stolen from earth by Pluto, became the queen of the nether world.

come conscious of my sin. But if the sin is with my judges, may nothing worse befall them than the wrong they do me.

(Creon returns.)

CHORUS: Look! the storm still rages in her soul.

CREON: Those who are guarding her shall pay for this delay.

ANTIGONE: Ah! those words bring death very near.

CREON: Yes, there shall be no reprieve.

ANTIGONE: (as the guards lead her away) O city of Thebes, my native land! Ye gods of my ancestors, see! They take me away! My hour has come! Look on me, princes of Thebes, the last of the royal house, see what I suffer, and at whose hands, because I gave the gods their due and would not disobey the laws of heaven.

(Exit Antigone and guards.)

CHORUS: So too, the lovely Danae[1]
Was hidden from the light of day,
Imprisoned in a brazen room
For a bridal bower.
Yet she came of a royal line
Like yours, my child, my child
And in her womb was the seed of Zeus
That fell in the golden rain.
Terrible is the power of Destiny,
Mysterious, invincible,
Man cannot escape it.
No wealth, nor arms, nor guarded tower,
Nor dark-prowed ship that fights the sea
Can save him when Fate calls.

And the hot-tempered son of Dryas, King of the Edonians, was brought under the yoke for his bursts of anger, being shut up by Dionysus in a rocky prison. Thus the terrible outbursts of his madness gradually diminished. He came to know the god whom he had provoked in his madness with taunts and mockery. For he tried to stop the god-possessed women and the Bacchanalian fire, and he insulted the Muses who love the flute.

There are also, near the Cyanean rocks of the double sea, the shores of the Bosphorus and the town of Thracian Salmydessus, where Ares, who dwells near them, saw the accursed blinding wound inflicted on the two sons of Phineus by his savage wife, making sightless their revengeful eyes, torn out by her bloody hands and the sharp point of a shuttle. And they, pining in their misery, wept for their wretched fate, having been born from an unhappily married mother. But she was descended from the ancient line of Erechtheus, and in far distant caves she was bred among her father's storms, that daughter of Boreas, swift as a steed over hills, a child of the gods; but on her also did the long-lived Fates press hard, O my daughter.

(The blind prophet, Tiresias, enters from left, led by a boy.)

TIRESIAS: Rulers of Thebes, we have come, with one to see for both of us, for this is the way the blind walk, with the help of a guide.

CREON: Aged Tiresias, what news have you brought?

TIRESIAS: Harken, my son, and mark well the prophet's words.

CREON: Have I ever in the past spurned your counsel?

TIRESIAS: That is why thou steerest aright this ship of state.

CREON: Your help I know, and will admit as much.

TIRESIAS: Know that once more thou standest on the razor-edge of doom.

CREON: What is that? Your words make me shudder.

TIRESIAS: Thou shalt learn all as thou hearest the warnings that my art reveals. As I took my place at the ancient seat of augury[2] where all the birds gather round me, I heard a strange noise among them, a weird and horrible jangle. As they screeched in frenzy, I knew that they were tearing at each other with murderous claws, for the whirring of their wings made it plain.

---

[1] Danae was shut up in a brazen tower by her father, the King of Argos, because the Delphic oracle had told him that he would be killed by his grandson. Zeus visited her in the likeness of a shower of golden rain. Her son was called Perseus.

---

[2] In ancient times the flight and cries of birds were interpreted by the augurs (or "prophets") as omens.

Straightaway in fear I made trial by sacrifice on an altar full kindled, but no flame rose from my offerings, Only a dripping moisture oozed from the thigh bones and smoked and sputtered among the embers. The gall shot into the air, and the streaming bones lay bare of the fat that covered them. But no flame!

So failed the rites by which I vainly sought a sign. I have it from this boy, for he is guide to me as I am to others. The state I say is sick, sick though your folly. All our shrines and altars are tainted and polluted by vultures and dogs with carrion flesh torn from the corpse of the ill-fated son of Oedipus. No longer do the gods accept our prayers and sacrifices. Our burnt offerings abominate. No more does a bird's clear note give a fair omen, for all are gorged with the thick blood of a slain man.

Ponder then on these things, my son. All men at times do wrong, but wrongs can be repaired, if men will overcome the folly of their stubborn wills. For obstinacy often proclaims the fool.

So give the dead his due, and do not stab a corpse. Is it bravery to kill a man who is dead?

I have sought thy good, and for thine own good speak. 'Tis sweet to learn from one who brings good counsel—the more so, if therein lies gain.

CREON: Aged priest, you and your kind shoot at me like archers at a target, and now you dare to try your fortune-telling on me. For years I have been bought and sold like merchandise by your tribe of prophets. Go, do your trading, drive your bargains in silver from Sardis or gold from India, but that man's burial you shall never buy, no, not even if the eagles[1] of Zeus should bear him morsel by morsel to their master's throne. No, not even fear of such a pollution will make me bury him. For I know full well that no mortal man can pollute the gods. Terrible is the fall, aged Tiresias, of even the wisest of men, when he disguises wicked thoughts in eloquence for the sake of gain.

TIRESIAS: Oh! does no man know, does no man pause to think …

CREON: What platitude is this?

TIRESIAS: How precious beyond gold is good counsel?

CREON: As much as folly is the worst of evils.

TIRESIAS: That is the very disease thou are tainted with.

CREON: I do not wish to cast your insults in your teeth.

TIRESIAS: But thou dost, when thou sayest that my prophecies are lies.

CREON: The prophet tribe is always out for gold.

TIRESIAS: Ill-gotten lucre is the curse of tyrants.

CREON: Do you know you are speaking of your king?

TIRESIAS: I know it. For 'tis through my counsel thou hast kept thy kingdom safe.

CREON: Wise you may be in counsel, but treacherous at heart.

TIRESIAS: Take heed, lest I reveal the locked secret in my soul.

CREON: Out with it! Speak, but let not bribery sway you!

TIRESIAS: Bribery! Is this your thought of me?

CREON: Know this. You cannot make me sell my fixed resolve.

TIRESIAS: Now hear the truth and mark it well. Thou shalt not see many more courses of the chariot of the sun before one born from thine own loins shall be sent to death, a life for a life, a corpse for a corpse, paid in due requital, for the life thou didst deny told still live—thou who didst so shamefully entomb her, a living soul.

Nay more, there is another whose soul thou keepest imprisoned on this earth, whose corpse lies naked, unblessed, without a tomb. Thou hast no right to keep him so. Wouldst thou set thyself up as a god? For this affront to heaven, the Avenging Furies lie in wait for thee to entrap thee in the net that thou hast spread for others.

---

[1] The eagle as sacred to Zeus and Apollo.

Now consider well whether I have been bribed to speak these words. Before many days have passed, thy palace will re-echo to the cries of men and women's wailings. Already a league of hate is formed against thee of all those cities whose mangled sons were not buried save by dogs or beasts, or by some winged bird that brought pollution to the dead men's hearths and homes.

These barbs I discharge against thy heart, for thou hast provoked my wrath; yea and they fly true; thou shalt not escape their sting.

(To the boy.)

Boy, lead me home, that this man may vent his wrath on younger men, and learn to keep a tongue more bridled, and in his breast to nurse better thoughts than now he holds.

(Tiresias goes out right, led by the boy.)

LEADER: O King, the man has gone. His prophecies affright me.

Through all the years in which my hair has turned from dark to grey, I have never known him prophesy falsely to this city.

CREON: I know that, too, and am troubled. My pride forbids me to yield, but if I stand by my decision and so bring ruin on my head.... To have to make the choice is terrible.

LEADER: Creon, son of Menoeceus, listen to wise counsel.

CREON: What would you have me do? Tell me. I will listen.

LEADER: Go, free the girl from her rocky prison, and make a tomb for the outcast dead.

CREON: Is this your counsel? You would have me yield?

LEADER: Yes, King, and at once. Swift are the feet of the gods upon the path of foolish men.

CREON: Ah me! 'tis hard. I will give up my heart's resolve. It is vain to fight with destiny.

LEADER: Go now, and do these things yourself. Leave them not to others.

CREON: I will go as I am. Quick, my servants, wherever you are, take axes in your hands, and hasten to that hill that you see yonder (pointing).

I have reversed my will. I imprisoned her; I will set her free. Fear impels me, for 'tis best to keep the eternal laws, even to the last day of life.

(Creon goes out right.)

CHORUS *(joyfully)*. Dionysus, god of many
   names,
Child of loud-thundering Zeus,
The pride of Theban Semele,
Thou guardest Italy's famous land,
And hast thy throne beside Eleusis bay
That welcomes all to Queen Demeter's shrine.
This is thy city, where thy Maenads dwell,
And Ismenus' stream glides softly,
Where the dragon's teeth were sown.
Where the smoking torches glare
Above the double crested rock,
The nymphs have seen thee, as they dance
Above Castalia's spring.
From Nysa's ivy-mantled slopes
Thou camest, from Euboea's shore
Green with many-clustered vines,
Thou art hymned with strains divine
Though the streets of thy city.
As of old thou lov'dst this city,
Thou and thy mother whom the lightning
   slew,
Come thou to succor us plague-stricken,
Come with healing feet from Parnassus's
   height,
Fly over the moaning strait.
Thou leader of the stars whose breath is fire,
Lord of wild voices of the night,
Appear, O Zeus-born, King;
Come with thy frenzied Maenad band,
Who dance before thee all night long,
Giver of life, Iacchus, come.

(Enter Messenger from right.)

MESSENGER. Listen, you who dwell beside the palaces of Cadmus and Amphion. There is no condition of human life which I would consider fixed or stable, be it good or bad, for fortune raises up and fortune throws down the prosperous and unfortunate alike. There is no sure way for a man to foretell his destiny. Once I thought Creon a King to be envied, when he saved this land of Cadmus from its foes, and took into his hands the rule of the city, absolute and supreme. Proud father, too, was he of noble children. And now he has lost all. When life is robbed of joy, I count it but as living death. Even if a man amasses in his house great wealth, and lives in royal pomp— if gladness once is gone, the rest compared with it is but a puff of smoke.

LEADER: What further evil has beset our royal house?

MESSENGER. They are dead. The guilty still live.

LEADER: Dead? Who? At whose hand? Speak!

MESSENGER. Haemon is dead, and by a hand he knew too well.

LEADER: What mean you? By his father's or his own?

MESSENGER. By his own, in anger at his father's murderous deed.

LEADER: Oh prophet! how fearfully your words have come true.

MESSENGER. These are the facts. The rest must lie with you.

(Enter Eurydice from the palace.)

LEADER: I see Eurydice, the Queen, coming forth from the palace. Is it by chance, or has she heard about her son?

EURYDICE. Citizens of Thebes, I was on my way to pray in Athena's temple, when I overheard your words. As I drew back the bolt to open the door, news of evil to our house fell upon my ears. Terrified, I reeled into my servants' arms and swooned. Tell me again what the news is—my ears are used to sorrow.

MESSENGER. Look, Madam, I will tell you the whole truth. I was there and saw it all ...why should I comfort you by saying things that may prove to be untrue. The truth is always best. I attended your lord as his guide to the edge of the plain, where the corpse of Polynices lay unpitied, mangled by dogs. We bathed it in holy water. We prayed to Pluto, and the Goddess of the Crossways to be merciful, and restrain their wrath. Then we cut fresh wood and burnt his poor remains, and over his ashes we built a high mound of his native earth. This done, we went straight to

the vault, Antigone's stony bridal-bower. From afar we heard a noise of wailing from the unhallowed chamber, and ran to tell the King. As he drew near, there reached him faint sounds of a bitter cry. At this he groaned and cried aloud, "Ah me! can my fears be true? Am I treading the most unhappy road of all that I have ever trod? It is my son's voice that greets me. Haste my servants, go near, past the place where the stones are torn away. Look into the mouth of the vault and tell me, if it is Haemon's voice I hear, or if some god is cheating me."

We looked, as the unhappy king bade us, and saw Antigone at the far end of the tomb, a noose of fine linen about her neck. Haemon lay embracing her, mourning his dead love, the bride of Death, and cursing his father's cruel deed. When his father saw him, he uttered a terrible cry, and went in and called to him. "What have you done, my son? Why have you done it? What calamity has unhinged your mind? Come forth, my child, I beg, I implore you." But the boy stared at him, glowering with angry eyes, he spat in his face, and without a word drew his double-edged sword, and made to strike his father. But he ran out and escaped the blow. The Haemon, angry with himself, drove the sword into his own side, and as he breathed his life away, his red blood gushed forth and splashed upon her white cheek.

There they lie, two bodies side by side, wedded in death, witnesses before all mankind, that of all the curses that can fall on man, the worst curse is his own folly.

(Eurydice retires into the palace.)

LEADER: What do you understand by this? The Queen has gone inside again, without a word.

MESSENGER. I, too, am troubled, but I hope she has only gone within to share her bitter sorrow with her women beneath her roof, rather than make a public show of grief for a death so tragic. She is not without wisdom, and will do nothing that is not fitting.

LEADER: I do not know, but to me this silence is not natural. 'Tis more ominous than the sound of wailing.

MESSENGER. Yes, you are right. Unnatural silence may bode no good. I will go in, and find out if in her distraction she conceals within her heart some secret purpose.

(Messenger goes into the palace.)

(The body of Haemon is brought in. Creon walks by its side.)

LEADER: Lo! here comes the King himself. This burden tells too clear a tale. This deed of frenzy is no stranger's doing: nay—dare I say it?—the crime is his and his alone.

CREON: Alas for the sin of a blinded soul,
A deadly, stubborn sin.
Here you see a murdered son,
The murderer his father.
Oh! the blindness of all my wisdom!
Alas, my son, so young to die.
The guilt is mine, not yours, but mine.

LEADER: Too late, too late, you see the right.

Creon: Yea, taught by bitter sorrow,
On my head has fallen
A crushing blow from heaven,
God drives me along a cruel road,
Trampling on what I hold most dear,
Heavy are the sufferings of mortal man.

(Enter Second Messenger from the palace.)

MESSENGER: Sir, sorrow enough your hands bear already, but you are soon to find more within your house.

CREON: What is this? Can anything be more cruel than what is now cruel enough?

Messenger. The Queen is dead—your dead son's mother has stabbed herself.

Creon. Oh! jaws of Death! inexpiable,
Will you engulf me now?

(Turning to the Messenger)

Thou herald of evil,
What new tale of woe is this?
I was as dead—would'st kill me again?
What sayest thou, boy? My wife dead?
Death heaped on death?

LEADER: See for yourself.

(The doors of the palace are opened, disclosing the body of the Queen within.)

CREON: Oh! agony still greater.
What further woe can yet await me.

My son, my wife! Oh son, your mother!

MESSENGER: There at the altar she fell upon a sword,
And closed her eyes in darkness,
Crying aloud for her elder son
Long dead, and then for Haemon,
And lastly on you—the slayer of her child—
She breathed a curse.

CREON *(groaning and terror-struck)*: Will no one draw a sword and strike me to the heart?
My cup is full.

MESSENGER: Yes, she who lies here laid all the blame on you,
For the deaths of both.

CREON: Tell me how she died.

MESSENGER: When she learned her dear son's fate,
With her own hand she stabbed herself in the heart.

CREON: Ah me! the guilt is mine, I know it.
I blame no other.
Lead me away servants, away with all speed.
My life is now as death.

LEADER. You speak rightly, if there can be any right
'Mid so much wrong.
Briefest is best, when ills are past enduring.

CREON: Let it come, ay, let it come—
Death, the blessed doom to end my sufferings—
Let it come, that I may never see the sun again.

LEADER: Let be what may be.
The present concerns is now.

CREON: That prayer of mine holds all that I could wish.

LEADER: Then pray no more. Man has no escape from destiny.

CREON: Lead me away, a poor, rash, fool.
Who killed his son unwittingly, and killed his wife.
I know not where to look, or where to turn.
All is gone amiss. A fate intolerable has leapt upon my head.

(As Creon is being led into the palace, the
CHORUS speaks the closing lines to the
audience.)

LEADER: Wisdom is the key to happiness,
The wise know how to bow the will to God.
Proud men, chastened, pay the price for their
    proud words.
And in old age alone do they learn wisdom.

✝

V. Sophistry And Illusion

The Peloponnesian War (431-404 B.C.) and the Sophistic movement had a corrosive effect on both the Enlightenment and Greek traditions governing the relationship of citizen and state. PERICLES' idealized picture of the identity of interest between individual and state, evident in this excerpt from the FUNERAL ORATION he delivered early in the war, gave way to a growing sense of the difference between ruler and ruled. Passages in this section from THUCYDIDES (c. 460-396 B.C.), PLATO (428-347 B.C.) and ARISTOTLE (384-322 B.C.) show the effect on Greek life and thought; CLEANTHES (c. 331-231 B.C.) and EPICURUS (341-270 B.C.) show philosophical responses to the post-polis world.

❖   ❖   ❖

1. THE FUNERAL ORATION

PERICLES

In the first year of the war against Sparta, Pericles, a prominent Athenian statesman until his death in 429, was chosen to deliver the customary eulogy over those killed in battle. In the selection that follows, he speaks of the state, Athens, for which the citizens died. What features of the city does he choose to praise? What makes Athens so unique in his eyes? How does his view of the role of the individual in the state compare with that of the individual in those Near Eastern cultures we have studied? By the way, can you identify the method he uses to analyze his topic?

That part of our history which tells of the military achievements which gave us our several possessions, or of the ready valor with which either we or our fathers stemmed the tide of Hellenic or foreign aggression, is a theme too familiar to my hearers for me to dilate on, and I shall therefore pass it by. But what was the road by which we reached our position, what the form of government under which our greatness grew, what the national habits out of which it sprang? These are questions which I may try to solve before I proceed to my panegyric upon these men; since I think this to be a subject upon which on the present occasion a speaker may properly dwell, and to which the whole assemblage, whether citizens or foreigners, may listen with advantage.

[handwritten: why athens is special & great]

Our constitution does not copy the laws of neighboring states; we are rather a pattern to others than imitators ourselves. Its administration favors the many instead of the few; this is why it is called a democracy. If we look to the laws, they afford equal justice to all in their private differences; if to social standing, advancement in public life falls to reputation for capacity, class considerations not being allowed to interfere with merit; nor again does poverty bar the way: if a man is able to serve the state, he is not hindered by the obscurity of his condition.

The freedom which we enjoy in our government extends also to our ordinary life. There, far from exercising a jealous surveillance over each other, we do not feel called upon to be angry with our neighbor for doing what he likes, or even to indulge in those injurious looks which cannot fail to be offensive, although they inflict no positive penalty.

But all this ease in our private relations does not make us lawless as citizens. Against this fear is our chief safeguard, teaching us to obey the magistrates and the laws, particularly such as regard the protection of the injured, whether they are actually on the statute book, or belong to that code which, although unwritten, yet cannot be broken without acknowledged disgrace.

Further, we provide plenty of means for the mind to refresh itself from business. We celebrate games and sacrifices all the year round, and the elegance of our private establishments forms a daily source of pleasure and helps to banish the spleen; while the magnitude of our city draws the produce of the world into our harbor, so that to the Athenian the fruits of other countries are as familiar a luxury as those of his own.

why militarily great & diff.

If we turn to our military policy, there also we differ from our antagonists. We throw open our city to the world, and never by alien acts exclude foreigners from any opportunity of learning or observing, although the eyes of an enemy may occasionally profit by our liberality, since we trust less in system and policy than to the native spirit of our citizens.

In education, where our rivals from their very cradles by a painful discipline seek after manliness, at Athens we live exactly as we please, and yet are just as ready to encounter every legitimate danger. In proof of this it may be noticed that the Lacedaemonians do not invade our country alone, but bring with them all their confederates, while we Athenians advance unsupported into the territory of a neighbor, and when we fight upon a foreign soil usually vanquish with ease men who are defending their homes.

Our united force was never yet encountered by any enemy, because we have at once to attend to our marine and to despatch our citizens by land upon a hundred different services; so that, wherever they engage with some fraction of our strength, a success against a detachment is magnified into a victory over the nation, and a defeat into a reverse suffered at the hands of our entire people. And yet if with habits not of labor but of ease, and courage not of art but of nature, we are still willing to encounter danger, we have the double advantage of escaping the experience of hardships in anticipation and of facing them in the hour of need as fearlessly as those who are never free from them.

Nor are these the only points in which our city is worthy of admiration. We cultivate refinement without extravagance and knowledge without effeminacy; wealth we employ more for use than for show, and place the real disgrace of poverty not in owning to the fact but in declining the struggle against it.

The Indv. in Athens

Our public men have, besides politics, their private affairs to attend to, and our ordinary citizens, though occupied with the pursuits of industry, are still fair judges of public matters; for, unlike any other nation, regarding him who takes no part in these duties not as unambitious but as useless, we Athenians are able to judge at all events if we cannot originate, and instead of looking on discussion as a stumbling-block in the way of action, we think it an indispensable preliminary to any wise action at all.

Again, in our enterprises we present the singular spectacle of daring and deliberation, each carried to its highest point, and both united in the same persons, although usually decision is the fruit of ignorance, hesitation of reflection. But the palm of courage will surely be adjudged most justly to those who best know the difference between hardship and pleasure and yet are never tempted to shrink from danger.

In generosity we are equally singular, acquiring our friends by conferring not by receiving favors. Yet, of course, the doer of the favor is the firmer friend of the two, in order by continued kindness to keep the recipient in his debt; while the debtor feels less keenly from the very consciousness that the return he makes will be a payment, not a free gift. And it is only the Athenians who, fearless of consequences, confer their benefits not from calculations of expediency, but in the confidence of liberality.

Athens as a whole

In short, I say that as a city we are the school of Hellas; while I doubt if the world can produce a man who, where he has only himself to depend upon, is equal to so many emergencies and graced by so happy a versatility as the Athenian. And that this is no mere boast thrown out for the occasion but plain matter of fact, the power of the state acquired by these habits proves. For Athens alone of her contemporaries is found when tested to be greater than her reputation, and alone gives no occasion to her assailants to blush at the antagonist by whom they have been worsted, or to her subjects to question her title by merit to rule.

Rather, the admiration of the present and succeeding ages will be ours, since we have not left our power without witness, but have shown it by mighty proofs; and far from needing a Homer for our panegyrist, or other of his craft whose verses might charm for the moment only for the impression which they gave to melt at the touch of fact, we have forced every sea and land to be the highway of our daring, and everywhere, whether for evil or for good, have left imperishable monuments behind us.

Such is the Athens for which these men, in the assertion of their resolve not to lose her, nobly fought and died; and well may every one of their survivors be ready to suffer in her cause.

❖

2. THE PELOPONNESIAN WAR

THUCYDIDES

The Peloponnesian War, whose first casualties Pericles eulogized so well, dragged on for nearly three decades. Thucydides, an Athenian admiral who lived through the whole conflict, saw the war as a great drain on Greek resources and ultimately a corrupter of all the highest ideal of the polis.

Thucydides opened his book with a standard discussion of the greatness of his subject. Here he also discussed Historical Method, to show how his writing differed from that of his predecessors (the reference to the Persian War shows he included Herodotus). Can you see from this passage why he is called the "Father of Scientific History"?

The second selection, The Revolution in Corcyra, offers a chilling description of the meltdown of a polis under the stresses of war in 427.

The third selection, The Melian Dialogue, is an essay on the effects of power on both the powerful and the powerless. In 416 the Athenians mounted an expedition against the island of Melos. The reasons for the Athenian action, and the response by the Melians, are given in the passage below. But what is most significant are the arguments each side gives to justify its actions. What do the Athenians want? What is the Melian answer? Which side has the better argument? Are there principles or ideals that continue to have force and validity even in time of war? Or is everything fair?

What reasons does Thucydides give for this conflict? What exactly are its effects? How valid do you think Thucydides' observations are?

A. ON HISTORICAL METHOD

The way that most men deal with traditions, even traditions of their own country, is to receive them all alike as they are delivered, without applying any critical test whatever.

So little pains do the vulgar take in the investigation of truth, accepting readily the first story that comes to hand. On the whole, however, the conclusions I have drawn from the proofs quoted may, I believe, safely be relied on. Assuredly they will not be disturbed either by the lays of a poet displaying the exaggeration of his craft, or by the compositions of the chroniclers that are attractive at truth's expense; the subjects they treat of being out of the reach of evidence, and time having robbed most of them of historical value by enthroning them in the region of legend. Turning from these, we can rest satisfied with having proceeded upon the clearest data, and having arrived at conclusions as exact as can be expected in matters of such antiquity. To come to this war: despite the known disposition of the actors in a struggle to overrate its importance, and when it is over to return to their admiration of earlier events, yet an examination of the facts will show that it was much greater than the wars which preceded it.

With reference to the speeches in this history, *cross examination* some were delivered before the war began, others while it was going on; some I heard myself, others I got from various quarters; it was in all cases difficult to carry them word for word in one's memory, so my habit has been to make the speakers say what was in my opinion demanded of them by the various occasions, of course adhering as closely as possible to the general sense of what they really said.

With reference to the narrative of events, far from permitting myself to derive it from the first source that came to hand, I did not even trust my own impressions, but it rests partly on what I saw myself, partly on what others saw for me, the accuracy of the report being always tried by the most severe and detailed tests possible.

My conclusions have cost me some labour from the want of coincidence between accounts of the same occurrences by different

what its for

eye-witnesses, arising sometimes from imperfect memory, sometimes from undue partiality for one side or the other. The absence of romance in my history will, I fear, detract somewhat from its interest; but if it be judged useful by those inquirers who desire an exact knowledge of the past as an aid to the interpretation of the future, which in the course of human things must resemble if it does not reflect it, I shall be content. In fine, I have written my work, not as an essay which is to win the applause of the moment, but as a possession for all time.

The Persian War, the greatest achievement of past times, yet found a speedy decision in two actions by sea and two by land. The Peloponnesian War was prolonged to an immense length, and, long as it was, it was short without parallel for the misfortunes that it brought upon Hellas. Never had so many cities been taken and laid desolate, here by the barbarians, here by the parties contending (the old inhabitants being sometimes removed to make room for others); never was there so much banishing and blood-shedding, now on the field of battle, now in the strife of faction. Old stories of occurrences handed down by tradition, but scantily confirmed by experience, suddenly ceased to be incredible; there were earthquakes of unparalleled extent and violence; eclipses of the sun occurred with a frequency unrecorded in previous history; there were great droughts in sundry places and consequent famines, and that most calamitous and awfully fatal visitation, the plague.

All this came upon them with the late war, which was begun by the Athenians and Peloponnesians by the dissolution of the thirty years' truce made after the conquest of Euboea. To the question why they broke the treaty, I answer by placing first an account of their grounds of complaint and points of difference, that no one may ever have to ask the immediate cause which plunged the Hellenes into a war of such magnitude. The real cause I consider to be the one which was formally most kept out of sight. The growth of the power of Athens, and the alarm which this inspired in Lacedaemon, made war inevitable.

cause of ❖ war

B. REVOLUTION IN CORCYRA

The Peloponnesians accordingly at once set off in haste by night for home, coasting along shore; and hauling their ships across the Isthmus of Leucas, in order not to be seen doubling it, so departed.

The Corcyraeans, made aware of the approach of the Athenian fleet and of the departure of the enemy, brought the Messenians from outside the walls into town, and ordered the fleet which they had manned to sail round into the Hyllaic harbor; and while it was so doing, slew such of their enemies as they laid hands on, dispatching afterwards as they landed them those whom they had persuaded to go on board the ships. Next they went to the sanctuary of Hera and persuaded about fifty men to take their trial, and condemned them all to death. The mass of the suppliants who had refused to do so, on seeing what was taking place, slew each other there in the consecrated ground; while some hanged themselves upon the trees, and others destroyed themselves as they were severally able. During seven days that Eurymedon stayed with his sixty ships, the Corcyraeans were engaged in butchering those of their fellow-citizens whom they regarded as their enemies: and although the crime imputed was that of attempting to put down the democracy, some were slain also for private hatred, others for the monies owed to them by their creditors. Death thus raged in every shape; sons were killed by their fathers, and suppliants dragged from the altar or slain upon it; while some were even walled up in the temple of Dionysus and died there.

So bloody was the march of the revolution, and the impression which it made was the greater as it was one of the first to occur. Later on, one may say, the whole Hellenic world was convulsed; struggles being everywhere made by the popular chiefs to bring in the Athenians, and by the oligarchs to introduce the Lacedaemonians. In peace there would have been neither the pretext nor the wish to make such an invitation; but in war, with an alliance always at the command of either faction for the hurt of their adversaries and their own corresponding advantage, opportunities for bringing in the foreigner were never wanting to the revolutionary parties. The sufferings which revolution entailed upon the cities were many and terrible, such as have occurred and always will occur, as long as the nature of mankind remains the same; though in a severer or milder form, and varying in their symptoms, according to the variety of the particular cases. In peace and prosperity states and individuals have better sentiments, because they do not find themselves suddenly confronted with imperious necessities; but war takes away the easy supply of daily wants, and so proves a rough master, that brings most men's characters to a level with their fortunes.

Revolution thus ran its course from city to city, and the places which it arrived at last, from having heard what had been done before, carried to a still greater excess the refinement of their inventions, as manifested in the cunning of their enterprises and the atrocity of their reprisals. Words had to change their ordinary meaning and to take that which was now given them. Reckless audacity became courage staunch to its associates; prudent hesitation, specious cowardice; moderation was held to be a cloak for unmanliness; ability to see all sides of a question inaptness to act on any. Frantic violence became the attribute of manliness; safe plotting, a justifiable means of self-defense. The advocate of extreme measures was always trustworthy; his opponent a man to be suspected. To succeed in a plot was to have a shrewd head, to divine a plot a still shrewder; but to try to provide against having to do either was to break up your party and to be afraid of your adversaries. In fine, to forestall an intending criminal, or to suggest the idea of a crime where it was wanting, was equally commended, until even blood became a weaker tie than party, from the superior readiness of the latter to dare everything without reserve; such associations not having in view the blessings derivable from established institutions but being formed by ambition for their overthrow; while the confidence of their members in each other rested less on any religious sanction than upon complicity in crime. The fair proposals of an adversary were met with jealous precautions by the stronger of the two, and not with a generous confidence.

Revenge also was held of more account than self-preservation. Oaths of reconciliation, being only proffered on either side to meet an immediate difficulty, only held good so long as no other weapon was at hand; but when opportunity offered, he who first ventured to seize it and to take his enemy off his guard, thought this perfidious vengeance sweeter than an open one, since, considerations of safety apart, success by treachery won him the palm of knowingness. Indeed rogues are oftener called clever than simpletons honest, and men are as ashamed of being the one as they are proud of being the other.

The cause of all these evils was the lust for power felt by greed and ambition, and out of this the violence of parties once engaged in contention. The leaders in the cities, each provided with the fairest professions, on the one side with the cry of political equality of the people, on the other of an ordered aristocracy, sought prizes for themselves in those public interests which they pretended to cherish, and recoiling from no means in their struggles for ascendancy, dared and went through with the direst excesses; which were met in their turn by reprisals still more terrible, that, instead of stopping at what justice or the good of the state demanded, were only limited by the party caprice of the moment; unjust legal condemnations or the authority of the strong arm being with equal readiness invoked to glut the animosities of the hour. Thus religion was in honor with neither party; but the use of fair names to arrive at guilty ends was in high reputation. Meanwhile the moderate part of the citizens perished between the two, either for not joining in the quarrel, or because envy would not suffer them to escape.

Thus every form of iniquity took root in the Hellenic countries by reason of the troubles. The ancient simplicity into which honor so largely entered was laughed down and disappeared; and society became divided into camps in which no man trusted his fellow. To put an end to this, there was neither promise to be depended upon, nor oath that could command respect; but all parties dwelling rather in their calculation upon the hopelessness of a permanent state of things, were more intent upon self-defense than capable of confidence. In this contest the blunter wits were most successful. Apprehensive of their own deficiencies and of the cleverness of their antagonists, they feared to be worsted in debate and to be surprised by the combinations of their more versatile opponents, and so at once boldly had recourse to action: while their adversaries, arrogantly thinking that they should know in time, and that it was unnecessary to secure by action what policy afforded, often fell victims to their want of precaution.

Meanwhile Corcyra gave the first example of most of the crimes alluded to; of the reprisals exacted by the governed who had never experienced equitable treatment or indeed aught but insolence from their rulers—when their hour came; of the iniquitous resolves of those who desired to get rid of their accustomed poverty, and ardently coveted their neighbors' goods; and lastly, of the savage and pitiless excesses into which men who had begun the struggle not in a class but in a party spirit, were hurried by their ungovernable passions. In the confusion into which life was now thrown in the cities, human nature, always rebelling against the law and now its master, gladly showed itself ungoverned in passion, above respect for justice, and the enemy of all superiority; since revenge would not have been set above religion, and gain above justice, had it not been for the fatal power of envy. Indeed men too often in the prosecution of their laws to which all alike can look for salvation in adversity, instead of allowing them to subsist against the day of danger when their aid may be required.

❖

C. *THE MELIAN DIALOGUE*

The Melians are a colony from Sparta. They had refused to join the Athenian empire like the other islanders, and at first had remained neutral without helping either side; but afterwards, when the Athenians had brought force to bear on them, they had become open enemies of Athens.

[The Athenians try to negotiate a surrender.]

The Melians did not invite these representatives [of Athens] to speak before the people, but asked them to make the statement for which they had come in front of the governing body of the few. The Athenian representatives then spoke as follows:

ATHENIANS: So we are not to speak before the people, no doubt in case the mass of the people should hear once and for all and without interruption an argument from us which is both persuasive and incontrovertible, and so should be led astray.

MELIANS: No one can object to each of us putting forth our own views in a calm atmosphere. That is perfectly reasonable. What is scarcely consistent with such a proposal is the present threat, indeed, the certainty, of your making war on us. We see that you have come prepared to judge the argument yourselves, and the likely end of it will be either war, if we refuse to surrender, or else slavery.

ATHENIANS: If you are going to spend the time in enumerating your suspicions about the future, or if you have met here for any other reason except to look the facts in the face and on the basis of these facts to consider how you can save your city from destruction, there is no point in our going on with this discussion.

[The Melians agree to let the Athenians speak]

ATHENIANS: Then we on our side will use no fine phrases saying, for example, that we have a right to our empire because we defeated the Persians, or that we have moved against you now because of the injuries you have done us—a great mass of words that nobody would believe. And we ask you on your side not to imagine that you will influence us by saying that you, though a colony of Sparta, have not joined Sparta in the war, or that you have never done us any harm. Instead we recommend that you should try to get what it is possible for to you to get, taking into consideration what we both really do think; since you know as well as we do that, when these matters are discussed by practical people, the standard of justice depends on the equality of power to compel and that in fact the strong do what they have the power to do and the weak accept what they have to accept.

MELIANS: Then in our view (since you force us to leave justice out and to confine ourselves to self-interest)—in our view it is at any rate useful that you should not destroy a principle that is to the general good of all men: namely, that in the case of all who fall into danger there should be such a thing as fair play and just dealing, and that such people should be allowed to use and to profit by arguments that fall short of mathematical accuracy. And this is a principle which affects you as mush as anybody, since your own fall would be visited by the most terrible vengeance and would be an example to the whole world.

ATHENIANS: As for us, even assuming that our empire does come to an end, we are not despondent about what would happen next. One is not so much frightened of being conquered by a power which rules over others, as Sparta does, as of what would happen if a ruling power is attacked and defeated by its own subjects. So far as this point is concerned, you can leave it to us to face the risks involved. We do not want any trouble in bringing you into our empire, and we want you to be spared for the good of both yourselves and of ourselves.

MELIANS: And how could it be just as good for us to be the slaves as for you to be the masters?

ATHENIANS: You, by giving in, would save yourselves from disaster; we, by not destroying you, would be able to profit from you.

MELIANS: So you would not agree to our being neutral, friends instead of enemies, but allies of neither side?

ATHENIANS: No, because it is not so much your hostility that injures us; it is rather the case that, if we were on friendly terms with you, our subjects would regard that as a sign of weakness in us, whereas your hatred is evidence of our power.

MELIANS: Is that your subjects idea of fair play—that no distinction should be made between people who are quite unconnected with you and people who are mostly your own colonists, or else rebels whom you have conquered?

ATHENIANS: So far as right and wrong are concerned they think that there is no difference between the two, that those who still preserve their independence do so because they are strong, and that if we fail to attack them it is because we are afraid. So that by conquering you we shall increase not only the size but the security of our empire.

MELIANS: Do you think there is no security for you in what we suggest? Is it not certain that you will make enemies of all states who are at present neutral, when they see what is happening here and naturally conclude that in the course of time you will attack them too?

ATHENIANS: As a matter of fact, we are not so much frightened of states on the mainland. They have their liberty, and this means that it will be a long time before they begin to take precautions against us. We are more concerned about islanders like yourselves, who are still unsubdued, or subjects who have already become embittered by the constraint which our empire imposes on them. These are the people who are most likely to act in a reckless manner and to bring themselves and us, too, into the most obvious danger.

MELIANS: Then surely, if such hazards are taken by you to keep your empire and by your subjects to escape from it, we who are still free would show ourselves great cowards and weaklings if we failed to face everything that comes rather than submit to slavery.

ATHENIANS: No, not if you are sensible. This is no fair fight, with honor on one side and shame on the other. It is rather a question of saving your lives and not resisting those who are far too strong for you.

MELIANS: Yet we know that in war fortune sometimes makes the odds more level than could be expected from the difference in numbers of the two sides. And if we surrender, then all our hope is last at once, whereas, so long as we remain in action, there is still a hope that we may yet stand upright.

ATHENIANS: Hope, that comforter in danger! If one already has solid advantages to fall back upon, one can indulge in hope. It may do harm, but will not destroy one. But hope is by nature an expensive commodity, and those who are risking everything on one cast of the dice find out what it means only when they are already ruined; hope never fails them in the period when such a knowledge would enable them to take precautions. Do not let this happen to you, you who are weak and whose fate depends on a single movement of the scale. And do not be like those people who, as so commonly happens, miss the chance of saving themselves in a human and practical way, and, when every clear and distinct hope has left them in their adversity, turn to what is blind and vague, to prophecies and oracles and such things which, by encouraging men to hope, lead men to ruin.

MELIANS: It is difficult, and you may be sure that we know it, for us to oppose your power and fortune, unless the terms be equal. Nevertheless, we trust that the gods will give us fortune as good as yours, because we are standing for what is right against what is wrong; and as for what we lack in power, we trust that it will be made up for by our alliance with the Spartans, who are bound, if for no other reason, then for honor's sake, and because we are kinsmen, to come to our help. Our confidence, therefore, is not so entirely irrational as you think.

ATHENIANS: So far as the favor of the gods is concerned, we think we have as much right to that as you have. Our aims and our actions are perfectly consistent with the beliefs men hod about the gods and with the principles which govern their own conduct. Our opinion of the gods, and our knowledge of men, lead us to conclude that it is a general and necessary law of nature to rule wherever one can. This is not a law that we made ourselves, nor were we the first to act upon it when it was made. We found it already in existence, and we shall leave it to exist for ever among those who come after us. We are merely acting in accordance with it, and we know that you or anybody else with the same power as ours would be acting in precisely the same way. And therefore, so far as the gods are concerned, we see no good reason why we should fear to be at a disadvantage. But with regard to your views about Spartan aid and your confidence that she, out of a sense of honor, will come to your aid, we must say that we congratulate you on your simplicity but do not envy you your folly. In matters that concern themselves or their own constitution the Spartans are quite remarkably good; as for their relations with others, that is a long story, but it can be expressed shortly and clearly by saying that of all people we know the Spartans are most conspicuous for believing that what they like doing is honorable and what suits their interests is just. And this kind of attitude is not going to be of much help to you in your absurd quest for safety at the moment.

MELIANS: But this is the very point where we can feel most sure. Their own self-interest will make them refuse to betray their own colonists, the Melians, for that would mean losing the confidence of their friends among the Hellenes and doing good to their enemies.

ATHENIANS: You seem to forget that if one follows one's self-interest one wants to be safe, whereas the path of justice and honor involves one in danger. And, where danger is concerned, the Spartans are not, as a rule, very venturesome. You will therefore be showing an extraordinary lack of common sense if, after you have asked us to retire from this meeting, you still fail to reach a conclusion wiser than anything you have mentioned so far. Do not be led astray by a false sense of honor—a thing which often brings men to ruin when they are faced with an obvious danger that somehow affects their pride. For in many cases men have still been able to see the dangers ahead of them, but this thing called dishonor, this word, by its own force of seduction, has drawn them into a state where they have surrendered to an idea, while in fact they have fallen voluntarily into irrevocable disaster, in dishonor that is all the more dishonorable because it has come to them from their own folly rather than their misfortune. You should see that there is nothing disgraceful in giving way to the greatest city in Hellas when she is offering such reasonable terms: alliance on a tribute-paying basis and liberty to enjoy your own property. This is the safe rule—to stand up to one's equals, to behave with deference towards one's superiors, and to treat one's inferiors with moderation. Think it over again, when we have withdrawn from the meeting, and let this be a point that constantly recurs to your minds—that you are discussing the fate of your country, that you have only one country, and that its future for good or ill depends on this one single decision which you are going to make.

The Athenians then withdrew from the discussion. The Melians, left to themselves, reached a conclusion which was much the same as they had indicated in their previous replies. Their answer was as follows:

MELIANS: Our decision, Athenians, is just the same is it was at first. We are not prepared to give up in a short moment the liberty which our city has enjoyed from its foundation for 700 years. We put our trust in the fortune that the gods will send and which has saved us up to now, and the help of men—that is, of the Spartans; and so we shall try to save ourselves. But we invite you to allow us to be friends of yours and enemies to neither side, to make a treaty which shall be agreeable to both you and us, and so to leave our country.

The Melians made this reply, and the Athenians, just as they were breaking off the discussion, said:

ATHENIANS: Well, at any rate, judging from this decision of yours, you seem to us quite unique in your ability to consider the future as something more certain than what is before your eyes, and to see uncertainties as realities, simply because you would like them to be so.

The Athenian representatives then went back to the army, and the Athenian generals, finding that the Melians would not submit, immediately commenced hostilities and built a wall completely round the polis of Melos. [Somewhat later] the Melians captured a part of the Athenian lines where there were only a few of the garrison on guard. As a result of this, another force came out afterwards from Athens. Siege operations were now carried on vigorously and, as there was also some treachery from inside, the Melians surrendered unconditionally to the Athenians, who put to death all the men of military age whom they took, and sold the women and children as slaves. Melos itself they took over for themselves, sending out later a colony of 500 men.

❖

3. THE REPUBLIC: A SOPHISTIC ARGUMENT

PLATO

The sort of word-juggling Thucydides described briefly in his History Plato illustrated at length in the *Republic*, where the new radical interpretation of power is advocated by Thrasymachus. The basis of the discussion is the definition of "Justice." How does Thrasymachus define it? What are the implications of his definition? Why does Socrates disagree with him? Which of the two sides do you agree with? Why?

A DEFINITION OF JUSTICE

Several times in the course of the discussion Thrasymachus had made an attempt to get the argument into his own hands, and had been put down by the rest of the company, who wanted to hear the end. But when Polemarchus and I had done speaking and there was a pause, he could no longer hold his peace; and, gathering himself up, he came at us like a wild beast, seeking to devour us. We were quite panic-stricken at the sight of him.

He roared out to the whole company: What folly, Socrates, has taken possession of you all? And why, sillybillies, do you knock under to one another? I say that if you want really to know what justice is, you should not only ask but answer, and you should not seek honor to yourself from the refutation of an opponent, but have your own answer; for there is many a one who can ask and cannot answer. And now I will not have you say that justice is duty or advantage or profit or gain or interest, for this sort of nonsense will not do for me; I must have clearness and accuracy.

I was panic-stricken at his words, and could not look at him without trembling. Indeed I believe that if I had not fixed my eye upon him, I should have been struck dumb:[1] but when I saw his fury rising, I looked at him first, and was therefore able to reply to him.

Thrasymachus, I said with a quiver, don't be hard upon us. Polemarchus and I may have been guilty of a little mistake in the argument, but I can assure you that the error was not intentional. If we were seeking for a piece of gold, you would not imagine that we were "knocking under to one another," and so losing our chance of finding it. And why, when we are seeking for justice, a thing more precious than many pieces of gold, do you say that we are weakly yielding to one another and not doing our utmost to get at the truth? Nay, my good friend, we are most willing and anxious to do so, but the fact is that we cannot. And if

---

[1]Socrates, who has been comparing Thrasymachus to a wild animal, here makes use of a popular superstition that people are struck dumb if a wolf sees them before they see the wolf.

so, you people who know all things should pity us and not be angry with us.

How characteristic of Socrates! he replied with a bitter laugh; that's your ironical style! Did I not foresee, have I not already told you, that whatever he was asked he would refuse to answer, and try irony or any other shuffle, in order that he might avoid answering?

You are a philosopher, Thrasymachus, I replied, and well know that if you ask a person what numbers make up twelve, taking care to prohibit him whom you ask from answering twice six, or three times four, or six times two, or four times three, "for this sort of nonsense will not do for me,"—then obviously, if that is your way of putting the question, no one can answer you. But suppose that he were to retort, "Thrasymachus, what do you mean? If one of these numbers which you interdict be the true answer to the question, am I falsely to say some other number which is not the right one?—is that your meaning?"—How would you answer him?

Just as if the two cases were at all alike! he said.

Why should they not be? I replied; and even if they are not, but only appear to be so to the person who is asked, ought he not to say what he thinks, whether you and I forbid him or not?

I presume then that you are going to make one of the interdicted answers?

I dare say that I may, notwithstanding the danger, if upon reflection I approve of any of them.

But what if I give you an answer about justice other and better, he said, than any of these? What do you deserve to have done to you?

Done to me!—as becomes the ignorant, I must learn from the wise—that is what I deserve to have done to me.

What, and no payment! a pleasant notion!

I will pay when I have the money, I replied.

But you have, Socrates, said Glaucon: and you, Thrasymachus, need be under no anxiety about money, for we will all make a contribution for Socrates.

Yes, he replied, and then Socrates will do as he always does—refuse to answer himself, but take and pull to pieces the answer of some one else.

Why, my good friend, I said, how can any one answer who knows, and says that he knows, just nothing; and who, even if he has some faint notions of his own, is told by a man of authority not to utter them? The natural thing is, that the speaker should be some one like yourself who professes to know and can tell what he knows. Will you then kindly answer, for the edification of the company and of myself?

Glaucon and the rest of the company joined in my request and Thrasymachus, as any one might see, was in reality eager to speak; for he thought that he had an excellent answer, and would distinguish himself. But at first he affected to insist on my answering; at length he consented to begin. Behold, he said, the wisdom of Socrates; he refuses to teach himself, and goes about learning of others, to whom he never even says Thank you.

That I learn of others, I replied, is quite true; but that I am ungrateful I wholly deny. Money I have none, and therefore I pay in praise, which is all I have; and how ready I am to praise anyone who appears to me to speak well you will very soon find out when you answer; for I expect that you will answer well.

Listen, then, he said; I proclaim that justice is nothing else than the interest of the stronger. And now why do you not praise me? But of course you won't.

Let me first understand you, I replied. Justice, as you say, is the interest of the stronger. What, Thrasymachus, is the meaning of this? You cannot mean to say that because Polydamas, the pancratiast,[1] is stronger than we are, and finds the eating of beef conducive to his bodily strength, that to eat beef is therefore equally for our good who are weaker than he is, and right and just for us?

---

[1]Olympic boxing, which in ancient Greece was a sort of combination wrestling and kick-boxing.

That's abominable of you, Socrates; you take the words in the sense which is most damaging to the argument.

Not at all, my good sir, I said; I am trying to understand them; and I wish that you would be a little clearer.

Well, he said, have you never heard that forms of government differ: there are tyrannies, and there are democracies, and there are aristocracies?

Yes, I know.

And the government is the ruling power in each state?

Certainly.

And the different forms of government make laws democratical, aristocratical, tyrannical, with a view to their several interests; and these laws, which are made by them for their own interests, are the justice which they deliver to their subjects, and him who transgresses them they punish as a breaker of the law, and unjust. And that is what I mean when I say that in all states there is the same principle of justice, which is the interest of the government; and as the government must be supposed to have power, the only reasonable conclusion is, that everywhere there is one principle of justice, which is the interest of the stronger.

Now I understand you, I said; and whether you are right or not I will try to discover. But let me remark, that in defining justice you have yourself used the word "interest" which you forbade me to use. It is true, however, that in your definition the words "of the stronger" are added.

A small addition, you must allow, he said.

Great or small, never mind about that: we must first inquire whether what you are saying is the truth. Now we are both agreed that justice is interest of some sort, but you go on to say "of the stronger"; about this addition I am not so sure, and must therefore consider further.

Proceed.

I will; and first tell me, Do you admit that it is just for subjects to obey their rulers?

I do.

But are the rulers of states absolutely infallible, or are they sometimes liable to err?

To be sure, he replied, they are liable to err.

Then in making their laws they may sometimes make them rightly, and sometimes not?

True.

When they make them rightly, they make them agreeably to their interest; when they are mistaken, contrary to their interest; you admit that?

Yes.

And the laws which they make must be obeyed by their subjects,—and that is what you call justice?

Doubtless.

Then justice, according to your argument, is not only obedience to the interest of the stronger but the reverse?

What is that you are saying? he asked.

I am only repeating what you are saying, I believe. But let us consider: Have we not admitted that the rulers may be mistaken about their own interest in what they command, and also that to obey them is justice? Has not that been admitted?

Yes.

Then you must also have acknowledged justice not to be for the interest of the stronger, when the rulers unintentionally command things to be done which are to their own injury. For if, as you say, justice is the obedience which the subject renders to their commands, in that case, O wisest of men, is there any escape from the conclusion that the weaker are commanded to do, not what is for the interest, but what is for the injury of the stronger?

Nothing can be clearer, Socrates, said Polemarchus.

Yes, said Cleitophon, interposing, if you are allowed to be his witness.

But there is no need of any witness, said Polemarchus, for Thrasymachus himself acknowledges that rulers may sometimes command what is not for their own interest, and that for subjects to obey them is justice.

Yes, Polemarchus,—Thrasymachus said that for subjects to do what was commanded by their rulers is just.

Yes, Cleitophon, but he also said that justice is the interest of the stronger, and, while admitting both these propositions, he further acknowledged that the stronger may command the weaker who are his subjects to do what is not for his own interest; whence follows that justice is the injury quite as much as the interest of the stronger.

But, said Cleitophon, he meant by the interest of the stronger what the stronger thought to be his interest,—this was what the weaker had to do; and this was affirmed by him to be justice.

Those were not his words, rejoined Polemarchus.

Never mind, I replied, if he now says that they are, let us accept his statement. Tell me, Thrasymachus, I said, did you mean by justice what the stronger thought to be his interest, whether really so or not?

Certainly not, he said. Do you suppose that I call him who is mistaken the stronger at the time when he is mistaken?

Yes, I said, my impression was that you did so, when you admitted that the ruler was not infallible but might be sometimes mistaken.

You argue like an informer, Socrates. Do you mean, for example, that he who is mistaken about the sick is a physician in that he is mistaken? or that he who errs in arithmetic or grammar is an arithmetician or grammarian at the time when he is making the mistake, in respect of the mistake? True, we say that the physician or arithmetician or grammarian has made a mistake, but this is only a way of speaking; for the fact is that neither the grammarian nor any other person of skill ever makes a mistake in so far as he is what his name implies; they none of them err unless their skill fails them, and then they cease to be called artists. No artist or sage or ruler errs at the time when he is what his name implies; though he is commonly said to err, and I adopted the common mode of speaking. But to be perfectly accurate, since you are such a lover of accuracy, we should say that the ruler, in so far as he is a ruler, is unerring, and, being unerring, always commands that which is for his own interest; and the subject is required to execute his commands; and therefore, as I said at first and now repeat, justice is the interest of the stronger.

Indeed, Thrasymachus, and do I really appear to you to argue like an informer?

Certainly, he replied.

And do you suppose that I ask these questions with any design of injuring you in the argument?

Nay, he replied, "suppose" is not the word—I know it; but you will be found out, and by sheer force of argument you will never prevail.

I shall not make the attempt, my dear man; but to avoid any misunderstanding occurring between us in future, let me ask, in what sense do you speak of a ruler or stronger whose interest, as you were saying, he being the superior, it is just that the inferior should execute—is he a ruler in the popular or in the strict sense of the term?

In the strictest of all senses, he said. And now cheat and play the informer if you can; I ask no quarter at your hands. But you never will be able, never.

And do you imagine, I said, that I am such a madman as to try and cheat Thrasymachus? I might as well shave a lion.

Why, he said, you made the attempt a minute ago, and you failed.

Enough, I said, of these civilities. It will be better that I should ask you a question: Is the physician, taken in that strict sense of which you are speaking, a healer of the sick or a maker of money? And remember that I am now speaking of the true physician.

A healer of the sick, he replied.

And the pilot—that is to say, the true pilot—is he a captain of sailors or a mere sailor?

A captain of sailors.

The circumstance that he sails in the ship is not to be taken into account; neither is he to be called a sailor—the name pilot by which he is distinguished has nothing to do with sailing, but is significant of his skill and of his authority over the sailors.

Very true, he said.

Now, I said, every art has an interest.

Certainly.

For which the art has to consider and provide?

Yes, that is the aim of art.

And the interest of any art is the perfection of it—this and nothing else?

What do you mean?

I mean what I may illustrate negatively by the example of the body. Suppose you were to ask me whether the body is self-suffing or has wants, I should reply: Certainly the body has wants; for the body may be ill and require to be cured, and has therefore interests to which the art of medicine ministers; and this is the origin and intention of medicine, as you will acknowledge. Am I not right?

Quite right, he replied.

But is the art of medicine or any other art faulty or deficient in any quality in the same way that the eye may be deficient in sight or the ear fail of hearing, and therefore requires another art to provide for the interests of seeing and hearing—has art in itself, I say, any similar liability to fault or defect, and does every art require another supplementary art to provide for its interest, and that another and another without end? Or have the arts to look only after their own interests? Or have they no need either of themselves or of another? Having no faults or defects, they have no need to correct them, either by the exercise of their own art or of any other; they have only to consider the interest of their subject-matter. For every art remains pure and faultless while remaining true—that is to say, while perfect and unimpaired. Take the words in your precise sense, and tell me whether I am not right.

Yes, clearly.

Then medicine does not consider the interest of medicine, but the interest of the body?

True, he said.

Nor does the art of horsemanship consider the interests of the art of horsemanship, but the interests of the horse; neither do any other arts care for themselves, for they have no needs;

they care only for that which is the subject of their art?

True, he said.

But surely, Thrasymachus, the arts are the superiors and rulers of their own subjects?

To this he assented with a good deal of reluctance.

Then, I said, no science or art considers or enjoins the interest of the stronger or superior, but only the interest of the subject and weaker?

He made an attempt to contest this proposition also, but finally acquiesced.

Then, I continued, no physician, in so far as he is a physician, considers his own good in what he prescribes, but the good of his patient; for the true physician is also a ruler having the human body as a subject, and is not a mere money-maker; that has been admitted?

Yes.

And the pilot likewise, in the strict sense of the term, is a ruler of sailors and not a mere sailor?

That has been admitted.

And such a pilot and ruler will provide and prescribe for the interest of the sailor who is under him, and not for his own or the ruler's interest?

He gave a reluctant "Yes."

Then, I said, Thrasymachus, there is no one in any rule who, insofar as he is a ruler, considers or enjoins what is for his own interest, but always what is for the interest of his subject or suitable to his art; to that he looks, and that alone he considers in everything which he says and does.

When we had got to this point in the argument, and everyone saw that the definition of justice had been completely upset, Thrasymachus, instead of replying to me, said: Tell me, Socrates, have you got a nurse?

Why do you ask such a question, I said, when you ought rather to be answering?

Because she leaves you to snivel, and never wipes your nose: she has not even taught you to know the shepherd from the sheep.

What makes you say that? I replied.

Because you fancy that the shepherd or neatherd fattens or tends the sheep or oxen with a view to their own good and not to the good of himself or his master; and you further imagine that the rulers of states, if they are true rulers, never think of their subjects as sheep, and that they are not studying their own advantage day and night. Oh, no; and so entirely astray are you in your ideas about the just and unjust as not even to know that justice and the just are in reality another's good; that is to say, the interest of the ruler and stronger, and the loss of the subject and servant; and injustice the opposite; for the unjust is lord over the truly simply and just; he is the stronger, and his subjects do what is for his interest, and minister to his happiness, which is very far from being their own.

Consider further, most foolish Socrates, that the just is always a loser in comparison with the unjust. First of all, in private contracts: wherever the unjust is the partner of the just you will find that, when the partnership is dissolved, the unjust man has always more and the just less. Secondly, in their dealings with the State: when there is an income-tax, the just man will pay more and the unjust less on the same amount of income; and when there is anything to be received the one gains nothing and the other much. Observe also what happens when they take an office; there is the just man neglecting his affairs and perhaps suffering other losses, and getting nothing out of the public, because he is just; moreover he is hated by his friends and acquaintances for refusing to serve them in unlawful ways.

But all this is reversed in the case of the unjust man. I am speaking, as before, of injustice on a large scale in which the advantage of the unjust is more apparent; and my meaning will be most clearly seen if we turn to that highest form of injustice in which the criminal is the happiest of men, and the sufferers or those who refuse to do injustice are the most miserable—that is to say tyranny, which by fraud and force takes away the property of others, not little by little but wholesale; comprehending in one, things sacred as well as profane, private and public; for which acts of wrong, if he were detected perpetrating any one of them

singly, he would be punished and incur great disgrace—they who do such wrong in particular cases are called robbers of temples, and man-stealers and burglars and swindlers and thieves. But when a man besides taking away the money of the citizens has made slaves of them, then, instead of these names of reproach, he is termed happy and blessed, not only by the citizens but by all who hear of his having achieved the consummation of injustice. For mankind censure injustice, fearing that they may be the victims of it and not because they shrink from committing it. And thus, as I have shown, Socrates, injustice, when on a sufficient scale, has more strength and freedom and mastery than justice; and, as I said at first, justice is the interest of the stronger, whereas injustice is a man's own profit and interest.

Thrasymachus, when he had thus spoken, having, like a bathman, deluged our ears with his words, had a mind to go away. But the company would not let him; they insisted that he should remain and defend his position; and I myself added my own humble request that he would not leave us.

Thrasymachus, I said to him, excellent man, how suggestive are your remarks! And are you going to run away before you have fairly taught or learned whether they are true or not? Is the attempt to determine the way of man's life so small a matter in your eyes—to determine how life may be passed by each one of us to the greatest advantage?

And do I differ from you, he said, as to the importance of the inquiry?

You appear rather, I replied, to have no care or thought about us, Thrasymachus—whether we live better or worse from now knowing what you say you know is to you a matter of indifference. Prithee, friend, do not keep your knowledge to yourself; we are a large party; and any benefit which you confer upon us will be amply rewarded. For my own part I openly declare that I am not convinced, and that I do not believe injustice to be more gainful than justice, even if uncontrolled and allowed to have free play. For granting that there may be an unjust man who is able to commit injustice either by fraud or force, still this does not convince me of the superior advantage of injustice, and there may be others who are in the same predicament with myself. Perhaps we may be wrong; if so, you in your wisdom should convince us that we are mistaken in preferring justice to injustice.

And how am I to convince you, he said, if you are not already convinced by what I have just said; what more can I do for you? Would you have me put the proof bodily into your souls?

Heaven forbid! I said; I would only ask you to be consistent; or, if you change, change openly and let there be no deception. For I must remark, Thrasymachus, if you will recall what was previously said, that although you began by defining the true physician in an exact sense, you did not observe a like exactness when speaking of the shepherd; you thought that the shepherd as a shepherd tends the sheep not with a view to their own good, but like a mere diner or banquetter with a view to the pleasures of the table; or, again, as a trader for sale in the market, and not as a shepherd. Yet surely the art of the shepherd is concerned only with the good of his subjects: he has only to provide the best for them, since the perfection of the art is already ensured whenever all the requirements of it are satisfied. And that was what I was saying just now about the ruler. I conceived that the art of the ruler, considered as ruler, whether in a state or in private life, could only regard the good of his flock or subjects; whereas you seem to think that the rulers in states; that is to say, the true rulers, like being in authority.

Think! Nay, I am sure of it.

Then why in the case of lesser offices do men never take them willingly without payment, unless under the idea that they govern for the advantage not of themselves but of others? Let me ask you a question: Are not the several arts different, by reason of their each having a separate function? And, my dear illustrious friend, do say what you think, that we may make a little progress.

Yes, that is the difference, he replied.

And each art gives us a particular good and not merely a general one—medicine, for example, gives us health; navigation, safety at sea, and so on?

Yes, he said.

And the art of payment has the special function of giving pay; but we do not confuse this with other arts, any more than the art of the pilot is to be confused with the art of medicine, because the health of the pilot may be improved by a sea voyage. You would not be inclined to say, would you, that navigation is the art of medicine, at least, if we are to adopt your exact use of language?

Certainly not.

Or because a man is in good health when he receives pay you would not say that the art of payment is medicine?

I should say not.

Nor would you say that medicine is the art of receiving pay because a man takes fees when he is engaged in healing?

Certainly not.

And we have admitted, I said, that the good of each art is specially confined to the art?

Yes.

Then, if there by any good which all artists have in common, that is to be attributed to something of which they all have the common use?

True, he replied.

And when the artist is benefited by receiving pay the advantage is gained by an addition use of the art of pay, which is not the art professed by him?

He gave a reluctant assent to this.

Then the pay is not derived by the several artists from their respective arts. But the truth is, that while the art of medicine gives health, and the art of the builder builds a house, another art attends them which is the art of pay. The various arts may be doing their own business and benefiting that over which they preside, but would the artist receive any benefit from his art unless he were paid as well.

I suppose not.

But does he therefore confer no benefit when he works for nothing?

Certainly, he confers a benefit.

Then now, Thrasymachus, there is no longer any doubt that neither arts nor governments provide for their own interests; but, as we were before saying, they rule and provide for the interests of their subjects who are the weaker and not the stronger—to their good they attend and not to the good of the superior. And this is the reason, my dear Thrasymachus, why, as I was just now saying, no one is willing to govern: because no one lies to take in hand the reformation of evils which are not his concern without remuneration. For, in the execution of his work, and in giving his orders to another, the true artist does not regard his own interest, but always that of his subjects; and therefore in order that rulers may be willing to rule, they must be paid in one of three modes of payment—money, or honor, or a penalty for refusing.

What do you mean, Socrates? said Glaucon. The first two modes of payment are intelligible enough, but what the penalty is I do not understand, or how a penalty can be a payment.

You mean that you do not understand the nature of this payment which to the best men is the great inducement to rule? Of course you know that ambition and avarice are held to be, as indeed they are, a disgrace?

Very true.

And for this reason, I said, money and honor have no attraction for them; good men do not wish to be openly demanding payment for governing and so to get the name of hirelings, nor by secretly helping themselves out of the public revenues to get the name of thieves. And not being ambitious they do not care about honor. Wherefore necessity must be laid upon them, and they must be induced to serve from the fear of punishment. And this, as I imagine, is the reason why the forwardness to take office, instead of waiting to be compelled, has been deemed dishonorable. Now the worst part of the punishment is that he who refuses to rule is liable to be ruled by one who is worse than himself. And the fear of this, as I conceive, induces the good to take office, not because they would, but because they cannot help—not under the idea that they are going to have any benefit or enjoyment themselves, but as a necessity, and because they are not able to commit the task of ruling to anyone who is better than themselves, or indeed as good. For there is reason to think that if a city

were composed entirely of good men, then to avoid office would be as much an object of contention as to obtain office is at present; then we should have plain proof that the true ruler is not meant by nature to regard his own interest, but that of his subjects; and everyone who knew this would choose rather to receive a benefit from another than to have the trouble of conferring one. So far am I from agreeing with Thrasymachus that justice is the interest of the stronger.

❖

4. *PLATO STRIKES BACK*

PLATO

It was in the environment of revolution and moral relativism created by the war and the self-serving arguments of sophists like Thrasymachus that PLATO began writing, his first work probably being the Apology, an account of Socrates' trial. Around 380 B.C. he completed a master work, the Republic, a section of which you have just read. It is often forgotten, in the debate over the type of state Plato set up in this dialogue, that his concern—as the preceding passage shows—was to provide a realistic defense of "Justice." This was no easy task in an age made cynical by the type of distortion of moral values and fine phrases described by Thucydides. To make just conduct a thing desirable in itself, Plato had to put the argument on an entirely different plane. In so doing, he gave us the concept of Ideals.

Here are two readings to give you some idea of how Plato worked and what his motives were.

A. *THE REPUBLIC: ALLEGORY OF THE CAVE*

You probably have read this famous passage before in a literature class as an example of allegory (actually, it is an extended simile). As you read it again, pay attention to the details of the simile: what does the "cave" stand for? Who is the "philosopher-king"? What exactly is the point Plato is trying to make? Why does he use this method to make it? Do you think it was effective?

And now, I said, let me show in a figure how far our nature is enlightened or unenlightened:—Behold! human beings living in an underground den, which has a mouth open towards the light and reaching all along the den; here they have been from their childhood, and have their legs and necks chained so that they cannot move, and can only see before them, being prevented by the chains from turning round their heads. Above and behind them a fire is blazing at a distance, and between the fire and the prisoners there is a raised way; and you will see, if you look, a low wall built along the way, like the screen which marionette players have in front of them, over which they show the puppets.

I see.

And do you see, I said, men passing along the wall carrying all sorts of vessels, and statues and figures of animals made of wood and stone and various materials, which appear over the wall? Some of them are talking, others silent.

You have shown me a strange image, and they are strange prisoners.

Like ourselves, I replied; and they see only their own shadows, or the shadows of one another, which the fire throws on the opposite wall of the cave?

True, he said; how could they see anything but the shadows if they were never allowed to move their heads?

And of the objects which are being carried in like manner they would only see the shadows?

Yes, he said.

And if they were able to converse with one another, would they not suppose that they were naming what was actually before them?

Very true.

And suppose further that the prison had an echo which came from the other side, would they not be sure to fancy when one of the passers-by spoke that the voice which they heard came from the passing shadow?

No question, he replied.

To them, I said, the truth would be literally nothing but the shadows of the images.

That is certain. And now look again, and see what will naturally follow if the prisoners are released and disabused of their error. At first, when any of them is liberated and compelled

suddenly to stand up and turn his neck round and walk and look towards the light, he will suffer sharp pains; the glare will distress him, and he will be unable to see the realities of which in his former state he had seen the shadows; and then conceive someone saying to him, that what he saw before was an illusion, but that now, when he is approaching nearer to being and his eye is turned towards more real existence, he has a clearer vision,—what will be his reply? And you may further imagine that his instructor is pointing to the objects as they pass and requiring him to name them,—will he not be perplexed? Will he not fancy that the shadows which he formerly saw are truer than the objects which are now shown to him?

Far truer.

And if he is compelled to look straight at the light, will he not have a pain in his eyes which will make him turn away to take refuge in the objects of vision which he can see, and which he will conceive to be in reality clearer than the things which are now being shown to him?

True, he said.

And suppose once more, that he is reluctantly dragged up a steep and rugged ascent, and held fast until he is forced into the presence of the sun himself, is he not likely to be pained and irritated? When he approaches the light his eyes will be dazzled, and he will not be able to see anything at all of what are now called realities.

Not all in a moment, he said.

He will require to grow accustomed to the sight of the upper world. And first he will see the shadows best, next the reflections of men and other objects in the water, and then the objects themselves; then he will gaze upon the light of the moon and the stars and the spangled heaven; and he will see the sky and the stars by night better than the sun or the light of the sun by day?

Certainly.

Last of all he will be able to see the sun, and not mere reflections of him in the water, but he will see him in his own proper place, and not in another; and he will contemplate him as he is.

Certainly.

He will then proceed to argue that this is he who gives the season and the years, and is the guardian of all that is in the visible world, and in a certain way the cause of all things which he and his fellows have been accustomed to behold?

Clearly, he said, he would first see the sun and then reason about him.

And when he remembered his old habitation, and the wisdom of the den and his fellow-prisoners, do you not suppose that he would felicitate himself on the change, and pity them?

Certainly, he would.

And if they were in the habit of conferring honors among themselves on those who were quickest to observe the passing shadows and to remark which of them went before, and which followed after, and which were together; and who were therefore best able to draw conclusions as to the future, do you think that he would care for such honors and glories, or envy the possessors of them? Would he not say with Homer,

"Better to be the poor servant of a poor master,"

and to endure anything, rather than think as they do and live after their manner?

Yes, he said, I think that he would rather suffer anything than entertain these false notions and live in this miserable manner.

Imagine once more, I said, such an one coming suddenly out of the sun to be replaced in his old situation; would he not be certain to have his eyes full of darkness?

To be sure, he said.

And if there were a contest, and he had to compete in measuring the shadows with the prisoners who had never moved out of the den, while his sight was still weak, and before his eyes had become steady (and the time which would be needed to acquire this new habit of sight might be very considerable),

would he not be ridiculous? Men would say of him that up he went and down he came without his eyes; and that it was better not even to think of ascending; and if any one tried to loose another and lead him up to the light, let them only catch the offender, and they would put him to death.

No question, he said.

This entire allegory, I said, you may now append, dear Glaucon, to the previous argument; the prison-house is the world of sight, the light of the fire is the sun, and you will not misapprehend me if you interpret the journey upwards to be the ascent of the soul into the intellectual world according to my poor belief, which, at your desire, I have expressed—whether rightly or wrongly God knows. But, whether true or false, my opinion is that in the world of knowledge the idea of good appears last of all, and is seen only with an effort; and, when seen, is also inferred to be the universal author of all things beautiful and right, parent of light and of the lord of light in this visible world, and the immediate source of reason and truth in the intellectual; and that this is the power upon which he who would act rationally either in public or private life must have his eye fixed.

I agree, he said, as far as I am able to understand you.

Moreover, I said, you must not wonder that those who attain to this beatific vision are unwilling to descend to human affairs; for their souls are ever hastening into the upper world where they desire to dwell; which desire of theirs is very natural, if our allegory may be trusted.

Yes, very natural.

And is there anything surprising in one who passes from divine contemplations to the evil state of man, misbehaving himself in a ridiculous manner; if, while his eyes are blinking and before he has become accustomed to the surrounding darkness, he is compelled to fight in courts of law, or in other places, about the images or the shadows of images of justice, and is endeavoring to meet the conceptions of those who have never yet seen absolute justice?

Anything but surprising, he replied.

Anyone who has common sense will remember that the bewilderments of the eyes are of two kinds, and arise from two causes, either from coming out of the light or from going into the light, which is true of the mind's eye quite as much as of the bodily eye; and he who remembers this when he sees anyone whose vision is perplexed and weak, will not be too ready to laugh; he will first ask whether that soul of man has come out of the brighter life, and is unable to see because unaccustomed to the dark, or having turned from darkness to the day is dazzled by excess of light. And he will count the one happy in his condition and state of being, and he will pity the other; or, if he have a mind to laugh at the soul which comes from below into the light, there will be more reason in this than in the laugh which greets him who returns from above out of the light into the den.

That, he said, is a very just distinction.

But then, if I am right, certain professors of education must be wrong when they say that they can put a knowledge into the soul which was not there before, like sight into blind eyes.

They undoubtedly say this, he replied.

Whereas our argument shows that the power and capacity of learning exists in the soul already; and that just as the eye was unable to turn from darkness to light without the whole body, so too the instrument of knowledge can only by the movement of the whole soul be turned from the world of becoming into that of being, and learn by degrees to endure the sight of being, and of the brightest and best of being, or in other words, of the good.

Very true.

And must there not be some art which will effect conversion in the easiest and quickest manner; not implanting the faculty of sight, for that exists already, but has been turned in the wrong direction, and is looking away from the truth?

Yes, he said, such an art may be presumed.

And whereas the other so-called virtues of the soul seem to be akin to bodily qualities, for even when they are not originally innate they can be implanted later by habit and exercise, the virtue of wisdom more than anything else contains a divine element which always remains, and by this conversion is rendered useful and profitable; or, on the other hand, hurtful and useless. Did you never observe the narrow intelligence flashing from the keen eye of a clever rogue—how eager he is, how clearly his paltry soul sees the way to his end; he is the reverse of blind, but his keen eyesight is forced into the service of evil, and he is mischievous in proportion to his cleverness?

Very true, he said.

But what if there had been a circumcision of such natures in the days of their youth; and they had been severed from those sensual pleasures, such as eating and drinking, which, like leaden weights, were attached to them at their birth, and which drag them down and turn the vision of their souls upon the things that are below—if, I say, they had been released from these impediments and turned in the opposite direction, the very same faculty in them would have seen the truth as keenly as they see what their eyes are turned to now.

Very likely.

Yes, I said; and there is another thing which is likely, or rather a necessary inference from what has preceded, that neither the uneducated and uninformed of the truth, nor yet those who never make an end of their education, will be able ministers of State; not the former, because they have no single aim of duty which is the rule of all their actions, private as well as public; nor the latter, because they will not act at all except upon compulsion, fancying that they are already dwelling apart in the islands of the blest.

Very true, he replied.

Then, I said, the business of us who are the founders of the State will be to compel the best minds to attain that knowledge which we have already shown to be the greatest of all, they must continue to ascend until they arrive at the good; but when they have ascended and seen enough we must not allow them to do as they do now.

What do you mean?

I mean that they remain in the upper world: but this must not be allowed; they must be made to descend again among the prisoners in the den, and partake of their labors and honors, whether they are worth having or not.

But is not this unjust? he said; ought we to give them a worse life, when they might have a better?

You have again forgotten, my friend, I said, the intention of the legislator, who did not aim at making any one class in the State happy above all the rest; the happiness was to be in the whole State, and he held the citizens together by persuasion and necessity, making them benefactors of the State, and therefore benefactors of one another; to this end he created them, not to please themselves, but to be his instruments in binding up the State.

True, he said, I had forgotten.

Observe, Glaucon, that there will be no injustice in compelling our philosophers to have a care and providence of others; we shall explain to them that in other States, men of their class are not obliged to share in the toils of politics: and this is reasonable, for they grow up at their own sweet will, and the government would rather not have them. Being self-taught, they cannot be expected to show any gratitude for a culture which they have never received. But we have brought you into the world to be rulers of the hive, kings of yourselves and of the other citizens, and have educated you far better and more perfectly than they have been educated, and you are better able to share in the double duty. Wherefore each of you, when his turn comes, must go down to the general underground abode, and get the habit of seeing in the dark. When you have acquired the habit, you will see ten thousand times better than the inhabitants of the den, and you will know what the several images are, and what they represent, because you have seen the beautiful and just and good in their truth. And thus our State which is also yours will be a reality and not a dream only, and will be administered in a spirit unlike that of other States, in which men fight with one another about shadows only and are distracted in the struggle for power, which in their eyes is a great good. Whereas the truth is that the State in which the rulers are most reluctant to govern is always the best and most quietly governed, and the State in which they are most eager, the worst.

Quite true, he replied.

And will our pupils, when they hear this, refuse to take their turn at the toils of State, when they are allowed to spend the greater part of their time with one another in the heavenly light?

Impossible, he answered; for they are just men, and the commands which we impose upon them are just; there can be no doubt that every one of them will take office as a stern necessity, and not after the fashion of our present rulers of State.

Yes, my friend, I said; and there lies the point. You must contrive for your future rulers another and a better life than that of a ruler, and then you may have a well-ordered State; for only in the State which offers this will they rule who are truly rich, not in silver and gold but in virtue and wisdom, which are the true blessings of life. Whereas if they go to the administration of public affairs, poor and hungering after their own private advantage, thinking that hence they are to snatch the chief good, order there can never be; for they will be fighting about office, and the civil and domestic broils which thus arise will be the ruin of the rulers themselves and of the whole State.

Most true, he replied.

✝

B. *THE 7TH EPISTLE*

PLATO

Near the end of his long life, Plato wrote a lengthy letter to explain certain actions he had taken in Sicily. In the course of this letter, he describes his own youth in Athens, and the effect political conditions had on him. Although some scholars dispute the genuineness of the letter, it seems to offer real insight into the processes that turned Plato from politics to philosophy. Then as now, it would appear, manipulation of values and beliefs for political purposes led to disillusionment and cynicism among the young. Once it is assumed that Plato was writing for others like himself, the difficulty of his accomplishment in the Republic becomes clear.

When I was a young man, I was affected as the many are. I thought, if I became quickly my own master, to betake myself immediately to the public affairs of the state. Now some such circumstances as these fell out regarding to state affairs. When the polity existing at that time was abused by many, a change took place; and over the change fifty-one men presided as governors—eleven in the city, and ten in the Piraeus, each with jurisdiction over the marketplace and whatever else it was necessary to regulate in the cities; and thirty others who held supreme authority.

Some of these happened to be my relatives and acquaintances; and they forthwith invited me to participate in state-affairs, as being a suitable pursuit. And how I was affected is, on account of my youth, not at all surprising. For I thought that they would, by leading the city from an unjust mode of living to a just one, administer it properly. So I diligently gave my mind to what they did. But soon I saw these men prove that the previous form of government had been, by comparison, golden. They committed acts unjustly, and ordered my elderly friend Socrates—who I am not ashamed to say was nearly the most righteous of those then living—to go with certain others, to arrest one of the citizens, in order that he might be executed. They did this so that he might have a share in their deeds, whether he wished it or not. But he did not comply, but ran the risk of suffering every punishment rather than take part in their impious acts.

When I saw all this, and other similar acts of no trifling kind, I felt indignant, and withdrew myself from the evil men of that period. Not long after this, the power of the Thirty fell by a revolution, together with the whole of the then-existing form of government. Once again, therefore, but somewhat more slowly, did a desire still drag me on to engage in public and political affairs.

Now in these, as being in a troubled state, many things took place, at which anyone might be indignant; nor was it surprising that in revolutions the punishment of hostile factions would have been rather severe in the case of some, although they who returned acted with considerable clemency.

But by some chance some of those in power brought before a court of justice my friend Socrates, laying upon him a most unholy accusation, of which he was the least deserving. For some brought him to trial, and others gave their vote against him, and destroyed the man, who had been unwilling to share in the unholy act of a removal relating to one of his then-exiled friends, when the exiles themselves were unfortunate.

The more I reflected upon these matters, and on the persons who managed political affairs, and on the laws and customs, and the more I advanced in years, by so much the more difficult did it appear to me to administer state affairs correctly. For it is not possible to do so without friends and faithful associates; but at that time it was not easy to find such men, since our city was then no longer administered according to the manners and institutions of our forefathers. And it was impossible to acquire new ones with any facility; since the written laws and customs were corrupted and unholiness was increasing to an alarming degree.

So I, who had been at first full of ardor towards engaging in affairs of state, did, upon looking at these things and seeing them carried along in every way and on every side, became giddy. I did not cease from deliberating how improvements might be made in the laws and the whole form of government, but I did hold back until there was a prudent opportunity for acting.

At last I perceived that all states existing at present were badly governed and their laws virtually incurable, barring some wonderful arrangement and good fortune. I was therefore compelled to say, in praise of true philosophy, that through it we are enabled to perceive all that is just as regards the state and individuals; and hence that the human race will never cease from ills, until those who philosophize correctly and truthfully shall come to political power, or persons of power in states shall, by a certain divine allotment, truly philosophize.

❖

5. *ON THE CHANGING OF LAWS;*

ARISTOTLE

Plato's life spanned nearly a century of tumultuous developments. His student ARISTOTLE lived to see the city-states of Greece come under the control of Macedonian kings. In this passage from the *Politics*, he expresses a caution with regard to changing laws that comes as a surprise to our reform-minded age. Can you account for his concern? Do you think it is justified? Is it as valid today as it was for his day? Having seen the outcome, would you judge the Greek Enlightenment overall a good thing or a bad thing?

It is a difficult question to some people whether it is injurious or advantageous to states to alter their ancestral laws and customs where another better law or custom is possible....

But as we have alluded to the subject, it will be worthwhile to discuss it a little more fully. There is room, as we said, for a difference of opinion. At first sight there would seem to be an advantage in alteration, as it has certainly proved beneficial in the other sciences. Thus there has been a benefit in the departure from ancestral rules in medicine, gymnastic and the arts and faculties generally; and as politics deserves to be placed in this category, it is evident that the same must be true also of politics.

It may be said that there is an indication of this truth in the facts of history, as ancient customs are exceedingly rude and barbarous. For instance, the Greeks always carried daggers and purchased their wives from one another; in fact all such primitive institutions as survive in the world are quite absurd....As a general rule it is not what is ancient but what is good that the world wants. Nor is it likely that our first parents, whether they were the children of earth or the survivors of some catastrophe were any better than ordinary or unwise people, as in fact is the common notion of the earth-children or Giants. It is absurd therefore to abide by their decrees. We may add that it is not desirable to leave even the written laws unaltered. For as in the arts generally, so in the political system it is impossible that everything should be precisely specified in writing. The terms of the written law are necessarily general, whereas its practical application is to individual cases. It is evident then that an alteration is right in the case of certain laws and on particular occasions.

From another point of view however such alterations seem to require no little caution. Where the improvement is but slight compared with the evil of accustoming the citizens lightly to repeal the laws, it is undoubtedly our duty to pass over some mistakes whether of the legislature or of the executive, as the benefit we shall derive from the alteration will not be equal to the harm we shall get by accustoming ourselves to disobey authority. The illustration from the arts is fallacious. There is no parallel between altering an art and altering a law. For all the potency of the law to secure obedience depends upon habit, and habit can only be formed by lapse of time; so that the ready transition from the existing laws to others that are new is a weakening of the efficacy of law itself.

✝

6. *PHILOSOPHICAL RESPONSES*

The Macedonian conquerors of Greece—especially Alexander the Great—radically expanded the frontiers of the Greek world. A hundred years earlier, men had claimed to belong to this or that polis; now, some said they were citizens of a world-state, the cosmopolis. Such a drastic change in the social horizons meant that old beliefs had to be adjusted to a new universe. CLEANTHES (331-232 B.C.) and EPICURUS (341-270 B.C) were the leading exponents of two schools of thought, Stoicism (founded by Zeno of Citium, who taught in the Painted Porch, or Stoa Poikile, in Athens, and Epicureanism, associated with The Garden of Epicurus. Both were responses to this new world. What are they searching for? How do they propose to find it? Which is more important, their similarities or their differences? How do each compare to the older philosophies of Plato and Aristotle? (A hint: where do they find virtue and value?) What would Pericles have made of them?

A. *HYMN TO ZEUS*

CLEANTHES

Most glorious of immortals, O thou of many names, all-powerful ever, hail!

On thee it is fit all men should call. For we come forth from thee, and have received the gift of imitative speech alone of all that live and move on earth.

So will I make my song of thee and chant thy power forever. Thee all this ordered universe, circling around the earth, follows as thou dost guide and evermore is ruled by thee. For such an engine hast thou in thine unswerving hands-the two-edged, blazing, everliving bolt-that at its blow all nature trembles. herewith thou guidest universal Reason-the moving principle of all the world, joined with the great and lesser lights-which, being born so great, is highest lord of all.

Nothing occurs on earth apart from thee, O Lord, nor at the airy sacred pole nor on the sea, save what the wicked work through lack of wisdom.

But thou canst make the crooked straight, bring order from disorder, and what is worthless is in thy sight worthy. For thou has so conjoined to one all good and ill that out of all goes forth a single everlasting Reason. This all the wicked seek to shun, unhappy men, who, ever longing to obtain a good, see not nor hear God's universal law; which, wisely heeded, would assure them noble life. hey haste away, however, heedless of good, one here, one there; some showing unholy zeal in strife for honor, some turning recklessly toward gain, others to looseness and the body's pleasures.

But thou, O Zeus, giver of all, thou of the cloud, guide of the thunder, deliver men from baleful ignorance! Scatter it, father, from our souls, grant us to win that wisdom on which thou thyself relying suitably guidest all; that thus being honored, we may return to thee our honor, singing thy works unceasingly, because there is no higher office for a man—nor for a god—than ever rightly singing of universal law.

✝

B. PHILOSOPHICAL SAYINGS

EPICURUS

1. That which is happy and imperishable, neither has trouble itself, nor does it cause trouble to anything; so that it is not subject to the feelings of either anger or gratitude; for these feelings only exist in what is weak.

2. Death is nothing to us; for that which is dissolved is devoid of sensation, and that which is devoid of sensation is nothing to us.

3. The limit of the greatness of the pleasures is the removal of everything which can give pain. And where pleasure is, as long as it lasts, that which gives pain, or that which feels pain, or both of them, are absent.

5. It is not possible to live pleasantly without living prudently, and honourably, and justly; nor to live prudently, and honourably, and justly, without living pleasantly. But he to whom it does not happen to live prudently, honourably, and justly, cannot possibly live pleasantly.

7. No pleasure is intrinsically bad: but the efficient causes of some pleasures bring with them a great many perturbations of pleasure.

8. If every pleasure were condensed, if one may so say, and if each lasted long, and affected the whole body, or the essential parts of it, then there would be no difference between one pleasure and another.

9. If those things which make the pleasures of debauched men, put an end to the fears of the mind, and to those which arise about the heavenly bodies, and death, and pain;, and if they taught us what ought to be the limit of our desires, we should have no pretence for blaming those who wholly devote themselves to pleasure, and who never feel any pain or grief (which is the chief evil) from any quarter.

10. If apprehensions relating to the heavenly bodies did not disturb us, and if the terrors of death have no concern with us, and if we had the courage to contemplate the boundaries of pain and of the desires, we should have no need of physiological studies.

12. It would be no good for a man to secure himself safety as far as men are concerned, while in a state of apprehension as to all the heavenly bodies, and those under the earth, and in short, all those in the infinite.

13. Irresistible power and great wealth may, up to a certain point, give us security as far as men are concerned; but the security of men in general depends upon the tranquillity of their souls, and their freedom from ambition.

14. The riches of nature are defined and easily procurable; but vain desires are insatiable.

16. The just man is the freest of all men from disquietude; but the unjust man is a perpetual prey to it.

17. Pleasure in the flesh is not increased, when once the pain arising from want is removed; it is only diversified.

21 But reason, enabling us to conceive the end and dissolution of the body, and liberating us from the fears relative to eternity, procures for us all the happiness of which life is capable, so completely that we have no further occasion to include eternity in our desires. In this disposition of mind, man is happy even when his troubles engage him to quit life; and to die thus, is for him only to interrupt a life of happiness.

22. He who is acquainted with the limits of life knows, that that which removes the pain which arises from want, and which makes the whole of life perfect, is easily procurable; so that he has no need of those things which can only be attained with trouble.

28. Of all the things which wisdom provides for the happiness of the whole life, by far the most important is the acquisition of friendship.

29. The same opinion encourages man to trust that no evil will be everlasting, or even of long duration; as it sees that, in the space of life allotted to us, the protection of friendship is most sure and trustworthy.

31. Those desires which do not lead to pain, if they are not satisfied, are not necessary. It is easy to impose silence on them when they appear difficult to gratify, or likely to produce injury.

37. It is not possible for a man who secretly does anything in contravention of the agreement which men have made with one another, to guard against doing, or sustaining mutual injury, to believe that he shall always escape notice, even if he have escaped notice already ten thousand times; for, till his death, it in uncertain whether he will not be detected.

38. In a general point of view, justice is the same thing to every one; for there is something advantageous in mutual society. Nevertheless, the difference of place, and divers other circumstances, make justice vary.

39. From the moment that a thing declared just by the law is generally recognized as useful for the mutual relations of men, it becomes really just, whether it is universally regarded as such or not.

42. He who desires to live tranquilly without having any thing to fear from other men, ought to make himself friends; those whom he cannot make friends of, he should, at least, avoid rendering enemies; and if that is not in his power, be should, as far as possible, avoid all intercourse with them, and keep them aloof, as far as it is for his interest to do so.

43. The happiest men are they who have arrived at the point of having nothing to fear from those who surround them. Such men live with one another most agreeably, having the firmest grounds of confidence in one another, enjoying the advantages of friendship in all their fulness, and not lamenting, as a pitiable circumstance, the premature death of their friends.

✝

VI. Great Individuals

What is the role of the individual in history? Writers have always been aware of the tension between personal achievement and the simple, grinding momentum of events. Does a person seize and shape the forces of destiny, or does the past control the individual's fate? Selections in this chapter deal with two of the most decisive figures in all history—the Macedonian conqueror ALEXANDER THE GREAT (356-323 B.C.) and GAIUS JULIUS CAESAR (100-44 B.C.), whose fateful career ended the Roman Republic and began the Roman Empire. As you read, consider your own criteria for making a historical figure "great": Alexander and Caesar were both conquerors; is this why they are "great"? If so, would you call Attila the Hun "great," or Genghis Khan? What about Adolph Hitler?

❖ ❖ ❖

1. ON HEROES

THOMAS CARLYLE — *explains why things happened in history.*

The idea of "the great man" as a force in history derives from the thinking of the great German philosopher Georg Wilhelm Hegel, who spoke of individuals in various ages who had been instinctively in tune with the "World Soul," and thus able to make needed changes happen. For English audiences, his ideas were popularized by the great prose stylist THOMAS CARLYLE (1795-1881). In 1840, Carlyle delivered a series of public lectures On Heroes, Hero-Worship, and the Heroic in History that electrified his audiences and decisively influenced subsequent generations of historians. Consider the place of Alexander and Caesar in Carlyle's scheme. Did they mold their future and defy their fate? Are they worthy of adoration or emulation?

Society is founded on Hero-worship. All dignities of rank, on which human association rests, are what we may call a Hero-archy (Government of Heroes),—or a Hierarchy, for it is "sacred" enough withal! The Duke means *Dux*, Leader; King is Kon-ning, Kan-ning, Man that knows or can. Society everywhere is some representation, not n supportably inaccurate, of a graduated Worship of Heroes;—reverence and obedience done to men really great and wise. Not insupportably inaccurate, I say! They are all as bank-notes, these social dignitaries, all representing gold;—and several of them, alas, always are forged notes. We can do with some forged false notes; with a good many even; but not with all, or the most of them forged! No: there have to come revolutions then; cries of Democracy, Liberty and Equality, and I know not what:—the notes being all false, and no gold to be had for them, people take to crying in their despair that there is no gold, that there never was any!—Gold," Hero-worship, is nevertheless, as it was always and everywhere, and cannot cease till man himself ceases.

I am well aware that in these days Hero-worship, the thing I call Hero-worship, professes to have gone out, and finally ceased. This, for reasons which it will be worth while some time to inquire into, is an age that as it were denies the existence of great men; denies the desirableness of great men. Show our critics a great man, a Luther for example, they begin to what they call "account" for him; not to worship him, but take the dimensions of him,—and bring him out to be a little kind of man! He was the "creature of the Time," they say; the Time called him forth, the Time did everything, he nothing—but what we the little critic could have done too! This seems to me but melancholy work. The Time call forth? Alas, we have known Times *call* loudly enough for their great man; but not find him when they called! He was not there; Providence had not sent him; the Time, *calling* its loudest, had to go down to confusion and wreck because he would not come when called.

For if we will think of it, no Time need have gone to ruin, could it have *found* a man great enough, a man wise and good enough: wisdom to discern truly what the Time wanted, valor to lead it on the right road thither; these are the salvation of any Time. But I liken com-

135

mon languid Times, with their unbelief, distress, perplexity, with their languid doubting characters and embarrassed circumstances, impotently crumbling down into ever worse distress towards final ruin;—all this I liken to dry dead fuel, waiting for the lightning out of Heaven that shall kindle it. The great man, with his free force direct out of God's own hand, is the lightning. His word is the wise healing word which all can believe in. All blazes round him now, when he has once struck on it, into fire like his own. The dry mouldering sticks are thought to have called him forth. They did want him greatly; but as to calling him forth—!—Those are critics of small vision, I think, who cry: "See, is it not the sticks that made the fire?" No sadder proof can be given by a man of his own littleness than disbelief in great men. There is no sadder symptom of a generation than such general blindness to the spiritual lightning, with faith only in the heap of barren dead fuel. It is the last consummation of unbelief. In all epochs of the world's history, we shall find the Great Man to have been the indispensable savior of his epoch;—the lightning, without which the fuel never would have burnt. The History of the World, I said already, was the Biography of Great Men....

Yes, from Norse Odin to English Samuel Johnson, from the divine Founder of Christianity to the withered Pontiff of Encyclopedism, in all times and places, the Hero has been worshipped. It will ever be so. We all love great men; love, venerate and bow down submissive before great men: nay can we honestly bow down to anything else? Ah, does not every true man feel that he is himself made higher by doing reverence to what is really above him? No nobler or more blessed feeling dwells in man's heart. And to me it is very cheering to consider that no sceptical logic, or general triviality, insincerity and aridity of any Time and its influences can destroy this noble inborn loyalty and worship that is in man. In times of unbelief, which soon have to become times of revolution, much down-rushing, sorrowful decay and ruin is visible to everybody. For myself, in these days, I seem to see in this indestructibility of Hero-worship the everlasting adamant lower than which the confused wreck of revolutionary things cannot fall. The

confused wreck of things crumbling and even crashing and tumbling all round us in these revolutionary ages, will get down so far; *no* farther. It is an eternal corner-stone, from which they can begin to build themselves up again. That man, in some sense or other, worships Heroes; that we all of us reverence and must ever reverence Great Men: this is, to me, the living rock amid all rushings-down whatsoever,—the one fixed point in modern revolutionary history, otherwise as if bottomless and shoreless....

We come now to the last form of Heroism; that which we call Kingship. The Commander over men; he to whose will our wills are to be subordinated, and loyally surrender themselves, and find their welfare in doing so, may be reckoned the most important of Great Men. He is practically the summary for us of *all* the various figures of Heroism; Priest, Teacher, whatsoever of earthly or of spiritual dignity we can fancy to reside in a man, embodies itself here, to *command* over us, to furnish us with constant practical teaching, to tell us for the day and hour what we are to *do*. He is called *Rex*, Regulator, *Roi*; our own name is still better; King, *Könning*, which means *Can*-ning, Able-man.

I say here, that the finding of your *Ableman* and getting him invested with the *symbols of ability*, with dignity, worship (*worth* -ship), royalty, kinghood, or whatever we call it, so that *he* may actually have room to guide according to his faculty of doing it,—is the business, well or ill accomplished, of all social procedure whatsoever in this world!

- great man able to bring spirit of age b/c overcome conflict
- has to be intentional
- needs tools

2. ALEXANDER AND GREECE

The main test of a "great man" is to determine the extent to which he (or she—yes, women can be "great men," too) shaped events. We'll use Alexander as a test case: how much of his own success was he responsible for, and how much was due to events essentially beyond his control?

A. ON GREEK UNITY

ISOCRATES

As often in the study of history, the route to an answer to the problem of the "great man" leads back several generations. In the case of Alexander, we must go back at least to the Peloponnesian War, which dealt a knockout blow to the traditional values of the polis. After 404 B.C. a host of writers attempted to get the polis back on track. Plato, as you have already read, suggested creation of a well-regulated and regimented state. Another Athenian, ISOCRATES (436-338 B.C.), had a different idea. His *Panegyricus*, written about the same time as Plato's *Republic*, promotes a new policy for Athens and all Greece. What is he advocating? What is new in his approach? What does this indicate about the idea of the polis? Is this a harbinger of the search for a great man?

[50] So far has Athens left the rest of mankind behind in thought and expression that her pupils have become the teachers of the world, and she has made the name of Hellas distinctive no longer of race but of intellect, and the title of Hellene a badge of education rather than of common descent. *on way towards citizenship*

[120] The magnitude of the change [in the fortunes of the Greeks] can be best seen at a glance by reading over side by side the treaties entered into under our empire and those which now stand recorded. In those days [both Sparta and Athens] shall be found marking the limits of the King's rule,[1] assessing some of their tributes, and forbidding him to make use of the sea; whereas now it is he who manages the affairs of Hellas, dictates what each must do, and all but sets up governors in the cities. [121] For with this exception what else is left undone? Was he not master of the war, did he not direct peace negotiations, and has he not been established our chief-president at the present time? Are we not drifting into his hands as into those of a master, ready to blame

---

[1]Referring to the King of Persia.

each other for the result? Do we not address him as "The Great King," as if we were prisoners of war? Do we not in our wars against each other place in him our hopes of a safe issue, when he would gladly destroy us both?

[133] Now I think that if men were to come from some other region and be spectators of the present state of things, they would find both of us [Athens and Sparta] guilty of great madness, for thus incurring risk about trifles, when it is within our power to enjoy great possessions in security, and for ruining our own territory while neglecting to reap the fruits of Asia. [134] To the King of course nothing is more important than the consideration of means to prevent us ever ceasing from making war against each other; but we are so far from embroiling any of his affairs or causing revolts that even the troubles which by chance have come upon him we endeavor to help him to suppress...[166] And it is a much nobler thing to fight with him for his kingdom than to wrangle among ourselves for the leadership of Hellas.

[167] Now it is right to undertake the campaign in the present generation, that those who have had their share of troubles may also enjoy success and not spend all their life in evil days. Sufficient is the past, in which every form of calamity has taken place. Many as are the evils attached to the natural condition of men, we ourselves have invented more evils in addition to those which necessity imposes, creating wars and factions in our midst, [168] so that some are lawlessly put to death in their own states, while others wander with wives and children in a foreign land, and many, forced into mercenary service by the want of daily necessities, die fighting for foes against friends. At this no one has ever yet shown indignation, yet they see fit to weep over the tales of calamity composed by poets, while— beholding with indifference the real woes, many and terrible, which are caused by war— they are so far from feeling pity that they even rejoice more at one another's troubles than at their own good fortune. [169] Many perhaps would even ridicule my simplicity, were I to mourn over the misfortunes of individuals in times like these, in which Italy has become a wasted land, Sicily has been enslaved, and so many states have been given up to the barbar-

ians, while the remaining portions of Hellas are in the midst of the greatest dangers.

[170] I wonder that those who are in power in our states consider that it befits them to hold their heads high, when they have never yet been able by word or thought to help in matters of such importance. For, were they worthy of their present reputation, they ought, neglecting everything else, to have made proposals and taken counsel concerning the war against the barbarians. For by chance they might together have accomplished something; [171] and even had they abandoned the attempt from weariness, yet they would at least have left their words behind them as oracles for the future. But as it is, those who are in the highest positions of honor concern themselves with small matters and have left it to us who stand aloof from public life to give advice on such weighty affairs.

[172] Nevertheless, the more narrow-minded our leaders prove to be, the more vigorously must the rest of us consider how to be rid of our present enmity. As things are, it is to no purpose that we make our treaties of peace; for we do not settle our wars, but only defer them, and wait for the time when we shall be able to inflict some irremediable injury on one another. [173] Our duty, on the contrary, is to put aside these plottings and apply ourselves to those undertakings which will enable us both to dwell in greater security in our cities and to feel greater confidence in one another. Now the word to be said on this subject is a simple and easy one; we cannot enjoy a sure peace unless we make war in common against the barbarians, nor can Hellas be made of one mind until we secure our advantages from the same enemies and meet our perils in the face of the same foes. [174] When these things are achieved, when we have removed the poverty surrounding our life, which breaks up friendships, perverts to enmity the ties of kindred, and throws all mankind into wars and seditions, it must follow that we shall be of one mind and our mutual goodwill will be real. For these reasons we must consider it all-important as speedily as possible to banish our domestic war to the continent, since the one advantage we can derive from our internal struggles would be the resolve to use against

the barbarian the lessons of experience which we have gained from them.

❖

B. *THE SECOND OLYNTHIAC*

DEMOSTHENES

Another factor to consider when assessing Alexander is the role of his father, Philip of Macedon (359-336 B.C.), who raised Macedon from near-extinction and made it the dominant military power in Greece. Two remarkable Athenian orators, DEMOSTHENES (384?-322 B.C.) and ISOCRATES again, reached different opinions about the nature and scope of Macedon's entry into Hellenic politics. Here are excerpts from Demosthenes' *Second Olynthiac*, delivered in 349, and Isocrates' *Address to Philip*, given in 346. What views do the two men share? Where do they differ? Has the Greek outlook changed since the "golden age" a century earlier? Has Isocrates' search for help changed? How is his solution different from the one he offered in the *Panegyricus*? In the event, who turned out to be right, Isocrates or Demosthenes?

[1] Many as are the occasions, men of Athens, on which we may discern the manifestation of the goodwill of Heaven towards this city, one of the most striking is to be seen in the circumstances of the present time. For that men should have been found to carry on war against Philip; men whose territory borders on his and who possess some power; men, above all, whose sentiments in regard to the war are such that they think of the proposed compact with him, not only as untrustworthy, but as the very ruin of their country—this seems to be certainly the work of a superhuman, a divine, beneficence. [2] And so, men of Athens, we must take care that we do not treat ourselves less well than circumstances have treated us. For it is a shameful thing—nay, it is the very depth of shame—to throw away openly, not only cities and places which were once in our power, but even the allies and the opportunities which have been provided for us by Fortune.

[3] Now to describe at length the power of Philip, men of Athens, and to incite you to the performance of your duty by such a recital, is not, I think, a satisfactory proceeding; and for this reason—that while all that can be said on this subject tends to Philip's glory, it is a story of failure on our part. For the greater the ex-

tent to which his success surpasses his desserts, the greater is the admiration with which the world regards him; while, for your part, the more you have fallen short of the right use of your opportunities, the greater is the disgrace that you have incurred. [4] I will therefore pass over such considerations. For any honest inquirer must see that the causes of Philip's rise to greatness lie in Athens, and not in himself. Of the services for which he has to thank those whose policy is determined by his interest—services for which you ought to require their punishment—the present is not, I see, the moment to speak. But apart from these, there are things which may be said, and which it is better that you should all have heard—things which (if you will examine them aright) constitute a grave reproach against him; and these I will try to tell you.

[5] If I called him perjured and faithless, without giving his actions in evidence, my words would be treated as idle abuse, and rightly: and it happens that to review all his actions up to the present time, and to prove the charge in every case, requires only a short speech. It is well, I think, that the story should be told, for it will serve two purposes; first, to make plain the real badness of the man's character; and secondly, to let those who are over-alarmed at Philip, as if he were invincible, see that he has come to the end of all those forms of deceit by which he rose to greatness, and that his career is already drawing to its close. [6] For I, too, men of Athens, should be regarding Philip with intense fear and admiration, if I saw that his rise was the result of a righteous policy. But when I study and consider the facts, I find that originally, when certain persons wished to drive from your presence the Olynthians who desired to address you from this place, Philip won over our innocent minds by saying that he would deliver up Amphipolis to us, and by inventing the famous secret understanding; [7] that he afterwards conciliated the Olynthians by seizing Potidaea, which was yours, and injuring their former allies by handing it over to themselves; and that, last of all, he recently won over the Thessalians, by promising to give up Magnesia to them, and undertaking to carry on the war with the Phocians on their behalf. There is absolutely no one who has ever had dealings with him that he has not

deluded; and it is by deceiving and winning over, one after another, those who in their blindness did not realize what he was, that he has risen as he has done. [8] And therefore, just as it was by these deceptions that he rose to greatness, in the days when each people fancied that he intended to do some service to themselves; so it is these same deceptions which should drag him down again, now that he stands convicted of acting for his own ends throughout. Such, then, is the crisis, men of Athens, to which Philip's fortunes have now come. If it is not so, let any one come forward and show me (or rather you) that what I say is untrue; or that those who have been deceived at the outset trust him as regards the future; or that those who have been brought into unmerited bondage would not gladly be free.

[9] But if any of you, while agreeing with me so far, still fancies that Philip will maintain his hold by force, because he has already occupied fortified posts and harbors and similar positions, he is mistaken. When power is cemented by goodwill, and the interest of all who join in a war is the same, then men are willing to share the labor, to endure the misfortunes, and to stand fast. But when a man has become strong, as Philip has done, by a grasping and wicked policy, the first excuse, the least stumble, throws him from his seat and dissolves the alliance. [10] It is impossible, men of Athens, utterly impossible, to acquire power that will last, by unrighteousness, by perjury, and by falsehood. Such power holds out for a moment, or for a brief hour; it blossoms brightly, perhaps, with fair hopes; but time detects the fraud, and the flower falls withered about its stem. In a house or a ship, or any other structure, it is the foundations that must be strongest; and no less, I believe, must the principles, which are the foundation of men's actions, be those of truth and righteousness. Such qualities are not to be seen today in the past acts of Philip.

[22] Now if any of you, men of Athens, seeing Philip's good fortune, thinks that this makes him a formidable enemy to fight against, he reasons like a sensible man: for fortune weighs heavily in the scale—nay, fortune is everything, in all human affairs. And yet, if I were given the choice, it is the fortune of Athens that I should choose, rather than that of

Philip, provided that you yourselves are willing to act even to a small extent as you should act. For I see that there are far more abundant grounds for expecting the goodwill of Heaven on your side than on his. [23] But here, of course, we are sitting idle; and one who is sluggard himself cannot require his friends to help him, much less the gods. It is not to be wondered at that Philip, who goes on campaigns and works hard himself, and is always at the scene of action, and lets no opportunity go, no season pass, should get the better of us who delay and pass resolutions and ask for news; nor do I wonder at it. It is the opposite that would have been wonderful—if we, who do nothing that those who are at war ought to do, were successful against one who leaves nothing undone. [24] But this I do wonder at, that you once raised your hand against Sparta, in defense of the rights of the Hellenes—you, who with opportunities often open to you for grasping large advantages for yourselves, would not take them, but to secure for others their rights spent your own fortunes in war-contributions, and always bore the brunt of the dangers of the campaign—that you, I say, are now shrinking from marching, and hesitating to make any contribution to save your own possessions; and that, though you have often saved the rest of the Hellenes, now all together and now each in their turn, you are sitting idle, when you have lost what was your own. [25] I wonder at this; and I wonder also, men of Athens, that none of you is able to reckon up the time during which you have been fighting with Philip, and to consider what you have been doing while all this time has been going by. Surely you must know that it is while we have been delaying, hoping that someone else would act, accusing one another, bringing one another to trial, hoping anew—in fact, doing practically what we are doing now—that all the time has passed. [26] And have you now so little sense, men of Athens, as to hope that the very same policy, which has made the position of the city a bad one instead of a good, will actually make it a good one instead of a bad? Why, it is contrary both to reason and to nature to think so! It is always much easier to retain than to acquire. But now, owing to the war, none of our old possessions is left for us to retain; and so we must needs acquire. [27] This, therefore, is our own personal and immediate duty; and accordingly I say that you must contribute funds, you must go on service in person with a good will, you must accuse no one before you have become masters of the situation; and then you must honor those who deserve praise, and punish the guilty, with a judgment based upon the actual facts. You must get rid of all excuses and all deficiencies on your own part; you cannot examine mercilessly the actions of others, unless you yourselves have done all that your duty requires.

❖

C. THE ADDRESS TO PHILIP
ISOCRATES

In his *Panegyricus* (c. 380 B.C.), Isocrates had advocated a grand alliance of Greeks, led by Athens and Sparta, to wage war against Persia. Now, more than 30 years later (c. 346 B.C.), he turns for inspiration to the ruler of Macedon.

9. [I once thought that] the greatest *poleis* should resolve their differences and lead a war against Asia, deciding to extract from the barbarians the advantages that they now possess at the cost of the Greeks. Such was the course I advocated in my *Panegyricus*.

13. [Now I think that] those who wish to do anything useful, and who think they have developed a plan for the common good, if they want to have any influence, must leave public speaking to others and not prattle vainly in assemblies, but find a champion for their plans among those men of great repute who have the power to act as well as talk. 14. For this reason I chose to discourse with you, not selecting you for your favor. To be sure, I would do much to appear favorable in your eyes, but that is not my purpose here. For I saw that all the other men of note are subject to cities and customs, are unable to act except according to convention, and, moreover, that they were not up to the task I propose. 15. To you alone has Fortune given authority both to send and receive embassies to whomever and from whomever you choose, and to say whatever you think expedient. In addition, you have acquired beyond any other Greek wealth and power, the only things that are capable of either persuading or coercing, and that I think are necessary for my proposal. 16. For I am going to advise you to lead the cause of Greek

unity and the war against the barbarians. That is the sum and substance of my speech.

68. Consider how worthy it is to attempt deeds of this sort. Should you succeed, you will make a reputation for yourself to rival that of the greatest men, while if you should fall short of your expectations you will nevertheless win the esteem of the Greeks, a prize worth more than the capture of many Greek *poleis*....
71. Should you succeed, how could you not rightly take pride? how could your life not be continuous joy, knowing that you had been the leader of such a great enterprise? And who of even moderate sense would not firmly advise you to choose those actions that are capable of bearing two fruits at once—both incomparable pleasure and indelible honor?

132. Consider also how shameful it is to see Asia faring better than Europe and barbarians wealthier than Greeks, and those whose rule derives from a Cyrus whose own mother threw him out on the road being called Great Kings while rulers descended from Heracles, whose sire raised him up to the gods because of his virtue, being addressed by lowlier titles than those. Such conditions must no longer be allowed to prevail; they must be reversed and overturned completely.

154. [In sum,] I say you must show kindness to the Greeks, be king to the Macedonians, and rule over as many barbarians as possible. If you do these things they all will be grateful to you: the Greeks because of the benefits they experience, the Macedonians for being ruled by a true king and not a tyrant, and the other peoples because through you they would be released from barbarian despotism and enjoy the protection of Greeks.

✝

D. LIFE OF ALEXANDER

PLUTARCH

Philip of Macedon was assassinated before he began his Persian campaign; instead, that task fell to his son, Alexander (356-323 B.C.). Alexander was spectacularly successful, becoming a legend to his own as well as distant ages. PLUTARCH (A.D. 46?-102?), author of the famous series of *Parallel Lives*, paired Alexander with Julius Caesar, much to the detriment of the latter. How does Plutarch see Alexander? Does Plutarch offer any clues to why Alexander is nicknamed "the Great"?

It must be borne in mind that my design is not to write histories, but lives. And the most glorious exploits do not always furnish us with the clearest discoveries of virtue or vice in men; sometimes a matter of less moment, an expression or a jest, informs us better of their characters and inclination, than the most famous sieges, the greatest armaments, or the bloodiest battles whatsoever. Therefore as portrait-painters are more exact in the lines and features of the face, in which the character is seen, than in the other parts of the body, so I must be allowed to give my more particular attention to the marks and indications of the souls of men, and while I endeavor by these to portray their lives, may be free to leave more weighty matters and great battles to be treated of by others.

It is agreed on by all hands, that on the father's side, Alexander descended from Hercules by Caranus, and from Aeacus by Neoptolemus on the mother's side. His father Philip, being in Samothrace, when he was quite young, fell in love there with Olympias, in company with whom he was initiated in the religious ceremonies of the country, and her father and mother being both dead, soon after, with the consent of her brother Arymbas, he married her. The night before the consummation of their marriage, she dreamed that a thunderbolt fell upon her body, which kindled a great fire, whose divided flames dispersed themselves all about, and then were extinguished. And Philip some time after he was married, dreamt that he sealed up his wife's body with a seal, whose impression, as he fancied, was the figure of a lion. Some of the diviners interpreted this as a warning to Philip to look narrowly to his wife; but Aristander of Telmessus, considering how unusual it was to seal up any thing that was empty, assured him the meaning of his dream was, that the queen was with child of a boy, who would one day prove as stout and courageous as a lion. Once, moreover, a serpent was found lying by Olympias as she slept, which more than anything else, it is said, abated Philip's passion for her; and whether he feared her as an enchantress, or thought she had commerce with some god, and so looked on himself as excluded, he was ever after less fond of her conversation.

Just after Philip had taken Potidaea, he received these three messages at one time, that Parmenio had overthrown the Illyrians in a great battle, that his race-horse had won the course at the Olympic games, and that his wife had given birth to Alexander; with which being naturally well pleased, as an addition to his satisfaction, he was assured by the diviners that a son, whose birth was accompanied with three such successes, could not fail of being invincible.

ALEXANDER'S YOUTH

While he was yet very young, he entertained the ambassadors from the king of Persia, in the absence of his father, and entering much into conversation with them, gained so much upon them by his affability, and the questions he asked them, which were far from being childish or trifling, (for he inquired of them the length of the ways, the nature of the road into inner Asia, the character of their king, how he carried himself to his enemies, and what forces he was able to bring into the field,) that they were struck with admiration of him, and looked upon the ability so much famed of Philip, to be nothing in comparison with the forwardness and high purpose that appeared thus early in his son. Whenever he heard Philip had taken any town of importance, or won any signal victory, instead of rejoicing at it altogether, he would tell his companions that his father would anticipate every thing, and leave him and them no opportunities of performing great and illustrious actions.

Philonicus the Thessalian brought the horse Bucephalas to Philip, offering to sell him for thirteen talents; but when they went into the field to try him, they found him so very vicious and unmanageable, that he reared up when they endeavored to mount him, and would not so much as endure the voice of any of Philip's attendants. Upon which, as they were leading him away as wholly useless and untractable, Alexander, who stood by, said, "What an excellent horse do they lose, for want of address and boldness to manage him!" Philip at first took no notice of what he said; but when he heard him repeat the same thing several times,

and saw he was much vexed to see the horse sent away, "Do you reproach," said he to him, "those who are older than yourself, as if you knew more, and were better able to manage him than they?" "I could manage this horse," replied he, "better than others do." "And if you do not," said Philip, "what will you forfeit for your rashness?" "I will pay," answered Alexander, "the whole price of the horse." At this the whole company fell a laughing; and as soon as the wager was settled amongst them, he immediately ran to the horse, and taking hold of the bridle, turned him directly towards the sun, having, it seems, observed that he was disturbed at and afraid of the motion of his own shadow; then letting him go forward a little, still keeping the reins in his hand, and stroking him gently when he found him begin to grow eager and fiery, he let fall his upper garment softly, and with one nimble leap securely mounted him, and when he was seated, by little and little drew in the bridle, and curbed him without either striking or spurring him. Presently, when he found him free from all rebelliousness, and only impatient for the course, he let him go at full speed, inciting him now with a commanding voice, and urging him also with his heel. Philip and his friends looked on at first in silence and anxiety for the result, till seeing him turn at the end of his career, and come back rejoicing and triumphing for what he had performed, they all burst out into acclamations of applause; and his father, shedding tears, it is said, for joy, kissed him as he came down from his horse, and in his transport, said "O my son, look thee out a kingdom equal to and worthy of thyself, for Macedonia is too little for thee."

After this, considering him to be of a temper easy to be led to his duty by reason, but by no means to be compelled, he always endeavored to persuade rather than to command or force him to any thing; and now looking upon the instruction and tuition of his youth to be of greater difficulty and importance, than to be wholly trusted to the ordinary masters in music and poetry, and the common school subjects, and to require, as Sophocles says,

"The bridle and the rudder too,"

he sent for Aristotle, the most learned and most celebrated philosopher of his time, and rewarded him with a munificence proportionable to and becoming the care he took to instruct his son.

Alexander owed to Aristotle his interest in medical practice and medical theory. When any of his friends were sick, Alexander often prescribed their diet and medicines. He was a great lover of all kinds of learning and reading and constantly kept Homer's *Iliad*—a copy corrected by Aristotle (called the casket copy)—with his dagger under his pillow, declaring that he valued it as the perfect, portable treasure of all military virtue and knowledge. But he valued many books and once, from the upper provinces of Asia, Alexander wrote home for a variety of books, including history, a great many of the plays of Euripides, Sophocles, and Aeschylus, and some odes.

When Alexander was sixteen, his father made him regent in Macedonia, entrusting to him the charge of the great seal. While Philip was on his expedition against Byzantium, the Medari rebelled, and Alexander acted vigorously. He defeated them, took their city by storm, drove out the barbarians, and installed a colony of several nations. He renamed the city Alexandropolis in his own honor. Later, at the battle of Chaeronea, which Philip fought against the Greeks, Alexander is said to have been the first man to break through the defenses of the dedicated men known as "the sacred band of Thebans."

This early bravery made Philip very fond of Alexander. Nothing pleased him more than to hear the Macedonians call Alexander "king" and himself only "general." But later family disputes, caused chiefly by Philip's new marriages and love affairs, created a rift between Alexander and his father. Olympias, who was extremely jealous and stubborn, turned Alexander against his father. At Philip's wedding to an additional wife much too young for him, the bride's uncle, drunk with wine, proposed that the Macedonians ask the gods to grant to this new marriage a lawful successor to the kingdom. Alexander, outraged, threw his cup at the speaker, crying out: "You villain! What then, am I? A bastard?" Philip immediately took the side of his bride's uncle and would have stabbed his son with a spear.

Luckily, either because he moved too quickly or because he had drunk too much wine, his foot slipped and he fell to the floor. Alexander reproached and insulted his father, saying, "There is the man who plans to pass from Europe into Asia; he cannot even pass from one table to another!"

Alexander was but twenty years old when his father was murdered, and succeeded to a kingdom beset on all sides with great dangers, and rancorous enemies. For not only the barbarous nations that bordered on Macedonia, were impatient of being governed by any but their own native princes; but Philip likewise, though he had been victorious over the Grecians, yet, as the time had not been sufficient for him to complete his conquest and accustom them to his sway, had simply left all things in a general disorder and confusion. It seemed to the Macedonians a very critical time, and some would have persuaded Alexander to give up all thought of retaining the Grecians in subjection by force of arms, and rather to apply himself to win back by gentle means the allegiance of the tribes who were designing revolt, and try the effect of indulgence in arresting the first motions towards revolution. But he rejected this counsel as weak and timorous, and looked upon it to be more prudence to secure himself by resolution and magnanimity, than, by seeming to truckle to any, to encourage all to trample on him.

AT DELPHI

Then he went to Delphi, to consult Apollo concerning the success of the war he had undertaken, and happening to come on one of the forbidden days, when it was esteemed improper to give any answers from the oracle, he sent messengers to desire the priestess to do her office; and when she refused, on the plea of a law to the contrary, he went up himself, and began to draw her by force into the temple, until tired and overcome with his importunity, "My son," said she, "thou art invincible." Alexander taking hold of what she spoke, declared he had received such an answer as he wished for, and that it was needless to consult the god any further.

His army, by their computation who make the smallest amount, consisted of thirty thousand foot, and four thousand horse; and those who make the most of it, speak but of forty-three thousand foot, and three thousand horse. Aristobulus says, he had not a fund of above seventy talents for their pay, nor had he more than thirty days' provision, if we may believe Duris; Onesicritus tells us, he was two hundred talents in debt. However narrow and disproportionable the beginnings of so vast an undertaking might seem to be, yet he would not embark his army until he had informed himself particularly what means his friends had to enable them to follow him, and supplied what they wanted, by giving good farms to some, a village to one, and the revenue of some hamlet or harbor town to another. So that at last he had portioned out or engaged almost all the royal property; which giving Perdiccas an occasion to ask him what he would leave himself, he replied, his hopes. "Your soldiers," replied Perdiccas, "will be your partners in those," and refused to accept of the estate he had assigned him.

[Alexander crosses the Hellespont with his army, arriving at the legendary site of Troy in Asia Minor.]

In the mean time Darius's captains having collected large forces, were encamped on the further bank of the river Granicus, and it was necessary to fight, as it were, in the gate of Asia for an entrance into it. The depth of the river, with the unevenness and difficult ascent of the opposite bank, which was to be gained by main force, was apprehended by most, and some pronounced it an improper time to engage, because it was unusual for the kings of Macedonia to march with their forces in the month called Daesius. But Alexander broke through these scruples, telling them they should call it a second Artemisius. And when Parmenio advised him not to attempt any thing that day, because it was late, he told him that he should disgrace the Hellespont, should he fear the Granicus. And so without more saying, he immediately took the river with thirteen troops of horse, and advanced against whole showers of darts thrown from the steep opposite side, which was covered with armed multitudes of the enemy's horse and foot, notwithstanding the disadvantage of the ground and the rapidity of the stream; so that the action seemed to have more of frenzy and

desperation in it, than of prudent conduct. However, he persisted obstinately to gain the passage, and at last with much ado making his way up the banks, which were extremely muddy and slippery, he had instantly to join in a more confused hand-to-hand combat with the enemy, before he could draw up his men, who were still passing over, into any order. For the enemy pressed upon him with loud and warlike outcries; and charging horse against horse, with their lances, after they had broken and spent these, they fell to it with their swords. And Alexander, being easily known by his buckler, and a large plume of white feathers on each side of his helmet, was attacked on all sides, yet escaped wounding, though his cuirass was pierced by a javelin in one of the joinings. And Rhoesaces and Spithridates, two Persian commanders, falling upon him at once, he avoided one of them, and struck at Rhoesaces, who had a good cuirass on, with such force, that his spear breaking in his hand, he was glad to betake himself to his dagger. While they were thus engaged, Spithridates came up on one side of him, and raising himself upon his horse, gave him such a blow with his battle-axe on the helmet, that he cut off the crest of it, with one of his plumes, and the helmet was only just so far strong enough to save him, that the edge of the weapon touched the hair of his head. But as he was about to repeat his stroke, Clitus, called the black Clitus, prevented him, by running him through the body with his spear. At the same time Alexander despatched Phoesaces with his sword. While the horse were thus dangerously engaged, the Macedonian phalanx passed the river, and the foot on each side advanced to fight. But the enemy hardly sustaining the first onset, soon gave ground and fled, all but the mercenary Greeks, who, making a stand upon a rising ground, desired quarter, which Alexander, guided rather by passion than judgment, refused to grant, and charging them himself first, had his horse, (not Bucephalas, but another) killed under him. And this obstinacy of his to cut off these experienced desperate men, cost him the lives of more of his own soldiers than all the battle before, besides those who were wounded. The Persians lost in this battle twenty thousand foot, and two thousand five hundred horse. On Alexander's side, Aristobulus says there were not wanting above four and thirty, of whom nine were foot-soldiers....

GORDIAN'S KNOT

Intelligent

At Gordium, said to be the seat of the ancient Midas, Alexander saw the famous chariot tied with cords made of the bark of the cornel tree. The legend was that whoever untied this Gordian knot would be emperor of the entire world. Some say Alexander cut it asunder with his sword; others that he loosened it by withdrawing the pin from the yoke and then drawing out the yoke itself.

In one way or another, Alexander seized every opportunity to invoke the aid of fate.

[Alexander subsequently captures Darius' wife and family.]

But the most noble and regal part of this treatment of Darius' family was that Alexander did not permit these virtuous prisoners to hear or experience anything unbecoming. It was as if they were lodged in a temple, with sacred and uninterrupted privacy, rather than in the camp of an enemy. Darius was considered the tallest and handsomest man of his time, his wife was believed to be the most beautiful princess, and the daughters not unworthy of their parents. But Alexander sought no intimacy with any of them; he considered it more noble to control himself than to conquer his enemies. He took no notice of the rest of the female captives, though they were remarkably beautiful, other than to say jokingly that the Persian women were terrible eyesores. Displaying the equal beauty of his own temperance and self-control, Alexander ordered them removed from his presence. He severely reprimanded those who wanted to bring him youths who were famed for their beauty. He said that sleep and the act of generation reminded him that he was mortal, implying that both weariness and sensual pleasure reflect the frailty of man. Except for Barsine, Memnon's widow, who was taken prisoner at Damascus, Alexander was intimate with no woman prior to his marriage.

mercy & honor

Alexander did not indulge himself with food either. Every day the lady Ada, whom he fondly called mother, and whom he later made queen of Caria, sent him many different dishes, and would have also furnished him with skilled cooks and pastrymakers. But Alexander refused all, saying that his tutor Leonidas supplied the best: a march before daybreak to whet his appetite for the noon meal, and a light noon meal to whet his appetite for the evening meal. When any rare fish or fruits were sent him, he would give them to his friends, often keeping nothing for himself. But he always served a magnificent table for his guests. He was very careful that everyone was served equally and with proper attention. The cost of his hospitality constantly increased, as his fortune did, until it amounted to ten thousand drachmas a day. Alexander limited the expenditure to that amount and would not allow anyone else to spend more in entertaining him.

And to strengthen his precepts by example, he applied himself now more vigorously than ever to hunting and warlike expeditions, embracing all opportunities of hardship and danger, insomuch that a Lacedaemonian, who was there on an embassy to him, and chanced to be by when he encountered with and mastered a huge lion, told him he had fought gallantly with the beast, which of the two should be king. Craterus caused a representation to be made of this adventure, consisting of the lion and the dogs, of the king engaged with the lion, and himself coming in to his assistance, all expressed in figures of brass, some of which were by Lysippus, and the rest by Leochares; and had it dedicated in the temple of Apollo at Delphi. Alexander exposed his person to danger in this manner, with the object both of inuring himself, and inciting others to the performance of brave and virtuous actions.

MARCH INTO PARTHIA

From hence he marched into Parthia, where not having much to do, he first put on the barbaric dress, perhaps with the view of making the work of civilizing them the easier, as nothing gains more upon men than a conformity to their fashions and customs. Or it may have been as a first trial, whether the Macedonians might be brought to adore him, as the Persians did their kings, by accustoming them by little and little to bear with the alteration of his rule and course of life in other things. At first he wore this habit only when he conversed with the barbarians, or within doors, among his intimate friends and companions, but afterwards he appeared in it abroad, when he rode out, and at public audiences, a sight which the Macedonians beheld with grief; but they so respected his other virtues and good qualities that they felt it reasonable in some things to gratify his fancies and his passion of glory, in pursuit of which he hazarded himself so far, that besides his other adventures, he had but lately been wounded in the leg by an arrow, which had so shattered the shank-bone that splinters were taken out.

The king had a present of Grecian fruit brought him from the sea-coast, which was so fresh and beautiful, that he surprised at it, and called Clitus to him to see it, and to give him a share of it. Clitus was then sacrificing, but he stayed not to finish his devotions, but came straight to supper with the king, who had sacrificed to Castor and Pollux. And when they had drunk pretty hard, at last Clitus, who had drunk too much, and was besides of a forward and willful temper, was so nettled that he could hold no longer, saying, it was not well done to expose the Macedonians so before the barbarians and their enemies, since though it was their unhappiness to be overcome, yet they were much better men than those who laughed at them. And when Alexander remarked, that Clitus was pleading his own cause, giving cowardice the name of misfortune, Clitus started up; "This cowardice, as you are pleased to term it," said he to him, "saved the life of a son of the gods, when in flight from Spithridates's sword; and it is by the expense of Macedonian blood, and by these wounds, that you are now raised to such a height, as to be able to disown your father Philip, and call yourself the son of Ammon." "Thou base fellow," said Alexander, who was now thoroughly exasperated, "dost thou think to utter these things everywhere of me, and stir up the Macedonians to sedition, and not be punished for it?"

But Clitus for all this would not give over, desiring Alexander to speak out if he had any thing more to say, or else why did he invite men who were free-born and accustomed to speak their minds openly without restraint, to sup with him. He had better live and converse with barbarians and slaves who would not

speaks native langs.

scruple to bow the knee to his Persian girdle and his white tunic. Which words so provoked Alexander, that not able to suppress his anger any longer, he threw one of the apples that lay upon the table at him, and hit him, and then looked about for his sword. But Aristophanes, one of his life-guard, had hid that out of the way, and others came about him and besought him, but in vain. For breaking from them, he called out aloud to his guards in the Macedonian language, which was a certain sign of some great disturbance in him, and commanded a trumpeter to sound, giving him a blow with his clenched fist for not instantly obeying him; though afterwards the same man was commended for disobeying an order which would have put the whole army into tumult and confusion. Clitus still refusing to yield, was with much trouble forced by his friends out of the room. But he came in again immediately at another door, very irreverently and confidently singing the verses out of Euripides's Andromache—

"In Greece, alas! how ill things ordered are!"

Upon this, at last, Alexander, snatching a spear from one of the soldiers, met Clitus as he was coming forward and was putting by the curtain that hung before the door, and ran him through the body. He fell at once with a cry and a groan. Upon which the king's anger immediately vanishing, he came perfectly to himself, and when he saw his friends about him all in a profound silence, he pulled the spear out of the dead body, and would have thrust it into his own throat, if the guards had not held his hands, and by main force carried him away into his chamber, where all that night and the next day he wept bitterly, till being quite spent with lamenting and exclaiming, he lay as it were speechless, only fetching deep sighs.

Alexander now intent upon his expedition into India, took notice that his soldiers were so charged with booty that it hindered their marching. Therefore, at break of day, as soon as the baggage wagons were laden, first he set fire to his own, and to those of his friends, and then commanded those to be burnt which belonged to the rest of the army. An act which in the deliberation of it had seemed more dangerous and difficult than it proved in the execution, with which few were dissatisfied; for most of the soldiers, as if they had been inspired, uttering loud outcries and warlike shoutings, supplied one another with what was absolutely necessary, and burnt and destroyed all that was superfluous, the sight of which redoubled Alexander's zeal and eagerness for his design. And, indeed, he was now grown very severe and inexorable in punishing those who committed any fault. For he put Menander, one of his friends, to death, for deserting a fortress where he had placed him in garrison, and shot Orsodates, one of the barbarians who revolted from him, with his own hand.

Kills friends

[At the Hydaspes River, Alexander fights a bloody battle with the Indian king Porus.]

Porus himself was said to be over seven feet tall; and when he sat upon his elephant, which was one of the largest, he appeared, in proportion to the elephant, as the usual horseman on his horse. During the battle this elephant showed extraordinary wisdom and concern for the King, his rider. As long as Porus was strong enough to fight, the elephant courageously defended, repelling all who attacked him. When Porus was overpowered by the darts thrown at him, the elephant knelt down and began to pull out the darts from the King's body with his long trunk.

When Porus was captured, Alexander asked him how he expected to be treated, "As a king," replied Porus. When asked to be more specific, Porus said he had nothing more to request, "for everything is understood in the word king." Accordingly, Alexander not only allowed Porus to govern his own kingdom as a satrap under himself, but added to it several other territories of independent tribes.

But this last combat with Porus took off the edge of the Macedonians' courage, and stayed their further progress into India. For having found it hard enough to defeat an enemy who brought but twenty thousand foot and two thousand horse into the field, they thought they had reason to oppose Alexander's design of leading them on to pass the Ganges too, which they were told was thirty-two furlongs broad and a hundred fathoms deep, and the banks on the further side covered with multitudes of enemies. For they were told that the

kings of the Gandaritans and Praesians expected them there with eighty thousand armed chariots, and six thousand fighting elephants. Alexander at first was so grieved and enraged at his men's reluctancy, that he shut himself up in his tent, and threw himself upon the ground, declaring, if they would not pass the Ganges, he owed them no thanks for any thing they had hitherto done, and that to retreat now, was plainly to confess himself vanquished. But at last the reasonable persuasions of his friends and the cries and lamentations of his soldiers, who in a suppliant manner crowded about the entrance of his tent, prevailed with him to think of returning.

At Susa, he married Darius's daughter Statira, and celebrated also the nuptials of his friends, bestowing the noblest of the Persian ladies upon the worthiest of them, at the same time making it an entertainment in honor of the other Macedonians whose marriages had already taken place. At this magnificent festival, it is reported, there were no less than nine thousand guests, to each of whom he gave a golden cup for the libations. Not to mention other instances of his wonderful magnificence, he paid the debts of his army, which amounted to nine thousand eight hundred and seventy talents. As he was upon his way to Babylon, Nearchus, who had sailed back out of the ocean up the mouth of the river Euphrates, came to tell him he had met with some Chaldaean diviners, who had warned him against Alexander's going thither. Alexander, however, took no thought of it, and went on, and when he came near the walls of the place, he saw a great many crows fighting with one another, some of whom fell down just by him. After this, being privately informed that Apollodorus, the governor of Babylon, had sacrificed, to know what would become of him, he sent for Pythagoras, the soothsayer, and on his admitting the thing, asked him, in what condition he found the victim; and when he told him the liver was defective in its lobe, "A great presage indeed!" said Alexander. However, he offered Pythagoras no injury, but was sorry that he had neglected Nearchus's advice, and stayed for the most part outside the town, removing his tent from place to place, and sailing up and down the Euphrates. Besides this, he was disturbed by many other

• imatates the Persian empire, takes over but does not change anything there

prodigies. A tame ass fell upon the biggest and handsomest lion that he kept, and killed him by a kick.

When once Alexander had given way to fears of supernatural influence, his mind grew so disturbed and so easily alarmed, that if the least unusual or extraordinary thing happened, he thought it a prodigy or a presage. But upon some answers which were brought him from the oracle concerning Hephaestion, he laid aside his sorrow, and fell again to sacrificing and drinking; and having given Nearchus a splendid entertainment, after he had bathed, as was his custom, just as he was going to bed, at Medius's request he went to supper with him. Here he drank all the next day, and was attacked with a fever, which seized him, not as some write, after he had drunk of the bowl of Hercules; nor was he taken with any sudden pain in his back, as if he had been struck with a lance, for these are the inventions of some authors who thought it their duty to make the last scene of so great an action as tragical and moving as they could. Aristobulus tells us, he took a draught of wine, upon which he fell into delirium, and died on the thirtieth day of the month Daesius.

But the journals give the following record. On the eighteenth of the month, he slept in the bathing-room on account of his fever. The next day he bathed and removed into his chamber, and spent his time in playing at dice with Medius. In the evening he bathed and sacrificed, and ate freely, and had the fever on him through the night. On the twentieth, after the usual sacrifices and bathing, he lay in the bathing-room and heard Nearchus's narrative of his voyage, and the observations he had made in the great sea. The twenty-first he passed in the same manner, his fever still increasing, and suffered much during the night. The next day the fever was very violent, and he had himself removed and his bed set by the great bath, and discoursed with his principal officers about finding fit men to fill up the vacant places in the army. On the twenty-fourth he was much worse, and was carried out of his bed to assist at the sacrifices, and gave order that the general officers should wait within the court, whilst the inferior officers kept watch without doors. On the twenty-fifth he was removed to his palace on the other side the

river, where he slept a little, but his fever did not abate, and when the generals came into his chamber, he was speechless, and continued so the following day. The Macedonians, therefore, supposing he was dead, came with great clamors to the gates, and menaced his friends so they were forced to admit them, and let them all pass through unarmed along by his bedside. The same day Python and Seleucus were despatched to the temple of Serapis to inquire if they should bring Alexander thither, and were answered by the god, that they should not remove him. On the twenty-eighth, in the evening, he died. This account is most of it word for word as it is written in the diary.

✝

E. THE PRAYER AT OPIS
ARRIAN

Another account of Alexander, written about half a century after Plutarch's Life by Arrian of Nicomedia (c. A. D. 150) describes the wedding ceremony between Macedonian generals and Persian princesses that Alexander presided over shortly before his death.

Alexander celebrated the occasion by sacrificing to the gods he normally sacrificed to, and offering a public banquet. He sat down and so did everyone else, the Macedonians around him, the Persians next to them, then any of the other peoples who enjoyed precedence for their reputation or some other quality. Then he and those around him drew wine from the same bowl and poured the same libations, beginning with the Greek seers and the Magi. He prayed for other blessings and for harmony and partnership in rule between Macedonians and Persians. It is said that there were 9,000 guests at the banquet, who all poured the same libation and then sang the song of victory.

✝

F. THE LION IN OUR MIDST
ARISTOTLE

ARISTOTLE (384-322 B.C.) was, among other things, Alexander's tutor. He too confronted the new life of Greece, but in this selection from his *Politics* he is dealing with political organization instead of ethics. Who do you think Aristotle had in mind here? Why did he write this? Is the classical polis his idea of the state, or something else? Would Aristotle and Carlyle agree on the importance of the great man?

…Righteousness in regard to laws must be conceived as implying equality and, so conceived, it has reference to the interest of the state as a whole, or in other words to the common interest of the citizens. But while a citizen in general is one who is capable of being a ruler and a subject, yet in each several polity he is different; and relatively to the best polity he is one who has the ability and purpose so to live both as subject and ruler as will conduce to the life which is according to virtue.

If however there is an individual or more persons than one, although not enough to constitute the full complement of a state, so preeminent in their excess of virtue that neither the virtue of all the other citizens nor their political capacity is comparable to theirs, if they are several, or, if it is an individual, to his alone, such persons are not to be regarded any more as part of a state. It will be a wrong to them to treat them as worthy of mere equality when they are so vastly superior in virtue and political capacity, for any person so exceptional may well be compared to a deity upon the earth.

And from this it clearly follows that legislation can be applicable to none but those who are equals in race and capacity; while for persons so exceptional there is no law, as they are a law in themselves. For any attempt to legislate for them would be ridiculous; they would probably make the same reply as did the lions in Antisthenes's story to the declamation of the hares when they demanded universal equality.

❖

3. CAESAR AND ROME

Alexander is the Greek case for a "great man;" the Roman example is Julius Caesar. Caesar's case rests in part, like Alexander's, on sheer military success; but there is more to it than that. There is also the question of fulfilling, and then transcending, a society's vision of greatness. The following selections offer a glimpse of the ideal and the real in the career of Caius Julius Caesar.

A. THE AENEID

VERGIL

Aeneas, the hero of Vergil's great Roman epic, was the legendary founder of the Julian line, which traced its ancestry to Aeneas's son, Iulus. He was also meant by Vergil to be the model Roman. What Roman values can you identify in the following passages? Keep these in mind when you read the next passage on Julius Caesar, and consider how well you think he lived up to them.

Book IV: Dido and Aeneas

[A fugitive from Troy, Aeneas has been shipwrecked at Carthage, where he receives shelter from its queen, Dido. The goddess Juno wants to thwart the will of her husband, Jupiter (Jove) and keep Aeneas from founding a 'ruling race' in Italy. She has tricked Aeneas and Dido into a love affair, hoping this will keep him from leaving. But Jupiter learns of the affair and sends his messenger, Mercury, to get Aeneas back on track.]

Jove spake. Mercury now got ready to obey.
As soon as his winged feet had carried him to
    the shacks there,
He noticed Aeneas superintending the work
    on towers
And new buildings: he wore a sword studded
    with yellow
Jaspers, and a fine cloak of flowing Tyrian
    purple
Hung from his shoulders—the wealthy Dido
    had fashioned it,
Interweaving the fabric with threads of gold,
    as a present for him.
Mercury went for him at once:—
              So now you are laying
Foundations for lofty Carthage, building a
    beautiful city
To please a woman, lost to the interests of
    your realm?
The king of the gods, who directs heaven and
    earth with his deity,

Sends me to you from bright Olympus: the
  king of the gods
Gave me this message to carry express through
  the air:—What do you
Aim at or hope for, idling and fiddling here in
  Libya?
If you're indifferent to your own high destiny
And for your own renown you will make no
  effort at all,
Think of your young hopeful, Ascanius,
  growing to manhood,
The inheritance which you owe him—an Ital-
  ian kingdom, the soil of Rome.

Final Paper

Such were the words which Mercury delivered;
And breaking off abruptly, was manifest no
  more,
But vanished into thin air, far beyond human
  ken.
 Dazed indeed by that vision was Aeneas, and
  dumbfounded:
His hair stood on end with terror, the voice
  stuck in his throat.
Awed by this admonition from the great
  throne above,
He desired to fly the country, dear though it
  was to him.
But oh, what was he to do? What words could
  he find to get round
The temperamental queen? How broach the
  matter to her?
His mind was in feverish conflict, tossed from
  one side to the other,
Twisting and turning all ways to find a way
  past his dilemma.
So vacillating, at last he felt this the better de-
  cision:—
Sending for Mnestheus, Sergestus and brave
  Serestus, he bade them
Secretly get the ships ready, muster their
  friends on the beach,
Be prepared to fight: the cause of so drastic a
  change of plan
They must keep dark: in the meanwhile, as-
  suming that generous Dido
Knew nothing and could not imagine the end
  of so great a love,
Aeneas would try for a way to approach her,
  the kindest moment
For speaking, the best way to deal with this
  delicate matter. His comrades
Obeyed the command and did as he told them
  with cheerful alacrity.

But who can ever hoodwink a woman in love?
  The queen,
Apprehensive even when things went well,
  now sensed his deception,
Got wind of what was going to happen. That
  mischievous,
Whispering the fleet was preparing to sail, put
  her in a frenzy.
Distraught, she witlessly wandered about the
  city, raving
Like some Bacchante driven wild, when the
  emblems of sanctity
Stir, by the shouts of "Hail, Bacchus!" and
  drawn to Cithaeron
At night by the din of revellers, at the triennial
  orgies.
Finding Aeneas at last, she cried, before he
  could speak:—
 Unfaithful man, did you think you could do
  such a dreadful thing
And keep it dark? yes, skulk from my land
  without one word?
Our love, the vows you made me—do these
  not give you pause,
Nor even the thought of Dido meeting a
  painful death?
Now, in the dead of winter, to be getting your
  ships ready
And hurrying to set sail when northerly gales
  are blowing,
You heartless one! Suppose the fields were not
  foreign, the home was
Not strange that you are bound for, suppose
  Troy stood as of old,
Would you be sailing for Troy, now, in this
  stormy weather?
Am I your reason for going? By these tears, by
  the hand you gave me—
They are all I have left, to-day, in my misery—
  I implore you,
And by our union of hearts, by our marriage
  hardly begun,
If I have ever helped you at all, if anything
About me pleased you, be sad for our broken
  home, forgo
Your purpose, I beg you, unless it's too late for
  prayers of mine!
Because of you, the Libyan tribes and the
  Nomad chieftains
Hate me, the Tyrians are hostile: because of
  you I have lost
My old reputation for faithfulness—the one
  thing that could have made me

Immortal. Oh, I am dying! To what, my guest,
    are you leaving me?
"Guest"—that is all I may call you now, who
    have called you husband.
Why do I linger here? Shall I wait till my
    brother, Pygmalion,
Destroys this place, or Iarbas leads me away
    captive?
If even I might have conceived a child by you
    before
You went away, a little Aeneas to play in the
    palace
And, in spite of all this, to remind me of you
    by his looks, oh then
I should not feel so utterly finished and deso-
    late.
  She had spoken. Aeneas, mindful of Jove's
    words, kept his eyes
Unyielding, and with a great effort repressed
    his feeling for her.
In the end he managed to answer:—
                   Dido, I'll never pretend
You have not been good to me, deserving of
    everything
You can claim. I shall not regret my memories
    of Elissa
As long as I breathe, as long as I remember my
    own self.
For my conduct—this, briefly: I did not look
    to make off from here
In secret—do not suppose it; nor did I offer
    you marriage
At any time or consent to be bound by a mar-
    riage contract.
If fate allowed me to be my own master, and
    gave me
Free will to choose my way of life, to solve my
    problems,
Old Troy would be my first choice: I would
    restore it, and honor
My people's relics—the high halls of Priam
    perpetuated,
Troy given back to its conquered sons, a re-
    naissant city,
Had been my task. But now Apollo and the
    Lycian
Oracle have told me that Italy is our bourne.
There lies my heart, my homeland. You, a
    Phoenician, are held by
These Carthaginian towers, by the charm of
    your Libyan city:
So can you grudge us Trojans our vision of
    settling down

In Italy? We too may seek a kingdom abroad.
Often as night envelops the earth in dewy
    darkness,
Often as star-rise, the troubled ghost of my
    father, Anchises,
Comes to me in my dreams, warns me and
    frightens me.
I am disturbed no less by the wrong I am do-
    ing Ascanius,
Defrauding him of his destined realm in
    Hesperia.
What's more, must now the courier of heaven,
    sent by Jupiter—
I swear it on your life and mine—conveyed to
    me, swiftly flying,
His orders: I saw the god, as clear as day, with
    my own eyes,
Entering the city, and these ears drank in the
    words he uttered.
No more reproaches, then—they only torture
    us both.
God's will, not mine, says "Italy."
  All the while he was speaking she gazed at
    him askance,
Her glances flickering over him, eyes exploring
    the whole man
In deadly silence. Now, furiously, she burst
    out:—
 Faithless and false! No goddess mothered
    you, no Dardanus
Your ancestor! I believe harsh Caucasus begat
    you
On a flint-hearted rock and Hyrcanian tigers
    suckled you.
Why should I hide my feelings? What worse
    can there be to keep them for?
 Not one sigh from him when I wept! Not a
    softer glance!
Did he yield an inch, or a tear, in pity for her
    who loves him?
I don't know what to say first. It has come to
    this,—not Juno,
Not Jove himself can view my plight with the
    eye of justice.
Nowhere is it safe to be trustful. I took him, a
    castaway,
A pauper, and shared my kingdom with
    him—I must have been mad—
Rescued his lost fleet, rescued his friends from
    death.
Oh, I'm on fire and drifting! And now Apol-
    lo's prophecies,

Lycian oracles, couriers of heaven sent by
  Jupiter
With stern commands—all these order you to
  betray me.
Oh, of course this is just the sort of transaction
  that troubles the calm of
The gods. I'll not keep you, nor probe the dis-
  honesty of your words.
Chase your Italy, then! Go, sail to your realm
  overseas!
I only hope that, if the just spirits have any
  power,
Marooned on some mid-sea rock you may
  drink the full cup of agony
And often cry out for Dido. I'll dog you, from
  far, with the death-fires;
And when cold death has parted my soul from
  my body, my sceptre
Will be wherever you are. You shall pay for
  the evil you've done me.
The tale of your punishment will come to me
  down in the shades.
  With these words Dido suddenly ended, and
  sick at heart
Turned from him, tore herself away from his
  eyes, ran indoors,
While he hung back in dread of a still worse
  scene, although
He had much to say. Her maids bore up the
  fainting queen
Into her marble chamber and laid her down on
  the bed.
  [Dido sends her sister, Anna, to change Ae-
  neas' mind, but to no avail.]
  But hapless Dido, frightened out of her wits
  by her destiny,
Prayed for death: she would gaze no more on
  the dome of daylight.
And now, strengthening her resolve to act and
  to leave this world,
She saw, as she laid gifts on the incense-
  burning altars—
Horrible to relate—the holy water turn black
And the wine she poured changing uncannily
  to blood.
She told no one, not even her sister, of this
  phenomenon.
So when, overmastered by grief, she conceived
  a criminal madness
And doomed herself to death, she worked out
  the time and method
In secret; then, putting on an expression of
  calm hopefulness

To hide her resolve, she approached her sor-
  rowing sister with these words:—
 I have found out a way, Anna—oh, wish me
  joy of it—
To get him back or else get free of my love for
  him.
Near Ocean's furthest bound and the sunset is
  Aethiopia,
The very last place on earth, where giant Atlas
  pivots
The Wheeling sky, embossed with fiery stars,
  on his shoulders.
I have been in touch with a priestess from
  there, a Massylian, who once,
As warden of the Hesperides' sacred close, was
  used to
Feed the dragon which guarded their orchard
  of golden apples,
Sprinkling its food with moist honey and
  sedative poppy-seeds.
Now this enchantress claims that her spells
  can liberate
One's heart, or can inject love-pangs, just as
  she wishes;
Can stop the flow of rivers, send the stars fly-
  ing backwards,
Conjure ghosts in the night: she can make the
  earth cry out
Under one's feet, and elm trees come trooping
  down from the mountains.
Dear sister, I solemnly call to witness the gods
  and you whom
I love, that I do not willingly resort to her
  magic arts.
You must build up a funeral pyre high in the
  inner courtyard,
And keep it dark: lay on it the arms which that
  godless man
Has left on the pegs in our bedroom, all relics
  of him, and the marriage-bed
That was the ruin of me. To blot out all that
  reminds me
Of that vile man is my pleasure and what the
  enchantress directs.
 So Dido spoke, and fell silent, her face going
  deadly white.
Yet Anna never suspected that Dido was
  planning her own death
Through these queer rites, nor imagined how
  frantic a madness possessed her,
Nor feared any worse would happen than
  when Sychaeus had died.
So she made the arrangements required of her.

When in the innermost court of the palace
    the pyre had been built up
To a great height with pinewood and logs of
    ilex, the queen
Festooned the place with garlands and
    wreathed it with funeral
Foliage: then she laid on it the clothes, the
    sword which Aeneas
Had left, and an effigy of him; she well knew
    what was to happen.
Was night. All over the earth, creatures were
    plucking the flower
Of soothing sleep, the woods and the wild seas
    fallen quiet—
A time when constellations have reached their
    mid-career,
When the countryside is all still, the beasts
    and the brilliant birds
That haunt the lakes' wide waters or the tan-
    gled undergrowth
Of the champain, stilled in sleep under the
    quiet night—
Cares are lulled and hearts can forget for a
    while their travails.
Not so the Phoenician queen: death at her
    heart, she could not
Ever relax in sleep, let the night in to her eyes
Or mind: her agonies mounted, her love
    reared up again
And savaged her, till she writhed in a boiling
    sea of passion.
So thus she began, her thoughts whirling
    round in a vicious circle:—
What shall I do? Shall I, who've been jilted,
    return to my former
Suitors? go down on my knees for marriage to
    one of the Nomads
Although, time and again, I once rejected
    their offers?
Well then, am I to follow the Trojan's fleet
    and bow to
Their lightest word? I helped them once. Will
    that help me now?
Dare I think they remember with gratitude my
    old kindness?
But even if I wished it, who would suffer me,
    welcome me
Aboard those arrogant ships? They hate me.
    Ah, duped and ruined!—
Surely by now I should know the ill faith of
    Laomedon's people?
So then? Shall I sail, by myself, with those ex-
    ulting mariners,

Or sail against them with all my Tyrian folk
    about me—
My people, whom once I could hardly per-
    suade to depart from Sidon—
Bidding them man their ships and driving
    them out to sea again?
Better die—I deserve it—end my pain with
    the sword.
Sister, you started it all: overborne by my tears,
    you laid up
These evils to drive me mad, put me at the
    mercy of a foe.
Oh, that I could have been some child of na-
    ture and lived
An innocent life, untouched by marriage and
    all its troubles!
I have broken the faith I vowed to the memory
    of Sichaeus.
Such were the reproaches she could not re-
    frain from uttering.
High on the poop of his ship, resolute now for
    departure,
Aeneas slept; preparations for sailing were
    fully completed.
To him in a dream there appeared the shape of
    the god, returning
Just as he'd looked before, as if giving the same
    admonitions—
Mercury's very image, the voice, the complex-
    ion, the yellow
Hair and the handsome youthful body identi-
    cal:—
Goddess-born, can you go on sleeping at such
    a crisis?
Are you out of your mind, not to see what
    dangers are brewing up
Around you, and not to hear the favoring
    breath of the West wind?
Being set upon death, her heart is aswirl with
    conflicting passions,
Aye, she is brooding now some trick, some
    desperate deed.
Why are you not going, all speed, while the
    going is good?
If dawn finds you still here, delaying by these
    shores,
You'll have the whole sea swarming with hos-
    tile ships, there will be
Firebrands coming against you, you'll see this
    beach ablaze.
Up and away, then! No more lingering!
    Woman was ever
A veering, weathercock creature.

He spoke, and vanished in the darkness.
Then, startled by the shock of the apparition, Aeneas
Snatched himself out of sleep and urgently stirred up his comrades:—
Jump to it, men! To your watch! Get to the rowing benches!
Smartly! Hoist the sails! A god from heaven above
Spurs me to cut the cables, make off and lose not a moment:
This was his second warning. O blessed god, we follow you,
God indeed, and once more we obey the command joyfully!
Be with us! Look kindly upon us! Grant us good sailing weather!
Thus did Aeneas cry, and flashing his sword from its scabbard,
With the drawn blade he severed the moorings. The same sense of
Urgency fired his comrades all; they cut and ran for it.
The shore lay empty. The ships covered the open sea.
The oarsmen swept the blue and sent the foam flying with hard strokes.
And now was Aurora, leaving the saffron bed of Tithonus,
Beginning to shower upon earth the light of another day.
The queen, looking forth from her roof-top, as soon as she saw the sky
Grow pale and the Trojan fleet running before the wind,
Aware that the beach and the roadstead were empty, the sailors gone,
Struck herself three times, four times, upon her lovely breast,
Tore at her yellow hair, and exclaimed:—
In god's name! shall that foreigner
Scuttle away and make a laughing-stock of my country?
Will not my people stand to arms for a mass pursuit?
Will some not rush the warships out of the docks? Move, then!
Bring firebrands apace, issue the weapons, pull on the oars!
What am I saying? Where am I? What madness veers my mind?
Poor Dido, the wrong you have done—is it only now coming home to you?

You should have thought of that when you gave him your sceptre.
            So this is
The word of honor of one who, men say, totes round his home-gods
Everywhere, and bore on his back a doddering father!
Why could I not have seized him, torn up his body and littered
The sea with it? finished his friends with the sword, finished his own
Ascanius and served him up for his father to banquet on?
The outcome of battle had been uncertain?— Let it have been so:
Since I was to die, whom had I to fear? I should have stormed
Their bulwarks with fire, set alight their gangways, gutted the whole lot—
Folk, father and child—then flung myself on the conflagration.
O sun, with your beams surveying all that is done on earth!
Juno, the mediator and witness of my tragedy!
Hecate, whose name is howled by night at the city crossroads!
Avenging Furies, and you, the patrons of dying Elissa!—
Hear me! Incline your godheads to note this wickedness
So worthy of your wrath! And hear my prayer! If he,
That damned soul, must make port and get to land, if thus
Jove destines it, if that bourne is fixed for him irrevocably,
May he be harried in war by adventurous tribes, and exiled
From his own land; may Ascanius be torn from his arms; may he have to
Sue for aid, and see his own friends squalidly dying.
Yes, and when he's accepted the terms of a harsh peace,
Let him never enjoy his realm or the allotted span,
But fall before his time and lie on the sands, unburied.
That is my last prayer. I pour it out, with my lifeblood.
Let you, my Tyrians, sharpen your hatred upon his children

And all their seed for ever: send this as a present to

My ghost. Between my people and his, no love, no alliance!

Rise up from my dead bones, avenger! Rise up, one

To hound the Trojan settlers with fire and steel remorselessly,

Now, some day, whenever the strength for it shall be granted!

Shore to shore, sea to sea, weapon to weapon opposed—

I call down a feud between them and us to the last generation!

But Dido, trembling, distraught by the terrible thing she was doing,

Her bloodshot eyes restless, with hectic blotches upon

Her quivering cheeks, yet pale with the shade of advancing death,

Ran to the innermost court of the palace, climbed the lofty

Pyre, frantic at heart, and drew Aeneas' sword—

Her present to him, procured once for a far different purpose.

Then, after eyeing the clothes he had left behind, and the memoried

Bed, pausing to weep and brood on him for a little,

She lay down on the bed and spoke her very last words:—

O relics of him, things dear to me while fate, while heaven allowed it,

Receive this life of mine, release me from my troubles!

I have lived, I have run to the finish the course which fortune gave me:

And now, a queenly shade, I shall pass to the world below.

I built a famous city, saw my own place established,

Avenged a husband, exacted a price for a brother's enmity.

Happy I would have been, ah, beyond words happy,

If only the Trojan ships had never come to my shore!

These words; then, burying her face in the bed:—

Shall I die unavenged?

At least, let me die. Thus, thus! I go to the dark, go gladly.

May he look long, from out there on the deep, at my flaming pyre,

The heartless! And may my death-fires signal bad luck for his voyage!

She had spoken; and with these words, her attendants saw her falling

Upon the sword, they could see the blood spouting up over

The blade, and her hands spattered. Their screams rang to the roofs of

The palace; then rumor ran amok through the shocked city.

All was weeping and wailing, the streets were filled with a keening

Of women, the air resounded with terrible lamentations.

It was as if Carthage or ancient Tyre should be falling,

With enemy troops breaking into the town and a conflagration

Furiously sweeping over the abodes of men and of gods.

Anna heard it: half dead from extreme fear, she ran through

The crowd, tearing her cheeks with her nails, beating her breast

With her fists, and called aloud by name on the dying woman:—

So this was your purpose, Dido? You were making a dupe of me?

That pyre, those lighted altars—for me, they were leading to this?

How shall I chide you for leaving me? Were you too proud to let your

Sister die with you? You should have called me to share your end:

One hour, one pang of the sword could have carried us both away.

Did I build this pyre with my own hands, invoking our family gods,

So that you might lie on it, and I, the cause of your troubles, not be there?

You have destroyed more than yourself—me, and the lords

And commons and city of Sidon. Quick! Water for her wounds!

Let me bathe them, and if any last breath is fluttering from her mouth,

Catch it in mine!

So saying, she had scaled the towering pyre,

Taken the dying woman into her lap, was caressing her,

Sobbing, trying to staunch the dark blood with
    her own dress.
Dido made an effort to raise her heavy eyes,
Then gave it up: the sword-blade grated
    against her breast bone.
Three times she struggled to rise, to lift herself
    on an elbow,
Three times rolled back on the bed. Her wan-
    dering gaze went up
To the sky, looking for light: she gave a moan
    when she saw it.
  Then did almighty Juno take pity on her
    long-drawn-out
Sufferings and hard going, sent Iris down
    from Olympus
To part the agonised soul from the body that
    still clung to it.
Since she was dying neither a natural death
    nor from others'
Violence, but desperate and untimely, driven
    to it
By a crazed impulse, not yet had Proserpine
    clipped from her head
The golden tress, or consigned her soul to the
    Underworld.
So now, all dewy, her pinions the color of yel-
    low crocus,
Her wake a thousand rainbow hues refracting
    the sunlight,
Iris flew down, and over Dido hovering,
    said:—
  As I was bidden, I take this sacred thing, the
    Death-god's
Due: and you I release from your body.
              She snipped the tress.
Then all warmth went at once, the life was lost
    in air.

Book VI: The Underworld

[Guided by the Cumaean Sibyl, Aeneas has
reached the waters of the underground river
Acheron in his journey to the underworld.]

Here a whirlpool boils with mud and immense
    swirlings
Of water, spouting up all the slimy sand of
    Cocytus.
A dreadful ferryman looks after the river
    crossing,
Charon: appallingly filthy he is, with a bush of
    unkempt
White beard upon his chin, white eyes like jets
    of fire;

And a dirty cloak draggles down, knotted
    about his shoulders.
He poles the boat, he looks after the sails, he is
    all the crew
Of that rust-colored wherry which takes the
    dead across—
An ancient now, but a god's old age is green
    and sappy.
This way came fast and streaming up to the
    bank the whole throng:
Matrons and men were there, and there were
    great-hearted heroes
Finished with earthly life, boys and unmarried
    maidens,
Young men laid on the pyre before their par-
    ents' eyes;
Multitudinous as the leaves that fall in a forest
At the first frost of autumn, or the birds that
    out of deep-sea
Fly to land in migrant flocks, when the cold of
    the year
Has sent them overseas in search of a warmer
    climate.
So they all stood, each begging to be ferried
    across first,
Their hands stretched out in longing for the
    shore beyond the river.
But the surly ferryman embarks now this, now
    that group,
While others he keeps away at a distance from
    the shingle.
Aeneas, being astonished and moved by the
    great stir, said:—
  Tell me, O Sibyl, what means this rendezvous
    at the river?
What purpose have these souls? By what dis-
    tinction are some
Turned back, while other souls sweep over the
    wan water?
To which the long-lived Sibyl uttered this
    brief reply:—
  O son of Anchises' loins and true-born off-
    spring of heaven,
What you see is the mere of Cocytus, the Sty-
    gian marsh
By whose mystery even the gods, having
    sworn, are afraid to be forsworn.
All this crowd you see are the helpless ones,
    the unburied:
That ferryman is Charon: the ones he conveys
    have had burial.
None may be taken across from bank to awe-
    some bank of

the unburied could not cross

That harsh-voiced river until his bones are laid
    to rest.
Otherwise, he must haunt this place for a
    hundred years
Before he's allowed to revisit the longed-for
    stream at last.
 The son of Anchises paused and stood stock
    still, in deep
Meditation, pierced to the heart by pity for
    their hard fortune….
So they resumed their interrupted journey, and
    drew near
The river. Now when the ferryman, from out
    on the Styx, espied them
Threading the soundless wood and making
    fast for the bank,
He hailed them, aggressively shouting at them
    before they could speak:—
 Whoever you are that approaches my river,
    carrying a weapon,
Halt there! Keep your distance, and tell me
    why you are come!
This is the land of ghosts, of sleep and somno-
    lent night:
The living are not permitted to use the Stygian
    ferry.
Not with impunity did I take Hercules,
When he came, upon this water, nor Theseus,
    nor Pirithous,
Though their stock was divine and their pow-
    ers were irresistible.
Hercules wished to drag off on a leash the
    watch-dog of Hades,
Even from our monarch's throne, and dragged
    it away trembling:
The others essayed to kidnap our queen from
    her lord's bed-chamber.
 The priestess of Apollo answered him shortly,
    thus:—
There is no such duplicity here, so set your
    mind at rest;
These weapons offer no violence: the huge
    watch-dog in his kennel
May go on barking for ever and scaring the
    bloodless dead,
Proserpine keep her uncle's house, unthreat-
    ened in chastity.
Trojan Aeneas, renowned for war and a du-
    teous heart,
Comes down to meet his father in the shades
    of the Underworld.
If you are quite unmoved by the spectacle of
    such great faith,

This you must recognize—
    And here she disclosed the golden
Bough which was hid in her robe. His angry
    mood calms down.
No more is said. Charon is struck with awe to
    see
After so long that magic gift, the bough fate-
    given;
He turns his sombre boat and poles it towards
    the bank.
Then, displacing the souls who were seated
    along its benches
And clearing the gangways, to make room for
    the big frame of Aeneas,
He takes him on board. The ramshackle craft
    creaked under his weight
And let in through its seams great swashes of
    muddy water.
At last, getting the Sibyl and the hero safe
    across,
He landed them amidst wan reeds on a dreary
    mud flat.
 Huge Cerberus, monstrously couched in a
    cave confronting them,
Made the whole region echo with his three-
    throated barking.
The Sibyl, seeing the snakes bristling upon his
    neck now,
Threw him for bait a cake of honey and wheat
    infused with
Sedative drugs. The creature, crazy with
    hunger, opened
Its three mouths, gobbled the bait; then its
    huge body relaxed
And lay, sprawled out on the ground, the
    whole length of its cave kennel.
Aeneas, passing its entrance, the watch-dog
    neutralised,
Strode rapidly from the bank of that river of
    no return.
At once were voices heard, a sound of mewl-
    ing and wailing,
Ghosts of infants sobbing there at the thresh-
    old, infants
From whom a dark day stole their share of
    delicious life,
Snatched them away from the breast, gave
    them sour death to drink.
Next to them were those condemned to death
    on a false charge.
Yet every place is duly allotted and judgment is
    given.

[Handwritten margin notes:]
○ who has gone to the U.W. & why
○ why living can't be there
Why Aeneas is in the U.W.
In case who is there, (name of place is on next pg.)
why (name of place) is on next pg.)

Minos, as president, summons a jury of the dead: he hears

Every charge, examines the record of each; he shakes the urn.

Next again are located the sorrowful ones who killed

Themselves, throwing their lives away, not driven by guilt

But because they loathed living: how they would like to be

In the world above now, enduring poverty and hard trials!

God's law forbids: that unlovely fen with its glooming water

Corrals them there, the nine rings of Styx corral them in.

Not far from here can be seen, extending in all directions,

The vale of mourning—such is the name it bears: a region

Where those consumed by the wasting torments of merciless love

Haunt the sequestered alleys and myrtle groves that give them

Cover; death itself cannot cure them of love's disease.

Here Aeneas descried Phaedra and Procris, sad

Eriphyle displaying the wounds her heartless son once dealt her,

Evadne and Pasiphae; with them goes Laodamia;

Here too is Caeneus, once a young man, but next a woman

And now changed back by fate to his original sex.

Amongst them, with her death-wound still bleeding, through the deep wood

Was straying Phoenician Dido. Now when the Trojan leader

Found himself near her and knew that the form he glimpsed through the shadows

Was hers—as early in the month one sees, or imagines he sees,

Through a wrack of cloud the new moon rising and glimmering—

He shed some tears, and addressed her in tender, loving tones:—

Poor, unhappy Dido, so the message was true that came to me

Saying you'd put an end to your life with the sword and were dead?

Oh god! was it death I brought you, then? I swear by the stars,

By the powers above, by whatever is sacred in the Underworld,

It was not of my own will, Dido, I left your land.

Heaven's commands, which now force me to traverse the shades,

This sour and derelict region, this pit of darkness, drove me

Imperiously from your side. I did not, could not imagine

My going would ever bring such terrible agony on you.

Don't move away! Oh, let me see you a little longer!

To fly from me, when this is the last word fate allows us!

Thus did Aeneas speak, trying to soften the wild-eyed,

Passionate-hearted ghost, and brought the tears to his own eyes.

She would not turn to him; she kept her gaze on the ground,

And her countenance remained as stubborn to his appeal

As if it were carved from recalcitrant flint or a crag or marble.

At last she flung away, hating him still, and vanished

Into the shadowy wood where her first husband, Sychaeus,

Understands her unhappiness and gives her an equal love.

None the less did Aeneas, hard hit by her piteous fate,

Weep after her from afar, as she went, with tears of compassion.

Then he passed on the appointed way. They came to the last part

Of Limbo, the place set apart for men famous in war.

Here Tydeus met him, here that warrior of high renown

Parthenopaeus, here the pale spectre of Adrastus;

Those for whom lamentation had risen on earth—the fallen

Fighters of Troy; Aeneas groaned aloud when he saw those

Long ranks of death—Glaucus, Medon, Thersilochus,

the worst people, worst place

The three sons of Antenor, Polyphoetes the
    priest of Ceres,
Idaeus, still with the arms he bore, the chariot
    he drove once.
To right and left the spirits press thickly
    around Aeneas.

Troy soldiers

Not enough just to have seen him once—they
    want to detain him,
To pace along beside him and find out why he
    has come there.
But the Greek generals and the regiments of
    Agamemnon,

Grk. soldiers

When they beheld his armor glinting through
    the gloom,
Were seized with fear and trembling; some
    turned tail, even as
In the old days they had run for their ships;
    some uttered a wraith of
A war cry—they tried to shout, but their wide
    mouths only whimpered….
Aeneas looked back on a sudden: he saw to
    his left a cliff

place where people are at

Overhanging a spread of battlements, a three-
    fold wall about them,
Girdled too by a swift-running stream, a
    flaming torrent—
Hell's river of fire, whose current rolls clashing
    rocks along.
In front, an enormous portal, the door-posts
    columns of adamant,
So strong that no mortal violence nor even the
    heaven-dwellers
Can broach it: an iron tower stands sheer and
    soaring above it,
Whereupon Tisiphone sits, wrapped in a
    bloodstained robe,
Sleeplessly, day-long, night-long, guarding the
    forecourt there.

People in enormous pain

From within can be heard the sounds of
    groaning and brutal lashing,
Sounds of clanking iron, of chains being
    dragged along.
Scared by the din, Aeneas halted; he could not
    move:—
What kinds of criminals are these? Speak,
    lady! What punishments
Afflict them, that such agonised sounds rise up
    from there?
Then the Sibyl began:—
        O famous lord of the Trojans,
No righteous soul may tread that threshold of
    the damned:

who is there, why, & exs. of punishments

But, when Hecate appointed me to the Av-
    ernian grove,
She instructed me in heaven's punishments,
    showed me all.
Here Rhadamanthus rules, and most severe his
    rule is,
Trying and chastising wrongdoers, forcing
    confessions
From any who, on earth, went gleefully un-
    detected—
But uselessly, since they have only postponed
    till death their atonement.
Here are those who in life hated their own
    brothers,
Or struck their parents; those who entangled
    their dependents
In fraudulent dealing; and those who sat tight
    on the wealth they had won,
Setting none aside for their own kin—most
    numerous of all are these;
Then such as were killed for adultery, took
    part in militant treason,
Men who made bold to break faith with their
    masters:—all such await
Punishment, mewed up here. And seek not to
    know what punishment,
What kind of destined torment awaits each
    one in the Pit.
Some have to roll huge rocks; some whirl
    round, spreadeagled
On spokes of wheels: the tragic Theseus sits,
    condemned to
Spend eternity in that chair: the poor wretch,
    Phlegyas,
Admonishes all, crying out through the mirk
    in solemn avowal,
"Be warned by me! Learn justice, and not to
    belittle the gods!"
One sold his country for gold, putting her un-
    der the yoke of
Dictatorship, and corruptly made and unmade
    her laws;
One entered the bed of his daughter, forced an
    unholy mating:
All dared some abominable thing, and what
    they dared they did.
No, not if I had a hundred tongues, a hundred
    mouths
And a voice of iron, could I describe all the
    shapes of wickedness,
Catalogue all the retributions inflicted here.
They went on into the Happy Place, the green
    and genial

Glades where the fortunate live, the home of
the blessed spirits.
What largesse of bright air, clothing the vales
in dazzling
Light, is here! This land has a sun and stars of
its own.
Some exercise upon the grassy playing-fields
Or wrestle on the yellow sands in rivalry of
sport;
Some foot the rhythmic dances and chant po-
ems aloud.
Orpheus, the Thracian bard, is there in his
long robe,
To accompany their measures upon the seven-
stringed lyre
Which he plucks, now with his fingers, now
with an ivory plectrum.
Here is the ancient line of Teucer, a breed
most handsome,
Great-hearted heroes born in the happier days
of old,
Ilus, Assaracus, and Dardanus, founder of
Troy.
From afar Aeneas marveled at the arms, the
phantom chariots.
Spears stood fixed in the ground, everywhere
over the plain
Grazed the unharnessed horses. The pleasure
those heroes had felt,
When alive, in their arms and chariots, the
care they had taken to pasture
Their sleek horses—all was the same beyond
the tomb,
Aeneas noticed others to left and right on the
greensward
Feasting and singing a jovial paean in unison
Amidst a fragrant grove of bay trees, whence
the river
Eridanus springs, to roll grandly through
woods of the world above.
Here were assembled those who had suffered
wounds in defense of
Their country; those who had lived pure lives
as priests; and poets
Who had not disgraced Apollo, poets of true
integrity;
Men who civilized life by the skills they discovered, and men whose
Kindness to other people has kept their memory green—
All these upon their temples wore headbands
white as snow.

Deep in a green valley stood father Anchises,
surveying
The spirits there confined before they went up
to the light of
The world above: he was musing seriously,
and reviewing
His folk's full tally, it happened, the line of his
loved children,
Their destinies and fortunes, their characters
and their deeds.
Now, when he saw Aeneas coming in his direction
Over the grass, he stretched out both hands,
all eagerness,
And tears poured down his cheeks, and the
words were tumbling out—
So you have come at last? The love that your
father relied on
Has won through the hard journey? And I
may gaze, my son,
Upon your face, and exchange the old homely
talk with you?
Thus indeed I surmised it would be, believed
it must happen,
Counting the days till you came: I was not de-
ceived in my hopes, then.
Over what lands, what wide, wide seas you
have made your journey!
What dangers, my son, have beset you! And
now you are here with me.
How I dreaded lest you should come to some
harm at Carthage!
Aeneas replied:—
Your image it was, your troubled phantom
That, often rising before me, has brought me
to this place, father.
Our ships are riding at anchor in the Tyrrhene
sea. Oh, let me
Take your hand and embrace you, father! Let
me! Withdraw not!
Even as he spoke, his cheeks grew wet with a
flood of tears.
Three times he tried to put his arms round his
father's neck,
Three times the phantom slipped his vain em-
brace—it was like
Grasping a wisp of wind or the wings of a
fleeting dream.
Now did Aeneas descry, deep in a valley retiring,
A wood, a secluded copse whose branches
sloughed in the wind,

And Lethe river drifting past the tranquil
 places.
Hereabouts were flitting a multitude without
 number,
Just as, amid the meadows on a fine summer
 day,
The bees alight on flowers of every hue, and
 brim the
Shining lilies, and all the lea is humming with
 them.
Aeneas, moved by the sudden sight, asked in
 his ignorance
What it might mean, what was that river over
 there
And all that crowd of people swarming along
 its banks.
Then his father, Anchises, said:—
              They are souls who are destined for
Reincarnation; and now at Lethe's stream they
 are drinking
The waters that quench man's troubles, the
 deep draught of oblivion.
Long, long have I wanted to tell you of these
 and reveal them
Before your eyes, to count them over, the seed
 of my seed,
That you might the more rejoice with me in
 the finding of Italy.

When Anchises had finished, he drew his son
 and the Sibyl
Into the thick of the murmuring concourse as-
 sembled there
And took his stand on an eminence from
 which he could scan the long files
Over against him, and mark the features of
 those who passed.
 Listen, for I will show you your destiny, set-
 ting forth
The fame that from now shall attend the seed
 of Dardanus,
The posterity that awaits you from an Italian
 marriage—
Illustrious souls, one day to come in for our
 Trojan name.
That young man there—do you see him? who
 leans on an untipped spear,
Has been allotted the next passage to life, and
 first of
All these will ascend to earth, with Italian
 blood in his veins;
He is Silvius, an Alban name, and destined to
 be your last child,

The child of your late old age by a wife,
 Lavinia, who shall
Bear him in sylvan surroundings, a king and
 the father of kings
Through whom our lineage shall rule in Alba
 Longa.
Next to him stands Procas, a glory to the
 Trojan line;
Then Capys and Numitor, and one who'll
 revive your own name—
Silvius Aeneas, outstanding alike for moral
 rectitude
And prowess in warfare, if ever he comes to
 the Alban throne.
What fine young men they are! Look at their
 stalwart bearing,
The oak leaves that shade their brows—deco-
 rations for saving life!
These shall found your Nomentum Gabii and
 Fidenae,
These shall rear on the hills Collatia's citadel,
Pometii, and the Fort of Inuus, Bola and
 Cora—
All nameless sites at present, but then they
 shall have these names.
Further, a child of Mars shall go to join his
 grandsire—
Romulus, born of the stock of Assaracus by his
 mother,
Ilia. Look at the twin plumes upon his hel-
 met's crest,
Mars' cognizance, which marks him out for
 the world of earth!
His are the auguries, my son, whereby great
 Rome
Shall rule to the ends of the earth, shall aspire
 to the highest achievement,
Shall ring the seven hills with a wall to make
 one city,
Blessed in her breed of men: as Cybele, wear-
 ing her turreted
Crown, is charioted round the Phrygian cities,
 proud of
Her brood of gods, embracing a hundred of
 her children's children—
Heaven-dwellers all, all tenants of the realm
 above.
Now bend your gaze this way, look at that
 people there!
They are *your* Romans. Caesar is there and all
 Ascanius'
Posterity, who shall pass beneath the arch of
 day.

And here, here is the man, the promised one
    you know of—
Caesar Augustus, son of a god, destined to
    rule
Where Saturn ruled of old in Latium, and
    there
Bring back the age of gold: his empire shall
    expand
Past Garamants and Indians to a land beyond
    the zodiac
And the sun's yearly path, where Atlas the
    sky-bearer pivots
The wheeling heavens, embossed with fiery
    stars, on his shoulder.
Even now the Caspian realm, the Crimean
    country
Tremble at oracles of the gods predicting his
    advent,
And the seven mouths of the Nile are in a
    lather of fright.
Not even Hercules roved so far and wide over
    earth,
Although he shot the bronze-footed deer,
    brought peace to the woods of
Erymanthus, subdued Lerna with the terror of
    his bow;
Nor Bacchus, triumphantly driving his team
    with vines for reins,
His team of tigers down from Mount Nysa,
    traveled so far.
Do we still hesitate, then, to enlarge our
    courage by action?
Shrink from occupying the territory of Auso-
    nia?
Who is that in the distance, bearing the hal-
    lows, crowned with
A wreath of olive? I recognize—grey hair and
    hoary chin—
That Roman king who, called to high power
    from humble Cures,
A town in a poor area, shall found our system
    of law
And thus refound our city. The successor
    Numa, destined
To shake our land out of its indolence, stirring
    men up to fight
Who have grown unadventurous and lost the
    habit of victory,
Is Tullus. After him shall reign the too boast-
    ful Ancus,
Already over-fond of the breath of popular fa-
    vor.

Would you see the Tarquin kings, and arro-
    gant as they, Brutus
The avenger, with the symbols of civic free-
    dom he won back?
He shall be first to receive consular rank and
    its power of
Life and death: when his sons awake the dor-
    mant conflict,
Their father, a tragic figure, shall call them to
    pay the extreme
Penalty, for fair freedom's sake. However pos-
    terity
Look on that deed, patriotism shall prevail and
    love of
Honor. See over there the Decii, the Drusi,
    Torquatus
With merciless axe, Camillus with the stan-
    dards he recovered.
See those twin souls, resplendent in duplicate
    armor: now
They're of one mind, and shall be as long as
    the Underworld holds them;
Caesar descending from Alpine strongholds,
    the fort of Monoccus,
His son-in-law Pompey lined up with an
    Eastern army against him.
Lads, do not harden yourselves to face such
    terrible wars!
Turn not your country's hand against your
    country's heart!
You, be the first to renounce it, my son of
    heavenly lineage,
You be the first to bury the hatchet!...
That one shall ride in triumph to the lofty
    Capitol,
The conqueror of Corinth, renowned for the
    Greeks he has slain.
That one shall wipe out Argos and Agamem-
    non's Mycenae,
Destroying an heir of Aeacus, the seed of
    warrior Achilles,
Avenging his Trojan sires and the sacrilege
    done to Minerva.
Who could leave unnoticed the glorious Cato,
    Cossus,
The family of the Gracchi, the two Scipios—
    thunderbolts
In war and death to Libya; Fabricius, who had
    plenty
In poverty; Serranus, sowing his furrowed
    fields?
Fabii, where do you lead my lagging steps? O
    Fabius,

The greatest, you the preserver of Rome by
    delaying tactics!
Let others fashion from bronze more lifelike,
    breathing images—
For so they shall—and evoke living faces from
    marble;
Others excel as orators, others track with their
    instruments
The planets circling in heaven and predict
    when stars will appear.
But, Romans, never forget that government is
    your medium!
Be this your art—to practice men in the habit
    of peace,
Generosity to the conquered, and firmness
    against aggressor.
        So far and wide, surveying all,
They wandered through that region, those
    broad and hazy plains.
After Anchises had shown his son over the
    whole place
And fired his heart with passion for the great
    things to come,
He told the hero of wars he would have to
    fight one day,
Told of the Laurentines and the city of Lati-
    nus,
And how to evade, or endure, each crisis upon
    his way.
There are two gates of Sleep: the one is made
    of horn,
They say, and affords the outlet for genuine
    apparitions:
The other's a gate of brightly-shining ivory;
    this way
The Shades send up to earth false dreams that
    impose upon us.
Talking, then, of such matters, Anchises es-
    corted his son
And the Sibyl as far as the ivory gate and sent
    them through it.
Aeneas made his way back to the ships and his
    friends with all speed,
Then coasted along direct to the harbor of
    Caieta.
The ships, anchored by the bows, line the
    shore with their sterns.

B. LIFE OF JULIUS CAESAR

PLUTARCH

On anybody's list of Great Men, C. Julius Caesar (100-44 B.C.) is certain to appear. After reading the following passages from Plutarch's *Life of Caesar*, would you agree? What qualifies, or disqualifies, Caesar as a "Great Man"? How does he compare to Alexander the Great—can one be called "greater" than the other? Why?

After Sulla became master of Rome, he wished to make Caesar put away his wife Cornelia, daughter of Cinna, the late sole ruler of the commonwealth, but was unable to effect it either by promises or intimidation, and so contented himself with confiscating her dowry. The ground of Sulla's hostility to Caesar was the relationship between him and Marius; for Marius, the elder, married Julia, the sister of Caesar's father, and had by her the younger Marius, who consequently was Caesar's first cousin. And though at the beginning, while so many were to be put to death, and there was so much to do, Caesar was overlooked by Sulla, yet he would not keep quiet, but presented himself to the people as a candidate for the priesthood, though he was yet a mere boy. Sulla, without any open opposition, took measures to have him rejected, and in consultation whether he should be put to death, when it was urged by some that it was not worth his while to contrive the death of a boy, he answered, that they knew little who did not see more than one Marius in that boy.

[Hiding from Sulla in the East, Caesar is captured by pirates.]

When these men at first demanded of him twenty talents for his ransom, he laughed at them for not understanding the value of their prisoner, and voluntarily engaged to give them fifty. He presently despatched those about him to several places to raise the money, till at last he was left among a set of the most bloodthirsty people in the world, the Cilicians, only with one friend and two attendants. Yet he made so little of them, that when he had a mind to sleep, he would send to them, and order them to make no noise. For thirty-eight days, with all the freedom in the world, he amused himself with joining in their exercises and games, as if they had not been his keepers, but his guards. He wrote verses and speeches, and made them his auditors, and those who did not admire them, he called to their faces illiterate and barbarous, and would often, in raillery, threaten to hang them. They were greatly taken with this, and attributed his free talking to a kind of simplicity and boyish playfulness. As soon as his ransom was come from Miletus, he paid it, and was discharged, and proceeded at once to man some ships at the port of Miletus, and went in pursuit of the pirates, whom he surprised with their ships still stationed at the island, and took most of them. Their money he made his prize, and the men he secured in prison at Pergamus, and he made application to Junius, who was then governor of Asia, to whose office it belonged, as praetor, to determine their punishment. Junius, having his eye upon the money, for the sum was considerable, said he would think at his leisure what to do with the prisoners, upon which Caesar took his leave of him, and went off to Pergamus, where he ordered the pirates to be brought forth and crucified; the punishment he had often threatened them with whilst he was in their hands, and they little dreamt he was in earnest.

[After Sulla's death, Caesar returns to Rome.]

In his pleadings at Rome, his eloquence soon obtained him great credit and favor, and he won no less upon the affections of the people by the affability of his manners and address, in which he showed a tact and consideration beyond what could have been expected at his age; and the open house he kept, the entertainments he gave, and the general splendor of his manner of life contributed little by little to create and increase his political influence. His enemies slighted the growth of it at first, presuming it would soon fail when his money was gone; whilst in the meantime it was growing up and flourishing among the common people. When his power at last was established and not to be overthrown, and now openly tended to the altering of the whole constitution, they were aware too late that there is no beginning so mean, which continued application will not make considerable, and that despising a danger at first will make it at last irresistible.

There being two factions in the city, one that of Sulla, which was very powerful, the other that of Marius, which was then broken and in

a low condition, he undertook to revive this and to make it his own. And to this end, whilst he was in the height of his repute with the people for the magnificent shows he gave as aedile, he ordered images of Marius and figures of Victory, with trophies in their hands, to be carried privately in the night and placed in the capitol. Next morning when some saw them bright with gold and beautifully made, with inscriptions upon them, referring them to Marius's exploits over the Cimbrians, they were surprised at the boldness of him who had set them up, nor was it difficult to guess who it was. The fame of this soon spread and brought together a great concourse of people. Some cried out that it was an open attempt against the established government thus to revive those honors which had been buried by the laws and decrees of the senate; that Caesar had done it to sound the temper of the people whom he had prepared before, and to try whether they were tame enough to bear his humor, and would quietly give way to his innovations. On the other hand, Marius's party took courage, and it was incredible how numerous they were suddenly seen to be, and what a multitude of them appeared and came shouting into the capitol. Many, when they saw Marius's likeness, cried for joy, and Caesar was highly extolled as the one man, in the place of all others, who was a relation worthy of Marius. Upon this the senate met, and Catulus Lutatius, one of the most eminent Romans of that time, stood up and inveighed against Caesar, closing his speech with the remarkable saying that Caesar was now not working mines, but planting batteries to overthrow the state. But when Caesar had made an apology for himself, and satisfied the senate, his admirers were very much animated, and advised him not to depart from his own thoughts for any one, since with the people's good favor he would ere long get the better of them all, and be the first man in the commonwealth.

….Caesar, in the meantime, being out of his praetorship, had got the province of Spain, but was in great embarrassment with his creditors, who, as he was going off, came upon him, and were very pressing and importunate. This led him to apply himself to Crassus, who was the richest man in Rome, but wanted Caesar's youthful vigor and heat to sustain the opposition against Pompey. Crassus took upon him to satisfy those creditors who were most uneasy to him, and would not be put off any longer, and engaged himself to the amount of eight hundred and thirty talents, upon which Caesar was now at liberty to go to his province. In his journey, as he was crossing the Alps, and passing by a small village of the barbarians with but few inhabitants, and those wretchedly poor, his companions asked the question among themselves by way of mockery, if there were any canvassing for offices there; any contention which should be uppermost, or feuds of great men one against another. To which Caesar made answer seriously, "For my part, I had rather be the first man among these fellows, than the second man in Rome." It is said that another time, when free from business in Spain, after reading some part of the history of Alexander, he sat a great while very thoughtful, and at last burst out into tears. His friends were surprised, and asked him the reason of it. "Do you think," said he, "I have not just cause to weep, when I consider that Alexander at my age had conquered so many nations, and I have all this time done nothing that is remarkable?"

...Caesar, being doubly supported by the interests of Crassus and Pompey, was promoted to the consulship, and triumphantly proclaimed with Calpurnius Bibulus. When he entered on his office he brought in bills which would have been preferred with better grace by the most audacious of the tribunes than by a consul,[1] in which he proposed the plantation of colonies and the division of lands, simply to please the commonalty. The best and most honorable of the senators opposed it, upon which, as he had long wished for nothing more than for such a colorable pretext, he loudly protested how much it was against his will to be driven to seek support from the people, and how the senate's insulting and harsh conduct left no other course possible for him than to devote himself henceforth to the popular cause and interest. And so he hurried out of the senate, and presenting himself to the people, and there placing Crassus and Pompey, one on each side of him, he asked them whether they consented to the bills he had proposed. They owned their assent, upon which he desired them to assist him against those who had threatened to oppose him with their swords. They engaged they would, and Pompey added further, that he would meet their swords with a sword and buckler too. These words the nobles much resented, as neither suitable to his own dignity, nor becoming the reverence due to the senate, but resembling rather the vehemence of a boy or the fury of a madman. But the people were pleased with it. In order to get a yet firmer hold upon Pompey, Caesar having a daughter, Julia, who had been before contracted to Servilius Caepio, now betrothed her to Pompey.

THE WAR IN GAUL

Thus far have we followed Caesar's actions before the wars of Gaul. After this, he seems to begin his course afresh, and to enter upon a new life and scene of action. And the period of those wars which he now fought, and those many expeditions in which he subdued Gaul, showed him to be a soldier and general not in the least inferior to any of the greatest and most admired commanders who had ever appeared at the head of armies. For if we compare him with the Fabii, the Metelli, the Scipios, and with those who were his contemporaries, or not long before him, Sulla, Marius, the Luculli, or even Pompey himself, whose glory, it may be said, went up at that time to heaven for every excellence in war, we shall find Caesar's actions to have surpassed them all. One he may be held to have outdone in consideration of the difficulty of the country in which he fought, another in the extent of territory which he conquered; some, in the number and strength of the enemy whom he defeated; one man, because of the wildness and perfidiousness of the tribes whose goodwill he conciliated, another in his humanity and clemency to those he overpowered; others, again, in his gifts and kindnesses to his soldiers; all alike in the number of the battles which he fought and the enemies whom he killed. For he had not pursued the wars in Gaul full ten years when he had taken by storm above eight hundred towns, subdued three hundred states, and of the three millions

---

[1]Tribunes were very junior officials who often tried to build support for higher office by sponsoring reforms. In Plutarch's opinion, there was no need for a consul to do so.

of men, who made up the gross sum of those with whom at several times he engaged, he had killed one million and taken captive a second.

He was so much master of the good-will and hearty service of his soldiers that those who in other expeditions were but ordinary men displayed a courage past defeating or withstanding when they went upon any danger where Caesar's glory was concerned. Such a one was Acilius, who, in the sea-fight before Marseilles, had his right hand struck off with a sword, yet did not quit his buckler out of his left, but struck the enemies in the face with it, till he drove them off and made himself master of the vessel.

This love of honor and passion for distinction were inspired into them and cherished by Caesar himself, who, by his unsparing distribution of money and honors, showed them that he did not heap up wealth from the wars for his own luxury, or the gratifying of his private pleasure, but that all he received was but a public fund laid by the reward and encouragement of valor, and that he looked upon all he gave to deserving soldiers as so much increase to his own riches. Added to this also, there was no danger to which he did not willingly expose himself, no labor from which he pleaded an exemption.

Caesar had long ago resolved upon the overthrow of Pompey, as had Pompey, for that matter, upon his. For Crassus, the fear of whom had hitherto kept them in peace, having now been killed in Parthia, if the one of them wished to make himself the greatest man in Rome, he had only to overthrow the other; and if he again wished to prevent his own fall, he had nothing for it but to be beforehand with him whom he feared. Pompey had not been long under any such apprehensions, having till lately despised Caesar, as thinking it no difficult matter to put down him whom he himself had advanced. But Caesar had entertained this design from the beginning against his rivals, and had retired, like an expert wrestler, to prepare himself apart for the combat. Making the Gallic wars his exercise ground, he had at once improved the strength of his soldiery, and had heightened his own glory by his great actions, so that he was looked on as one who might challenge comparison with Pompey. Nor did he let go any of the advantages which were now given him both by Pompey himself and the times, and the ill-government of Rome, where all who were candidates for offices publicly gave money, and without any shame bribed the people, who, having received their pay, did not contend for their benefactors with their bare suffrages, but with bows, swords, and slings. So that after having many times stained the place of election with blood of men killed upon the spot, they left the city at last without a government at all, to be carried about like a ship without a pilot to steer her; while all who had any wisdom could only be thankful if a course of such wild and stormy disorder and madness might end no worse than in a monarchy. Some were so bold as to declare openly that the government was incurable but by a monarchy, and that they ought to take that remedy from the hands of the gentlest physician, meaning Pompey, who, though in words he pretended to decline it, yet in reality made his utmost efforts to be declared dictator. Cato, perceiving his design, prevailed with the senate to make him sole consul, that with the offer of a more legal sort of monarchy he might be withheld from demanding the dictatorship. They over and above voted him the continuance of his provinces, for he had two, Spain and all Africa, which he governed by his lieutenants, and maintained armies under him, at the yearly charge of a thousand talents out of the public treasury.

Upon this Caesar also sent and petitioned for the consulship and the continuance of his provinces. Pompey at first did not stir in it, but Marcellus and Lentulus opposed it, who had always hated Caesar, and now did everything, whether fit or unfit, which might disgrace and affront him. For they took away the privilege of Roman citizens from the people of New Comum, who were a colony that Caesar had lately planted in Gaul, and Marcellus, who was then consul, ordered one of the senators of that town, then at Rome, to be whipped, and told him he laid that mark upon him to signify he was no citizen of Rome, bidding him, when he went back again, to show it to Caesar.

[With civil war looming, Caesar offers a compromise: he will retire to private life if Pompey

[does likewise. But his enemies in the Senate block the vote.]

Afterwards there came other letters from Caesar, which seemed yet more moderate, for he proposed to quit everything else, and only to retain Gaul within the Alps, Illyricum, and two legions, till he should stand a second time for consul. Cicero, the orator, who was lately returned from Cilicia, endeavored to reconcile differences, and softened Pompey, who was willing to comply in other things, but not to allow him the soldiers. At last Cicero used his persuasions with Caesar's friends to accept of the provinces and six thousand soldiers only, and so to make up the quarrel. And Pompey was inclined to give way to this, but Lentulus, the consul, would not hearken to it, but drove Antony and Curio out of the senate house with insults, by which he afforded Caesar the most plausible pretense that could be, and one which he could readily use to inflame the soldiers, by showing them two persons of such repute and authority who were forced to escape in a hired carriage in the dress of slaves. For so they were glad to disguise themselves when they fled out of Rome.

There were not about him at that time above three hundred horse and five thousand foot; for the rest of his army, which was left behind the Alps, was to be brought after him by officers who had received orders for that purpose. But he thought the first motion towards the design which he had on foot did not require large forces at present, and that what was wanted was to make this first step suddenly, and so to astound his enemies with the boldness of it; as it would be easier, he thought, to throw them into consternation by doing what they never anticipated than fairly to conquer them, if he had alarmed them by his preparations. And therefore he commanded his captains and other officers to go only with their swords in their hands, without any other arms, and make themselves masters of Ariminum, a large city of Gaul, with as little disturbance and bloodshed as possible. He committed the care of these forces to Hortensius, and himself spent the day in public as a stander-by and spectator of the gladiators, who exercised before him. A little before night he attended to his person, and then went into the hall, and conversed for some time with those he had

invited to supper, till it began to grow dusk, when he rose from table and made his excuses to the company, begging them to stay till he came back, having already given private directions to a few immediate friends that they should follow him, not all the same way, but some one way, some another. He himself got into one of the hired carriages, and drove at first another way, but presently turned towards Ariminum. When he came to the river Rubicon, which parts Gaul within the Alps from the rest of Italy, his thought began to work, now he was just entering upon the danger, and he wavered much in his mind when he considered the greatness of the enterprise into which he was throwing himself. He checked his course and ordered a halt, while he revolved with himself, and often changed his opinion one way and the other, without speaking a word. This was when his purposes fluctuated most; presently he also discussed the matter with his friends who were about him (of which number Asinius Pollio was one), computing how many calamities his passing that river would bring upon mankind, and what a relation of it would be transmitted to posterity. At last, in a sort of passion, casting aside calculation, and abandoning himself to what might come, and using the proverb frequently in their mouths who enter upon dangerous and bold attempts. "The die is cast," with these words he took the river. Once over, he used all expedition possible, and before it was day reached Ariminum and took it. It is said that the night before he passed the river he had an impious dream, that he was unnaturally familiar with his own mother.

[Caesar's speed catches Pompey and the Senate by surprise. They flee to Greece, where Pompey is defeated at the Battle of Pharsalus in 48 B.C.]

Nevertheless his countrymen, conceding all to his fortune, and accepting the bit, in the hope that the government of a single person would give them time to breathe after so many civil wars and calamities, made him dictator for life. This was indeed a tyranny avowed, since his power now was not only absolute, but perpetual too. Cicero made the first proposals to the senate for conferring honors upon him, which might in some sort be said not to exceed the limits of ordinary human moderation. But others, striving which should deserve most, carried them so excessively high, that they made Caesar odious to the most indifferent and moderate sort of men, by the pretensions and extravagance of the titles which they decreed him. His enemies, too, are thought to have had some share in this, as well as his flatterers. It gave them advantage against him, and would be their justification for any attempt they should make upon him; for since the civil wars were ended, he had nothing else that he could be charged with. And they had good reason to decree a temple to Clemency, in token of their thanks for the mild use he made of his victory. For he not only pardoned many of those who fought against him, but, further, to some gave honors and offices; as particularly to Brutus and Cassius, who both of them were praetors. Pompey's images that were thrown down he set up again, upon which Cicero also said that by raising Pompey's statues he had fixed his own. When his friends advised him to have a guard, and several offered their services, he would not hear of it; but said it was better to suffer death once than always to live in fear of it. He looked upon the affections of the people to be the best and surest guard, and entertained them again with public feasting and general distributions of corn; and to gratify his army, he sent out colonies to several places, of which the most remarkable were Carthage and Corinth; which as before they had been ruined at the same time, so now were restored and repeopled together.

But that which brought upon him the most apparent and mortal hatred was his desire of being king; which gave the common people the first occasion to quarrel with him, and proved the most specious pretense to those who had been his secret enemies all along.

[Brutus and Cassius form a conspiracy and kill Caesar at a meeting of the Senate on the Ides of March 44 B.C. Caesar was 56 years old.]

❖

PART III

CAUSE AND EFFECT: THE FALL OF ROME

Sun God (c. A.D. 240)

VII. Rome's Mission

Thanks in no small part to the late-night movie, our picture of Rome is one of half-crazed emperors and military despots. But the Romans accomplished something for the Mediterranean region that no other state has done before or since: the unification of these peoples into a single state, dwelling in peace for several hundred years. How did the Romans accomplish this, and what was its effect? The readings in this section suggest answers other than the standard one of military barbarism. What are they?

POLYBIUS (C. 200-c. 118 B. C.), a Greek who was a hostage in Rome for some twenty years, provides an idealized, but highly influential view at the constitution of the Roman Republic CICERO (106-43 B. C.), Roman orator and politician presents a lawsuit that demonstrates both the bad and good side of Rome's treatment of conquered provinces, while the emperor CLAUDIUS (A.D. 41-54) gives an eloquent speech to the senate defending Rome's assimilation of foreigners. The selections that follow, from APPIAN OF ALEXANDRIA (c. A.D. 90–160), AELIUS ARISTIDES (c. A.D. 117–181), JUVENAL (c. A.D. 65–130), and from the Christian BOOK OF REVELATION (c. 110?) all give different views of Rome. It's worth bearing in mind that none of these authors came from Rome (though Juvenal came from Italy): Their perspectives are those of outsiders brought into the Roman world. What do they see? What explains their different perspectives? Are there points on which all would agree?

❖ ❖ ❖

1. THE ROMAN CONSTITUTION

POLYBIUS

1. What is really educational and beneficial to students of history is the clear view of the causes of events and the consequent power of choosing the better policy in a particular case. Now in every practical undertaking by a state we must regard as the most powerful agent for success or failure the form of its constitution: for from this as from a fountainhead all conceptions and plans of action not only proceed, but attain their consummation.

7. In old times, then, those who were once thus selected and obtained this office grew old in their royal functions, making magnificent strongholds and surrounding them with walls and extending their frontiers, partly for the security of their subjects, and partly to provide them with an abundance of the necessaries of life. And while engaged in these works they were exempt from all vituperation or jealousy, because they did not make their distinctive dress, food, or drink at all conspicuous, but lived very much like the rest and joined in the everyday employments of the common people.

[handwritten note: When kings became tyrants]

But when their royal power became hereditary in their family, and they found every necessary for security ready to their hands, as well as more than was necessary for their personal support, then they gave the rein to their appetites: imagined that rulers must needs wear different clothes from those of subjects; have different and elaborate luxuries of the table; and must even seek sensual indulgence, however unlawful the source, without fear of denial. These things having given rise in the one case to jealousy and offence, in the other to outbursts of hatred and passionate resentment, the kingship became a tyranny. The first step in disintegration was taken, and plots began to be formed against the government which did not now proceed from the worst men but from the noblest, most high-minded, and most courageous, because these are the men who can least submit to the tyrannical acts of their rulers.

[handwritten note: How king was taken out of power]

[handwritten note: How republic started]

8. But as soon as the people got leaders, they cooperated with them against the dynasty for the reasons I have mentioned. Then *kingship* and *despotism* were alike entirely abolished, and *aristocracy* once more began to revive and

start afresh. For in their immediate gratitude to those who had deposed the despots, the people employed them as leaders and entrusted their interests to them. The leaders, looking upon this charge at first as a great privilege, made the public advantage their chief concern and conducted all kinds of business, public or private, with diligence and caution. But when the sons of these men received the same position of authority from their fathers—having had no experience of misfortunes, and none at all of civil equality and freedom of speech, but having been bred up from the first under the shadow of their fathers' authority and lofty position—some of them gave themselves up with passion to avarice and unscrupulous love of money, others to drinking and the boundless debaucheries which accompany it, and others to the violation of women or the forcible appropriation of boys: and so they turned an *aristocracy* into an *oligarchy*. But it was not long before they roused in the minds of the people the same feelings as before; and their fall therefore was very like the disaster which befell the tyrants.

9. For no sooner had the knowledge of the jealousy and hatred existing in the citizens against them emboldened someone to oppose the government by word or deed, than he was sure to find the whole people ready and prepared to take his side. Having rid themselves of these rulers by assassination or exile, they do not venture to set up a king again, being still in terror of the injustice to which this led before; nor dare they entrust the common interests again to more than one, considering the recent example of their misconduct. Therefore, as the only sound hope left them is that which depends upon themselves, they are driven to take refuge in that, and so change the constitution from an oligarchy to a *democracy* and take upon themselves the superintendence and charge of the state. And as long as any survive who have had experience of oligarchical supremacy and domination, they regard their present constitution as a blessing and hold equality and freedom as of the utmost value. But as soon as a new generation has arisen, and the democracy has descended to their children's children, long association weakens their value for equality and freedom, and some seek to become more powerful than

the ordinary citizens; and the most liable to this temptation are the rich. So when they begin to be fond of office and find themselves unable to obtain it by their own unassisted efforts and their own merits, they ruin their estates, while enticing and corrupting the common people in every possible way. By this means, when in their senseless mania for reputation they have made the populace ready and greedy to receive bribes, the virtue of democracy is destroyed, and it is transformed into a government of violence and the strong hand. For the mob, habituated to feed at the expense of others and to have its hopes of a livelihood in the property of its neighbors, as soon as it has got a leader sufficiently ambitious and daring, being excluded by poverty from the sweets of civil honors, produces a reign of mere violence. Then come tumultuous assemblies, massacres, banishments, and redivisions of land until, after losing all trace of civilization, it has once more found a master and a despot.

This is the regular cycle of constitutional revolutions, and the natural order in which constitutions change, are transformed, and return again to their original stage. If a man have a clear grasp of these principles, he may perhaps make a mistake as to the dates at which this or that will happen to a particular constitution; but he will rarely be entirely mistaken as to the stage of growth or decay at which it has arrived, or as to the point at which it will undergo some revolutionary change. However, it is in the case of the Roman constitution that this method of inquiry will most fully teach us its formation, its growth, and zenith, as well as the changes awaiting it in the future; for this, if any constitution ever did, owed, as I said just now, its original foundation and growth to natural causes, and to natural causes will owe its decay. My subsequent narrative will be the best illustration of what I say.

As for the Roman constitution, it had three elements, each of them possessing sovereign powers; and their respective share of power in the whole state had been regulated with such a scrupulous regard to equality and equilibrium that no one could say for certain, not even a native, whether the constitution as a whole were an aristocracy or democracy or despotism. And no wonder, for if we confine our observation to the power of the consuls, we should be inclined to regard it as despotic: if on that of the Senate, as aristocratic; and if finally one looks at the power possessed by the people, it would seem a clear case of a democracy....

18. The result of this power of the several estates for mutual help or harm is a union sufficiently firm for all emergencies, and a constitution than which it is impossible to find a better. For whenever any danger from without compels them to unite and work together, the strength which is developed by the State is so extraordinary that everything required is unfailingly carried out by the eager rivalry shown by all classes to devote their whole minds to the need of the hour and to secure that any determination come to should not fail for want of promptitude; while each individual works, privately and publicly alike, for the accomplishment of the business in hand. Accordingly, the peculiar constitution of the State makes it irresistible and certain of obtaining whatever it determines to attempt. Nay, even when these external alarms are past, and the people are enjoying their good fortune and the fruits of their victories and, as usually happens, growing corrupted by flattery and idleness, show a tendency to violence and arrogance-it is in these circumstances, more than ever, that the constitution is seen to possess within itself the power of correcting abuses. For when any one of the three classes becomes puffed up and manifests an inclination to be contentious and unduly encroaching, the mutual interdependency of all the three and the possibility of the pretensions of anyone being checked and thwarted by the others, must plainly check this tendency. And so the proper equilibrium is maintained by the impulsiveness of the one part being checked by its fear of the other....

How the const. works

✝

2. AGAINST VERRES

CICERO

In Chapter VI you read about Vergil's idealized vision of Rome. After the great conquests of the second century B.C., Roman senators proved themselves all too susceptible to bribery and corruption. In 70 B.C., a particularly unscrupulous governor, Gaius Verres, returned from a three-year binge in Sicily convinced he could buy

acquittal from any court. For political and personal reasons, pillars of the establishment rallied around Verres, but he reckoned without the persistence of a rising trial attorney, Marcus Tullius Cicero (106-43 B.C.). Verres tried elaborate maneuvers to stack the jury, to rig the court calendar, and even to have Cicero replaced by a more friendly prosecutor. But the orator persisted, and on a fact-finding trip to Sicily discovered that Verres had arranged for a forged record to be submitted to the court. Because it was so late in the year before the trial opened, Verres remained confident: Roman lawyers customarily used the opening days of a trial to show off their rhetorical skills, and his own counsel, Hortensius (at that time the most famous attorney in Rome), was certain Cicero would not be able to resist the opportunity. Thus, the trial would drag on until a new magistrate favorable to Verres would be able to take over.

Cicero was desperate to avoid this trap. Therefore, he abandoned his opening speech and began immediately to produce witnesses for interrogation, catching Hortensius off guard and completely unprepared. Seeing the handwriting on the wall, Verres went into voluntary exile after the first day. Later, Cicero wrote up the full body of evidence and published it all in a series of six orations, just as if the trial had continued (only the first of these was ever delivered). The result is a detailed picture of the extent to which provinces during the Republic were at the mercy of a corrupt governor.

Partly because of the number of influential persons involved, the Verres case became a *cause célèbre*, something like our own "Watergate." Then as now, though, more proved to be at fault than bad people doing bad things. How is it that the Roman system tolerated people like Verres? Can you find any answers in Cicero's account? (It may help to know that the juries who tried cases of provincial maladministration were made up exclusively of senators, creating a potential for conflict of interest roughly similar to what our government faces when the administration is responsible for investigating charges against itself.)

Remember, Cicero was a prosecutor: He was trying to win a case, not to be fair to Verres. He also was one of the great masters of rhetoric of all time. Can you spot some of his techniques? How effective do you think they are? Could you have defended Verres?

THE FIRST HEARING

1.1 That which was above all things to be desired, O judges, and which above all things was calculated to have the greatest influences towards allaying the unpopularity of your order, and putting an end to the discredit into which your judicial decisions have fallen, appears to have been thrown in your way and given to you not by any human contrivances, but almost by the interposition of the gods, at a most important crisis of the republic. For an opinion has now become established, pernicious to us, and pernicious to the republic, which has been the common talk of every one, not only at Rome, but among foreign nations also,—that in the courts of law as they exist at present, no wealthy man, however guilty he may be, can possibly be convicted. Now at this time of peril to your order and to your tribunals, when men are ready to attempt by harangues, and by the proposal of new laws, to increase the existing unpopularity of the senate, Caius Verres is brought to trial as a criminal, a man condemned in the opinion of every one by his life and actions, but acquitted by the enormousness of his wealth according to his own hope and boast. I, O judges, have undertaken this cause as prosecutor with the greatest good wishes and expectation on the part of the Roman people, not in order to increase the unpopularity of the senate, but to relieve it from the discredit which I share with it.

For I have brought before you a man, by acting justly in whose case you have an opportunity of retrieving the lost credit of your judicial proceedings, of regaining your credit with the Roman people, and of giving satisfaction to foreign nations; a man, the embezzler of the public funds, the petty tyrant of Asia and Pamphylia, the robber who deprived the city of its rights, the disgrace and ruin of the province of Sicily. And if you come to a decision about this man with severity and a due regard to your oaths, that authority which ought to remain in you will cling to you still; but if that man's vast riches shall break down the sanctity and honesty of the courts of justice, at least shall achieve this, that it shall be plain that it was rather honest judgment that was wanting to the republic, than a criminal to the judges, or an accuser to the criminal.

1.2. I, indeed, that I may confess to you the truth about myself, O judges, though many snares were laid for me by Caius Verres, both by land and sea, which I partly avoided by my own vigilance, and partly warded off by the zeal and kindness of my friends, yet I never

seemed to be incurring so much danger, and I never was in such a state of great apprehension, as I am now in this very court of law. Nor does the expectation which people have formed of my conduct of this prosecution, nor this concourse of so vast a multitude as is here assembled, influence me (though indeed I am greatly agitated by these circumstances) so much as his nefarious plots which he is endeavoring to lay at one and the same time against me, against you, against Marcus Glabrio the praetor,[1] and against the allies, against foreign nations, against the senate, and even against the very name of senator; whose favorite saying it is that they have got to fear who have stolen only as much as is enough for themselves, but that he has stolen so much that it may easily be plenty for many; that nothing is so holy that it cannot be corrupted, or so strongly fortified that it cannot be stormed by money.

But if he were as secret in acting as he is audacious in attempting, perhaps in some particular he might some time or other have escaped our notice. But it happens very fortunately that to his incredible audacity there is joined a most unexampled folly. For as he was unconcealed in committing his robberies of money, so in his hope of corrupting the judges he has made his intentions and endeavors visible to everyone.

He says that only once in his life has he felt fear, at the time when he was first impeached as a criminal by me; because he was only lately arrived from his province, and was branded with unpopularity and infamy, not modern but ancient and of long standing; and, besides that, the time was unlucky, being very ill-suited for corrupting the judges. Therefore, when I had demanded a very short time to prosecute my inquiries in Sicily, he found a man to ask for two days less to make investigations in Achaea; not with any real intention of doing the same with his diligence and industry that I have accomplished by my labor, and daily and nightly investigations. For the Achaean inquisitor never even arrived at Brundisium. I in fifty days so traveled over the

---

[1]Praetors were annually elected officials, second in rank to consuls. One of their duties was to preside over trials.

whole of Sicily that I examined into the records and injuries of all the tribes and of all private individuals, so that it was easily visible to everyone, that he had been seeking out a man not really for the purpose of bringing the defendant whom he accused to trial, but merely to occupy the time which ought to belong to me.

[Cicero describes Verres' entire career, from his first election as quaestor,[1] as marked by greed and cowardice.]

But now he has established great and numerous monuments and proofs of all his vices in the province of Sicily, which he for three years so harassed and ruined that it can by no possibility be restored to its former condition, and appears scarcely able to be at all recovered after a long series of years, and long succession of virtuous praetors. While this man was praetor the Sicilians enjoyed neither their own laws, nor the decrees of our senate, nor the common rights of every nation. Every one in Sicily has only so much left as either escaped the notice or was disregarded by the satiety of that most avaricious and licentious man.

V. No legal decision for three years was given on any other ground but his will; no property was so secure to any man, even if it had descended to him from his father and grandfather, but he was deprived of it at his command; enormous sums of money were exacted from the property of the cultivators of the soil by a new and nefarious system. The most faithful of the allies were classed in the number of enemies. Roman citizens were tortured and put to death like slaves; the greatest criminals were acquitted in the courts of justice through bribery; the most upright and honorable men, being prosecuted while absent, were condemned and banished without being heard in their own defense; the most fortified harbors, the greatest aid strongest cities, were laid open to pirates and robbers; the sailors and soldiers of the Sicilians, our own allies and friends, died of hunger; the best built fleets on the most important stations were lost and destroyed to the great disgrace of the Roman

people. This same man while praetor plundered and stripped those most ancient monuments, some erected by wealthy monarchs and intended by them as ornaments for their cities ; some, too, the work of our own generals, which they either gave or restored as conquerors to the different states in Sicily. And he did this not only in the case of public statues and ornaments, but he also plundered all the temples consecrated in the deepest religious feelings of the people. He did not leave, in short, one god to the Sicilians which appeared to him to be made in a tolerably workmanlike manner, and with any of the skill of the ancients. I am prevented by actual shame from speaking of his nefarious licentiousness as shown in rapes and other such enormities ; and I am unwilling also to increase the distress of those men who have been unable to preserve their children and their wives unpolluted by his wanton lust. But, you will say, these things were done by him in such a manner as not to be notorious to all men. I think there is no man who has heard his name who cannot also relate wicked actions of his; so that I ought rather to be afraid of being thought to omit many of his crimes, than to invent any charges against him. And indeed I do not think that this multitude which has collected to listen to me wishes so much to learn of me what the facts of the case are, as to go over it with me, refreshing its recollection of what it knows already.

1.14 And what do you suppose will be my thoughts, if I find in this very trial any violation of the laws committed in any similar manner? especially when I can prove by many witnesses that Caius Verres often said in Sicily, in the hearing of many persons, that he had a powerful friend, in confidence in whom he was plundering the province; and that he was not seeking money for himself alone, but that he had so distributed the three years of his Sicilian praetorship, that he should say he did exceedingly well if he appropriated the gains of one year to the augmentation of his own property, those of the second year to his patrons and defenders, and reserved the whole of the third year, the most productive and gainful of all, for the judges.

From which it came into my mind to say that which I perceived the Roman people greatly

the bad shit he did

---

[1]Quaestors were junior officials on a governor's staff who paid bills and kept records. Normally, this would be the first position for a young, aspiring politician.

moved by: that I thought that foreign nations would send ambassadors to the Roman people to procure the abrogation of the law, and of all trials, about extortion. For if there were no trials, they think that each man would only plunder them of as much as he would think sufficient for himself and his children; but now, because there are trials of that sort, everyone carries off as much as it will take to satisfy himself, his patrons, his advocates, the praetor, and the judges. And that is an enormous sum. They may be able to satisfy the cupidity of one most avaricious man, but they are quite unable to incur the expense of his most guilty victory over the laws.

Would that man [Verres] ever have had a favorable hope of his own safety if he had not conceived in his mind a bad opinion of you? on which account he ought, if possible, to be still more hated by you than he is by the Roman people, because he considers you like himself in avarice and wickedness and perjury.

THE SECOND HEARING

2.12 I will pass by that first act of his life, most infamous and most wicked as it was. He shall hear nothing from me of the vices and offences of his childhood, nothing about his most dissolute youth: how that youth was spent, you either remember, or else you can recognize it in the son whom he has brought up to be so like himself. I will pass over everything which appears shameful to be mentioned; and I will consider not only what that fellow ought to have said of himself, but also what it becomes me to say. Do you, I entreat you, permit this, and grant to my modesty, that it may be allowed to pass over in silence some portion of his shamelessness. All that time which passed before he came into office and became a public character, he may have free and untouched as far as I am concerned. Nothing shall be said of his drunken nocturnal revels; no mention shall be made of his pimps, and dicers, and panders; his losses at play, and the licentious transactions which the estate of his father and his own age prompted him to shall be passed over in silence. He may have lived in all infamy at that time with impunity, as far as I am concerned; the rest of his life has been such that I can well afford to put up with the loss of not mentioning those enormities.

[As governor of Sicily, Verres even makes money by letting recruits buy leaves from duty, until his fleet—abandoned by Verres' hand-picked commander, Cleomenes, is burned by pirates.]

6.35 While all this was going on, in the meantime Cleomenes had already arrived at Elorum, already he had hastened on land from the ship, and had left the quadrireme tossing about in the surf. The rest of the captains of ships, when the commander-in-chief had landed, as they had no possible means either of resisting or of escaping by sea, ran their ships ashore at Elorum, and followed Cleomenes. Then Heracleo, the captain of the pirates, being suddenly victorious, beyond all his hopes, not through any valor of his own, but owing to the avarice and worthlessness of Verres, as soon as evening came on, ordered a most beautiful fleet belonging to the Roman people, having been driven on shore and abandoned, to be set fire to and burnt.

O what a miserable and bitter time for the province of Sicily! O what an event, calamitous and fatal to many innocent people! O what unexampled worthlessness and infamy of that man! On one and the same night, the praetor was burring with the flame of the most disgraceful love, a fleet of the Roman people with the fire of pirates.

It was a stormy night when the news of this terrible disaster was brought to Syracuse—men run to the praetor's house, to which his women had conducted him back a little while before from his splendid banquet with songs and music. Cleomenes, although it was night, still does not dare to show himself in public. He shuts himself up in his house, but his wife was not there to console her husband in his misfortunes.

But the discipline of this noble commander-in-chief was so strict in his own house, that though the event was so important, the news so serious, still no one could be admitted; no one dared either to wake him if asleep, or to address him if awake. But now, when the affair had become known to everybody, a vast multitude was collecting in every part of the city; for the arrival of the pirates was not given notice of, as had formerly been the custom, by a fire raised on a watchtower, or a hill, but both the disaster that had already been sustained, and the danger that was impending, were notified by the conflagration of the fleet itself.

6.36. When the praetor was inquired for, and when it was plain that no one had told him the news, a rush of people towards his house takes place with great impetuosity and loud cries. Then, he himself being roused, comes forth; he hears the whole news from Timarchides; he takes his military cloak. It was now nearly dawn. He comes forth into the middle of the crowd, bewildered with wine, and sleep, and debauchery. He is received by all with such a shout that it seemed to bring before his eyes a remembrance to the dangers of Lampsacus.[1] But this present appeared greater than that, because, though both the mobs hated him equally, the numbers here were much greater....

6.39. Verres is informed that nothing is done in the forum and in the assembly all that day, except putting questions to the naval captains how the fleet was lost. That they made answer, and informed every one that it was owing to the discharge of the rowers, the want of food of the rest, the cowardice and desertion of Cleomenes. And when he heard this, he began to form this design. He had long since made up his mind that a prosecution would be instituted against him, long before this happened, as you have heard him say himself at the former pleading. He saw that if those naval captains were produced as witnesses against him, he should not be able to stand against so serious an accusation. He forms at first a plan, foolish indeed, but still merciful. He orders Cleomenes and the naval captains to be summoned before him. They come. He accuses them of having held this language about himself; he begs then, to cease from holding it; and begs everyone there to say that he had had in his ship as large a crew as he ought to have had, and that none had been discharged.

They promise him to do whatever he wished. He does not delay. He immediately summons his friends. He then asks of all the captains separately how many sailors each had had on board his ship. Each of them answers as he had been enjoined to. He makes an entry of their answers in his journal. He seals it up, prudent man that he is, with the seals of his friends; in order, forsooth, to use this evidence against this charge, if ever it should be necessary. I imagine that senseless man must have been laughed at by his own counselors, and warned that these documents would do him no good; that if the charge were made, there would be even more suspicion, owing to these extraordinary precautions of the praetor. He had already behaved with such folly in many cases, as even publicly to order whatever he pleased to be expunged out of, or entered in the records of different cities. All which things he now finds out are of no use to him, since he is convicted by documents, and witnesses, and authorities which are all undeniable.

6.40. When he sees that their confession, and all the evidence which he has manufactured, and his journals, will be of no use to him, he then adopts the design, not of a worthless praetor, for even that might have been endured, but an inhuman and senseless tyrant. He determines, that if he wishes to palliate that accusation, for he did not suppose that he could get rid of it altogether, all the naval captains, the witnesses of his wickedness, must be put to death.

The next consideration was—"What am I to do with Cleomenes? Can I put those men to death whom I placed under his command, and spare him whom I placed in command and authority over them? Can I punish those men who followed Cleomenes, and pardon Cleomenes who bade them fly with him, and follow him? Can I be severe to those men who had vessels not only devoid of crews, but devoid of decks, and be merciful to him who was the only man who had a decked ship, and whose ship, too, was not stripped bare like those of the others?"

Cleomenes must die too. What signify his promises? what do the curses that he will heap on him, the pledges of friendship and mutual embraces, that comradeship in the service of a woman on that most luxurious sea-shore signify? It was utterly impossible that Cleomenes could be spared. He summons Cleomenes. He tells him that he has made up his mind to exe-

---

[1]Referring to an earlier incident in Verres' career when, according to Cicero, his actions touched off a riot.

cute all the naval captains; that considerations of his own personal danger required such a step. "I will spare you alone, and I will endure the blame of all that disaster myself, and all possible reproaches for my inconsistency, rather than act cruelly to you on the one hand, or, on the other hand, leave so many and such important witnesses against me in safety and in life."

[The captains are tried and executed. One, however, Junius of Heraclea, writes an account of the whole affair before his death, in which he itemizes Verres' misdeeds.]

6.61. How shall I speak of Publius Gavius, a citizen of the municipality of Cosa, O judges? or with what vigor of language, with what gravity of expression, with what grief of mind shall I mention him? But, indeed, that indignation fails me. I must take more care than usual that what I am going to say be worthy of my subject,—worthy of the indignation which I feel. For the charge is of such a nature that when I was first informed of it I thought I should not avail myself of it. For although I knew that it was entirely true, still I thought that it would not appear credible. Being compelled by the tears of all the Roman citizens who are living as traders in Sicily, being influenced by the testimonies of the men of Valentia, most honorable men, and by those of all the Rhegians, and of many Roman knights who happened at that time to be at Messana, I produced at the previous pleading only just that amount of evidence which might prevent the matter from appearing doubtful to any one.

What shall I do now? When I have been speaking for so many hours of one class of offences, and of that man's nefarious cruelty, —when I have now expended nearly all my treasures of words of such a sort as are worthy of that man's wickedness on other matters, and have omitted to take precautions to keep your attention on the stretch by diversifying my accusations, how am I to deal with an affair of the importance that this is? There is, I think, but one method, but one line open to me. I will place the matter plainly before you, which is of itself of such importance that there is no need of my eloquence—and eloquence,

indeed, I have none, but there is no need of anyone's eloquence to excite your feelings.

This Gavius of whom I speak, a citizen of Cosa, when he (among the vast number of Roman citizens who had been treated in the same way) had been thrown by Verres into prison, and somehow or other had escaped secretly out of the stone-quarries, and had come to Messana, being now almost within sight of Italy and of the walls of Rhegium,[1] and being revived, after that fear of death and that darkness, by the light, as it were, of liberty and of the fragrance of the laws, began to talk at Messana, and to complain that he, a Roman citizen, had been thrown into prison. He said that he was now going straight to Rome, and that he would meet Verres on his arrival there.

6.62. The miserable man was not aware that it made no difference whether he said this at Messana or before the man's face in his own praetorian palace. For, as I have shown you before, Verres had selected this city as the assistant in his crimes, the receiver of his thefts, the partner in all his wickedness. Accordingly, Gavius is at once brought before the Mamertine magistrates; and, as it happened, Verres came on that very day to Messana. The matter is brought before him. He is told that the man was a Roman citizen, who was complaining that at Syracuse he had been confined in the stone-quarries, and who, when he was actually embarking on board ship, and uttering violent threats against Verres, had been brought back by them, and reserved in order that he himself might decide what should be done with him.

Verres thanks the men and praises their goodwill and diligence in his behalf. He himself, inflamed with wickedness and frenzy, comes into the forum. His eyes glared; cruelty was visible in his whole countenance. All men waited to see what steps he was going to take, —what he was going to do; when all of a sudden he orders the man to be seized, and to be stripped and bound in the middle of the forum, and the rods to be got ready. The miserable man cried out that he was a Roman citizen, a citizen, also, of the municipal town of Cosa,—that he had served with Lucius Pretius,

---

[1] A city on the Italian mainland, directly across the narrow Straits of Messana from Sicily, and easily visible from the island.

a most illustrious Roman knight, who was living as a trader at Panormus, and from whom Verres might know that he was speaking the truth.

Then Verres said that he had ascertained that he had been sent into Sicily by the leaders of the runaway slaves, in order to act as a spy; a matter as to which there was no witness, no trace, nor even the slightest suspicion in the mind of any one. Then he orders the man to be most violently scourged on all sides.

In the middle of the forum of Messana a Roman citizen, O judges, was beaten with rods; while in the meantime no groan was heard, no other expression was heard from that wretched man, amid all his pain, and between the sound of the blows, except these words, "I am a citizen of Rome." He fancied that by this one statement of his citizenship he could ward off all blows, and remove all torture from his person. He not only did not succeed in averting by his entreaties the violence of the rods, but as he kept on repeating his entreaties and the assertion of his citizenship, a cross—a cross, I say—was got ready for that miserable man, who had never witnessed such abuse of power.

6.63. O the sweet name of liberty! O the admirable privileges of our citizenship! O Porcian law! O Sempronian laws! O power of the tribunes, bitterly regretted by, and at last restored to the Roman people! Have all our rights fallen so far that in a province of the Roman people,—in a town of our confederate allies,—a Roman citizen should be bound in the forum and beaten with rods by a man who only had the fasces and the axes through the kindness of the Roman people?

What shall I say, when fire and red-hot plates and other instruments of torture were employed? If the bitter entreaties and the miserable cries of that man had no power to restrain you, were you not moved even by the weeping and loud groans of the Roman citizens who were present at that time? Did you dare to drag any one to the cross who said that he was a Roman citizen?

I was unwilling, O judges, to press this point so strongly at the former pleading; I was unwilling to do so. For you saw how the feelings of the multitude were excited against him with indignation, and hatred, and fear of their common danger. I at that time fixed a limit to my oration, and checked the eagerness of Caius Numitorius, a Roman knight, a man of the highest character, one of my witnesses. And I rejoiced that Glabrio had acted (and he had acted most wisely) as he did in dismissing that witness immediately, in the middle of the discussion. In fact he was afraid that the Roman people might seem to have inflicted that punishment on Verres by tumultuary violence which he was anxious he should only suffer according to the laws and by your judicial sentence.

Now since it is made clear beyond a doubt to everyone in what state your case is and what will become of you, I will deal thus with you: I will prove that the very same Gavius whom you all of a sudden assert to have been a spy had been confined by you in the stone-quarries at Syracuse; and I will prove that not only by the registers of the Syracusans—lest you should be able to say that, because there is a man named Gavius mentioned in those documents, I have invented this charge, and picked out this name so as to be able to say that this is the man,—but in accordance with your own choice I will produce witnesses, who will state that that identical man was thrown by you into the stone-quarries at Syracuse. I will produce, also, citizens of Cosa, his fellow-citizens and relations, who shall teach you, though it is too late, and who shall also teach the judges, (for it is not too late for them to know) that that Publius Gavius whom you crucified was a Roman citizen, and a citizen of the municipality of Cosa, not a spy of runaway slaves.

And you, O Verres, say the same thing. You confess that he did cry out that he was a Roman citizen; but that the name of citizenship did not avail with you even so much as to cause the least hesitation in your mind, or even any brief respite from a most cruel and ignominious punishment. This is the point I press, this is what I dwell upon, O judges; with this single fact I am content. I give up, I am indifferent to all the rest. By his own confession he must be entangled and destroyed.

You did not know who he was; you suspected that he was a spy. I do not ask you what were your grounds for that suspicion, I impeach you by your own words. He said that he was a Roman citizen. If you, O Verres, being taken among the Persians or in the remotest parts of India, were being led to execution, what else would you cry out but that you were a Roman citizen? And if that name of your city, honored and renowned as it is among all men, would have availed you, a stranger among strangers, among barbarians, among men placed in the most remote and distant corners of the earth, ought not he, whoever he was, whom you were hurrying to the cross, who was a stranger to you, to have been able, when he said that he was a Roman citizen, to obtain from you, the praetor, if not an escape, at least a respite from death by his mention of and claims to citizenship?

6.65. Men of no importance, born in an obscure rank, go to sea; they go to places which they have never seen before; where they can neither be known to the men among whom they have arrived, nor always find, people to vouch for them. But still, owing to this confidence in the mere fact of their citizenship, they think that they shall be safe, not only among our own magistrates, who are restrained by fear of the laws and of public opinion, nor among our fellow-citizens only, who are united with them by community of language, of rights, and of many other things; but wherever they come they think that this will be a protection to them.

Take away this hope, take away this protection from Roman citizens, establish the fact that there is no assistance to be found in the words "I am a Roman citizen;" that a praetor, or any other officer, may with impunity order any punishment he pleases to be inflicted on a man who says that he is a Roman citizen, though no one knows that it is not true; and at one blow, by admitting that defense, you cut off from the Roman citizens all the provinces, all the kingdoms, all free cities, and indeed the whole world, which has hitherto been open most especially to our countrymen....

6.66. But why need I say more about Gavius? as if you were hostile to Gavius, and not rather an enemy to the name and class of citizens, and to all their rights. You were not, I say, an enemy to the individual, but to the common cause of liberty. For what was your object in ordering the Mamertines, when, according to their regular custom and usage, they had erected the cross behind the city in the

Pompeian road, to place it where it looked towards the strait; and in adding, what you can by no means deny, what you said openly in the hearing of everyone, that you chose that place in order that the man who said that he was a Roman citizen might be able from his cross to behold Italy and to look towards his own home?

And accordingly, O judges, that cross, for the first time since the foundation of Messana, was erected in that place. A spot commanding a view of Italy was picked out by that man, for the express purpose that the wretched man who was dying in agony and torture might see that the rights of liberty and of slavery were only separated by a very narrow strait, and that Italy might behold her son murdered by the most miserable and most painful punishment appropriate to slaves alone.

It is a crime to bind a Roman citizen; to scourge him is a wickedness; to put him to death is almost parricide. What shall I say of crucifying him? So guilty an action cannot by an possibility be adequately expressed by any name bad enough for it. Yet with all this that man was not content. "Let him behold his country," said he; "let him die within sight of laws and liberty." It was not Gavius, it was not one individual, I know not whom,—it was not one Roman citizen,—it was the common cause of freedom and citizenship that you exposed to that torture and nailed on that cross....

6.67. If I were to choose to make these complaints and to utter these lamentations not to Roman citizens, not to any friends of our city, not to men who had heard of the name of the Roman people—if I uttered them not to men, but to beasts—or even, to go further if I uttered them in some most desolate wilderness to the stones and rocks, still all things, mute and inanimate as they might be, would be moved by such excessive, by such scandalous atrocity of conduct.

But now, when I am speaking before senators of the Roman people the authors of the laws, of the courts of justice, and of all right, I ought not to fear other than that Verres will be judged the only Roman citizen deserving of that cross of his, and that all others will be judged most undeserving of such a danger.

A little while ago, O judges, we did not restrain our tears at the miserable and most unworthy death of the naval captains; and it was right for us to be moved at the misery of our innocent allies; what now ought we to do when the lives of our relations are concerned? For the blood of all Roman citizens ought to be accounted kindred blood; since the consideration of the common safety and truth requires it. All the Roman citizens in this place, both those who are present and those who are absent in distant lands, require your severity, implore the aid of your good faith, look anxiously for your assistance. They think that all their privileges, all their advantages, all their defenses, in short their whole liberty, depends on your sentence.

✝

3. ROMAN CITIZENSHIP

EMPEROR CLAUDIUS CAESAR

The Verres case shows the strains that were developing as the Romans tried to adjust their Republican form of government to the realities of being a world power. Barely twenty years later—in 49 B.C.—the civil war began that brought Julius Caesar to power and eventually resulted in a responsible Imperial government—at the price of Republican freedom. One of Caesar's successors, the Emperor Claudius (A.D. 41-54), illustrates the type of change that was taking place in the following exchange with the Roman Senate, recorded by the historian Tacitus in his *Annals* (c. A.D. 110). What is the issue involved? How does the senate's attitude compare with that of the Emperor? Which do you agree with? Why?

23. In the consulship of Aulus Vitellius and Lucius Vipsantus the question of filling up the Senate was discussed, and the chief men of Gallia Comata, as it was called, who had long possessed the rights of allies and of Roman citizens, sought the privilege of obtaining public offices at Rome. There was much talk of every kind of the subject, and it was argued before the emperor with vehement opposition. "Italy," it was asserted, "is not so feeble as to be unable to furnish its own capital with a senate. Once our native-born citizens sufficed for peoples of our own kin, and we are by no means dissatisfied with the Rome of the past. To this day we cite examples, which under our old customs the Roman character exhibited as to valor and renown. Is it a small thing that Veneti and Insubres have already burst into the Senate-house, unless a mob of foreigners, a troop of captives, so to say, is now forced upon us? What distinctions will be left for the remnants of our noble houses, or for any impoverished senators from Latium? Every place will be crowded with these millionaires, whose ancestors of the second and third generations at the head of hostile tribes destroyed our armies with fire and sword, and actually besieged the divine Julius at Alesia. These are recent memories. What if there were to rise up the remembrance of those who fell in Rome's citadel and at her altar by the hands of these same barbarians! Let them enjoy indeed the title of citizens, but let them not vulgarize the distinctions of the Senate and the honors of office."

24. These and like arguments failed to impress the emperor. He at once addressed himself to answer them, and thus harangued the assembled Senate. "My ancestors, the most ancient of whom was made at once citizen and a noble of Rome, encourage me to govern by the same policy of transferring to this city all conspicuous merit, wherever found. And indeed I know, as facts, that the Julii came from Alba, the Coruncanii from Camerium, the Porcii from Tusculum, and not to inquire too minutely into the past, that new members have been brought into the Senate from Etruria and Lucania and the whole of Italy, that Italy itself was at last extended to the Alps, to the end that not only singly persons but entire countries and tribes might be united under our name. We had unshaken peace at home; we prospered in all our foreign relations, in the days when Italy beyond the Po was admitted to share our citizenship, and when, enrolling in our ranks the most vigorous of the provincials, under color of settling our legions throughout the world, we recruited our exhausted empire. Are we sorry that the Balbi came to us from Spain, and other men not less illustrious from Narbonnese Gaul? Their descendants are still among us, and do not yield to us in patriotism.

"What was the ruin of Sparta and Athens, but this, that mighty as they were in war, they spurned from them as aliens those whom they had conquered? Our founder Romulus, on the other hand, was so wise that he fought as enemies and then hailed as fellow-citizens several nations on the very same day. Strangers have reigned over us. That freedmen's sons should be entrusted with public offices is not, as many wrongly think, a sudden innovation, but was a common practice in the old commonwealth. But, it will be said, we have fought with the Senones. I suppose then that the Volsci and Aequi never stood in array against us. Our city was taken by the Gauls. Well, we also gave hostages to the Etruscans, and passed under the yoke of the Samnites. On the whole, if you review all our wars, never has one been finished in a shorter time than that with the Gauls. Thenceforth they have preserved an unbroken and loyal peace. United as they now are with us by manners, education, and intermarriage, let them bring us their gold and their wealth rather than enjoy it in isolation. Everything, Senators, which we now hold to be of the highest antiquity, was once new. Plebeian magistrates came after patrician; Latin magistrates after plebeian; magistrates of other Italian peoples after Latin. This practice too will establish itself, and what we are this day justifying by precedents, will be itself a precedent."

25. The emperor's speech was followed by a decree of the Senate, and the Aedui were the first to obtain the right of becoming senators at Rome. This compliment was paid to their ancient alliance, and to the fact that they alone of the Gauls cling to the name of brothers of the Roman people.

✝

4. THE VOICE OF THE PEOPLE

The policy represented by Claudius in his letter won out (the senate always found the emperor's control of the armies a persuasive point), and helped create the cosmopolitan culture we now call "Graeco-Roman." But how was this new order received? Here are four views.

First, a description of the empire by a Greek scholar, Appian of Alexandria, in the Preface to his *Roman History*, written around A.D. 160 (can you come up with this date yourself from what Appian tells you?). Second, the *Panegyric to Rome* delivered by another Greek, Aelius Aristides, around A.D. 143. Although they are Greeks, both men speak favorably of the Empire. Why? How do they distinguish Rome's Empire

from those which have gone before? What are their criteria for claiming Rome's is better? Do their standards differ from each other in any way?

The final two comments are by the satirist Juvenal, writing in Rome about A.D. 100, and the author of the *Book of Revelation*, writing about the same time, whose references to "Babylon" on the Last Day are really a veiled comment on contemporary Rome.

Are there any statements in these writings that surprise you? If so, why? Can you identify any differences in attitude between the authors? If so, how do you account for them?

A. THE ROMAN HISTORY

APPIAN OF ALEXANDRIA

6. Although holding the empire of so many and such great nations the Romans labored five hundred years with toil and difficulty to establish their power firmly in Italy itself. Half of this time they were under kings, but having expelled them and sworn to have kingly rule no longer, they henceforward adopted aristocracy, and chose their rulers yearly. In about the two hundred years next succeeding the five hundred their dominion increased greatly, they acquired unexampled foreign power, and brought the greater part of the nations under their sway. Gaius [Julius] Caesar having got the upper hand of his rivals possessed himself of the sovereignty, which he strengthened, systematized, and secured, and, while preserving the form and name of the republic, made himself the absolute ruler of all. In this way the government, from that time to this, has been a monarchy; but they do not call their rulers kings, out of respect, as I think, for the ancient oath. They call them imperators [emperors], that being the title also of those who formerly held the chief command of the armies for the time being. Yet they are very kings in fact.

7. From the advent of the emperors to the present time is nearly two hundred years more, in the course of which the city has been greatly embellished, its revenue much increased, and in the long reign of peace and security everything has moved towards a lasting prosperity. Some nations have been added to the empire by these emperors, and the revolts of others have been suppressed. Possessing the best part

of the earth and sea they have, on the whole, aimed to preserve their empire by the exercise of prudence, rather than to extend their sway indefinitely over poverty-stricken and profitless tribes of barbarians, some of whom I have seen at Rome offering themselves, by their ambassadors, as its subjects, but the emperor would not accept them because they would be of no use to him. They give kings to a great many other nations whom they do not wish to have under their own government. On some of these subject nations they spend more than they receive from them, deeming it dishonorable to give them up even though they are costly. They surround the empire with great armies and they garrison the whole stretch of land and sea like a single stronghold.

8. No empire down to the present time ever attained to such size, and duration. As for the Greeks, even if we reckon as one the successive periods of Athenian, Spartan, and Theban supremacy, which followed that most glorious epoch of Greek history, the invasion of Darius, and further include with them the Greek hegemony of Philip, son of Amyntas, we see that their empire lasted comparatively but few years. Their wars were waged not so much for the sake of acquisition of empire, as out of mutual rivalry, and the most glorious of them were fought in defense of Greek freedom against the aggression of foreign powers. Those of them who invaded Sicily, with the hope of extending their dominion failed, and whenever they marched into Asia they accomplished small results and speedily returned. In short the Greek power, ardent as it was in fighting for the hegemony, never established itself beyond the boundaries of Greece; and although they succeeded wonderfully for a long period, their history since the time of Philip, the son of Amyntas, and Alexander, the son of Philip, is in my opinion most inglorious and unworthy of them.

9. The empire of Asia is not to be compared, as to achievements and bravery, with that of the smallest of the countries of Europe, on account of the effeminacy and cowardice of the Asiatic peoples, as will be shown in the progress of this history. Such of the Asiatic nations as the Romans hold, they subdued in a few battles, though even the Macedonians joined in the defense, while the conquest of

Africa and of Europe was in many cases very exhausting. Again, the duration of the Assyrians, Medes, and Persians taken together (the three greatest empires before Alexander), does not amount to nine hundred years, a period which that of Rome has already reached, and the size of their empire, I think, was not half that of the Romans, whose boundaries extend from the setting of the sun and the Western ocean to Mount Caucasus and the river Euphrates, and through Egypt up country to Ethiopia and through Arabia as far as the Eastern ocean, so that their boundary is the ocean both where the sun-god rises and where he sinks, while they control the entire Mediterranean, and all its islands as well as Britain in the ocean. But the greatest sea-power of the Medes and Persians included only the gulf of Pamphylia and the single island of Cyprus or perhaps some other small islets belonging to Ionia in the Mediterranean. They controlled the Persian gulf also, but how much of that is open sea?

10. Again, the history of Macedonia before Philip, the son of Amyntas, was of very small account; there was a time, indeed, when the Macedonians were a subject race. The reign of Philip himself was full of toil and struggles which were not contemptible, yet even his deeds concerned only Greece and the neighboring country. The empire of Alexander was splendid in its magnitude, in its armies, in the success and rapidity of his conquests, and it wanted little of being boundless and unexampled, yet in its shortness of duration it was like a brilliant flash of lightning. Although broken into several satrapies even the parts were splendid. The kings of my own country [Egypt] alone had an army consisting of 200,000 foot, 40,000 horse, 300 war elephants, and 2,000 armed chariots, and arms in reserve for 300,000 soldiers more. This was their force for land service. For naval service they had 2,000 barges propelled by poles, and other smaller craft, 1,500 galleys with from one and a half to five benches of oars each, and galley furniture for twice as many ships, 800 vessels provided with cabins, gilded on stem and stern for the pomp of war, with which the kings themselves were wont to go to naval combats; and money in their treasuries to the amount of 740,000 Egyptian talents. Such was the state

of preparedness for war shown by the royal accounts as recorded and left by the king of Egypt, second in succession after Alexander, a monarch remarkable for his skill in raising money, for the lavishness of his expenditure, and for the magnificence of his public works. It appears also that many of the other satrapies were not much inferior in these respects. Yet all these resources were wasted under their successors through civil war, by which alone great empires are destroyed.

11. Through prudence and good fortune has the empire of the Romans attained to greatness and duration; in gaining which they have excelled all others in bravery, patience, and hard labor. They were never elated by success until they had firmly secured their power, nor were they ever cast down by misfortune, although they sometimes lost 20,000 men in a single day, at another time 40,000 and once 50,000, and although the city itself was often in danger. Neither famine, nor frequently recurring plague, nor sedition, nor all these falling upon them at once could abate their ardor; until, through the doubtful struggles and dangers of seven hundred years, they achieved their present greatness, and won prosperity as the reward of good counsel.

✝

B. TO ROME

AELIUS ARISTIDES

10. Some chronicler, speaking of Asia, asserted that one man ruled as much land as the sun passed, and his statement was not true because he placed all Africa and Europe outside the limits where the sun rises in the East and sets in the West. It has now however turned out to be true. Your possession is equal to what the sun can pass, and the sun passes over your land. Neither the Chalcidonean nor the Cyanean promontories limit your empire, nor does the distance from which a horseman can reach the sea in one day, nor do you reign within fixed boundaries, nor does another dictate to what point your control reaches; but the sea like a girdle lies extended, at once in the middle of the civilized world and of your hegemony.

14. I blush now: after such great and impressive matters have been mentioned, my argument reaches a point where it is without great and impressive material; I shall distinguish myself ingloriously by recalling some barbarian empire or Hellenic power and it will seem that I intend to do the opposite of what the Aeolic poets did. For they, when they wished to disparage any work of their contemporaries, compared it with something great and famous among the ancients, thinking in this way best to expose its deficiency. Yet having no other way to show the degree of your empire's superiority, I shall compare it with petty ancient ones. For you have made all the greatest achievements appear very small by your success in surpassing them. Selecting the most important, I shall discuss them, though you perhaps will laugh at them then.

15. On the one hand, let us look at the Persian Empire, which in its day had indeed reputation among the Hellenes and gave to the king who ruled it the epithet "great"–for I shall omit the proceeding empires which were even less ideal–and let us see all in succession, both its size and the things which were done in its time. Therefore we must examine in conjunction how they themselves enjoyed what they had acquired and how they affected their subjects.

16. First then, what the Atlantic now means to you, the Mediterranean was to the "King" in that day. Here his empire stopped, so that the Ionians and Aeolians were at the end of the world. Once when he, "the King of those from the Sunrise to the Sunset, " tried to cross into Greece, he evoked wonder less for his own greatness than for the greatness of his defeat, and he exhibited his splendor in the enormity of his losses. He who failed by so much to win control over Hellas, and who held Ionia as his most remote possession, is, I think, left behind by your empire not by a mere discus throw or an arrow's flight, but by a good half of the civilized world and by the sea in addition.

17. Moreover, even within these boundaries he was not always king with full authority, but as the power of Athens or the fortunes of Lacedaemon varied, now king as far as Ionia, Aeolis and the sea, and then again no longer down to Ionia and the sea, but as far as Lydia

without seeing the sea west of the Cyanean Islands, being a king while he stayed upcountry just like a king in a game of children, coming down again with the consent of those who would let him be king. This the army of Agesilaus revealed, and before him that of the Ten Thousand with Clearchus, the one marching as through its own country, all the way to Phrygia, the other penetrating, as through a solitude, beyond the Euphrates.

19. In truth such were deeds of men, as it were, dared not trust that the empire was their own. They did not mind it as their own, nor did they raise either the urban or the rural areas to beauty and full size, but like those who have laid violent hands on property not their own they consumed it without conscience or honor, seeking to keep their subjects as weak as possible, and as if, in the feat of the five exercises, vying with each other in murders, the second ever tried to outdo the man before. It was a contest to slaughter as many people, to expel as many families and villages, and to break as many oaths as possible.

20. Those then are the enjoyments they derived from their famous power. The consequences of these enjoyments were what a law of nature ordained, hatreds and plots from those who were so used, and defections and civil wars and constant strife and ceaseless rivalries.

23. Fundamentally two things were wrong. The Persians did not know how to rule and their subjects did not cooperate, since it is impossible to be good subjects if the rulers are bad rulers. Government and slave-management were not yet differentiated, but king and master were equivalent terms. They certainly did not proceed in a reasonable manner and with great objectives. For the word "master" (*despótēs*) applies properly within the circle of a private household; when it extends to cities and nations, the role is hard to keep up.

24. Again Alexander, who acquired the great empire—so it looked until yours arose—by overrunning the earth, to tell the truth, more closely resembled one who acquired a kingdom than one who showed himself a king. For what happened to him, I think, is as if some ordinary person were to acquire much good

land but were to die before receiving the yield of it.

25. He advanced over most of the earth and reduced all who opposed him; and he had absolutely all the hardships. But he could not establish the empire nor place the crown upon the labors he had endured, but died midway in the course of his affairs. So one might say that he won very many battles but, as a king, he did very little, and that he became a great contender for kingship, but never received any enjoyable result worthy of his genius and skill. What happened to him was much as if a man, while contending in an Olympic contest, defeated his opponents, then died immediately after the victory before rightly adjusting the crown upon his head.

26. After all, what laws did he ordain for each of his peoples? Or what contributions in taxes, men or ships did he put on a permanent basis? Or by what routine administration with automatic progress and fixed periods of time did he conduct his affairs? In civil administration what successes did he achieve among the people under his rule? He left only one real memorial of his endowment as a statesman, the city by Egypt which bears his name; he did well in founding this for you, the greatest city after yours, for you to have and to control. Thus he abolished the rule of the Persians, yet he himself all but never ruled.

28. Now, however, the present empire has been extended to boundaries of no mean distance, to such, in fact, that one cannot even measure the area within them. On the contrary, for one who begins a journey westward from the point where at that period the empire of the Persian found its limit, the rest is far more than the entirety of his domain, and there are no sections which you have omitted, neither city nor tribe nor harbor nor district, except possibly some that you condemned as worthless. The Red Sea and the Cataracts of the Nile and Lake Maeotis, which formerly were said to lie on the boundaries of the earth, are like the courtyard walls to the house which is this city of yours. On the other hand, you have explored Ocean. Some writers did not believe that Ocean existed at all, or did not believe that it flowed around the earth; they thought that poets had invented the name and

had introduced it into literature for the sake of entertainment. But you have explored it so thoroughly that not even the island therein has escaped you.

29. Vast and comprehensive as is the size of it, your empire is much greater for its perfection than for the area which its boundaries encircle. There are no pockets of the empire held by Mysians, Sacae, Pisidians, or others, land which some have occupied by force, others have detached by revolt, who cannot be captured. Nor is it merely called the land of the *King*, while really the land of all who are able to hold it. Nor do satraps fight one another as if they had no king; nor are cities at variance, some fighting against these and some against those, with garrisons being dispatched to some cities and being expelled from others. But for the eternal duration of this empire the whole civilized world prays all together, emitting, like an aulos after a thorough cleaning, one note with more perfect precision than a chorus; so beautifully is it harmonized by the leader in command.

31. All directions are carried out by the chorus of the civilized world at a word or gesture of guidance more easily than at some plucking of a chord; and if anything need be done, if suffices to decide and there it is already done. The governors sent out to the city-states and ethnic groups are each of them rulers of those under them, but in what concerns themselves and their relations to each other they are all equally among the ruled, and in particular they differ from those under their rule in that it is they—one might assert—who first show how to be the right kind of subject. So much respect has been instilled in all men for him who is the great governor, who obtains for them their all.

32. They think that he knows what they are doing better than they do themselves. Accordingly they fear his displeasure and stand in greater awe of him than one would of a despot, a master who was present and watching and uttering commands. No one is so proud that he can fail to be moved upon hearing even the mere mention of the Ruler's name, but, rising, he praises and worships him and breathes two prayers in a single breath, one to the gods on the Ruler's behalf, one for his own affairs to the Ruler himself. And if the

governors should have even some slight doubt whether certain claims are valid in connection with either public or private lawsuits and petitions from the governed, they straightway send to him with a request for instructions what to do, and they wait until he renders a reply, like a chorus waiting for its trainer.

33. Therefore, he has no need to wear himself out traveling around the whole empire nor, by appearing personally, now among some, then among others, to make sure of each point when he has the time to tread their soil. It is very easy for him to stay where he is and manage the entire civilized world by letters, which arrive almost as soon as they are written, as if they were carried by winged messengers.

34. But that which deserves as much wonder and admiration as all the rest together, and constant expression of gratitude both in word and action, shall now be mentioned. You who hold so vast an empire and rule it with such a firm hand and with so much unlimited power have very decidedly won a great success, which is completely your own.

36. For of all who have ever gained empire you alone rule over men who are free. Caria has not been given to Tissaphernes, nor Phrygia to Pharnabazus, nor Egypt to someone else; nor is the country said to be enslaved, as household of so-and-so, to whomsoever it has been turned over, a man himself not free. But just as those in states of one city appoint the magistrates to protect and care for the governed, so you, who conduct public business in the whole civilized world exactly as if it were one city-state, appoint the governors, as is natural after elections, to protect and care for the governed, not to be slave masters over them. Therefore governor makes way for governor unobtrusively, when his time is up, and far from staying too long and disputing the land with his successor, he might easily not stay long enough to meet him.

59. But there is that which very decidedly deserves as much attention and admiration now as all the rest together. I mean your magnificent citizenship with its grand conception, because there is nothing like it in the records of all mankind. Dividing into two groups all those in your empire--and with this word I

have indicated the entire civilized world—you have everywhere appointed to your citizenship, or even to kinship with you, the better part of the world's talent, courage, and leadership, while the rest you recognized as a league under your hegemony.

60. Neither sea nor intervening continent are bars to citizenship, nor are Asia and Europe divided in their treatment here. In your empire all paths are open to all. No one worthy of rule or trust remains an alien, but a civil community of the World has been established as a Free Republic under one, the best, ruler and teacher of order; and all come together as into a common civic center, in order to receive each man his due.

61. What another city is to its own boundaries and territory, this city is to the boundaries and territory of the entire civilized world, as if the latter were a country district and she had been appointed common town. It might be said that this one citadel is the refuge and assembly place of all perioeci or of all who dwell in outside demes.

63. Let this passing comment, which the subject suggested, suffice. As we were saying, you who are "great greatly" distributed your citizenship. It was not because you stood off and refused to give a share in it to any of the others that you made your citizenship an object of wonder. On the contrary, you sought its expansion as a worthy aim, and you have caused the word Roman to be the label, not of membership in a city, but of some common nationality, and this not just one among all, but one balancing all the rest. For the categories into which you now divide the world are not Hellenes and Barbarians, and it is not absurd, the distinction which you made, because you show them a citizenry more numerous, so to speak, than the entire Hellenic race. The division which you substituted is one into Romans and non-Romans. To such a degree have you expanded the name of your city.

64. Since these are the lines along which the distinction has been made, many in every city are fellow-citizens of yours no less than of their own kinsmen, though some of them have not yet seen this city. There is no need of garrisons to hold their citadels, but the men of

greatest standing and influence in every city guard their own fatherlands for you. And you have a double hold upon the cities, both from here and from your fellow citizens each.

65. No envy sets foot in the empire, for you yourselves were the first to disown envy, when you placed all opportunities in view of all and offered those who were able a chance to be governed more than they governed in turn. Nor does hatred either steal in from those who are not chosen. For since the constitution is a universal one and, as it were, of one state, naturally your governors rule not as over the property of others but as over their own. Besides, all the masses have as a share in it the permission to <take refuge with you> from the power of the local magnates, <but there is> the indignation and punishment from you which will come upon them immediately, if they themselves dare to make any unlawful change.

68. It is not safe for those to rule who have not power. The second best way to sail, they say, is to be governed by one's betters, but by you now it has been shown to be actually the first best way. Accordingly, all are held fast and would not ask to secede any more than those at sea from the helmsman. As bats in caves cling fast to each other and to the rocks, so all from you depend with much concern not to fall from this cluster of cities, and would sooner conceive fear of being abandoned by you, than abandon you themselves.

69. They no longer dispute over the right to rule and to have first honors, which caused the outbreak of all the wars of the past. Instead, the rulers of yore do not even recall with certainty what domain they once had, while the others, like water in silent flow, are most delightfully at rest. They have gladly ceased from toil and trouble, for they have come to realize that in the other case they were fighting vainly over shadows.

70. Wars, even if they once occurred, no longer seem to have been real; on the contrary, stories about them are interpreted more as myths by the many who hear them.

90. It appears to me that in this state you have established a constitution not at all like any of those among the rest of mankind. Formerly there seemed to be three constitutions in hu-

man society. Two were tyranny and oligarchy, or kingship and aristocracy, since they were known under two names each according to the view one took in interpreting the character of the men in control. A third category was known as democracy whether the leadership was good or bad. The cities had received one or the other constitution as choice or chance prevailed for each. Your state, on the other hand, is quite dissimilar; it is such a form of government as if it were a mixture of all the constitutions without the bad aspects of any one. That is why precisely this form of constitution has prevailed. So when one looks at the strength of the People and sees how easily they get all that they want and ask, he will deem it a complete democracy except for the faults of democracy. When he looks at the Senate sitting as a council and keeping the magistracies, he will think that there is no aristocracy more perfect than this. When he looks at the Ephor and Prytanis, who presides over all of these, him from whom it is possible for the People to get what they want and for the Few to have the magistracies and power, he will see in this one, the One who holds the most perfect monarchic rule, One without a share in the vices of a tyrant and One elevated above even kingly dignity.

91. It is not strange that you alone made these distinctions and discoveries how to govern both in the world and in the city itself. For you alone are rulers, so to speak, according to nature. Those others who preceded you established an arbitrary, tyrannical rule. They became masters and slaves of each other in turn, and as rulers they were a spurious crew. They succeeded each other as if advancing to the position in a ball game. Macedonians had a period of enslavement to Persians, Persians to Medes, Medes to Assyrians, but as long as men have known you, all have known you as rulers. Since you were free right from the start and had begun the game as it were in the rulers' position, you equipped yourselves with all that was helpful for the position of rulers, and you invented a new constitution such as no one ever had before, and you prescribed for all things fixed rules and fixed periods.

✝

C. THE THIRD SATIRE

JUVENAL

ROME IS NO PLACE FOR HONEST MEN

Though troubled at an old friend's departure, I however congratulate him since he proposes to fix his home in deserted Cumae, and present one townsman to the Sibyl. It is the approach to Baiae, and a pleasant seaside for agreeable retirement. I prefer even Prochyta to the crowded city. For what spot have we ever seen so wretched and desolate that one would not hold it a worse thing to stand in dread of fires, constant collapses to houses, with all the thousand perils of the heartless city and poets spouting in the hot August month?

But while his entire effects were being packed upon a single coach, my friend halted by the time-worn arches and dripping Capena gate. At the place where by night Numa used to make appointments with his mistress (now the grove of the hollowed spring and temple is leased out to Jews whose worldly wealth is a basket and a wisp of hay; for every tree is by law ordained to pay rent to the nation, and the Muses are evicted and the wood is turned beggar), down we went into the valley of Egeria and grottoes from nature transformed. How far more real would have been the spirit of the stream, if lawn had enclosed the waters with a green fringe, and no marble slabs done outrage to the ground!

Here then Umbricius spoke: "Since there is no room in the city for honest men, no wages for our efforts, and my means today are less than they were yesterday, and will tomorrow lose somewhat of the little that remains, I purpose to go to the place where Daedalus put off his tired wings, while my gray hairs are still fresh, and I am still at the outset of old age, still upright, while there is still some thread of life left for Fate to spin, and I bear myself on my own proper feet with no wretched stick to prop my right hand.

"Farewell, my native town. There let your villains live of low and high degree; there let them stay who swear that black is white, who scruple not to contract for farming the tolls on rivers and harbors, clearing flood water, neatly executing funerals, and come at last themselves beneath the hammer that assigns ownership.

CIRCUS CLOWNS

"These men, musicians once, familiar figures from circuses, whose puffed cheeks are well known through all the country towns, now exhibit pageants, and to curry favor, decree the death of those the mob orders with a twist of the thumb; then they are back to private parties: and why should they not try all trades? For it is men such as these that chance elevates from low estate to high pinnacles of success, whenever it has pleased her to make merry.

"What can I do at Rome? I know not how to lie; I cannot praise a book if it is bad, and cry 'Oh, let me read it'; the movements of the stars are beyond my knowledge; I have neither the will nor the power to hire a father's death; I have never pried into the entrails of frogs; to bring her paramour's presents and messages to the young wife I leave to others; I will not be a robber's tool, and so that's why, like a cripple whose right hand is palsied, I am a useless trunk, not marching forth in any governor's train. Who is now in favor, except the confidant and he whose heart boils and seethes with secrets which must never be revealed? Nothing does that man think he owes you, nothing will he ever bestow upon you who has shared with him his honorable secret.

"Dear to Verres will be the man that can bring Verres to justice whenever he will. Prize not so highly all the sand of shady Tagus and all the gold it rolls down to the sea, as for such to forego your sleep and take bribes you must soon relinquish with a sigh, and be ever a terror to your patron.

"What race now is chiefly beloved by our wealthy men, and what persons I mainly avoid, I will hasten to disclose, and consideration will not check me. Men of Rome, it is our Rome turned Greek I cannot stomach. Yet how small a portion of our scum hail from Achaea? Long ago has Syrian Orontes turned its tide into the Tiber, bringing too its language and customs and flute-players and slanting harp-strings, and with itself its foreign timbrels and daughters of dishonor in the circus. Hither hasten all who delight in an Eastern harlot with broidered cap. Romulus,

behold your yeoman dons his Greek dress-shoes, and wears his Greek medals on his neck smeared with Greek ointment. This one has left steep Sicyon, or that one Amydon, this Andros and that Samos, another Tralles or Alabanda, and to the Esquiline they flock and the hill that's named from the osier, soon to be bosom friends and masters in the houses of the great.

"Theirs is quick talent, reckless impudence, words ready and more impetuous than Isaeus. Conceive him if you can. A many-sided person he has brought in himself: schoolmaster, professor, mathematician, painter, masseur, tight-rope dancer, doctor, wizard, yon hungry Greek knows all things alike: bid him fly, and fly he will. In a word, no Moor or Sarmatian or Thracian was he that got him wings, but a true Greek born in the heart of Athens. Shall I not scorn the gaudy robes that such men wear?

"Shall the foreign seal before me as witness, and sit at meat in a more honorable place that I, though he came sailing to Rome before the wind that brings our damson plums and figs? Is it so utterly of no account that in childhood I breathed the air of Aventine and fed on Sabine olives?

"Or mark how that race of flatterers most adroit extols the talk of an unlettered man or looks of an ugly friend, and compares the long throat of some weakling to the brawny neck of Hercules holding Antaeus aloft from earth, and is in ecstatic joy at some feeble voice whose tone is as wretched as the squeak of her mate that pecks the hen. We too may try our hand at like compliments, but they convince. Or has he a rival when your Greek in comedy plays a Thais or a wife or a Doris not in mantle attired: why, a real female seems to be speaking, not the player. They look the woman to the life.

"Still in their own land Antiochus or Stratocles or Demetrius and mincing Haemus will excite no wonder: the whole race are actors born. You smile, he is convulsed with a louder laugh; he weeps if he has caught sight of his friend in tears, yet feels no real grief; if in mid-winter you should ask for a bit of fire he draws his rug round him; if you say, 'I am hot,' he is in a perspiration.

"We are not then equally matched; the advantage is with the man who can take his expression from another's face, and throw up his hands, ready to congratulate on any common act successfully performed, or if the master's drinking-scoop falls with a crash bottom upwards.

NOTHING SACRED

"Also there's nothing sacred from him or safe from his lechery: not the lady of the household, or maiden daughter, or beardless son-in-law that is to be, or son hitherto uncorrupted—in default of these he debauches the old grandmother. These men wish to learn the secrets of the home and thence be feared.

"Now since the topic of Greeks is my theme, glance at their philosophers and learn a crime of one who wore the ampler gown. A Stoic was the informer that did Barea to death; his own friend and pupil that old man did to death, who was reared on the river-bank where dropped to earth the wing of the hack that bore the Gorgon's head. There is no place here for any Roman where the monarch is some Protogenes or Diphilus or Hermarchus; such an one never shares his friend but keeps him to himself—it is the failing of blood. For as soon as he has dropped into the receptive ear a little of the poison of his character and country, I am ousted from the door; the years of my long service count as nothing: nowhere do men think less of the sacrifice of a dependent.

"Further, since our countrymen must not be screened, of what use to him here in Rome can be his attention or service on the poor man's part, if in full dress he should be at pains to bestir himself, for some praetor is bustling his lictor, bidding him haste with headlong speed, as the childless old ladies have been up some time, for fear his colleague be before him in paying his respects to Mistress Albina or Mistress Modia? Here in Rome the son of freeborn parents gives the place of honor to the rich man's slave; for that other spends the whole salary of a gallant captain in presents to some Calvina or Catiena to enjoy for once or twice her favors, while you, poor friend, when some dressy frail one's face takes your fancy, waver and hesitate to hand your choice from her high sedan.

"Even if you produce in town a witness as stainless as was he who housed the goddess of Ida, though even Numa come forward or the man that rescued trembling Minerva from the blazing temple, instantly to his income we direct our inquiries, his character is the last thing about which we ask. 'How many servants does he keep; how many acres of land does he hold; how many and how large are the dishes off which he dines?' Each man's credit is gauged by his balance at the bank.

"Swear if you will by the altars of the gods of Samothrace and our own, the poor man is supposed to make light of thunderbolts and gods, and the gods themselves forgive him. Besides, your poor man too is a butt and subject for jests if his cloak is dirty and torn, if his robe is a little shabby and one of his shoes shows a hole where the leather is split, or if where a rent has been stitched more than one patch exhibits some coarse fresh linen. The cruelest sting of all that luckless poverty feels is the mockery of men.

"'Outside,' is the word, 'for very shame, and move from the cushioned stalls of the knights you whose income falls below the law's demands; and there must sit the pander's lads born in some nameless stew, there the sleek broker's hopeful must clap his hands beside some bruiser's strapping sons and sons of some trainer.' This is the ordinance of senseless Otho, who gave us each our place.

HARD TO RISE

"Who was ever here accepted for son-in-law whose income is inferior and no match for the lady's portion? What poor man is named as heir? When is he appointed magistrates' assessor? The needy Romans should in days gone by have left the city once and for all in a body. It is hard to rise when straitened means at home conceal men's merits, but harder still is their struggle in city, where deplorable quarters are dear, and dear the servant's keep, and dear the modest little dinner. You dare not dine off earthenware, though this you will call demeaning no more if suddenly you are transported to some Sabine repast, content too there with your coarse Venetian cape.

"If we confess the truth, through the chief portion of Italy no one wears full dress except for burial. Even when the pomp of public festivals is observed in the grass-grown theater, and at last the familiar farce has reappeared on the stage, when the village baby on its mother's lap shudders at the gaping mouth of the ghastly mask, there you will see dresses of one pattern, no difference between stalls and gallery, white doublets serve the highest magistrates for robes of their exalted office. In town our dress is smart beyond our means, in town we sometimes borrow from our neighbor's pocket rather more than we require.

"The fault is general: in town we all live in pretentious poverty. In short, everything in town is costly. What are you prepared to give for the privilege of at last paying your respects to a Cossus, or that a Veiento may deign to look at you though he never open his lips? Suppose one great man is shaving the beard, another cutting off the hair of his favorite: the house is full of cakes, but they must be paid for. Take yours and keep it to stir the leaven of your rage. We dependents must perforce pay blackmail, and swell the perquisites of dandified domestics.

"Who fears or ever feared the collapse of a house at bracing Praeneste, or Volsinii lying amid its woody hills, or old-world Gabii, or on the height of sloping Tibur? The city we dwell in is mainly propped with frail supports; for by such sorry means the agent stays the tumbling piles, and having patched up the fissure of an ancient crack, bids us sleep at ease though threatened with collapse. Where never are conflagrations and never alarms by night, there let me live. Your ground-floor friend is already bawling 'Fire!' and shifting his lumber; already, alack! your third story is smoking, yet you know it not: for if the alarm begins at the bottom of the staircase, the last to burn will be the man whom the tiles alone shield from the rain, aloft where the gentle doves lay their tale of eggs.

"Codrus owned one bed too small for any dwarf, six jugs the service of his sideboard, and beneath a tiny beaker, and a Centaur standing under the same marble slab; and a poor old basket contained his library of Greek poets, and those Vandal mice would gnaw the glorious verses. Poor Codrus owned nothing (I know), still all that nothing the poor thing has

lost. While the last drop in his cup of woe is that, when penniless and begging for scraps, nobody will help him with food or lodging or a roof. If my lord duke's palatial mansion is destroyed, each lady wears mourning, peers are prostrate, and my lord chancellor closes his court.

"Then we deplore the accidents of the town and curse its fires. It is still smoldering, when up rushes someone with a present of marbles and offer of materials; one will give undraped white statues, another some masterpiece of Euphranor and Polyclitus, another some glories in days gone by of eastern temples, another books and a dwarf bookcase, and a bust of Minerva, another a bushel of money. Your Croesus replaces what he lost with objects choicer and better, most prosperous of bachelors, and suspected now with good reason of having set fire to his own house.

"If you can drag yourself from the city pageants, you may buy a capital house at Sora or Fabrateria or Frusino for the yearly sum you now pay for your dingy den. Here you have a little garden, and a well that is not deep and needs no rope to work it besprinkles your tiny slips with water easily drawn. Enjoy life, devoted to your mattock, tending your well-kept garden from which you could provide a meal for a hundred vegetarians. It is worthwhile, however insignificant the place of the retreat, to have made oneself the owner of a single lizard.

"Many a sick man here in town dies from sleeplessness (though the actual ailment was caused by the undigested food clogging the fevered stomach), for where can one sleep well in lodgings? Night's rest costs a princely fortune in town. That's the source of illness. The traffic of traps through the narrow winding streets and shouts at the standstill herd will rob even a Drusus and the sea-calves of their sleep.

"When a call takes him from home, the rich man will be carried through the retiring crowd and speed above our heads in a spacious Liburnian litter, and read as well on the way or write or sleep maybe inside; for a litter with window closed induces sleep. Yet he will arrive before us poor folk: speed as we may the surging crowd in front arrests us, the throng behind jostles our backs in dense array; there's a knock now from this fellow's elbow, now another knock from that one's hard pole; now this lout bangs my head with a plank, and that one with an oil-jar. My legs are coated with mud; before long I am trampled upon every side by heavy feet, and find some soldier's hobnail sticking in my toe.

"Note the thick smoke rising around men crowding to the club banquet. There are a hundred diners, each attended by his own chafing-dish. A Corbulo could scarcely have carried so many big basins, so many articles upon his head, as those that the luckless wretched servant bears with neck unbent, running to fan the flame. Doublets just mended are torn, a big beam comes swinging along in a lumbering lorry, and another kind of dray is conveying a whole fir tree: aloft they sway and threaten the public. For if a wagon that is carrying blocks of Luna marble suddenly overturns and pours its spilt avalanche upon the living masses, what is left of their bodies? Who identifies the limbs or bones? Each pauper's corpse when crushed vanishes away utterly like his soul.

"Meanwhile the unsuspecting servants are already washing the plates for dinner, and with puffed cheek blowing up the fire and making a clatter with the greasy flesh-scrapers and laying out the towels after filling the oil flask. These are the different tasks upon which the slaves are busy, but the victim is already seated on the riverbank, and fresh-arrived is shuddering at the grim ferryman, and dares not hope, poor soul! for the skiff to cross the oozy flood, and has no copper between his teeth to proffer.

"Regard now the different perils of the night: how high are the tall roofs from whence a tile comes crashing on your head; how often cracked and broken pots tumble from the windows, with what weight they dent and damage the basalt as they strike it. You might be considered careless and heedless of sudden accident if you go out to dinner with your will unmade: indeed there are as many chances of death as there are watchful windows open this night as you walk by.

"Therefore you should pray and never omit this plaintive petition, that they may be satisfied with emptying the contents of the footpans on you. The drunk and disorderly, who has not had the luck to maul his man, suffers torments, and spends the night like Achilles bemoaning his friend, lying now on his face and now in turn on his back: we find this is the sole condition on which he will be able to rest: it's only a brawl that ensures some people sleep. But although insolent with youth and flushed with wine, he keeps clear of the personage whom a scarlet cloak, and extensive file of retainers, and blaze of torches as well, and a bronze lantern marks as one to be avoided. But he cares not for me, who am generally escorted to bed by the moon or scanty light of a candle, whose wick I husband and economize.

"Mark the preliminaries for the sorry fray, if fray it can be called, where you deal the blows and I am merely beaten. He confronts me and bids me stop: I must needs obey. For what can you do when a wild fellow stronger than yourself compels you? 'Where do you come from?' he cries. 'With whose vinegar and beans are you gorged? What cobbler has been eating cut leeks with you or boiled sheep's lips? Won't answer? Speak, or I will kick you. Tell me where is your beat, in what Jew's praying-shop am I to look for you?'

"If you venture a word or silently make off, it makes no difference: they lay on just the same; next in a passion want to arrest you for it. This is the poor man's boasted freedom: after a thrashing he begs and after a sound punching he implores to be allowed to leave the scene with a few teeth left. Still this is not all you have to fear. You'll find plenty to rob you, when the houses are barred, and each chained up shop's fittings are everywhere secured and have ceased to jangle.

"Sometimes too the footpad starts forth and plies his knife—whenever the Pontine marshes and Gallinarian pine-forest are safely guarded by armed patrols: that's the reason why the brigands all hurry thence to town as a happy hunting ground.

"What furnace and what anvil is not busy with forging heavy fetters? The best part of our iron goes to make chains, so you may well fear that ploughshares will fail, and pickaxes and hoes run short. Happy our forefathers remote, happy you may call the generation that in by-gone days when kings and tribunes ruled saw Rome served well enough by a single prison!

"To these reasons I could have added many others also, but my beasts want me and the sun is setting: I must start, for my driver has long been signaling to me with a crack of his whip. So good-bye, forget me not, and whenever Rome sends you back on a hurried trip for health to your native Aquinium, send for me too from Cumae to Ceres Helvina and your Diana. Unless they scorn me, I will come to your cool country to listen to your satires in my farmer's boots."

✝

D. THE BOOK OF REVELATION

Chapter 17: Then one of the seven angels who had the seven bowls came and said to me, "Come, I will show you the judgment of the great harlot who is seated upon many waters, 2 with whom the kings of the earth have committed fornication, and with the wine of whose fornication the dwellers on earth have become drunk." 3 And he carried me away in the Spirit into a wilderness, and I saw a woman sitting on a scarlet beast which was full of blasphemous names, and it had seven heads and ten horns. 4 The woman was arrayed in purple and scarlet, and bedecked with gold and jewels and pearls, holding in her hand a golden cup full of abominations and the impurities of her fornication; 5 and on her forehead was written a name of mystery: "Babylon the great, mother of harlots and of earth's abominations." 6 And I saw the woman, drunk with the blood of the saints and the martyrs of Jesus.

When I saw her I marveled greatly. 7 But the angel said to me, "Why marvel? I will tell you the mystery of the woman and of the beast with seven heads and ten horns that carries her. 8 The beast that you saw was, and is not, and is to ascend from the bottomless pit and go to perdition; and the dwellers on earth whose names have not been written in the book of life from the foundation of the world, will marvel to behold the beast, because it was

and is not and is to come. 9 This calls for a mind with wisdom: the seven heads are seven hills on which the woman is seated; 10 they are also seven kings, five of whom have fallen, one is, the other has not yet come, and when he comes he must remain only a little while. 11 As for the best that was and is not, it is an eighth but it belongs to the seven, and it goes to perdition. 12 And the ten horns that you saw are ten kings who have not yet received royal power, but they are to receive authority as kings for one hour, together with the beast. 13 These are of one mind and give over their power and authority to the beast; 14 they will make war on the Lamb, and the Lamb will conquer them, for he is Lord of lords and King of kings, and those with him are called and chosen and faithful."

15 And he said to me, "The waters that you saw, where the harlot is seated, are peoples and multitudes and nations and tongues. 16 And the ten horns that you saw, they and the beast will hate the harlot; they will make her desolate and naked, and devour her flesh and burn her up with fire, 17 for God has put it into their hearts to carry out his purpose by being of one mind and giving over their royal power to the beast, until the words of God shall be fulfilled. 18 And the woman that you saw is the great city which has dominion over the kings of the earth."

Chapter 18: After this I saw another angel coming down from heaven, having great authority; and the earth was made bright with his splendor. 2 And he called out with a mighty voice,

"Fallen, fallen is Babylon the great!
It has become a dwelling place of demons,
a haunt of every foul spirit,
a haunt of every foul and hateful bird;
3 for all nations have drunk the wine of her
    impure passion,
and the kings of the earth have committed
    fornication with her,
and the merchants of the earth have grown
    rich with the wealth of her wantonness."
4 Then I heard another voice from heaven
    saying,
"Come out of her, my people,
'lest you take part in her sins,
lest you share in her plagues;

5 for her sins are heaped high as heaven,
and God has remembered her iniquities.
6 Render to her as she herself has rendered,
and repay her double for her deeds;
mix a double draught for her in the cup she
     mixed.
7 As she glorified herself and played the wan-
     ton,
so give her a like measure of torment and
     mourning.
Since in her heart she says, 'A queen I sit,
I am no widow, mourning I shall never see,'
8 so shall her plagues come in a single day,
pestilence and mourning and famine,
and she shall be burned with fire;
for mighty is the Lord God who judges her."
9 And the kings of the earth, who committed
fornication and were wanton with her, will
weep and wail over her when they see the
smoke of her burning; 10 they will stand far
off, in fear of her torment, and say,

"Alas! alas! thou great city,
thou mighty city, Babylon!
In one hour has thy judgment come."

11 And the merchants of the earth weep and
mourn for her, since no one buys their cargo
any more, 12 cargo of gold, silver, jewels and
pearls, fine linen, purple silk and scarlet, all
kinds of scented wood, all articles of ivory, all
articles of costly wood, bronze, iron and
marble, 13 cinnamon, spice, incense, myrrh,
frankincense, wine, oil, fine flour and wheat,
cattle and sheep, horses and chariots, and
slaves, that is, human souls.

14 "The fruit for which thy soul longed has
     gone from thee,
and all thy dainties and thy splendor are lost to
     thee, never to be found again!"
15 The merchants of these wares, who gained
     wealth from her, will stand far off, in fear
     of her torment, weeping and mourning
     aloud,
16 "Alas, alas, for the great city
that was clothed in fine linen, in purple and
     scarlet,
bedecked with gold, with jewels, and with
     pearls!
17 In one hour all this wealth has been laid
     waste."
And all shipmasters and seafaring men, sailors
and all whose trade is on the sea, stood far off

18 and cried out as they saw the smoke of her
burning,

"What city was like the great city?"
19 And they threw dust on their heads, as they
     wept and mourned, crying out,
"Alas, alas, for the great city
where all who had ships at sea grew rich by her
     wealth!
In one hour she has been laid waste.
20 Rejoice over her, O heaven,
O saints and apostles and prophets,
for God has given judgment for you against
     her!"
21 Then a mighty angel took up a stone like a
great millstone and threw it into the sea, saying,

"So shall Babylon the great city be thrown
     down with violence, and shall be found no
     more;
22 and the sound of harpers and minstrels, of
     flute players and trumpeters, shall be heard
     in thee no more;
and a craftsman of any craft shall be found in
     thee no more;
and the sound of the millstone shall be heard
     in thee no more;
23 and the light of a lamp shall shine in thee
     no more;
and the voice of bridegroom and bride shall be
     heard in thee no more; for thy merchants
     were the great men of the earth,
and all nations were deceived by thy sorcery.
24 And in her was found the blood of
     prophets and of saints,
and of all who have been slain on earth."

✝

VIII. The Christian Message

How and why did Christianity succeed? A common answer, from a religious viewpoint, would be that it was God's will. Even a less religious person today would probably assume that Christianity was morally superior, ethically more appealing, somehow "better" than pagan beliefs. Yet these aren't, at least to historians, very satisfying answers (which does not mean that they are false, merely that they rely on supernatural and a priori assumptions–and historians are skittish about things like that). The following readings present some evidence from the first three centuries of the Christian era. The core of the Christian message comes, of course, from JESUS OF NAZARETH (c. 4 B.C.–A.D. 30). While there is much in Jesus' teaching that is revolutionary, a careful look at the teachings of EPICTETUS (c. A.D. 55-135) can reveal some surprising comparisons. The remaining readings deal with the conflict between paganism and Christianity. For example, CELSUS (c. A.D.180) shows an educated pagan's understanding of Christianity. THE BOOK OF JAMES illustrates some practical solutions to the complex question of how Christians should live. The story of the LYONS MARTYRS (A.D.170) and the letter of DIONYSUS OF ALEXANDRIA (c. A.D. 260) show the paradoxical effects of persecution, while DIONYSIUS'S recounting of Christian behavior during a plague shows the immense practical benefit of Christian values in action.

❖ ❖ ❖

1. PAGAN AND CHRISTIAN CONCORD

Although Christian and pagan beliefs usually are put in opposition to each other, there were broad areas of agreement.

The Christian message is contained in a series of remembrances and letters that were put together early in the second century in a document that Christians called *The New Testament*, to distinguish it from the Hebrew Bible, which they called *The Old Testament*. The core of the Christian message is contained in the sayings of Jesus of Nazareth excerpted below. After reading them, see if you can define what was new or different about Christianity. Would you call anything in them 'revolutionary'?

Epictetus (c. A.D. 55-135) was a former slave who became a major Stoic philosopher. How would you compare his teachings to those of Jesus? Is there a major difference between the two? Are there similarities? Are the similarities superficial or fundamental? The differences? For whom was Epictetus writing? Is his audience the same as Jesus'?

A. SAYINGS OF JESUS

i. THE SERMON ON THE MOUNT

Chapter 5: Seeing the crowds, he went up on the mountain, and when he sat down his disciples came to him. 2 And he opened his mouth and taught them, saying:

3 "Blessed are the poor in spirit, for theirs is the kingdom of heaven.

4 "Blessed are those who mourn, for they shall be comforted.

5 "Blessed are the meek, for they shall inherit the earth.

6 "Blessed are those who hunger and thirst for righteousness, for they shall be satisfied.

7 "Blessed are the merciful, for they shall obtain mercy.

8 "Blessed are the pure in heart, for they shall see God.

9 "Blessed are the peacemakers, for they shall be called sons of God.

10 "Blessed are those who are persecuted for righteousness' sake, for theirs is the kingdom of heaven.

11 "Blessed are you, when men revile you and persecute you and utter all kinds of evil against you falsely on my account. 12 Rejoice and be glad, for your reward is great in heaven, for so men persecuted the prophets who were before you.

13 "You are the salt of the earth; but if salt have lost its taste, how shall its saltness be restored? It is no good for anything except to be thrown out and trodden under foot by men.

14 "You are the light of the world. A city set on a hill cannot be hid. 15 Nor do men light a lamp and put it under a bushel, but on a stand, and it gives light to all the house. 16 Let your light so shine before men, that they may see your good works and give glory to your Father who is in heaven.

17 "Think not that I have come to abolish the law and the prophets; I have come not to abolish them but to fulfill them. 18 For truly, I say to you, till heaven and earth pass away, not an iota, not a dot, will pass from the law until all is accomplished. 19 Whoever then relaxes one of the least of these commandments and teaches men so, shall be called least in the kingdom of heaven; but he who does them and teaches them shall be called great in the kingdom of heaven. 20 For I tell you, unless your righteousness exceeds that of the scribes and Pharisees, you will never enter the kingdom of heaven.

21 "You have heard that it was said to the men of old, You shall not kill; and whoever kills shall be liable to judgment.' 22 But I say to you that every one who is angry with his brother shall be liable to judgment; whoever insults his brother shall be liable to the council, and whoever says, 'You fool!' shall be liable to the hell of fire. 23 So if you are offering your gift at the altar, and there remember that your brother has something against you, 24 leave your gift there before the altar and go; first be reconciled to your brother, and then come and offer your gift. 25 Make friends quickly with your accuser, while you are going with him to court, lest your accuser hand you over to the judge, and the judge to the guard, and you be put in prison. 26 Truly, I say to you, you will never get out till you have paid the last penny.

27 "You have heard that it was said, 'You shalt not commit adultery.' 28 But I say to you that every one who looks at a woman lustfully has already committed adultery with her in his heart. 29 If your right eye causes you to sin, pluck it out and throw it away; it is better that

you lose one of your members than that your whole body be thrown into hell. 30 And if your right hand causes you to sin, cut it off, and throw it away; for it is better that you lose one of your members than that your whole body go into hell.

31 "It was also said, 'Whoever divorces his wife, let him give her a certificate of divorce.' 32 But I say to you that every one who divorces his wife, except on the ground of unchastity, makes her an adulteress; and whoever marries a divorced woman commits adultery.

33 "Again you have heard that it was said to the men of old, 'You shalt not swear falsely, but shall perform to the Lord what you have sworn.' 34 But I say to you, Do not swear at all, either by heaven, for it is the throne of God, 35 or by the earth, for it is his footstool, or by Jerusalem, for it is the city of the great King. 36 And do not swear by your head, because you cannot make one hair white or black. 37 Let what you say be simply 'Yes' or 'No'; anything more than this comes from evil.

38 "You have heard that it was said, 'An eye for an eye and a tooth for a tooth.' 39 But I say to you, Do not resist one who is evil. But if any one strikes you on the right cheek, turn to him the other also; 40 and if any one would sue you and take your coat, let him have your cloak as well; 41 and if any one forces you to go one mile, go with him two miles. 42 Give to him that begs from you, and do not refuse him who would borrow from you.

43 "You have heard that it was said, 'You shall love your neighbor and hate your enemy.' 44 But I say to you, Love your enemies and pray for those who persecute you, 45 so that you may be sons of your Father who is in heaven; for he makes his sun rise on the evil and on the good, and sends rain on the just and on the unjust. 46 For if you love those who love you, what reward have you? Do not even the tax collectors do the same? 47 And if you salute only your brethren, what are you doing than others? Do not even the Gentiles do the same? 48 You, therefore, must be perfect, as your heavenly Father is perfect.

Chapter 6 "Beware of practicing your piety before men in order to be seen by them; for then you will have no reward from your Father who is in heaven.

2 "Thus, when you give alms, sound no trumpet before you, as the hypocrites do in the synagogues and in the streets, that they may be praised by men. Truly, I say to you, they have their reward. 3 But when you give alms, do not let your left hand know what your right hand is doing, 4 so that your alms may be in secret; and your Father who sees in secret will reward you.

5 "And when you pray, you must not be like the hypocrites; for they love to stand and pray in the synagogues and at the street corners, that they may be seen by men. Truly, I say to you, they have their reward. 6 But when you pray, go into your room and shut the door and pray to your Father who is in secret; and your Father who sees in secret will reward you.

7 "And in praying do not heap up empty phrases as the Gentiles do; for they think that they will be heard for their many words. 8 Do not be like them, for your Father knows what you need before you ask him. 9 Pray then like this:

Our Father who art in heaven,
Hallowed be thy name.
Thy kingdom come,
Thy will be done,
On earth, as it is in heaven.
Give us this day our daily bread;
And forgive us our debts,
As we also have forgiven our debtors;
And lead us not into temptation,
But deliver us from evil.

14 For if you forgive men their trespasses, your heavenly Father also will forgive you; 15 but if you do not forgive men their trespasses, neither will your Father forgive your trespasses.

16 "And when you fast, do not look dismal, like the hypocrites, for they disfigure their faces that their fasting may be seen by men. Truly, I say to you, they have their reward. 17 But when you fast, anoint your head and wash your face, 18 that your fasting may not be seen by men but by your Father who is in secret; and your Father who sees in secret will reward you.

19 "Do not lay up for yourselves treasures on earth, where moth and rust consume and where thieves break in and steal, 20 but lay up for yourselves treasures in heaven, where neither moth nor rust consumes and where thieves do not break in and steal. 21 For where your treasure is, there will your heart be also.

22 "The eye is the lamp of the body. So, if therefore your eye is sound, your whole body will be full of light; 23 but if your eye is not sound, your whole body will be full of darkness. If then the light in you is darkness, how great is the darkness!

24 "No one can serve two masters; for either he will hate the one and love the other, or he will be devoted to the one and despise the other. You cannot serve God and mammon.

25 "Therefore I tell you, do not be anxious about your life, what you shall eat or what you shall drink, nor about your body, what you shall put on. Is not life more than food, and the body more than clothing? 26 Look at the birds of the air; they neither sow nor reap nor gather into barns, and yet your heavenly Father feeds them. Are you not of more value than they? 27 And which of you by being anxious can add one cubit to his span of life? 28 And why are you anxious about clothing? Consider the lilies of the field, how they grow; they neither toil nor spin; 29 yet I tell you, even Solomon in all his glory was not arrayed like one of these. 30 But, if God so clothes the grass of the field, which today is alive and tomorrow is thrown into the oven, will he not much more clothe you, O men of little faith? 31 Therefore do not be anxious, saying, 'What shall we eat?' or 'What shall we drink?' or 'What shall we wear?' 32 For the Gentiles seek all these things; and your heavenly Father knows that you need them all. 33 But seek first his kingdom and his righteousness, and all these things shall be yours as well.

34 "Therefore do not be anxious about tomorrow, for tomorrow will be anxious for itself. Let the day's own trouble be sufficient for the day.

Chapter 7 "Judge not, that you not be judged. 2 For with the judgment you pronounce you will be judged, and the measure you give will be the measure you get. 3 And why do you see the speck that is in your brother's eye, but do not notice the log that is in your own eye? 4 Or how can you say to your brother, 'Let me take the speck out of your eye,' when there is the log in your own eye? 5 You hypocrite, first take the log out of your own eye, and then you will see clearly to take the speck out of your brother's eye.

6 "Do not give dogs what is holy; and do not throw your pearls before swine, lest they trample them under foot and turn to attack you.

7 "Ask, and it will be given you; seek, and you will find; knock, and it will be opened to you. 8 For every one who asks receives, and he who seeks finds, and to him who knocks it will be opened. 9 Or what man of you, if your son asks him for bread, will give him a stone? 10 Or if he asks for a fish, will give him a serpent? 11 If you then, who are evil. know how to give good gifts to your children, how much more will your Father who is in heaven give good things to those who ask him! 12 So whatever you wish that men would do to you, do so to them; for this is the law and the prophets.

13 "Enter by the narrow gate, for the gate is wide and the way is easy, that leads to destruction, and those who enter by it are many. 14 For the gate is narrow and the way is hard, that leads to life, and those who find it are few.

15 "Beware of false prophets, who come to you in sheep's clothing but inwardly are ravening wolves. 16 You will know them by their fruits. Are grapes gathered from thorns, or figs from thistles? 17 So, every sound tree bears good fruit, but the bad tree bears evil fruit. 18 A sound tree cannot bear evil fruit, nor can a bad tree bear good fruit. 19 Every tree that does not bear good fruit is cut down and thrown into the fire. 20 Thus you will know them by their fruits.

21 Not everyone who says to me, 'Lord, Lord,' shall enter into the kingdom of heaven, but he who does the will of my Father who is in heaven. 22 On that day many will say to me, 'Lord, Lord, did we not prophesy in your name, and cast out demons in your name, and do many mighty works in your name? 23 And

then will I declare to them, 'I never knew you; depart from me, you evildoers.

24 "Every one then who hears these words of mine and does them will be like a wise man, who built his house upon the rock: 25 And the rain fell, and the floods came, and the winds blew and beat upon that house, but it did not fall, because it had been founded on the rock. 26 And every one who hears these words of mine and does not do them will be like a foolish man who built his house upon the sand; 27 and the rain fell, and the floods came, and the winds blew and beat against that house, and it fell; and great was the fall of it."

28 And when Jesus finished these sayings, the crowds were astounded at his teaching, 29 for he taught them as one who had authority, and not as their scribes.

✝

ii.   THE LAST JUDGMENT

25.31 "When the Son of man comes in his glory, and all the angels with him, then he will sit on his glorious throne. 32 Before him will be gathered all the nations, and he will separate them one from another as a shepherd separates the sheep from the goats, 33 and he will place the sheep at his right hand, but the goats at the left. 34 Then the King will say to those at his right hand, 'Come, O blessed of my Father, inherit the kingdom prepared for you from the foundation of the world; 35 for I was hungry and you gave me food, I was thirsty and you gave me drink, I was a stranger and you welcomed me, 36 I was naked and you clothed me, I was sick and you visited me, I was in prison and you came to me.' 37 Then the righteous will answer him, 'Lord, when did we see thee hungry and feed thee, or thirsty and give thee drink? 38 And when did we see thee a stranger and welcome thee, or naked and clothe thee? And when did we see thee sick or in prison and visit thee?' 40 And the King will answer them, 'Truly, I say to you, as you did it to one of the least of these my brethren, you did it to me.' 41 Then he will say to those at his left hand, 'Depart from me, you cursed, into the eternal fire prepared for the devil and his angels' 42 for I was hungry and you gave me no food, I was thirsty and you gave me no drink, 43 I was a stranger and you did not welcome me, naked and you did not clothe me, sick and in prison and you did not visit me.' 44 Then they also will answer, 'Lord, when did we see thee hungry or thirsty or a stranger or naked or sick or in prison, and did not minister to thee? 45 Then he will answer them, 'Truly, I say to you, as you did it not to one of the least of these, you did it not to me.' 46 And they will go away into eternal punishment, but the righteous into eternal life."

✝

iii. SELECTED SAYINGS

"Do not think that I have come to bring peace on earth; I have not come to bring peace, but a sword. For I have come to set a man against his father, and a daughter against her mother, and a daughter-in-law against her mother-in-law; and a man's foes will be those of his own household. He who loves father or mother more than me is not worthy of me; and he who loves son or daughter more than me is not worthy of me. And he who takes not his cross and follow me is not worthy of me. He who finds his life will lose it, and he who loses his life for my sake will find it." [Matt. 10:34-39]

"I thank thee, Father, Lord of heaven and earth, that thou hast hidden these things from the wise and understanding and revealed them to babes." [Matt. 11:25]

While he was still speaking to the people, behold, his mother and his brothers stood outside, asking to speak to him. But he replied to the man who told him, "Who is my mother, and who are my brothers?" And stretching out his hand toward his disciples, he said, "Here are my mother and my brothers! For whoever does the will of my Father in heaven is my brother, and sister, and mother." [Matt 12:46-50]

"...so will be the coming of the Son of man. Then two men will be in the field; one is taken and one is left. Two women will be grinding at the mill; one is taken and one is left." [Matt. 24:39-41]

"You know that those who are supposed to rule over the Gentiles lord it over them, and their great men exercise authority over them. But it shall not be so among you; but whoever would be great among you must be your servant, and whoever would be first among you must be slave of all. For the Son of man came not to be served, but to serve, and to give his life as a ransom for many." [Mark 10:42-45]

"When you are invited by any one to a marriage feast, do not sit down in a place of honor, lest a more eminent man than you be invited by him; and he who invited you both will come and say to you, 'Give place to this man' and then you will begin with shame to take the lowest place. But when you are invited, go and sit in the lowest place, so that when your host comes he may say to you, 'Friend, go up higher'; then you will be honored in the presence of all who sit at table with you. For every one who exalts himself will be humbled, and he who humbles himself will be exalted." [Luke 14:8-11]

"If any one comes to me and does not hate his father and mother and wife and children and brothers and sisters, yes, and even his own life, he cannot be my disciple. Whoever does not bear his own cross and come after me, cannot be my disciple. For which of you, desiring to build a tower, does not first sit down and count the cost, whether he has enough to complete it? Otherwise, when he has laid a foundation, and is not able to finish, all who see it begin to mock him, saying, 'This man began to build, and was not able to finish.' Or what king, going to encounter another king in war, will not sit down first and take counsel whether he is able with ten thousand to meet him who comes against him with twenty thousand? And if not, while the other is yet a great way off, he sends an embassy and asks terms of peace. So therefore, whoever of you does not renounce all that he has cannot be my disciple." [Luke 14:26-33]

✝

B. THE MANUAL OF PHILOSOPHY

EPICTETUS

audience-aristocrats

1 Of all existing things some are in our power, and others not in our power. In our power are thought, impulse, will to get and will to avoid, and, in a word, everything which is our own doing. Things not in our power include the body, property, reputation, office, and, in a word, everything which is not our own doing. Things in our power are by nature free, unhindered, untrammeled; things not in our power are weak, servile, subject to hindrance, dependent on others. Remember then that if you imagine that what is naturally slavish is free, and what is naturally another's is your own, you will be hampered, you will mourn, you will be put to confusion, you will blame gods and men; but if you think that only your own belongs to you, and that what is another's is indeed another's, no one will ever put compulsion or hindrance on you, you will accuse none, you will do nothing against your will, no one will harm you, you will have no enemy, for no harm can touch you.

Aiming then at these high matters, you must remember that to attain them requires more than ordinary effort; you will have to give up some things entirely, and put off others for the moment. And if you would have these also—office and wealth—it may be that you will fail to get them, just because your desire is set on the former, and you will certainly fail to attain those things which alone bring freedom and happiness.

Make it your study then to confront every harsh impression with the words, 'You are but an impression, and not at all what you seem to be.' Then test it by those rules that you possess; and first by this—the chief test of all—"Is it concerned with what is in our power or with what is not in our power?' And if it is concerned with what is not in our power, be ready with the answer that it is nothing to you.

3 When anything, from the meanest upwards, is attractive or serviceable or an object of affection, remember always to say to yourself, 'What is its nature?' If you are fond of a jug, say you are fond of a jug; then you will not be disturbed if it be broken. If you kiss your child or your wife, say to yourself that you are kissing a human being, for then if death strikes you will not be disturbed.

5 What disturbs men's minds is not events but their judgments on events. For instance, death is nothing dreadful, or else Socrates would have thought it so. No, the only dreadful thing about it is men's judgment that it is dreadful. And so when we are hindered, or disturbed, or distressed, let us never lay the blame on others, but on ourselves, that is, on our own judgments. To accuse others for one's own misfortunes is a sign of want of education; to accuse oneself shows that one's education has begun; to accuse neither oneself nor others shows that one's education is complete.

7 When you are on a voyage, and your ship is at anchorage, and you disembark to get fresh water, you may pick up a small shellfish or a truffle by the way, but you must keep your attention fixed on the ship, and keep looking towards it constantly, to see if the Helmsman calls you; and if he does, you have to leave everything, or be bundled on board with your legs tied like a sheep. So it is in life. If you have a dear wife or child given you, they are like the shellfish or the truffle, they are very well in their way. Only, if the Helmsman call, run back to your ship, leave all else, and do not look behind you. And if you are old, never go far from the ship, so that when you are called you may not fail to appear.

8 Ask not that events should happen as you will, but let your will be that events should happen as they do, and you shall have peace.

9 Sickness is a hindrance to the body, but not to the will, unless the will consent. Lameness is a hindrance to the leg, but not to the will. Say this to yourself at each event that happens, for you shall find that though it hinders something else it will not hinder you.

11 Never say of anything, 'I lost it', but say, 'I gave it back'. Has your child died? It was given back. Has your wife died? She was given back. Has your estate been taken from you? Was not this also given back? But you say, 'He who took it from me is wicked'. What does it matter to you through whom the Giver asked it back? As long as He gives it you, take care of it, but not as your own; treat it as passers-by treat an inn.

A diffs & sames of StM & E

revealed truth by god — reason by epictetus

16 When you see a man shedding tears in sorrow for a child abroad or dead, or for loss of property, beware that you are not carried away by the impression that it is outward ills that make him miserable. Keep this thought by you: 'What distresses him is not the event.' Therefore do not hesitate to sympathize with him so far as words go, and if it so chance, even to groan with him; but take heed that you do not also groan in your inner being.

17 Remember that you are an actor in a play, and the Playwright chooses the manner of it: if he wants it short, it is short; if long, it is long. If he wants you to act a poor man you must act the part with all your powers; and so if your part be a cripple or a magistrate or a plain man. For your business is to act the character that is given you and act it well; the choice of the cast is Another's.

25 Has some one had precedence of you at an entertainment or a levée[1] or been called in before you to give advice? If these things are good you ought to be glad that he got them; if they are evil, do not be angry that you did not get them yourself. Remember that if you want to get what is not in your power, you cannot earn the same reward as others unless you act as they do. How is it possible for one who does not haunt the great man's door to have equal shares with one who does, or one who does not go in his train equality with one who does; or one who does not praise him with one who does? You will be unjust then and insatiable if you wish to get these privileges for nothing, without paying their price. What is the price of a lettuce? An obol perhaps. If then a man pays his obol and gets his lettuces, and you do not pay and do not get them, do not think you are defrauded. For as he has the lettuces so you have the obol you did not give. The same principle holds good too in conduct. You were not invited to some one's entertainment? Because you did not give the host the price for which he sells his dinner. He sells it for compliments, he sells it for attentions. Pay him the price then, if it is to your profit. But if you wish to get the one and yet not give up the other, nothing can satisfy you in your folly.

What! you say, you have nothing instead of the dinner?

Nay, you have this, you have not praised the man you did not want to praise, you have not had to bear with the insults of his doorstep.

29 In everything you do consider what comes first and what follows, and so approach it. Otherwise you will come to it with a good heart at first because you have not reflected on any of the consequences, and afterwards, when difficulties have appeared, you will desist to your shame. Do you wish to win at Olympia? So do I, by the gods, for it is a fine thing. But consider the first steps to it, and the consequences, and so lay your hand to the work. You must submit to discipline, eat to order, touch no sweets, train under compulsion, at a fixed hour, in heat and cold, drink no cold water, nor wine, except by order; you must hand yourself over completely to your trainer as you would to a physician, and then when the contest comes you must risk getting hacked, and sometimes dislocate your hand, twist your ankle, swallow plenty of sand, sometimes get a flogging, and with all this suffer defeat. When you have considered at this well, then enter on the athlete's course, if you still wish it. If you act without thought you will be behaving like children, who one day play at wrestlers, another day at gladiators, now sound the trumpet, and next strut the stage. Like them you will be now an athlete, now a gladiator, then an orator, then philosopher, but nothing with all your soul. Like an ape, you imitate every sight you see, and one thing after another takes your fancy. When you undertake a thing you do it casually and half-heartedly, instead of considering it and looking at it all round. In the same way some people, when they see a philosopher and hear a man speaking like Euphrates (and indeed who can speak as he can?), wish to be philosophers themselves.

31 For piety towards the gods know that the most important thing is this: to have right opinions about them—that they exist, and that they govern the universe well and justly—and to have set yourself to obey them, and to give way to all that happens, following events with a free will, in the belief that they are fulfilled by the highest mind. For thus you will never blame the gods, nor accuse them of neglecting you. But this you cannot achieve, unless you

---

[1] A formal reception, at which the clients or retainers of a great person saluted his rising.

apply your conception of good and evil to those things only which are in our power, and not to those which are out of our power. For if you apply your notion of good or evil to the latter, then, as soon as you fail to get what you will to get or fail to avoid what you will to avoid, you will be bound to blame and hate those you hold responsible. For every living creature has a natural tendency to avoid and shun what seems harmful and all that causes it, and to pursue and admire what is helpful and all that causes it. It is not possible then for one who thinks he is harmed to take pleasure in what he thinks is the author of the harm, any more than to take pleasure in the harm itself. That is why a father is reviled by his son, when he does not give his son a share of what the son regards as good things; thus Polynices and Eteocles were set at enmity with one another by thinking that a king's throne was a good thing. That is why the farmer, and the sailor, and the merchant, and those who lose wife or children revile the gods. For men's religion is bound up with their interest. Therefore he who makes it his concern rightly to direct his will to get and his will to avoid, is thereby making piety his concern. But it is proper on each occasion to make libation and sacrifice and to offer first-fruits according to the custom of our fathers, with purity and not in slovenly or careless fashion, without meanness and without extravagance.

33 Lay down for yourself from the first a definite stamp and style of conduct, which you will maintain when you are alone and also in the society of men. Be silent for the most part, or, if you speak, say only what is necessary and in a few words. Talk, but rarely, if occasion calls you, but do not talk of ordinary things—of gladiators, or horse-races, or athletes, or of meats or drinks—these are topics that arise everywhere—but above all do not talk about men in blame or compliment or comparison. If you can, turn the conversation of your company by your talk to some fitting subject; but if you should chance to be isolated among strangers, be silent. Do not laugh, nor at many things, nor without restraint.

Refuse to take oaths, altogether if that be possible, but if not, as far as circumstances allow.

For your body take just so much as your bare need requires, such as food, drink, clothing, house, servants, but cut down all that tends to luxury and outward show.

Avoid impurity to the utmost of your power before marriage, and if you indulge your passion, let it be done lawfully. But do not be offensive or censorious to those who indulge it, and do not be always bringing up your own chastity. If some one tells you that so and so speaks ill of you, do not defend yourself against what he says, but answer, 'He did not know my other faults, or he would not have mentioned these alone.'

It is not necessary for the most part to go to the games; but if you should have occasion to go, show that your first concern is for yourself; that is, wish that only to happen which does happen, and him only to win who does win, for so you will suffer no hindrance. But refrain entirely from applause, or ridicule, or prolonged excitement. And when you go away do not talk much of what happened there, except so far as it tends to your improvement. For to talk about it implies that the spectacle excited your wonder.

Do not go lightly or casually to hear lectures; but if you do go, maintain your gravity and dignity and do not make yourself offensive. When you are going to meet any one, and particularly some man of reputed eminence, set before your mind the thought, 'What would Socrates or Zeno have done?' and you will not fail to make proper use of the occasion.

When you go to visit some great man, prepare your mind by thinking that you will not find him in, that you will be shut out, that the doors will be slammed in your face, that he will pay no heed to you. And if in spite of all this you find it fitting for you to go, go and bear what happens and never say to yourself, 'It was not worth all this'; for that shows a vulgar mind and one at odds with outward things.

In your conversation avoid frequent and disproportionate mention of your own doings or adventures; for other people do not take the same pleasure in hearing what has happened to you as you take in recounting your adventures.

Avoid raising men's laughter; for it is a habit that easily slips into vulgarity, and it may well suffice to lessen your neighbor's respect.

It is dangerous too to lapse into foul language; when anything of the kind occurs, rebuke the offender, if the occasion allow, and if not, make it plain to him by your silence, or a blush or a frown, that you are angry at his words.

34 When you imagine some pleasure, beware that it does not carry you away, like other imaginations. Wait a while, and give yourself pause. Next remember two things: how long you will enjoy the pleasure, and also how long you will afterwards repent and revile yourself. And set on the other side the joy and self-satisfaction you will feel if you refrain. And if the moment seems come to realize it, take heed that you be not overcome by the winning sweetness and attraction of it; set in the other scale the thought how much better is the consciousness of having vanquished it.

When you do a thing because you have determined that it ought to be done, never avoid being seen doing it, even if the opinion of the multitude is going to condemn you. For if your action is wrong, then avoid doing it altogether, but if it is right, why do you fear those who will rebuke you wrongly?

41 It is a sign of a dull mind to dwell upon the cares of the body, to prolong exercise, eating, drinking, and other bodily functions. These things are to be done by the way; all your attention must be given to the mind.

42 When a man speaks evil to you, remember that he does or says it because he thinks it is fitting for him. It is not possible for him to follow what seems good to you, but only what seems good to him, so that, if his opinion is wrong, he suffers, in that he is the victim of deception. In the same way, if a composite judgment which is true is thought to be false, it is not the judgment that suffers, but the man who is deluded about it. If you act on this principle you will be gentle to him who reviles you, saying to yourself on each occasion, 'He thought it right.'

44 It is illogical to reason thus, 'I am richer than you, therefore I am superior to you', 'I am more eloquent than you, therefore I am superior to you.' It is more logical to reason, 'I am richer than you, therefore my property is superior to yours', 'I am more eloquent than you, therefore my speech is superior to yours.' You are something more than property or speech.

45 If a man wash quickly, do not say that he washes badly, but that he washes quickly. If a man drink much wine, do not say that he drinks badly, but that he drinks much. For till you have decided what judgment prompts him, how do you know that he acts badly? If you do as I say, you will assent to your apprehensive impressions and to none other.

46 On no occasion call yourself a philosopher, nor talk at large of your principles among the multitude, but act on your principles. For instance, at a banquet do not say how one ought to eat, but eat as you ought. Remember that Socrates had so completely got rid of the thought of display that when men came and wanted an introduction to philosophers he took them to be introduced; so patient of neglect was he. And if a discussion arise among the multitude on some principle, keep silent for the most part; for you are in great danger of blurting out some undigested thought. And when some one says to you, 'You know nothing', and you do not let it provoke you, then know that you are really on the right road. For sheep do not bring grass to their shepherds and show them how much they have eaten, but they digest their fodder and then produce in the form of wool and milk. Do the same yourself; instead of displaying your principles to the multitude, show them the results of the principles you have digested.

47 When you have adopted the simple life, do not pride yourself upon it, and if you are a water-drinker do not say on every occasion, 'I am a water-drinker.' And if you ever want to train laboriously, keep it to yourself and do not make a show of it. Do not embrace statues. If you are very thirsty take a good draught of cold water, and rinse your mouth and tell no one.

48 The ignorant man's position and character is this; he never looks to himself for benefit or harm, but to the world outside him. The philosopher's position and character is that he always look to himself for benefit and harm.

The signs of one who is making progress are: he blames none, praises none, complains of none, accuses none, never speaks of himself as if he were somebody, or as if he knew anything. And if any one compliments him he laughs in himself at his compliment; and if one blames him, he makes no defense. He goes about like a convalescent, careful not to disturb his constitution on its road to recovery, until it has got firm hold. He has got rid of the will to get, and his will to avoid is directed no longer to what is beyond our power but only to what is in our power and contrary to nature. In all things he exercises his will without strain. If men regard him as foolish or ignorant he pays no heed. In one word, he keeps watch and guard on himself as his own enemy, lying in wait for him.

50 Whatever principles you put before you, hold fast to them as laws which it will be impious to transgress. But pay no heed to what any one says of you; for this is something beyond your own control.

53 On every occasion we must have these thoughts at hand:

> *Lead me, O Zeus, and lead me, Destiny,*
> *Whither ordained is by your decree.*
> *I'll follow, doubting not, or if with will*
> *Recreant I falter, I shall follow still.'*

> —*CLEANTHES*

> *Who rightly with necessity complies*
> *In things divine we count him skilled and wise.*

> —*EURIPIDES, Fragment 965*

> *Well, Crito, if this be the gods' will, so be it.'*

> —*PLATO, Crito, 43D*

> *'Anytus and Meletus have power to put me to death, but not to harm me.'*

> —*PLATO, Apology, 30C*

2. PAGAN AND CHRISTIAN CONFLICT

Despite areas of agreement where we would least expect them, pagans and Christians came into frequent conflict during the first three centuries of the new faith. The task now is to identify reasons for that conflict.

This section begins with selections from Celsus' *Alethes Logos* (*True Word*), written about A.D. 180. Celsus' anti-Christian polemic was so strident that it survives only as quoted in a refutation (written about 250) by the great Christian theologian, Origen. What is Celsus attacking? How does he characterize the Christian God? For whom is he writing? Are any of these criticisms of Christianity still around? What does Celsus indicate about the pagan reaction to Christianity? How would he react to the idea that Christianity was "better" than paganism?

The second selection is from a letter of James, one of the apostles, who tried to explain to Christians how to turn their faith into action. How would you characterize his ideas? What light does *The Letter of James* shed on the success of Christianity?

Celsus ended his attack on Christianity with a pathetic picture of a people whose own God could not save them from torture and death. He might have had in mind the event described in the third selection by Eusebius of Caesarea (c. 260-339)—an account of a persecution which occurred in Lyons in southern Gaul during the reign of the philosopher Emperor Marcus Aurelius (A.D. 161-180). The report was composed shortly afterward by the surviving congregation in Lyons to inform their brethren in Asia Minor. As you read it, consider in what ways, if any, your own reaction differs from that of Celsus. Can you find here material which helps explain the eventual success of Christianity? What motivated the "pagans"?

The final two selections in this chapter, from letters written by Bishop Dionysus of Alexandria in the mid-third century, also come from the *History of the Church* written by Eusebius at the end of that century.

In the first, Dionysus describes what happened during an martyr trial, in order to answer a critic named Germanus. The thought of martyrdom scared off some potential converts, but this letter suggests that martyrs also could produce a positive effect. How? Can you explain it?

In the last selection, Dionysius describes a Christian community in action during a plague in the 260s. Compare their acts with James' advice and Jesus' sayings. What effect do you suppose this had on pagans living through the plague?

What are the strengths shown by this Christian community?

A. *THE TRUE WORD*

CELSUS

Why Jesus looks the way he is?

I.28 [Jesus] fabricated the story of his birth from a virgin.... He came from a Jewish village and from a poor country woman who earned her living by spinning....She was driven out by her husband, who was a carpenter by trade, as she was convicted of adultery.... After she had been driven out by her husband and while she was wandering about in a disgraceful way she secretly gave birth to Jesus... Because he was poor he hired himself out as a workman in Egypt, and there tried his hand at certain magical powers on which the Egyptians pride themselves; he returned full of conceit because of these powers, and on account of them gave himself the title of God. 39. Then was the mother of Jesus beautiful? And because she was beautiful did God have sexual intercourse with her, although by nature He cannot love a corruptible body? It is not likely that God would have fallen in love with her since she was neither wealthy nor of royal birth; for nobody knew her, not even her neighbors.

II.54. What led you to believe, except that he foretold that after his death he would rise again? 55. Come now, let us believe your view that he actually said this. How many others produce wonders like this to convince simple hearers whom they exploit by deceit?... Moreover, they say that Orpheus did this among the Odrysians, and Protesilaus in Thessaly, and Heracles at Taenarum, and Theseus. But we must examine the question whether anyone who really died ever rose again with the same body. Or do you think that the stories of these others really are the legends which they appear to be, and yet that the ending of your tragedy is to be regarded as noble and convincing— his cry from the cross when he expired, and the earthquake and the darkness? While he was alive he did not help himself, but after death he rose again and showed the marks of his punishment and how his hands had been pierced. But who saw this? A hysterical female, as you say, and perhaps some other one of those who were deluded by the same sorcery, who either dreamt in a certain state of mind and through wishful thinking had a hallucination due to some mistaken notion (an experience which has happened to thousands), or, which is more likely, wanted to impress the others by telling this fantastic tale, and so by this cock-and-bull story to provide a chance for other beggars. 63. If Jesus really wanted to show forth divine power, he ought to have appeared to the very men who treated him despitefully and to the man who condemned him and to everyone everywhere. 68. But if he was so great he ought, in order to display his divinity, to have disappeared suddenly from the cross.

III.44. Their injunctions are like this. 'Let no one educated, no one wise, no one sensible draw near. For these abilities are thought by us to be evils. But as for anyone ignorant, anyone stupid, anyone uneducated, anyone who is a child, let him come boldly.' By the fact that they themselves admit that these people are worthy of their God, they show that they want and are able to convince only the foolish, dishonorable and stupid, and only slaves, women, and little children. 50. Moreover, we see that those who display their trickery in the marketplaces and go about begging would never enter a gathering of intelligent men, nor would they dare to reveal their noble beliefs in their presence; but whenever they see adolescent boys and a crowd of slaves and a company of fools they push themselves in and show off. 55. In private houses also we see wool-workers, cobblers, laundry-workers, and the most illiterate and bucolic yokels, who would not dare to say anything at all in front of their elders and more intelligent masters. But whenever they get hold of children in private and some stupid women with them, they let out some astounding statements as, for example, that they must not pay any attention to their father and school-teachers, but must obey them; they say that these talk nonsense and have no understanding, and that in reality they neither know nor are able to do anything good, but are taken up with mere empty chatter. But they alone, they say, know the right way to live, and if the children would believe them, they would become happy and make their home happy as well. And if just as they are speaking they see one of the school-teachers coming, or some intelligent person, or even the father himself, the more cautious of them flee in all directions; but the more reckless urge the children on to rebel. They whisper to them that in the presence of their father and their schoolmasters they do not feel able to explain anything to the children, since they do not want to have anything to do with the silly and obtuse teachers who are totally corrupted and far gone in wickedness and who inflict punishment on the children. But, if they like, they should leave father and their schoolmasters, and go along with the women and little children who are their playfellows to the wooldresser's shop, that they may learn perfection. And by saying this they persuade them. 59. And that I am not criticizing them any more bitterly than the truth compels me, anyone may see also from this. Those who summon people to the other mysteries make this preliminary proclamation: Whosoever has pure hands and a wise tongue. And again, others say: Whosoever is pure from all defilement, and whose soul knows nothing of evil, and who has lived well and righteously. Such are the preliminary exhortations of those who promise purification from sins. But let us hear what folk these Christians call. Whosoever is a sinner, they say, whosoever is unwise, whosoever is a child, and, in a word, whosoever is a wretch, the kingdom of God will receive him. Do you not say that a sinner is he who is dishonest, a thief, a burglar, a poisoner, a sacrilegious fellow, and a grave-robber? What others would a robber invite and call? 62. But why was he not sent to those without sin? What evil is it not to have sinned?

IV.2. The assertion made both by some of the Christians and by the Jews, the former saying that some God or son of God has come down to the earth as judge of mankind, the latter saying that he will come, is most shameful, and no lengthy argument is required to refute it. 3. What is the purpose of such a descent on the part of God? Was it in order to learn what was going on among men? Does not he know everything? If, then, he does know, why does he not correct men, and why can he not do this by divine power?

VI.73. And if he did wish to send down a spirit from himself, why did he have to breathe it into the womb of a woman? He already knew how to make men. He could have

formed a body for this one also without having to thrust his own spirit into such foul pollution. In that case he would not have been disbelieved, had he been begotten directly from above. 75. If a divine spirit was in a body, it must certainly have differed from other bodies in size or beauty or strength or voice or striking appearance or powers of persuasion. For it is impossible that a body which had something more divine than the rest should be no different from any other. Yet Jesus' body was no different from any other, but, as they say, was little and ugly and undistinguished. 78. Furthermore, if God, like Zeus in the comic poet, woke up out of his long slumber and wanted to deliver the human race from evils, why on earth did he sent this spirit that you mention into one corner? He ought to have breathed into many bodies in the same way and sent them all over the world. The comic poet wrote that Zeus woke up and sent Hermes to the Athenians and Spartans because he wanted to raise a laugh in the theater. Yet do you not think it is more ludicrous to make the Son of God to be sent to the Jews?

VII.18. If the prophets of the God of the Jews foretold that Jesus would be his son, why did he give them laws by Moses that they were to become rich and powerful and to fill the earth and to massacre their enemies, children and all, and slaughter their entire race, which he himself did, so Moses says, before the eyes of the Jews? And besides this, if they were not obedient, why does he expressly threaten to do to them what he did to their enemies? Yet his son, the man of Nazareth, gives contradictory laws, saying that a man cannot come forward to the Father if he is rich or loves power or lays claim to any intelligence or reputation, and that he must not pay attention to food or to his storehouse any more than the ravens, or to clothing any more than the lilies, and that to a man who has struck him once he should offer himself to be struck once again. Who is wrong? Moses or Jesus? Or when the Father sent Jesus had he forgotten what commands he gave to Moses? Or did he condemn his own laws and change his mind, and send his messenger for quite the opposite purpose?

VIII.12. If these men worshipped no other God but one, perhaps they would have had a valid argument against the others. But in fact they worship to an extravagant degree this man who appeared recently, and yet think it is not inconsistent with monotheism if they also worship His servant. 14. If you taught them that Jesus is not his Son, but that God is father of all, and that we really ought to worship him alone, they would no longer be willing to listen to you unless you included Jesus as well, who is the author of their sedition. Indeed, when they call him Son of God, it is not because they are paying very great reverence to God, but because they are exalting Jesus greatly. 39. Do you not see, my excellent man, that anyone who stands by your daemon not only blasphemes him, but proclaims his banishment from every land and sea, and after binding you who have been dedicated to him like an image takes you away and crucifies you; but the daemon or, as you say, the son of God, takes no vengeance on him? 68. We ought not to disbelieve the ancient man who long ago declared

Let there be one king, him to whom the son of crafty Kronos gave the power. [Iliad II.205]

For, if you overthrow this doctrine, it is probable that the emperor will punish you. If everyone were to do the same as you, there would be nothing to prevent him from being abandoned, alone and deserted, while earthly things would come into the power of the most lawless and savage barbarians, and nothing more would be heard among men either of your worship or of the true wisdom. 69. You will surely not say that if the Romans were convinced by you and were to neglect their customary honors to both gods and men and were to call upon your Most High, or whatever name you prefer, He would come down and fight on their side, and they would have no need for any other defense. In earlier times also the same God made these promises and some far greater than these, so you say, to those who pay regard to him. But see how much help he has been to both them and you. Instead of being masters of the whole world, they have been left no land or home of any kind. While in your case, if anyone does still wander about in secret, yet he is sought out and condemned to death.

✝

B. THE LETTER OF JAMES

1 James, a servant of God and of the Lord Jesus Christ, to the twelve tribes in the Dispersion: Greeting.

2 Count it all joy, my brethren, when you meet various trials, 3 for you know that the testing of your faith produces steadfastness. 4 And let steadfastness have its full effect, that you may be perfect and complete, lacking in nothing.

5 If any of you lacks wisdom, let him ask God, who gives to all men generously and without reproaching, and it will be given him. 6 But let him ask in faith, with no doubting, for he who doubts is like a wave of the sea that is driven and tossed by the wind. 7, 8 For that person must not supposed that a double-minded man, unstable in all his ways, will receive anything from the Lord.

9 Let the lowly brother boast in his exaltation, 10 and the rich in his humiliation, because like the flower of the grass he will pass away. 11 For the sun rises with its scorching heat and withers the grass; its flower falls, and its beauty perishes. So will the rich man fade away in the midst of his pursuits.

12 Blessed is the man who endures trial, for when he has stood the test he will receive the crown of life which God has promised to those who love him. 13 Let no one say when he is tempted, "I am tempted by God"; for God cannot be tempted with evil and he himself tempts no one; 14 but each person is tempted when he is lured and enticed by his own desire. 15 Then desire when it has conceived gives birth to sin; and sin when it is full-grown brings forth death....

22 But be doers of the word, and not hearers only, deceiving yourselves. 23 For if any one is a hearer of the word and not a doer, he is like a man who observes his natural face in a mirror; 24 for he observes himself and goes away and at once forget what he was like. 25 But he who looks into the perfect law, the law of liberty, and perseveres, being no hearer that forgets but a doer that acts, he shall be blessed in his doing.

26 If any one thinks he is religious, and does not bridle his tongue but deceives his heart,

this man's religion is vain. 27 Religion that is pure and undefiled before God and the Father is this: to visit orphans and widows in their affliction, and to keep oneself unstained from the world.

Chapter 2: My brethren, show no partiality as you hold the faith of our Lord Jesus Christ, the Lord of glory. 2 For if a man with gold rings and in fine clothing comes into your assembly, and a poor man in shabby clothing also comes in, 3 and you pay attention to the one who wears the fine clothing and say, "Have a seat here, please," while you say to the poor man, "Stand there," or, "Sit at my feet," 4 Have you not made distinctions among yourselves, and become judges with evil thoughts? 5 Listen, my beloved brethren. Has not God chosen those who are poor in the world to be rich in faith and heirs of the kingdom which he has promised to those who love him? 6 But you have dishonored the poor man. Is it not the rich who oppress you, is it not they who drag you into court? 7 Is it not they who blaspheme that honorable name by which you are called?

8 If you really fulfill the royal law, according to the scripture, "You shall love your neighbor as yourself," you do well. 9 But if you show partiality, you commit sin, and are convicted by the law as transgressors. 10 But whoever keeps the whole law but fails in one point has become guilty of all of it. 11 For he who said, "Do not commit adultery," said also, "Do not kill." If you do not commit adultery but do kill, you have become a transgressor of the law. 12 So speak and so act as those who are to be judged under the law of liberty. 13 For judgment is without mercy to one who has shown no mercy; yet mercy triumphs over judgment.

14 What does it profit, my brethren, if a man says he has faith but has not works? Can his faith save him? 15 If a brother or sister is ill-clad and in lack of daily food, 16 and one of you says to them, "Go in peace, be warmed and filled," without giving them the things needed for the body, what does it profit? 17 So faith by itself, if it has no works, is dead.

Chapter 5: Come now, you rich, weep and how for the miseries that are coming upon you. 2 Your riches have rotted and your gar-ments are moth-eaten. 3 Your gold and silver have rusted, and their rust will be evidence against you and will eat your flesh like fire. You have laid up treasure for the last days. 4 Behold, the wages of the laborers who mowed your fields, which you kept back by fraud, cry out; and the cries of the harvesters have reached the ears of the Lord or hosts. 5 You have lived on the earth in luxury and in pleasure; you have fattened your hearts in a day of slaughter. 6 You have condemned, you have killed the righteous man; he does not resist you.

7 Be patient, therefore, brethren, until the coming of the Lord. Behold the farmer waits for the precious fruit of the earth, being patient over it until it received the early and the late rain. 8 You also be patient. Establish your hearts, for the coming of the Lord is at hand. 9 Do not grumble, brethren, against one another, that you may not be judged; behold, the Judge is standing at the doors. 10 As an example of suffering and patience, brethren, take the prophets who spoke in the name of the Lord. 11 Behold, we call those happy who were steadfast. You have heard of the steadfastness of Job, and you have seen the purpose of the Lord, how the Lord is compassionate and merciful.

✝

C. THE LYONS MARTYRS

EUSEBIUS OF CAESAREA

First of all, they endured nobly the injuries heaped upon them by the populace; clamors and blows and draggings and robberies and stonings and imprisonments, and all things which an infuriated mob delight in inflicting on enemies and adversaries. Then, being taken to the forum by the chiliarch[1] and the authorities of the city, they were examined in the presence of the whole multitude, and having confessed, they were imprisoned until the arrival of the governor.

When, afterwards, they were brought before him, and he treated us with the utmost cruelty,

---

[1] A Greek term, literally meaning the commander of a thousand men. Commonly used by Greeks to translate the Latin *tribunus militum,* or military tribune.

Vettius Epagathus, one of the brethren, and a man filled with love for God and his neighbor, interfered. His life was so consistent that, although young, he had attained a reputation equal to that of the elder Zacharias: for he "walked in all the commandments and ordinances of the Lord blameless,"[1] and was untiring in every good work for his neighbor, zealous for God and fervent in spirit. Such being his character, he could not endure the unreasonable judgment against us, but was filled with indignation, and asked to be permitted to testify in behalf of his brethren, that there is among us nothing ungodly or impious.

But those about the judgment seat cried out against him, for he was a man of distinction; and the governor refused to grant his just request, and merely asked if he also were a Christian. And he, confessing this with a loud voice, was himself taken into the order of the martyrs, being called the Advocate of the Christians, but having the Advocate in himself, the Spirit, more abundantly than Zacharias. He showed this by the fullness of his love, being well pleased even to lay down his life in defense of the brethren. For he was and is a true disciple of Christ, "following the Lamb whithersoever he goeth."[2]

Then the others were divided, and the protomartyrs were manifestly ready, and finished their confession with all eagerness. But some appeared unprepared and untrained, weak as yet, and unable to endure so great a conflict. About ten of these proved abortions, causing us great grief and sorrow beyond measure, and impairing the zeal of the others who had not yet been seized, but who, though suffering all kinds of affliction, continued constantly with the martyrs and did not forsake them. Then all of us feared greatly on account of uncertainty as to their confession; not because we dreaded the sufferings to be endured, but because we looked to the end, and were afraid that some of them might fall away. But those who were worthy were seized day by day, filling up their number, so that all the zealous persons, and those through whom especially our affairs had been established, were collected together out of the two churches.

And some of our heathen servants also were seized, as the governor had commanded that all of us should be examined publicly. These, being ensnared by Satan, and fearing for themselves the tortures which they beheld the saints endure, and being also urged on by the soldiers, accused us falsely of Thyestean banquets and Oedopean intercourse,[3] and of deeds which are not only unlawful for us to speak of or to think, but which we cannot believe were ever done by men. When these accusations were reported, all the people raged like wild beasts against us, so that even if any had before been moderate on account of friendship, they were now exceedingly furious and gnashed their teeth against us. And that which was spoken by our Lord was fulfilled: "The time will come when whosoever killeth you will think that he doeth God service."[4] Then finally the holy martyrs endured sufferings beyond description, Satan striving earnestly that some of the slanders might be uttered by them also.

But the whole wrath of the populace, and governor, and soldiers was aroused exceedingly against Sanctus, the deacon from Vienne, and Maturus, a late convert, yet a noble combatant, and against Attalus, a native of Pergamum, where he had always been a pillar and foundation, and Blandina, through whom Christ showed that things which appear mean and obscure and despicable to men are with God of great glory,[5] through love toward him manifested in power, and not boasting in appearance. For while we all trembled, and her earthly mistress, who was herself also one of the martyrs, feared that on account of the weakness of her body she would be unable to make bold confession, Blandina was filled with such power as to be delivered and raised above those who were torturing her by turns from morning till evening in every manner, so that they acknowledged that they were conquered, and could do nothing more to her. And they were astonished at her endurance, as her entire body was mangled and broken; and they tes-

---

[3] I.e., cannibalism and incest. According to legend, Thyestes had unwittingly eaten his own sons served to him at a banquet by an enemy, and Oedipus had unwittingly married his own mother.
[4] John 16:2.
[5] Cf. I Corinthians 1:27-8.

---

[1] Luke 1:6.
[2] Revelation 14:4.

tified that one of these forms of torture was sufficient to destroy life, not to speak of so many and so great sufferings. But the blessed woman, like a noble athlete, renewed her strength in her confession; and her comfort and recreation and relief from the pain of her sufferings was in exclaiming, "I am a Christian, and there is nothing vile done by us."

But Sanctus also endured marvelously and superhumanly all the outrages which he suffered. While the wicked men hoped, by the continuance and severity of his tortures to wring something from him which he ought not to say, he girded himself against them with such firmness that he would not even tell his name, or the nation or city to which he belonged, or whether he was bond or free, but answered in the Roman tongue to all their questions, "I am a Christian." He confessed this instead of name and city and race and everything besides, and the people heard from him no other word. There arose therefore on the part of the governor and his tormentors a great desire to conquer him; but having nothing more that they could do to him, they finally fastened red-hot brazen plates to the most tender parts of his body. And these indeed were burned, but he continued unbending and unyielding, firm in his confession, and refreshed and strengthened by the heavenly fountain of the water of life, flowing from the bowels of Christ. And his body was a witness of his sufferings, being one complete wound and bruise, drawn out of shape, and altogether unlike a human form. Christ, suffering in him, manifested his glory, delivering him from her adversary, and making him an example for the others, showing that nothing is fearful where the love of the Father is, and nothing painful where there is the glory of Christ. For when the wicked men tortured him a second time after some days, supposing that with his body swollen and inflamed to such a degree that he could not bear the touch of a hand, if they should again apply the same instruments, they would overcome him, or at least by his death under his sufferings others would be made frail, not only did not this occur, but, contrary to all human expectation, his body arose and stood erect in the midst of the subsequent torments, and resumed its original appearance and the use of its limbs, so that, through the grace of Christ, these second suf-

ferings became to him, not torture, but healing.

But the devil, thinking that he had already consumed Biblias, who was one of those who had denied Christ, desiring to increase her condemnation through the utterance of blasphemy, brought her again to the torture, to compel her, as already feeble and weak, to report impious things concerning us. But she recovered herself under the suffering, and as if awaking from a deep sleep, and reminded by the present anguish of the eternal punishment in hell, she contradicted the blasphemers. "How," she said. "could those eat children who do not think it lawful to taste the blood even of irrational animals?" And thenceforward she confessed herself a Christian, and was given a place in the order of the martyrs.

But as the tyrannical tortures were made by Christ of none effect through the patience of the blessed, the devil invented other contrivances,–confinement in the dark and most loathsome parts of the prison, stretching of the feet to the fifth hole in the stocks, and the other outrages which his servants are accustomed to inflict upon the prisoners when furious and filled with the devil. A great many were suffocated in prison, being chosen by the Lord for this manner of death, that he might manifest in them his glory. For some, though they had been tortured so cruelly that it seemed impossible that they could live, even with the most careful nursing, yet, destitute of human attention, remained in the prison, being strengthened by the Lord, and invigorated both in body and soul; and they exhorted and encouraged the rest. But such as were young, and arrested recently, so that their bodies had not become accustomed to torture, were unable to endure the severity of their confinement, and died in prison.

The blessed Pothinus, who had been entrusted with the bishopric of Lyons, was dragged to the judgment seat. He was more than ninety years of age, and very infirm, scarcely indeed able to breathe because of physical weakness; but he was strengthened by spiritual zeal through his earnest desire for martyrdom. Though his body was worn out by old age and disease, his life was preserved that Christ might triumph in it. When he was brought by the soldiers to the tribunal, accompanied by the civil magistrates and a multitude who shouted against him in every manner as if he were Christ himself, he bore noble witness. Being asked by the governor, Who was the God of the Christians, he replied, "If thou art worthy, thou shalt know." Then he was dragged away harshly, and received blows of every kind. Those near him struck him with their hands and feet, regardless of his age; and those at a distance hurled at him whatever they could seize; all of them thinking that they would be guilty of great wickedness and impiety if any possible abuse were omitted. For thus they thought to avenge their own deities. Scarcely able to breathe, he was cast into prison and died after two days.

Then a certain great dispensation of God occurred, and the compassion of Jesus appeared beyond measure, in a manner rarely seen among the brotherhood, but not beyond the power of Christ. For those who had recanted at their first arrest were imprisoned with the others, and endured terrible sufferings, so that their denial was of no profit to them even for the present. But those who confessed what they were imprisoned as Christians, no other accusation being brought against them. But the first were treated afterwards as murderers and defiled, and were punished twice as severely as the others. For the joy of martyrdom, and the hope of the promises, and love for Christ, and the Spirit of the Father, supported the latter; but their consciences so greatly distressed the former that they were easily distinguishable from all the rest by their very countenances when they were led forth. For the first went out rejoicing, glory and grace being blended in their faces, so that even their bonds seemed like beautiful ornaments, as those of a bride adorned with variegated golden fringes; and they were perfumed with the sweet savor of Christ, so that some supposed they had been anointed with earthly ointment. But the others were downcast and humble and dejected and filled with every kind of disgrace, and they were reproached by the heathen as ignoble and weak, bearing the accusation of murderers, and having lost the one honorable and glorious and life-giving Name. The rest, beholding this, were strengthened, and when apprehended, they confessed with-

out hesitation, paying no attention to the persuasions of the devil....

VARIOUS TORTURES

After these things, finally, their martyrdoms were divided into every form. For plaiting a crown of various colors and of all kinds of flowers, they presented it to the Father. It was proper therefore that the noble athletes, having endured a manifold strife, and conquered grandly, should receive the crown, great and incorruptible.

Maturus, therefore, and Sanctus and Blandina and Attalus were led to the amphitheater to be exposed to the wild beasts, and to give to the heathen public a spectacle of cruelty, a day for fighting with wild beasts being specially appointed on account of our people. But Maturus and Sanctus passed again through every torment to the amphitheater, as if they had suffered nothing before, or rather, as if, having already conquered their antagonist in many contests, they were now striving for the crown itself. They endured again the customary running of the gauntlet and the violence of the wild beasts, and everything which the furious people called for or desired, and at last, the iron chair in which their bodies being roasted, tormented them with the fumes. And not with this did the persecutors cease, but were yet more mad against them, determined to overcome their patience. But even thus they did not hear a word from Sanctus except the confession which he had uttered from the beginning. These, then, after their life had continued for a long time through the great conflict, were at last sacrificed, having been made throughout that day a spectacle to the world, in place of the usual variety of combats.

But Blandina was suspended on a stake, and exposed to be devoured by the wild beasts who should attack her. And because she appeared as if hanging on a cross, and because of her earnest prayers, she inspired the combatants with great zeal. For they looked on her in her conflict, and beheld with their outward eyes, in the form of their sister, him who was crucified for them, that he might persuade those who believe on him, that every one who suffers for the glory of Christ has fellowship always with the living God. As none of the wild beasts at that time touched her, she was taken down from the stake, and cast again into prison. She was preserved thus for another contest, that, being victorious in more conflicts, she might make the punishment of the crooked serpent irrevocable; and, though small and weak and despised, yet clothed with Christ the mighty and conquering Athlete, she might arouse the zeal of the brethren, and, having overcome the adversary many times might receive, through her conflict, the crown incorruptible.

But Attalus was called for loudly by the people, because he was a person of distinction. He entered the contest readily on account of a good conscience and his genuine practice in Christian discipline, and as he had always been a witness for the truth among us. He was led around the amphitheater, a table being carried before him on which was written in the Roman language "This is Attalus the Christian," and the people were filled with indignation against him. But when the governor learned that he was a Roman, he commanded him to be taken back with the rest of those who were in prison concerning whom he had written to Caesar, and whose answer he was awaiting.

[The emperor orders that all the prisoners be re-examined by the governor, and any who deny Christ be set free. The others are to be beaten to death.]

Therefore, at the beginning of the public festival which took place there, and which was attended by crowds of men from all nations, the governor brought the blessed ones to the judgment seat, to make of them a show and spectacle for the multitude. Wherefore also he examined them again, and beheaded those who appeared to possess Roman citizenship, but he sent the others to the wild beasts.

And Christ was glorified greatly in those who had formerly denied him, for, contrary to the expectations of the heathen, the confessed. For they were examined by themselves, as about to be set free; but confessing, they were added to the order of the martyrs. But some continued without, who had never possessed a trace of faith, nor any apprehension of the wedding garment, nor an understanding of the fear of God; but as sons of perdition, they blasphemed the Way through their apostasy. But all the others were added to the Church.

While these were being examined, a certain Alexander, a Phrygian by birth, and physician by profession, who had resided in Gaul for many years, and was well known to all on account of his love of God and boldness of speech (for he was not without a share of apostolic grace), standing before the judgment seat, and by signs encouraging them to confess, appeared to those standing by as if in travail. But the people being enraged because those who formerly denied now confessed, cried out against Alexander as if he were the cause of this. Then the governor summoned him and inquired who he was. And when he answered that hew as a Christian, being very angry he condemned him to the wild beasts. And on the next day he entered along with Attalus. For the please the people, the governor had ordered Attalus again to the wild beasts.

And they were tortured in the amphitheater with all the instruments contrived for that purpose, and having endured a very great conflict, were at last sacrificed. Alexander neither groaned nor murmured in any manner, but communed in his heart with God. But when Attalus was placed in the iron seat, and the fumes arose from his burning body, he said to the people in the Roman language: "Lo! this which ye do is devouring men; but we do not devour men; nor do any other wicked thing." And being asked, what name God has, he replied, "God has not a name as man has."

BLANDINA SUFFERS

After all these, on the last day of the contests, Blandina was again brought in, with Ponticus, a boy about fifteen years old. They had been brought every day to witness the sufferings of the others, and had been pressed to swear by the idols. But because they remained steadfast and despised them, the multitude became furious, so that they had no compassion for the youth of the boy nor respect for the sex of the woman. Therefore they exposed them to all the terrible sufferings and took them through the entire round of torture, repeatedly urging them to swear, but being unable to effect this; for Ponticus, encouraged by his sister so that even the heathen could see that she was confirming and strengthening him, having nobly endured every torture, gave up the ghost.

But the blessed Blandina, last of all, having, as a noble mother, encouraged her children and sent them before her victorious to the King, endured herself all their conflicts and hastened after them, glad and rejoicing in their departure as if called to a marriage supper, rather than cast to wild beasts. And, after the scourging, after the wild beasts, after the roasting seat, she was finally enclosed in a net, and thrown before a bull. And having been tossed about by the animal, but feeling none of the things which were happening to her, on account of her hope and firm hold upon what had been entrusted to her, and her communion with Christ, she also was sacrificed. And the heathen themselves confessed that never among them had a woman endured so many and such terrible tortures.

But not even thus was their madness and cruelty toward the saints satisfied. For, incited by the Wild Beast, wild and barbarous tribes were not easily appeased, and their violence found another peculiar opportunity in the dead bodies.... For they cast to the dogs those who had died of suffocation in the prison, carefully guarding them by night and day, lest any one should be buried by us. And they exposed the remains left by the wild beasts and by fire, mangled and charred, and placed the heads of the others by their bodies, and guarded them in like manner from burial by a watch of soldiers for many days. And some raged and gnashed their teeth against them, desiring to execute more severe vengeance upon them; but others laughed and mocked at them, magnifying their own idols, and imputed to them the punishment of the Christians. Even the more reasonable, and those who had seemed to sympathize somewhat, reproached them often, saying, "Where is their God, and what has their religion, which they have chosen rather than life, profited them?"

So various was their conduct toward us; but we were in deep affliction because we could not bury the bodies. For neither did night avail us for this purpose, nor did money persuade, nor entreaty move to compassion; but they kept watch in every way, as if the prevention of the burial would be of some great advantage to them.

The bodies of the martyrs, having thus in every manner been exhibited and exposed for six days, were afterward burned and reduced to ashes, and swept into the Rhone by the wicked men, so that no trace of them might appear on the earth. And this they did, as if able to conquer God, and prevent their new birth; "that," as they said, "they may have no hope of a resurrection, through trust in which they bring to us this foreign and new religion, and despise terrible things, and are ready even to go to death with joy. Now let us see if they will rise again, and if their God is able to help them, and to deliver them out of our hands."

†

D. A MARTYR TRIAL

DIONYSUS OF ALEXANDRIA

But as regards the persecution which prevailed so fiercely in his reign,[1] and the sufferings which Dionysus with others endured on account of piety toward the God of the universe, his own words shall show, which he wrote in answer to Germanus, a contemporary bishop who was endeavoring to slander him. His statement is as follows:

"Truly I am in danger of falling into great folly and stupidity through being forced to relate the wonderful providence of God toward us. But since it is said that 'it is good to keep close the secret of a king, but it is honorable to reveal the works of God,'[2] I will join issue with the violence of Germanus.

"I went not alone to Aemilianus;[3] but my fellow-presbyter, Maximus, and the deacons Faustus, Eusebius, and Chaeremon, and a brother who was present from Rome, went with me. But Aemilianus did not at first say to me: 'Hold no assemblies'; for this was superfluous to him, and the last thing to one who was seeking to accomplish the first. For he was not concerned about our assembling, but that we ourselves should not be Christians. And he commanded me to give this up, supposing if I

---

[1] Of the Emperor Valerian (253-260).
[2] Tobit 12:7.
[3] Prefect of Egypt under Valerian.

turned from it the others also would follow me. But I answered him, neither unsuitably nor in many words: 'We must obey God rather than men.' And I testified openly that I worshipped the one only God, and no other; and that I would not turn from this nor would I ever cease to be a Christian. Thereupon he commanded us to go to a village near the desert, called Cephro.

"But listen to the very words which were spoken on both sides, as they were recorded:[1]

Dionysus, Faustus, Maximus, Marcellus, and Chaeremon being arraigned, Aemilianus the prefect said: "I have reasoned verbally with you concerning the clemency which our rulers have shown to you; for they have given you the opportunity to save yourselves, if you will turn to that which is according to nature, and worship the gods that preserve their empire, and forget those that are contrary to nature. What then do you say to this? For I do not think that you will be ungrateful for their kindness, since they would turn you to a better course."

Dionysus replied: "Not all people worship all gods; but each one those whom he approves. We therefore reverence and worship the one God, the Maker of all; who hath given the empire to the divinely favored and august Valerian and Gallienus;[2] and we pray to him continually for their empire, that it may remain unshaken."

Aemilianus, the prefect, said to them: "But who forbids you to worship him, if he is a god, together with those who are gods by nature. For ye have been commanded to reverence the gods, and the gods whom all know."

Dionysus answered: We worship no other."

Aemilianus, the prefect said to them: "I see that you are at once ungrateful and insensible to the kindness of our sovereigns. Wherefore ye shall not remain in this city. But ye shall be sent into the regions of Libya, to a place called Cephro. For I have chosen this place at the command of our sovereigns, and it shall by no

means be permitted you or any others, either to hold assemblies or to enter into the so-called cemeteries.[3] But if any one shall be seen outside of the place which I have commanded, or be found in any assembly, he will bring peril on himself. For suitable punishment shall not fail. Go, therefore, where ye have been ordered.'

"And he hastened me away, though I was sick, not granting even a day's respite….But through the help of the Lord we did not give up the open assembly. But I called together the more diligently those who were in the city, as if I were with them; being, so to speak, 'absent in body but present in spirit.'[4] But in Cephro a large church gathered with us of the brethren that followed us from the city, and those that joined us from Egypt; and there 'God opened unto us a door for the Word.'[5] At first we were persecuted and stoned; but afterwards not a few of the heathen forsook the idols and turned to God. For until this time they had not heard the Word, since it was then first sown by us. And as if God had brought us to them for this purpose, when we had performed this ministry he transferred us to another place."

✝

E. THE PLAGUE AT ALEXANDRIA

DIONYSUS OF ALEXANDRIA

After these events a pestilential disease followed the war, and at the approach of the feast he wrote again to the brethren, describing the sufferings consequent upon this calamity.

"To other men the present might not seem to be a suitable time for a festival. Nor indeed is this or any other time suitable for them; neither sorrowful times, nor even such as might be thought especially cheerful. Now, indeed, everything is tears and every one is mourning, and wailings resound daily through the city because of the multitude of the dead and dy-

---

[1]Scribes kept records of proceedings in Roman courts.; as today, transcripts could be purchased by interested parties, and one such is what Dionysus evidently quotes here.
[2]Valerian's son and co-ruler.

[3]*Coemeteria*, "literally, 'sleeping-places.' The word was used only in this sense in classic Greek; but the Christians, looking upon death only as a sleep, early applied the name to their burial places, hence Aemilian speaks of them as 'so-called' cemeteries." (A. McG.)
[4]I Corinthians 5:3.
[5]Colossians 4:3.

ing. For as it was written of the firstborn of the Egyptians, so now 'there has arisen a great cry, for there is not a house where there is not one dead.' And would that this were all! For many terrible things have happened already. First, they drove us out; and when alone, and persecuted, and put to death by all, even then we kept the feast. And every place of affliction was to us a place of festival: field, desert, ship, inn, prison; but the perfected martyrs kept the most joyous festival of all, feasting in heaven. After these things war and famine followed, which we endured in common with the heathen. But we bore alone those things with which they afflicted us, and at the same time we experienced also the effects of what they inflicted upon and suffered from one another; and again, we rejoiced in the peace of Christ, which he gave to us alone.

"But after both we and they had enjoyed a very brief season of rest this pestilence assailed us; to them more dreadful than any dread, and more intolerable than any other calamity; and, as one of their own writers has said, the only thing which prevails over all hope. But to us this was not so, but no less than the other things was it an exercise and probation. For it did not keep aloof even from us, but the heathen it assailed more severely."

"The most of our brethren were unsparing in their exceeding love and brotherly kindness. They held fast to each other and visited the sick fearlessly, and ministered to them continually, serving them in Christ. And they died with them most joyfully, taking the affliction of others, and drawing the sickness from their neighbors to themselves and willingly receiving their pains. And many who cared for the sick and gave strength to others died themselves, having transferred to themselves their death. And the popular saying which always seems a mere expression of courtesy, they then made real in action, taking their departure as the others' 'offscouring.'

"Truly the best of our brethren departed from life in this manner, including some presbyters and deacons and those of the people who had the highest reputation; so that this form of death, through the great piety and strong faith it exhibited, seemed to lack nothing of martyrdom. And they took the bodies of the saints in their open hands and in their bosoms, and closed their eyes and their mouths; and they bore them away on their shoulders and laid them out; and they clung to them and embraced them; and they prepared them suitably with washings and garments. And after a little they received like treatment themselves, for the survivors were continually following those who had gone before them.

"But with the heathen everything was quite otherwise. They deserted those who began to be sick, and fled from their dearest friends. And they cast them out into the streets when they were half dead, and left the dead like refuse, unburied. They shunned any participation or fellowship with death; which yet, with all their precautions, it was not easy for them to escape."

✝

IX. Faith and Identity

After centuries as outcasts, Christians after Constantine suddenly found themselves first an accepted, then an official, part of the state. How were they to keep from being swallowed up by a government in which the emperor had traditionally been the head of the state religion? On a wider issue, a church which had grown up with adversity now had the splendors of the world within its grasp. How was it to react? The basic question is, Could a religion of outcasts and sinners become "official" without losing something of its nature?

ST. DANIEL THE STYLITE (A.D. 409-493) represents a new type of hero: a Christian in an age of toleration. But toleration hid temptations of its own: How does Daniel deal with a world that no longer persecutes Christians? A passage from the LIFE OF ST. JOHN THE ALMSGIVER (c. A.D. 560-630) illustrates another problem Christianity faced now that it had replaced the pagan gods. The way John deals with it shows something about the Christian message. Can you tell what? Both Daniel and John were Eastern Christians. ST. JEROME (c. A.D. 340-419) and ST. AUGUSTINE (A.D. 354-430) lived in the Western half of the empire at a time when major upheavals were occurring. They, too, were forced to think about rethought the proper relationship between Christians and matters of this world.

The success of Christianity also brought with it a new problem: what is the appropriate role for a Christian Roman emperor? Two answers are provided by the subsequent readings. LACTANTIUS (c. A.D. 240-320) and EUSEBIUS OF CAESAREA illustrate the enthusiastic reaction of Christians coming out of an age of persecution, while the writings of Bishop OSSIUS OF CORDOBA, an early adviser of the emperor Constantine, and POPE GELASIUS I (A.D. 492-496) propose a different relationship.

In the seventh century, Islam burst forth from the Arabian peninsula to become a major world religion and rival to Christianity. This chapter ends with excerpts from the *KORAN*, the holy book of Islam as written by Mohammad; you ought to be able to make useful comparisons and contrasts with western civilization's other great monotheistic religions. Last are the writings of AL-GHAZALI, who lived in Persia in the eleventh century A.D. and who is widely regarded as one of the most brilliant Muslim scholars. See if you can construct a Muslim hero from his writings, then compare and contrast this hero with his Christian counterparts.

❖   ❖   ❖

1. WILL SUCCESS SPOIL CHRISTIAN-ITY?

Christians already had developed their own type of hero in the person of the martyrs who suffered during the centuries of persecution. After the end of persecutions, this role was taken up by the "holy men," who reenacted the suffering of the martyrs through voluntary acts of abstinence and endurance. To these "athletes in Christ" even Emperors had to yield. St. Daniel the Stylite (A.D. 409-493) is a good example of the type. In reading this account of his life, can you isolate the traits of the Christian hero? How does he compare to the Greek, Roman, and Near-Eastern heroes you already have studied? How is he different? What gives him his power? How does he exercise it? What does the *Life of Daniel* indicate about the impact of Christianity on the later Roman Empire? What motivates Daniel?

The next selection is an incident from the *Life of St. John the Almsgiver*. John was bishop of Alexandria in the seventh century. The passage illustrates one way that Christians dealt with adversity. What is the problem John faced, and how does he resolve it?

The final two passages also represent Christian reactions to adversity, these from the Western half of the empire. St. Jerome was studying in

Jerusalem when word reached him that Rome had been taken by the Visigoths in a.d. 410. The following letter to a friend indicates his reaction. Is there anything in it which surprises you? If so, what?

St. Augustine began his major work, *The City of God* in the aftermath of the sack of Rome in A.D. 410 by Alaric and the Visigoths. He had a major problem to address. What was it? How well does this passage handle it?

A. THE LIFE OF ST. DANIEL THE STYLITE

Before all things it is right that we should give glory to Jesus Christ our God, Who for us was made man and for our salvation endured all things according to the Dispensation; for His sake, too, prophets were killed, and just men crucified themselves because of this faith in Him and by His grace, after having kept patience under their sufferings unswervingly unto the end, they received a crown of glory. These men our Master and Savior Christ gave us as an example that we might know that it is possible for a man by the patient endurance of his sufferings to please God and be called His faithful servant.

For this reason I thought it good to take in hand a recital of the labors of St. Daniel, yet I do so with fear; for this man's way of life was great and brilliant and marvelous, whereas I am but a witless and humble person. I will put down truthfully everything I heard from the men who were the Saint's disciples before me and I will also relate truly all the things I saw with my own eyes.

This father among saints was the son of a father named Elias and a mother Martha; he came from a small village called Meratha (which is, being interpreted, 'the Caves') in the territory of Samosata in Mesopotamia. As his mother was barren and was reproached for this by her husband and kinsfolk, she went out one day secretly at midnight unbeknown to her husband and stretching forth her hands to heaven, prayed saying, 'Oh Lord Jesus Christ, Who art long-suffering towards the sins of men, Thou Who didst in the beginning create woman to increase the race of men, do Thou Thyself take my reproach from me and grant me fruit of my womb that I may dedicate him

to Thee, the Lord of All.' After weeping bitterly and afflicting her soul with many lamentations, she came in to her husband and whilst sleeping beside him saw in a vision of the night two great circular lights coming down from heaven and resting near her. Next morning she related the vision to her husband and kinsfolk and each one interpreted differently the things she had told them. But she sighed and said to herself, 'My God to Whom I prayed will do what is best for my unhappy soul.' And not many days later she conceived the holy man of whom we spoke.

TO THE MONASTERY

So he was born; and when in course of time he had reached the age of five years his parents took him with offerings of fruit to a monastery near the village and the abbot asked them, 'By what name is the child called?' And when the parents mentioned some other name, the old man said, 'He shall not be called that, but whatever the Lord shall reveal to us, that shall his name be.' And the archimandrite said to the child in the Syrian dialect, 'Go, child, and fetch me a book from the table.' For it is a custom in monasteries that many different books should be laid in front of the sanctuary, and whichever book a brother wants he takes and reads. So the child went and fetched the book of the prophet Daniel, and from this he got that name.

Now when he was twelve years old he heard his mother say, 'My child, I have dedicated you to God.' Thereupon one day without saying anything to anybody he went out of the village for a distance of about ten miles where there was a monastery containing fifty brethren. And entering the monastery he fell at the abbot's feet and begged to be received by him. But the abbot said to him, 'Child, you are still very young in years and are not able to endure so hard a discipline; you know nothing of the monks' life; go home, stay with your parents and after some time when you are able both to fast and to sing and to endure discipline, then come back to us.' But the child answered, 'Father, I should prefer to die in these hardships than to quit the shelter of your flock!' And when, in spite of all he could do, the archimandrite was unable to persuade the child, he said to the brethren, 'In truth, my children, let us receive this boy for he seems to me to be very much in earnest.' And they all yielded to the abbot's counsel, and thus Daniel remained in the brotherhood.

[Daniel eventually becomes abbot himself, at which time he quits the monastery in order to devote himself to asceticism. He spends two weeks with the great pillar saint Simeon and then leaves, intending to visit the Holy Land. But a mysterious monk meets him on the road and warns him to avoid the Holy Land because of rioting there, and to go instead to Constantinople. The monk disappears when Daniel arrives at a monastery, where he spends the night.]

Then saying nothing to anybody about this, but bidding them all farewell after the psalm-singing in the night and having received their 'God speed you!' he left the monastery and started on the road to Byzantium. When he reached a place called Anaplus where there was an oratory dedicated to the archangel Michael he spent seven days there in his oratory.

Once he heard some men conversing in the Syrian dialect and saying that there was a church in that place inhabited by demons who often sank ships and had injured, and still were injuring, many of the passers-by, and that it was impossible for anyone to walk along that road in the evening or even at noonday.

As everybody was continually complaining about the destructive power which had occupied the place, the divine spirit came upon Daniel and he called to mind that great man, Antony, the model of asceticism [and Paul, his disciple]; he remembered their struggles against demons and the many temptations they suffered from them and how they had overcome them by the strength of Christ and were deemed worthy of great crowns. Then he asked a man who understood the Syrian dialect about this church and begged him to show him the spot.

On reaching the porch of the church, just as a brave soldier strips himself for battle before venturing against a host of barbarians, so he, too, entered the church reciting the words spoken by the prophet, David, in the Psalms: The Lord is my light and my savior, whom shall I fear? the Lord is the defender of my life, of whom shall I be afraid?' and the rest.

And holding the invincible weapon of the Cross, he went round into each corner of the church making genuflections and prayers.

When night fell, stones, they say, were thrown at him and there was the sound of a multitude knocking and making an uproar; but he persevered in prayer. In this way he spent the first night and the second; but on the third night sleep overpowered him, as it might overtake any man bearing the weakness of the flesh. And straightway many phantoms appeared as of giant shapes some of whom said, 'Who induced you to take possession of this place, poor wretch? do you wish to perish miserably? Come, let us drag him out and throw him into the water!' Again, others carrying, as it seemed, large stones stood at his head, apparently intending to crush it to pieces. On waking, the athlete of Christ again went round the corners of the church praying and singing and saying to the spirits, 'Depart from hence! if you do not, then by the strength of the Cross you shall be devoured by flames and thus be forced to flee.' But they made a still greater uproar and howled the louder. But he despised them and taking not the slightest notice of their uproar, he bolted the door of the church and left a small window through which he would converse with the people that came up to see him.

In the meantime his fame had spread abroad in those regions, and you could see men and women with their children streaming up to see the holy man and marveling that the place formerly so wild and impassable lay in such perfect calm, and that where demons danced lately, there by the patience of the just man Christ was now glorified day and night.

After a space of nine years had elapsed, the servant of God fell into ecstasy, as it were, and saw a huge pillar of cloud standing opposite him and the holy and blessed Simeon standing above the head of the column and two men of goodly appearance, clad in white, standing near him in the heights. And he heard the voice of the holy and blessed Simeon saying to him, 'Come here to me, Daniel.' And he said, 'Father, father, and how can I get up to that height?' Then the Saint said to the young men standing near him, 'Go down and bring him up to me.' So the men came down and brought Daniel up to him and he stood there. Then Simeon took him in his arms and kissed him with a holy kiss, and then others called him away, and escorted by them he was borne up to heaven leaving Daniel on the column with the two men. When holy Daniel saw him being carried up to heaven he heard the voice of Saint Simeon, 'Stand firm and play the man.' But he was confused by fear and by that fearful voice, for it was like thunder in his ears. When he came to himself again he declared the vision to those around him. Then they, too, said to the holy man, 'You must mount on to a pillar and take up Saint Simeon's mode of life and be supported by the angels.' The blessed one said, 'Let the will of God, our Master, be done upon His servant.' And taking the holy Gospel into his hands and opening it with prayer he found the place in which was written 'And thou, child, shalt be called the prophet of the Highest, for thou shalt go before the face of the Lord to prepare His ways.' And he gave thanks and closed the book.

[A monk, Sergius, arrives with word that St. Simeon has died.]

From that day he remained near the blessed Daniel, and Sergius saw the following vision. Three young men, it seemed, came to him and said, 'Arise, say unto father Daniel "The appointed time of thy discipline in this church is now fulfilled, form henceforth leave the church, come hither and begin thy contest".' When he awoke he related what he had seen. The blessed Daniel said to him, 'Brother, the Lord has revealed quite clearly to us what should be done, for this dream which your Piety saw fits in with the vision which I saw; be ready therefore to endure hardships for the Lord and come up on the hill and we will search out the more desolate and higher-lying spots in these parts and judge where we ought to set up a column. For it was not without a purpose that God guided you to bring to my unworthiness the father's garment.'

Sergius went up to view the spot where the column was to be set; and a short distance away he saw a white dove fluttering and then settling again. Thinking it was caught in a snare he ran towards it, and then it flew up and away out of his sight. Seeing that the

place was solitary and considering the incident of the dove that it had not been shown to him casually or by chance, he gave thanks to the Lord and returned to the holy man in the church bringing him the glad tidings that the Lord had prepared for them a suitable place. Then he, too, gave thanks to the Lord Who brings all things to pass according to His will.

And it came to pass after three days when night had fallen they opened the church in which Daniel was shut up, and taking the brother he went up to the spot—for Sergius had departed to another place Thrace-wards—and they found a long plank lying there which the inhabitants of the suburb had prepared for knocking down the column. This they bound with a rope and stood it up against the column, and then went up and put the balustrade on the column, for that column was not really high, only about the height of two men. When they had fitted the balustrade and bound it firmly with a rope they knelt and prayed to God. And the blessed Daniel went up and stood on the column inside the balustrade and said, 'Oh Lord Jesus Christ, in Thy holy name, I am entering upon this contest; do Thou approve my purpose and help me to accomplish my course.' And he said to the brother, 'Take away the plank and the rest of the rope and get away quickly so that if anybody comes he may not find you.' And the brother did as he was told.

The next morning the husbandmen came and when they saw Daniel they were amazed; for the sight was a strange one, and they came near him, and when they looked on him they recognized him as the man who had formerly been in the church. After having received the Saint's blessing they left him and went to the City and reported to Gelanius, the owner of the property. On hearing their news he was very angry with them for not having guarded that part of his land; and he was also annoyed with the blessed Daniel for having done this without his consent. And he went and reported the matter to the blessed Emperor Leo and the Archbishop Gennadius, for the blessed Anatolius had already gone to his rest. The Emperor for his part said nothing. But the Archbishop said to him, 'As master of the property, fetch him down; for where he was he had no right to be, but he was not there on my authority.'

A COMPROMISE

Then Gelanius took several men with him and went up to the servant of God, and, although it was a calm day and the air was still, yet it came to pass that suddenly the clouds gathered and a storm arose accompanied with hail so that all the fruit of the vineyards was destroyed and the leaves were stripped from the vines, for it was the time of the vintage. And it was only with difficulty that the men who were with Gelanius got away, and they muttered amongst themselves, for they were astonished at the strangeness of the sight.

Gelanius then approached the blessed man and said, 'Who gave you permission to take up your stand on land belonging to me? Was it not better for you in the church?—but since you have shown contempt of me, the owner of the property, and have taken no account of the Emperor and the Archbishop, let me tell you that I have been empowered by them to fetch you down.'

But when he persisted and repeated his demands it seemed an unjust and illegal proceeding to his companions and they opposed its being done, 'Because', said they, 'the Emperor himself is a pious man and this man is orthodox and this spot lies at a distance from your field.' When Gelanius perceived that there would be a disturbance he said to the Saint in the Syrian language—for by birth he was a Syro-Persian from Mesopotamia—'Please pretend to come down for the sake of those who ordered you to descend, and then I will not allow you really to touch the ground.' So then a ladder was brought and Daniel came down about six rungs from the column. There were still several rungs before he actually reached the ground, when Gelanius ran forward and prevented his coming down the last rungs, saying, 'Return to your dwelling and your place and pray for me.' For as Daniel was coming down he had noticed that sores and swellings had begun to appear on his feet, and he was distressed. And the blessed man went up the rungs of the ladder down which he had come, and stood inside the balustrade on the column; and after offering prayer, all received

his blessing and went down from the hill in peace. So Gelanius, when he had reached the capital, reported everything to the Emperor telling him of the patience and endurance of the man so that he won the Emperor's pity for him.

Not many days later Gelanius went up to the Saint asking him to allow him to change the column and have a very large one placed for him. And lo! while they were conversing a certain Sergius arrived from the parts about Thrace, a lawyer by profession, bringing with him a very young boy, his only son, by name John, who was grievously tormented by a demon. This man came and threw himself to the ground in front of the column, weeping and lamenting and crying out, saying, 'Have pity upon my son, oh servant of God; it is now thirty days since the unclean spirit first called upon the name of your Holiness; and after inquiring for you through eight long days, we have come to claim your blessing.' When Gelanius heard this and saw the old man afflicting himself thus out of pity, he, too, was affected and burst into tears. And the holy Daniel said to the old man, 'He that asketh in faith receives all from God; if therefore you believe that through me a sinner, God will heal your son, according to your faith it shall be given unto you.' And he bade the young man approach; and he drew near and stood before the column. And the Saint bade them give him a drink of the oil of the saints. And it came to pass when they gave him to drink that the demon threw him to the ground and there he rolled in their midst. Then the evil spirit rose up and shouted swearing that he would go out on that very day a week hence.

DANIEL TRADES UP

And it came to pass on the following day, Saturday, Gelanius came with a large company to remove the Saint to the larger column; and as they were about to transfer the servant of God from pillar to pillar, the demon in Sergius' son became agitated, for he was being forced to go out of him, and he cried with a loud voice saying, 'Oh, the violence of this false magician! When he was still in the church he drove me out of Cyrus' daughter; so I went away to Thrace and found a dwelling in this young man; and behold, he has brought me here from Thrace and now he persecutes me. What have you to do with me, Daniel?—oh violence! I must come out from this one, too!' and after reviling the Saint furiously and afflicting the young man he came out of him by the power of the Lord. As the demon came out, he created such a stench that all the crowds present could not endure the stench and had to cover their noses; and the young man lay on the ground with his mouth open so that all said he was dead and his father beat his breast as if over a corpse. Then the holy Daniel said to Sergius, 'make him sit up and give him to drink of the oil of the saints.' And as the boy drank, vomiting came upon him and he brought up black clotted blood. Then the servant of God cried from above with a loud voice saying, 'John, what ails you? stand up!' And immediately, as if awakened from sleep, the boy said, 'What is your will, master?' and He ran forward and embraced the column, giving thanks to God and the Saint. And fear seized upon them all and for a long space of time they stretched out their hands to heaven and with tears kept shouting the 'Kyrie, eleeson' (Lord, have mercy!).

Then with great ceremony and with an escort to guard him Daniel moved on to the taller column. And Gelanius, having seen the wonderful works of God, went down from the hill and related everything in detail to the Emperor and to all the great folk of the Court. The young man who had been cured fell at his father's feet and implored him to entreat the servant of God to grant him the holy robe of a monk and, as the old man could not be persuaded because he wished to keep his son near him, the son protested saying, 'If you will not do this, then I shall go away secretly to some other place where you will not even be able to see me.' In this way he persuaded his father who then petitioned the holy man who received his son and bade him live with the brethren. After a year had been fulfilled and the young man by the grace of God was making progress towards the good way of life the holy man sent for his father and gave the son the holy robe. The father was content and returned to his home rejoicing and glorifying God. After three years the young man passed away and went to the Lord after having lived a good life.

Now the blessed Emperor Leo of pious memory had heard from many of these things and desired for a long time to see the man. Therefore he sent for the pious Sergius, who carried the Saint's messages, and through him he asked that the Saint would pray and beseech God to grant him a son. And Daniel prayed, and through God's good pleasure the Emperor's wife, the Empress Verina, thereafter conceived and begot a son—whereupon the Emperor immediately sent and had the foundations laid of a third column.

Now the demon of envy could not control his envy so he found an instrument worthy of his evil designs. A certain harlot, Basiane, who had lately come to Constantinople from the East, entrapped many of those who hunted after women of her sort. The sons of some heretics summoned her and made the following suggestion to her: 'If you can in any way bring a scandal upon the man who stands on the pillar in Anaplus or upon any of those who are with him, we will pay you a hundred gold pieces.' The shameless woman agreed and went up to the holy man with much parade and took with her a crowd of young men and prostitutes and simulated illness and remained in the suburb opposite the Saint's enclosure. And though she stayed there no little time she spent her time in vain. As she was anxious to get possession of the money she went down to the city and plotted after this fashion. To her lovers she said, 'I managed to seduce the man, for he became enamored of my beauty and ordered his disciples to bring me up to him by means of the ladder; but as I would not consent, the men there planned to lie in wait and kill me; and it is with difficulty that I have escaped from their hands.' When her lovers heard this they thought they had gained their object and imparted the news to all their fellow conspirators. And thereupon as the report spread you could have seen a war between the believers and unbelievers. While matters were in this state, God Who rejoices in the truth and ever defends His servants, brought it about that the abandoned woman, Basiane, should be tormented by an evil demon in the middle of the City and then and there should proclaim her plot and the wrong which the licentious men had suggested to her against the righteous Daniel, promising her money if she were successful. And not only did she make public their names, shouting them for all to hear, but their rank also. Then could be seen a change in the ordering of affairs, for the faithful now rejoiced, whilst the faithless who had threatened to throw stones against the just man were put to shame.

And it came to pass shortly afterwards that there was a great fire in the capital. So all the inhabitants were in great distress and the majority had to flee from the city. They made their way to the holy man and each of them implored him to placate God's anger so that the fire should cease. At the same time they would relate to him the personal misfortunes they had suffered; one would say, 'I have been stripped bare of great possessions'; another, 'As the fire was far off I felt no uneasiness but slept with my wife and children; but suddenly the catastrophe overtook me and now I am a widower and childless, and have barely escaped being burnt alive.' Or again another, 'I ran away from that terrible danger only to suffer shipwreck of my scanty belongings.' The holy man wept with them and said, 'The merciful God wished to spare you in His goodness and made these things known beforehand and He did not keep silence concerning it; you should therefore have importuned God and escaped His terrible wrath. For once upon a time when the Ninevites were warned by the prophet that destruction threatened them, they escaped it by repenting. I was not vexed by the thought that God's mercy might prove me to be a false prophet; for I had as an example the prophet who was angry because of the gourd; and now I beg you bear with gratitude that which God has sent. For a master is most truly served when he sees his servant bearing chastisement gratefully; and then he deems him worthy not only of his former honor but even of greater by reason of his good will towards him.' And many other words of counsel he spoke unto them and turned their hopelessness into hopefulness and then dismissed them saying, 'The city will be afflicted for seven days.'

It happened about the same time that Gubazius, the king of the Lazi, arrived at the court of the Emperor Leo, who took him up to visit the holy man. When he saw this strange sight Gubazius threw himself on his face and said, 'I thank Thee, heavenly King, that by means of an earthly king Thou hast deemed me worthy to behold great mysteries; for never before in this world have I seen anything of this kind.' And these kings had a point of dispute touching the Roman policy; and they laid the whole matter open to the servant of God and through the mediation of the holy man they agreed upon a treaty which satisfied the claims of each. After this the Emperor returned to the city and dismissed Gubazius to his native land, and when the latter reached his own country he related to all his folk what he had seen. Consequently the men who later on came up from Lazica to the City invariably went up to Daniel. Gubazius himself, too, wrote to the holy man and besought his prayers and never ceased doing so to the end of his life.

[When the remains of St. Simeon arrive in Constantinople from Antioch, the Emperor and all the people go to the church at Anaplus to celebrate.]

After the service which followed the whole populace streamed out into the enclosure to the holy man in order to be blessed. And the Archbishop with all the clergy went there likewise; and a throne was placed in front of the column; and when the Archbishop had taken his seat he said to the holy man, 'Behold the Lord has fulfilled all your desires; and now bless your children with your counsel.' After the deacon had said the 'Let us attend,' the holy man from his pillar said to the people: 'Peace be upon you!' and then opening his mouth taught them, saying nothing rhetorical or philosophical, but speaking about the love of God and the care of the poor and almsgiving and brotherly love and of the everlasting life which awaits the holy, and the everlasting condemnation which is the lot of sinners. And by the grace of God the hearts of the faithful people were so touched to the quick that they watered the ground with their tears. After this the Archbishop offered a prayer, and then the holy man dismissed them all, and each man returned to his house in peace.

THE STORY OF TITUS

At that time the blessed Emperor Leo heard from many about a certain Titus, a man of vigor who dwelt in Gaul and had in his service a number of men well trained for battle; so he sent for him and honored him with the rank of Count that he might have him to fight on his behalf if he were forced to go to war. This Titus he sent to the holy man for his blessing; on his arrival the Saint watered him with many and divers counsels from the Holy writings and proved him to be an ever-blooming fruit-bearing tree; and Titus, beholding the holy man, marveled at the strangeness of his appearance and his endurance and just as good earth when it has received the rain brings forth much fruit, so this admirable man Titus was illuminated in mind by the teaching of the holy and just man and no longer wished to leave the enclosure, for he said, 'The whole labor of man is spent on growing rich and acquiring possessions in this world and pleasing men; yet the single hour of his death robs him of all his belongings, therefore it is better for us to serve God rather than men.' With these words he threw himself down before the holy man begging him to receive him and let him be enrolled in the brotherhood. And Daniel, the servant of the Lord, willingly accepted his good resolve. Thereupon that noble man Titus sent for all his men and said to his soldiers, 'From now on I am the soldier of the heavenly King; aforetime my rank among men made me your captain and yet I was unable to benefit either you or myself, for I only urged you on to slaughter and bloodshed. From to-day, however, and henceforth I bid farewell to all such things; therefore those of you who wish it, remain here with me, but I do not compel any one of you, for what is done under compulsion is not acceptable. See, here is money, take some, each of you, and go to your homes.' Then he brought much gold and he took and placed it in front of the column and gave to each according to his rank. Two of them, however, did not choose to take any, but remained with him. All the rest embraced Titus and went their ways.

When the Emperor heard this he was very angry and sent a messenger up to the holy man to say to Titus, 'I brought you up from your country because I wanted to have you quite near me and I sent you to the holy man to pray and receive a blessing, but not that you should separate yourself from me.' Titus replied to the messenger, 'From now on, since I have listened to the teaching of this holy man, I am

dead to the world and to all the things of the world. Whatever the just man says about me do you tell to the Emperor, for Titus, your servant, is dead.' Then the messengers went outside into the enclosure to the holy man and told him everything. And the holy man sent a letter of counsel by them to the Emperor, beseeching him and saying, 'You yourself need no human aid; for owing to your perfect faith in God you have God as your everlasting defender; do not therefore covet a man who to-day is and tomorrow is not; for the Lord doeth all things according to His will. Therefore dedicate thy servant to God Who is able to send your Piety in his stead another still braver and more useful; without your approval I never wished to do anything.'

And the Emperor was satisfied and sent and thanked the holy man and said, 'To crown all your good deeds there yet remained this good thing for you to do. Let the man, then, remain under your authority, and may God accept his good purpose.' Not long afterwards they were deemed worthy of the holy robe, and both made progress in the good way of life; but more especially was this true of Titus, the former Count.

Next the Devil, the hinderer of good men, imbued Titus with a spirit of inquisitiveness and suggested that he should watch the holy man in order to see if he ate and what he took to eat. So one day he waited till about the time of lamp-lighting and then unnoticed by all the brethren he remained outside in the enclosure hidden behind the column. When the nightly psalmody took place in the oratory the brothers imagined he had stayed behind because he was sick. The following day he spent with all the others. Although he did the same thing for seven nights, he found out nothing. Finally he openly conjured the holy man to explain his manner of life to him. And the holy man granted him his wish saying, 'Believe me, brother, I both eat and drink sufficiently for my needs; for I am not a spirit nor disembodied, but I too am a man and am clothed with flesh. And the business of evacuation I perform like a sheep exceedingly dryly, and if ever I am tempted to partake of more than I require, I punish myself, for I am unable either to walk about or to relieve myself to aid my digestion; therefore in proportion as I struggle to be temperate, to that degree I benefit and the pain in my feet becomes less intense.' Titus answered, 'If you, your Holiness, who are in such a state of body and standing in such a wind-swept spot, struggle in that manner to be temperate for your own good, what ought I to do who am young in years and vigorous in body?' The Saint replied, 'Do whatever your flesh can endure; neither force it beyond measure nor on the other hand abandon it to slackness; for if you load a ship beyond its usual burden, it will readily be sunk by its weight, but if on the contrary you leave it too light, it is easily overturned by the winds. By the grace of God, brother, I understand my natural capacity and know how to regulate my food.' After hearing this Titus went away to the oratory, took his place in one corner and hung himself up by ropes under his armpits so that his feet did not rest upon the ground, and from one evening to another he would eat either three dates or three dried figs and drink the ration of wine. He also fixed a board against his chest on which he would sometimes lay his head and sleep and at others place a book and read.

And he did this for some long time and benefited all those who visited him; amongst these was the most faithful Emperor, Leo, for whenever he went up to the holy man, after taking leave of him, he would go in to the blessed Titus; and beholding his inspired manner of life he marveled at this endurance and besought him to pray for him. And it pleased the Lord to call him while he was at prayer, with his eyes and his face turned upwards and heavenwards, and thus it was that he breathed his last. The brethren looking at him thought he was praying as usual. When evening had fallen, the two brethren came who had formerly been his servants and now ministered unto him and brought him all he required, and they discovered that he was dead. And when they began to lament all recognized that he had gone to his rest. His head lay back on his neck, his hands were crossed and supported by the plank and since the weight of the body was borne by the shoulder ropes his legs hung down straight and were not bent up. And as one looked on the corpse of this saintly champion it showed the departed soul's longing for God. The brethren went and told the elders who came out to the holy man's enclosure and announced to him the death of the glorious saint. When he heard of it he thanked the Lord and bade them carry out the corpse to him after the time of lamp-lighting and put it in front of the column and hold an all-night service there in his memory. The next day Titus was buried in the tomb of the elders by command of the holy man.

[Leo is succeeded by the Emperor Zeno, who is driven out by a palace conspiracy led by Basiliscus, a heretic who attempts to remove the archbishop of Constantinople, Acacius.]

After some consideration the Archbishop ordered all the churches to be draped as a sign of mourning, and going up into the pulpit he addressed the crowds and explained the blasphemous attempt which was being made. 'Brethren and children', he said, 'the time of martyrdom is at hand; let us therefore fight for our faith and for the Holy Church, our mother, and let us not betray our priesthood.' A great shout arose and all were overcome by tears, and since the Emperor remained hostile and refused to give them any answer, the Archbishop and the archimandrites determined to send to the holy man, Daniel, and give him an account of these things, and this they did.

And it happened by God's providence that on the following day Basiliscus sailed to Anaplus, and sent a chamberlain named Daniel, to the holy man to say, 'Do those things which the Archbishop Acacius is practicing against me seem just to your angelic nature? for he has roused the city against me and alienated the army and rains insults on me! I beg you, pray for us that he may not prevail against us.' After listening to him the holy man said to Daniel, 'Go and tell him who sent you, "You are not worthy of a blessing for you have adopted Jewish ideas and are setting at nought the incarnation of our Lord Jesus Christ and upsetting the Holy Church and despising His priests. For it is written 'Give not that which is holy unto the dogs, neither cast your pearls before the swine.' Know therefore and see, for the God Who rendeth swiftly will surely rend your tyrannous royalty out of your hands". When the chamberlain heard this answer he said he dared not himself say these things to the Emperor and besought Daniel to send the message in writing, if he would, and to seal it with his seal. The holy man yielded to the eunuch's entreaties, wrote a note and after sealing it, gave it to Daniel and dismissed him; and he returned and delivered the sealed note to the Emperor. He opened it and when he learnt the purport of the message he was very angry and immediately sailed back to the city. These things were not hidden from the Archbishop Acacius and his most faithful people; therefore on the following day almost the whole city was gathered together in the Great Church and they kept shouting, 'The holy man for the Church! let the new Daniel save Susanna in her peril! another Elijah shall put Jezebel and Ahab to shame! in you we have the priest of orthodoxy; he that standeth for Christ will protect His bride, the Church.' And other such exclamations they poured forth with tears.

[Acacius sends an embassy to beg Daniel to descend from his column and protect the church.]

And they went and did as they were bid and threw themselves down before the column; and the holy man seeing them lying from above, 'What are you doing, holy fathers, mocking my unworthiness? What is it that you bid me do?' Then they stood up and said, 'That you with God's help should save the faith which is being persecuted, save a storm-tossed church and a scattered flock, and save our priest who, despite his grey hairs, is threatened with death.' And Daniel said to them, 'He is truthful that said, "The gates of hell shall not prevail against the Holy Church"; wait patiently therefore where you are and the will of God shall be done.' And it came to pass that Daniel was praying in the middle of the night, and as the day dawned—it was a Wednesday—he heard a voice saying distinctly to him, 'Go down with the fathers and do not hesitate; and afterwards fulfill your course in peace!' Obedient therefore to the counsel of the Lord he woke his servants. And they placed the ladder and went up and took away the iron bars round him. And Daniel came down with difficulty owing to the pain he suffered in his feet, and in that same hour of the night he took the pious archimandrites

with him and they sailed to the City and entered the church before the day had begun.

THE PEOPLE GREET DANIEL

And thus it was that when the people came to God's house while, according to custom, the fiftieth psalm was being sung, they saw the holy man in the sanctuary with the Bishop and marveled; and the report ran through the City that he had come. All the City, and even secluded maidens, left what they had in hand and ran to the Holy Church to see the man of God. And the crowds started shouting in honor of the Saint saying, 'To you we look to banish the grief of the Church; in you we have a high priest; accomplish that for which you came; the crown of your labors is already yours.' But the holy man beckoned with his hand to the people to be silent and addressed them through the deacon, Theoctistus, 'The stretching forth of the hands of Moses, God's servant, utterly destroyed all those who rose up against the Lord's people, both kings and nations; some He drowned in the depths of the sea, others He slew on dry land with the sword and exalted His people; so to-day, too, your faith which is perfect towards God has not feared the uprising of your enemies, it does not know defeat nor does it need human help; for it is founded on the firm rock of Christ. Therefore do not grow weary of praying; for even on behalf of the chief of the apostles earnest prayer was offered to God, not as if they thought he was deserted by God but because God wishes the flock to offer intercessions for its shepherd. Do you, therefore, do likewise, and amongst us, too, the Lord will quickly perform marvelous things to His glory.' After he had said this they took down all the mourning draperies from the sanctuary and the whole church. Daniel also wrote a letter to the Emperor saying, 'Does this angering of God do you any service? is not your life in His hands? What have you to do with the Holy Church to war against its servants, and prove yourself a second Diocletian?' And many other things like these he wrote both by way of counsel and of blame. When the Emperor received the letter and found that Daniel had come down and was in the church he was stung by the prick of fear and sent back word to him, 'All your endeavor has been to enter the City and stir up the citizens against me;

now see, I will hand the City, too, over to you.' And he left the palace and sailed to the Hebdomon.

When the holy man heard this news, he took the cross-bearers and the faithful people and bidding the monks guard the Church and the Archbishop he went out. As they reached Ammi, close to the chapel of the prophet the holy Samuel, the just man being carried by the crowd of the Christ-loving people, behold, a leper approached and cried aloud saying, 'I beseech you, the servant of the God Who healed lepers, to pray Him that I may be healed!' On hearing him the holy man ordered his bearers to halt; and when the leper had drawn near, the holy man said to him, 'Brother, how came you to think of asking me things that are beyond my power? for I, too, am a man encompassed with weakness even as you are.' The leper replied, 'But I beg you, I know that you are a man of God; and I believe that the God Whom you serve will grant me cleansing in answer to your prayers; for the apostles too were but men and yet through their prayers the Lord healed many.' The holy man marveling at his faith said to him, 'Do you then believe in Him Who gave healing to many through His saints?' The leper said, 'Yes, and I believe that even now if you pray I shall be healed.' Then Daniel turning to the East asked the people to stretch forth their hands to heaven and with tears to cry aloud the 'Kyrie eleeson' (Lord, have mercy!). And when he deemed that they had done this long enough, he said to the men near him, 'In the name of Jesus Christ, Who cleansed lepers, take him and wash him in the sea and wipe him clean and bring him back.' They ran off with the man, washed him in the sea and by the power of Jesus Christ the leper was healed on the spot. When the multitudes saw this astonishing miracle they shouted unceasingly the 'Kyrie eleeson.' Then the crowds took the man that was healed, all naked as he was, and returned to the City and brought him into the Holy Church and leading him up to the pulpit declared this wondrous miracle to all. The whole city ran together and beholding him who had been a leper cleansed by God through the holy man's prayers they glorified God for making the leper spotless. And so all those in the City who had sick folk ran to the

servant of God. And the Lord gave healing abundantly to them all.

Thereafter as the holy man with the crowd approached the palace of Hebdomon, a Goth leant out of a window and seeing the holy man carried along, he dissolved with laughter and shouted, 'See here is our new consul!' And as soon as he said this he was hurled down from the height by the power of God and burst asunder. Then sentinels, or the palace guards, prevented those who had seen the fall from entering into the palace, saying they should have an answer given them through a window. But when the people insisted with shouts that the holy man should enter the palace but received no answer, the servant of God said to them, 'Why do you trouble, children? You shall have the reward promised to peacemakers from God; and since it seems good to this braggart to send us away without achieving anything, let us do to him according to the word of the Lord. For He said to His disciples and apostles, "Into whatsoever city or village ye shall enter and they do not receive you, shake off the dust of your feet against them as a testimony to them"; let us therefore do that.' And he first of all shook out his leather tunic and incited the whole crowd to do likewise; and a noise as of thunder arose from the shaking of garments. When the guards who were on duty saw this and heard all the marvelous things God had wrought by Daniel most of them left all and followed him.

When all these things had been thus auspiciously accomplished by the grace of the Lord, and when Basiliscus of ill-omened name had heard from his legal secretary of the Saint's condemnation of him and of the sudden fall of the palace tower, it did not seem to him to augur any good. And immediately without a moment's delay he entered a boat and sailed from the Hebdomon to the City; and the next day he sent senators to the very holy Cathedral to beseech the Saint to take the trouble to come as far as the palace. But he would not consent to go but said, 'Let him come himself to the Holy Church and make his recantation before the precious Cross and the holy Gospel which he has insulted; for I am but a sinful man.' The senators went back and gave this message to the Emperor, whereupon in solemn procession he at once went to the

Church. The Archbishop met him with the holy Gospel in the sanctuary and was received by the Emperor with dissimulation; then after the customary prayer had been offered Basiliscus went in with the Archbishop to the holy man. And they both fell at his feet before all the people, both Basiliscus and the Archbishop Acacius. And Daniel greeted them and counseled them to seek the way of peace and for the future to refrain from enmity towards each other. 'For if you are at variance', he said, 'you cause confusion in the holy churches and throughout the world you stir up no ordinary unrest.' The Emperor then made a full apology to the holy man and the people cried out saying, 'Oh Lord, protect both father and sons; it is in Thy power to grant us concord between them; let us now hear the Emperor's confession of faith! why are the canons of orthodoxy upset? why are the orthodox bishops exiled? To the Stadium with Theoctistus, the Master of the Offices! the Emperor is orthodox! burn alive the enemies of orthodoxy! send the disturbers of the world into exile! a Christian Emperor for the world! let us hear what your faith is, Emperor!'

These and countless other exclamations the people kept shouting, and all the time the Emperor and the Archbishop lay prostrate on the ground at the holy man's feet.

Then the holy man summoned Strategius, the imperial secretary, and bade the Emperor make a proclamation to the people by way of justification, and this he did.

Having in this way appeased the holy man and the people, the Emperor was reconciled to them. And having been reconciled to the Archbishop in the sight of them all the Emperor returned to his palace. Thus did our Master God bring the enemy of His Holy Church to His feet.

When all minds were set at rest and the people were moving off to their own homes the servant of God returned to his usual practice of asceticism.

So great a grace of prophecy was granted to this holy man that three months before his falling asleep he foretold to us that within a few days he would quit the dwelling of his body and go to dwell with the Lord. And from that time on he did not converse with those that resorted to him about present-day matters only, but by foreknowledge he also announced future events to them, strengthening them with words of good counsel, and he gave injunctions to his usual attendants and to us how his precious body was to be brought down from the column.

And in every instance in which we obeyed him things turned out propitiously for us; but if perchance we did anything contrary to his command, or as we thought fit, being satisfied with our human planning, it was sure to turn out contrariwise for us; for he had been deemed worthy by God of the prophetic gift.

DANIEL'S LAST DAYS

Seven days before his falling asleep he summoned the whole brotherhood, from chiefest to least, and some he bade stand quite near him on the top of the ladder and listen to his words. When he knew they were assembled, he said, 'My brothers and children, behold, I am going to our Master and Lord, Jesus Christ....He will strengthen you and will guard you safe from evil and will keep your faith in Him firm and immovable if you continue in unity with each other and perfect love until you draw your last breath. May He give you grace to serve him blamelessly and to be one body and one spirit continuing in humanity and obedience. Do not neglect hospitality; never separate yourselves from your holy mother, the Church, turn away from all causes of offense and the tares of heretics, who are the enemies of Christ, in order that ye may become perfect even as also your heavenly Father is perfect. And now, I bid you Farewell, my beloved children, and I embrace you all with the love of a father; the Lord will be with you.' These words he ordered to be read aloud to the brethren by those who had stood nearest to him and caught the words, for he was lying down. When this had been done, and the brethren had heard the holy father's prayer and farewell they burst into such weeping and wailing that the noise of their lamentation sounded like unto a clap of thunder. Once again the holy man prayed over us and then dismissed us telling us not to be faint-hearted but bear up bravely, 'and make mention of me in your prayers!'

From that hour on, as if moved by some divine providence, the body of faithful people came up of their own accord. And they would not move from the holy man's enclosure until Euphemius, the most holy Archbishop of this imperial city, arrived. He mounted the column and looked, and then standing high up on the ladder, announced to all the people, 'The holy man is still alive and with us; do not be troubled; for it is impossible for his holy body to be consigned to the grave before news of his death has been published to everyone and all the holy churches everywhere have been informed.' And this was done.

But I must not forget to mention the greatest thing of all which was indeed worthy of wonder. Three days before his falling asleep in the middle of the night he was allowed to see at one time all those who had been well-pleasing to God. They came down and when they had greeted him they bade him celebrate the divine and august sacrament of the Eucharist, and two brethren standing by were allowed to be hearers of the words and to make the due responses. And directly he had completed the liturgy of God he woke up from his trance and coming to himself he asked for the holy communion to be administered to him; this was done and he partook of the Holy Mysteries just as if he had been administering to us the holy sacrament. Then, bidding farewell to the crowds who surrounded him, he bade the brethren present throw incense into the censer without ceasing.

When they took down the railing they found his knees drawn up to his chest, and his heels and legs to his thighs. And whilst his body was being forcibly straightened, his bones creaked so loudly that we thought his body would be shattered; yet when he was laid out, he was quite entire except that his feet had been worn away by inflammation and the gnawing of worms. The weight of the hair of his head was divided into twelve plaits, each of which was four cubits long; likewise his beard was divided into two and each plait was three cubits long. Most of the Christ-loving men saw this.

They clad him, as was his wont, in a leather tunic, and a plank was brought up and laid on the column and he was placed on it.

But the people demanded that the holy man should be shown to them before his burial, and in consequence an extraordinary tumult arose. For by the Archbishop's orders the plank was stood upright—the body had been fixed to it so that it could not fall—and thus, like an icon, the holy man was displayed to all on every side; and for many hours the people all looked at him and also with cries and tears besought him to be an advocate with God on behalf of them all. When this had been done, behold, all the people suddenly saw clearly with the naked eye three crosses in the sky above the corpse and white doves flying round it.

And Daniel was brought into the oratory and laid to rest underneath the holy martyrs as he had wished.

Now let us in a short summary review his whole life down to the end of his time on earth.

Our all-praiseworthy father Daniel bade adieu to his parents when he was twelve years old, then for twenty-five years he lived in a monastery; after that during five years he visited the fathers and from each learned what might serve his purpose, making his anthology from their teaching. At the time when the crown of his endurance began to be woven the Saint had completed his forty-second year, and at that age he came by divine guidance, as we have explained above, to this our imperial city. He dwelt in the church for nine years, standing on the capital of a column, thus training himself beforehand in the practice of that discipline which he was destined to bring to perfection. For he had learned from many divine revelations that his duty was to enter upon the way of life practiced by the blessed and sainted Simeon.

For three and thirty years and three months he stood for varying periods on the three columns, as he changed from one to another, so that the whole span of his life was a little more than eighty-four years.

During these he was deemed worthy to receive 'the prize of his high calling'; he blessed all men, he prayed on behalf of all, he counseled all not to be covetous, he instructed all in the things necessary to salvation, he showed hospitality to all, yet he possessed nothing on earth beyond the confines of the spot on which the enclosure and religious houses had been built. And though many, amongst whom were sovereigns and very distinguished officials occupying the highest posts, wished to present him with splendid possessions he never consented, but he listened to each one's offer and then prayed that he might be recompensed by God for his pious intention.

While we bear in mind our holy father's spiritual counsels, let us do our utmost to follow in his steps and to preserve the garment of our body unspotted and to keep the lamp of faith unquenched, carrying the oil of sympathy in our vessels that we may find mercy and grace in the day of judgment from the Father, the Son and the Holy Ghost now and henceforth and to all eternity, Amen.

✝

B. THE LIFE OF ST. JOHN THE ALMSGIVER

A man came one day bringing seven and a half pounds of gold and told the holy man that was all the gold he possessed; then he begged him with many a genuflection to pray to God to preserve his son (for he had an only boy about fifteen years old), and also to bring back his ship safely from Africa, to which country it had sailed.

The Patriarch took the money from his hand and marveled at the man's magnanimity in bringing him all the money he possessed, then on the man's behalf he offered up a lengthy prayer in his presence and so dismissed him. Yet because of the man's great faith he placed the bag containing the money under the holy table in the oratory of his own bed-chamber and at once celebrated the whole liturgy over it, earnestly importuning God on behalf of the giver to save the latter's son and to bring back the ship safely, as the man had begged him to do.

Before thirty days had passed the son of him who had brought the seven and a half pounds to the Patriarch died, and three days after the boy's death the ship arrived from Africa, on which the man's own brother sailed as 'Master', but near the Pharos it suffered ship-

wreck, all the cargo was lost and only the lives of the crew and the empty ship were saved.

When the ship-owner, the father of the boy, heard of this further catastrophe which had befallen him, then in the words of the Psalmist: 'His soul had almost dwelt in Hades.' For before his grief for his son had been assuaged he was further thrown into despair by the loss of the ship.

All these occurrences were reported to the Patriarch who grieved almost more than the sufferer himself, especially over the loss of the man's only son. And as he did not know what to do, he besought God in His mercy to comfort the man through His boundless pity; for he was ashamed to send for the man and comfort him face to face; yet he did send him a message not to let his spirits fail, reminding him that 'God does nothing without judgment, but all is to our profit though we know it not.' To show him that he would not lose the reward for the seven and a half pounds and for the trust which he had placed in the holy Patriarch—and further to teach us, too, to remain untroubled and thankful to God in any trials that may befall us after doing a good deed—this true lover of Christ saw in a vision the following night a man in the likeness of the most holy Patriarch saying to him: 'Why are you so distressed and despondent, brother? Did you not ask me to implore God to save your son? Well, he is saved! For had he lived he would have turned out a most pernicious and unclean fellow. Then as regards the ship, had not God been touched by your good deed and my unworthiness, since it had been determined that the vessel, souls and all, should go to the bottom, you would have lost your brother also. Rise and glorify God Who has granted you his life and has kept your son unspotted from this vain world.'

When the man awoke he felt his soul comforted and freed from all sorrow; so he put on his clothes and went in haste to the most venerable Patriarch and, throwing himself at his feet, gave thanks to God and to him and related the vision which he had seen. The just man heard his story and then said: 'Glory to Thee, oh merciful Lover of men, for listening to my prayer, sinner though I be.' And turning to the ship-owner he said, 'Do not by any means ascribe your blessings wholly to my prayers but rather to God and your own faith, for this it is which effected all.' For the Saint was exceedingly humble-minded both in words and thought.

†

C. *LETTER CXXVII: ON ROME*

St. Jerome

While these things were happening in Jerusalem, from the west a terrible rumor came to us, that Rome is besieged, that the safety of the citizens is redeemed by gold; despoiled and again surrounded, they lost their wealth and now are losing their lives. My voice cannot continue, sobs interrupt its words. Captured is the city that captured the world; it perished by famine before it died; and few were found to be captured. The rage of the hungry sought nefarious food: men tore one another's limbs; while the mother did not spare her infant at the breast—she ingested into herself what before she had pushed out. "By night was Moab captured, by night her walls fell." (Isaiah 15.1) "O God, the heathen have come into thy inheritance; they have defiled thy holy temple; they have laid Jerusalem in ruins. They have given the bodies of thy servants to the birds of the air for food, the flesh of thy saints to the beasts of the earth. They have poured out their blood like water round about Jerusalem, and there was none to bury them." (Psalm 79:1-3)

Who can describe the horror of that night,
who can shed enough tears for those deaths?
Ruined is that ancient city that for many years
ruled.
Bodies in the streets! countless images of death!
          (Virgil, Aeneid, ll. 361-65)

† "let gov. be your medium"

D. *THE CITY OF GOD*

St. Augustine

Rome had been invaded by the Goths under King Alaric and was staggered by the impact of this great disaster; and the worshippers of false gods, whom we customarily call pagans, working to turn this invasion into an accusation against the Christian religion, began to curse the true God more sharply and more bitterly than ever. Upon which I, burning with the zeal of the house of God, decided to confute their blasphemies and errors in these books on the city of God.

The first five books of *The City of God* rebut those who think that the safety of mankind depends on the cult of the gods whom the pagans worshipped, and who contend that these disasters happened, and were as bad as they were, because of the prohibition of that worship. The next five books answer those who, while saying that mortals never have and never will be spared evils—some greater, some lesser, varying with time and place and person—still argue that the cult of many gods, in which sacrifices are made to them, is useful because of the life to be after death. In these ten books, then, are refuted those two false notions that are contrary to the Christian religion.

Of the twelve books following, the first four contain the beginning of the two cities, of which the one is of God, the other of man; the second four, their course or progress; the third, which is the last four, their ends. And all twenty-two books, whether they are about one city or the other, took their title from the better of the two, with the result that they were called by preference *The City of God*.

I place humanity into two groups, one that lives following man, the other that lives according to God; and about which I might call two cities, that is, two societies, of which one is predestined to reign eternally with God and the other to undergo eternal punishment with the devil. But this is their end, which is to be spoken of later. Now I must detail the paths of the two cities from the time when two people first reproduced to the time when reproduction will come to an end. For the history of the two cities consists of the whole era or age in which the dying give way to the born.

Cain was born first among these two parents of mankind, a member of the city of men; Abel afterwards, of the city of God. It is known by experience that in every individual, as the Apostle has said, "it is not the spiritual which is first but the physical, and then the spiritual" (1 Corinthians 15.46)—and this is true in the whole of humanity as well. When the two cities began their history through birth and death, first was born was the citizen of this world, and after him the alien in this world who belongs to the city of God, predestined by grace, made elect by grace, a pilgrim below by grace, a citizen above by grace. So in himself a person first is reprobate, which by necessity is the beginning–but where we must not remain–and later becomes virtuous, to which we come as we progress and in which we may remain when we arrive. Consequently, not each bad person will be good, but no one will be good who was not first bad.

So it is written that Cain established a city, but Abel, being a foreigner, did not establish one. For in heaven is the city of the saints, although it produces its citizens here, in whom it waits until its kingdom shall come.(CD XV.i)

The earthly city has its good here, and its society delights in it with such delight as it can. But this kind of good is not the sort that causes no difficulties for those who admire it, so the earthly city is generally divided against itself by lawsuits; or by fights and battles; or by victories that are deadly or temporary. And when one part has risen up in war against the other, it seeks to be victorious over other peoples while itself a captive of vices. And it cannot dominate forever those it may overcome by conquest.

But it is not correct to say that the good things that this earthly city desires are not good, for it is made better, in a human fashion, by these. It desires an earthly peace for these lowest of things, a peace it hopes to come by through war; and if it wins and, no one may resist it, there will be peace. This is a peace that requires hard fighting, this is a peace that "glorious" war can win. But if, neglecting the better things that pertain to the supernatural city (where there will be eternal victory and secure perpetual peace), while other things are desired because they are either believed the only good things or are loved more than better ones, it follows by necessity that new misery will augment the old. (CD XV.iv)

Now the household of a person who doesn't live by faith seeks an earthly peace through the things of this earth; while a household of people who live by faith expects those blessings that are promised in eternity, and they use earthly and temporal things like a wanderer, not being captured by them, or diverted by them, from those things that tend towards God. On that account, the things necessary for mortal life are used by both types of people and households; but the purpose of using such differs with each. So the earthly city, which does not live by faith, desires only an earthly peace, securing civil obedience and authority so that there may be a consensus about things useful in this mortal life. But the heavenly city, or that bit of it that sojourns in this mortal life and lives by faith, needs to use such peace only until this weak necessity shall pass. And so, while in the earthly city it leads its life as if in captivity, it does not balk at complying with the laws of the earthly city in the administration of those things that sustain and accommodate this mortal life, since life is common to both.

While this heavenly city is traveling on earth, it finds citizens among all peoples and collects a pilgrim society of all tongues and in all tongues, not caring anything about differing customs, laws, institutions, not rescinding or destroying them, but serving and following them (because it allows diversity in different peoples) to the same earthly peace as they tend–as long as the religion which advises the following of the most true high God is not impeded. So the heavenly city uses the earthly peace for itself during its pilgrimage; it makes this earthly peace work for that peace of heaven which alone is truly peace, namely the most orderly and harmonious society in the enjoyment of God and of one another in God. And when we come there, there will be life, certainly, but not mortal life; no animal body corrupting the soul; but a spiritual one, one without wants and one subject in all parts to the will. While on earth the heavenly city has this peace through faith; and by this faith it lives justly, and makes the winning of this peace the goal of every good action in which it done for the sake of God and neighbors; for the life of every city is certainly a social life. (CD XIX.xvii)

†

2. THE EMPEROR AND THE CHURCH

For three centuries, Christianity had been an outcast religion. When it became the official religion of the state, Christians had to rethink their duties and allegiances. Christian Roman emperors continued to regard oversight of the state religion as one of their responsibilities. Christian bishops, on the other hand, asserted that the Church had an independent role. This conflict between Church and State became a fundamental issue in western history for more than a millennium; it is not fully resolved today.

The first two selections come from writers during the Age of Constantine. LACTANTIUS was a Christian rhetorician who became tutor to Constantine's sons. He wrote *On the Deaths of the Persecutors* around the year 315, in the aftermath of a great ten-year persecution. There is a thesis about Church and State in his work. What is it? To whom do you think he was he making the argument—Christians? Or pagans?

About twenty years after Lactantius wrote, EUSEBIUS OF CAESAREA (the author of the *History of the Church* that you encountered in the previous chapter, delivered an oration to celebrate the dedication of the Church of the Holy Sepulchre in Jerusalem in A.D. 335. Here, too, is a theory of Church and State. Does any of his argument sound familiar to you? What is new about it? What are the implications?

Only a few years after Eusebius, other Christians began to assert a different view of the emperor's role. Here are excerpts from protests to Roman emperors by two early Christian bishops. The first was written around A.D. 342 to the emperor Constantius II by BISHOP OSSIUS (or Hosius) OF CORDOBA (c. 250-c. 345), who had been an adviser to Constantius's father, Constantine the Great. The second was written 152 years later, in A.D. 494, by Gelasius I, bishop of Rome from 492-496, to the Emperor Anastasius I in Constantinople. Gelasius's letter has been called "one of the most important pronouncements in the history of political thought."[1] What is this theory of authority presented by Gelasius? What criteria does he give to support it? How does it compare with the relationship of Church and State asserted by Hosius? How is it different?

[1]N. Cantor, *The Medieval World: 300-1300* (New York, 1963), p. 95.

A. ON THE FATE OF PERSECUTORS

LACTANTIUS

The Lord has heard those supplications which you, my best beloved Donatus pour forth in His presence all the day long, and the supplications of the rest of our brethren, who by a glorious confession have obtained an everlasting crown, the reward of their faith. Behold, all the adversaries are destroyed, and tranquillity having been re-established throughout the Roman empire, the late oppressed Church arises again, and the temple of God, overthrown by the hands of the wicked, is built with more glory than before. For God has raised up princes to rescind the impious and sanguinary edicts of the tyrants and provide for the welfare of mankind; so that now the cloud of past times is dispelled, and peace and serenity gladden all hearts. And after the furious whirlwind and black tempest, the heavens are now become calm, and the wished-for light has shone forth; and now God, the hearer of prayer, by His divine aid has lifted His prostrate and afflicted servants from the ground, has brought to an end the united devices of the wicked, and wiped off the tears from the faces of those who mourned. They who insulted over the Divinity, lie low; they who cast down the holy temple, are fallen with more tremendous ruin; and the tormentors of just men have poured out their guilty souls amidst plagues inflicted by Heaven, and amidst deserved tortures. For God delayed to punish them, that, by great and marvelous examples, He might teach posterity that he alone is God, and that with fit vengeance He executes judgment on the proud, the impious, and the persecutors.

Of the end of those men I have thought good to publish a narrative, that all who are afar off, and all who shall arise hereafter, may learn how the Almighty manifested His power and sovereign greatness in rooting out and utterly destroying the enemies of His name. And this will become evident, when I relate who were the persecutors of the Church from the time of its first constitution, and what were the punishments by which the divine Judge, in His severity, took vengeance on them.

In the latter days of the Emperor Tiberius, in the consulship of Ruberius Geminus and Fufius Geminus, and on the tenth of the Kalends of April, as I find it written, Jesus Christ was crucified by the Jews. After He had risen again on the third day, He gathered together His apostles, whom fear, at the time of His being laid hold on, had put to flight; and while He sojourned with them forty days, He opened their hearts, interpreted to them the Scripture, which hitherto had been wrapped up in obscurity, ordained and fitted them for the preaching of His word and doctrine, and regulated all things concerning the institutions of the New Testament; and this having been accomplished, a cloud and whirlwind enveloped Him, and caught Him up from the sight of men unto heaven.

His apostles were at that time eleven in number, to whom were added Matthias, in the room of the traitor Judas, and afterwards Paul. Then were they dispersed throughout all the earth to preach the Gospel, as the Lord their Master had commanded them; and during twenty-five years, and until the beginning of the reign of the Emperor Nero, they occupied themselves in laying the foundations of the Church in every province and city. And while Nero reigned, the Apostle Peter came to Rome, and, through the power of God committed unto him, wrought certain miracles, and, by turning many to the true religion, built up a faithful and steadfast temple unto the Lord. When Nero heard of those things, and observed that not only in Rome, but in every other place, a great multitude revolted daily from the worship of idols, and, condemning their old ways, went over to the new religion, he, an execrable and pernicious tyrant, sprung forward to raze the heavenly temple and destroy the true faith. He it was who first persecuted the servants of God; he crucified Peter, and slew Paul: nor did he escape with impunity; for God looked on the affliction of His people; and therefore the tyrant, bereaved of authority, and precipitated from the height of empire, suddenly disappeared, and even the burial-place of that noxious wild beast was nowhere to be seen. This has led some persons of extravagant imagination to suppose that, having been conveyed to a distant region, he is

still reserved alive; and to him they apply the Sibylline verses concerning

"The fugitive, who slew his own mother, being to come from the uttermost boundaries of the earth;"

as if he who was the first should also be the last persecutor, and thus prove the forerunner of Antichrist! But we ought not to believe those who, affirming that the two prophets Enoch and Elias have been translated into some remote place that they might attend our Lord when He shall come to judgment, also fancy that Nero is to appear hereafter as the forerunner of the devil, when he shall come to lay waste the earth and overthrow mankind.

CHAPTER III

After an interval of some years from the death of Nero, there arose another tyrant no less wicked (Domitian), who, although his government was exceedingly odious, for a very long time oppressed his subjects, and reigned in security, until at length he stretched forth his impious hands against the Lord. Having been instigated by evil demons to persecute the righteous people, he was then delivered into the power of his enemies, and suffered due punishment. To be murdered in his own palace was not vengeance ample enough: the very memory of his name was erased. For although he had erected many admirable edifices, and rebuilt the Capitol, and left other distinguished marks of his magnificence, yet the senate did so persecute his name, as to leave no remains of his statues, or traces of the inscriptions put up in honor of him; and by most solemn and severe decrees it branded him, even after death, with perpetual infamy. Thus, the commands of the tyrant having been rescinded, the Church was not only restored to her former state, but she shone forth with additional splendor, and became more and more flourishing. And in the times that followed, while many well-deserving princes guided the helm of the Roman empire, the Church suffered no violent assaults from her enemies, and she extended her hands unto the east and unto the west, insomuch that now there was not any the most remote corner of the earth to which the divine religion had not penetrated, or any nation of manners so barbarous that did not, by being converted to the worship of God, become mild and gentle.

CHAPTER IV

This long peace, however, was afterwards interrupted. Decius appeared in the world, an accursed wild beast, to afflict the Church,–and who but a bad man would persecute religion? It seems as if he had been raised to sovereign eminence, at once to rage against God, and at once to fall; for, having undertaken an expedition against the Carpi, who had then possessed themselves of Dacia and Moesia, he was suddenly surrounded by barbarians, and slain, together with great part of his army; nor could he be honored with the rites of sepulture, but, stripped and naked, he lay to be devoured by wild beasts and birds,–a fit end for the enemy of God.

CHAPTER V

And presently Valerian also, in a mood alike frantic, lifted up his impious hands to assault God, and, although his time was short, shed much righteous blood. But God punished him in a new and extraordinary manner, that it might be a lesson to future ages that the adversaries of Heaven always receive the just recompense of their iniquities. He, having been made prisoner by the Persians, lost not only that power which he had exercised without moderation, but also the liberty of which he had deprived others; and he wasted the remainder of his days in the vilest condition of slavery: for Sapores, the king of the Persians, who had made him prisoner, whenever he chose to get into his carriage or to mount on horseback, commanded the Roman to stoop and present his back; then, setting his foot on the shoulders of Valerian, he said, with a smile of reproach, "This is true, and not what the Romans delineate on board or plaster." Valerian lived for a considerable time under the well-merited insults of his conqueror; so that the Roman name remained long the scoff and derision of the barbarians: and this also was added to the severity of his punishment, that although he had an emperor for his son, he found no one to revenge his captivity and most abject and servile state; neither indeed was he ever demanded back. Afterward, when he had finished this shameful life under so great dishonor, he was flayed, and his skin, stripped from the flesh, was dyed with vermilion, and placed in the temple of the gods of the barbarians, that the remembrance of a triumph so signal might be perpetuated, and that this spectacle might always be exhibited to our ambassadors, as an admonition to the Romans, that, beholding the spoils of their captive emperor in a Persian temple, they should not place too great confidence in their own strength. Now since God so punished the sacrilegious, is it not strange that any one should afterward have dared to do, or even to devise, aught against the majesty of the one God, who governs and supports all things?

✝

B. ON CHRIST'S SEPULCHRE

EUSEBIUS OF CAESAREA

(2) Now formerly all the peoples of the earth were divided, and the whole human race cut up into provinces and tribal and local governments, states ruled by despots or by mobs. Because of this, continuous battles and wars, with their attendant devastations and enslavements, gave them no respite in countryside or city. Hence the topics of countless histories–adultery and rape of the womenfolk–in particular the evils of Ilium and the tragedies of the ancients, so well remembered among all men. (3) If you should ascribe the reason for these evils to polytheistic error, you would not miss the mark. For once the salutary instrument–that is, specifically, the All-Holy Body of Christ– had been seen to be stronger than all demonic error and the adversary of evil-doing, whether by deed or word; once it had been raised as a victory trophy over the demons and a safeguard against ancient evils, then at once all the acts of the demons also were undone. No longer were there localized governments and states ruled by many, tyrannies and democracies, and the devastations and sieges that resulted from these, but One God was proclaimed to all. (4) At the same time, one empire also flowered everywhere, the Roman, and the eternally implacable and irreconcilable enmity of nations was completely resolved. And as the knowledge of One God was imparted to all men and one manner of piety, the salutary teaching of Christ, in the same way at one and the same time a single sovereign arose for the entire Roman Empire and a deep peace

took hold of the totality. Together, at the same critical moment, as if from a single divine will, two beneficial shoots were produced for mankind: the empire of the Romans and the teachings of true worship. (5) Before this, at least, independently, one dynasty ruled Syria, while another held sway over Asia Minor, and others yet over Macedonia. Still another dynasty cut off and possessed Egypt, and likewise others the Arab lands. Indeed, even the Jewish race ruled over Palestine. And in city and country and everyplace, just as if possessed by some truly demonic madness, they kept murdering each other and spent their time in wars and battles.

But two great powers–the Roman Empire, which became a monarchy at that time, and the teaching of Christ–proceeding as if from a single starting point, at once tamed and reconciled all to friendship. Thus each blossomed at the same time and place as the other. (6) For while the power of Our Savior destroyed the polyarchy and polytheism of the demons and heralded the one kingdom of God to Greeks and barbarians and all men to the farthest extent of the earth, the Roman Empire, now that the causes of the manifold governments had been abolished, subdued the visible governments, in order to merge the entire race into one unity and concord. Already it has united most of the various peoples, and it is further destined to obtain all those not yet united, right up to the very limits of the inhabited world. For with divine power the salutary instruction prepares the way for it and causes everything to be smooth. (7) This, if nothing else, must be a great miracle to those who direct their attention to the truth and do not wish to belittle these blessings. For at one and the same time that the error of the demons was refuted, the eternal enmity and warfare of the nations was resolved. Moreover, as One God and one knowledge of this God was heralded to all, one empire waxed strong among men, and the entire race of mankind was redirected into peace and friendship as all acknowledged each other brothers and discovered their related nature. All at once, as if sons of one father, the One God, and children of one mother, true religion, they greeted and received each other peaceably, so that from that time the whole inhabited world differed

in no way from a single well-ordered and related household. It became possible for anyone who pleased to make a journey and to leave home for wherever he might wish with all ease. Thus some from the West moved freely to the East, whole others went from here back there, as easily as if traveling to their native lands. Thus the predictions of the ancient oracles and utterances of the prophets were fulfilled–countless of them not time now to quote, but including those which said of the saving Logos that "He shall have dominion from sea to sea, and from the rivers unto the ends of the earth." And again, "In his days shall the righteous flourish and abundance of peace." "And they shall beat their swords into ploughshares, and their spears into pruning hooks: nation shall not lift up sword against nation, neither shall they learn war any more."

At this point, then, it is appropriate to consider the accomplishments of Our Savior in our day and to survey the living God. Or do not achievements such as these indicate living acts of one alive and living in very truth the life of God? What, precisely, you ask, are these? Now you will learn. (2) Only yesterday certain persecutors, infected with love of strife and too much power and force, began to raze the houses of His worship, tearing them up from the foundations and trying to eradicate His congregations. With every device they kept warring with the One who cannot be seen with the eyes, pricking and jabbing with their countless verbal darts. But the Invisible One defended Himself invisibly. (3) And it happened that these men, who shortly before had been luxurious and thrice-happy, who had been praised in song by all equal to the gods, who had governed the Empire with distinction for long periods of years when they maintained peace and friendship with the One whom they later opposed, by a single nod of His head ceased to exist. For as soon as they changed their minds and dared to make war on God, arraying their own divine defenders and champions against our God, than at once with a single turn of the scale and by the nod and power of the God they had attacked they all paid the penalty for their cruel and audacious acts. Forced to yield and bend their backs to their enemy, they acknowledged, consented to, and supported His divinity in complete reversal of their former temerity. (4) In contrast, He at once erected victory trophies everywhere on earth, adorning the entire inhabited world once again with holy temples and the solemn dedication of oratories. In cities and villages, in all regions and the barbarian wastes He dedicated temples and precincts to the One God the Ruler of All, surely the Master of the Universe. For which reasons the dedications are deemed worthy of the Master's title, since they came into their surname not from men but from the Lord of the Universe, and so they are deemed worthy of the title "Lord's houses," or "churches."

✝

C. LETTER TO CONSTANTIUS

OSSIUS, BISHOP OF CORDOBA

"I was a Confessor at first, when a persecution arose in the time of your grandfather Maximian; and if you shall persecute me, I am ready now, too, to endure anything rather than shed innocent blood and to betray the truth. But I cannot approve of your conduct in writing after this threatening matter. Cease to write thus; adopt not the cause of Arius, nor listen to those in the East, nor give credit to Ursacius, Valens, and their fellows…Cease these proceedings, I beseech you, and remember that you are a mortal man. Be afraid of the day of judgment, and keep yourself pure thereunto. Intrude not yourself into Ecclesiastical matters, neither give commands unto us concerning them; but learn them from us. God has put into your hands the kingdom; to us He has entrusted the affairs of His Church; and as he who would steal the empire from you would resist the ordinance of God, so likewise fear on your part lest by taking upon yourself the government of the Church, you become guilty of a great offense. It is written, 'Render unto Caesar the things that are Caesar's, and unto God the things that are God's.' Neither therefore is it permitted unto us to exercise an earthly rule, nor have you, Sire, any authority to burn incense. These things I write unto you out of a concern for your salvation…Cease then, I beseech you, O Constantius, and be persuaded by me. These things it becomes me to write, and you not to despise."

Such were the sentiments, and such the letter, of the Abraham-like old-man, Hosius, truly so called. But the Emperor desisted not from his designs, nor ceased to seek an occasion against him; but continued to threaten him severely, with a view either to bring him over by force, or to banish him if he refused to comply.

✝

D. LETTER TO ANASTASIUS

GELASIUS I

I beg Your Piety not to judge the use of divine reckoning as arrogance. Far be it, I pray, for a Roman emperor to deem the most profound truth injurious to his interests. Indeed, August Emperor, two forces rule this world—the sacred authority [*auctoritas*] of the bishops and the royal power [*potestas*]. Of these the heavier burden is that of the priests, inasmuch as they will render an account to the Lord even for kings themselves during divine judgment. Know, most clement son, that though you are preeminent among humankind by virtue of your honorable office, nevertheless you need bend your neck in devotion to those who are in charge of divine offices, and from whom you seek your own salvation.

Well you know that in matters pertaining to the heavenly sacraments it is fitting that you be subject to the dictates of religion, rather than dictate to it. So you know that you should not wish those on whose judgment you depend to submit to your will on these matters. For if the bishops themselves recognize that governance over matters regarding the proper arrangement of public discipline was conferred on you by the Divine Disposition, and obey your laws lest they seem to exercise a counter-jurisdiction over worldly affairs, then, I ask, with what willingness should you obey those who have been charged with administering the Divine mysteries?

In the same vein, just as no light burden lies on Popes to observe what is fitting for divine worship, so is there no small danger—may God forbid!—to those who show contempt when they ought to obey. If, as a rule, it is fitting for the hearts of the faithful to yield to all priests who properly perform their divine tasks, then is it not all the more fitting to respect the opinion of the bishop of that See which the Supreme God wished to take precedence over all priests, and which has ever since received the constant devotion of the entire Church?

✝

3. MUSLIM WISDOM

A. THE KORAN

Islam was yet another of the world's great religions born in the deserts of southwest Eurasia. Muhammad (571?-632 C.E.), the founder of Islam, preached the relatively simple message that devotees must submit to the will of Allah, the one and only Creator and merciful and benevolent god of Islam, and also recognize that Muhammad was a prophet of God. The Qu'ran—the "remembrances"—is the central text of the Moslem religious canon, records the Prophet's utterances as they were dictated to him by the angel Gabriel. This sacred book is literally revered as the word of God. The text is divided into 114 chapters of varying length and complexity; but regardless of the subject matter of a *sura*, or chapter, each one has essentially the same message: can you determine the nature of that message? The sequence in which the suras appear below mirrors that which scholars construe as the proper chronological order of Muhammad's revelations.

I.   NIGHT (SURA 92)

In the Name of Allah, the Compassionate, the Merciful.

By the night, when it covers all things with darkness; by the day, when it shines forth; by him who has created the male and the female: verily your endeavor is different. Know whosoever is obedient, and fears God, and professes the truth of that faith which is most excellent; unto him will we facilitate the way to happiness: but whosoever shall be covetous, and shall be wholly taken up with this world, and shall deny the truth of that which is most excellent; unto him will we facilitate the way to misery; and his riches shall not profit him, when he shall fall headlong into hell. Verily unto us appertains the direction of mankind: and ours is the life to come and the present life. Wherefore I threaten you with fire which burns fiercely, which none shall enter to be burned except the most wretched; who shall have disbelieved, and turned back. But he who

strictly bewares idolatry and rebellion, shall be removed far from the same; who gives his substance in alms, and by whom no benefit is bestowed on any, that it may be recompensed, but who bestows the same for the sake of his Lord, the most High: and hereafter he shall be well satisfied with is reward.

II. THE PROOF (SURA 98)

In the Name of Allah, the Compassionate, the Merciful.

The unbelievers among those to whom the scriptures were given, and among the idolaters, did not stagger, until the clear evidence had come unto them: an apostle from God, rehearsing unto them pure books or revelations; wherein are contained right discourses. Neither were they unto whom the scriptures were given divided among themselves, until after the clear evidence had come unto them. And they were commanded no other in the scriptures than to worship God, exhibiting unto him the pure religion, and being orthodox; and to be constant at prayer, and to give alms: and this is the right religion. Verily those who believe not, among those who have received the scriptures, and among the idolaters, shall be cast into the fire of hell, to remain therein for ever. These are the worst of creatures. But they who believe, and do good works; these are the best of creatures: their reward with their Lord shall be gardens of perpetual abode, through which rivers flow; they shall remain therein for ever. God will be well pleased in them; and they shall be well pleased in him. This is prepared for him who shall fear his Lord.

III. THE COW (SURA 2)

In the Name of Allah, the Compassionate, the Merciful.

This book is not to be doubted; it is a direction to the pious who believe in the mysteries of faith, who observe the appointed times of prayer, and distribute alms out of what we have bestowed on them; and who believe in that revelation, which has been sent down unto you and unto the prophets before you, and have firm assurance in the life to come: these are directed by their Lord, and they shall prosper. . . .

Surely those who believe, and those who Judaize, and the Christians, and Sabians, whoever believes in God, and the last day, and does that which is right, they shall have their reward with the Lord; there shall come no fear on them, neither shall they be grieved.

. . . And when Moses said unto his people, Verily God commands you to sacrifice a cow; they answered, Do you make jest of us? Moses said, God forbid that I should be one of the foolish. They said, Pray for us unto your Lord, that he would show us what cow it is. Moses answered, He says, She is neither an old cow nor a young heifer, but of a middle age between both: do you therefore that which you are commanded. They said, Pray for us unto your Lord, that he would show us what color she is. Moses answered, He says, She is a red cow, intensely red, her color rejoices the beholders. They said, Pray for us unto your Lord, that he would further show us what cow it is, for several cows with us are like one another, and we, if God please, will be directed. Moses answered, He says, She is a cow not broken to plough the earth, or water the field, a sound one with no blemish in her. They said, Now have you brought the truth. Then they sacrificed her; yet they wanted little of leaving it undone. . . .

We formerly delivered the book of the law unto Moses, and caused apostles to succeed him, and gave evident miracles to Jesus the son of Mary, and strengthened him with the holy spirit. Do you therefore, whenever an apostle comes unto you with that which your souls desire not, proudly reject him, and accuse some of imposture, and slay others? The Jews say, Our hearts are uncircumcised: but God has cursed them with their infidelity, therefore few shall believe. And when a book came unto them from God, confirming the scriptures which were with them, although they had before prayed for assistance against those who believed not, yet when that came unto them which they knew to be from God, they would not believe therein: therefore the curse of God shall be on the infidels. For a vile price have they sold their souls, that they should not be-

lieve in that which God sends down his favors to such of his servants as he pleases: therefore they brought on themselves indignation on indignation; and the unbelievers shall suffer an ignominious punishment. . . .

It is not the desire of the unbelievers, either among those unto whom the scriptures have been given, or among the idolaters, that any good should be sent down unto you from your Lord: but God will appropriate his mercy unto whom he pleases; for God is exceeding beneficent. Whatever verse we shall abrogate, or cause you to forget, we will bring a better than it, or one like unto it. Do you not know that God is almighty? Do you not know that unto God belongs the kingdom of heaven and earth? Neither have you any protector or helper except God. . . .

Who will be adverse to the religion of Abraham, but he whose mind is infatuated? Surely we have chosen him in this world, and in that which is to come he shall be one of the righteous. When his Lord said unto him, Resign yourself unto me; he answered, I have resigned myself unto the Lord of all creatures. And Abraham bequeathed this religion to his children, and Jacob did the same, saying, My children, verily God has chosen this religion for you, therefore die not, unless you also be resigned. . . .

They say, become Jews or Christians that you may be directed. Say, No, we follow the religion of Abraham the orthodox, who was no idolater. Say, we believe in God, and that which has been sent down unto us, and that which has been sent down unto Abraham, and Ismael, and Isaac, and Jacob, and the tribes, and that which was delivered unto Moses, and Jesus, and that which was delivered unto the prophets from their Lord: We make no distinction between any of them, and to God we are resigned. . . .

As we have sent unto you an apostle from among you, to rehearse our signs unto you, and to purify you, and to teach you the book of the *Koran* and wisdom, and to teach you the that which you knew not: therefore remember me, and I will remember you, and give thanks unto me, and be not believers. O true believers, beg assistance with patience and prayer,

for God is with the patient. And say not of those who are slain in fight for the religion of God, that they are dead; yea, they are living. . .
.

It is not righteousness that you turn your faces in prayer towards the east and the west, but righteousness is of him who believes in God and the last day, and the angels and the scriptures, and the prophets; who gives money for God's sake unto his kindred, and unto orphans and the needy and the stranger, and to those who ask and for redemption of captives; who is constant at prayer, and gives alms; and of those who perform their covenant, when they have covenanted, and who behaved themselves patiently in adversity and hardships and in time of violence: these are they who are true, and these are they who fear God. . . .

O true believers, a fast is ordained you, as it was ordained unto those before you, that you may fear God. A certain number of days shall you fast: but he among you who shall be sick, or on a journey, shall fast an equal number of other days. And those who can keep it, and do not, must redeem their neglect by maintaining of a poor man. And he who voluntarily deals better with the poor man than is obligated, this shall be better for him. But if you fast it will be better for you, if you knew it. The month of Ramadan shall you fast, in which the *Koran* was sent down from heaven, a direction unto men, and declarations of direction, and the distinction between good and evil. Therefore let those among you who shall be present in this month, fast the same month,
. . .

And fight for the religion of God against those who fight against you, but transgress not by attacking them first, for God loves not the transgressor. And kill them wherever you find them, and turn them out of that whereof they have dispossessed you; for temptation to idolatry is more grievous than slaughter: yet fight not against them in the holy temple, until they attack you therein; but if they attack you, slay them there. This shall be the reward of the infidels. But if they desist, God is gracious and merciful. Fight therefore against them, until there be no temptation to idolatry, and the religion be God's: but if they desist, then let

there be no hostility, except against the ungodly. . . .

Contribute out of your substance towards the defense of the religion of God, and throw not yourselves with your own hands into perdition; and do good, for God loves those who do good. Perform the pilgrimage of Mecca, and the visitation of God; and if you be besieged, send that offering which shall be the easiest; and shave not your heads, until your offering reaches the place of sacrifice. But whoever among you is sick, or is troubled with any distemper of the head, must redeem the shaving of his head by fasting, or alms, or some offering. . . .

Carefully observe the appointed prayers, and the middle prayer, and be assiduous of therein, with devotion towards God. But if you fear any danger, pray on foot or on horseback; and when you are safe, remember God, how he has taught you what as yet you knew not. . . .

God! there is no God but he; the living, the self-subsisting: neither slumber nor sleep seizes him; to him belongs whatsoever is in heaven, and on earth. Who is he that can intercede with him, but through his good pleasure? He knows that which is past, and that which is to come unto them, and they shall not comprehend anything of his knowledge, but so far as he pleases. His *Corsi* (throne) is extended over heaven and earth, and the preservation of both is no burden unto him. He is the high, the mighty.

Let there be no violence in religion. Now is right direction manifestly distinguished from deceit: whoever therefore shall deny *Tagut* [idols], and believe in God, he shall surely take hold on a strong handle, which shall not be broken; God is he who hears and sees. God is the patron of those who believe; he shall lead them out of darkness into light; but as to those who believe not, their patrons are Tagut; they shall lead them from the light into darkness; they shall be the companions of hell fire, and they shall thus remain therein forever. . . .

Whatever is in heaven and on earth is God's; and whether you manifest that which is in your minds, or conceal it, God will call you to account for it, and will forgive whom he pleases, and will punish whom he pleases; for

God is almighty. The apostle believes in that which has been sent down unto him from his Lord, and the faithful also. Every one of them believes in God, and his angels, and his scriptures, and his apostles: we make no distinction at all between his apostles. And they say, we have heard, and do obey: we implore your mercy, O Lord, for unto you we must return. God will not force any soul beyond its capacity: it shall have the good which it gains, and it shall suffer the evil which it gains. O Lord, punish us not, if we forget, or act sinfully: O Lord, lay not on us a burden like that which you have laid on those who have been before us; neither make us, O Lord, to bear what we have not strength to bear, but be favorable unto us, and spare us, and be merciful unto us. You are our patron, help us therefore against the unbelieving nations.

IV. WOMEN (SURA 4)

In the Name of Allah, the Compassionate, the Merciful.

O men, fear your Lord, who has created you out of one man, and out of him created his wife, and from the two has multiplied many men and women: and fear God by whom you beseech one another; and respect women, who have borne you, for God is watching over you. And give the orphans when they come to age their substance; and render them not in exchange bad for good: and devour not their substance, by adding it to your substance; for this is a great sin. And if you fear that you shall not act with equity towards orphans of the female sex, take in marriage of such other women as please you, two, or three, or four, and not more. But if you fear that you cannot act equitably towards so many, marry one only, or the slaves that you shall have acquired. This will be easier, that you swerve not from righteousness. And give women their dowry freely; but if they voluntarily remit unto you any part of it, enjoy it with satisfaction and advantage. . . .

If any of your women be guilty of whoredom, produce four witnesses from among you against them, and if they bear witness against

them, imprison them in separate apartments until death release them, or God affords them a way to escape. . . .

O true believers, it is not lawful for you to be heirs of women against their will, nor to hinder them from marrying others, that you may take away part of what you have given them in dowry; unless they have been guilty of a manifest crime: but converse kindly with them. And if you hate them, it may happen that you may hate a thing wherein God has placed much good. . . . You are also forbidden to take to wife free women who are married, except those women whom your right hands shall possess as slaves. This is ordained you from God. Whatever is beside this, is allowed you; that you may with your substance provide wives for yourselves, acting that which is right, and avoiding whoredom. And for the advantage which you receive from them, give them their reward, according to what is ordained: but it shall be no crime in you to make any other agreement among yourselves, after the ordinance shall be complied with; for God is knowing and wise. . . .

Men shall have the preeminence above women, because of those advantages wherein God has caused the one of them to excel the other, and for that which they expend of their substance in maintaining their wives. The honest women are obedient, careful in the absence of their husbands, for that God preserves them, by committing them to the care and protection of the men. But those, whose perverseness you shall be apprehensive of, rebuke; and remove them into separate apartments, and chastise them. But if they shall be obedient unto you, seek not an occasion of quarrel against them; for God is high and great. . . . Who is better in point of religion than he who resigns himself unto God, and is a worker of righteousness, and follows the law of Abraham the orthodox? since God took Abraham for his friend: and to God belongs whatsoever is in heaven and on earth; God comprehends all things. They will consult you concerning women; Answer, God instructs you concerning them, and that which is read unto you in the book if the Koran concerning female orphans, to whom you give not that which is ordained them, neither will you marry them, and concerning weak infants, and that you observe justice towards orphans: whatever good you do, God knows it. If a woman fear ill usage, or aversion, from her husband, it shall be no crime in them if they agree the matter amicably between themselves; for a reconciliation is better than a separation. Men's souls are naturally inclined to covetousness: but if you be kind towards women, and fear to wrong them, God is well acquainted with what you do. You can by no means carry yourselves equally between women in all respects, although you study to do it; therefore turn not from a wife with all manner of aversion, nor leave her like one in suspense: if you agree, and fear to abuse your wives, God is gracious and merciful; but if they separate, God will satisfy them both of his abundance; for God is extensive and wise, and unto God belongs whatsoever is in heaven and on earth. . . .

God is witness of that revelation which he has sent down unto you; he sent it down with is special knowledge; the angels were also witnesses thereof; but God is a sufficient witness. They who believe not, and turn aside others from the way of God, have erred in a wide mistake. Verily those who believe not, and act unjustly, God will by no means forgive, neither will he direct them into any other way than the way of hell; they shall remain therein forever: and this is easy with God. O men, now is the apostle come unto you, with truth from your Lord; believe therefore, it will be better for you. But if you disbelieve, verily unto God belongs whatsoever is in heaven and on earth; and God is knowing and wise. O you who have received the scriptures, exceed not the just bounds in your religion, neither say of God any other than the truth. Verily Christ Jesus the son of Mary is the apostle of God, and his Word, which he conveyed into Mary, and a spirit proceeding from him. Believe therefore in God, and his apostles, and say not, There are three Gods; forbear this; it will be better for you. God is but one God. Far be it from him that he should have a son! Unto him belongs whatsoever is in heaven and on earth; and God is a sufficient protector. Christ does not proudly disdain to be a servant unto God; neither the angels who approach near to his presence; and whoso disdains his service, and is puffed up with pride, God will gather them all to himself, on the last day. Unto those who believe, and do that which is right, he shall give their rewards, and shall superabundantly add unto them of his liberality: but those who are disdainful and proud, he will punish with a grievous punishment; and they shall not find any to protect or to help them, besides God.

✝

B. THE CALL OF ISLAM

Abu Hamid al-Ghazali

At the age of 37, Abu Hamid Muhammad AL-GHAZALI (A.D. 1058-1111, A.H. 450-505) resigned from the prestigious position of professor at the University of Baghdad and took up the life of a wandering ascetic. Later, he wrote *Deliverance from Error*, a sort of spiritual autobiography, and *The Beginning of Guidance*, a handbook for practicing the ideal Muslim life.

INTRODUCTION

You must know—and may God most high perfect you in the right way and soften your hearts to receive the truth—that the different religious observances and religious communities of the human race and likewise the different theological systems of the religious leaders, with the multiplicity of sects and variety of practices, constitute ocean depths in which the majority drown and only a minority reach safety. Each separate group thinks that it alone is saved, and "each party is rejoicing in what they have" (Q. 32,55; 30,31). This is what was foretold by the prince of the Messengers[1] (God bless him), who is true and trustworthy, when he said, "My community will be split up into seventy-three sects, and but one of them is saved"; and what he founded has indeed almost come about.

From my early youth, since I attained the age of puberty before I was twenty, until the present time when I am over fifty, I have ever recklessly launched out into the midst of these

---

[1] I.e., Muhammad.

ocean depths, I have ever bravely embarked on this open sea, throwing aside all craven caution; I have poked into every dark recess, I have made an assault on every problem, I have plunged into every abyss, I have scrutinized the creed of every sect, I have tried to lay bare the inmost doctrines of every community. All this I have done that I might distinguish between true and false, between sound tradition and heretical innovation. Whenever I have met one of the Batiniyah,[1] I like to study his creed; whenever I meet one of the Zahiriyah, I want to know the essentials of his belief. If it is a philosopher, I try to become acquainted with the essence of his philosophy; if a scholastic theologian I busy myself in examining his theological reasoning; if a Sufi,[2] I yearn to fathom the secret of his mysticism; if an ascetic (muta'abbid), I investigate the basis of his ascetic practices; if one of the Zanadiqah or Mu'attilah, I look beneath the surface to discover the reasons for his bold adoption of such a creed.

To thirst after a comprehension of things as they really are was my habit and custom from a very early age. It was instinctive with me, a part of my God-given nature, a matter of temperament and not of my choice or contriving. Consequently as I drew near the age of adolescence the bonds of mere authority (taqulid) ceased to hold me and inherited beliefs lost their grip upon me, for I saw that Christian youths always grew up to be Christians, Jewish youth to be Jews and Muslim youths to be Muslims. I heard, too, the Tradition related of the Prophet of God according to which he said: "Everyone who is born is born with a sound nature; it is his parents who make him a Jew or a Christian or a Magian." My inmost being was moved to discover what his original nature really was and what the beliefs derived from the authority of parents and teachers really were. The attempt to distinguish between these authority-based opinions and their principles developed the mind, for in distinguishing the true in them from the false differences appeared.

---

[1] Muslim theologians who held that the sayings of the Imam, or priest, were infallible. The official ideology of the Fatimid caliphate whose capital was Cairo.
[2] A Muslim mystic.

I therefore said within myself: "To begin with, what I am looking for is knowledge of what things really are, so I must undoubtedly try to find what knowledge really is." It was plain to me that sure and certain knowledge is that knowledge in which the object is disclosed in such a fashion that no doubt remains along with it, that no possibility of error or illusion accompanies it, and that the mind cannot even entertain such a supposition. Certain knowledge must also be infallible; and this infallibility or security from error is such that no attempt to show the falsity of the knowledge can occasion doubt or denial, even though the attempt is made by someone who turns stones into gold or a rod into a serpent. Thus, I know that ten is more than three. Let us suppose that someone says to me: "No, three is more than ten, and in proof of that I shall change this rod into a serpent"; and let us suppose that he actually changes the rod into a serpent and that I witness him doing so. No doubts about what I know are raised in me because of this. The only result is that I wonder precisely how he is able to produce this change. Of doubt about my knowledge there is no trace.

After these reflections I knew that whatever I do not know in this fashion and with this mode of certainty is not reliable and infallible knowledge; and knowledge that is not infallible is not certain knowledge.

BEGINNING OF GUIDANCE

With eager desire you are setting out to acquire knowledge, my friend; for yourself you are making clear how genuine is your longing and how passionate your thirst for it. Be sure that, if in your quest for knowledge your aim is to gain something for yourself and to surpass your fellows, to attract men's attention to yourself and to amass this-worldly vanities, then you are on the way to bring your religion to nothing and destroy yourself, to sell your eternal life for this present one; your bargain is dead loss, your trading without profit. Your teacher abets you in your disobedience and is partner in your loss. He is like one who sells a sword to a highwayman, for in the words of the Prophet (God bless and preserve him), "whoever aids and abets a sin, even by half a word, is partner with the sinner in it."

On the other hand, if in seeking knowledge your intention and purpose between God most high and yourself is to receive guidance and not merely to acquire information, then rejoice. The angels will spread out their wings for you when you walk, and the denizens of the sea will ask pardon from God for you when you run. Above all, however, you must realize that the guidance which is the fruit of knowledge has a beginning and an ending; no one can discover the inward aspect until he has mastered the outward.

Here, then, I give you counsel about the Beginning of Guidance, so that thereby you may test yourself and examine your heart. If you find your heart drawn towards it and your soul docile and receptive, go ahead, make for the end, launch out into the oceans of knowledge. If, on the other hand, you find that when you turn to the matter seriously, your heart tends to procrastinate and to put off actually doing anything about it, then you may be sure that the part of your soul which is drawn to seek knowledge is the evil-inclined irrational soul. It has been aroused in obedience to Satan, the accursed, in order that he may lower you into the well by the rope of his deception, and by his wiles lure you to the abyss of destruction. His aim is to press his evil wares upon you in the place where good wares are sold, so that he may unite you with those "who most lose their works, whose effort goes astray in this present life though they think they are doing well" (Q. 18, 103f.).

Moreover Satan, to impress you, rehearses the excellence of knowledge, the high rank of scholars and the Traditions about knowledge from the Prophet and others. He thus diverts your attention from sayings of the Prophet (God bless and preserve him) such as the following: "Whoever increases in knowledge and does not increase in guidance, only increases in distance from God"; "the most severe punishment on the day of Resurrection is that of the scholar to whom God gave no benefit from his knowledge"; "O God, I take refuge with Thee from knowledge which does not benefit, from the heart which does not humble itself, from the act which is not lifted up to God, and from the prayer which is not heard"; "during my night-journey I passed some groups of people whose lips were cut by fiery scissors,

and I said to them, Who are you? and they replied, We used to command others to do good and yet ourselves did not do it, and to prohibit others from doing evil and yet ourselves did it."

Beware then, unfortunate man, of listening to his fair words, lest he lower you into the well by the rope of his deception. Woe to the ignorant man, when he has not learned even once, and woe to the learned man when he has not put into practice what he learned a thousand times!

People who seek knowledge are of three types. There is the man who seeks knowledge to take it as his traveling-provision for the life to come; he seeks thereby only the Countenance of God and the mansion of eternity; such a man is saved. Then there is the man who seeks it for the help it gives in his transitory life in obtaining power, influence and wealth, and at the same time is aware of that ultimate truth and in his heart has some perception of the worthlessness of his condition and the vileness of his aim. Such a man is in jeopardy, for if his appointed term comes upon him suddenly before he repents, a bad end of life is to be feared for him and his fate will depend upon the will (of God); yet, if he is given grace to repent before the arrival of the appointed term, and adds practice to theory, and makes up for the matters he has neglected, he will join the ranks of the saved, for "the man who repents of sin is like the man who has none".

A third man has been overcome by Satan. He has taken his knowledge as a means to increase his wealth, the boast of his influence and to pride himself on his numerous following. By his knowledge he explores every avenue which offers a prospect of realizing what he hopes for from this world. Moreover he believes in himself that he has an important place in God's eyes because with his garb and jargon he bears the brand and stamp of the scholar despite his mad desire of this world both openly and in secret. Such men will perish, being stupid and easily deceived, for there is no hope of their repentance since they fancy that they are acting well. They are unmindful of the words of God most high, "O ye who have believed, why do ye say what ye do not do?" (Q.61,2). To them may be applied the saying of the Messenger of God (God bless and preserve him), "I fear on your account one who is not the Dajjal (or Antichrist) more than I fear the Dajjal", and when someone said to him, "Who is that?" he replied, "An evil scholar."

The point of this is that the aim of the Dajjal is to lead men astray. The scholar is similar. If he turns men from this world by what he says, yet he calls them to it by what he is and what he does. A man's conduct speaks more eloquently than his words. Human nature is more inclined to share in what is done than to follow what is said. The corruption caused by the acts of this misguided man is greater than the improvement effected by his words, for the ignorant man does not venture to set his desire on this world till the scholars have done so. Thus the man's knowledge has become a cause of God's servants venturing to disobey Him. Despite that his ignorant soul remains confident; it fills him with desire and hope, and urges him to expect a reward from God for his knowledge. It suggests to him that he is better than many of God's servants.

Be of the first group, then, O seeker of knowledge. Avoid being of the second group, for many a procrastinator is suddenly overtaken by his appointed term before repenting, and is lost. But beware, above all, beware of being in the third group and perishing utterly without any hope or expectation of salvation.

IN THE MOSQUE

When the imam commences the obligatory Worship, do nothing but follow him in it, as will be explained to you in (the chapter on) the Manner and Conduct of Worship. When you have finished say, "O God, bless and preserve Muhammad and the house of Muhammad. O God, Thou art peace, and from Thee is peace, and to Thee peace returns. Greet us with peace, O Lord, and bring us into Thy house, the house of peace. Blessed art thou, O Lord of majesty and honor. Praise to my Lord, the high, the most high; there is no god save God alone; He has no partner; His is the kingdom and His is the praise; He makes alive and causes to die, yet He is ever living never dying. From His hand comes all our good, and He has power over all things. There is no God

save God, the beneficent, the excellent, the praiseworthy. There is no God, save God, and Him alone do we worship, serving Him in sincerity, though the infidels refuse."

Then, after that, repeat the general comprehensive prayer which the Messenger of God (God bless and preserve him) taught to 'A'ishah (may God be pleased with her), saying: "O God, I beseech Thee to grant me all good things, both earlier and later, both those I know and those I do not know; I take refuge with Thee from all evil, both earlier and later, both what I know and what I do not know; I ask Thee to grant me Paradise and every word and deed, every intention and belief, that brings me near it; I take refuge with Thee from Hell, and from every word and deed, every intention and belief, that brings me near it. I ask Thee to grant me the good for which Thy servant and messenger, Muhammad (God bless and preserve him) asked Thee; and I take refuge with Thee from the evil from which Thy servant and messenger, Muhammad (God bless and preserve him) took refuge with Thee. O God, whatever Thou hast ordained for me, may its outcome be for my true weal."

Then repeat the words the Messenger of God (God bless and preserve him) prescribed to Fatimah (may God be pleased with her), saying; "O Living and Steadfast One, Lord of majesty and honor, there is no god save Thee; of Thy mercy succor me, from Thy punishment protect me, leave me not to my own care one moment; make all my life upright, as Thou didst for the righteous ones."

Then repeat the words of Jesus (God bless and preserve both our prophet and him): "O God, I here this morning am unable to repel what I loathe and to gain what I hope for; by Thy hand has this morning come, not by the hand of any other; I this morning am obliged to do my work, and no needy man is in greater need than I am of Thee, while no rich man is less in need than Thou art of me. O God, let not my enemy rejoice over me, and let not my friend think evil of me; May I not come into misfortune in my religion. May this world not be the greatest of my cares nor the sum of my knowledge. Let not him who has no mercy for me prevail over me by my sin."

Then repeat any of the well-known prayers you think fit; for this purpose learn some of those we have given in the book on "Prayers" of *The Revival of the Religious Sciences* (sc. the ninth book of the first "quarter")...our conception of useful knowledge is what we have already expounded in *The Revival of the Religious Sciences*. If you accept this conception, study it and practice it, then teach it and preach it. When a man knows these things and practices them, that man shall be called great in the kingdom of heaven, according to the witness of Jesus (peace be upon him.)

THE WORSHIP

...Make your heart attentive, emptying it of all evil suggestions. Consider in front of Whom you stand and speak, and shrink from addressing your Patron with negligent heart and breast laden with worldly suggestions and evil passions. God most high is aware of your inmost thoughts and sees your heart. God accepts your worship only according to the measure of your humility, submissiveness, modesty, and lowliness. Serve Him in your Worship as if you see Him, for, even if you do not see Him, yet He sees you....

The pillars of the Worship are humility and recollectedness of heart, together with the recital of the Qur'an with understanding and the making of acts of adoration with understanding. Al-Hasan al-Basri (God most high have mercy on him) said, "Every Worship at which the heart is not present is more likely to bring punishment that reward." Muhammad (God bless and preserve him) said "A man may perform the Worship so that he is given credit only for that amount of his Worship which he understands."

THE AVOIDANCE OF SINS

Religion consists of two parts, the leaving undone of what is forbidden and the performance of duties. Of these the setting aside of what is forbidden is the weightier, for the duties or acts of disobedience (as described in Part I) are within the power of everyone, but only the upright are able to set aside the appetites. For that reason Muhammad (may God bless and preserve him) said: "The true Flight or Hijrah is the flight from evil, and the real Holy War or Jihad is the warfare against one's passions."

You disobey or sin against God only through the parts of your body. Yet these are a gift to you from God and a trust committed to you. To employ God's gift in order to sin against Him is the height of ingratitude; to betray the trust which God committed to you is the height of presumption. The parts of your body are your subjects; see to it, then, how you rule over them. "Each of you is a ruler, and each of you is responsible for those he rules over."

All the parts of your body will bear witness against you in the courts of the resurrection, with voluble and sharp, that is, eloquent, tongue, declaring your faults before the chiefs of the creatures. God most high says (Q. 24,24): "On a day when their tongues and hands and feet will bear witness against them for what they have been doing"; and also (Q. 36,65):"Today We shall set a seal upon their mouths, and their hands will speak to Us, and their feet will testify what they have been piling up." Then guard all your body, and especially the seven parts, for Hell has seven gates, to each of which is allotted a portion of the people of Hell. To these gates are appointed only those who have sinned against God with these seven parts of the body, namely, the eye, the ear, the tongue, the stomach, the genitals, the hand, the foot.

✝

X. Change and Continuity

The "Fall of Rome" is a traditional, but complicated, subject. Unfortunately, one of the complications is our stereotyped picture of decadent Romans destroyed on a given day or year by waves of savage, barbarian invaders. Beneath this facile image lies a centuries-long process that transformed the ancient world and created, in western Europe, a new synthesis. The readings in this chapter indicate some of the ways in which Rome continued to influence history even after its "fall." The Roman historian TACITUS (c. A.D.55-110) gives an early glimpse into Germanic society. SUETONIUS (A.D.69?-140?) and EINHARD (A.D. 775?-838?) offer portraits of two emperors separated by 800 years. The THEODOSIAN CODE and the LOMBARD LAWS show both a late Roman and a post-Roman society at work. The CAPITULARY OF MEERSEN illustrates one element of medieval society. Finally, THE SONG OF ROLAND shows a new hero, the synthesis of the Roman, Christian, and Germanic elements that make the Middle Ages. After reading these documents, can you say what it was that fell, or when it happened?

❖   ❖   ❖

1. ON GERMANY

TACITUS

Rome was threatened by invaders throughout its history, but from about 100 B.C. to A.D. 250 most of the barbarians, as the Romans called them, lived safely outside the frontiers. Because the Germans were pre-literate and left none of their own records, much of what we know about early Germanic society (before they made extensive inroads into the empire) comes from the pen of the brilliant Roman historian Tacitus (A.D. 55?-117?). Why did Tacitus write this? What are the main differences between Roman and Germanic civilization? If you were a Roman reading this account in A.D.100, would you have guessed that these Germans were destined to overthrow your empire? Did Tacitus?

4. For my own part, I agree with those who think that the tribes of Germany are free from all taint of inter-marriages with foreign nations, and that they appear as a distinct, unmixed race, like none but themselves. Hence, too, the same physical peculiarities throughout so vast a population. All have fierce blue eyes, red hair, huge frames, fit only for a sudden exertion. They are less able to bear laborious work. Heat and thirst they cannot in the least endure; to cold and hunger their climate and their soil inure them.

5. Their country, though somewhat various in appearance, yet generally either bristles with forests or reeks with swamps; it is more rainy on the side of Gaul, bleaker on that of Noricum and Pannonia. It is productive of grain, but unfavorable to fruit-bearing trees; it is rich in flocks and herds, but these are for the most part undersized, and even the cattle have not their usual beauty or noble head. It is number that is chiefly valued; they are in fact the most highly prized, indeed the only riches of the people. Silver and gold the gods have refused to them, whether in kindness or in anger I cannot say. I would not, however, affirm that no vein of German soil produces gold or silver, for who has ever made a search? They care but little to possess or use them. You may see among them vessels of silver, which have been presented to their envoys and chieftains, held as cheap as those of clay. The border population, however, value gold and silver for their commercial utility, and are familiar with, and show preference for, some of our coins. The tribes of the interior use the simpler and more ancient practice of the barter of commodities. They like the old and well-known money, coins milled, or showing a two-horse chariot. They likewise prefer silver to gold, not from any special liking, but because a large number of silver pieces is more convenient for use among dealers in cheap and common articles.

6. Even iron is not plentiful with them, as we infer from the character of their weapons. But few use swords or long lances. They carry a spear (*framea* is their name for it), with a narrow and short head, but so sharp and easy to wield that the same weapon serves, according to circumstances, for close or distant conflict. As for the horse-soldier, he is satisfied with a shield and spear; the foot-soldiers also scatter showers of missiles, each man having several and hurling them to an immense distance, and being naked or lightly clad with a little cloak. There is no display about their equipment: their shields alone are marked with very choice colors. A few only have corslets, and just one or two here and there a metal or leathern helmet. Their horses are remarkable neither for beauty nor for fleetness. Nor are they taught various evolutions after our fashion, but are driven straight forward, or so as to make one wheel to the right in such a compact body that none is left behind another. On the whole, one would say that their chief strength is in their infantry, which fights along with the cavalry; admirably adapted to the action of the latter is the swiftness of certain foot-soldiers, who are picked from the entire youth of their country, and stationed in front of the line. Their number is fixed—a hundred from each canton; and from this they take their name among their countrymen, so that what was originally a mere number has now become a title of distinction. Their line of battle is drawn up in a wedge-like formation. To give ground, provided you return to the attack, is considered prudence rather than cowardice. The bodies of their slain they carry off even in indecisive engagements. To abandon your shield is the basest of crimes; nor may a man thus disgraced be present at the sacred rites, or enter their council; many, indeed, after escaping from battle, have ended their infamy with the halter.

GERMANIC TRADITION

7. They choose their kings by birth, their generals for merit. These kings have not unlimited or arbitrary power, and the generals do more by example than by authority. If they are energetic, if they are conspicuous, if they fight in the front, they lead because they are admired. But to reprimand, to imprison, even to flog, is permitted to the priests alone, and that not as a punishment, or at the general's bid-

ding, but, as it were, by the mandate of the god whom they believe to inspire the warrior. They also carry with them into battle certain figures and images taken from their sacred groves. And what most stimulates their courage is, that their squadrons or battalions, instead of being formed by chance or by a fortuitous gathering, are composed of families and clans. Close by them, too, are those dearest to them, so that they hear the shrieks of women, the cries of infants. *They* are to every man the most sacred witnesses of his bravery—*they* are his most generous applauders. The soldier brings his wounds to mother and wife, who shrink not from counting or even demanding them and who administer both food and encouragement to the combatants.

8. Tradition says that armies already wavering and giving way have been rallied by women who, with earnest entreaties and bosoms laid bare, have vividly represented the horrors of captivity, which the Germans fear with such extreme dread on behalf of their women, that the strongest tie by which a state can be bound is the being required to give, among the number of hostages, maidens of noble birth. They even believe that the sex has a certain sanctity and prescience, and they do not despise their counsels, or make light of their answers.

11. About minor matters the chiefs deliberate, about the more important the whole tribe. Yet even when the final decision rests with the people, the affair is always thoroughly discussed by the chiefs. They assemble, except in the case of a sudden emergency, on certain fixed days, either at new or at full moon; for this they consider the most auspicious season for the transaction of business. Instead of reckoning by days as we do, they reckon by nights, and in this manner fix both their ordinary and their legal appointments. Night they regard as bringing on day. Their freedom has this disadvantage, that they do not meet simultaneously or as they are bidden, but two or three days are wasted in the delays of assembling. When the multitude think proper, they sit down armed. Silence is proclaimed by the priests, who have on these occasions the right of keeping order. Then the king or the chief, according to age, birth, distinction in war, or eloquence, is heard, more because he has influence to persuade than because he has

power to command. If his sentiments displease them, they reject them with murmurs; if they are satisfied, they brandish their spears. The most complimentary form of assent is to express approbation with their weapons.

12. In their councils an accusation may be preferred or a capital crime prosecuted. Penalties are distinguished according to the offence. Traitors and deserters are hanged on trees; the coward, the unwarlike, the man stained with abominable vices, is plunged into the mire of the morass, with a hurdle put over him. This distinction in punishment means that crime, they think, ought, in being punished, to be exposed, while infamy ought to be buried out of sight. Lighter offences, too, have penalties proportioned to them; he who is convicted, is fined in a certain number of horses or of cattle. Half of the fine is paid to the king or to the state, half to the person whose wrongs are avenged and to his relatives. In these same councils they also elect the chief magistrates, who administer law in the cantons and the towns. Each of these has a hundred associates chosen from the people, who support him with their advice and influence.

13. They transact no public or private business without being armed. It is not, however, usual for anyone to wear arms till the state has recognized his power to use them. Then in the presence of the council one of the chiefs, or the young man's father, or some kinsman, equips him with a shield and a spear. These arms are what the "toga" is with us, the first honor with which youth is invested. Up to this time he is regarded as a member of a household, afterwards as a member of the commonwealth. Very noble birth or great services rendered by the father secure for lads the rank of a chief; such lads attach themselves to men of mature strength and of long approved valor. It is no shame to be seen among a chief's followers. Even in his escort there are gradations of rank, dependent on the choice of the man to whom they are attached. These followers vie keenly with each other as to who shall rank first with his chief, the chiefs as to who shall have the most numerous and the bravest followers. It is an honor as well as a source of strength to be thus always surrounded by a large body of picked youths; it is an ornament in peace and a defense in war. And not only in

his own tribe but also in the neighboring states it is the renown and glory of a chief to be distinguished for the number and valor of his followers, for such a man is courted by embassies, is honored with presents, and the very prestige of his name often settles a war.

PRACTICE IN WAR

14. When they go into battle, it is a disgrace for the chief to be surpassed in valor, a disgrace for his followers not to equal the valor of the chief. And it is an infamy and a reproach for life to have survived the chief, and returned from the field. To defend, to protect him, to ascribe one's own brave deeds to his renown, is the height of loyalty. The chief fights for victory; his vassals fight for their chief. If their native state sinks into the sloth of prolonged peace and repose, many of its noble youths voluntarily seek those tribes which are waging war, both because inaction is odious to their race, and because they win renown more readily in the midst of peril, and cannot maintain a numerous following except by violence and war. Indeed, men look to the liberality of their chief for their war-horse and their blood-stained and victorious lance. Feasts and entertainments, which, though inelegant, are plentifully furnished, are their only pay. The means of this bounty come from war and rapine. Nor are they as easily persuaded to plough the earth and to wait for the year's produce as to challenge an enemy and earn the honor of wounds. Nay, they actually think it tame and stupid to acquire by the sweat of toil what they might win by their blood.

15. Whenever they are not fighting, they pass much of their time in the chase, and still more in idleness, giving themselves up to sleep and to feasting, the bravest and the most warlike doing nothing, and surrendering the management of the household, of the home, and of the land, to the women, the old men, and all the weakest members of the family. They themselves lie buried in sloth, a strange combination in their nature that the same men should be so fond of idleness, so averse to peace. It is the custom of the states to bestow by voluntary and individual contribution on the chiefs a present of cattle or of grain, which, while accepted as a compliment, supplies their wants. They are particularly delighted by gifts

from neighboring tribes, which are sent not only by individuals but also by the state, such as choice steeds, heavy armor, trappings, and neck-chains. We have now taught them to accept money also.

16. It is well known that the nations of Germany have no cities, and that they do not even tolerate closely contiguous dwellings. They live scattered and apart, just as a spring, a meadow, or a wood has attracted them. Their villages they do not arrange in our fashion, with the buildings connected and joined together, but every person surrounds his dwelling with an open space, either as a precaution against the disasters of fire, or because they do not know how to build. No use is made by them of stone or tile; they employ timber for all purposes, rude masses without ornament or attractiveness. Some parts of their buildings they stain more carefully with a clay so clear and bright that it resembles painting, or a colored design. They are wont also to dig out subterranean caves, and pile on them great heaps of dung, as a shelter from winter and as a receptacle for the year's produce, for by such places they mitigate the rigor of the cold. And should an enemy approach, he lays waste the open country, while what is hidden and buried is either not known to exist, or else escapes him from the very fact that it has to be searched for.

21. It is a duty among them to adopt the feuds as well as the friendships of a father or a kinsman. These feuds are not implacable; even homicide is expiated by the payment of a certain number of cattle and of sheep, and the satisfaction is accepted by the entire family, greatly to the advantage of the state, since feuds are dangerous in proportion to a people's freedom.

Justice →

No nation indulges more profusely in entertainments and hospitality. To exclude any human being from their roof is thought impious; every German, according to his means, receives his guest with a well-furnished table. When his supplies are exhausted, he who was but now the host becomes the guide and companion to further hospitality, and without invitation they go to the next house. It matters not; they are entertained with like cordiality. No one distinguishes between an acquaintance and a stranger, as regards the rights of hospi-

tality. It is usual to give the departing guest whatever he may ask for, and a present in return is asked with as little hesitation. They are greatly charmed with gifts, but they expect no return for what they give, nor feel any obligation for what they receive.

22. On waking from sleep, which they generally prolong to a late hour of the day, they take a bath, oftenest of warm water, which suits a country where winter is the longest of the seasons. After their bath they take their meal, each having a separate seat and table of his own. Then they go armed to business, or no less often to their festal meetings. To pass an entire day and night in drinking disgraces no one. Their quarrels, as might be expected with intoxicated people, are seldom fought out with mere abuse, but commonly with wounds and bloodshed. Yet it is at their feasts that they generally consult on the reconciliation of enemies, on the forming of matrimonial alliances, on the choice of chiefs, finally even on peace and war, for they think that at no time is the mind more open to simplicity of purpose or more warmed to noble aspirations. A race without either natural or acquired cunning, they disclose their hidden thoughts in the freedom of the festivity. Thus the sentiments of all having been discovered and laid bare, the discussion is renewed on the following day, and from each occasion its own peculiar advantage is derived. They deliberate when they have no power to dissemble; they resolve when error is impossible.

23. A liquor for drinking is made out of barley or other grain, and fermented into a certain resemblance to wine. The dwellers on the river-bank also buy wine. Their food is of a simple kind, consisting of wild-fruit, fresh game, and curdled milk. They satisfy their hunger without elaborate preparation and without delicacies. In quenching their thirst they are not equally moderate. If you indulge their love of drinking by supplying them with as much as they desire, they will be overcome by their own vices as easily as by the arms of an enemy.

†

2. THE ROLE OF THE KING

Augustus (31 B.C.-A.D. 14) and Charlemagne (A.D. 768-814) were ideals to later ages: what an emperor or king ought to be was often defined in terms of what they were. Gaius Suetonius Tranquillus (A.D. 69?-140?) and Einhard (A.D. 775?-838?) have left important biographies of these rulers; indeed, Einhard adapted Charlemagne to fit Suetonius's portrait of Augustus. Still, both rulers and both writers had distinctive personalities which are clear, even if Einhard borrowed much from Suetonius. How do these rulers compare to ideal rulers in other periods? How do Charlemagne and Augustus differ from each other? What makes them great? How does Einhard's Charlemagne measure up against the legendary king in Roland? Has the king's function changed? Is it a change for the better or worse? Can you compare these two monarchs with Alexander the Great?

A. LIFE OF AUGUSTUS

SUETONIUS

21. In part as leader, and in part with armies serving under his auspices, he subdued Cantabria, Aquitania, Pannonia, Dalmatia, and all Illyricum, as well as Raetia and the Vindelici and Salassi, which are Alpine tribes. He also put a stop to the inroads of the Dacians, slaying great numbers of them, together with three of their leaders, and forced the Germans back to the farther side of the river Albis, with the exception of the Suebi and Sigambri, who submitted to him and were taken into Gaul and settled in lands near the Rhine. He reduced to submission other peoples, too, that were in a state of unrest.

But he never made war on any nation without just and due cause, and he was so far from desiring to increase his dominion or his military glory at any cost that he forced the chiefs of certain barbarians to take oath in the temple of Mars the Avenger that they would faithfully keep the peace for which they asked; in some cases, indeed, he tried exacting a new kind of hostages, namely women, realizing that the barbarians disregarded pledges secured by males; but all were given the privilege of reclaiming their hostages whenever they wished. On those who rebelled often or under circumstances of especial treachery he never inflicted any severer punishment than that of selling the prisoners, with the condition that they should not pass their term of slavery in a country near their own, nor be set free within thirty years.

The reputation for prowess and moderation which he thus gained led even the Indians and the Scythians, nations known to us only by hearsay, to send envoys of their own free will and sue for his friendship and that of the Roman people. The Parthians, too, readily yielded to him, when he laid claim to Armenia, and at his demand surrendered the standards which they had taken from Marcus Crassus and Marcus Antonius;[1] they offered him hostages besides, and once when there were several claimants of their throne, they would accept only the one whom he selected.

22. The temple of Janus Quirinus, which has been closed but twice before his time since the founding of the city,[2] he closed three times in a far shorter period, having won peace on land and sea. He twice entered the city in an ovation, after the war of Philippi, and again after that in Sicily, and he celebrated three regular triumphs for his victories in Dalmatia, at Actium, and at Alexandria, all on three successive days.

23. He suffered but two severe and ignominious defeats, those of Lollius and Varus, both of which were in Germany. Of these the former was more humiliating than serious, but the latter was almost fatal, since three legions were cut to pieces with their general, his lieutenants, and all the auxiliaries. When the news of this came, he ordered that watch be kept by night throughout the city, to prevent any outbreak, and he prolonged the terms of the governors of the provinces, that the allies might be held to their allegiance by experienced men with whom they were acquainted. He also vowed great games to Jupiter Optimus Maximus, in case the condition of the commonwealth should improve, a thing which had been done in the Cimbric and Marsic wars. In fact, they say that he was so greatly affected that for several months in succession he cut neither his beard nor his hair, and sometimes he would dash his head against a door, crying:

---

[1] Crassus lost his standards at the battle of Carrhae in 53, and Antony through the defeat of his lieutenants in 40 and 36 B.C. [J. C. R.]

[2] In the reign of Numa (second king of Rome), and in 235 B.C., after the first Punic war. [J. C. R.]

"Quintilius Varus, give me back my legions!" And he observed the day of the disaster each year as one of sorrow and mourning.

26. He received offices and honors before the usual age, and some of a new kind and for life. He usurped the consulship in the twentieth year of his age, leading his legions against the city as if it were that of any enemy, and sending messengers to demand the office for him in the name of his army; and when the Senate hesitated, his centurion, Cornelius, leader of the deputation, throwing back his cloak and showing the hilt of his sword, did not hesitate to say in the House, "This will make him consul, if you do not." He held his second consulship nine years later, and a third after a year's interval; the rest up to the eleventh were in successive years, then after declining a number of terms that were offered him, he asked of his own accord for a twelfth after a long interval, no less than seventeen years, and two years later for a thirteenth, wishing to hold the highest magistracy at the time when he introduced each of his sons Gaius and Lucius to public life upon their coming of age.

CONSULSHIPS

The five consulships from the sixth to the tenth he held for the full year, the rest for nine, six, four, or three months, except the second, which lasted only a few hours; for after sitting for a short time on the curule chair in front of the temple of Jupiter Capitolinus in the early morning, he resigned the honor on the Kalends of January and appointed another in his place. He did not begin all his consulships in Rome, but the fourth in Asia, the fifth on the Isle of Samos, the eighth and ninth at Tarraco.

29. He built many public works, in particular the following: his forum with the temple of Mars the Avenger, the temple of Apollo on the Palatine, and the face of Jupiter the Thunderer on the Capitol. His reason for building the forum was the increase in the number of the people and of cases at law, which seemed to call for a third forum, since two were no longer adequate. Therefore it was opened to the public with some haste, before the temple of Mars was finished, and it was provided that the public prosecutions be held there apart

from the rest, as well as the selection of jurors by lot. He had made a vow to build the temple of Mars in the war of Philippi, which he undertook to avenge his father; accordingly he decreed that in it the senate should consider wars and claims for triumphs, from it those who were on their way to the provinces with military commands should be escorted, and to it victors on their return should bear the tokens of their triumphs.

He reared the temple of Apollo in that part of his house on the Palatine for which the soothsayers declared that the god had shown his desire by striking it with lightning. He joined to it colonnades with Latin and Greek libraries, and when he was getting to be an old man he often held meetings of the senate there as well, and revised the lists of jurors. He dedicated the shrine to Jupiter the Thunderer because of a narrow escape; for on his Cantabrian expedition during a march by night, a flash of lightning grazed his litter and struck the slave dead who was carrying a torch before him. He constructed some works too in the name of others, his grandsons to wit, his wife and his sister, such as the colonnade and basilica of Gaius and Lucius; also the colonnades of Livia and Octavia, and the theater of Marcellus.

More than that, he often urged other prominent men to adorn the city with new monuments or to restore and embellish old ones, each according to his means. And many such works were built at that time by many men; for example, the temple of Hercules of the Muses by Marcius Philippus, the temple of Diana by Lucius Cornificius, the Hall of Liberty by Asinius Pollio, the temple of Saturn by Munatius Plancus, a theater by Cornelius Balbus, an amphitheater by Statilius Taurus, and by Marcus Agrippa in particular many magnificent structures.

33. He himself administered justice regularly and sometimes up to nightfall, having a litter placed upon the tribunal, if he was indisposed, or even lying down at home. In his administration of justice he was both highly conscientious and very lenient; for to save a man clearly guilty of parricide from being sewn up in the

sack,[1] a punishment which was inflicted only on those who pleaded guilty, he is said to have put the question to him in this form: "You surely did not kill your father, did you?" Again, in a case touching a forged will, in which all the signers were liable to punishment by the Cornelian Law, he distributed to the jury not merely the two tablets for condemnation or acquittal, but a third as well, for the pardon of those who were shown to have been induced to sign by misrepresentation or misunderstanding. Each year he referred appeals of cases involving citizens to the city praetor, but those between foreigners to ex-consuls, of whom he had put one in charge of the business affairs of each province.

41. He often showed generosity to all classes when occasion offered. For example, by bringing the royal treasures to Rome in his Alexandrian triumph he made ready money so abundant that the rate of interest fell, and the value of real estate rose greatly; and after that, whenever there was an excess of funds from the property of those who had been condemned, he loaned it without interest for fixed periods to any who could give security for double the amount. He increased the property qualification for senators, requiring one million two hundred thousand sesterces, instead of eight hundred thousand, and making up the amount for those who did not possess it. He often gave largess to the people, but usually of different sums: now four hundred, now three hundred, now two hundred and fifty sesterces a man; and he did not even exclude young boys, though it had been usual for them to receive a share only after the age of eleven. In times of scarcity too he often distributed grain to each man at a very low figure, sometimes for nothing, and he doubled the money tickets.[2]

SURPASSING ALL OTHERS

43. He surpassed all his predecessors in the frequency, variety, and magnificence of his public shows. He says that he gave games four times in his own name and twenty-three times

for other magistrates who were either away from Rome or lacked means. He gave them sometimes in all the wards and on many stages with actors in all languages, and combats of gladiators not only in the Forum or the amphitheater, but in the Circus and in the Saepta; sometimes, however, he gave nothing except a fight with wild beasts. He gave athletic contests too in the Campus Martius, erecting wooden seats; also a sea-fight, constructing an artificial lake near the Tiber, where the grove of the Caesars now stands. On such occasions he stationed guards in various parts of the city to prevent it from falling a prey to footpads because of the few people who remained at home.

In the Circus he exhibited charioteers, runners, and slayers of wild animals, who were sometimes young men of the highest rank. Besides he gave frequent performances of the Trojan Games by older and younger boys, thinking it a time-honored and worthy custom for the flower of the nobility to become known in this way. When Nonius Asprenas was lamed by a fall while taking part in this game, he presented him with a golden necklace and allowed him and his descendants to bear the surname Torquatus. But soon afterwards he gave up that form of entertainment, because Asinius Pollio the orator complained bitterly and angrily in the senate of an accident to his grandson Aeserninus, who also had broken his leg.

He sometimes employed even Roman knights in scenic and gladiatorial performances, but only before it was forbidden by decree of the senate. After that he exhibited no one of respectable parentage, with the exception of a young man named Lycius, whom he showed merely as a curiosity; for he was less than two feet tall, weighed but seventeen pounds, yet had a stentorian voice. He did however on the day of one of the shows make a display of the first Parthian hostages that had ever been sent to Rome, by leading them through the middle of the arena and placing them in the second row above his own seat. Furthermore, if anything rare and worth seeing was ever brought to the city, it was his habit to make a special exhibit of it in any convenient place on days when no shows were appointed. For example a

---

[1]Traditional law called for those who killed their fathers to be sewn up in a sack with a dog, a cock, a snake, and a monkey and thrown into the sea.
[2]Tablets distributed to the poor entitling the holder to receive the amount written on them in cash.

rhinoceros in the Saepta, a tiger on the stage and a snake of fifty cubits in the Comitium.

It chanced that at the time of the games which he had vowed to give in the circus he was taken ill and headed the sacred procession lying in a litter; again, at the opening of the games with which he dedicated the theater of Marcellus, it happened that the joints of his curule chair gave way and he fell on his back. At the games for his grandsons, when the people were in a panic for fear the theater should fall, and he could not calm them or encourage them in any way, he left his own place and took his seat in the part which appeared most dangerous.

65. But at the height of his happiness and his confidence in his family and its training, Fortune proved fickle. He found the two Julias, his daughter and granddaughter, guilty of every form of vice, and banished them. He lost Gaius and Lucius within the span of eighteen months, for the former died in Lycia and the latter at Massilia. He then publicly adopted his third grandson Agrippa and at the same time his stepson Tiberius by a bill passed in the assembly of the *curiae*; but he soon disowned Agrippa because of his low tastes and violent temper, and sent him off to Surrentum.

He bore the death of his kin with far more resignation than their misconduct. For he was not greatly broken by the fate of Gaius and Lucius, but he informed the senate of his daughter's fall through a letter read in his absence by a quaestor, and for very shame would meet no one for a long time, and even thought of putting her to death.

76. He was a light eater (for I would not omit even this detail) and as a rule ate of plain food. He particularly liked coarse bread, small fishes, handmade moist cheese, and green figs of the second crop; and he would eat even before dinner, wherever and whenever he felt hungry…. Because of this irregularity he sometimes ate alone either before a dinner party began or after it was over, touching nothing while it was in progress.

77. He was by nature most sparing also in his use of wine. Cornelius Nepos writes that in camp before Mutina it was his habit to drink not more than three times at dinner. After-

wards, when he indulged most freely he never exceeded a pint; or if he did, he used to throw it up. He liked Raetian wine best, but rarely drank before dinner. Instead he would take a bit of bread soaked in cold water, a slice of cucumber, a sprig of young lettuce, or an apple with a tart flavor, either fresh or dried.

PHYSICAL APPEARANCE

79. He was unusually handsome and exceedingly graceful at all periods of his life, though he cared nothing for personal adornment. He was so far from being particular about the dressing of his hair that he would have several barbers working in a hurry at the same time, and as for his beard he now had it clipped and now shaved, while at the very same time he would either be reading or writing something. His expression, whether in conversation or when he was silent, was so calm and mild that one of the leading men of the Gallic provinces admitted to his countrymen that it had softened his heart and kept him from carrying out his design of pushing the emperor over a cliff when he had been allowed to approach him under the pretense of a conference as he was crossing the Alps.

He had clear, bright eyes, in which he liked to have it thought that there was a kind of divine power, and it greatly pleased him, whenever he looked keenly at anyone, if he let his face fall as if before the radiance of the sun; but in his old age he could not see very well with his left eye. His teeth were wide apart, small, and ill-kept; his hair was slightly curly and inclining to golden; his eyebrows met. His ears were of a moderate size, and his nose projected a little at the top and then bent slightly inward. His complexion was between dark and fair. he was short of stature (although Julius Maratus, his freedman and keeper of his records, says that he was five feet and nine inches in height[1]), but this was concealed by the fine proportion and symmetry of his figure, and was noticeable only by comparison with some taller person standing beside him.

84. From early youth he devoted himself eagerly and with the utmost diligence to oratory and liberal studies. During the war at Mutina,

---

[1] Roman measure, equal to about five foot seven in English measurement.

amid such a press of affairs, he is said to have read, written and declaimed every day. In fact he never afterwards spoke in the senate or to the people or the soldiers except in a studied and written address, although he did not lack the gift of speaking off-hand without preparation. Moreover, to avoid the danger of forgetting what he was to say, or wasting time in committing it to memory, he adopted the practice of reading everything from a manuscript. Even his conversations with individuals and the more important of those with his own wife Livia he always wrote out and read from a note-book, for fear of saying too much or too little if he spoke offhand. He had an agreeable and rather characteristic enunciation, and he practiced constantly with a teacher of elocution; but sometimes because of weakness of the throat he addressed the people through a herald.

85. He wrote numerous works of various kinds in prose, some of which he read to a group of his intimate friends, as others did in a lecture-room, for example, his "Reply to Brutus on Cato." At the reading of these volumes he had all but come to the end when he grew tired and handed them to Tiberius to finish, for he was well on in years. He also wrote "Exhortations to Philosophy" and some volumes of an Autobiography, giving an account of his life in thirteen books up to the time of the Cantabrian war, but no farther. His essays in poetry were but slight. One book has come down to us written in hexameter verse, of which the subject and the title is "Sicily." There is another, equally brief, of "Epigrams," which he composed for the most part at the time of the bath. Though he began a tragedy with much enthusiasm, he destroyed it because his style did not satisfy him, and when some of his friends asked him what in the world had become of Ajax, he answered that his Ajax had fallen on his sponge.[1]

SPEAKING STYLE

86. He cultivated a style of speaking that was chaste and elegant, avoiding the vanity of attempts at epigram and an artificial order and, as he himself expresses it, "the noisomeness of

---

[1] That is, the sponge used to wipe a slate clean. The mythical Ajax took his own life by falling on his sword.

far-fetched words," making it his chief aim to express his thoughts as clearly as possible. With this end in view, to avoid confusing and checking his reader or hearer at any point, he did not hesitate to use prepositions with names of cities, nor to repeat conjunctions several times, the omission of which causes some obscurity, though it adds grace. He looked on innovators and archaizers with equal contempt as faulty in opposite directions, and he sometimes had a fling at them, in particular his friend Maecenas, whose "unguent-dripping curls," as he calls them, he loses no opportunity of belaboring and pokes fun at them by parody. He did not spare even Tiberius, who sometimes hunted up obsolete and pedantic expressions; and as for Mark Antony, he calls him a madman for writing rather to be admired than to be understood.... And in a letter praising the talent of his granddaughter Agrippina he writes: "But you must take great care not to write and talk affectedly."

88. He does not strictly comply with orthography, that is to say the theoretical rules of spelling laid down by the grammarians, seeming to be rather of the mind of those who believe that we should spell exactly as we pronounce. Of course his frequent transposition or omission of syllables as well as of letters are slips common to all mankind. I should not have noted this, did it not seem to me surprising that some have written that he cashiered a consular governor as an uncultivated and ignorant fellow because he observed that he had written *ixi* for *ipsi*. Whenever he wrote in cipher, he wrote B for A, C for B, and the rest of the letters on the same principle, using AA for X.

89. He was equally interested in Greek studies, and in these too he excelled greatly. His teacher of declamation was Apollodorus of Pergamon, whom he even took with him in his youthful days from Rome to Apollonia, though Apollodorus was an old man at the time. Later he became versed in various forms of learning through association with the philosopher Areus and his sons Dionysus and Nicanor. Yet he never acquired the ability to speak Greek fluently or to compose anything in it; for if he had occasion to use the language, he wrote what he had to say in Latin and gave it to someone else to translate. Still

he was far from being ignorant of Greek poetry, even taking great pleasure in the Old Comedy and frequently staging it at his public entertainments. In reading the writers of both tongues there was nothing for which he looked so carefully as precepts and examples instructive to the public or to individuals; these he would often copy word for word and send to the members of his household or to his generals and provincial governors, whenever any of them required admonition. He even read entire volumes to the senate and called the attention of the people to them by proclamations—for example, the speeches of Quintus Metellus "On Increasing the Family," and of Rutilius "On the Height of Buildings"—to convince them that he was not the first to give attention to such matters, but that they had aroused the interest even of their forefathers.

He gave every encouragement to the men of talent of his own age, listening with courtesy and patience to their readings, not only of poetry and history but of speeches and dialogues as well. But he took offense at being made the subject of any composition except in serious earnest and by the most eminent writers, often charging the praetors not to let his name be cheapened in prize declamations.

†

B. LIFE OF CHARLEMAGNE

EINHARD

15....He so nobly increased the kingdom of the Franks, which was great and strong when he inherited it from his father Pippin, that the additions he made almost doubled it. For before his time the bower of the Frankish kingdom extended only over that part of Gaul which is bounded by the Rhine, the Loire, and the Balearic Sea; and that part of Germany which is inhabited by the so-called eastern Franks, and which is bounded by Saxony, the Danube, the Rhine, and the river Saal, which stream separates the Thuringians and the Sorabs; and, further, over the Alamanni and the Bavarians. But Charles, by the wars that have been mentioned, conquered and made tributary the following countries. First, Aquitania and Gascony, and the whole Pyrenean range, and the country of Spain as far as the

Ebro, which, rising in Navarre and passing through the most fertile territory of Spain, falls into the Balearic Sea, beneath the walls of the city of Tortosa ; next, all Italy from Augusta Pretoria as far as lower Calabria, where are the frontiers of the Greeks and Beneventans, a thousand miles and more in length; next, Saxony, which is a considerable portion of Germany, and is reckoned to be twice as broad and about as long as that part of Germany which is inhabited by the Franks; then both provinces of Pannonia and Dacia, on one side of the river Danube, and Histria and Liburnia and Dalmatia, with the exception of the maritime cities which he left to the Emperor of Constantinople on account of their friendship and the treaty made between them; lastly, all the barbarous and fierce nations lying between the Rhine, the Vistula, the Ocean, and the Danube, who speak much the same language, but in character and dress are very unlike. The chief of these last are the Welatabi, the Sorabi, the Abodriti, and the Bohemians; against these he waged war, but the others, and by far the larger number, surrendered without a struggle.

17. Though he was so successful in widening the boundaries of his kingdom and subduing the foreign nations he, nevertheless, put on foot many works for the decoration and convenience of his kingdom, and carried some to completion. The great church dedicated to Mary, the holy Mother of God, at Aix, and the bridge, five hundred feet in length, over the great river Rhine near Mainz, may fairly be regarded as the chief of his works. But the bridge was burnt down a year before his death, and though he had determined to rebuild it of stone instead of wood it was not restored, because his death so speedily followed. He began also to build palaces of splendid workmanship—one not far from the city of Mainz, near a town called Ingelheim; another at Nimeguen, on the river Waal, which flows along the south of the Batavian island. And he gave special orders to the bishops and priests who had charge of sacred buildings that any throughout his realm which had fallen into ruin through age should be restored, and he instructed his agents to see that his orders were carried out.

He built a fleet, too, for the war against the Northmen, constructing ships for this purpose near those rivers which flow out of Gaul and Germany into the northern ocean. And because the Northmen laid waste the coasts of Gaul and Germany by their constant attacks he planted forts and garrisons in all harbors and at the mouths of all navigable rivers, and prevented in this way the passage of the enemy. He took the same measures in the South, on the shore of Narbonne and Septimania, and also along all the coasts of Italy as far as Rome, to hold in check the Moors, who had lately begun to make piratical excursions. And by reason of these precautions Italy suffered no serious harm from the Moors, nor Gaul and Germany from the Northmen, in the days of Charles; except that Centumcellae, a city of Etruria, was betrayed into the hands of the Moors and plundered, and in Frisia certain islands lying close to Germany were ravaged by the Northmen.

18. I have shown, then, how Charles protected and expanded his kingdom and also what splendor he gave to it. I shall now go on to speak of his mental endowments, of his steadiness of purpose under whatever circumstances of prosperity or adversity, and of all that concerns his private and domestic life.

As long as, after the death of his father, he shared the kingdom with his brother he bore so patiently the quarreling and restlessness of the latter as never even to be provoked to wrath by him. Then, having married at his mother's bidding the daughter of Desiderius, King of the Lombards, he divorced her, for some unknown reason, a year later. He took in marriage Hildigard, of the Suabian race, a woman of the highest nobility, and by her he had three sons—viz. Charles and Pippin and Ludovicus, and three daughters—Hrotrud and Bertha and Gisla. He had also three other daughters—Theoderada and Hiltrud and Hruodhaid. Two of these were the children of his wife Fastrada, a woman of the eastern Franks or Germans; the third was the daughter of a concubine, whose name has escaped my memory. On the death of Fastrada he married Liutgard, of the Alemannic race, by whom he had no children. After her death he had four concubines-namely, Madelgarda, who bore him a daughter of the name of

Ruothild; Gersuinda, of Saxon origin, by whom he had a daughter of the name of Adolthrud; Regina, who bore him Drogot and Hugo; and Adallinda; who was the mother of Theoderic.

His mother Bertrada lived with him to old age in great honor. He treated her with the utmost reverence, so that no quarrel of any kind ever arose between them—except in the matter of the divorce of the daughter of King Desiderius, whom he had married at her bidding. Bertrada died after the death of Hildigard, having lived to see three grandsons and as many granddaughters in her son's house. Charles had his mother buried with great honor in the same great church of St Denys in which his father lay.

He had only one sister, Gisla, who from childhood was dedicated to the religious life. He treated her with the same affectionate respect as his mother. She died a few years before Charles's own death in the monastery in which she had passed her life.

19. In educating his children he determined to train them, both sons and daughters, in those liberal studies to which he himself paid great attention. Further, he made his sons, as soon as their age permitted it, learn to ride like true Franks, and practice the use of arms and hunting. He ordered his daughters to learn wool work and devote attention to the spindle and distaff, for the avoidance of idleness and lethargy, and to be trained to the adoption of high principles.

He lost two sons and one daughter before his death—namely, Charles, his eldest; Pippin, whom he made King of Italy; and Hruotrud, his eldest daughter, who had been betrothed to Constantine, the Emperor of the Greeks. Pippin left one son, Bernard, and five daughters— Adalheid, Atula, Gundrada, Berthaid, and Tfieoderada. In his treatment of them Charles gave the strongest proof of his family affection, for upon the death of his son he appointed his grandson Bernard to succeed him, and had his granddaughters brought up with his own daughters.

He bore the deaths of his two sons and of his daughters with less patience than might have been expected from his usual stoutness of heart, for his domestic affection, a quality for which he was as remarkable as for courage, forced him to shed tears. Moreover, when the death of Hadrian, the Roman Pontiff, whom he reckoned as the chief of his friends, was announced to him, he wept for him as though he had lost a brother or a very dear son. For he showed a very fine disposition in his friendships: he embraced them readily and maintained them faithfully, and he treated with the utmost respect all whom he had admitted into the circle of his friends.

He had such care of the upbringing of his sons and daughters that he never dined without them when he was at home, and never traveled without them. His sons rode along with him, and his daughters followed in the rear. Some of his guards, chosen for this very purpose, watched the end of the line of march where his daughters traveled. They were very beautiful, and much beloved by their father, and, therefore, it is strange that he would give them in marriage to no one, either among his own people or of a foreign state. But up to his death he kept them all at home, saying that he could not forego their society. And hence the good fortune that followed him in all other respects was here broken by the touch of scandal and failure. He shut his eyes, however, to everything, and acted as though no suspicion of anything amiss had reached him, or as if the rumor of it had been discredited.

20. He had by a concubine a son called Pippin—whom I purposely did not mention along with the others—handsome, indeed, but deformed. When Charles, after the beginning of the war against the Huns, was wintering in Bavaria, this Pippin pretended illness, and formed a conspiracy against his father with some of the leaders of the Franks, who had seduced him by a vain promise of the kingdom. When the design had been detected and the conspirators punished Pippin was tonsured and sent to the monastery of Prussia, there to practice the religious life, to which in the end he was of his own will inclined.

Another dangerous conspiracy had been formed against him in Germany at an earlier date. The plotters were some of them blinded and some of them maimed, and all subsequently transported into exile. Not more than

three lost their lives, and these resisted capture with drawn swords, and in defending themselves killed some of their opponents. Hence, as they could not be restrained in any other way, they were cut down.

The cruelty of Queen Fastrada is believed to be the cause and origin of these conspiracies. Both were caused by the belief that, upon the persuasion of his cruel wife, he had swerved widely from his natural kindness and customary leniency. Otherwise his whole life long he so won the love and favor of all men both at home and abroad that never was the slightest charge of unjust severity brought against him by anyone.

21. He had a great love for foreigners, and took such pains to entertain them that their numbers were justly reckoned to be a burden not only to the palace but to the kingdom at large. But, with his usual loftiness of spirit, he took little note of such charges, for he found in the reputation of generosity and in the good fame that followed such actions a compensation even for grave inconveniences.

22. His body was large and strong; his stature tall but not ungainly, for the measure of his height was seven times the length of his own feet. The top of his head was round; his eyes were very large and piercing His nose was rather larger than is usual; he had beautiful white hair; and his expression was brisk and cheerful; so that, whether sitting or standing, his appearance was dignified and impressive. Although his neck was rather thick and short and he was somewhat corpulent this was not noticed owing to the good proportions of the rest of his body. His step was firm and the whole carriage of his body manly; his voice was clear, but hardly so strong as you would have expected. He had good health, but for four years before his death was frequently attacked by fevers, and at last was lame of one foot. Even then he followed his own opinion rather than the advice of his doctors, whom he almost hated, because they advised him to give up the roast meat to which he was accustomed, and eat boiled instead. He constantly took exercise both by riding and hunting. This was a national habit; for there is hardly any race on the earth that can be placed on equality with the Franks in this respect. He took

delight in the vapor of naturally hot waters, and constantly practiced swimming, in which he was so proficient that no one could be fairly regarded as his superior. Partly for this reason he built his palace at Aix, and lived there continuously during the last years of his life up to the time of his death. He used to invite not only his sons to the bath but also his nobles and friends, and at times even a great number of his followers and bodyguards.

23. He wore the national—that is to say, the Frankish dress. His shirts and drawers were of linen, then came a tunic with a silken fringe, and hose. His legs were cross-gartered and his feet enclosed in shoes. In wintertime he defended his shoulders and chest with a jerkin made of the skins of otters and ermine. He was clad in a blue cloak, and always wore a sword, with the hilt and belt of either gold or silver. Occasionally, too, he used a jeweled sword, but this was only on the great festivals or when he received ambassadors from foreign nations. He disliked foreign garments, however beautiful, and would never consent to wear them, except once at Rome on the request of Pope Hadrian, and once again upon the entreaty of his successor, Pope Leo, when he wore a long tunic and cloak, and put on shoes made after the Roman fashion. On festal days he walked in procession in a garment of gold cloth, with jeweled boots and a golden girdle to his cloak, and distinguished further by a diadem of gold and precious stones. But on other days his dress differed little from that of the common people.

24. He was temperate in eating and drinking, but especially so in drinking; for he had a fierce hatred of drunkenness in any man, and especially in himself or in his friends. He could not abstain so easily from food, and used often to complain that fasting was injurious to his health. He rarely gave large banquets, and only on the high festivals, but then he invited a large number of guests. His daily meal was served in four courses only, exclusive of the roast, which the hunters used to bring in on spits, and which he ate with more pleasure than any other food. During the meal there was either singing or a reader for him to listen to. Histories and the great deeds of men of old were read to him. He took delight also in the books of Saint Augustine, and especially in those which are entitled the City of God. He was so temperate in the use of wine and drink of any kind that he rarely drank oftener than thrice during dinner.

In summer, after his midday meal, he took some fruit and a single draught, and then, taking off his clothes and boots, just as he was accustomed to do at night, he would rest for two or three hours. At night he slept so lightly that he would wake, and even rise, four or five times during the night.

When he was putting on his boots and clothes he not only admitted his friends, but if the Count of the Palace told him there was any dispute which could not be settled without his decision he would have the litigants at once brought in, and hear the case, and pronounce on it just as if he were sitting on the tribunal. He would, moreover, at the same time transact any business that had to be done that day or give any orders to his servants.

25. In speech he was fluent and ready, and could express with the greatest clearness whatever he wished. He was not merely content with his native tongue but took the trouble to learn foreign languages. He learnt Latin so well that he could speak it as well as his native tongue; but he could understand Greek better than he could speak it. His fluency of speech was so great that he even seemed sometimes a little garrulous.

He paid the greatest attention to the liberal arts, and showed the greatest respect and bestowed high honors upon those who taught them. For his lessons in grammar he listened to the instruction of Deacon Peter of Pisa, an old man; but for all other subjects Albinus, called Alcuin, also a deacon, was his teacher—a man from Britain, of the Saxon race, and the most learned man of his time. Charles spent much time and labor in learning rhetoric and dialectic, and especially astronomy, from Alcuin. He learnt, too, the art of reckoning, and with close application scrutinized most carefully the course of the stars. He tried also to learn to write, and for this purpose used to carry with him and keep under the pillow of his couch tablets and writing-sheets that he might in his spare moments accustom himself to the formation of letters. But he made little advance in this strange task, which was begun too late in life.

26. He paid the most devout and pious regard to the Christian religion, in which he had been brought up from infancy. And, therefore, he built the great and most beautiful church at Aix, and decorated it with gold and silver and candelabras and with wicket-gates and doors of solid brass. And, since he could not procure marble columns elsewhere for the building of it, he had them brought from Rome and Ravenna. As long as his health permitted it he used diligently to attend the church both in the morning and evening, and during the night, and at the time of the Sacrifice. He took the greatest care to have all the services of the church performed with the utmost dignity, and constantly warned the keepers of the building not to allow anything improper or dirty either to be brought into or to remain in the building. He provided so great a quantity of gold and silver vessels, and so large a supply of priestly vestments, that at the religious services not even the doorkeepers, who form the lowest ecclesiastical order, had to officiate in their ordinary dress. He carefully reformed the manner of reading and singing; for he was thoroughly instructed in both, though he never read publicly himself, nor sang except in a low voice, and with the rest of the congregation.

27. He was most devout in relieving the poor and in those free gifts which the Greeks call alms. For he gave it his attention not only in his own country and in his own kingdom, but he also used to send money across the sea to Syria, to Egypt, to Africa—to Jerusalem, Alexandria, and Carthage—in compassion for the poverty of any Christians whose miserable condition in those countries came to his ears. It was for this reason chiefly that he cultivated the friendship of kings beyond the sea, hoping thereby to win for the Christians living beneath their sway some succor and relief. Beyond all other sacred and venerable places he loved the church of the holy Apostle Peter at Rome, and he poured into its treasury great wealth in silver and gold and precious stones. He sent innumerable gifts to the Pope; and during the whole course of his reign he strove with all his might (and, indeed, no object was nearer to his heart than this) to restore to the city of Rome her ancient authority, and not merely to defend the church of Saint Peter but to decorate and enrich it out of his resources above all other churches. But although he valued Rome so much, still, during all the forty-seven years that he reigned, he only went there four times to pay his vows and offer up his prayers.

29. When he had taken the imperial title he noticed many defects in the legal systems of his people; for the Franks have two legal systems, differing in many points very widely form one another, and he, therefore, determined to add what was lacking, to reconcile the differences, and to amend anything that was wrong or wrongly expressed. He completed nothing of all his designs beyond adding a few capitularies, and those unfinished. But he gave orders that the laws and rules of all nations comprised within his dominions which were not already written out should be collected and committed to writing.

✝

3.   THE FORCE OF LAW

At the end, as at the beginning, a society reveals itself through its laws. Laws are passed for a reason, a response to crimes and pressures a society has faced. And if justice, in its broadest sense, is the core and reason for a society, then law is the key to that realm's concept of justice. Here are excerpts from the Theodosian Code, compiled in Constantinople in the early fifth century A.D. at the behest of the emperor Theodosius II (grandson of Theodosius the Great) and the Lombard Laws, from c. 700, whose land lay in Northern Italy. How do these codes differ from one another? Do they present differing, perhaps competing, ideas of justice? Finally, a *capitulary* (literally, a decree divided into chapters) from the reign of Charles the Bald (840-877), one of Charlemagne's grandsons. Does a study of these laws shed any light on the "fall of Rome"?

A.   THE THEODOSIAN CODE

I.1.5. Emperors Theodosius and Valentinian Augustuses to the Senate:

We decree that, after the pattern of the Gregorian and Hermogenian Codes, a collection shall be made of all the constitutions that were issued by the renowned Constantine, which rest upon the force of edicts or sacred imperial law of general force.

First, the titles, which are the definite designations of the matters therein shall be so divided that, when the various headings have been expressed, if one constitution should pertain to several titles, the materials shall be assembled wherever is fitting. Second, if any diversity should cause anything to be stated in two ways, it shall be tested by the order of the readings, and not only shall the year of the consulship be considered and the time of the reign be investigated, but also the arrangement of the work itself shall show that the laws which are later are more valid. Furthermore, the very words themselves of the constitutions, in so far as they pertain to the essential matter, shall be preserved, but those words which were added not from the very necessity of sanctioning law shall be omitted.

Although it would be simpler and more in accordance with law to omit those constitutions which were invalidated by later constitutions and to set forth only those which must be valid, let us recognize that this code and the previous ones were composed for more diligent men, to whose scholarly efforts it is granted to know those laws also which have been consigned to silence and have passed into desuetude, since they were destined to be valid for the cases of their own time only.

Moreover, from these three codes and from the treatises and responses of the jurists which are attached to each of the titles, through the services of the same men who shall arrange the third code, there shall be produced another code of Ours. This code shall permit no error, no ambiguities; it shall be called by Our name and shall show what must be followed and what must be avoided by all.

For the consummation of so great a work and for the composition of the codes—the first of which shall collect all the diversity of general constitutions, shall omit none outside itself which are now permitted to be cited in court, and shall reject only an empty copiousness of words, the other shall exclude every contradiction of the law and shall undertake the guidance of life—men must be chosen of singular trustworthiness, of the most brilliant genius.

When they have presented the first code to Our Wisdom and to the public authority, they shall undertake the other, which must be worked over until it is worthy of publication. Let Your Magnificence acknowledge the men who have been selected; We have selected the Illustrious Antiochus, Ex-Quaestor and Ex-Prefect, the Illustrious Antiochus, Quaestor of the sacred imperial palace, the Respectable Theodorus, Count and Master of the Bureau of Memorials, the Respectable Eudicius and Eusebius, Masters of the Bureaus, the Respectable Johannes, ex-Count of Our sacred imperial sanctuary, the Respectable Comazon and Eubulus, Ex-Masters of the Bureaus, and Apelles, most eloquent jurist.

We are confident that these men who have been selected by Our Eternity will employ every exceptionally learned man, in order that by their common study a reasonable plan of life may be apprehended and fallacious laws may be excluded.

Furthermore, if in the future it should be Our pleasure to promulgate any new law in one part of this very closely united Empire, it shall be valid in the other part on condition that it does not rest upon doubtful trustworthiness or upon a private assertion; but from that part of the Empire in which it will be established, it shall be transmitted with the sacred imperial letters, it shall be received in the bureaus of the other part of the Empire also, and it shall be published with the due formality of edicts. For a law that has been sent must be accepted and must undoubtedly be valid, and the power to emend and to revoke shall be reserved to Our Clemency. Moreover, the laws must be mutually announced, and they must not be admitted otherwise. (Etc.)

Given on the seventh day before the kalends of April at Constantinople in the year of the consulship of Florentius and Dionysus.—March 26, 429.

†

I.4.3. Emperors Theodosius and Valentinian Augustuses to the Senate of the City of Rome.:

(After other matters.) We confirm all the writings of Papinian, Paulus, Gaius, Ulpian and Modestinus, so that the same authority shall attend Gaius as Paulus, Ulpian and the others, and passages from the whole body of his writings may be cited. 1. We also decree to be valid the learning of those persons whose treatises and opinions all the aforesaid jurisconsults have incorporated in their own works, such as Scaevola, Sabinus, Julianus, and Marcellus, and all others whom they cite, provided that, on account of the uncertainty of antiquity, their books shall be confirmed by a collation of the codices. 2. Moreover, when conflicting opinions are cited, the greater number of the authors shall prevail, or if the numbers should be equal, the authority of that group shall take precedence in which the man of superior genius, Papinian, shall tower above the rest, and as he defeats a single opponent, so he yields to two. 3. As was formerly decreed, We also order to be invalidated the notes which Paulus and Ulpian made upon the collected writings of Papinian. 4. Furthermore, when their opinions as cited are equally divided and their authority is rated as equal, the regulation of the judge shall choose whose opinion he shall follow. 5. We order that the Sentences of Paulus also shall be valid. (Etc.)

Given on the eighth day before the Ides of November at Ravenna in the year of the twelfth consulship of Our Lord Theodosius Augustus and the second consulship of Our Lord Valentinian Augustus–November 6 (7), 426.

✝

I.16.4. *Emperor Constantine Augustus to Maximus:*

If any very powerful and arrogant person should arise, and the governors of the provinces are not able to punish him or to examine the case or to pronounce sentence, they must refer his name to Us, or at least to the knowledge of Your Gravity. Thus provision shall be made for consulting the interests of public discipline and the oppressed lower classes. (Etc.)

Given on the fourth day before the kalends of January at Trier in the year of the consulship of Januarinus and Justus–December 29, 328 (?)

I.16.7. *Emperor Constantine Augustus to the Provincials:*

The rapacious hand of the apparitors[1] shall immediately cease, they shall cease, I say; for if after due warning they do not cease, they shall be cut off by the sword. The chamber curtain of the judge shall not be venal; entrance shall not be gained by purchase, the private council chamber shall not be infamous on account of the bids. The appearance of the governor shall not be at a price; the ears of the judge shall be open equally to the poorest as well as to the rich. There shall be no despoiling on the occasion of escorting persons inside by the one who is called chief of the office staff. The assistants of the aforesaid chiefs of office staff shall employ no extortion on litigants; the intolerable onslaught of the centurions and other apparitors who demand small and great sums shall be crushed; and the unsated greed of those who deliver the records of a case to litigants shall be restrained. 1. Always shall the diligence of the governor guard lest anything be taken from a litigant by the aforesaid classes of men. If they should suppose that anything ought to be demanded by them from those involved in civil cases, armed punishment will be at hand, which will cut off the heads and necks of the scoundrels. Opportunity shall be granted to all persons who have suffered extortion to provide for an investigation by the governors. If they should dissemble, We hereby open to all persons the right to express complaints about such conduct before the counts of the provinces or before the praetorian prefects, if they are closer at hand, so that We may be informed by their references to Us and may provide punishment for such brigandage.

Given on the kalends of November at Constantinople in the year of the consulship of Bassus and Ablavius–November 1, 331.

II.14.1. *Emperors Arcadius and Honorius Augustuses to Messala, Praetorian Prefect:*

We have observed that many men, in desperation because of the injustice of their cases, oppose to those by whom they are summoned into court notices of title of powerful persons

---

[1]Staff officers who controlled access to provincial governors.

and the prerogatives of the Most Noble dignity. 1. Lest in fraud of the laws and to the terror of adversaries, they misuse these names and notices of title, those persons who knowingly connive at trickery of this kind shall be branded with infamy by public sentence. 2. But if such powerful persons have in no wise given their consent that statements of claim or notices of title in their names should be affixed to the houses of others, such punishment shall be inflicted on those who commit such acts that they shall be flogged with leaden scourges and consigned to the perpetual punishment of labor in the mines. 3. Therefore, when a person is sued at law, if he believes that the name of another should be inserted in the answering statements or notices of title, although he is himself the possessor of the property in dispute and of the legal right thereto and although he himself receives the notice of the legal action which is formally brought against him, he shall be penalized by the forfeiture of the possession and of the case that he has tried to maintain or to evade under cover of this fraud. He shall not have the right to renew the action, even though the merits of a good case support him. 4. Those persons shall certainly be branded as prodigal of their reputation and as trafficking in chicanery who willingly allow their names to be inserted in lawsuits of others, although they are legally entitled to neither ownership nor possession.

Given on the fifth day before the kalends of December at Milan in the year of the consulship of the Most Noble Stilicho.—November 27, 400.

†

III.1.9. Emperors Honorius and Theodosius Augustuses to the People:

We command that sales, gifts, and compromises which have been extorted through the exercise of power shall be invalidated.

Given on the thirteenth day before the kalends of March at Constantinople in the year of the tenth consulship of Honorius Augustus and the sixth consulship of Theodosius Augustus—February 17, 415.

†

IX.1.1. Emperor Constantine Augustus to Octavianus, Count of Spain:

If any person of Most Noble rank should rape a maiden or invade the boundaries of another or be apprehended in any wrongdoing or crime, he shall immediately be subjected to the public laws, within the province wherein he perpetrated the offense. Neither shall his name be referred to Our knowledge nor shall he make use of any prescription of forum, for an accusation excludes all prerogatives of rank when a criminal case, not a civil or pecuniary suit, is brought.

Given on the day before the nones of December at Sofia (Serdica) —December 4, (316). Received on the fifth day before the nones of March at Cordoba in the year of the consulship of Gallicanus and Bassus.—March 3, 317.

†

XVI.1.2. Emperors Gratian, Valentinian, and Theodosius Augustuses: An Edict to the People of the City of Constantinople:

It is Our will that all the peoples who are ruled by the administration of Our Clemency shall practice that religion which the divine Peter the Apostle transmitted to the Romans, as the religion which he introduced makes clear even unto this day. It is evident that this is the religion that is followed by the Pontiff Damasus and by Peter, Bishop of Alexandria, a man of apostolic sanctity; that is, according to the apostolic discipline and the evangelic doctrine, we shall believe in the single Deity of the Father, the Son, and the Holy Spirit, under the concept of equal majesty and of the Holy Trinity.

1. We command that those persons who follow this rule shall embrace the name of Catholic Christians. The rest, however, whom We adjudge demented and insane, shall sustain the infamy of heretical dogmas, their meeting places shall not receive the name of churches, and they shall be smitten first by divine vengeance and secondly by the retribution of Our own initiative, which We shall assume in accordance with the divine judgment.

Given on the third day before the kalends of March at Thessalonica in the year of the fifth consulship of Gratian Augustus and the first consulship of Theodosius Augustus.—February 28, 380.

†

XVI.5.26. Emperors Arcadius and Honorius Augustuses to Rufinus, Praetorian Prefect:

None of the heretics, who are now restrained by innumerable laws of our sainted father, shall dare to assemble unlawful gatherings and to contaminate with profane mind the mystery of Almighty God, either publicly or privately, secretly or openly. None shall dare to appropriate the title of bishop or, with polluted mind, to arrogate to himself the ecclesiastical order and their most sacred titles.

Given on the third day before the kalends of April at Constantinople in the year of the consulship of Olybrius and Probinus.—March 30, 395.

†

B. THE LOMBARD LAWS

1. That man who conspires or gives counsel against the life of the king shall be killed and his property confiscated.

2. He who receives counsel from the king concerning another's death or kills a man by the king's order, shall be entirely without blame. Neither he nor his heirs shall suffer any payment or trouble at any time from that one [the man conspired against] or his heirs. For since we believe that the heart of the king is in the hand of God, it is inconceivable that anyone whose death the king has ordered could be entirely free of guilt.

3. He who tries to flee outside of the country shall be killed and his property confiscated.

4. He who invites or introduces enemies into our land shall be killed and his property confiscated.

5. He who hides a spy (*scamaras*) within the land or gives him provisions shall either be killed or shall pay 900 solidi as compensation to the king.

6. That one who while on campaign raises a revolt against his duke or against him appointed by the king to command the army, or

the one who raises a revolt in any part of the army, shall be killed.

7. He who during a battle with the enemy abandons his comrade or betrays him and does not remain with him, shall be killed.

13. He who kills his lord (*dominus*) shall be killed himself. The man who tries to defend this murderer who killed his lord shall pay 900 solidi as compensation, half to the king and half to the relatives of the dead man. And he who refuses aid in avenging the man's death, if his aid is sought, shall pay fifty solidi as compensation, half to the king and half to the man to whom he refused aid.

15. On grave breaking (*crapworfin*). He who breaks into the grave of a dead man and despoils the body and throws it out shall pay 900 solidi to the relatives of the dead. And if there are no near relatives, then the king's gestald or schultheis shall exact this penalty and collect it for the king's court.

17. If one of our men wishes to come to us, let him come in safety and return to his home unharmed; let none of his enemies presume to cause any injury or harm to him on the journey. It shall be done thus in order that he who hastens to come to the king may come openly and receive no injury or damage of any sort on that journey while coming to the king and returning. He who does cause such injury shall pay compensation as is provided below in this code [Rothair 148].

18. He who, in order to avenge some injury or damage, attacks with arms one of his enemies who is on his way to the king, shall pay 900 solidi, half to the king and half to him who bore the injury.

35. On breach of the peace (*scandalum*). He who creates a disturbance (*scandalum*) in a church shall pay forty solidi to that venerable place in addition to [the composition paid] him who suffered the wounds or injuries. The abovementioned forty solidi shall be collected by the schultheis or judge of the district and laid on the holy altar of that church where the offense occurred.

36. He who dares to create a disturbance (*scandalum*) within the king's palace when the

king is present shall lose his life unless he can redeem his life from the king.

40. The slave who creates a disturbance in another district [where the king is not present] shall pay three solidi to the royal fisc. That one, however, who inflicts wounds or injuries shall pay six solidi to the fisc in addition to paying compensation for the wounds or injuries to him who suffered them.

41. Concerning the beating of a freeman. If anyone, by himself or with the aid of someone else, plans an ambush against some freeman who is simply standing or walking along unprepared, and if they seize him disgracefully and beat him without the king's command, then, since they treated the man shamefully and with derision, they shall pay as compensation half of the wergeld which they would have paid had they killed him.

49. On cutting off noses. He who cuts off another man's nose shall pay half of that one's wergeld as compensation.

50. On cutting off lips. He who cuts off another man's lip shall pay sixteen solidi as compensation. And if one, two or three teeth are thereby exposed, he shall pay twenty solidi as compensation.

51. Concerning the front teeth. He who knocks out another man's tooth—one of those which appear when smiling—shall pay sixteen solidi as compensation for one tooth. If two or more of such teeth which appear in smiling are knocked out, the compensation shall be computed to this assessment for each one.

52. Concerning the jaw teeth. He who knocks out one or more molars shall pay eight solidi as compensation for each tooth.

75. Concerning the death of a child in its mother's womb. If a child is accidentally killed while still in its mother's womb, and if the woman is free and lives, then her value shall be measured in accordance with her rank, and compensation for the child shall be paid at half the sum at which the mother is valued. But if the mother dies, then compensation must be paid for her according to her rank in addition to the payment of compensation for the child killed in her womb. But thereafter the feud shall cease since the deed was done unintentionally.

76. Concerning the half-free (*aldii*) and the household slaves (*servi ministeriales*). We call those "household slaves" who have been taught, nourished, and trained in the home.

77. He who strikes another's aldius or household slave so that the wound or bruise is apparent shall pay one solidus as compensation for one blow. He who strikes two blows shall pay two solidi. He who strikes three, three solidi. He who strikes four shall pay four solidi. If, however, more blows than this were endured, they shall not be counted.

78. He who strikes another's aldius or household slave on the head so that the bones are not broken shall pay two solidi compensation for one blow. He who strikes two blows shall pay four solidi; in addition he shall pay for the work lost and the doctor's fee. If, however, he inflicts more blows than this against the head, they shall not be counted.

328. In the case where an animal kills or injures someone else's animal—that is, if an ox injures or kills an ox or any other animal— we order that the man whose animal was injured or incapacitated or otherwise weakened turn the injured animal over to him whose animal injured it. And he shall receive in return from that one whose animal caused the injury another animal of the same kind and value as the injured one was at the time it was hurt.

329. On stolen dogs. He who steals a dog shall return it nine-fold.

330. If a man in defending himself kills another man's dog with a broad sword or with a staff or with any other weapon which is held in the hand, nothing shall be required of him so long as the weapon is simply a staff or medium-sized sword. But the man who throws a weapon at a dog and kills it shall return it singlefold, that is, he shall return a dog of similar sort.

331. If a man finds another man's dog causing damage in his house by day or night and kills it, nothing shall be required from him. If it is not killed, its master shall restore the damage which it caused.

332. On cows in calf. He who strikes a cow in calf and causes a miscarriage shall pay one tremissus as compensation. If the cow dies, he shall pay for it the price at which it is valued, and in addition he shall pay for the calf.

333. On mares in foal. He who strikes a mare in foal and causes a miscarriage shall pay one solidus as compensation. If the mare dies, he shall pay as above for it and its young.

334. On pregnant woman slaves. He who strikes a woman slave large with child and causes a miscarriage shall pay three solidi as compensation. If, moreover, she dies from the blow, he shall pay compensation for her and likewise for the child who died in her womb.

13.VII. On the killing of freemen. If a Lombard is killed by another man (which God forbid), and according to law it is a case where compensation should be paid and if he who is killed does not leave a son: although we have [earlier] established that daughters could be heirs, just as if they were boys, to all the property of their father or mother [Liutprand 1], nevertheless we decree here [in this case] that the nearest [male] relatives of him who was killed–those who can succeed him within the proper degree of relationship–shall receive that compensation. For daughters, since they are of the feminine sex, are unable to raise the feud. Therefore we provide that the daughters not receive that compensation, but, as we have said, the above-mentioned [male] relatives [ought to have it]. If there are no near [male] relatives, then the daughters themselves shall receive half of that compensation, whether there is one or more of them, and half [shall be received] by the king's treasury.

✝

C. THE CAPITULARY OF MEERSEN

In 847, the Frankish kingdom, enduring civil war and foreign invasion, faced a problem with refugees: vagabonds were a major social problem. The difficulty was how to control this rootless population in a world with virtually no police and almost nothing we would recognize as "social services." The three grandsons of Charlemagne hit on this solution. How is it similar to arrangement you have seen in the Theodosian Code and the Lombard Laws? What does it tell you about government and society in the medieval west?

We will moreover that each free man in our kingdom shall choose a lord, from us or our faithful, such a one as he wishes.

We command moreover that no man shall leave his lord without just cause, nor should any one receive him, except in such a way as was customary in the time of our predecessors.

And we wish you to know that we want to grant right to our faithful subjects and we do not wish to do anything to them against reason. Similarly we admonish you and the rest of our faithful subjects that you grant right to your men and do not act against reason toward them.

And we will that the man of each one of us in whosoever kingdom he is, shall go with his lord against the enemy, or in his other needs unless there shall have been (as may there not be!) such an invasion of the kingdom as is called a *landwer*, so that the whole people of that kingdom shall go together to repel it.

✝

4. THE SONG OF ROLAND

The last hero you will meet in this book is a product of the new civilization that emerged in western Europe after the fall of Rome. The "Song of Roland" is based on events that occurred in A.D. 778, but the version we have was not composed until several hundred years later, at the very end of our period of study. As usual, history has taken a beating in the process: Charlemagne, for instance, who appears here as a venerable 200-year-old figure, was only 38 at the time it occurred, and he was fighting in Spain as an ally, not an enemy, of the Moslem princes. The treacherous attack on Roland was carried out by Christian Basques, not perfidious Moslems. But we do not study heroic tales for historical evidence of this sort. Rather, we do so to extrapolate values and concerns that will help us to distinguish and understand the society that produced the tale. What evidence of this sort can you find in the *Song of Roland*?

1. Charles the King, our great emperor, has been in Spain for seven full years; he has conquered all the upland right down to the seashore and not a castle can stand before him; neither wall nor city remains to be destroyed except Saragossa, which is built in a mountain. King Marsilie rules in Saragossa; he does not love God, he worships Mahomet and calls

upon Apollin.[1] He has no protection against all the evil which is about to come upon him.

2. King Marsilie was in Saragossa. He has gone into an orchard beneath the shade and has laid himself down on a slab of blue marble, and round about him are more than twenty thousand of his men. He calls his dukes and his counts to him: "Listen, my lords, what a calamity threatens us: The emperor Charles of fair France has come into this land to destroy us. I have no army capable of giving him battle, nor are my people such that they can break his to pieces. Counsel me, as wise men, and save me from death and dishonor." Not a heathen replied a single word save Blancandrin of the Castle of Valfonde.

3. Blancandrin was one of the wisest of the heathen. He was a good knight for his valor and a prudent man to counsel his lord. And he said to the king: "Now be not dismayed! Send a message of faithful service and very great friendship to Charles, the proud and arrogant one; say that you will give him bears and lions and dogs, seven hundred camels and a thousand moulted falcons, four hundred mules laden with gold and silver and fifty wagons wherewith to form the convoy, and he will have the wherewithal in plenty to pay his soldiers. He has been fighting in this land long enough and he ought to return to Aix in France. Say that you will follow him at the feast of St. Michael and you will accept the Christian faith and will be his vassal in all loyalty. If he ask you for hostages you will send them, whether ten or twenty, as a pledge of your good faith. Let us send the sons of our own wives. It is far better that they should lose their heads than that we should lose our honor and our dignity and be reduced to beggary."

4. Blancandrin spake: "By this my right hand and by the beard that waves over my breast, you will very soon see the army of the Frenchmen brought to nought. The Franks will return to France, their own land, and when each one is at the abode of his choice, Charles will be at Aix in his chapel and he will be holding high revel at Michaelmastide. The day will come and the appointed time will pass, but of us no word and no news shall he

hear. The king is proud and his heart is wrathful, he will have our hostages beheaded. But it is far better that they lose their heads than that we should lose Spain, the bright and fair, and suffer evils and deprivations thereto." The heathen say: "Perhaps he speaks truth."

[Ambassadors from Marsilie make the offer to Charles at Cordoba; his knights oppose it, especially Count Roland, his nephew, who warns of treachery.]

14. The emperor has finished speaking. Count Roland, who does not agree with him, leaps up and begins to contradict him. He said to the king: "To your misfortune will you trust Marsilie! We came into Spain seven full years ago; I conquered Noples and Commibles for you, I took Valterne and the land of Pine and Balaguer, Tuele and Sezille. King Marsilie acted in very treacherous wise. He sent fifteen of his heathen, each one carrying an olive branch, and they said these very same words to you. You took counsel with your Frenchmen and they advised you very unwisely. You sent two of your counts to the heathen; one was Basan and the other Basille. He took off both their heads in the mountains beneath Haltilie. Carry on the war as you have begun it. Lead your army in battle array to Saragossa, besiege it for the rest of your life and avenge those whom the felon had murdered."

15. The emperor sat with bowed head. He stroked his beard and smoothed his moustache and gave his nephew no answer, either good or bad. The Frenchmen are silent—save Ganelon only. He jumped to his feet and came before Charles and began to speak very fiercely. And he said to the king: "To your misfortune you will listen to a fool, whether me or any other man, if it be not to your profit. When Marsilie tells you that he will become your vassal with clasped hands, and will hold all Spain as a gift from you; that he will accept the faith that we hold—whoever he be who advises you to reject this offer, sire, little he cares by what death we die. It is no right that a counsel of pride proceed any further; let us leave the fools and listen only to the wise."

16. Then Naimes came forward; in all the court there was no better vassal than he. And he said to the king: "You have heard the answer that Ganelon the count has given you.

---

[1] I.e., Apollo.

There is wisdom in it if it be rightly understood. King Marsilie is defeated in war: you have taken all his strongholds, you have broken down his walls with your stonethrowers, you have burnt his cities and defeated his army. Now that he requests you to have mercy on him, it would be a crime to do anything further against him…. And since he is willing to give you hostages as a pledge, this great war ought not to go on any longer." The Frenchmen say: "The duke has spoken well."

[On Roland's advice, Charles chooses Ganelon as his ambassador to Marsilie–a dangerous mission. Irate, Ganelon vows revenge.]

25. The emperor hands him the glove from his right hand but count Ganelon would gladly not have been there. When he should have taken it, he let it fall to the ground. The Frenchmen say "God, what can this mean? Great loss will come to us from this message." "Sirs," said Ganelon, "you will hear tidings of it."

27. Ganelon the count goes to his dwelling and begins to get ready his armor, the very best that he can find. He has fixed golden spurs to his feet and he girds his sword Murgleis to his side. He has mounted Tachebrun, his battle-steed, and his uncle Guinemer held the stirrups for him. And there you might have seen many knights weeping, and they say to him: "Your valor was ill-fated. You have been long at the king's court and you have always been acclaimed a noble warrior. The one who proposed that you should go will not be saved or protected by Charlemaine. Count Roland ought not to have thought of it, for you are descended from a right noble stock." And then they say: "Sire, take us with you!" But Ganelon replies: "God forbid! It is better that I should die alone than that so many good knights should lose their lives. Go back to dear France, my lords; salute my wife for me and Pinabel my friend and peer, and Baldwin my son whom you all know; protect him and consider him your lord." And so he gets on his way and begins his journey.

28. Ganelon is riding beneath a high olive-grove. He has joined himself to the Saracen messengers, and he and Blancandrin fall a little way behind. And they talk to each other in

very cunning wise. Says Blancandrin: "Charles is a wonderful man. He has conquered Apulia and all Calabria, he has crossed the salt sea to England and has taken tribute for the use of St. Peter; what does he want here in our country?" Ganelon replies: "Such is his pleasure. There will never be a man who can stand against him."

29. Said Blancandrin: "The Franks are very gallant men. But these dukes and counts do much harm to their lord when they advise him such things. Both he himself and others are worn out and ruined thereby." Ganelon replies: "Indeed I know of no one except Roland who is to blame, and it will be to his confusion. Yesterday the emperor was sitting in the shade, and up comes his nephew, still clad in his byrnie[1] and bringing the booty which he had obtained round about Carcassone. In his hand he held a crimson apple, and he said to his uncle: 'Take it, fair sir. I present you with the crowns of all the kings.' His own pride will bring him to nought, for he risks his own life everyday. If someone else would only kill him, then we should have universal peace."

30. Said Blancandrin: "What a bad man is this Roland who wishes to defeat all nations and challenges all other lands. By what people does he hope to accomplish so much?" Ganelon replies: "By the French people. They love him so much that they will never fail him; he gives them so many gifts of gold and silver, mules and warhorses, silken cloths and armor. The emperor himself gets all that he wants from him, for he will conquer the lands for him from here to the East."

31. Ganelon and Blancandrin rode along together until they had pledged their faith each to the other that they would do their utmost to kill Roland. They rode along the main roads and the by-paths until they dismounted beneath a yew-tree in Saragossa. There was a throne placed there beneath the shadow of a pine; it was enveloped in the silken cloth of Alexandria, and upon it was seated the king who held all Spain. Round about him are twenty thousand Saracens, and not one of them uttered a sound or a word, so anxious were they for the news they were about to

---

[1] A coat of mail.

hear. And now Ganelon and Blancandrin approach.

[Ganelon delivers Charles' terms, and Blancandrin tells Marsilie of their plot.]

42. Spake the Saracen: "I am much surprised concerning Charlemaine, who is white and hoary! To my knowledge he is more than two hundred years old. He has been a conqueror in so many lands, he has received so many blows from good sharp-edged lances, he has slain so many strong kings or conquered them in battle; when will he be tired of waging warfare?" "Never," replied Ganelon, "as long as Roland lives, for there is not such a vassal from here to the East. Exceedingly valiant too is Oliver, his companion, and the twelve peers whom Charles loves so dearly and who form the vanguard with twenty thousand Franks. Charles is safe for he need fear no man alive."

43. "Fair Sir Ganelon," said King Marsilie, "my people are such that you will never see a nobler race; I can put four hundred thousand knights into the field—can I fight against Charles and the Frenchmen?" Ganelon replies: "You have no chance this time! You would lose a great many of your heathen. Put aside foolish counsel and cleave to wisdom. Give the emperor such great gifts that there will not be a Frenchman who does not marvel at them. By reason of twenty hostages whom you will send to him the king will return to fair France; but he will leave his rearguard behind him, and count Roland his nephew will be in it—of this I am certain—and Oliver the brave and courteous. The counts are dead men, if my words are believed, and Charles will see the fall of his great pride. He will never wish to fight against you anymore."

44. "Fair Sir Ganelon.... How can I destroy Roland?" "I can easily tell you that," replied Ganelon. "The king will be at the major passes of Sizer; he will have left behind him his rearguard in which is his nephew, the powerful Roland, and Oliver in whom he has such faith. They have twenty thousand Franks in their company. Now do you send a hundred thousand of your heathen and let these engage them first in battle. The men of France will be wounded and harassed, and of yours too (for I must not hide the fact) there will be great

slaughter. Then you will attack them a second time and in the same way, and Roland will not escape in whichever battle he perish. Then you will have accomplished a noble piece of knighthood and you will have no more war all your life."

45. "If anyone could compass Roland's death Charles would lose the right arm from his body and the marvelous armies would cease to exist. Charles would never get together so large a force again and the Land of the Ancients would rest in peace." When Marsilie heard this he kissed him on the neck, and straightaway he began to have his treasures brought out.

46. Then said Marsilie: "An agreement is of no use unless (it be pledged)....You will have to swear to me that you will betray Roland." Ganelon replied: "Let this be as you wish." On the relics of his sword Murgleis he swore to the treason, and thus the crime was committed.

[Ganelon returns to Charles and gets him to appoint Roland to hold the pass; meanwhile, twelve pagan champions, led by Marsilie's nephew, are chosen to lead the Saracen horde.]

68. Charlemaine cannot keep himself from weeping. A hundred thousand Frenchmen are filled with tenderness for him and with a dreadful fear for Roland. Ganelon the traitor has betrayed him; he has received large gifts in payment from the heathen king, gold and silver, rugs and silken cloths, mules and horses and camels and lions. Marsilie calls together the barons of Spain, the counts, the viscounts, the dukes, the almaçours,[1] the amirafles and the sons of the contors.[2] Four hundred thousand he puts in battle array in three days. Then he has tambours sounded throughout Saragossa and he hoists Mahomet up to the highest tower; there is not a heathen who does not pray to him and adore him. Then they set out and ride at full speed, across the Terre Certeine and the valley and the mountains until they see the banners of those of France. The rearguard of the twelve companions will not fail to give them battle.

---

[1]Saracen grandees.
[2]I.e., conders, ships' pilots.

79. The heathen arm themselves with their Saracen hauberks, most of which are of triple thickness. They lace their good helmets of Saragossa and they gird their swords of Viennese steel. They have noble shields and Valencian lances, and battle standards of white and blue and red. They leave their mules and ride in serried ranks. The day was fair and the sun shone brightly and they have not a piece of armor that does not reflect its rays. A thousand trumpets sound to make the scene yet more beautiful. The noise is great and the Frenchmen hear it. Said Oliver: "Sir comrade, I feel sure that we shall have battle with the Saracens." Roland replies: "And may God grant it! For one's lord one ought to suffer hardship and endure both great heat and great cold and lose one's skin and one's hair. Now let each see that he strikes hard blows, that an evil song never be sung about us! The heathens are in the wrong and the Christians in the right. Never shall a bad example come from me."

80. Oliver is mounted on a hillock and he looks towards the right through a grassy valley and sees the heathen army approaching. He calls Roland his comrade: "I see such a commotion coming from the direction of Spain, so many bright hauberks and shining helmets! This army will bring much anguish upon our Frenchmen. Ganelon knew it—the felon, the traitor, who chose us out before the emperor." "Be silent, Oliver," count Roland replies; "He is my stepfather, I do not wish you to say a word about it."

81. Oliver has mounted on a hillock and he can clearly see the kingdom of Spain and the Saracens who are assembled in such large numbers. Their helmets, which are set with gold, glisten, their shields too and their embroidered hauberks, their lances and their folded pennons. He cannot even count their formations, for there are so many that one cannot number them. He is much disturbed in mind as he looks at them; as quickly as possible he descends the hill and comes to the Frenchmen and tells them all.

82. Said Oliver: "I have seen the heathen; never has any man on earth seen a greater number of them. There are a hundred thousand of them in front of us, with shields and laced helmets, and clad in shining hauberks; their polished lances glitter as they hold the hafts erect. You will have a battle such as there never was before. Sir Frenchmen, may you have strength from God! Stand firm, that we be not vanquished!" The Frenchmen say: "Cursed be he who flees! Never will one of us fail you for fear of death."

83. Said Oliver: "The heathen are in great force, and it seems to me there are very few of our Frenchmen! Comrade Roland, sound your horn; Charles will hear it and the army will return." Roland replies: "I should act like a madman! I should lose my renown in sweet France. I will strike hard blows with Durendal without delay; the blade will be stained with blood right up to the golden hilt. To their misfortune the felon heathen came to the passes; I warrant you that they are all appointed to death."

86. Said Oliver: "I know of no reproach in this. I myself have seen the Saracens of Spain: the valleys and the mountains are covered with them, the open country and all the plains. Great are the armies of this foreign people and we have but a very small company." Roland replies: "My desire grows greater on that account. May it not please God nor His angels that France ever lose her worth on my account! I would rather die than be overtaken by dishonor. The better we strike the more the emperor will love us."

87. Roland is valiant and Oliver is wise. Both of them have marvelous courage. When once they are mounted and armed they will never avoid the battle for fear of death. They are noble counts and their words are bold. The felon heathen are riding fiercely. Said Oliver: "Roland, look in front of you now. The heathen are close to us, but Charles is far away. You did not deign to sound your horn; if the king were here we should take no harm. Look up towards the Spanish passes; you can see, the rearguard is in a sad plight. He who fights in the rearguard today will never fight in another one." Roland replies: "Speak not so rashly! Cursed be the heart which quakes within the breast! We will make a firm stand on the spot, and we shall be the ones to strike and attack."

88. When Roland sees that the battle will take place he becomes fiercer than a lion or a leopard. He calls aloud to the French, and he summons Oliver: "Sir comrade, friend, say no such thing! The emperor who left the French with us put ten thousand men on one side amongst whom he knew there was not a single coward. For one's lord one ought to suffer great hardships and be able to endure excessive cold or heat—yea, one ought to be ready to lose one's blood and one's flesh. Strike with thy lance and I will strike with Durendal, my good sword that the king gave me. If I die on the battlefield, he who has it after me will be able to say that it belonged to a noble vassal."

89. Elsewhere in the field is the archbishop Turpin. He spurs his horse and mounts a bare spot of high ground; he calls the Frenchmen to him and these are the words he spake: "Sir barons, Charles has left us here; it is fitting that we should die for our king. Help to maintain the Christian faith! You will have battle, you are quite certain of it with your own eyes you see the Saracens. Confess your sins and pray God for His mercy. I will absolve you for the salvation of your souls. If you die you will be holy martyrs; you will have seats in greater paradise." The Frenchmen dismount and kneel on the ground; the archbishop has blessed them in God's name and he bids them strike hard as penance for their sins.

[The battle begins.]

93. The nephew of Marsilie—Aelroth by name—rides first in advance of the army. And as he rides he says evil words of our Frenchmen: "Ye felon Franks, today you shall joust with us. The one who should have protected you has betrayed you and the king was mad to leave you behind in the passes. Today sweet France will lose her reputation and Charlemaine will lose the right arm from his body." When Roland heard this, God! how angry he was! He spurs his horse and puts it to the gallop and strikes at the heathen to the utmost of his force. He breaks his shield and tears open his hauberk, he cuts open his breast and breaks all his bones and cleaves him to the chine. He makes an exit for the soul with his lance. He has driven it in deeply and made the heathen's body totter and the length of his haft he has hurled him dead from his horse.

He has broken his neck in two halves; but he cannot refrain from speaking to him: "Begone, son of a slave! Charles is by no means mad, nor did he ever tolerate treason. He acted like a brave man when he left us at the passes. Sweet France will not lose her reputation today. Strike, Frenchmen, the first blow is ours! The right is on our side and these felons are in the wrong."

[More people die.]

95. There is a king there, Corsablix by name, from Barbary a distant land. He called to the rest of the Saracens: "We can well sustain this battle for there are very few Frenchmen, and we need only have contempt for those who are here. Not one of them will ever have any protection from Charles; this is the day on which they must die." Archbishop Turpin heard him distinctly, and there is no man beneath the sky for whom his hatred could be greater. He pricks his horse with the spurs of fine gold and rides to strike him with all his force. He breaks his shield and tears his hauberk to pieces and drives his great lance right through the body. He has his lance firmly in his grasp and he shakes the dead man on it; then the length of his haft he hurls him on the path. He looks down and sees the felon lying on the ground and he will not refrain from addressing him: "Heathen, son of a slave," says he, "you have lied! Charles, my master, is our protection at all times. Our men of France have no desire to flee until all your companions remain on this spot. I tell you this news, you will have to suffer death. Strike men of France! Let no one forget himself. This first blow is ours, God be thanked!" And he cries Montjoie so as to hold the field.

[Lots more people die.]

128. Count Roland sees the great slaughter of his men and he calls his companion Oliver and he says to him: "Fair sir, dear comrade, for God's sake, what do you think? You see so many good vassals lying on the ground; we ought to weep for the sweet land of fair France! Henceforward it will be destitute of such barons. Ah! king, friend, why are you not here? Oliver, my brother, how can we do it? How can we send him news?" Said Oliver: "I

do not know how to set about it. Better that we die than that we be spoken of shamefully."

129. Roland said: "I will sound the horn, and Charles will hear it as he crosses the defiles; I warrant you the Franks will return." Said Oliver: "It would be a great disgrace and a reproach to all your family and the shame of it would last all their lives. When I told you to do it, you would not; and now you will not do it with my consent! If you sound your horn now it will not be an act of courage and already both your arms are covered with blood." The count replied: "I have struck some noble blows."

130. Roland said: "It is a hard battle. I will blow the horn and Charles the king will hear it." Said Oliver: "It would not be an act of valor. When I told you to do it comrade, you thought it unworthy. If the king had been here we should have suffered no loss—but we cannot blame those who are over there for it." And Oliver spoke again: "By this my beard, if I see my gentle sister Aude, you shall never lie in her embrace!"

131. Then said Roland: "Why are you angry with me?" And he replied: "Comrade, it was your fault, for valor tempered with sense is not a foolish thing and moderation is worth more than pride. The French are dead because of your thoughtlessness and Charles will never have service from us again. If you had listened to me, my lord had been here. This battle would have been won and king Marsilie either dead or a prisoner. Your prowess, Roland, has been our undoing. We shall not fight again for Charles, the great emperor, who will never have his equal till the day of judgment. You will die here and France will be disgraced. Today our faithful comradeship must end; there will be a sorrowful parting before the fall of night."

132. The archbishop heard them disputing, so he pricked his horse with his spurs of pure gold and came up to them and began to rebuke them: "Sir Roland, and you, Sir Oliver, for God's sake I beg you not to blame each other. Sounding the horn could not save you now; nevertheless it is better that you do it, that the king may come and be able to avenge us. The Spaniards must never return home

rejoicing. Our Frenchmen will dismount from their horses; they will find us dead and mutilated; they will place us on biers on beasts of burdens and will bury us in the cloisters of their chapels. We shall not be devoured by wolves and pigs and dogs." Roland replies: "Sir, you speak well."

133. Roland has put the horn to his mouth; he grasps it firmly and sounds it with all his might. High are the hills, and the voice carries a long way—a good thirty away the echo was heard. Charles heard it and all his companies. And the king said: "Our men are fighting!" But Ganelon answered: "If anyone else had said that, I should have called it a lie."

134. Count Roland, with difficulty and effort and much suffering sounds his horn. The bright blood leaps forth from his mouth and he has broken the temple of his forehead. The sound of the horn he holds carries very far and Charles hears it as he crosses the border. Duke Naimes heard it too, and the French listened to it. Then said the king: "I hear the horn of Roland! He would never sound it unless he were fighting!" Ganelon replies: "There is no battle! You are old and hoary and white; by words such as these you resemble a child. You know well Roland's great pride. It is amazing that God suffers it so long. He captured Noples without your permission—the Saracens came forth out of the town and fought a battle with good vassal Roland, and afterwards he washed the bloodstained meadows with water in order to remove all trace of it! He sounds his horn all day for nothing more than a hare; he is boasting now before his peers that there is not an army under the sky that would dare meet him in the field. Ride on; why are you stopping here? The Land of the Ancients is still far in front of us."

135. Count Roland's mouth is bleeding and he has burst the temple of his forehead; he sounds his horn with pain and difficulty. Charles has heard it and the French have heard it too. The king said: "That horn has a long breath." Duke Naimes replies: "There is a baron in distress. A battle is going on, I know that well. It is the one who has betrayed him that bids you hesitate now. Arm yourself and sound your battle-cry, and go to the rescue of

your noble household. You can hear well enough that Roland is in difficulty."

137. The day has been fine and the evening glows brightly. Their armor flashes in the sunlight, hauberks and helmets shine like firs, their shields too which are painted with flowers, and the lances with their gilded pennons. The emperor rides in great wrath and the Frenchmen also are sad and angry; they all weep bitterly and are in great fear on account of Roland. The king commands that Ganelon be seized, and he hands him over to the cooks of his house. He calls Besgon, the head cook, and says to him: "Guard him well for me as such a felon deserves, for he has betrayed my household." Besgon receives him and set upon him with a hundred of his companions of the best and the worst of the kitchen. They tear out his beard and his moustache and each one strikes him four blows with his fist. They have beaten him well with stakes and sticks, then they put a chain on his neck and chained him up like a bear. They mounted him shamefully on a beast of burden and thus they kept him until such time as they should give him back to Charles.

[Meanwhile, back at the battle, lots more people die.]

157. The heathen say: "The emperor is returning. Listen to the trumpets of the men of France. If Charles comes we shall suffer great loss. If Roland lives, he will renew this war and we shall have lost Spain, our native land." Four hundred helmeted men, of those who are considered best on the battlefield, band themselves together, and deliver a very terrible attack on Roland. Now the count has enough to do on his own account.

158. Count Roland, when he sees them approaching, shows himself strong and proud and ready for the conflict. He will not turn in flight as long as he lives. He is seated on his horse called Veillantif; he spurs it forward with his golden spurs and rushes into the thick of the fight to attack them. Archbishop Turpin is close behind him, and they say to one another: "Forward, friend! we have heard the horns of those of France; Charles the mighty king, is on his way back."

159. Count Roland never loved a coward, nor a proud man, nor an ill-conditioned man—nor even a knight if he were not courageous. He called to archbishop Turpin: "Sire, you are on foot and I on horseback; out of love to you I will take my stand here and together we will suffer either good or evil. I will not abandon you for any mortal man. Even this attack of the heathen we will repulse, and the best blows shall be those of Durendal." Said the archbishop: "Dishonored be he who does not strike hard! Charles is returning and he will avenge us well."

160. The heathen say: "To our misfortune were we born! What a dreadful day has dawned for us today. We have lost our lords and our peers and now Charles the warrior, is returning with his great army. We can hear the trumpets of the Frenchmen quite distinctly and loud is the noise of their battle-cry Montjoie. Count Roland's spirit is so fierce that he will never be vanquished by mortal man. Let us aim at him from a distance and leave him on the field of battle." And so they aimed at him with their darts and their arrows, their spears and lances and feathered shafts. They have broken and pierced Roland's shield and torn and dismailed his hauberk; but his body within they have not touched. But they have wounded Veillantif in thirty places and have struck him dead beneath the count. Then the heathen flee and leave him standing there. Count Roland remains there dismounted and on foot.

161. The heathen flee in wrath and evil humour; they strive their utmost to make their way towards Spain. Count Roland has not the wherewithal to pursue them, for he has lost Veillantif, his warhorse and, will he nill he, he has to remain on foot. He went to the assistance of archbishop Turpin; he unlaced the gilded helmet from his head, he took off his white, supple hauberk, he tore his jerkin to pieces and stuffed the strips into his gaping wounds. Then he lifted him, pressing him gently against his breast, and laid him down tenderly on the green grass. Then in a gentle voice he said to him: "Noble lord, give me your permission to go! All our comrades whom we loved so dearly are dead and we cannot leave them there. I must go and search for them and pick them out and gather them

together here and range them before you."
The archbishop replied: "Go and return
hither! The field is yours, thank God, and
mine."

162. Roland departs and wanders over the
field by himself. He searches the valleys and
the hills....There he found Gerin and his
companion Gerier, and Berenger and Aton;
there too he found Anseis and Samson, and
the aged Girard de Roussillon. One by one the
baron brought them and came with them to
the archbishop and placed them in a row before his knees. The archbishop cannot refrain
from weeping; he raises his hand and gives
them his benediction. Then he says: "Ill-fated
you have been, lords! May the God of glory
receive your souls and place them in paradise
among the holy flowers! And now my own
death is causing me anguish; I shall never see
the great emperor again."

164. Count Roland, when he sees all his peers
dead, and Oliver too whom he loved so much,
was overcome with tenderness and he began to
weep. The color left his face and his grief was
so great that he could not stand. Whether he
will or no, he falls down in a swoon. The
archbishop said: "You have had an evil fate,
baron!"

165. The archbishop, when he saw that
Roland had fainted, was filled with such great
grief that never has there been greater. He
stretched out his hand and picked up the horn.
There is some running water in Roncevaux; he
tried to go to it that he might give some to
Roland. He sets out tottering, with little steps
and slow, he is so weak that he cannot go any
further. He has lost so much blood that he has
no strength. In shorter time than one would
take to cross an acre of ground, his heart failed
him and he fell to the ground. His death is
causing him great anguish.

166. Count Roland recovers from his swoon;
he gets up on his feet but his suffering is very
great. He looks down the valley and up the
slope; on the green grass, a little beyond his
comrades, he sees the noble baron lying, the
archbishop whom God placed here in his
name. He is confessing his sins and looking
upwards; with his hands clasped towards
heaven he prays God to grant him paradise.

Both by great battles and by very fine sermons
he was always a champion against the heathen.
May God grant him his holy benediction.

167. Count Roland sees the archbishop on the
ground; he sees his bowels lying outside his
body and his brains in a heap upon his forehead. Upon his breast, between the two shoulder blades, he has crossed his beautiful white
hands. Deeply Roland makes lament according to the custom of the land: "Ah! noble lord,
knight of gentle birth, today I commend thee
to the glorious God of heaven. Never will
there be a man who serves him more willingly.
Since the days of the apostles never has there
been such a prophet for upholding the faith
and for attracting men to it, May your soul
know no lack and may the door of paradise be
open to it!"

168. Roland feels that his own death is near;
his brain is issuing forth out of his ears. Concerning his peers he prays God that he will call
them to him, then on his own behalf he prays
to the angel Gabriel. He takes the horn that
he may have no reproach, and in the other
hand he takes Durendal his sword. Somewhat
further than a crossbow can shoot an arrow he
walks on the plough land in the direction of
Spain; he mounts on a hillock and there under
a fine tree there are four steps made of marble.
He has fallen face downwards on the green
grass and there he has lost consciousness for
death is very near.

177. Roland is dead; God has his soul in
heaven. The emperor arrives in Roncevaux—
there is not a road, not a path, not an ell nor a
square foot of free ground but either a
Frenchman or a heathen is lying on it. Charles
cries out: "Where are you, fair nephew? Where
is the archbishop? and Count Oliver? Where is
Gerin and his companion Gerier? Where is
Oton and the count Berenger? Where are Ivon
and Ivoire whom I loved so much? What has
become of Engelier the Gascon? Of Samson
the duke and the valiant warrior Anseis?
Where is the aged Girard of Roussillon, and
where are the twelve peers I left behind?" Of
what avail are his cries, for no one replies to
them? "God," said the king, "I am full of dis-
may that I was not here at the beginning of
the battle." He pulls his beard like a man in
great anguish, and all his baron knights weep;

twenty thousand of them swoon and fall to the ground. Naimes the duke is filled with pity for them.

[Charles pursues the retreating pagans.]

179. The emperor causes his trumpets to be sounded, then he rides forward valiantly with his great army. Those of Spain have their back turned towards them; the French pursue after them as one man. When the king sees that evening is falling, he dismounts in a meadow upon the green grass, lies down upon the ground and prays to the Lord God that he will cause the sun to stop in its course for him, that the night might tarry and the day remain. And behold, an angel, the one that was accustomed to speak to him, quickly gave him the command: "Ride, Charles, for the light shall not fail thee. Thou hast lost the flower of France—God knows this. But you may take your vengeance on these wicked people." At these words the emperor mounted his horse again.

180. God performed a very great miracle for Charlemaine, for the sun stood still. The heathen flee, the French pursue them; they come up to them in the Val Ténébreux, then force them fighting towards Saragossa. They slay them with mighty blows and cut them off from the tracks and the high roads. Now the river Ebro is in front of them; it is a very deep river, mysterious and swift, and no barge, nor swift galley, nor sloop is seen upon it. The heathen call but there is no protection for them. The armed men are the heaviest and they go straight down to the bottom in numbers; the others float down stream. The most fortunate have drunk in great abundance and at last they are all drowned in great anguish. The French cry out: "To your misfortune you saw Roland."

[Charles camps for the night; he is armed with his sword, "Joyeuse" (also called "Montjoie.")]

183. The emperor has lain down in a meadow. Beside his head the baron has put his great lance, for he did not wish to disarm himself that night. He is clothed in his white broidered hauberk, he has laced his helmet which is studded with gold, and he has girded on "Joyeuse," which never had its peer and each day reflects a score of different shades of light.

We know well the history of the lance wherewith our Lord was wounded on the cross; Charles has the point of it, by God's grace, and he has had it encased into the golden pommel of his sword. On account of this honor and this favor the name of "Joyeuse" was given to the sword. The French barons ought never to forget it; from that they have their battle-cry, Montjoie; and it is for this reason that no people can withstand them.

[Meanwhile, a great pagan force assembles, led by the emir Baligant from Babylon.]

190. Large are the armies of this accursed people. They set sail; they navigate and direct their course forward steadily; on the tops of the masts and on the high yardarms there are many lanterns, and stones which reflect the light. Up there, on high, they give forth such light by night that they make the sea more beautiful, and when they arrive at the land of Spain all the countryside is illuminated and lighted up by them. The news of their arrival reaches Marsilie.

191. The heathen army brook no delay. They leave the high sea, they reach the calm waters, they leave Marbrise and Marbrose behind them, right up to the Ebro they steer their ships. There are lanterns and brilliant stones in abundance, which give a bright light all the night, and in the morning they arrive in Saragossa.

192. The day is bright and the sun is shining. The emir has disembarked from his vessel. Espaneliz advances at his right hand, seventeen kings follow behind him, and I know not how many dukes and counts. Beneath a laurel in the middle of a field they throw a white silken rug upon the green grass. On it they place an ivory seat and the heathen Baligant takes his seat thereon. All the others remain standing. Their lord spoke first: "Charles the king, the emperor of the Franks, has no right to eat unless I give him leave. Throughout the whole of Spain he has carried on a great war against me. Now I intend to go and find him in fair France, and I will not give up the quest all my life until he is either dead or a fugitive." In pledge thereof he strikes his right glove upon his knee.

193. Now that he has said it, he is fixed in his determination that for all the gold beneath the sky he will not desist from going to Aix where Charles is wont to hold his court. His men applaud it and give him the same advice. Then he called two of his knights, one Clarifan the other Clarien by name: "you are the sons of king Maltraien who used to be a willing messenger. I command you to go to Saragossa. Tell Marsilie from me that I am come to help him against the French. If I come across their army there will be a great battle; give him as a pledge this glove pleated with gold and let him put it on his right hand. Take him this little staff of pure gold and bid him come to acknowledge his fief. I shall go to wage war on Charles in France. If he does not lie down at my feet and beg for mercy, and if he will not abandon the Christian faith, I will take the crown from his head." The heathen reply: "Sire, you have spoken well."

[Finding Marsilie in Saragossa, the messengers learn that Charles is still in Spain. Baligant determines to meet him in battle, and catches up with Charles as he visits the dead in Roncevaux.]

226. The emperor has dismounted from his horse and laid himself flat down upon the green grass. He turns his face towards the rising sun and calls upon God from his heart: "True father, defend me this day: Thou who didst deliver Jonas from the whale which had him in its body, and didst spare the king of Nineveh, and deliver Daniel from horrible suffering in the lion's den where he had been put, and the three youths from the fiery furnace! Let thy love be present with me this day! By thy mercy, if it please thee, grant that I may avenge my nephew Roland!" When he had prayed, he arose and made upon his head the sign that has such power. Then the king mounted on his swift steed; Naimes and Jozeran held his stirrup for him. He seizes his shield and his sharp-edged lance; he has a noble form, handsome and comely, and his countenance is open and good to look upon. Then he rides forward, firmly seated in his saddle, and a thousand trumpets sound behind him and before. The sound of the horn reverberates above all the others, and the French weep out of grief for Roland.

227. Very nobly the emperor rides. He has placed his beard outside his byrnie, and the others all do the same for the love of their lord; by this his hundred thousand Frenchmen can be recognized. They pass the mountains and the high rocks, the deep valleys and the terrible defiles; they traverse the passes and the deserted land, and enter into the region of Spain, where they establish themselves on an open piece of land. Baligant's advance-guards return to him and a Syrian told him the tidings: "We have seem the proud king Charles. His men are resolute and they will not fail him. Arm yourselves, we shall have battle before long!" Said Baligant: "These are the tidings of good vassals! Sound your horns that my heathen may know of it."

228. Then are the drums sounded throughout the army, and the bugles and the clear-voiced trumpets. The heathen dismount to arm themselves. The emir will not be behind them. He dons a byrnie with broidered lappets, he laces his helmet studded with gold; then he girds his sword to his left side. He has found a name for his sword in his pride: because of the sword of Charlemaine of which he has heard tell [he calls it "Précieuse"], and this is his battle-cry in the field which he has told his knights to shout. Round his neck he hangs one of his shields; it is large and wide, its buckle is of gold broidered with crystal; the strap is of good silk cloth ringed round. He grasps his spear which he calls "Maltet": the handle is as large as a club and the iron part alone would load a mule. Baligant has mounted his charger; Marcules from over-seas held the stirrup for him. A very large stride has the baron; he is slender at the thighs, but wide at the ribs. His chest is broad and he is well moulded; his shoulders are wide, his complexion is very clear, his face is proud and his waving hair is as white as the flowers in summer; concerning valor he is well proven. God! what a warrior, if he had been a Christian! He spurs his horse so that the bright blood pours forth; it bounds forward and leaps across a ditch a good fifty feet wide. The heathen cry: "This man ought to defend the borders! There is not a Frenchman who would not willy nilly lose his life if he met him in the fight. Charles is mad not to have departed ere now."

229. The emir looks a true baron. His beard is as white as a flower and he is very learned in the law of the land; in battle he is both fierce and proud. Very chivalrous too is his son Malpramis—he is tall and strong and takes after his ancestors. He said to his father: "Sire, let us advance! If we see Charles, I shall be much surprised." Said Baligant: "We shall see him, for he is very valiant. Many honorable things are told of him in several chronicles. But he no longer has his nephew Roland. He will not have the strength to hold out against us."

[Baligant surveys the pagan host.]

232. The emir rides amongst his troops and his son, tall of stature, follows him. The kings Torleu and Dapamort quickly form thirty army corps; each contains a marvelous number of knights and in the least of them there are fifty thousand. The first is formed of men of Butentrot; the next of large-headed men of Micenes who have bristles like pigs all along the backbone. The third is formed of Nuples and of Blos, the fourth of Bruns and Esclavons, the fifth of Sorbres and of Sors, the sixth of Armenians and Moors, the seventh of men of Jericho, the eighth is of Nigres and the ninth of Gros, the tenth is of men from the stronghold of Balide. It is a troop of evil-intentioned men. The emir swears with all his might by Mahomet and his miracles: "Charles of France is mad to advance. There will be a battle unless he takes himself off and he will never wear a golden crown upon his head again."

233. Then they form another ten army corps. The first is of hideous Chananeans who have come across from Val-Fuit. The second is of Turks, the third of Persians, the fourth is of Pinceneis and Persians, the fifth of Solteras and Avers, the sixth of Ormaleus and Eugiez, the seventh of the people of Samuel, the eighth of those of Bruise, the ninth of Claviers, and the tenth is of men from desert Occian. It is a troop of men who serve not God; you will never hear tell of greater felons—their skins are as hard as iron so that they have no need of helmet or hauberk, and they are evil and fierce in the battle.

234. The emir has adjusted ten more army corps. The first is of the giants of Malprose, the second of Huns, the third of Hungarians, the fourth is of men of Baldise la Longue, the fifth of those of Val Penose, the sixth of those of Marose, the seventh of Lens and Astrimoines, the eighth of those of Argoilles and the ninth of Clarbonne, the tenth of bearded men of Fronde. It is a troop of men who never loved God; in the annals of the French the thirty army corps are numbered. Great are the armies where the bugles are sounding, and the heathen ride forward after the manner of valiant men.

235. The emir is a very important person. He commands that his dragon be carried before him and the standard of Termagant and Mahomet and a statue of the felon Apollin. The Chananeans are riding around and they exhort the others loudly: "Let him who wishes our gods to protect him pray and do homage to them with great humility." The heathen bow their heads and cast their faces down so that their bright helmets are all lowered. The French say: "Your hour is come, ye scoundrels! A curse upon you this day! Do thou, our God, protect Charles and let this battle be won in his name!"

[The battle is joined, with great slaughter on both sides.]

253. The French and the Arabs fight hard. Many are the lances and the polished spears that come to grief! It was a sight to see the mangled shields; and anyone who heard the white hauberks rattling and the shields grating on the helmets and saw the knights rattling all round, and heard the groans of men as they died upon the ground, would always have a memory of great grief. This was a battle grievous to be borne. The emir calls upon Apollin and Termagant, and Mahomet too: "My lord gods, I have served you faithfully. I will make images of you all in pure gold...."

[The two leaders meet in combat.]

258. The day passes and evening comes on. French and heathen both strike with their swords. Great was the courage of the ones who joined these two armies in battle. Neither of them has forgotten their battle cry: the emir shouts "Précieuse" and Charles cries "Montjoie!" the well known signal. Each rec-

ognized the other by his loud, clear voice and they met in the middle of the field. They advance to the attack and they gave each other terrific blows on their circle-marked shields. Both their shields are broken beneath the wide bosses and the flaps are torn from their hauberks; but neither of them is touched as yet in the body. Their girths are broken, their saddles roll over and the kings fall to the ground....Quickly they rise again to their feet and undaunted they draw their swords. The combat will never be averted now; it will not come to an end till one of them be slain.

259. Very valiant is Charles of sweet France; but the emir neither fears nor dreads him. They brandish their naked swords and give each other great blows upon their shields; they cut through the skins and the double staves, the nails fall out and the bosses are broken in pieces. Then, unprotected, they rain blows on their coats of mail and fire flashes from their bright helmets. This battle cannot cease until one or other of them acknowledges that he is to blame.

260. Said the emir: "Charles, bethink thyself now and make up thy mind to repent towards me! Thou hast killed my son as I know for a truth; without any right thou dost lay claim to my land. Become my liege man now...and come hence as my vassal to the East." Charles replies: "A base proposal dost thou make to me. Neither peace nor love ought I to accord to a heathen. Accept the law which God has given us, the Christian law, and then I will love thee straightaway; then serve and adore the King omnipotent." Baligant answered: "Thou preachest an evil sermon." And they renew the fight with the swords that hang at their sides.

261. The emir is a powerful man. He strikes Charlemagne on his burnished helmet and he has broken and split it on his head. The sword has reached his hair and has taken a large handful and more of his flesh so that the bone is bare where he struck him. Charles tottered and all but fell, but God willed not that he should be killed or conquered. Saint Gabriel appeared to him and asked him: "Great king, what are thou doing?"

262. When Charles heard the holy voice of the angel he no longer had any fear or dread of death. Strength and consciousness came back to him and he struck the emir with the sword of France. He has shattered the helmet with its sparkling gems, he has cloven his head so that the brains are scattered, and his face down to the white beard, and he has struck him down dead without hope of recovery. Then he shouts "Montjoie" for a signal, and at the word duke Naimes comes up. He takes Tencendur and the great king mounts upon him. The heathen flee, for God wills not that they remain and the Frenchmen have attained their desire.

263. The heathen flee for God has willed it. The French pursue and the emperor with them. Then said the king: "Lords, avenge your losses; by so doing you will assuage your desires and your hearts, for this very morning I saw you weeping." The French reply: "Sire, it behooves us to do so." Each strike as hard blows as he can and very few of those who were there escaped.

264. The heat is great and the dust rises up. The heathen flee and the French harass them. The pursuit lasted from there to Saragossa. Bramimonde[1] has mounted to the top of her tower; with her are the clerks and canons of the false law which God never loved; they have neither orders nor tonsured heads. When she saw the rout of the Arabs with a loud voice she cried: "Help us, Mahomet!...Ah, noble king, our men are defeated, and the emir shamefully slain. When Marsilie heard her words, he turned his face to the wall; tears flowed from his eyes and his head sank down. He died of grief for sin lay heavy on him. He renders up his soul to living demons.

265. The heathens are dead...And Charles has been victorious. He has beaten down the gate of Saragossa and he knows that now it will be defended no longer. He takes possession of the city and his army has entered it and they lie in it that night as conquerors. The white-bearded king is a proud man. And Branimonde has handed over the towers to him; ten of them are large and fifty are small. He whom God helps achieves much.

---

[1] Marsilie's queen.

266. The day passes and the night has fallen; the moon is bright and the stars are shining. The emperor has taken Saragossa. A thousand Frenchmen have to search the town with care, and the synagogues and the mosques. With iron mallets and hatchets they break the images and every one of the idols. No trace of sorcery or fraud will they leave in place. The king worships God and desires to serve him; his bishops bless the waters and take the heathen to the baptistry. If there is anyone there who refuses to obey, Charles bids that he be hung, or burnt, or killed by the sword. More than a hundred thousand were baptized and became true Christians; the queen alone was not among them. She is to be led captive to sweet France for the king wishes her to be converted by love.

[Charles and his army return to France.]

271. It is told in the old chronicle that Charles summoned his men from many lands. They assembled in Aix, at the chapel. It was the high day of a solemn festival–some say it was the day of Saint Sylvester, the baron. Now begins the trial and the account of the fate of Ganelon, who committed the treason. The emperor has had him brought before him.

272. "Sir barons," said Charlemaine the king, "now give me right judgment concerning Ganelon! He went to Spain with me, in my army; he robbed me of twenty thousand of my Frenchmen and my nephew whom you will never see again, and of Oliver the valiant and the knightly. The twelve peers too he betrayed for gain." Said Ganelon: "May I be accursed if I conceal it! Roland wronged me in money and in possessions; that is why I sought his death and his destruction; but I do not admit that there was any treason." "Now we will take counsel concerning the matter."

276. The barons come back to Charlemaine and say to him: "Sire, we beseech you, acquit count Ganelon and let him serve you hereafter in loyalty and love. Let him live, for he is a very noble man." The king replied: "You are traitors to me."

277. When Charles sees that none of his barons support him, his face and his expression grow dark and he groans aloud in his grief. Then up came a knight and stood before him. It was Thierry, brother of Geoffroy duke of Anjou. His body was spare and slim, his hair was black and his skin rather dark; he was not large of stature but neither was he too small. He spoke courteously to the emperor: "Fair sir king, grieve not so much! You know well that I have served you faithfully. By reason of my lineage I have a right to speak thus: Whether or not Roland acted wrongly towards Ganelon, he was in your service and that ought to have protected him. Ganelon is a traitor in that he betrayed him; he has perjured himself and committed a crime towards you. Therefore my verdict is that he be hung and put to death...inasmuch as he is a felon and has committed felony. If now he has a kinsman who wishes to give me the lie, I will forthwith defend my judgment with the sword that I have girded to my side." The French reply: "You have spoken well indeed."

278. Then Pinabel came and stood before the king. He is tall and strong, courageous and swift. Anyone who received a blow from him has no longer to live. And he said to the king: "Sire, this trial is yours! Bid then that all this commotion cease! I see here Thierry, who has given his judgment. I declare it to be false and I will defend my view against him." His right glove of deerskin he placed in the king's hand. The emperor said: "I require good hostages." Thirty kinsmen offer themselves as loyal pledges, and the king said: "I for my part accept your surety." He put them into custody until the right be vindicated.

[Thierry also offers hostages, and the combat begins.]

283. Pinabel said: "Thierry, withdraw your words! I will be thy man in love and loyalty, I will give of my possessions as much as thou desirest, provided that thou wilt make Ganelon's peace with the king!" Thierry replied: "I will not consider it. May I be accursed if I agree to such a thing! May God vindicate the right between us two this day!" Thierry spoke: "Pinabel, thou are a valiant knight; thou art tall and strong and thy limbs are well fashioned. Thy peers take account of thy courage. Now withdraw from this combat; I will make thy peace with Charlemaine and such justice shall be done concerning Ganelon that it shall be spoken of continually." Said

Pinabel: "May it not please the Lord God! I will support my kin; I will not yield for any mortal man. I would rather die than bear reproach for that." Then they begin to strike each other on their gold-decked helmets so that bright sparks fly upwards towards the sky. There is no way now by which they can be separated; by a man's death alone can the combat end.

286. Thierry sees that he is wounded in the face. The bright blood flows down on to the grassy meadow. He strikes Pinabel on his polished helmet; he has broken and split it as far as the nose-piece, he has scattered the brains from his head. He has delivered his stroke and has hurled him down dead. This stroke has decided the battle. The French say: "God has shown us a sign! It is right that Ganelon be hung, both he and his kinsmen who have pleaded for him."

288. Charles calls his counts and his dukes: "What do you counsel me to do with those I kept in custody? They came hither for Ganelon's trial and I received them as hostages for Pinabel." The French reply: "Let not one of them remain alive!" Then the king gave his order to his provost Basbrun: "Go and hang them all on the tree of the accursed wood. By the beard of which the hairs are hoary, if one escapes thou are a dead and ruined man!" He replies: "How could I do otherwise?" With a hundred sergeants he took them by force and thirty of them were hung on the spot. A traitor brings both himself and others to destruction.

289. Then the Bavarians and the Germans, the Poitevins, the Bretons and the Normans departed. The French more than all the others have decreed that Ganelon shall die a death of special torment. They order four chargers to be brought up, and they bind him to them by his hands and feet. The horses are spirited and swift; four sergeants drive them forwards towards a mare in the middle of a field. Ganelon has come to a terrible end. All his nerves are stretched and his limbs break asunder from his body; the bright blood spurts forth onto the green grass. Ganelon is dead like the felon traitor that he is. It is not right that he who betrays another should live to boast of it.

†

EPILOGUE

CROSSING THE LINE

The Philosopher (Third Century B.C.)

Crossing the Line

Most of you probably have thought of history as "names and dates." In a certain mind-numbing way, this concept has its satisfactions. History might be boring, perhaps, but it is real: just know the facts, and you know history. You know if a statement is true or false by checking the names and dates.

Now, with some experience of how historians define problems and use dates—especially a problem as big and amorphous as the "Fall of Rome"—at least some of you must be wondering if there is any truth in history at all. Can there be, when so many different and contradictory conclusions about the same event are possible?

Students uniformly loathe the following reading, from Plato's *Republic*, and for good reason. It's very abstract, and certainly it has nothing to do with "names and dates." But it is a good way to end this book, because it provides a means of pulling together what you have learned about the study of history.

At this point in the dialogue, Plato (speaking, as usual, through Socrates) is making a technical case for his theory of Ideas, or Forms. As you know by now, what he is talking about is a conceptual world, a world that exists only in the mind but which, he argues, is more real than that shadow world of the Cave that most of us think of as reality.

As usual, therefore, you have to turn his argument on its head to get the point. There is the "thing," and there is the idea of the thing: the one is real, or at least tangible; the other abstract. It is this latter that Plato calls "real." Whether you agree with him or not, the point is to see that he is drawing a distinction between things as they exist, and things as we conceive them in the human mind.

You may still loathe this passage. But in terms of your mental growth—your awareness of that "self" in you that is in constant and increasingly conscious conflict with everything else—this statement of the role of perception is one of the most important passages you will read in college.

THE 'DIVIDED LINE'

PLATO

Plato's concern is to distinguish between "absolute" and "relative" truth. He does this by distinguishing between two worlds–the "visible" world, by which he means the world of the senses, and the "intelligible" world, by which he means the world of the mind, which is where underlying causes and principles can be abstracted and thus basic truths for the first time perceived. This latter world is to Plato the "real" world, and he rates various mental activities according to the level of "reality" with which they correspond: true Knowledge, at the top of the scale, is concerned with Ideal Good and the study of the "intelligible" world; at the bottom of the scale come mere "sense impressions" (here translated "imagining") which only look at the surface of things without trying to understand causes. Through the middle of the scale he draws a line which separates the "visible" from the "intelligible" world. His discussion has been diagrammed by Francis Cornford as follows:

	OBJECTS		STATES OF MIND
	The Good		Intelligence (*noesis*)
INTELLIGIBLE WORLD	Forms	**D**	Knowledge (*episteme*)
	Mathematical objects	**C**	Thinking (*dianoia*)
	Visible Things	**B**	Belief (*pistis*)
WORLD OF APPEARANCES			
	IMAGES	**A**	Imagining (*eikasia*)

Historians are not philosophers, but there is something useful the student of history can extract from this classic discussion: Where along the line does the study of history fall? How "real" is the study of history, then? Would your own definition of "reality" be the same as Plato's? Should it be?

In the following passage, Socrates is the speaker. The names of his respondents–who, as usual, are limited to saying "Yes, Socrates," "No, Socrates," and "Of course, Socrates"–are omitted.

You have to imagine, then, that there are two ruling powers, and that one of them is set over the intellectual world, the other over the visible. I do not say heaven, lest you should fancy that I am playing upon the name.[1] May I suppose that you have this distinction of the visible and intelligible fixed in your mind?

I have.

Now take a line which has been cut into two unequal parts, and divide each of them again in the same proportion, and suppose the two main divisions to answer, one to the visible and the other to the intelligible, and then compare the subdivisions in respect of their clearness and want of clearness, and you will find that the first section in the sphere of the visible [A] consists of images. And by images I mean, in the first place, shadows, and in the second place, reflections in water and in solid, smooth and polished bodies and the like. Do you understand?

Yes, I understand.

Imagine, now, the other section [B], of which this is only the resemblance, to include the animals which we see, and everything that grows or is made.

Very good.

---

[1]Some connected the word for "heaven" with the verb "to see." It is sometimes used for the whole of the visible universe.

Would you not admit that both the sections of this division have different degrees of truth, and that the copy is to the original as the sphere of opinion is to the sphere of knowledge?

Most undoubtedly.

Next proceed to consider the manner in which the sphere of the intellectual is to be divided.

In what manner?

Thus:–There are two subdivisions, in the lower of which [C] the soul uses the figures given by the former division as images; the inquiry can only be hypothetical, and instead of going upwards to a principle descends to the other end; in the higher of the two [A], the soul passes out of hypotheses, and goes up to a principle which is above hypotheses, making no use of images as in the former case, but proceeding only in and through the ideas themselves.[1]

I do not quite understand your meaning, he said.

Then I will try again; you will understand me better when I have made some preliminary remarks. You are aware that students of geometry, arithmetic, and the kindred sciences assume the odd and the even and the figures and three kinds of angles and the like in their several branches of science; these are their hypotheses, which they and everybody are supposed to know, and therefore they do not deign to give any account of them either to themselves or others; but they begin with them, and go on until they arrive at last, and in a consistent manner, at their conclusion?

Yes, he said, I know.

And do you not know also that although they make use of the visible forms and reason about time, they are thinking not of these, but of the ideals which they resemble; not of the figures which they draw, but of the absolute square and the absolute diameter, and so on–the forms which they draw or make, and which have shadows and reflections in water of their own, are converted by them into images, but they are really seeking to behold the things themselves, which can only be seen with the eye of the mind?

That is true.

And of this kind I spoke as the intelligible [C], although in the search after it the soul is compelled to use hypotheses; not ascending to a first principle, because she is unable to rise above the region of hypothesis, but employing the objects of which the shadows below are resemblances in their turn as images, they having in relation to the shadows and reflections of them a greater distinctness, and therefore a higher value.

I understand, he said, that you are speaking of the province of geometry and the sister arts.

And when I speak of the other division of the intelligible [D], you will understand me to speak of that other sort of knowledge which reason herself attains by the power of dialectic, using the hypotheses not as first principles, but only as hypotheses–that is to say, as steps and points of departure into a world which is above hypotheses, in order that she may soar beyond them to the first principle of the whole; and clinging to this and then to that which depends on this, by successive steps she descends again without the aid of any sensible object, from ideas, through ideas, and in ideas she ends.

---

[1]A difficult passage. Here is the way Cornford translates it: "Now consider how we are to divide the part which stands for the intelligible world. There are two sections. In the first (C) the mind uses as images those actual things which themselves had images in the visible world; and it is compelled to pursue its inquiry by starting from assumptions and traveling, not up to a principle, but down to a conclusion. In the second (D) the mind moves in the other direction, from an assumption up towards a principle which is not hypothetical; and it makes no use of the images employed in the other section, but only of Forms, and conducts its inquiry solely by their means."

I understand you, he replied; not perfectly, for you seem to me to be describing a task which is really tremendous; but, at any rate, I understand you to say that knowledge and being, which the science of dialectic contemplates, are clearer than the notions of the arts, as they are termed, which proceed from hypotheses only: these are also contemplated by the understanding, and not by the senses: yet, because they start from hypotheses and do not ascend to a principle, those who contemplate them appear to you not to exercise the higher reason upon them, although when a first principle is added to them they are cognizable by the higher reason. And the habit which is concerned with geometry and the cognate sciences I suppose that you would term understanding and not reason, as being intermediate between opinion and reason.

You have quite conceived my meaning, I said; and now, corresponding to these four divisions, let there be four faculties in the soul—reason answering to the highest, understanding to the second, faith (or conviction) to the third, and perception of shadows to the last—and let there be a scale of them, and let us suppose that the several faculties have clearness in the same degree that their objects have truth.

I understand, he replied, and give my assent, and accept your arrangement.

✝

Postscript

The following work, slightly modified, was forwarded by a student in Western Civ several years ago. She got it from a friend in the Midwest, whose student newspaper got it from a graduate student in East Lansing who had found it a year earlier in the University of Minnesota *Daily*. The *Daily* said it had gotten it from the Wesleyan College paper *Town and Country*, which stole it from the University of Tennessee's *Daily Beacon*. The *Beacon* claims to have taken it from the *Daily Tar Heel*, which attributed it to a geology professor who said it first appeared in the *Daily Illini* about 1963. The author is unknown.

GOOD LUCK ON ALL THOSE FINALS!

And it came to pass,
Early in the morning toward the last day of
    the semester,
There arose a great multitude smiting the
    books and wailing
And there was much weeping and gnashing of
    teeth
For the day of judgment was at hand
And they were sore afraid, for they had left
    undone
Those things which they ought to have done,
And they had done
Those things which they ought not to have
    done
And there was no help for it.
And there were many abiding in the dorm
Who had kept watch over their books by
    night,
But it had availed them naught.
But some there were who arose peacefully,
For they had prepared themselves the way
And made straight paths of knowledge.
And these were known
As wise burners of the midnight oil.
But to others they were known as "curve rais-
ers"
And other things not fit even for unclean ears.
And the multitude arose
And ate a hearty breakfast
And they came unto the appointed place
And their hearts were heavy within them.
And they had come to pass,
But some to pass out. And some of them
Repented of their riotous living and bemoaned
    their fate,
But they had not a prayer.

And at the last hour there came among them
One known as the instructor; and they feared
    exceedingly.
He was of the diabolical smile.
And he passed papers among them and went
    his way.
And many and varied
Were the answers that were given,
For some of his teachings had fallen among
    fertile minds,
While others had fallen flat.
And some there were who wrote for one hour,
Others for two.
But some were turned away sorrowfully, and
    many of these
Offered up a little bull
In hopes of pacifying the instructor.
And these were the ones who had not a
    prayer.
And when they finished
They gathered up their belongings
And went their way quietly, each in his own
    direction,
And each one vowing unto himself in this
    manner,
"I shall not pass this way again!"

Apollo from the Temple of Zeus at Olympia (c. 460 B.C.)

Suggestions for Further Reading

The Ancient Near East

Assmann, Jan. *Moses the Egyptian: The Memory of Egypt in Western Monotheism*. Cambridge, Mass., 1997.

Bartlett, J. R., ed. *Archaeology and Biblical Interpretation*. London, 1997.

Beaulieu, P.-A. *The Reign of Nabonidus, King of Babylon (556-539 B.C.)*. New Haven, 1989.

Bernstein, Alan. *The Formation of Hell. Death and Retribution in the Ancient and Early Christian Worlds*. Ithaca, 1993.

Bottéro, Jean. *Mesopotamia: Writing Reasoning, and the Gods*. Tr. Z. Bahrani. Chicago, 1992.

Bottéro, Jean. *Everyday Life in Ancient Mesopotamia*. Tr. A. Nevil. Baltimore, 2001.

Boyce, Mary. *A History of Zoroastrianism*. 2 vols. Leiden, 1982-96.

Ceram, C.W. *Gods, Graves and Scholars: The Story of Archaeology*. 2d edn. New York, 1967.

Curtis, Vesta. *Persian Myths*. Austin, 1993.

Dalley, Stephanie, ed. *The Legacy of Mesopotamia*. Oxford, 1998.

Dundes, Alan, ed. *The Flood Myth*. Berkeley, 1988.

Frankfort, H. *The Birth of Civilization in the Near East*. Indiana, 1951; repr Garden City, 1956.

Hallo, William. *Origins. The Ancient Near Eastern Background of Some Modern Western Institutions*. Leiden, 1996.

Hexter, J. H. *The Judaeo-Christian Tradition*. 2d edn. New Haven, 1995.

Hillers, D. *Covenant: The History of a Biblical Idea*. Baltimore, 1969.

James, E.O. *The Ancient Gods: The History and Diffusion of Religion in the Ancient Near East and the Eastern Mediterranean*. New York, 1964.

James, T. G. H. *Howard Carter: The Path to Tutankhamun*. London, 1992.

Keller, Werner. *The Bible As History*. 2d edn. New York, 1981.

Kramer, S.N. *History Begins at Sumer: 27 'Firsts' in Man's Recorded History*. Garden City, 1959.

Malek, Jaromir, ed. *Egypt*. Norman, Okla., 1993.

McCall, Henrietta. *Mesopotamian Myths*. Austin, 1990.

Modrzejewski, J. M. *The Jews of Egypt: From Rameses II to Emperor Hadrian*. Princeton, 1995.

Moscati, Sabatino. *The Face of the Ancient Orient*. Garden City, 1962.

Parkinson, Richard. *The Rosetta Stone and Decipherment*. Berkeley, 1999.

Saggs, H. W. F. *The Encounter with the Divine in Mesopotamia and Israel*. London, 1978.

Schmandt-Besserat, Denise. *How Writing Came About*. Austin, 1997.

Shafer, B., ed. *Religion in Ancient Egypt: Gods, Myths and Personal Practice*. Ithaca, 1991.

Shanks, H. & J. Meinhardt, eds. *Aspects of Monotheism: How God Is One.* Washington, D.C., 1997.

Tyldesley, Joyce. *Hatchepsut: The Female Pharaoh.* New York, 1996.

Tyldesley, Joyce. *Nefertiti: Egypt's Sun Queen.* New York, 1999.

Greece

Allen, Susan. *Finding the Walls of Troy: Frank Calvert and Heinrich Schliemann at Hisarlik.* Berkeley, 1999.

Blundell, Sue. *Women in Ancient Greece.* Cambridge, Mass., 1995.

Boedeker, Deborah, ed. *The World of Troy: Homer, Schliemann and the Treasures of Priam.* Washington, D. C., 1997.

Borza, Eugene, ed. *The Impact of Alexander the Great: Civilizer or Destroyer?* Hinsdale, Ill. 1974.

Brickhouse, T. & N. Smith. *Socrates on Trial.* paper edn. Princeton, 1990.

Brunschwig, J. & G. E. R. Lloyd, eds. *Greek Thought: A Guide to Classical Knowledge.* Cambridge, MA, 2000.

Burstein, Stanley. *Graeco-Africana: Studies in the History of Greek Relations with Egypt and Nubia.* New Rochelle, 1993.

Bury, J. B. & R. Meiggs. *A History of Greece to the Death of Alexander the Great.* 4th edn. New York, 1978.

Connolly, P. & H. Dodge. *The Ancient City: Life in Classical Athens and Rome.* Oxford, 1998.

Donlan, Walter. *The Aristocratic Ideal in Ancient Greece: Attitudes of Superiority from Homer to the End of the Fifth Century B.C.* Lawrence, Kans., 1980.

Farrar, Cynthia. *The Origins of Democratic Thinking: The Invention of Politics in Classical Athens.* Cambridge, 1989.

Frost, Frank J. *Greek Society.* 5 edn. Boston, 1997.

Hanson, Victor, ed. *Hoplites: The Classical Greek Battle Experience.* London, 1991.

Mogens, Herman. *The Trial of Sokrates— from the Athenian Point of View.* Copenhagen, 1995.

Powell, C.A. *Athens and Sparta: Constructing Greek Political and Social History, 478-371 B.C.* Portland, Ore., 1988.

Rawson, Elizabeth. *The Spartan Tradition in European Thought.* Oxford, 1969.

Reeder, Ellen D., ed. *Pandora: Women in Classical Greece.* Princeton, 1995.

Rich, John and G. Shipley, eds. *War and Society in the Greek World.* New York, 1995.

Sage, Michael. *Warfare in Ancient Greece: A Sourcebook.* New York, 1996.

Samuel, Alan. *The Greeks in History.* Buffalo, 1992.

Sealey, R. *A History of the Greek City States, 700-338 B.C.* Berkeley, 1976.

Snodgrass, Anthony. *Archaeology and the Rise of the Greek State.* Cambridge, 1977.

Walbank, F. W. *The Hellenistic World.* Cambridge, Mass., 1981.

Rome

Adcock, F. E. *Roman Political Ideas and Practice.* Ann Arbor, 1959.

Bauman, Richard A. *Women and Politics in Ancient Rome.* New York, 1992.

Bauman, Richard A. *Crime and Punishment in Ancient Rome.* New York, 1996.

Beard, M. and J. North, edd. *Pagan Priests: Religion and Power in the Ancient World.* Ithaca, 1990.

Beard, Mary & M. Crawford. *Rome in the Late Republic.* Ithaca, 1985.

Bradley, K. R. *Slavery and Rebellion in the Roman World, 140 B.C.-70 B.C.* Bloomington, 1989.

Bradley, K. R. *Slaves and Masters in the Roman Empire: A Study in Social Control.* New York, 1987.

Brantlinger, Patrick. *Bread and Circuses: Theories of Mass Culture as Social Decay.* Ithaca, 1984.

Brown, P.R.L. *Augustine of Hippo.* London, 1967.

Brown, P.R.L. *The World of Late Antiquity, A.D. 150-750.* New York, 1971.

Cameron, Av. *The Later Roman Empire, AD 284-430.* Cambridge, Mass., 1993.

Cameron, Av. *The Mediterranean World in Late Antiquity, AD 395-600.* New York, 1993.

Cary, M. & H. H. Scullard, *A History of Rome down to the Reign of Constantine.* 3d edn., New York, 1975.

Chitty, D. *The Desert a City. An Introduction to the Study of Egyptian & Palestinian Monasticism Under the Christian Empire.* Oxford, 1966.

Crook, J.A. *Law and Life of Rome, 90 BC-AD 212.* Ithaca, 1984.

Drake, H. A. *Constantine and the Bishops: The Politics of Intolerance.* Baltimore, 2000.

Errington, R. M. *The Dawn of Empire: Rome's Rise to World Power.* Ithaca, 1973.

Finley, M. I. *Politics in the Ancient World.* Cambridge, 1983.

Garnsey, P. and Saller, R. *The Roman Empire: Economy, Society and Culture.* Berkeley, 1987.

Garnsey, Peter. *Social Status and Legal Privilege in the Roman Empire.* Oxford, 1970.

Gelzer, M. *Caesar: Politician and Statesman.* Oxford, 1968.

Gibbon, E. *The Decline & Fall of the Roman Empire,* ed. J. Bury. 7 vols. London, 1909-14.

Grant, M. *The Collapse and Recovery of the Roman Empire.* New York, 1999.

Green, P. *Alexander to Actium: The Historical Evolution of the Hellenistic Age.* Berkeley, 1990.

Greene, Kevin. *The Archaeology of the Roman Economy.* Berkeley, 1986.

Gruen, E. *The Hellenistic World and the Coming of Rome.* 2 vols. Berkeley, 1984.

Gurval, R. *Actium and Augustus: the Politics and Emotions of Civil War.* Ann Arbor, 1995.

Jenkyns, R., ed. *The Legacy of Rome: A New Appraisal.* Oxford, 1992.

Jones, A.H.M. *The Decline of the Ancient World.* New York, 1975.

Lane Fox, R. *Pagans and Christians: Religion and the Religious Life from the Second to the Fourth Century A.D.* New York, 1987.

Lewis, A. & D. Ibbetson, eds. *The Roman Law Tradition.* Cambridge, 1994.

MacMullen, R. *Roman Social Relations, 50 BC to AD 284.* New Haven, 1974.

Markus, R.A. *Christianity in the Roman World.* London, 1974.

Mellor, R., ed. *From Augustus to Nero: The First Dynasty of Imperial Rome.* East Lansing, 1990.

Nicolet, C. *Space, Geography and Politics in the Early Roman Empire.* Ann Arbor, 1991.

Nicolet, C. *The World of the Citizen in Republican Rome.* Berkeley, 1980.

Rawson, B., ed. *Marriage, Divorce and Children in Ancient Rome.* Oxford, 1991.

Riesenberg, Peter. *Citizenship in the Western Tradition: Plato to Rousseau.* Chapel Hill, 1992.

Scullard, H.H. *From the Gracchi to Nero.* 2d edn. London, 1963.

Shelton, J.-A. *As the Roman Did: A Sourcebook in Roman Social History.* New York, 1988.

Southern, Pat. *Augustus.* New York, 1998.

Syme, R. *The Roman Revolution.* Oxford, 1939.

Wallace-Hadrill, A. *Augustan Rome.* Bristol, 1993.

Wilken, Robert L. *The Christians as the Romans Saw Them.* New Haven, 1984.

Wolfram, Herwig. *The Roman Empire and Its Germanic Peoples.* Tr. Thomas Dunlap. Berkeley, 1997.

Zanker, Paul. *The Power of Images in the Age of Augustus.* Tr. Alan Shapiro. Ann Arbor, 1988.

Byzantium, Islam, Medieval Europe

Ahsan, M. M. *Social Life Under the Abbasids.* London. 1979

Angold, Michael. *The Byzantine Empire, 1025-1204: A Political History.* New York and London. 1997

Ausenda, Giorgio. *After Empire: Towards an Ethnology of Europe's Barbarians.* New York and London. 1995

Bachrach, Bernard S. *Fulk Nerra, the Neo-Roman Consul, 987-1040: A Political Biography of the Angevin Count.* Berkeley. 1993

Blankinship, Khalid Yahya. *The End of the Jihad State: The Reign of Hisham Ibn Abd Al-Malik and the Collapse of the Umayyads.* Albany. 1994

Bowersock, G. et al., eds. *Late Antiquity: A Guide to the Postclassical World.* Cambridge, MA, 1999.

Davids, Adelbert, ed. *The Empress Theophano: Byzantium and the West at the Turn of the First Millennium.* Cambridge. 1995

El-Hibri, Tayeb. *Reinterpreting Islamic Historiography: Harun Al-Rashid and the Narrative of the Abbasid Caliphate.* Cambridge. 1999

Evans, J. A. S. *The Age of Justinian: The Circumstances of Imperial Power.* London. 1996

Fichtenau, Heinrich. *Living in the Tenth Century: Mentalities and Social Orders.* Chicago. 1993

Fletcher, Richard. *The Barbarian Conversion: From Paganism to Christianity.* Boston and New York. 1998

Frassetto, M. & D. R. Blanks, eds. *Western Views of Islam in Medieval and Early Modern Europe.* New York, 1999.

Garland, Lynda. *Byzantine Empresses: Women and Power in Byzantium, A.D. 527-1204.* London. 1999

Geary, Patrick J. *Before France and Germany: The Creation and Transformation of the Merovingian World.* London and New York. 1988

Haldon, J.F. *Byzantium in the Seventh Century: The Transformation of a Culture.* Cambridge. 1991

Harvey, Susan Ashbrook. *Asceticism and Society in Crisis: John of Ephesus and the Lives of the Eastern Saints.* Berkeley. 1990

Herrin, Judith. *The Formation of Christendom.* Princeton. 1989

Hillgarth, J.N. (Editor). *Christianity and Paganism, 350–750: The Conversion of Western Europe.* University of Pennsylvania Press. 1986

Hodges, Richard. *Light in the Dark Ages: The Rise and Fall of San Vincenzo Al Volturno.* Ithaca. 1997

Holt, P. M. *The Age of the Crusades: The Near East from the Eleventh Century to 1517.* New York and London. 1986

Horden, P. & N. Purcell. *The Mediterranean World: Man and Environment in Antiquity and the Middle Ages.* Oxford, 1995.

Humphreys, R. Stephen. *Islamic History: A Framework for Inquiry.* Princeton. 1991

James, Edward. *Origins of France: From Clovis to the Capetians 500–1000.* St Martins Pr. 1989

Jones, Gwyn. *A History of the Vikings.* Oxford Univ Pr. 1984

Kaegi, Walter E. *Byzantium and the Early Islamic Conquests.* London. 1995

Kennedy, Hugh. *The Prophet and the Age of the Caliphates: The Near East from the 6th to the 11th Century.* New York and London. 1986

Madelung, Wilferd. *The Succession to Muhammad: A Study of the Early Caliphate.* Cambridge. 1996

Mathisen, Ralph Whitney. *Roman Aristocrats in Barbarian Gaul: Strategies for Survival in an Age of Transition.* Austin. 1993

Mayr-Harting, Henry. *The Coming of Christianity to Anglo-Saxon England.* Philadelphia. 1991

McKitterick, Rosamond. *Carolingian Culture: Emulation and Innovation.* Cambridge. 1994

Mernissi, Fatima (tr. Mary Jo Lakeland). *The Forgotten Queens of Islam.* Minneapolis. 1993

Nelson, Janet L. *Charles the Bald.* New York and London. 1992

Nelson, Janet L. *The Frankish World 750–900.* Hambledon Pr. 1996.

Pohl, W. et al., eds. *The Transformation of Frontiers from Late Antiquity to the Carolingians.* Leiden, 2001.

Reynolds, Susan. *Fiefs and Vassals: The Medieval Evidence Reinterpreted.* London and New York. 1996

Reynolds, Susan. *Kingdoms and Communities in Western Europe, 900–1300.* London and New York. 1997

Rosenthal, Franz. *The Classical Heritage in Islam.* Tr. E. & J. Marmorstein. New York, 1994.

Rosenwein, Barbara H. *Negotiating Space: Power, Restraint, and Privileges of Immunity in Early Medieval Europe.* Ithaca. 1999

Sanders, J. J. *A History of Medieval Islam.* London. 1990

Schiavone, Aldo. *The End of the Past: Ancient Rome and the Modern West.* Tr. M. Schneider. Cambridge, MA, 2000.

Schick, Robert. *The Christian Communities of Palestine from Byzantine to Islamic Rule: A Historical and Archaeological Study.* New York. 1996

Shahid, Irfan. *Byzantium and the Arabs in the Fifth Century.* Washington;. 1989

Treadgold, Warren. *Byzantium and Its Army, 284-1081*. Stanford. 1995

Wallace-Hadrill , J. M. The Barbarian West 400-1000. Oxford. 1960

Wasserstrom, Steven M. *Between Muslim and Jew: The Problem of Symbiosis Under Early Islam*. Princeton. 1995

Whittow, Mark. *The Making of Byzantium, 600-1025*. Berkeley. 1996

Williams, Stephen and Friell, Gerard. *The Rome That Did Not Fall: The Survival of the East in the Fifth Century*. London. 1998

Wood, I. N. *The Merovingian Kingdoms, 450-751*. New York and London. 1994

Watt, W.M. *The Influence of Islam on Medieval Europe*. Edinburgh, 1972.

Acknowledgments

Chapter 1: Getting Started

"In Praise of Stark Lucidity." Bruce D. Price, *Princeton Alumni Weekly* (March 14, 1977), pp. 12-14. Reprinted by permission of the author.

"A Handy Guide." was written by Paul St. Pierre for the Williams Lake *Tribune* in 1977. The "Handy Guide" is from Betty H. Zisk, "The Compleat Jargoner: How to Obfuscate the Obvious Without Half Trying," *Western Political Quarterly,* 23:1 (March 1970), 55-56. Reprinted by permission of the *University of Utah,* Copyright Holder.

"Truth and Education." Rick Kennedy, *UCSB Daily Nexus* (April 19, 1984). Reprinted by permission of the author.

"Getting Even: How to Write a Convincing Analytical Essay." Laura Wertheimer, "Analytical Essays." Reprinted by permission of the author.

Roberts, Paul William. "My Translation Problem. One Man's Protest Against the Desecration of Dead Languages." *Lingua Franca* 7 (Dec/Jan 1997): 69-75. The extract is from pp. 71-73.

Chapter 2: In the Beginning

"Complex Societies." Patricia Crone, *Pre-Industrial Societies*, pp. 2-5. © 1989. Reprinted by permission of Blackwell Publishers, Oxford, England.

"The Descent of Ishtar." From Morris Jastrow, ed., *The Civilization of Babylonia and Assyria,* © 1915, pp. 453-59. Public domain.

"The Code of Hammurabi." Excerpts from *The Code of Hammurabi*, tr. R. F. Harper and ed. P. Handcock, London, © 1920, pp. 5-45, with emendations by H. A. Drake and J. W. Leedom. Public Domain.

"Hebrew Law." *Exodus* 19.7-23.33 and *Deuteronomy* 4:5–31, *The New Revised Standard Version Bible.* Public Domain.

"The Institutes of Justinian." Excerpts from *The Institutes of Justinian*, tr. T. C. Sandars, © 1910, pp. 1-13. Public Domain.

"Another Version of Hammurabi's Code." Doug Kenney, "The Code of Hammurabi," *The National Lampoon* (August 1975), pp. 56-7. Reprinted by permission.

Chapter 3: Monotheism

"Enuma Elish." Tr. E. A. Speiser in *Ancient Near Eastern Texts Relating to the Old Testament*, ed. James Pritchard, 2 ed. (Princeton, 1955), pp. 60-72 (abridged). Copyright © 1950, 1955, © renewed 1983 by Princeton University Press.

Reprinted by permission of Princeton University Press.

"Hymn to the Nile" and "Hymn to the Sun" Tr. A. Erman, *The Literature of the Ancient Egyptians*, tr. A. Blackman (New York, 1927), pp. 138-40, 1146-9.

"Hymn to Aton." Tr. J. A. Wilson in *Ancient Near Eastern Texts Relating to the Old Testament*, ed. James Pritchard, 2 ed. (Princeton, 1955), pp. 370-71. Copyright © 1950, 1955, © renewed 1983 by Princeton University Press. Reprinted by permission of Princeton University Press.

Plutarch, "On Isis and Osiris," 12-20 (356a-358e) (abridged), tr. J. Gwyn Griffiths

"Creation." *Genesis* 1:1-2.4. *The New Revised Standard Version Bible.* Public Domain.

"The Flood." *Genesis* 6:5-9.15. *The New Revised Standard Version Bible.* Public Domain.

"Abraham and Isaac" [From: *Genesis*, 17-18, 21-22; *New International Version*.]

"Jonah and the Whale" [From: *Jonah*, 1-4; *New International Version*.]

"The Book of Job." *Genesis* 10:23-33. *The New Revised Standard Version Bible.* Public Domain.

"Nabonidus and His God," tr. A. Leo Oppenheim in J. Pritchard, ed., *Ancient Near Eastern Texts* (1955): 562-3.

"The Verse Account of Nabonidus," tr. A. Leo Oppenheim in J. Pritchard, ed., *Ancient Near Eastern Texts* (1955): 312-13.

Yasna 30, 49, 46, tr. M. Boyce, *Textual Sources for the Study of Zoroastrianism* (Manchester University Press, 1984), pp. 35, 40-2.

"The Scrolls." Woody Allen, *The New Republic* (August 31, 1974), 18-19. Reprinted by permission of The New Republic, Inc.

Chapter 4: Greek Heroes

The Iliad of Homer, tr. Richard Lattimore, The University of Chicago Press, © 1968, pp. 59-100, 153-67, 198-217, 475-496. Reprinted by permission.

Greek Lyrics, 2 ed, tr. Richard Lattimore, The University of Chicago Press, © 1960, pp. 1-2, 13, 32, 41-42, 45, 50. Reprinted by permission.

Antigone. Sophocles. Tr. F. Kinchin Smith. London: Sidgwick and Jackson, Ltd., 1950.

"Heroic Action." Keightly, David N., "Early Civilization in China: Reflections of How It Became Chinese." From *Heritage of China: Contempo-*

rary Perspectives on Chinese Civilization, ed. Paul S. Ropp, © 1990, pp. 16-21. Reprinted by permission of the Regents of the University of California and the University of California Press.

Chapter 5: Sophistry and Illusion

"The Funeral Oration of Pericles." Thucydides, *History of the Peloponnesian War* II.6.36-41, tr. Richard Crowley (London, 1876), pp. 121-25.

"On Historical Method." Thucydides, *History of the Peloponnesian War* I.20-23, tr. Richard Crowley (London, 1876), pp. 20-22 (abridged and slightly emended).

"Revolution on Corcyra." Thucydides, *History of the Peloponnesian War* III.10.81-84, tr. Richard Crowley (London, 1876), pp. 223-37.

"The Melian Dialogue." Thucydides, *History of the Peloponnesian War* V.17.85-116, tr. Richard Crowley (London, 1876), pp. 396-403 (abridged).

"A Sophistic Argument." Plato, *The Republic*, Book I (336b-347e), tr. Benjamin Jowett, 1871. Public domain.

"The Allegory of the Cave." Plato, *The Republic*, Book VII (514a-521b), tr. Benjamin Jowett, 1871. Public domain.

"The 7th Epistle." Plato, *The Works of Plato*, tr. Georges Burges (London, 1855), IV, 500-502. Public domain.

"On the Changing of Laws." Aristotle, *The Politics* II.8, tr. J. E. C. Welldon (London, 1901), pp. 72-4. Public Domain.

Chapter 6: Great Individuals

"On Heroes." Thomas Carlyle, *On Heroes, Hero-Worship, and the Heroic in History* (London, 1940). Selections from Lecture One, "The Hero as Divinity", (Tuesday, May 5, 1840), and Lecture Six, "The Hero as King" (Friday, May 22, 1840). Public Domain.

"On Greek Unity." Isocrates,"Panegyricus." tr. J. H. Freese In M. Miller, ed., *The Classics: Greek and Latin*, v. 6 (New York, 1909), 145, 162-3, 166, 175-7.]

"The Second Olynthiac." Demosthenes, *The Public Orations of Demosthenes*, tr. Arthur Wallace, © 1912. Public domain.

"Address to Philip." Isocrates, "Address to Philip," 9.14-16. 68-71, tr. H. A. Drake.

"Life of Alexander." Plutarch, *Parallel Lives*, tr. John Dryden (abridged, with slight modifications). Public domain.

"The Prayer at Opis." Arrian, *Anabasis*, VII.11.8-9, tr. M. M. Austen, Livius webpage (www.livius.org).

"The Lion in Our Midst." Aristotle, *The Politics of Aristotle* 3.13, tr. J. E. C. Welldon (London,1901), pp. 140-42. Public Domain.

"A Roman Hero." Vergil, *The Aeneid*, Books IV and VI (abridged), tr. C. Day Lewis. Reprinted by permission of Sterling Lord Literistic, Inc. © 1953 by C. Day Lewis.

"Life of Julius Caesar." Plutarch, *Parallel Lives*, tr. John Dryden (abridged, with slight modification). Public domain.

Chapter 7: Rome' s Mission

"The Roman Constitution." Polybius, *The Histories*, Book VI.1, 7-9, 11-18, tr. E. S. Shuckburgh, (London,1889). public domain.

"Against Verres." *The Orations of Marcus Tullius Cicero*, tr. C. D. Yonge, I (London, 1893), 132-7, 146-7, 164-5, 388, 501-7, 509-11, 532-39. Public domain.

"Roman Citizenship." A Speech of the Emperor Claudius. Tacitus, *The Annals* 11.23-25, tr. A. Church and W. Brodribb, 1871. Public domain.

The Roman History. Appian, *The Roman History* I.6-11, tr. Horace White, Loeb Classical Library, 1912. Public domain.

"To Rome." Panegyric of Aelius Aristides, tr. James H. Oliver, *The Ruling Power,* Transactions of the American Philosophical Society, n.s. 43:4, pp. 895-907. © 1953. Reprinted by permission of the American Philosophical Society.

"The Third Satire", Juvenal, *Thirteen Satires of Juvenal*, tr. S. G. Owen, pp. 9-21. © 1903. Public domain.

"The Book of Revelation." *Revelation* 17-18, *The New Revised Standard Version Bible*. Public Domain.

Chapter 8: The Christian Message

"The Sermon on the Mount." The Gospel of Matthew 5:1-7.28. The New Revised Standard Version Bible. Public Domain.

"The Last Judgment." The Gospel of Matthew 25:31-46. The New Revised Standard Version Bible. Public Domain.

"Selected Sayings." The New Revised Standard Version Bible. Public Domain.

"The Manual of Philosophy.", Epictetus, The Discourses and Manual, tr. P. E. Matheson, selections. © 1917. Reprinted by permission of Oxford University Press.

"The True Word." Celsus in Origen, Contra Celsum I.28, 39; II.5455, 63. 68; III.44, 50, 55, 59, 62; IV.2-3; VI.73, 75, 78; VII.18; VIII.12, 14, 39, 68, tr. H. Chadwick, © 1955 by Cambridge University Press. Reprinted with the permission of Cambridge University Press.

"The Letter of James." The New Revised Standard Version Bible. Public Domain.

"The Lyons Martyrs." In Eusebius of Caesarea,, The Church History 5.1.7-63. tr. A. McGiffert (with slight modifications), in A Select Library of Nicene and Post-Nicene Fathers of the Christian

Church, 2 ser., v. 1, 212-17, ed. P. Schaff and H. Wace, 1890. Public domain.

"A Martyr Trial." Dionysius of Alexandria, "Letter to Germanus," in Eusebius of Caesarea, The Church History 7.11.1-14, tr. A. McGiffert, in A Select Library of Nicene and Post-Nicene Fathers of the Christian Church, 2 ser., v. 1, 299-300, ed. P. Schaff and H. Wace, 1890. Public domain.

"The Plague at Alexandria." Dionysius of Alexandria in Eusebius of Caesarea, The Church History 7.22.1-10, tr. A. McGiffert, in A Select Library of Nicene and Post-Nicene Fathers of the Christian Church, 2 ser, v. 1, 306-7, ed. P. Schaff and H. Wace, 1890. Public domain.

Chapter 9: Faith and Identity

"The Life of Daniel the Stylite." *Three Byzantine Saints*, tr. E. Dawes and N. H. Baynes, pp. 7-71 (abridged), © 1948. Reprinted by permission of Blackwell Publishers, England.

"The Life of St. John the Almsgiver." *Three Byzantine Saints*, tr. E. Dawes and N. H. Baynes, pp. 236-7, © 1948. Reprinted by permission of Blackwell Publishers, England.

"Letter CXXVII: On Rome." St. Jerome, tr. David Tipton, 1993. Reprinted by permission of David Tipton.

"The City of God." St. Augustine, *Retractations* 2.43; *The City of God* 15.1, 15.4, 19.17, tr. M. Dods in *A Select Library of the Nicene and Post-Nicene Fathers of the Christian Church*, ser. 1, v. 11, xi, 284-85, 286, 412-13, ed. P. Schaff and H. Wace, 1886. Public domain.

On the Fate of the Persecutors." Lactantius, *De Mortibus Persecutorum*, I-V, tr. William Fletcher in *The Ante-Nicene Fathers of the Christian Church*, v. 7, 301-3. ed. A. Roberts and J, Donaldson, 1886. Public domain.

"On Christ's Sepulchre.", Eusebius of Caesarea, *De sepulchro Christi*, XVI-XVII, from *In Praise of Constantine*, tr. H. A. Drake, pp. 119-24. © 1976. The Regents of the University of California. Reprinted by permission of the University of California Press.

"Letter to Constantius." Ossius of Cordoba, in Athanasius of Alexandria, "History of the Arians"44-45, tr. M. Atkinson and A. Robertson in *A Select Library of the Nicene and Post-Nicene Fathers of the Christian Church*, 2 ser., v. 4, 285-6. ed. P. Schaff and H. Wace, 1891. Public domain.

"Letter to Anastasius."Gelasius I, *Epistle VIII*, in *Patrologia Latina*, by J. P. Migne. Tr. Kathleen Drake. Reprinted by permission of Kathleen Drake.

The Koran, George Sale, trans., Frederick Warne and Co., [London: 1900]. The translation has been slightly modernized.

"Muslim Wisdom." Abu Haid Al-Ghazali, *The Faith and Practice of Al-Ghazali*, tr. W. Montgomery Watt, pp. 20-22, 86-90, 103-5, 106, 108, 123, 131-2. © 1963 by Routledge, England.

Chapter 10: Change and Continuity

"On Germany." Tacitus, *Germania* 4-16, 21-23, tr. A. Church and W. Brodribb, 1871. Public domain.

"Life of Augustus." Suetonius, *The Lives of Caesars*, tr. J. C. Rolfe, The Loeb Classical Library, 1913. For permission to photocopy this section, please contact Harvard University Press. Reprinted by permission of the publisher and the Loeb Classical Library, Harvard University Press.

"Life of Charlemagne." *Early Lives of Charlemagne by Eginhard and the Monk of St. Gall*, ed. A. J. Grant, 1905. Public domain.

Excerpts from *The Theodosian Code*, tr. Clyde Pharr. Copyright © 1952 by Clyde Pharr, © renewed by Roy Pharr 1980. Published and reprinted by permission of Princeton University Press.

Excerpts from *The Lombard Laws*, tr. K. F. Drew, copyright © 1964 and 1970 by the University of Pennsylvania Press. Reprinted by permission of the publisher.

"The Capitulary of Meersen." Tr. E. P. Cheyney, *Translations and Reprints from the Original Sources of European history*, IV, No. 3, 5. (Philadelphia, University of Pennsylvania Press,1898). Public domain.

Excerpt from *The Song of Roland*, tr. Jessie Crosland, copyright © 1927 by The Medieval Library, London, renewed © 1970 by Coopers Square Publishers, Inc.

Epilogue: Crossing the Line

"The Divided Line." Plato, *The Republic*, Book VI 509d-511e, tr. Benjamin Jowett, 1871. Public domain.

"Postscript: Good Luck on All those Finals!" Anonymous.